CRITICAL COMPANION TO

Jack London

CRITICAL COMPANION TO

Jack London

A Literary Reference to His Life and Work

JEANNE CAMPBELL REESMAN

Facts On File
An Infobase Learning Company

Critical Companion to Jack London
A Literary Reference to His Life and Work

Facts On File, Inc.
An imprint of Infobase Learning
132 West 31st Street
New York NY 10001

Library of Congress Cataloging-in-Publication Data

Reesman, Jeanne Campbell.
Critical companion to Jack London / Jeanne Campbell Reesman.
    p. cm.
Includes bibliographical references and index.
ISBN 978-0-8160-8084-7 (acid-free paper) 1. London, Jack, 1876–1916—
Handbooks, manuals, etc. I. Title.
PS3523.O46Z8664 2011
813'.52—dc22   2010014297

Facts On File books are available at special discounts when purchased in bulk
quantities for businesses, associations, institutions, or sales promotions.
Please call our Special Sales Department in New York at (212) 967-8800
or (800) 322-8755.

You can find Facts On File on the World Wide Web at http://www.factsonfile.com

Text design by Erika K. Arroyo
Composition by Hermitage Publishing Services
Cover printed by Sheridan Books, Inc., Ann Arbor, Mich.
Book printed and bound by Sheridan Books, Inc., Ann Arbor, Mich.
Date printed: February 2011

Printed in the United States of America

10 9 8 7 6 5 4 3 2 1

This book is printed on acid-free paper.

CONTENTS

INTRODUCTION

Both during his lifetime (1876–1916) and today, Jack London has been one of the most popular American writers the world over. Having been translated into more than 100 languages, his work is that of the American writer most likely to have been read abroad. Though London was once snubbed by critics at home as too popular, too socialist, too Western, and too prolific to be considered a serious subject for university study, today book after book is being published in the field of Jack London studies. There are few writers who are both the subject of 6th-grade reading assignments and doctoral dissertations. Perhaps because his adventurous life is such a part of his appeal, most readers, both scholarly and general, regard London as primarily a writer of adventures, mostly featuring dogs and gold prospectors in the Klondike. The critical and popular success of such novels as *The Call of the Wild* and *White Fang* notwithstanding, London is a writer whose true range of subject matter requires readers to put aside the macho stereotypes they may entertain of him. Despite his exciting explorations, war correspondence, and South Seas sailing trips, London was primarily a writer, spending each morning of his career writing his 1,000 words a day. He read voraciously on nearly every subject, from science to missionary accounts to the poetry of Oscar Wilde and Alfred, Lord Tennyson—as a young man he made a special study of Greek and Roman classics, especially Homer.

London wrote on an astonishing array of topics in his brief but remarkably productive career.

His work presents a diverse and experimental array of subjects and styles, including characters drawn from cavemen, lepers, the desperately poor, the homeless, prisoners, the mentally retarded, Solomon Islanders, Native Americans, and so on, focusing for the most part on characters who suffer some form of oppression, including colonization by whites; a great number of his short stories feature nonwhite and non-Western narrators and characters. Though London could sometimes reflect the racialism of his day, for the most part he challenges his white, middle-class readers to revise their unrealistic view of the world and, in privileging the downtrodden, recognize shared humanity. This is in keeping, of course, with his socialist politics. London both included socialist themes in his work and gave numerous speeches for the cause. Finally, London's subjects often reflect some ideas not usually associated with him, such as feminism, androgyny as an ideal, psychoanalytic theory, temperance.

Just as London's characters and subject matter are quite diverse, so are his settings; they range from the Arctic Circle to the South Seas, from the streets of San Francisco and the docks of Oakland to the slums of the East End of London. London traveled by sailboat, dogsled, and boxcar. He spent time in prison and a spell as an oyster pirate on San Francisco Bay. Because the majority of his settings are on the West Coast, the Pacific Northwest, Japan, Korea, China, Polynesia, Melanesia, and Australia, he may be described as America's first Pacific Rim writer. Because he wrote about so many different peoples, a constant element in his work is race. Toward the end of his life, he joined a movement called the Pan-Pacific Union, which was composed of businessmen determined to achieve strong connections with all Pacific Rim countries, especially Japan. London advocated that American children be taught Japanese and Japanese children English.

London's major themes include three that pervade especially his short fiction: the Imagination, Community, and Justice. It is imagination that allows for adaptivity to environment and hence survival. It is community that keeps a man or woman with a trail mate, so that both may survive. And it is justice that is usually at issue, whether in a stifling courtroom in Tahiti or in a miners' meeting in the goldfields of the far North. London's style is most often called naturalistic, that is, focused on physical survival and struggle against natural forces, but it is also described as romantic, as any reader of *The Call of the Wild* can attest. London is difficult to pigeonhole because he wrote so much (50 books in 16 years) and wrote on such diverse topics. What remains constant is a devotion to realism, to opening readers' eyes to things they fail to see every day (the plight of the poor at the hands of the era's robber baron capitalists) or things they had never imagined (cannibalism in Fiji). London was open to life and to people and to characters of all types; a restless man, he seemed never to slow down or stop working, stop traveling, stop creating. Indeed, it is fair to say that London's early death at the age of 40 was in part brought on by his excesses of one kind or another. Nevertheless, his spirit of adventure and human curiosity lives on in his extraordinary body of work.

Although much has been written about London, the vast majority of published criticism dwells on only a handful of works, especially the Klondike stories, *The Call of the Wild*, *Martin Eden*, *The Iron Heel*, and *The Sea-Wolf*. This book, for the first time, offers a near-total look at London's entire literary oeuvre, from famous novels such as *The Call of the Wild* to lesser-known but significant works such as his Hawaiian short fiction. It provides context for understanding London's enormous popularity among readers—in his own day and in ours—by providing information on American literature and culture at the turn of the last century, especially literary naturalism; the ferment of ideas at the time from such thinkers as Marx, Darwin, and Freud; London's influences and connections to other writers; his family; his main themes, ideas, characters, and settings. This book is intended for the student and casual reader who wishes to learn more about London's life and work, as well as for the serious scholar-researcher looking for a convenient and comprehensive reference tool.

Portions of the entries on *The Call of the Wild* and *The Cruise of the* Snark appeared in different form in Jeanne Campbell Reesman's *Jack London's Racial Lives* (Athens: University of Georgia Press, 2009).

How to Use This Book

Part I of the volume offers an overview of London's life and career. Part II provides detailed synopses and commentaries for nearly all of London's 198 short stories, his 23 novels, and a generous selection of his nonfiction. It omits some little-read works, including three of his four plays, as they are truly obscure. Each entry for a work of fiction contains subentries describing the individual characters in the work, listed in the order of importance. Part III includes entries on people, places, and topics that are important to London's work. It covers biographical background and historical, literary, and intellectual influences on London. Throughout the text, references to entries in Part III are presented in SMALL CAPITAL LETTERS to indicate a cross-reference. Part IV contains a chronology of London's life and a bibliography of London's works and secondary sources.

A Note on Editions

All page numbers from London works cited in this book are from the following editions:

Novels
A Daughter of the Snows. Philadelphia, Pa.: J. B. Lippincott, 1902.
The Call of the Wild [novella]. New York: Macmillan, 1903.
The Kempton-Wace Letters (with Anna Strunsky). New York: Macmillan, 1903.
The Sea-Wolf. New York: Macmillan, 1904.
The Game [novella]. New York: Macmillan, 1905.

White Fang. New York: Macmillan, 1906.

Before Adam. New York: Macmillan, 1907.

The Iron Heel. New York: Macmillan, 1908.

Martin Eden. New York: Macmillan, 1909.

Burning Daylight. New York: Macmillan, 1910.

Adventure. New York: Macmillan, 1911.

The Abysmal Brute [novella]. New York: Century, 1913.

The Valley of the Moon. New York: Macmillan, 1913.

The Mutiny of the Elsinore. New York: Macmillan, 1914.

The Scarlet Plague. New York: Macmillan, 1915.

The Star Rover. New York: Macmillan, 1915.

The Little Lady of the Big House. New York: Macmillan, 1916.

Cherry [unfinished last novel by Jack London]. Edited by James Williams. *Jack London Journal* 6 (1999): 4–76.

Nonfiction

The People of the Abyss. New York: Macmillan, 1903.

War of the Classes. New York: Macmillan, 1905.

The Road. New York: Macmillan, 1907.

The Cruise of the Snark. New York: Macmillan, 1911.

John Barleycorn: Alcoholic Memoirs. New York: Century, 1913.

Jack London Reports: War Correspondence, Sports Articles, and Miscellaneous Writings. Edited by King Hendricks and Irving Shepard. Garden City, N.Y.: Doubleday, 1970.

No Mentor but Myself: A Collection of Articles, Essays, Reviews, and Letters, by Jack London, on Writing and Writers. New York: Kennikat Press, 1979. Reprinted in an expanded edition as *No Mentor but Myself: Jack London on Writers and Writing.* Edited by Dale L. Walker and Jeanne Campbell Reesman. Stanford, Calif.: Stanford University Press, 1999.

Fiction and Nonfiction

Revolution and Other Essays. New York: Macmillan, 1910.

Short Fiction

The Complete Short Stories of Jack London. Edited by Earle Labor, Robert C. Leitz, III, and I. Milo Shepard. 3 vols. Stanford, Calif.: Stanford University Press, 1993. (cited as *Stories*)

Letters

London, Jack. *The Letters of Jack London.* Edited by Earle Labor, Robert C. Leitz, III, and I. Milo Shepard. 3 vols. Stanford, Calif.: Stanford University Press, 1988. (cited as *Letters*)

Play

The Acorn Planter: A California Forest Play—Planned to Be Sung by Efficient Singers Accompanied by a Capable Orchestra. New York: Macmillan, 1916.

PART I

Biography

Jack London

(1876–1916)

Jack London was born John Griffith Chaney on January 18, 1876. His parents, FLORA WELLMAN (later LONDON) and WILLIAM HENRY CHANEY, lived together in a common-law marriage in the bohemian world of San Francisco. Thus, London was born out of wedlock, a fact he did not discover until he was 21. He thought all along that the man Flora had married when he was nine months old, JOHN LONDON, was his true father. Actually, no one really knows who his biological father was, but Flora named Chaney, an itinerant astrologer who called himself "Professor" Chaney. His specialty was reading a couple's horoscope to determine the most auspicious time for mating to create the most gifted children; ironically, when Flora told him she was pregnant, he told her to have an abortion. When she refused, he left her, and she responded with a possibly faked suicide attempt, grazing her head with a bullet fired from a gun. Flora had been brought up in the upper middle class of Massillon, Ohio, but had moved west as a young woman. Despite her unconventional beliefs (she led séances to earn part of her living), when she became pregnant she expected to be supported.

When her son was nine months old, Flora met John London, a Civil War veteran who had brought his three children west to CALIFORNIA following the death of his wife. His son, Charles, died soon after the move, and he put his two girls, Ida and Eliza, in school while he sought out what work he could get in OAKLAND; the war had left him partially disabled. He most likely met Flora through a mutual acquaintance, a fellow construction worker named Alonzo Prentiss, a biracial man who passed as white but who had a wife who was African American, whom he kept secret from most of his white friends. Flora knew Alonzo through his wife, VIRGINIA PRENTISS, for on the night London was born, Flora struggled terribly and was left seriously weakened by a difficult delivery and then afterward was unable to nurse her son. That same evening, Mrs. Prentiss lost a baby, and so the doctor suggested to Flora that Mrs. Prentiss help her

Portrait of Jack London by Arnold Genthe, ca. 1903 *(Huntington Library)*

as a wet nurse. This was the beginning of a close and loving relationship between little "Johnny," as he was called, and Mrs. Prentiss, with whom he lived until he was weaned and also at times later. London found his own mother cold and undemonstrative. By the time he was 21, he had had, so to speak, two fathers and two mothers, and the fact that one of these mothers was black and herself a former slave helped London later on to write about nonwhite heroes even as he valorized the English and Welsh stock of his "own" parents.

Despite the warm maternal care of Mrs. Prentiss nearly always available to him (the Prentisses sometimes moved to follow the Londons, as the latter tried out numerous ventures to make money, both in business in Oakland and farming in the countryside), London felt lonely and deprived as a child. Flora's restless temperament resulted in some disastrous business decisions, so that she was having to

A young Jack London with his dog, Rollo *(Huntington Library)*

give séances to earn a living, as well as having to rent out her son's bed. London himself was sent to work by the age of 10, and he was later to write movingly about the plight of the child laborer. London hated the fakery of the séance sessions and how his mother pretended to channel a Native American chief named "Plume," whose shrieks would drive him from the house. But mainly he felt rejected by his mother; according to him, he never received a caress from her, and she once called him "my badge of shame." She did, however, encourage his first efforts at writing. For his part, John London did his best, but he was never a reliable support for his family. Besides Mrs. Prentiss, London received loving and maternal attention from Eliza London, his stepsister, and the two remained very close until his death.

For someone who would later deeply value his home in SONOMA VALLEY, London as a boy was subjected to numerous moves from one rented

house to another in the Bay Area as his parents tried to make a living from contracting, selling sewing machines, farming, storekeeping, and raising livestock. London hated the countryside and, as a solitary youth, turned to books. He recalled being excited by WASHINGTON IRVING's romantic sketches in *Tales of the Alhambra* and OUIDA's *Signa.* He thrilled to CAPTAIN JAMES COOK's adventures in his *Voyages* and to Horatio Alger's stories of poor boys who become millionaires. When the family moved back to Oakland in 1885 after they lost their farm in Livermore, London discovered that he could check out all the books he wanted for free from the Oakland Public Library. These books gave him the basis for his education. He completed Cole Grammar School in Oakland and Oakland High School, which he attended at the age of 21, after his KLONDIKE and seafaring adventures, working as a school janitor to make ends meet. He ended up only attending one semester of college at the UNIVERSITY OF CALIFORNIA, BERKELEY, a lack of finances forcing him to drop out.

As a child and adolescent in Oakland, he knew well the factory, the saloon, and the docks. After school and odd jobs such as selling newspapers, working on an ice wagon, setting pins in a bowling alley, sweeping saloon floors, and doing yards, he resorted to gang life on the docks, leaving him little time for reading. Upon graduating from grammar school in 1889, he worked in a cannery to help support the family. He merely endured his life as one only of toil, a portrait he would later paint in his story "The Apostate." At one point he worked 18 hours a day stuffing pickles into jars; this experience in particular led to his lifelong hatred of physical labor. He would come to learn that as a youth of the lower class he was destined to be no more than a WORK-BEAST, an industrial slave. A growing sense of wanting to escape this life formed within him. At the age of 15, he borrowed $300 from Mrs. Prentiss to buy his first boat, a little sloop the *Razzle Dazzle,* he got cheap from one of his gang friends on the waterfront. Now calling himself "Jack" and not "Johnny," London joined a gang of oyster pirates who stole oysters from the company-owned beds to sell on the Bay Area docks. Though stealing oysters may sound a little trivial as a life of crime, London found himself among hardened criminals, some of whom were murderers, and he began to drink with them in the saloons, becoming a man by showing he could stand up to them and launching a lifelong habit of heavy drinking that would take a terrible toll on his health. He earned the sobriquet "Prince of the Oyster Pirates" and kept a mistress on his boat. Eventually, after a near-death by suicide in the cold waters of the Bay, he realized he had to leave the pirating life, and he joined the California Fish Patrol, capturing his former pirate friends. This was not something he wanted to do, but he was frightened by the prospect of an early death or prison. About these escapades he wrote juvenilia such as *The Cruise of the Dazzler* (1902) and *Tales of the Fish Patrol* (1905).

Just before he turned 17, London sailed on the sealing schooner SOPHIA SUTHERLAND as an able seaman. Hunting seals in the stormy North Pacific, London once again had to become a man, this time with the seasoned and gritty sailors he found

Jack London at age 17 as a sailor in Yokohama
(Huntington Library)

himself among. This seven-month voyage inspired his first published story, "A Typhoon Off the Coast of Japan" (1893), which won first place in a story-writing contest held by the SAN FRANCISCO MORN-ING CALL, in which London beat out graduates of Stanford and the University of California, netting the (back then) handsome sum of $25. This experience is also reflected in his novel, *The Sea-Wolf* (1904). Returning home, he got work—grueling work—in a jute mill and at the power plant of the Oakland Electric Railway, but, as he records in *John Barleycorn* (1913), this life repulsed him, and he headed out on the adventure trail again, this time as a hobo riding the rails east as part of a workers' army marching on Washington, D.C. Deserting COXEY'S ARMY, as it was called, at Hannibal, Missouri, he hoboed northeast on his own, finally being arrested for vagrancy and put in the Erie County, New York, penitentiary for a month for sleeping outside near Niagara Falls. It was in prison that London felt he woke up. Reflecting over his tramping experiences, he realized more than a few of the bare facts of life and realized he occupied the bottom tier of society. How to climb up? Physical labor, as he could see from John London's example, would only wear out the body and soul and leave an older worker with nothing. London resolved to return to California and hit the books—acquire an education and finish high school. His prison experience in New York also turned him into a socialist.

By 1895, he was back home reading everything he could get his hands on, CHARLES DARWIN's *On the Origin of Species*, HERBERT SPENCER's *First Principles*, KARL MARX's *The Communist Manifesto*. In high school, he began contributing sketches and essays to the student literary magazine, the *Aegis*. He joined the local branch of the Socialist Party, soon becoming one of its most popular speakers; he was called the "Boy Socialist" of Oakland and regularly exhorted passersby from street corners. In the summer of 1896, having crammed two years of high school into a few months, he took entrance exams and was accepted to the UNIVERSITY OF CALIFORNIA. However he found the curriculum disconnected from what he thought of as real life, its canons and theories either dry as dust or clearly being articulated only to support the interests of the ruling class. He dropped out, however, because he ran out of money. London never thought much of higher education. That, he believed, he could do on his own observing the facts of the environment around him and reading countless books. London was also never much of a sleeper and instead read well into the night, smoking his packs of unfiltered cigarettes and marking passages in books with burnt matches and using his endless supply of pencils and Big Chief notebooks. When he decided to launch his writing career, as he notes in *John Barleycorn,* he wrote everything: ". . . ponderous essays, scientific and sociological, short stories, humorous verse, verse of all sorts from triolets and sonnets to blank verse tragedy and elephantine epics in Spenserian stanzas. On occasion I composed steadily, day after day, for fifteen hours a day. At times I forgot to eat, or refused to tear myself away from my passionate outpouring in order to eat" (*John Barleycorn,* 221). But he earned nothing but rejection slips and repeatedly pawned his coat, his bicycle, even his typewriter. He was forced to return to manual labor, as in his stint in the laundry at the Belmont Academy, a private boys' school. It was intense, unremitting, thankless labor, as he relates of Martin Eden's service in a laundry in the novel by that name.

In 1897, another call to the road came in the dramatic form of the Alaska GOLD RUSH. His sister Eliza had married a much older man, CAPTAIN JAMES SHEPARD, who mortgaged his house and with his nephew headed for the gold country. This was the turning point in London's life and career. As he put it, "It was in the Klondike that I found myself. There, nobody talks, and everyone listens. There you get your perspective. I got mine" (*Jack London by Himself,* n.p.). After some prospecting and more loitering in the saloons of DAWSON to hear old-timers' tales in the spring, London, suffering from scurvy, departed the NORTHLAND on a 1,500-mile river-rafting trip from Dawson to ST. MICHAEL on the Bering Sea. On the way, he began to keep a notebook, commenting on people and situations he witnessed on the trip, including the lives of the NATIVES forever compromised by their contact with the invading whites, first RUSSIANS, then Americans and British. He recorded experiences there that would enrich his imagination and fuel his writing for the rest of his life.

In the fall of 1898, London returned to Oakland to find that John London had died and that he was now the main support of his family. He began to write even more furiously than before, turning out story after story, as he relates in *Martin Eden.* He had found his subject, and he finally got a break when the West Coast literary magazine OVERLAND MONTHLY accepted a story in 1899. By the next year, his work was appearing widely in prestigious literary magazines, including ATLANTIC MONTHLY, which published "An Odyssey of the North" in its January 1900 issue, a fitting way to acknowledge the new literature of a new age. In 1900, his first book, the short story collection *The Son of the Wolf,* was published by the Boston house of Houghton Mifflin.

On April 7, 1900, London married BESSIE MAE MADDERN, a young woman he had met through her former fiancé, who was killed in the Spanish-American War. Maddern tutored London in math for his university entrance exams. London had been having a love affair with a young Stanford graduate ANNA STRUNSKY, but when she seemed coy at the moment he asked her to marry him, London angrily turned away and abruptly decided to marry for biological purposes and not for love. This debate is the subject of the book London and Strunsky had coauthored, *The Kempton-Wace Letters.* He told Bessie he was marrying her to produce sturdy ANGLO-SAXON children and not for love, and for some reason she agreed. The couple had two daughters, Joan and Becky, soon after.

Though he was receiving acclaim for his writing, London's personal life was undergoing strain. Bessie, serious and steady, did not like Jack's bohemian artist friends. They began to draw apart. Just before he left for LONDON, ENGLAND, in 1902, he told Anna that his marriage was a sham and that he wanted to run away with her to be married in Australia or some other exotic place, to which she agreed. However, as letters between them reveal, once in England, London received the unwelcome news that she was done with him, for, having thought that he and Bessie were truly apart in the months before, Anna was angry and shocked to discover that Bessie was pregnant with their sec-

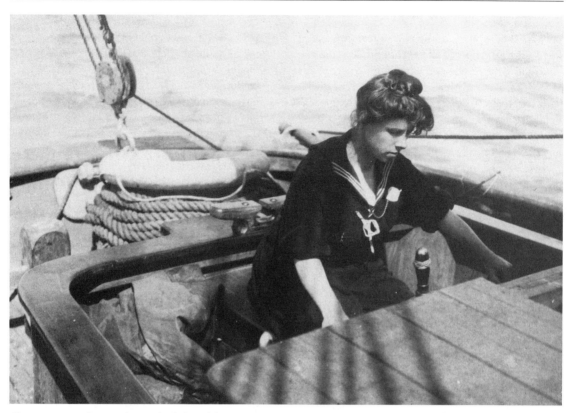

Charmian Kittredge London at the helm of the *Snark,* ca. 1908 *(Huntington Library)*

ond child. When in 1904 Bessie finally filed divorce papers while London was in KOREA as a war correspondent in the RUSSO-JAPANESE WAR, she named Anna as another kind of "correspondent," but she had missed the fact that London and Anna were no more. Instead, he had fallen in love with CHARMIAN KITTREDGE, a niece of a woman who interviewed him for the *Overland Monthly.* Theirs was an immediate, torrid, and lifelong love affair. As soon as his divorce was final in 1905, he married Charmian. Although she made him happy, his access to his daughters was restricted: he could only see them when he visited Bessie's home. Bessie forbade them to go to the ranch in Sonoma Valley the Londons bought as long as Charmian, whom she called "the Beauty," was there. Ironically, the ranch in GLEN ELLEN, CALIFORNIA, was named the BEAUTY RANCH. Strunsky and the Londons remained lifelong friends, Strunsky writing about London in reviews, obituaries, and her personal memoirs.

London's fame spread farther and wider. Known for his Northland saga of novels and stories, such as *Children of the Frost, The God of His Fathers and Other Stories, The Faith of Men and Other Stories,* and the world classics *The Call of the Wild* and *White Fang,* London added to his locales the high seas with his sensationalistic novel of brutality and love, *The Sea-Wolf.* He advanced themes of ATAVISM, primitivism, DETERMINISM, race battles, and SOCIALISM. He mingled REALISM and NATURALISM with folk motifs, myth, and supernaturalism. His reading of such thinkers as Darwin, Marx, SIGMUND FREUD, Spencer, THOMAS HENRY HUXLEY, JOHN FISKE, and ERNST HAECKEL lent intellectual depth and nuance to his writing, as did his broad background in reading literary classics. He defined himself as a "materialistic monist," or thoroughgoing determinist, but he often betrayed a more romantic, spiritual, or even religious side. London could not accept conventional CHRISTIANITY because he saw, like MARK TWAIN, the church as only another support for the power structure and of little aid to the poor, and because he detested the "spiritual" side of his mother's nature. Later in his life, he would read the works of CARL JUNG, who with his "collective unconscious" and "archetypes" of myth drew London out spiritually and influenced his last short stories of 1916, among his finest and most psychologically and culturally keen writings.

A sense of London's romantic or spiritual side is perhaps most memorably expressed in the following passage from his haunting story "The White Silence":

> The afternoon wore on, and with the awe, born of the White Silence, the voiceless travelers bent to their work. Nature has many tricks wherewith she convinces man of his finity,—the ceaseless flow of the tides, the fury of the storm, the shock of the earthquake, the long roll of heaven's artillery,—but the most tremendous, the most stupefying of all, is the passive phase of the White Silence. All movement ceases, the sky clears, the heavens are as brass; the slightest whisper seems sacrilege, and man becomes timid, affrighted at the sound of his own voice. Sole speck of life journeying across the ghostly wastes of a dead world, he trembles at his audacity, realizes that his is a maggot's life, nothing more. Strange thoughts arise unsummoned, and the mystery of all things strives for utterance. And the fear of death, of God, of the universe, comes over him,—the hope of the Resurrection and the Life, the yearning for immortality, the vain striving of the imprisoned essence,—it is then, if ever, man walks alone with God (*Stories*, 143–144).

Toward the middle of his career, another memorable passage showing his descriptive powers and sense of myth occurs in "Koolau the Leper":

> The far head of Kalalau Valley had been well chosen as a refuge. Except Kiloliana, who knew back-trails up the precipitous walls, no man could win to the gorge save by advancing across a knife-edged ridge. This passage was a hundred yards in length. At best, it was a scant

twelve inches wide. On either side yawned the abyss. A slip, and to right or left the man would fall to his death. But once across he would find himself in an earthly paradise. A sea of vegetation laved the landscape, pouring its green billows from wall to wall, dripping from the cliff-lips in great vine-masses, and flinging a spray of ferns and air-plants into the multitudinous crevices. During the many months of Koolau's rule, he and his followers had fought with this vegetable sea. The choking jungle, with its riot of blossoms, had been driven back from the bananas, oranges, and mangoes that grew wild. In little clearings grew the wild arrowroot; on stone terraces, filled with soil scrapings, were the taro patches and the melons; and in every open space where the sunshine penetrated, were papaia trees burdened with their golden fruit. (*Stories*, 442)

The very last story he wrote, "The Water Baby," only weeks before he died, contains much that he drew from ancient Hawaiian MYTHOLOGY, such as this passage spoken by an old Hawaiian fisherman, Kohokumu, whose name means "tree of knowledge," and who speaks to a dissipated and doubtful white interlocutor named "Lakana," London's Hawaiian name. Kohokumu speaks of the mythic life and of spiritual existence outside Lakana's experience:

> "But listen, O Young Wise One, to my elderly wisdom. This I know: as I grow old I seek less for the truth from without me, and find more of the truth from within me. Why have thought this thought of my return to my mother and of my rebirth from my mother into the sun? You do not know. I do not know, save that, without whisper of man's voice or printed word, without prompting from otherwhere, this thought has arisen from within me, from the deeps of me that are as deep as the sea. I am not a god. I do not make things. Therefore I have not made this thought. I do not know its father or its mother. It is of old time before me, and therefore it is true. Man does not make truth. Man, if he be not blind, only recognizes truth when he sees it. Is this thought that I have thought a dream?" (*Stories*, 2,488–2,489)

London's combination of naturalism and romance is never more powerful, however, than in *The Call of the Wild*, wherein the tame dog Buck transforms himself into a wild wolf through his experiences of struggle in the Northland as a sled dog. A classic in world literature, *The Call of the Wild* is a poetic journey of life and death with a near-universal Western thematic pattern of the myth of the hero. This hero finds himself being called to adventure, departing his homeland, suffering the initiations of numerous ordeals of survival, undertaking perilous journeys, and finding transformation and a final apotheosis as his true wild self in the end. Perhaps London was struggling to escape his marriage and longing for the adventure trail once again, but he created a work of enduring greatness read by the young and the old. It is the story of discovering who you were meant to be. In the end, despite his love for his master, John Thornton, Buck must sever all ties with man and join the pack of his fellows, becoming a legend among the Natives, "a great, gloriously coated wolf, like, and yet unlike, all other wolves . . . running at the head of the pack through the pale moonlight or glimmering borealis, leaping gigantic above his fellows, his great throat a-bellow as he sings a song of the younger world, which is the song of the pack" (*The Call of the Wild*, 231). In a different way, *White Fang* explores some of these naturalistic and romantic ideas, this time in the story of a wild wolf dog who is tamed by the love of a master who understands his wild nature.

The Call of the Wild was also shaped by his urgent need to escape from the work-beast class. This sense was intensified when, in 1902, London journeyed to London, England, en route to cover the Boer War in South Africa. The war having been concluded, he found himself at loose ends. He decided to disguise himself as an AWOL American sailor and, with clothes purchased off the street, entered the East End ghettos of London to write his sociological exposé, *The People of*

"A Chill, Raw Wind Was Blowing, and These Creatures Huddled There Sleeping or Trying to Sleep." Spitalfields Garden, London, England, 1902 *(Huntington Library)*

the Abyss, for which he also took photographs. As he wrote to Strunsky, "Am settled down and hard at work. The whole thing, all the conditions of life, the immensity of it, everything is overwhelming," both from a personal and a socialist point of view. How could the greatest empire in the world allow people to live in such degrading and hopeless slum conditions, to shiver homelessly in the cold streets, to starve their children? As he continues, "I never conceived such a mass of misery in the world before." The next week he wrote to say that his book was one-fifth done: "Am rushing, for I am made sick by this human hellhole called London Town. I find it almost impossible to believe that some of the horrible things I have seen are really so" (*Letters*, 306). His book was a pioneering work of sociological analysis combined with personal account, reflecting his immersion in his subject but also his American perspective on what he saw of

England. He urged English slum dwellers to emigrate to the American West where they could lead healthy, productive lives. He called *The People of the Abyss* his favorite among his books.

Returning home, his marriage collapsed, he fell in love with Charmian; he rented a small cabin near her in Sonoma Valley (the landlords were NINETTA and ROSCOE EAMES, Charmian's aunt and uncle and publishers of the *Overland Monthly*). Charmian knew how to make the most of herself and was sexually uninhibited. They fell deeply in love, and, unlike Bessie, though she sometimes resented London's lively "Crowd," as he called them, nearly all artists and writers, she put up with them and impressed them with her independent spirit. For him she became the "mate-woman" he had dreamed of, a true comrade for his adventures and a love-mate for life. Moving into an apartment in Oakland away from Bessie, he finished *The Sea-*

Russo-Japanese war correspondent Jack London, holding camera, with Japanese officers, Korea, 1904 *(Huntington Library)*

Wolf and left its proofs in the hands of Charmian and his poet-friend, GEORGE STERLING, to accept an assignment for the Hearst syndicate to cover the Russo-Japanese War brewing in Korea. Perhaps again he felt he needed to get away from events unfolding at home.

In early January 1904, London sailed on the SS *Siberia* for Yokohama, Japan, familiar to him from his days frequenting its dockside bars when he was on the *Sophia Sutherland*. He had written some touching stories about the lives of ordinary Japanese there, but this time he was met with official resistance. Within days of his arrival in Japan, he was arrested for accidentally photographing what he learned was a military installation in Moji. He was eventually released with a fine and his camera was returned. On the battlefields of Korea and Manchuria, he went on to return battlefield dispatches and photographs to Hearst, while also, since he was often prevented from getting to the front, taking photographs and writing dispatches about the people behind the lines, ordinary Japanese soldiers with bleeding feet, exasperated Korean villagers down to their last provisions, lines of refugees moving up and down the frozen roads, beggar children and old men on the streets of Seoul. He returned home in June, after an incident in which London struck a Korean stable worker and was arrested. President THEODORE ROOSEVELT intervened to obtain his release, which was conditioned on his leaving the country.

In spring 1905, London ran unsuccessfully for the mayor of Oakland on the Socialist ticket; in June, he purchased the 130-acre Hill Ranch, near GLEN ELLEN, the first parcel of what would grow over the years into his 1,400-acre model ranch, where he practiced scientific horticulture and land management, including organic farming, and raised wheat, grapes, sorghum, and other crops, as well as breeding champion pigs, bulls, and horses. Charmian and Jack were married, and he produced some of his best fiction that same year, "All Gold Canyon," "The Unexpected," and *White Fang.* Later in the fall, he embarked on a lecture tour for the INTERCOLLEGIATE SOCIALIST SOCIETY and toured the country, rousing the privileged students of Yale and Harvard to embrace his cause (if only momen-

The ruins of San Francisco City Hall after the earthquake of 1906 *(Huntington Library)*

tarily): Either fight for us, he declaimed, "or fight against us—of course, sincerely fight against us, believing that the right conduct lies in combating socialism because socialism is a great growing force. But what we do not want is that which obtains today and has obtained in the past of this university, a mere deadness and unconcern and ignorance so far as socialism is concerned. Fight for us or fight against us! Raise your voice one way or the other; be alive!" *(Jack London at Yale,* 19–20). That year he was elected president of the society, with UPTON SINCLAIR as vice president.

London's socialist speeches led to the character of revolutionary leader Ernest Everhard in the novel

The Iron Heel. London gave all of his best speeches to Everhard. The story is told in retrospect by his widow, Avis Everhard; the combination of her sentimental devotion and Ernest's harangues causes the book to lose some dramatic drive, but it is a compelling DYSTOPIAN look at what London imagined as the American 1930s and a chilling portrayal of the lengths capital went to suppress labor in his day. Perhaps also the apocalyptic theme of this novel was in part inspired by the 1906 SAN FRANCISCO EARTHQUAKE, which London covered for *Collier's.*

London's next novel is described by critics as his masterpiece, *Martin Eden.* The book tells of a young sailor, resembling London, who becomes a famous writer and wins the love of his impossible dream, Ruth Morse, an ethereal blonde from the top tier of society. However, Martin is disillusioned with success when he realizes she prizes him only for his fame, and he commits suicide (which has led to confusion over whether London did as well).

London said many times that Martin failed because he did not become a socialist when he was offered the opportunity and so died from the disease of Nietzschean INDIVIDUALISM. Most readers do not seem to focus on this, instead mourning his death as the hero of a tragic bildungsroman aimed at the notion of success in modern, materialistic America.

Martin Eden was written while London, Charmian, and a small crew had embarked on what was proposed as a seven-year, around-the-world cruise on a sailboat London had had built, the 42-foot ketch SNARK. Having been inspired by their reading of CAPTAIN JOSHUA SLOCUM's book about his round-the-world sail, they decided to embark on what would prove to be the most personally and artistically fulfilling passage of London's life and career. Though the voyage ended after nearly two years due to tropical illnesses, it was a tremendous education for London on the lives of diverse and fascinating peoples. Again he photographed pro-

Snark at anchor, 1907 *(Huntington Library)*

digiously and illustrated his many magazine travel pieces and essays as well as his volume of travel narrative, *The Cruise of the* Snark, alongside his dramatic descriptions of the lives of the islanders they encountered, from HAWAI'I south to the MARQUESAS, the Society Islands, including TAHITI and BORA BORA, SAMOA, FIJI, the Gilbert Islands, the SOLOMON ISLANDS, and other spots. The farther west they went in the South Pacific, the wilder the cultures were, with head-hunting, constant war, and CANNIBALISM. But London generally writes of even the most savage protagonists with a sympathetic point of view; one thing the islanders all had in common were the results of white invasion and colonization, including more wars, being kidnapped as slaves, having their chiefs deposed, having lands taken from them, and suffering imported illnesses and diseases.

The *Snark* voyage was fraught with difficulties, from the unseaworthiness of the boat to the incompetence of the captain, Roscoe Eames, on the way to Hawai'i, to the later dangerous crossing from Hawai'i to the Marquesas. But the most lasting problem that arose from the voyage was the tropical diseases London and his crew contracted. London seemed to suffer the most, especially from a type of flesh-eating bacteria he contracted in the Solomons called yaws or Solomon Island sores. The treatment was to apply corrosive sublimate of mercury, which London used in great amounts, never one not to go to excess. It is now the opinion of medical doctors who have researched his untimely death from uremia, or kidney failure, eight years after the *Snark* voyage, that his death was caused by mercury damage to his kidneys. Nevertheless, in his fiction, the South Seas holds forth the promise of regeneration in a climate of warmth, beauty, and life abundant; he fell in love with the Hawaiian Islands in particular and returned there twice in 1915–16 for health reasons. He saw in Hawai'i both the toll taken by whites and the possibility of a true melting pot of racial identities in a place that was for him a flower-swept paradise of good health. Yet his Hawaiian stories do not tell a happy tale: From "The House of Pride" to "Koolau the Leper" to "Shin Bones," they relate the decline of ancient Hawaiian ways and with them the sense of community post-coloniza-

Jack London and French Frank, an oyster pirate friend, reunited *(Huntington Library)*

tion. He was especially sympathetic to the lepers of Molokai, whom he visited twice and wrote about as human beings and not monsters.

Returning to his Sonoma Valley ranch, London healed from his illnesses and devoted most of his time to fulfilling his agrarian dream on the ranch. He increased the size of the ranch and carefully put in terraces, such as he had observed in the Orient, manure pits, a "pig palace," and planted grapes, prunes, and alfalfa on land thought to be hopeless. He built the first concrete-block silos in California and befriended the famous horticulturalist Luther Burbank. He began a series of Sonoma novels, *Burning Daylight*, *The Valley of the Moon*, and *The Little Lady of the Big House*, all of which urged the modern, urban man to rediscover himself by going back to the land and finding the love

Portrait of Jack London by Arnold Genthe, ca. 1904
(Huntington Library)

of a woman. By 1913, London's drinking having upset Charmian beyond her limit, especially on a trip they took to New York City in 1912, their marriage was in trouble. She nearly had two affairs, but she and London managed to overcome their problems. Thus, London developed the strong and healing heroines of the first two of these novels, Dede Mason and Saxon Brown Roberts, and the woman who sacrifices herself for her men, Paula Forrest of *The Little Lady of the Big House.*

His failing health—he suffered from edema, swollen ankles, bloated body, kidney stones, rheumatism—stemmed from his increasing kidney failure. He would not listen to his physicians and get more rest, stop drinking and smoking, and eat a healthier diet. The signal event of his last year was his discovery of the work of Carl Jung, which, to a dying man, held special resonance. He used the Polynesian myths he knew combined with Jung's archetypal insights to create some of his most powerful work. London died on the morning of November 22, 1916, on his wife's sleeping porch. Unable to rouse him for breakfast, his servant, Sekine, summoned Charmian and his stepsister Eliza London Shepard. Even though they walked him up and down the cottage's small corridor, he was paralyzed on one side probably due to a stroke brought on by kidney failure, and he did not regain consciousness. He was cremated, and his ashes were buried under a stone placed on a hillhock at the ranch, one too big for the builders of his dream house, Wolf House. With him, sealed beneath this rock, is an ilima lei from his friends in Hawai'i, symbolizing the importance of people in faraway places. Today, we not only remember him but continue to read his works. He is truly a writer for everyone, of whatever age, background, sex, or nationality. Jack London is America's best claim to a world author.

FURTHER READING

London, Jack. *Jack London by Himself.* Undated promotional pamphlet.
———. *John Barleycorn.* New York: Century, 1913.
———. *The Call of the Wild.* New York: Macmillan, 1903.
"Jack London to Yale Men." *Yale Alumni Weekly,* January 31, 1906. In *Jack London at Yale.* Edited by State Secretary of the Socialist Party of Connecticut. Westwood, Mass.: Connecticut State Committee, 1906.

PART II

Works A–Z

The *Abysmal Brute* (1913)

This tale of a handsome young BOXING sensation who not only wins all of his fights but takes on the corrupt boxing "game" itself was published as a book by CENTURY COMPANY in 1913; it first appeared in *Popular Magazine* in 1911. According to CHARMIAN LONDON, it was "hardly more than a long-short story, but subsequently published as a novelette—a cleanly conceived bit of propaganda for the purifying of the prize-ring" (*Book of Jack London*, 204).

Evidently, its plot was one of those London purchased from SINCLAIR LEWIS; on December 13, 1910, London wrote Lewis, "Remember your dress-suit pugilist story? Tomorrow I finish it. . . . But to save my own life I don't know what to make of it" (*Letters*, 957). He wrote Lewis again when the periodical version appeared, confessing that he modeled the character Sam Stubner on Sam Berger, a member of JIM JEFFRIES's training camp in Reno for the 1910 world heavyweight fight with JACK JOHNSON, which London covered for the HEARST SYNDICATE. London says of Berger, "I hear [he] is looking to punch my head off" (*Letters*, 1,022–1,023). London was also locked in a dispute with Century Company, to which he had turned after a spat with MACMILLAN; now he wished to return to Macmillan. Among other problems with Century, London was infuriated by the cheap appearance of *The Abysmal Brute* next to all his other books: "it is the two-by-four publisher trying to publish the stuff of an eight-by-ten writer." It is "the measliest, cheapest, scrubbiest book of all my books" (*Letters*, 1,175).

SYNOPSIS

Boxing promoter Sam Stubener receives a letter from a retired four-time world heavyweight champion "Old" Pat Glendon offering to introduce him to a new fighter he describes as "The greatest unknown that ever happened" (5), his son, Young Pat Glendon. Stubener travels to Glendon's home in the rugged logging country of northern CALIFORNIA. Old Pat describes his son: "'What do you think of a lad of twenty-two that's never had a drink in

his life nor tasted tobacco? That's him. He's a giant, and he's lived natural all his days. . . . He's a child of the open air, an' winter nor summer has he slept under a roof. The open for him, as I taught him'" (15). He praises his son's size, "Irish" strength, and boxing ability as well as his love of nature and poetry; but he adds that his son is "woman-shy." Glendon worries about how the city life will affect his son but urges Stubener to promote him.

Stubener's first glimpse of Young Pat Glendon impresses him deeply: "[A] young giant walk[ed] into the clearing . . . He seemed a creature of the wild, more a night-roaming figure from some old fairy story or folk tale than a twentieth-century youth" (21–22). Reluctantly—for despite his ability he doesn't really like boxing—Pat agrees to accompany Stubener to San Francisco to train. Before they depart, Old Pat warns Stubener:

> "The boy's clean an' he's honest. He knows nothing of the rottenness of the game. I kept it all away from him, I tell you. He don't know the meanin' of fake. . . . He don't know a man ever lay down or threw a fight. So don't turn the boy's stomach. . . . [Play] it square or you lose. Understand?" (31–32)

Despite his homesickness for the country, Pat is eager to fight, beginning with the champion Jim Hanford, but Stubener counsels him to start with some lesser names first to build his reputation. This he does, and in his first fight he knocks out his opponent with one blow to the jaw. The same thing happens in his subsequent fights, and he earns the nickname "One Punch Glendon." Stubener advises him to stop "'putting your men out so quickly'" (45). Audiences want a show, and other fighters will refuse to fight him. Pat apologizes to Stubener and explains that his is a natural gift that he can't help, but the two agree to let the next fight go for 15 rounds.

After an evening of attending a lecture on Browning at the Academy of Sciences, Pat faces the Flying Dutchman, who has never been knocked out, and defeats him: "It was after this battle that Pat Glendon started on his upward rush to fame" (60). In his second year of fighting, after finishing up the "second-raters," Pat moves on to the tier just under the champions. He travels around the country and the world, earning larger and larger purses and money from film rights. Pat and Stubener begin to grow rich; despite this, Pat remains aloof from the sporting world, taking up photography in addition to his other interests. He maintains his clean reputation and is dubbed by a newspaper reporter "the abysmal brute" because his reserve is perceived as "sullen and unsocial" and even "an ox-muscled and dumbly stupid brute" (66–67).

Pat becomes more interested in boxing as his opponents grow more difficult to defeat. He looks forward to the chance to fight the heavyweight champion, Hanford. "And all would have been well had not a certain society girl gone adventuring into journalism, and had not Stubener agreed to an interview with the woman reporter of the San Francisco 'Courier-Journal'" (70). This beautiful and wealthy young woman, Maud Sangster, represents the NEW WOMAN of the day; like Pat she is athletic and unconventional. She is also an artist. Their first meeting is a shock to them both, as they instantly connect with each other: "Here was a woman, a WOMAN. He had not known that such a creature could exist" (80). For her part, "To her it was delicious. A shy young man, with the body of a giant, who was one of the kings of bruisers, and who read poetry, and went to art exhibits, and experimented with color photography!" (87). However, during their conversation Maud reveals that she has heard from an editor that Pat would end the fight with Nat Powers in the 16th round, meaning that Stubener has told others of their private plans. He tells Maud that the fight will not end in that round, and she agrees not to publish the interview. Pat and Stubener fall out.

On the night of the Powers fight, Maud sneaks into the ringside disguised as a man; she sees in Pat "the thoroughbred" and in Powers "the abysmal brute": "Both looked their parts—Glendon, clean cut in face and form, softly and massively beautiful, Powers almost asymmetrically rugged and heavily matted with hair" (109). But in the 16th round, after a hit from Pat, Powers pretends to be knocked out, defeating Pat's plan. A beaming Stubener raises Pat's right glove and says, "'Good boy, Pat. I knew you'd do it.'" Pat responds, "'You go to hell'" (117).

Confronting Maud, Pat explains what happened. Then they truly fall in love. Against his growing awareness of the crooked nature of "the game," Pat realizes how naïve he has been. He and Maud leave the city and are married in Sacramento. Upon their return, Pat plans his revenge on Stubener by putting out his next opponent, Tom Cannam, in the first round. When he does, the crowd nearly riots, and a graft investigation of "the whole fight game" commences (142). Before the fight, Pat gives a speech to the crowd condemning the corruption in fighting; he is rushed by an infuriated Jim Hanford, whom Pat has accused of fixing their upcoming fight. Pat knocks him out easily and then knocks out Cannam quickly too once they begin to fight. Glendon is the city's hero, and he announces he will retire from the game for good. The story ends with Maud looking approvingly at her "young Hercules" (169).

COMMENTARY

One of the first boxing stories, *The Abysmal Brute* employs all the action of a blow-by-blow, round-by-round reporting technique for boxing London learned covering the Jack Johnson world heavyweight fights in 1908 and 1910, as well as the newspaper reportage he turned in as a young sports reporter for the EXAMINER (SAN FRANCISCO). A classic tale of purity against corruption, the novel pits its innocent but incredibly strong and morally upright hero against the corrupt betting machine of prizefighting, engaging in some muckraking as well as allowing its hero a splendid revenge against the boxing promoters. It is also a love story. As in "The Night-Born," an innocent young man is pitted against a corrupt world, but in this case he prevails. London creates an ideal hero in Pat, like himself a lover of literature and a sportsman, and an ideal woman in Maud, modeled on his wife Charmian. It thus combines a romantic hero with the gritty realism of the ring. The very title of the book indicates London's preoccupation with the concept of the "abysmal brute," which underlies the social behavior of men and animals alike. However, as he used the term, he means that his "brute" is uncivilized in the sense of being pure and unspoiled by society, a "natural" man who has little patience with the false values of money and fame. It also compares with such novels as *Burning Daylight* and *The Valley of the Moon,* in which a man is saved by the love of a woman he sees as his equal.

CHARACTERS

Pat Glendon Raised in the mountains of northern California, Pat is the son of "Old" Pat Glendon, a retired heavyweight champion, who trains his son to be the best fighter in the world. Pat is immensely strong but completely innocent of the world at the beginning of the story; he is devoted to art, poetry, and nature. Over the course of the story, he experiences an awakening into knowledge of the evil of the world when he realizes that his manager is fixing his fights. He retaliates by exposing the corruption and, after his last victory, retiring forever from the "game." He is an ideal London hero.

"Old" Pat Glendon At 81 years of age, the retired heavyweight champion has trained his son to be his successor and contacts a boxing manager to launch his son's career. He dies of a heart attack, but not until he realizes his dream has come true in his son.

Sam Stubener Stubener is an acquaintance of "Old" Pat Glendon and agrees to promote his son, Pat, which he does very successfully until Pat realizes that Stubener is crooked and has been telling other bettors how he and Pat have determined between them the round each fight will end in. He is humiliated and defeated at the end of the story, and he will doubtless be prosecuted for his crimes.

Maud Sangster Pat's love interest, Maud, is a beautiful, wealthy, adventurous young reporter in her 20s who meets him when she interviews him for a newspaper. She works at the paper because she resents her father's inheritance, and she has been bored by all the potential husbands she has seen. She is aroused by his reputation as the Abysmal Brute. She falls in love with Pat and helps him toward his final victory.

Tim Donovan A boxing colleague and friend of Stubener's who directs him to the Glendon home.

Jim Hanford World champion boxer Pat dreams of fighting but never does, as he retires before the match can be set. Probably modeled on Jim Jeffries, the "Great White Hope," who was defeated by Jack Johnson in 1910.

Chub Collins, Rough-House Kelly, the Flying Dutchman Low-level boxers Pat must fight before he can move up the ladder; they are called "little local dubs" by Stubener. Pat gets his first fight with Rough-House Kelly. He boasts to Pat, "'I'll eat yeh up, you pup!'" (40) but is felled with one blow to the jaw. Chub Collins is Pat's third fight, and he is down in 12 seconds. The Flying Dutchman, a young Swede with "phenomenal endurance" (56) who has never been knocked out, is Pat's first fight in which he agrees to prolong things until the last round.

Spider Walsh A trainer Stubener hires for Pat when he first starts out in the city's boxing world; he trains Pat in Contra Costa County across the bay from San Francisco.

Rufe Mason Pat's third fight, over in seconds.

Pete Sosso Pat's fourth match, a Portuguese from Butchertown known for his amazing tricks. Pat tries to prolong the fight for the exhibition but knocks Sosso out in the fourth round after Sosso tries to trick him.

Ben Menzies, Bill Tarwater Fighters referred to as "second-raters" whom Pat fights on the road and defeats.

Will King, Tom Harrison Accomplished fighters Pat defeats in England and Australia, respectively.

Henderson, Sulzberger, Kid McGrath, Philadelphia Jack McBride, Nat Powers, Tom Cannam Very accomplished fighters Pat has more trouble defeating on his way up. Powers is the opponent who makes a deal with Stubener without Pat's knowledge. Cannam is the fighter whom Pat defeats in his last fight.

Billy Morgan Fight announcer at the Golden Gate Arena, site of the Cannam match.

FURTHER READING

London, Charmian Kittredge. *The Book of Jack London.* 2 vols. New York: Century, 1921.

London, Jack. *The Letters of Jack London.* 3 vols. Edited by Earle Labor, Robert C. Leitz, III, and I. Milo Shepard. Stanford, Calif.: Stanford University Press, 1988.

————. *Sporting Blood: Selections from Jack London's Greatest Sports Writing.* Edited by Howard Lachtman. Novato, Calif.: Presidio Press, 1981, 15–24.

The Acorn Planter: A California Forest Play— Planned to Be Sung by Efficient Singers Accompanied by a Capable Orchestra (1916)

In his last year, London faced daunting challenges, the most significant being the decline in his health; in November of that year he would die of kidney failure. But he was also troubled by lawsuits over film rights, a loss of sales due to World War I, and his overall fears about the state of a world at war. In addition, the financial and physical demands of the BEAUTY RANCH and the support of several households wore on him. He jumped at the opportunity when San Francisco's BOHEMIAN CLUB invited him to write a play for their summer "Jinks" at their redwood grove near the Russian River. Unfortunately, London never saw his last and, today, his best-known play performed; the club rejected it ostensibly because it had no singers or orchestra, but probably more so because of its peculiar nature. Macmillan, as a favor to London, published the play, but printed only 1,350 copies, making it a collector's prize.

SYNOPSIS

The play is a mythic fantasy beginning "in the morning of the world" and concluding in its "Epilogue, or Apotheosis" with a celebration of the death of war, just as Red Cloud advocates. Though California is an ideal, even gardenlike setting, "[t]he warm and golden California land" (74), Red Cloud and his tribe, having visited the grove in different personas over thousands of years, are killed off by the whites and their land taken from them. The whites are called the "Sun Men" since they come from the south, and they prove inexorable enemies despite Indian attempts to drive their exploring parties away and even massacring them. The play ends on a note of affirmation, "The New Day dawns / The day of brotherhood / The day of man!" (81).

COMMENTARY

London brings together his two most troubling concerns of the time, the ranch and the war in his "nature play." However, its lack of action (it was to be chanted) and the strange paradox of praising the whites who destroy the original inhabitants of the forest, the Nishinam Indians, weaken it considerably, to say the least. London's racialist Anglo-Saxonism comes through, despite the play's ostensible optimism about the future, since, as Red Cloud surmises, now that the warrior whites have come they will also send their planters, and the land will be "honored." Since most of it is recited by NATIVES, it is hard to see the coming of the whites in California and the destruction of the Indians' world as a good thing. It may remind readers of Frank Norris's flimsy conclusion of *The Octopus* (1901), in which the annual planting of the wheat—no matter by whom and no matter the cost to small ranchers—is seen as hope for the future by Presley, heading to Asia to try to arrange the distribution of U.S. wheat. There are also the problems of its stylistic eccentricity, its contrived song lyrics, its stereotypes of Indians, and its glaring SOCIAL DARWINISM. However, one note that is sounded may surprise: Red Cloud praises the Sun Men because they allow the wisdom of women to be admitted to their councils, unlike the Indians. Yet the reader is mostly left with the amoral triumph of the whites: as the Sun Men chant,

> Our brothers will come after,
> On our trail to farthest lands;
> Our brothers will come after
> With the thunder in their hands.

Loud will be the weeping,
Red will be the reaping,
High will be the heaping
Of the slain their law commands. (53)

Though there is some sense of tragedy in the passing of the Indians, the tone of ANGLO-SAXON triumph is unsettling.

CHARACTERS

Red Cloud The philosopher, "the first man of men, and the first man of the Nishinam" (v), which seems to be a hereditary title passed down to generation after generation. Red Cloud argues against war and for agrarianism.

War Chief Like Red Cloud, a mythic figure represented by men of each generation, who "sings that war is the only way to life" (v).

Shaman The medicine man, who "sings of foreboding and prophecy" (v) and who eventually sides with the War Chief.

Dew Woman Like the three preceding characters, a type who represents religion and the interests of women.

Sun Men The whites who migrate to California and usurp the Indians.

People Made up of hunters, squaws, artisans—the entire Native community of the Nishinam.

FURTHER READING

Labor, Earle. "From 'All Gold Canyon' to *The Acorn-Planter*: Jack London's Agrarian Vision." *Western American Literature* 11 (Summer 1976): 83–102.

Adventure (1911)

This novel should have been an embarrassment for a writer whose direction seemed to be, during the voyage of the SNARK, toward a sense of brotherhood of humankind against the racialist projects

of white "others" who were colonizing the Pacific. Ill with multiple tropical diseases (especially yaws, or "Solomon Island sores," a flesh-eating bacterial infection of the skin and muscle) and contemplating the abandonment of their seven-year voyage after only two years, the Londons and their crew spent five months in the SOLOMON ISLANDS, with a home base at PENDUFFRYN PLANTATION on the island of GUADALCANAL. London grew discouraged as his illnesses multipled—but it is interesting that they spent the same amount of time in this hostile environment as they did in the balmy clime of HAWAI'I, only at the last possible moment ending the voyage in Sydney, Australia, in December 1908. The copra plantation they stayed on was managed by TOM HARDING and his partner GEORGE DARBISHIRE and their wives. (The Londons learned in 1914 that the Darbishires had been killed and eaten by plantation workers.) In a letter to Charles A. MacLean, publisher of the *Popular Magazine,* an action and adventure journal that serialized *Adventure* (after London had much trouble placing it), London says he wrote the major portion of *Adventure* while "right on the ground, so that the red raw savagery I have described is the real thing. After getting part-way through the book, I fell victim to a multiplicity of ills which sent me to the hospital in Sydney and compelled me to abandon the voyage. To this day my wife and I, and the cabin-boy of the *Snark* who is still with us, are fighting the fever we contracted in the Solomons" (*Letters,* 863).

London hated the Solomons for their brutality, CANNIBALISM, crushing colonialism, and disease. If his REALISM, NATURALISM, and sense of humor could portray the races as equally worthy in *A Son of the Sun,* here he justified the white man's actions as part of a grand race drama enacted within Western progress, despite its costs to blacks and whites. As Clarice Stasz observes, London "did not require consistency of himself" and wrote for different audiences, sometimes playing to popular notions of adventure: his "vacillation reflected that of the age" (139). In contrast to *A Son of the Sun, Adventure* has all the negative aspects of naturalism and ROMANTICISM as literary modes and none of their positive attributes. Its white "heroes" are unadmirable in the extreme; it is hard to believe they were created by the same person who wrote the short stories. It is a negative, bitter book, as though London wished to strike back at the Solomons for their deleterious effects upon his body and his plans.

SYNOPSIS

The novel tells of Berande Plantation in the Solomon Islands, owned by fever-stricken Dave Sheldon, whose partner dies and leaves him to manage the NATIVE contract workers who tend the coconut trees and make copra (dried coconut flesh used for fuel) from them, who are stirring toward revolt. He is saved by the arrival of Joan Lackland, a brave and beautiful young tomboy raised in Hawai'i, armed and self-sustaining. She becomes Sheldon's new partner, and together they try to maintain Berande and suppress the workers. In the end, they fall in love, despite the hopes of a second man, the adventurer John Tudor; the book concludes with Lackland telling Sheldon, "'I am ready, Dave.'"

Chapters 1–7

Sheldon is first seen riding on the back of one of his workers, too weak with fever to walk, ironically reflecting the white man's "dominance" in the Solomons. Sheldon is hardly presented as admirable, despising his workers sick with fever (as he is) even as he depends upon them. Weak as he is, he manages to have some workers beaten for their infringements. He awaits the return of Hughie Drummond, his partner, but is shocked when Drummond is brought home after a recruiting trip to MALAITA on a stretcher; he dies of black-water fever, which is also killing his workers. Sheldon collapses with fever as a terrible storm rages. Just in time, Joan Lackland appears in a whale boat with a crew of Tahitians, having been shipwrecked. She helps nurse Sheldon back to health, and he in turn educates her about the realities of the plantation. She tells of her upbringing on a ranch on the BIG ISLAND and displays her shooting skills. As they become acquainted, Sheldon is nonplussed by her independence; when he tells her he won't allow her to go to Guvutu, she is incensed at his masculine presumption and goes anyway. She also takes over the management of the house and to some extent the plantation, including burning down "the pes-

tilential hospital" (89). One evening, they rescue two female workers from being beaten to death by a gang of men. Challenged by the ringleaders, Bellin-Jama and his brother Carin-Jama, Sheldon fights with them, knocking Bellin out while Lackland shoots Carin. She is very disturbed by what she has witnessed and what she has done.

Sheldon disabuses Lackland of her view of workers as romantic primitives: "'You are used to Polynesians. These boys are Melanesians. . . . Really, you know, there is a vast difference. They possess no gratitude, no sympathy, no kindliness. If you are kind to them they think you are a fool. If you are gentle with them they think you are afraid. And when they think you are afraid, watch out, for they will get you'" (98–99). Even though Sheldon is right in his assessment of their hostility to whites (for their own very good reasons), Lackland again doesn't listen to Sheldon and embarks on her own trading and recruiting trips.

Chapters 8–19

Berande has a visit from a *Bounty* descendent, Christian Young, who dazzles Lackland but reports the dangerous news of a Native revolt against the plantations and the murder of Sheldon's trader at Ugi. Joan decides to leave Berande and start her own plantation, but Sheldon persuades her to stay. Then she says she'll go recruiting instead, over his protests. One night she is menaced by two boat carriers and the next day one's father, Telepasse, arrives with armed companions from Port Adams to demand payment for what he sees as insults against his son Gogoomy, whom Sheldon has punished. Lackland solves the crisis by throwing a stick of dynamite at Telepasse and his men. Sheldon unleashes his workers on them, who are "saltwater men" and who delight in beating the bushmen intruders. The final insult is Lackland's forcibly giving Telepasse a bath.

Sheldon plans to sell Berande. But instead, he and Lackland decide to partner in blackbirding and running the plantation. John Tudor's party arrives on a schooner; they leave on a gold-hunting expedition to the interior. Two months go by with no word of Tudor. Lackland leaves for a trip to Sydney to buy a schooner, and Sheldon realizes he has fallen in love with her. Captain Auckland of the *Martha* informs Sheldon that she has gone to Guvutu and has bought the *Martha* at auction, as it was stranded and looted on a reef near Poonga-Poonga. She also steals the *Flibberty-Gibbet* from Captain Oleson. Using her new ships, she sends horses, saddles, fruit trees, and corn to Berande. Joan returns to Berande with bushmen recruits, which surprises Sheldon, since bushmen don't usually recruit. Captain Munster of the *Flibberty-Gibbet* is amazed at Lackland's bravery: "'Gritty! She's the grittiest thing, man or woman, that ever blew into the Solomons'" (260). She calls her wheeling and dealing "'hustling American methods'" (268).

Chapters 20–27

Dave's desire for Joan grows, but he makes a mistake when he confesses to her that his dearest wish is "'for you, someday, when you are ready, to be my wife.'" She angrily accuses him of "'This taking for granted! When I am ready!'" (284). She rejects the idea and cries because it will spoil their partnership; she says she wants to be left alone and not hear "'marriage' and 'I want, I want,'" and Sheldon calls her "'positively soulless'" (288). But they make up and agree not to discuss it further. A series of thefts distracts them; the ringleader is Gogoomy, who avoids a beating at Lackland's insistence but is furious that he is fined three pounds. Lackland overhears Gogoomy making plans to murder them in their sleep; she confronts him and has to be rescued by Sheldon on horseback. Several workers depart with Gogoomy into the bush. Following with Lackland's Tahitians, they find that Gogoomy has killed a foreman named Kwaque and taken his head. Most of the runaways are captured. Binu Charley returns to Berande with the news that Tudor's expedition has been decimated by bushmen and that he has hidden an ailing Tudor in the jungle.

The climax occurs when Lackland, Sheldon, Lackland's Tahitians, some of the bushmen Berande workers, and a party of Poonga-Poonga saltwater men set off to rescue Tudor. Once in the bush, the narrator's tone changes to irony. Now the whites are off the plantation, and the jungle is in charge. As they penetrate farther and farther,

"their task was to carry the situation off with careless bravado as befitted 'big fella marsters' of the dominant breed" (337). As is so common in *Adventure*, here superiority is not earned but performed according to racial expectations.

A bushman is captured smoking a white head over a fire. The Poonga-Poonga men require little encouragement: "Their faces were keen and serious, their eyes eloquent with the ecstasy of living that was upon them; for this was living, this game of life and death, and to them it was the only game a man should play, withal they played it in low and cowardly ways, killing from behind in the dim forest gloom and rarely coming out into the open" (340). The "eloquent eyes" and "serious" faces almost justify them, and their "ecstasy of living" weirdly echoes the passage in *The Call of the Wild* when Buck experiences the ecstasy in the chase of the snowshoe rabbit. When the Poonga-Poonga boys find the head of Gogoomy, they laugh at "the funniest incident that had come under their notice in many a day. . . . Gogoomy had completed the life-cycle of the bushman. He had taken heads, and now his own head had been taken. He had eaten men, and now he had been eaten by men" (342).

In the end, Tudor is rescued, the only member of his nine-man party not to have had his head taken, and, his fever abated by Lackland's ministrations, he tries to make love to her. She refuses him but consents to marry Sheldon after he fights a duel with Tudor. The book ends back on the seacoast, traditional racial and gender order having been restored. Despite its sentimental ending, the confusion and bitterness of this book are what the reader remembers.

COMMENTARY

Stasz, one of the few critics to analyze *Adventure*, calls it "the nadir of London's longer tales, lacking character development and suspense," presenting racialism "without apology." As a parallel, Lackland sacrifices her criticisms of Sheldon and her female independence for marriage. Stasz attributes London's failure in *Adventure* to his view of it as a money-making diversion, his illnesses, and the general "vacillation and ambiguity of the age" when it came to gender and race. *Adventure* lacks "the most productive part of his creativity, his ability to identify with the character so completely that the reader participates in the character's journey" (Stasz, 132, 139–140). It is possible that *Adventure* is meant to be a satire, but this is hard to sustain given the novel's racism.

For example, early in the novel Sheldon is moved to share with Joan his vision of the South Seas of the future:

> "Give us fifty years, and when all the bush is cleared off back to the mountains fever will be stamped out, everything will be far healthier. There will be cities and towns here, for there's an immense amount of good land going to waste."
>
> "But it will never become a white man's climate, in spite of all of that," Joan reiterated. "The white men will always be unable to perform the manual labor."
>
> "That is true."
>
> "It will mean slavery," she dashed on.
>
> "Yes, like all the tropics. The black, the brown, and the yellow will have to do the work, managed by white men. The black labor is too wasteful, however, and in time Chinese or Indian coolies will be imported. The planters are already considering the matter. I, for one, am heartily sick of black labor."
>
> "Then the blacks will die off?"
>
> Sheldon shrugged his shoulders and retorted:
>
> "Yes, like the North American Indian, who was a far nobler type than the Melanesian. The world is only so large, you know, and it is filling up—"
>
> "And the unfit must perish?"
>
> "Precisely so. The unfit must perish." (*Adventure*, 113–114)

One thing London was proud of in *Adventure* was its realism and sense of place—a place virtually no Americans really knew. He was careful in his descriptions and made ample use of dialect with BÊCHE-DE-MER ENGLISH; for example, this exchange between Sheldon and a worker,

> "'What name you sing out alla time?' he demanded.

> 'Him fella my brother belong me,' was the answer. 'Him fella die too much.'
>
> 'You sing out, him fella brother belong you die too much,' the white man went on in threatening tones. 'I cross too much along you. What name you sing out, eh? You fat-head make um brother belong you die dose up too much. You fella finish sing out, savvee? You fella no finish sing out I make finish damn quick. . . . Sing out no good little bit,' the white man went on, more gently. 'You no sing out. You chase um fella fly. Too much strong fella fly. You catch water, washee brother belong you; washee plenty too much, bime bye brother belong you all right. Jump!'" (7)

CHARACTERS

Dave Sheldon   An Englishman, he is the proprietor of Berande Plantation on Guadalcanal who falls prey to fever and is rescued by and eventually marries a wayfarer to the island, Joan Lackland. He is convinced of his right as a white man to dominate the Native workers.

Joan Lackland   Modeled on London's friend Armine von Tempsky, from a great ranch on Maui, the American Joan is a Hawaiian kamaʻāina haole and a fearless tomboy. With Dave she matures into a partner—though one equal to her "mate"—and helps Dave reestablish the plantation. She is able to command a crew of Hawaiians and Tahitians and wears her independence with her Baden-Powell hat, breeches, and Colt revolver. She is a model of the NEW WOMAN.

John Tudor   A gold-hunter and adventurer who visits Berande and Guadalcanal. He tries to make love to Joan but has to be rescued and tended by her after he is attacked by bushmen and then fights with Sheldon. Altogether a foolish figure of the gentleman adventurer.

Angara   A sick plantation worker. Dave demands of him, "'What for talk long you, eh? I knock seven bells out of you, too much, quick!'" (5).

Seelee   Chief of Balesuna village who shelters runaways from Berande and is punished.

Berande workers Many plantation workers in the Solomon Islands were "recruited" to a particular plantation from other nearby islands, and most of them were saltwater men from the villages near the water. They were ancient enemies of the bushmen. In one scene, Sheldon orders three of his workers, Billy, Narada, and Astoa, to beat Arunga, who has displeased Sheldon. Noa Noah is a trusted worker. Manonmie is fined for stealing. Others, like Gogoomy, are more of a problem, but all are threatening.

bushmen Living in the highlands and mountains of the Solomon Islands and almost never interacting with whites. When whites do penetrate the bush, they rarely come back. Bushmen were the enemies of the saltwater men and raided plantations to capture them.

house servants Lalaperu, Ornfiri, and Viaburi, who are sent after Gogoomy.

Hughie Drummond Dave's partner who dies of black-water after after a recruiting trip to Malaita.

Captain Oleson Captain of the *Jessie*, a BLACK-BIRDER (or "recruiting") ship. His brother Pete Oleson is another boat captain, stricken like Sheldon with fever. Joan steals his new ship, the *Flibberty-Gibbet*.

Bellin-Jama A fieldworker who is the leader of the men beating the two women. He challenges and fights with Sheldon along with his brother, Carin-Jama.

Christian Young *Bounty* descendant who visits Berande and brings news of a workers' uprising nearby.

Aroa Boat-carrier who demands trade goods from Lackland in exchange for taking his fever medicine.

Gogoomy Also makes demands of Lackland and swears revenge on her and Sheldon for fining him for stealing. Gogoomy leads the runaway workers into the bush but has her head taken by bushmen.

Morgan and Raff Visitors who arrive at Berande on the schooner *Malakula* to whom Sheldon has offered the sale of the plantation.

Von Blix Partner of John Tudor; a German, "rough and boorish" (185).

Utami/Joe One of Lackland's Tahitian sailors who knows Tudor, having once saved his life.

Captain Auckland Skipper of the *Malakula*.

Welshmere Missionary doctor.

Lackland's recruits Tagari, Ogu. Most, like Ogu, are bushmen.

Captain Munster Lackland's captain aboard the *Flibberty-Gibbet*.

Sparrowhawk Mate of the *Flibberty-Gibbet*.

Mahua Body servant to Lackland.

Kwaque Sheldon's gang-boss, decapitated by Gogoomy.

Binu Charley A saltwater man who accompanies the Tudor party to the interior.

Babatani One of Kwaque's men who tells Sheldon of Kwaque's death.

Papehara One of Lackland's Tahitians who tracks Gogoomy.

Koogoo Spokesman of the Poonga-Poonga saltwater men.

FURTHER READING

Ellis, Juniper. "'A Wreckage of Races' in Jack London's South Pacific." *Arizona Quarterly* 57, no. 3 (2001): 57–75.

Furer, Andrew. "'Zone-Conquerors' and 'White Devils': The Contradictions of Race in the Works of Jack London." In *Rereading Jack London*, edited by Leonard Cassuto and Jeanne Campbell Reesman,

158–171. Stanford, Calif.: Stanford University Press, 1996.

Phillips, Lawrence. "Violence in the South Sea Fiction of Jack London." *Jack London Newsletter* 16 (January–April 1983): 1–35.

———. "The Indignity of Labor: Jack London's *Adventure* and Plantation Labor in the Solomon Islands." *Jack London Journal* 6 (1999): 175–205.

Reesman, Jeanne Campbell. Chapter 4: "Jack London and the Past-Colonial Southern Pacific" in *Jack London's Racial Lives*. Athens: University of Georgia Press, 2009.

———. "Re-Visiting *Adventure:* Jack London in the Solomon Islands." *Excavatio* 17, nos. 1–2 (2002): 209–237.

Stasz, Clarice. "Social Darwinism, Gender, and Humor in *Adventure*." In *Rereading Jack London,* edited by Leonard Cassuto and Jeanne Campbell Reesman, 130–140. Stanford, Calif.: Stanford University Press, 1996.

"All Gold Canyon" (1905)

First published in the *Century Magazine* 71 (November 1905), "All Gold Canyon" appeared in *Moon-Face and Other Stories* (1906). In the weeks before he finished it, London and his second wife, Charmian, had been engaged in buying an adjacent ranch and making new plans for a barn and a house. Soon, he would begin writing *White Fang.* "All Gold Canyon" reflects, in beautiful prose, London's awakening sense of beauty in nature, especially in California, as well as his growing determination as a rancher to farm organically and preserve the land through practices such as terracing. The conflict that takes place in this story involves humankind's relationship to the land.

SYNOPSIS

Into a Sierra valley's peaceful somnolence, Bill, a "pocket-miner," intrudes. He sings songs about "them sweet hills of grace" and his steel-soled shoes ring out loudly in the small and lush valley. He is delighted with the scene, which he calls "a cayuse's paradise" (1,019) (*cayuse:* skilled horseman named after the Cayuse Indians). Bill "had the habit of soliloquy," and he talks admiringly about what he sees in his test of the stream for gold. He keeps working farther and farther up the mountain, and as he keeps telling "Mr. Pocket" he will find him, he starts to find greater and greater concentrations of gold in his pan. Obsessively, he works, long after sunset, looking for the apex of the inverted V with tireless and careful crosscutting that will lead him to the heart of the gold vein. Somewhat crazed, he digs "with pick and shovel gouging and mauling the soft brown earth. . . . Before him was the smooth slope, spangled with flowers and made sweet with their breath. Behind him was devastation. It looked like some terrible eruption breaking out on the smooth skin of the hill. His slow progress was like that of a slug, befouling beauty with a monstrous trail" (1,026). The next morning, he slides down a side of the canyon and finds his mine, with huge nuggets of gold; he christens the canyon "All Gold Canyon." Suddenly, he feels a premonition of danger and realizes someone is behind him. When the man jumps into the hole, Bill hits him, and they fight for the man's gun. Bill kills the stranger and realizes he has been shot in the back. He buries the body, eulogizing: "'An' you shot me in the back!'" (1,033). "The measly skunk," he thinks, as she forces his horses back down the mountain and out of the valley with his treasure and his aching back. As his song fades down the mountain, the canyon returns to its silence and peace: "Only remained the hoof-marks in the meadow and the torn hillside to mark the boisterous trail of the life that had broken the peace and passed on" (1,034).

COMMENTARY

The opening two paragraphs of the story are some of London's most evocative nature writing:

> It was the green heart of the canyon, where the walls swerved back from the rigid plan and relieved their harshness of line by making a little sheltered nook and filling it to the brim with sweetness and roundness and softness. Here all things rested. Even the narrow stream ceased its turbulent down-rush long enough to form a

quiet pool. Knee-deep in the water, with drooping head and half-shut eyes, drowsed a red-coated, many-antlered buck.

On one side, beginning at the very lip of the pool, was a tiny meadow, a cool, resilient surface of green that extended to the base of the frowning wall. Beyond the pool a gentle slope of earth ran up and up to meet the opposing wall. Fine grass covered the slope—grass that was spangled with flowers, with here and there patches of color, orange and purple and golden. Below, the canyon was shut in. There was no view. The walls leaned together abruptly and the canyon ended in a chaos of rocks, moss-covered and hidden by a green screen of vines and creepers and boughs of trees. Up the canyon rose far hills and peaks, the big foothills, pine-covered and remote. And far beyond, like clouds upon the border of the sky, towered minarets of white, where the Sierra's eternal snows flashed austerely the blazes of the sun. (1,017)

A primal act of murder takes place in this idyllic setting, but because Bill respects the mountain he is spared and he restores, with his departure, the canyon to its peace. The idea seems to be that condemnable as the act of despoiling the mountains of gold might be, there are still codes of behavior among men and the ability of the natural world to restore itself once the deeds of men are done. There is a lack of communion with nature, as Bill's song rudely interrupts the canyon as his pick and shovel disembowel the mountain. Still, he seems through his lack of guile to be closer to the spirit of the canyon than the man who tries to kill him from behind in cold blood to steal his gold. Nevertheless, one is left with the sense that "raping" nature for gold at all is man's sin, and that nature would be better off without his technological interruptions or his sins. The sense that nature looks on disapprovingly at the attempted murder between the men is reinforced by the narrator's constant references to the position of the SUN as heaven's witness and the deliberate description of the canyon as symbolic of female sexuality. The very next tale London wrote, "Planchette," tells of the mysterious death of a young man determined to marry a SONOMA VALLEY

woman; however, he somehow fails the "test" the land puts on him.

CHARACTERS

Bill   The pocket-miner who prospects in the canyon: "He was a sandy-complexioned man in whose face geniality and humor seemed the salient characteristics. It was a mobile face, quick-changing to inward mood and thought. Thinking was in him a visible process. Ideas chased across his face like wind-flows across the surface of a lake. His hair, sparse and unkempt of growth, was as indeterminate and colorless as his complexion. It would seem that all the color of his frame had gone into his eyes, for they were startlingly blue. Also, they were laughing and merry eyes" (1,019). Bill is attacked from behind by a stranger but kills him and escapes with his find.

stranger   Follows Bill and tries to kill him but instead is killed by Bill. His cowardly approach includes shooting Bill in the back.

"Aloha Oe" (1908)

This tale of love thwarted on racial grounds was first published in *Lady's Realm* (December 1908) in Britain and then in *Smart Set* 28 (May 1909) in the United States; it was included in *The House of Pride and Other Stories* (1912).

SYNOPSIS

On the dock at HONOLULU, the Royal Hawaiian Band plays "Aloha Oe" to the accompaniment of Hawaiian singers as a group of U.S. senators prepares to depart after a month's junket in the Islands. Beside her father, Senator Jeremy Sambrooke, Dorothy Sambrooke must say good-bye to her companion while in the Islands, Stephen Knight, a member of the entertainment committee for the congressional party. The two have fallen in love, but their union is forbidden by her father because Stephen, though well-placed in Honolulu society, is one-quarter Hawaiian: "He could have dinner with her and her father, dance with her, and be a member of the entertainment committee; but because there was tropic sunshine in his veins he could not marry her" (1,472). In their last moments together on the gangway, as "[s]tewards were going about nervously begging shore-going persons to be gone," Steve reaches for her hand. "When she felt the grip of the fingers that had gripped hers a thousand times on surf-boards and lava slopes, she heard the words of the song with a new understanding as they sobbed in the Hawaiian woman's silver throat. . . . Steve had taught her air and words and meaning, so she had thought, till this instant; and in this instant of the last finger clasp and warm contact of palms she divined for the first time the real meaning of the song" (1,469). "When would they ever meet again," she desperately wonders. At the end, seeing him below on the dock, she trembles as the words of the song speak of "my love to you." Seeing other passengers throw their garlands to friends below, she tries to throw hers, but it becomes entangled in her pearls. Without hesitating, she snaps the string of pearls "and, amid a shower of pearls, the flowers fell to the waiting lover." The crowd sings on: "Aloha oe, Aloha oe, e ke onaona no ho ika lipo / A fond embrace, ahoi ae au, until we meet again." But now, "still melting with the sensuous love-langor of Hawaii, the words [bit] into her heart like acid because of their untruth" (1,473).

COMMENTARY

Many of the stories in *The House of Pride* angered London's friends among the white elite of Honolulu. Some exposed leprosy and others criticized the white powers that ruled HAWAI'I at the expense of its NATIVES and Asian laborers. London wrote several stories about mixed-blood Hawaiians sympathetic to their struggles against racism. In this story, he both offers a touching romantic portrait of two "star-crossed" lovers and at the same time clearly shows the limited point of view and careless racism of the senator and the white Honolulu establishment. It also forecasts the end of the old Hawai'i replaced by the modern invasion of U.S. business interests and CAPITALISM. But he does not neglect to note how many prominent white Hawai-

ians have married Hawaiian women, which was not frowned upon—a white woman marrying a Hawaiian man is considered differently. Thus, there are two hypocritical double standards at work, both in race and in gender.

CHARACTERS

Dorothy Sambrooke The young daughter of a U.S. senator, Dorothy, is becoming a woman. Upon her arrival she is pale and tired, but her "cheeks were touched by the sun. . . . The tropics had entered into her blood, and she was aglow with the warmth and color and sunshine" (1,468), and her thoughts are only for her companion over the past month, Stephen Knight.

Senator Jeremy Sambrooke Dorothy's father, who forbids her union with Stephen Knight. The senator has a "stout neck and portly bosom" and a "sunburned and perspiring face." He has only a "statistical eye" for Hawai'i and even hates the flower leis around his neck; he sees only the opportunity for "the labor power, the factories, the railroads, and the plantations" the "multitude" of Hawaiians represent.

Stephen Knight A young and athletic man who is one-quarter Hawaiian, thus making him suitable as a temporary companion to teach Dorothy surfing but unsuitable for marriage.

"The Apostate" (1906)

Based on London's own experiences with CHILD LABOR, this moving story of a young boy's struggle to escape the life of the WORK-BEAST, as London called it, was first published in *Woman's Home Companion* 33 (September 1906) and later included in the collection *When God Laughs and Other Stories* (1911). Like *The Call of the Wild*, it displays features of the slave narrative in the sense that the main character, Johnny, must realize the hope of freedom within before he can physically escape the evils of the city and its factories; his, like Buck's, is a spiritual quest.

SYNOPSIS

With the opening words of the story, "'If you don't git up, Johnny, I won't give you a bite to eat!'" the reader immediately learns that Johnny is at the mercy of a hard world. His response to being dragged out of bed in the dark is "a cry that began, muffled, in the deeps of sleep, that swiftly rushed upward, like a wail, into passionate belligerence, and that died away and sank down into an inarticulate whine. It was a bestial cry, as of a soul in torment, filled with infinite protest and pain" (1,112). He rises and eats his meager breakfast after halfway washing himself at the cold and dirty sink. The factory whistle blows at 5:30, and he trudges in the dark toward his work; the narrator mentions that as he also leaves work after dark, he never sees daylight. He listens apathetically to the praise of the foreman, for he can repeat his movements over and over again at the bobbins without being conscious of it: "He was the perfect worker. He knew that. He had been told so, often. It was a commonplace, and besides it didn't seem to mean anything to him any more." Though some of the other boys resist and complain, "He had a way of accepting things" (1,116). He easily fools the inspector as to his real age, but the inspector does notice his skinny legs and arms: "'Pipe stems,'" he observes, "'look at those legs. The boy's got the rickets—incipient, but he's got them. If epilepsy doesn't get him in the end, it will be because tuberculosis gets him first'" (1,117).

At supper that night, the only time of day he spends with his brothers and sisters, he resents his younger brother Will because the mother has chosen to keep Will in school and out of the factory, placing the entire burden on Johnny: "It partook of the nature of an encounter, to him, for he was very old, while they were distressingly young. He had no patience with their excessive and amazing juvenility" (1,118). His mother's constant whining about how she is doing her best also irritates him. When Will teases his exhausted brother, he gets a beating and Johnny gets a scolding. He does not understand their youth, for he had none, having gone to work at seven: "No child works on the night shift and remains a child" (1,122). His only happy memories are of a girl he once longed for, those rare evenings

when there was some extra food like prunes and custard, or even better "Floating Island," which she promises one day to make (this was London's favorite dessert). Once he found a silver quarter on the sidewalk and bought candy, a great "sin" against his family, who usually got all his wages.

Thus, Johnny has no life of his own; he is only a replacement for the missing father. His distant memory of his father is not a happy one:

> This particular memory never came to Johnny in broad daylight when he was wide awake. It came at night, in bed, at the moment that his consciousness was sinking down and losing itself in sleep. It always aroused him to frightened wakefulness, and for the moment, in the first sickening start, it seemed to him that he lay crosswise on the foot of the bed. In the bed were the vague forms of his father and mother. He never saw what his father looked like. He had but one impression of his father, and that was that he had savage and pitiless feet. (1,123)

The years pass, but never is there any "joyousness of life for him." He never sees "the procession of days," and "[t]he nights he slept away in twitching unconsciousness." Working nearly round the clock, "his consciousness was machine consciousness. Outside this his mind was a blank. He had no ideals. . . . He was a work-beast. He had no mental life whatever" (1,124).

However, "deep down in the crypts of his mind, unknown to him, were being weighed and sifted every hour of his toil, every movement of his hands, every twitch of his muscles, and preparations were making for a future course of action that would amaze him and all his little world" (1,124). That night, his mother proudly presents him with a surprise, Floating Island, but he is too tired to eat it: "All his bones ached. He ached everywhere. And in his head began the shrieking, pounding, crashing, roaring of a million looms" (1,125). Johnny has come down with a severe case of grippe, or influenza. He does not go to work the next day. Instead, during his long convalescence, he changes. Calculating the number of moves he has made as the perfect machine, he realizes that he will not go back to work, over the sobs of his mother. As he sits on the stoop doing his calculations, he becomes "greatly absorbed in the one tree that grew across the street. He studied it for hours at a time, and was unusually interested when the wind swayed its branches and fluttered its leaves. Throughout the week he seemed lost in a great communion with himself" (1,126). This vision of even a tiny slice of nature heals him. He tells his mother he is leaving them, and that Will can now go to work. He hits the road, the vision of the spindly tree in his mind, and in the sunshine he begins to revive. Boarding a freight car, Johnny lies down, "and in the darkness he smiled" (1,129).

COMMENTARY

"The Apostate" was one of London's first socialist stories, and it is the most provocative. It also reflects his troubled relationship with his mother, whose poverty meant that he was forced to go to work at the age of 10; she even rented out his bed to boarders. At the London home, he was called "Johnny." But if the story exposes the life he led as a child laborer, it also sounds the call to the open road he responded to as a youth, when he hit the road as a hobo, a romantic American escape. Though he has little idea of freedom when the story begins, he becomes a believer in it and in himself, if an "apostate" to the laws of wage slavery. Johnny's basic physical needs are not being met, let alone his spiritual ones. The motif of darkness runs throughout the story, emphasizing his lack of a real life. But sudden awareness of his situation hits him like a thunderbolt when he at last is able to sit in the SUN. As in other stories, London uses the sun here as a symbol of divine justice and rebirth. Some readers question his decision to force his brother Will into the hellish world of the mills, as many also question the mother's decision to spare one of her sons. But few can resist the impact of Johnny's finally freeing himself from a world that cares little for him into a new world of sunshine and possibilities.

CHARACTERS

Johnny At age 12 Johnny looks as though he is an old man. Actually born on the floor of the factory, Johnny performs unceasing and backbreak-ing work. Also, working in the looms has filled his chest with lint. He is the best worker in the mill. He is little more than a machine until he realizes there can be more to life. Several years pass with him never ceasing to work, until he has an epiphany of freedom and leaves home when he is 18.

Johnny's Mother "A sad-eyed, tired-faced woman" who struggles to feed and house her children and can spare little affection, though she starves herself to feed especially Johnny, since without a husband Johnny is her breadwinner. Johnny resents her decision to keep his younger brother Will away from factory work.

Will Will is Johnny's 10-year-old brother who taunts him and in return gets kicked in the shins and his face rubbed in the dirt. His mother babies Will and makes Johnny work to feed them all.

superintendent Covers up the fact that he is employing underage boys in his jute mill and exploits them without mercy.

inspector Though he realizes how many of the boys are underage and comments on their illnesses and malnourishment, he only removes one boy from the factory floor, a one-legged child who is working because his siblings are dying of starvation, reflecting his own lack of sympathy despite his official action.

"Bâtard" (1902)

"Bâtard," the story of a deadly feud between a KLON-DIKE gold hunter and his dog, was composed in the first two weeks of January 1902, at the beginning of one of London's most powerful periods of short story writing, culminating in the collection *Children of the Frost* (1902). Though "Bâtard" appears in a different collection, like those tales it reflects London's deepening pessimism about human life. At this time, suffering depression, he wrote his friend CLOUDESLEY JOHNS, "But after all, what . . . means anything? . . . I have at last discovered what I am. I am a materialist monist, and there's dam [sic] little satisfaction in it" (*Letters*, 270). However, later that winter London would sign a contract with MACMILLAN for all of his future books, thus ensuring their success, and his philosophy would develop beyond MATERIALISM and DETERMINISM toward a more spiritual and affirmative orientation.

SYNOPSIS

"Bâtard was a devil. This was recognized throughout the Northland. 'Hell's Spawn' he was called by many men, but his master, Black Leclère, chose for him the shameful name 'Bâtard.' Now Black Leclère was also a devil, and the twain were well matched. There is a saying that when two devils come together, hell is to pay" (*Stories*, 729).

In the very first lines of London's first dog story, the narrator describes the immediate hatred between a dog and his new owner. Indeed "Bâtard" is an anatomy of hatred, and its canine protagonist is the antithesis of everything that man's best friend is supposed to be. But it is clear that such devils are not merely born; they are also made. His sadistic treatment at the hands of Leclère, the dissolute voyageur, transforms Bâtard: Half-starved, tortured, beaten, and cursed, the dog grows progressively more vicious and cunning, yet he refuses to leave his master because he waits for revenge, just like his master. Even after Bâtard has attacked him in his sleep, Leclère scorns the old-timers who advise him to shoot the dog. Near the end of the story, unjustly convicted of murdering a gold miner, he is forced to mount a large box, hands tied and noose around his neck. He gets a last-minute reprieve, but the miners leave him alone, standing precariously on the box, to meditate upon his sinful ways while they go downriver to apprehend the real murderer. When they have gone, the dog, grinning "with a fiendish levity," casually retreats a few yards—then hurls himself against the box. "Fifteen minutes later, Slackwater Charley and Webster Shaw, returning, caught a glimpse of a ghostly pendulum swinging back and forth in the dim light. As they hurriedly drew in closer, they made out the man's inert body, and a live thing that clung to it, and shook and worried, and gave to it the swaying motion" (*Stories*, 741).

COMMENTARY

First published as "Diable, a Dog" in COSMOPOLITAN (1902), this tale was written before *The Call of the Wild* and *White Fang*, London's classic dog stories. London later told his wife he wrote these "to redeem the species"; perhaps to him it reflected too clearly his embrace of mere MATERIALISM during his 1902 depression. In *The Call of the Wild*, Buck, a pet dog, is kidnapped and taken northward as a sled dog, but reverts to his primitive self when he escapes men. In *White Fang*, a wolf is domesticated. Both show the power of adaptability. Does "Bâtard"? We are told "It was a primordial setting and a primordial scene, such as might have been in the savage youth of the world" (*Stories*, 733). Perhaps not, as the dog and man cannot leave each other alone until one of them is dead, but it shares with these works London's use of fable, literary NATURALISM, and themes of hereditary and environmental Darwinism. It also shares, if in reverse, the moral theme of the NORTHLAND CODE, that BROTHERHOOD is necessary for survival.

In its naturalism and Darwinism, the story makes clear the stakes involved: "Often the man felt that he had bucked against the very essence of life—the unconquerable essence that swept the hawk down out of the sky like a feathered thunderbolt, that drove the great gray goose across the zones, that hurled the spawning salmon through two thousand miles of boiling Yukon flood" (*Stories*, 737). Yet if it is a Darwinian tour de force, it is also a story of not only unnatural but immoral cruelty repaid.

In "Bâtard," the moral fault lies with Leclère, for while Bâtard is vicious, he is naturally so but made much worse by Leclère: "The first time they met, Bâtard was a part-grown puppy, lean and hungry, with bitter eyes; and they met with snap and snarl, and wicked looks, for Leclère's upper lip had a wolfish way of lifting and showing the white, cruel teeth." The narrator notes that "With a proper master Bâtard might have made an ordinary, fairly efficient sled-dog. He never got the chance" (*Stories*, 730). The dog's heritage is legitimately wild, while his master's reveals the real "bastard," a drunken, psychotic abuser of men and dogs. While Bâtard's mother was a "snarling, bickering, obscene, husky, full-fronted and heavy-chested, with a malign eye, a cat-like grip on life, and a genius for trickery and evil," and his father was "a great grey timberwolf," Leclère has no hereditary claim to the primitive, but rather the civilization of men (*Stories*, 730). His lack of brotherhood with his fellow miners, however, removes him from that community. When Leclère is accused of the murder of Timothy Brown, "there was nothing to atone for Black Leclère, . . . [for] he was as well hated as the other was beloved" (*Stories*, 738). This is one reason the men leave him on his box—it would have only taken them a couple of seconds to get him down.

Note how moral values are assigned in the story. For Bâtard, "out of his terrible struggle for life developed a preternatural intelligence. His were the stealth and cunning of the husky, his mother, and the fierceness and valor of the wolf, his father" (*Stories*, 730). Value-laden words such as "valor" and "intelligence" appear. In contrast, Leclère's deepest sin is the sin of pride. After their great battle, when Leclère takes himself and his dog to the camp surgeon, he insists on their treating the dog first, to thus torture him into life only so he can one day kill him, perhaps an echo of London's early science fiction story "A Thousand Deaths," in which a scientist father experiments with killing and then reviving his son.

London ties Leclère's brutality to a broader moral problem: the whites' destruction of the Natives through the sin of greed for gold. Toward the conclusion, in the background of the drama between Bâtard and Leclère, we learn "A strike had been made at Sunrise, and things had changed considerably. With the infusion of several hundred gold-seekers, a deal of whiskey, and half a dozen equipped gamblers, the missionary had seen the page of his years of labor with the Indians wiped clean." The missionary "took to his bed, said 'bless me' several times, and departed to his final accounting in a rough-hewn, oblong box" (*Stories*, 738). The missionary's is the fourth death in the story attributable to the sins of men.

CHARACTERS

Bâtard His father a wolf and his mother a vicious husky, Bâtard is born into the rugged YUKON environment equipped to survive. But when he is taken

as a "part-grown puppy, lean and hungry, with bitter eyes" by his first owner, Black Leclère, frightened of Leclère's "wolfish" upper lip and "white, cruel teeth," roughly dragged from among his litter, he bites. Leclère chokes him nearly to death in response (*Stories*, 729). This meeting foreshadows the burning hatred dog and man will develop for one another over the course of the next five years, wandering for gold across the NORTHLAND from ST. MICHAEL to the Great Slave Lake. At the story's end, Bâtard's hatred of his master reaches its climax, and by using both instinct and careful calculation, he takes his revenge.

Leclère, "Black" A French-Canadian voyageur who not only deliberately turns his dog into a monster but who is known to all in the Klondike as a something of a monster himself. Leclère's nickname "Black" symbolizes his terrible reputation. Leclère's ethnicity is demonstrated in the heavy dialect London assigns him, but this is not the reason the other men distrust him; rather, it is because his violent, cruel nature runs counter to the brotherhood of the trail London praises elsewhere. When he is brutally killed by his dog, no one mourns his passing.

John Hamlin Storekeeper at the Sixty Mile post who sells Bâtard to Leclère.

missionary Stationed at Sunrise, he is a newcomer in the country and tries to caress Bâtard, for which he receives a terrible bite and blood poisoning.

surgeon Stationed at McQuestion, the surgeon travels to Sunrise to save the missionary from blood poisoning who tried to be kind to Bâtard and nearly lost his hand. He later treats Bâtard after he has been severely beaten by Leclère.

Timothy Brown Leclère quarrels with him, and he is later shot by a Native on the river where he is in a poling boat with Leclère, who is (wrongly) accused of the murder.

Webster Shaw, Slackwater Charley The miners who prepare Leclère for hanging but leave him standing on the box while they investigate news of the shooting on the river.

Before Adam (1907)

Published first in *Everybody's Magazine* in fall 1906, the novel was issued in book form the next year by MACMILLAN. One of London's most unusual novels, it is set in prehistory among cavemen and women, written in a spurt of mythic vision in only 40 days. It reflects London's interests in dream-life, in the primordial human past, and in ATAVISM. Among his other experiences, the narrator's dream-vision of the "Younger World" includes evocative descriptions of Earth eons ago: "We climbed and descended mighty canyons and gorges; and ever, from every view point, there spread out before us, in all directions, range upon range, the unceasing mountains. . . . And then, at last, one hot mid-day, dizzy with hunger, we gained the divide. From this high backbone of earth, to the north, across the diminishing, down-falling ranges, we caught a glimpse of a far lake. The sun shone upon it, and about it were open, level grass-lands, while to the eastward we saw the dark line of a wide-stretching forest" (155–156).

SYNOPSIS

Chapters 1–7

"Pictures! Pictures! Pictures!" begins the narrator: "Often, before I learned, did I wonder whence came the multitudes of pictures that thronged my dreams; for they were pictures the like of which I had never seen in real wake-a-day life. They tormented my childhood, making of my dreams a procession of nightmares and a little later convincing me that I was different from my kind, a creature unnatural and accursed" (1). The narrator has a recurrent dream that takes him back in time as one of his remote ancestors in the mid-Pleistocene age. In his dreams, he is Big-Tooth, a member of the "Folk" caught between the apelike Tree People and the more advanced Fire People (*Homo sapiens*). Childhood fears are replaced by naturalistic threats: "Ogres and bugaboos and I had been happy

bed-fellows, compared with these terrors that made their bed with me throughout my childhood, and that still bed with me, now, as I write this, full of years" (11). He learns of "racial memory" and "dissociation of personality" while in college and concludes that his dream-self is actually a progenitor from the distant past.

Big-Tooth describes his mother as a large orangutan or chimpanzee, but different. She is strong and agile, as when she saves her baby from a wild boar, and his father as half-ape, half-human, with prehensile feet. He describes their simple "language" of sounds. His life is not all danger: he enjoys "the peace of the cool caves in the cliffs, the circus of the drinking-places at the end of the day, . . . the bite of the morning wind in the tree-tops, . . . the taste of young sweet bark" (2). Mainly he enjoys the freedom to adventure and explore.

Big-Tooth separates from his mother, who, with the disappearance of his father, has chosen a new mate, whom Big-Tooth calls The Chatterer; because of him, Big-Tooth leaves. He stumbles upon a "village" of the Folk. Red-Eye, their leader, terrifies him; he is huge and can leap 20 feet in the air. He runs on all fours—which to Big-Tooth makes him an atavism. While the Tree People are moving more and more to the ground, Red-Eye is a reversion. Big-Tooth is befriended by Lop-Ear; together, they fend off a saber-toothed tiger. One day while playing, the two youths encounter a Fire Man, whom they think is a beast; though he has less hair than they, he wears a bearskin. He also carries a bow and arrow, which he fires at them. He kills Broken-Tooth and wounds Big-Tooth and Lop-Ear.

Chapters 8–18

The Folk survive a cold winter. They improve their technology by using gourds or woven baskets to hold berries. Red-Eye has been growing more and more violent, and he murders not only his wives but those of others and their children. Lop-Ear and Big-Tooth are attacked, and Big-Tooth strikes him with a rock. The two friends continue to pelt him and are able to escape to the lands of the Tree People. They play and explore and learn to make boats. Big-Tooth longs for the Swift One,

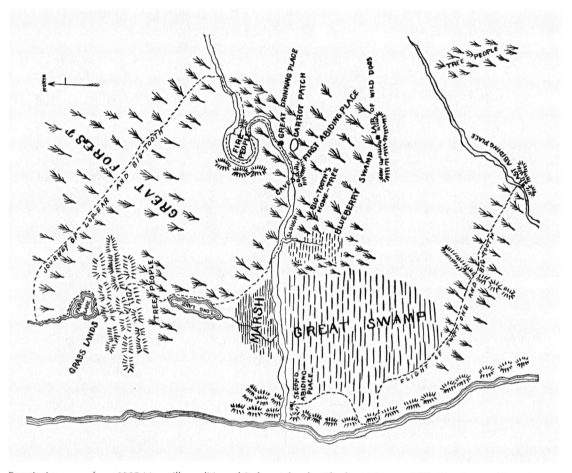

Frontispiece map from 1905 Macmillan edition of *Before Adam* by Charles Livingston Hill *(Huntington Library)*

who seems different than the other women of the Tree People; he speculates based on her features that she is related to the Fire People. While "boating" the two friends are attacked by Red-Eye. They attack an old Tree Man and are chased by the Tree People. They run across a settlement of Fire People and note their superiority in development. Again they flee, this time back to the Folk, where Red-Eye tries to capture a new wife, Singing One, but the Folk band together to resist him. They hold a "hee-hee council," which soothes their anger; it involves chattering in unison and banging on a log. The narrator observes how this illustrates "the inconsecutiveness and inconsequentiality of the Folk. Here were we, drawn together by mutual rage and the impulse toward cooperation, led off

into forgetfulness by the establishment of a rude rhythm" (182).

Lop-Ear mates with Big-Tooth's sister, but she is killed by Fire Men, who are increasingly raiding the Folk. Big-Tooth has to save Swift One from being raped and murdered by Red-Eye; as they fight, the narrator knows he will die, but he is saved by a saber-toothed tiger who eats Big-Face and frightens off Red-Eye. Big-Tooth mates with Swift One, and they have many children. Finally the Fire Men come in numbers to kill the Folk. They kill the Chatterer and Red-Eye's most recent wife. Red-Eye defends himself, while Lop-Ear, the Swift One, and the narrator escape into a swamp, where they rear their families. At the close of the story, the narrator finds that Red-Eye, maimed from all his injuries, has mated with an old woman of the Tree People, and is, at last, subdued.

COMMENTARY

This novel shows the influence of such writers as H. G. Wells, Jules Verne, H. Rider Haggard, and Stanley Waterloo, and it in turn was an influence on GEORGE ORWELL and Edgar Rice Burroughs. And there is an almost Poelike quality to the narrator's repeated descriptions of being possessed by fear: "From my earliest recollection my sleep was a period of terror. Rarely were my dreams tinctured with happiness. As a rule, they were stuffed with fear—and with a fear so strange and alien that it had no ponderable quality . . ." (3–4).

The novel is most clearly drawn from London's interest in the ideas of EVOLUTION of CHARLES DARWIN and of psychology of SIGMUND FREUD. The narrator tells us that when he confesses to a playmate his dream-world, he is laughed at, leading the narrator to the conclusion that "I was different from my kind. I was abnormal with something they could not understand" (10), in other words, a mutation. While in college, he learns that the falling-through-air dream is a "racial memory" of remote ancestors who lived in trees (13). The narrator describes himself as a "freak" like a two-headed calf (17): "I am a freak of heredity, an atavistic nightmare—call me what you will; but here I am, real and alive, eating three hearty meals a day, and what are you going to do about it?" (20). Also learning about psychology in college, he uses the term "disassociation of reality" to describe himself (13). As he notes, he is not describing reincarnation; it is not the narrator who roams the primeval past but "one that is only remotely a part of me, and my father and grandfather are parts of me less remote" (19), like a racial unconscious. Such a twin scientific focus on evolution and psychology makes *Before Adam* more than a tour de force. Indeed, as Earle Labor and Jeanne Campbell Reesman note, the novel "is rich with Freudian implications," and Big-Tooth achieves a "rebirth" by returning to his tribe and mating with Swift One; his story is, in mythological terms, "a recreation of the 'rites of passage' archetype, . . . our universal compulsion to return to the beginning of things and to the . . .

simplicity of the childhood of the race" (Labor and Reesman, 69).

CHARACTERS

Big-Tooth The primordial ancestor of the narrator of the novel who visits the mid-Pleistocene era in his ancestral identity. Big-Tooth's journey from child to man and father, escaping horrifying threats to his life, is a story of maturation.

Red-Eye "The atavism," Red-Eye is the leader of the Folk and the antagonist to Big-Tooth; he is a terrifying, violent, and unbelievably strong adversary. Red-Eye is constantly killing, especially his wives. He is the major threat to Big-Tooth throughout the story.

Lop-Ear Big-Tooth's loyal friend, affectionate and protective. Lop-Ear behaves like a parent, once even risking his own life to save Big-Tooth from the arrows of the Fire Men.

Swift One Mate to Big-Tooth. He woos her for a long time, but they finally mate after he saves her from being raped and murdered by Red-Eye.

Broken-Tooth A "youngster" of the Folk who is thrust away from his mother when more babies come; lives with Lop-Ear and Big-Tooth. Killed by the arrow of a Fire Man.

Old Marrow-Bone Oldest member of the folk who manages to survive constant threats to his life; perhaps a figure of the Wise Old Man archetype.

Singing One Red-Eye, having killed his latest wife, decides to catch her. She is the daughter of Hairless One and granddaughter of Old Marrow-Bone. She is killed by Red-Eye.

Hairless One Father of Singing One who unsuccessfully tries to defend her from Red-Eye.

Crooked-Leg Mate of Singing One.

Big-Face A participant in the "hee-hee council."

Hair-Face Escapes the Fire Men with his mate, the narrator, Lop-Ear, and Swift One.

FURTHER READING

Berkove, Lawrence I. *"Before Adam* and *The Scarlet Plague:* Two Novels of Evolution by Jack London."* In *ALN: The American Literary Naturalism Newsletter* 2, no. 1 (2007): 13–16.

Hensley, John R. "Eugenics and Social Darwinism in Stanley Waterloo's *The Story of Ab* and Jack London's *Before Adam.*" In *Studies in Popular Culture* 25, no. 1 (October 2002): 22–37.

"The Bones of Kahekili"
(1919)

Completed in July 1916 after London's last visit to HAWAI'I, "The Bones of Kahekili" was published posthumously in COSMOPOLITAN 67 (July 1919) and then included in *On the Makaloa Mat* (1919). It begins with a bantering tone but turns darker, as a plantation owner pries a sacred story from one of his retainers. Implicit are a sense of Hawaiian traditional MYTHOLOGY and a satire on white dominance.

SYNOPSIS

In the 1880s, a wealthy HAOLE rancher below the high Koolau Mountains of OAHU, Hardman Pool, has a habit of calling his workers together with his numerous part-Hawaiian sons and answering their monetary requests. He also uses these times to demonstrate his mastery over them. The Hawaiian cowboys among them, called *paniolos*, wear large Spanish spurs and cowboy hats, leather leggings, knives, and wreaths of flowers around the crowns of their hats. Kanaka Oolea (Pool's Hawaiian name) orders a gin and milk, and, before the day is done, he manages to find out the secret of the location of a famous chief's bones from an old man, Kumuhana, whom he has plied with gin and milk.

Kumuhana reluctantly tells of an event that occurred at the death of an *ali'i* (or noble) in his village. Kumuhana was in love with Malia, who was the chief of Kahekili's household, as was his friend Anapuni, and they were drunk the night Kahekili died. Chief Konukalani dragged Malia away by her hair; the high priest Eoppo decided that Anapuhi and Kumuhana would be the sacrifices (*moepuu*) to go with Kahekili and his bones and "to care for him afterward and for ever in the shadowy other world" (2,368).

Ironically, Pool resembles the arrogant chiefs who demanded sacrifice from the people: "He knew his Hawaiians from the outside and the in, knew them better than themselves—their Polynesian circumlocutions, faiths, customs, and mysteries" (*Stories* 2,357). Such presumption, to know a "people" better than they know themselves, is typical of men of Pool's rank: "'All this is life for you, because you think but one day at a time, while we, your chiefs, think for you all days and far days ahead'" (2,366). Despite his certainty about life and his position in it, Pool is obsessed with Kumuhana's knowledge of a Maori death chant:

> But death is nothing new.
> Death is and has been ever since old Maui died
> Then Pata-tai laughed loud
> And woke the goblin-god,
> Who severed him in two, and shut him in,
> So dusk of eve came on. (2,372)

Maui is a rising and dying god and also a trickster. It is thus appropriate that what saves Kumuhana from death is a series of strange accidents: The priests must catch some fish to sacrifice along with him and Kumuhana, and they cannot. Their plan to do the sacrifice at sea then return to shore to bury the chief in a secret cave is completely foiled when they heave the (new, haole-made) coffin overboard. Instead of floating properly, it floats vertically, so that they can see the frightening face of Kahekili through a glass panel. One of them tries to move the coffin with an oar but he shatters the glass, and it sinks to the bottom of the Molokai channel. Kumuhana is spared. At the end, Pool gives the old man $6.50 to buy a donkey, a bridle, and saddle, as Kumuhana has asked.

COMMENTARY

"The Bones of Kahekili" is a frame story with the outer setting the plantation system and the inner the world of Kumuhana with its secrets. This is probably the first story London wrote under the direct influence of his reading of the psychoanalytic and mythic theories of CARL JUNG in his last summer. In its opposition of "outer" and "inner" worlds and truths it reflects the basic ideas of Jung's conscious and unconscious, as well as his sense of world myth, as London demonstrates with his references to Maui. Pool seems in need of the truths of the old myths, even as he denigrates the tellers of the past, symbolized in his bartering and paying to get the stories revealed to him. But not everything is one-sided. Though Pool is the dominant figure in the story, his worker-audience is able to play him by doubling their requisitions. Kumuhana flatters him, negotiating with him on the side for the best possible deal: "'Great is your haole wisdom'" (2,362).

CHARACTERS

Kumuhana An old retainer of Hardman Pool's plantation, chosen as a youth to be sacrificed upon the death of a chief, Kahekili. Through a series of accidents, he escapes death and lives to tell the tale. In Hawaiian, "Kumuhana" means literally "knowledge work."

Hardman Pool "New Beford born," he has been in Hawai'i over 50 years and has married into Hawaiian royalty and inherited a large plantation, which he rules like a god. Pool is a figure who suggests the fortunes garnered by Americans in Hawai'i and their unearned sense of "understanding" the NATIVES.

Kalama Pool's Hawaiian wife, descended from chiefs and an owner of land; by marrying her he receives not only her riches but "her own chief rank, and the fealty owed to her by virtue of her genealogy" (2,357).

Ahuhu A cowboy whose name means "poisonwood," he asks from Pool the price of a pair of dungarees: "I have ridden much and hard after your cattle, Kanaka Oolea, and . . . [i]t is not well that it be said that a Kanaka Oolea cowboy, who is also a cousin of Kanaka Oolea's wife's half-sister, should be shamed to be seen out of the saddle" (2,360).

Eoppo High priest or *kahuna* overseeing the funeral rituals of Kahekili and would-be executioner of Kumuhana.

"Brown Wolf" (1906)

"Brown Wolf" first appeared in *Everybody's Magazine* in August 1906 and was included in the collection *Love of Life and Other Stories* (1907). It is a slightly fantastic tale of a contest of affections for a very special animal.

SYNOPSIS

Walt and Madge Irvine are enjoying a morning on their SONOMA VALLEY, CALIFORNIA, mountain meadow with its fresh, "dew-wet grass," orchards, blackberries, and redwoods (*Stories*, 1,073). Their half-wolf, half-dog, Wolf, chases a rabbit, and as they stroll after him they call to him. He appears on a ridge above them, a huge red-brown animal who once strayed onto their property hurt from the south. At first, he is wild and menacing, but they gradually earn his trust. As he recovers his strength, he slowly becomes their companion. They suspect he is a former KLONDIKE sled dog, as their neighbor, Mrs. Johnson, whose brother is a Klondiker, suggests. Wolf again and again escapes and heads north, running hundreds of miles—the last time getting as far as Washington, before he is returned to the Irvines' address on his collar. As the three rest, a stranger approaches, Mrs. Johnson's brother, Skiff Miller, returned to visit her. Wolf instantly recognizes him, and Miller claims he is his long-lost lead sled dog. The three humans debate ownership, as Wolf eagerly looks on, and they decide to let the dog decide. Miller walks away down the path, and, after agonized attempts to pull both Walt and Madge down the trail after him, Wolf gives the Irvines one last look and runs after Miller, back to the heady if hard life of a Klondike work dog.

COMMENTARY

Written just after the eerie story "Planchette," in which a young man's decision to join his lover and move from the city to the pastoral life of Sonoma Valley results in his strange death, "Brown Wolf" also reflects London's ambivalence about leaving San Francisco and his friends there to move to a ranch in Sonoma with his fiancé CHARMIAN KITTREDGE. London suffered a depression in 1905–06 following his divorce from his first wife BESS LONDON and separation from his daughters. Interestingly, in both stories, the main character is not able to remain in the valley and its peaceful life, though London himself chose to do so.

CHARACTERS

Walt Irvine   A successful poet whose earnings he transmutes into farm animals, crops, and ranch improvements: "I am no attic singer, no ballroom warbler. And why? Because I am practical. Mine is no squalor of song that cannot transmute itself, with proper exchange value, into a flower-crowned cottage, a sweet mountain-meadow, a grove of redwoods, an orchard of thirty-seven trees, one long row of blackberries and two short rows of strawberries, to say nothing of a quarter of a mile of gurgling brook. I am a beauty-merchant, a trader in song" (1,073–1,074).

Madge Irvine   Walt's wife, who begins the story by asking Walt where Wolf is, and insisting on trailing after him, calling out again and again. She teases her husband about his vanities but devotes herself to his happiness—and to Wolf.

Skiff Miller   A returning Klondiker, Miller comes across the Irvines and Wolf and is shocked to see his own dog, who had been stolen. He is "bare-headed and sweaty. With a handkerchief in one hand he mopped his face, while in the other hand he carried a new hat and a wilted starched collar which he had removed from his neck. He was a well-built man, and his muscles seemed on the point of bursting out of the painfully new and ready-made black clothes he wore" (1,078). In the contest between the three "owners" of Wolf (whom he named "Brown"), he wins back his dog.

Burning Daylight (1910)

"Get up, Jack, daylight's burning!" With these words, one of London's KLONDIKE companions, Elam Harnish, would make a quick breakfast and try to rouse his hard-to-wake friend. Harnish was the model for the hero of *Burning Daylight*; London did not even change his name. Like London, Harnish climbed the CHILKOOT PASS in fall 1897; he met London when he arrived at the upper Yukon. Harnish praised his friend as a good companion, if one hard to get out of bed. He remained a gold miner in the Klondike long after London went home. He was said to do the work of three men, but he never became rich, though he was regarded as one of the last true gold rush pioneers (Bykov, chapter 30). In the novel, Harnish becomes enormously wealthy from his gold prospecting and returns to San Francisco to become a captain of industry and finance. However, because he falls in love with a woman who despises what his wealth has done to his character, he gives it all up, marries her, and moves to the bucolic Valley of the Moon to farm and enrich the land, instead of asking it to enrich him. *Burning Daylight* is the first of London's trilogy of SONOMA novels: Each follows a similar pattern in which a man is saved from the evils of the city by the love of a good woman. The other two are *The Valley of the Moon* (1913) and *The Little Lady of the Big House* (1916).

SYNOPSIS

Part I

In the Tivoli Saloon in Circle City, YUKON TERRITORY, bored gold prospectors drink and gamble during the long Arctic night when no work can be done. To cries of "Daylight!" Elam Harnish comes in from the cold and announces his birthday, makes a winning bet at faro, and spreads cheer. Harnish, given his nickname because he always complains of those who "burn daylight," is liked and respected; for 12 years he has been seeking his fortune in the NORTHLAND: "He was a striking figure of a man. . . . His face, lean and slightly long, with the suggestion of hollows under the cheek-bones, seemed almost Indian. The burnt skin and keen dark eyes contributed to this effect, though the bronze of the skin and the eyes themselves were essentially those of a white man. He looked older than thirty, and yet, smooth-shaven and without wrinkles, he was almost boyish." And yet some of his features hint at other qualities: "The lips themselves were thin, and prone to close tightly over the even, white teeth. But their harshness was retrieved by the upward curl at the corners of his mouth. This curl gave to him sweetness, as the minute puckers at the corners of the eyes gave him laughter. These necessary graces saved him from a nature that was essentially savage and that otherwise would have been cruel and bitter" (7–8).

Though he is cleaned out at poker, Daylight, adored by the Virgin, resents her demand for more dances: "he did not want any woman running him," and he prefers the comradeship of men (10). Since he has lost his $8,000, he earns some back by having the miners bet on his lifting 900 pounds of flour sacks and arm wrestling, and he also bets on his speedy return from his run. He boasts that he will one day find millions in gold:

> "I sure will. I first come over Chilcoot in '83. . . . in a fall blizzard, with a rag of a shirt and a cup of raw flour. I got my grub-stake in Juneau that winter, and in the spring I went over the Pass once more. And once more the famine drew me out. Next spring I went in again, and I swore then that I'd never come out till I made my stake. Well, I ain't made it, and here I am. And I ain't going out now. . . . And so I swear once more, by the mill-tails of hell and the head of John the Baptist, I'll never hit for the Outside till I make my pile. And I tell you-all, here and now, it's got to be an almighty big pile." (31–32)

On the trail, Daylight and Kama and their dogs make excellent progress, though the landscape they must traverse is forbidding: "It was a dead world, and furthermore, a gray world. . . . [T]he sky was a gray pall. . . . [T]here was no sun to give brightness. Far to the south the sun climbed steadily to meridian, but between it and the frozen Yukon intervened the bulge of the earth. The Yukon lay in a night shadow, and the day itself was in reality a long twilight-light" (38). Just before they reach DYEA and begin the climb up the CHILKOOT PASS, Kama is unable to keep up with Daylight's unrelenting pace and collapses; Daylight carries him to Dyea, where they part. Daylight and another NATIVE climb the pass, but in the rapids on their way to DAWSON they lose their dog team and must themselves pull the sled 200 miles to Selkirk.

The Tivoli welcomes Daylight home after his 2,000-mile journey. He agrees to partner with three other men to prospect on the STEWART RIVER, even though the region is still in darkness. This they do, facing such challenges as losing their food to wolverines. When they are no longer able to sustain themselves on wild food, they attempt to launch a boat to Sixty Mile on the spring flood. Daylight decides to prospect on Indian River and engages some new partners; he has heard of the great strike made by George Carmack and is determined to make one himself. He stakes claims all over the upper NORTHLAND and makes millions; he also plans a town site—in the newly burgeoning Dawson. He becomes a legend: "Not alone was he the richest man in the country, but he was Burning Daylight, the pioneer, the man who, almost in the midst of antiquity of that young land, had crossed the Chilcoot and drifted down the Yukon[,] . . . the man who carried word to the ice-bound whaling fleet across the tundra wilderness to the Arctic Sea, who raced the mail from Circle to Salt Water and back again in sixty days, who saved the whole Tanana tribe from perishing in the winter of '91—in short, the man who smote the chechaquos' imaginations more violently than any other dozen men rolled into one" (108). His pleasure in success is marred by the suicide—supposedly over him—of the Virgin. He cashes in his holdings and leaves for points south.

Part II

Daylight meets other magnates and begins to learn how the financial game is played. He visits New York to advance his interests. There, three wealthy men he admires conspire to swindle him; when he learns what has happened he demands his $10 million from them at gunpoint, and he prevails. Daylight returns to San Francisco to "gamble" in speculative finance, which makes him even richer. He acquires a stenographer, Dede Mason, who begins her tenure by correcting his grammar in a document. Daylight's fortune grows vast and vaster, but he begins to deteriorate physically and to drink heavily. He notices that he is beginning to look soft like the club men he despises for their lack of masculinity.

For a respite, he travels to a country retreat in GLEN ELLEN; there, he is struck by nature's beauty and sense of peace: "This was different. No room for contempt and evil here. This was clean and fresh and beautiful—something he could respect. It was like a church. The atmosphere was one of holy calm. Here man felt the prompting of nobler things" (184). He realizes what he has lost: "'A sweet land, an almighty sweet land'" (198).

On his return, he begins more and more to feel drawn to Mason. He buys a horse, "Bob," and begins riding. One day, while riding in the Piedmont Hills, he encounters Mason and finds out more about her, and she expertly rides the temperamental Bob. When he suddenly proposes, she refuses him because she does not approve of his way of living, which he characterizes as playing "the cards he could see in his hand, and they were BATTLE, REVENGE, AND COCKTAILS. And Luck sat over all and grinned" (210). She challenges him: "'In ancient Greece,'" she began pedantically, "a man was judged a good citizen who built houses, planted trees—' She did not complete the quotation, but drew the conclusion hurriedly. 'How many houses have you built? How many trees have you planted?'" (250). Unless he gives up the "game" of money-making, she will refuse him. He decides to try to satisfy her by buying up land around OAKLAND and making the necessary improvements in water and transportation to attract settlers there. But still she refuses, so he shows up at her lodging and demands: "'Dede Mason, I want you, I just want you.' While he spoke he advanced upon her, his black eyes burning with bright fire, his aroused blood swarthy in his cheek" (278). He says he'll give her everything her heart desires, to which she responds, "'Except yourself. . . . Instead of giving yourself to your wife, you would give yourself . . . to everything business—and—and to all that that means'" (282).

Discouraged, Daylight turns more feverishly to business and relaxes with double martinis. But one evening in a bar he challenges the local arm-wrestling champion and loses: "Dede was right. He was not the same man" (313). In the end, he chooses Mason and the ranch in Glen Ellen, and he gets rid of all his wealth and most of his property. They marry and move onto a small ranch. One afternoon, fixing a leaking pipe, Daylight stumbles onto a huge gold vein. Feverishly, he works at it until he holds a big chunk of quartz filled with gold. However, the sound of Mason calling to her baby chickens comes to his ears, and he carefully covers up all traces of the find. The book ends with him prosaically going with a pail to milk the cows.

COMMENTARY

Having just returned from the voyage of the SNARK, London and his wife were delighted to resume life on their BEAUTY RANCH, which had expanded considerably in their absence. London had given instructions to his managers to buy adjoining properties, adding nearly 200 acres to the 129 existing acres. As Earle Labor has noted, "Due mainly to the disastrous physical consequences of his *Snark* voyage, Jack's 'seeking' drive was no longer aimed seaward, but landward." During the next seven years, with the help of ELIZA SHEPARD, who became his ranch superintendent as well as his business manager in early 1910, "he would fulfill an agrarian dream that had perhaps been latent in his vision ever since his childhood on the land JOHN LONDON had unsuccessfully farmed" (Labor, *American Life*, chapter 24). London spoke of a return to the soil as the true basis of economics, and he would increasingly come to believe that AGRARIANISM and careful husbandry of the land was a foundation for human virtue. He found that careless predecessors had worn out the soil on the ranch, and he began his plans to revitalize the soil, which included using organic fertilizer (manure) and terracing the hillsides as he saw in Korea, as well as tillage and crop rotation. Beauty Ranch thus became a model farm producing three crops a year of alfalfa, barley, hay, prunes, and vetch; its livestock regularly won blue ribbons at state fairs. He read intensively in agricultural journals and worked with his friend LUTHER

BURBANK on farm innovations. More important, as Labor observes, "The relationship between London's farming and writing was symbiotic." Much of what he envisioned for Beauty Ranch he incorporated into his fiction, and his fiction in turn fueled his agrarian ideals. This "vital interaction" is most evident in the Sonoma novels, of which *Burning Daylight* is the first, and, for Labor, perhaps the most interesting: "It is the only novel in American literature in which all three major icons of our mythic hero are incarnated in one character: the hero as frontiersman (i.e., James Fenimore Cooper's Leatherstocking saga), the hero as businessman (i.e., William Dean Howells's Silas Lapham and THEODORE DREISER's Frank Algernon Cowperwood), and the hero as yeoman farmer (i.e., the Jeffersonian ideal)" (Labor, *American Life*, chapter 24).

Charles N. Watson, Jr., has noted that "in his metamorphosis from frontier hero to financial magnate to rural homesteader, Elam Harnish reflects some of London's perennial tribulations as well as fulfilling three of his most cherished fantasies: his early dream of a big strike in the Klondike, his later success as a literary entrepreneur, and his final vision of a return to the land" (Watson, *Novels*, 169). Harnish's decline, due in large part, ironically, to his success, mirrors London's "Long Sickness," as he called his depression in 1905–06 following his divorce from BESS LONDON. He is, Labor remarks, "properly attired in a Brooks Brothers suit, . . . a rich but flabby Wolf Larsen—or what Martin Eden might have become had he decided to stay and play the cynic's game." Labor goes on to describe him as "a Wall Street prototype of Lt. Frederick Henry twenty years before Hemingway valorizes his hero's naturalistic pessimism in *A Farewell to Arms.* Here is Jay Gatsby stripped of all lovely romantic illusions about Daisy and the Dream of Success" (Labor, *American Life,* chapter 24). For Harnish, the love of Dede Mason was the key to victory, just as the love of CHARMIAN LONDON was for the author.

CHARACTERS

Elam Harnish Having made a fortune in the Klondike, Harnish returns to the United States intent on becoming a captain of finance, which he does. However, he declines both morally and physically: "Daylight's coming to civilization had not improved him. True, he wore better clothes, had learned slightly better manners, and spoke better English. . . . But he had hardened, and at the expense of his old-time, whole-souled geniality. . . . Power had its effect on him that it had on all men. Suspicious of the big exploiters, despising the fools of the exploited herd, he had faith only in himself. This led to an undue and erroneous exaltation of his ego, while kindly consideration of others—nay, even simple respect—was destroyed, until naught was left for him but to worship at the shrine of self." At the same time, "Physically, he was not the man of iron muscles who had come down out of the Arctic. He did not exercise sufficiently, ate more than was good for him, and drank altogether too much. His muscles were getting flabby. . . . The lean Indian visage was suffering a city change. . . . The beginning of puff-sacks under the eyes was faintly visible. The . . . first crease and fold of a double chin were becoming plainly discernible. The old effect of asceticism, bred of terrific hardships and toil, had vanished; the features had become broader and heavier, betraying all the stigmata of the life he lived, advertising the man's self-indulgence, harshness, and brutality" (180–181). Only when he renounces his fortune and fortune-hunting ways does Mason consent to marry him. He finds in the country the answer to his need for a meaningful life.

Dede Mason A well-bred young woman of the monied class from Siskiyou County, she appears in Part II of the novel after Harnish has won his fortune and entered into financial dealings in San Francisco. Like her model CHARMIAN LONDON, Mason is a skilled stenographer with a trim and well-dressed figure and an independent turn of mind. At first, Harnish barely notices her, but soon he falls in love, makes a pass, and proposes; she refuses him because she believes his wealth is destroying him, body and soul. She only agrees to marry him when he rids himself of his millions.

the Virgin A "young, dark-eyed woman, comely of face and figure, who was known from Juneau to

Fort Yukon as the Virgin," she appears in the opening scene. She is annoyed by a lack of business: "If something don't happen soon, I'm gin' to bed. What's the matter with the camp, anyway? Everybody dead?" (1). This is ironic because she later shoots herself in the head over Daylight.

Charley Bates A miner the Virgin complains to about the "dead" camp.

Dan MacDonald The "pioneer saloonman and gambler on the upper Yukon, owner and proprietor of the Tivoli and all its games" (1).

Olaf Henderson and French Louis They are "partners together on Bone Creek, . . . the two largest men in the country" (1).

Ben Davis Faro dealer at the Tivoli Saloon. Daylight plays a "dancing" game with him and throws him down.

Jack Kearns Poker player, "a big, bluff-featured man" who, failing at founding a trading post in the Arctic Circle, turns instead to running a sawmill (9). Kearns scores a huge pot off of Daylight when they play poker.

Bettles Jack Kearns's partner in the failed trading post and another of the poker players.

Hal Campbell Poker player who made a big strike at Moosehide.

Kama Kama is Daylight's dog-driver—"a Tananaw Indian, far-wandered from his tribal home in the service of the invading whites[,] . . . tall, lean, muscular, and fur-clad, the pick of his barbaric race and barbaric still" (22). Daylight outlasts him on the trail.

Pat Hanrahan and Doc Watson Men defeated at arm wrestling by Daylight.

Joe Hines "[C]oming in from consulting the spirit thermometer outside the door," he counsels Daylight not to go on his mail run: "'We're in for a good cold snap. It's sixty-two below now, and still goin' down. Better wait till she breaks'" (33). Daylight partners with him and Elijah Davis to try to mine in the darkness at the Stewart River.

Elijah Davis Partners with Daylight and Joe Hines for a risky mining adventure on the Stewart River.

Henry Finn A lumberjack from Wisconsin who partners with Daylight, Hines, and Davis. Presumably dies while on a trip for new food supplies.

Harper and Joe LaDue Miners who "had faith in the Upper Country" and who suggest that Daylight prospect on Indian River (87). The real Joseph LaDue was a prospector and the founder of Dawson City.

Skookum Jim Mason (Keish) Based on the real Skookum Jim, who was a member of the Tagish First Nation in what became the Yukon Territory. In the mid-1880s, he worked as a packer over the Chilkoot Pass carrying supplies for miners, where he earned his nickname because of his extraordinary strength. *Skookum* means "strong," "big," and "reliable" in Chinook. Keish is today credited with making the gold discovery that led to the Klondike gold rush, although it was originally attributed to George Carmack, his brother-in-law.

George Carmack The character is based on the actual Carmack, said to have made the first Alaskan gold rush strike, though it was really made by his brother-in-law Skookum Jim.

Bob Henderson Character based on the actual Patsy Henderson, nephew of Skookum Jim, and the only surviving member of the original party who struck gold on BONANZA CREEK; he recorded its history.

Curly Parson A miner skeptical of the claims of riches by Carmack, but who joins Daylight prospecting on Bonanza Creek.

Pat Monahan Partners with Daylight on Bonanza Creek.

Long Jim Harney A sourdough who invests a claim in Daylight's venture on Bonanza Creek.

Jacob Wilkins Sourdough who scoffs at Daylight's hopes for riches in the upper North.

Freda Dance-hall girl in Dawson whom Daylight saves from starvation and suicide; she is abandoned by a lover. Observing her misery, he is put off love.

John Dowsett, Nathaniel Letton, Leon Guggenhammer Financial magnates Daylight seeks advice from; however, they conspire to swindle him.

Jones Daylight's accountant in San Francisco—Daylight spurns his overly cautious advice.

Bunny McIntosh A club man and former footballer Daylight knows and consults on grammar.

Morrison Daylight's clerk, whom he asks for information about Mason: "'She comes from Siskiyou County. She's very nice to work with in the office, of course, but she's rather stuck on herself—exclusive, you know'" (170).

Larry Hegan A talented and unscrupulous lawyer Daylight hires to help him understand labor politics and commercial and corporation law.

Ferguson A small farmer in Napa who charms Daylight with his country life.

Swiftwater Bill A former Klondiker Daylight meets up with in San Francisco; with Bill he encounters Mason riding on the road.

Slosson A young arm-wrestling champion in San Francisco whom Daylight challenges and is defeated by.

FURTHER READING

Bykov, Vil. *In the Steps of Jack London.* Edited by Earle Labor, Susan Nuernberg, and Hensley Woodbridge. Translated by Julia Istomina. In The World of Jack London. Available online. URL: http://www.jack-londons.net. Accessed May 6, 2010.

Cole, Terrence. "Go Up, O Elam: The Story of Burning Daylight." *Alaska Journal* 6, no. 4 (1976): 235–239.

Labor, Earle. *Jack London: An American Life* (manuscript). New York: Farrar, Straus & Giroux, forthcoming, chapter 24.

———. "Jack London's Symbolic Wilderness: Four Versions." In *Nineteenth-Century Fiction* 17, no. 2 (1962): 149–161. Reprinted in *Jack London: Essays in Criticism.* Edited by Ray Wilson Ownbey. Santa Barbara, Calif.: Peregrine Smith, 1978, 31–42.

Stasz, Clarice. *American Dreamers: Charmian and Jack London.* New York: St. Martin's, 1988.

Walker, Franklin. *Jack London and the Klondike: The Genesis of an American Writer.* San Marino, Calif.: Huntington Library, 1966.

Watson, Charles N., Jr. *The Novels of Jack London: A Reappraisal.* Madison: University of Wisconsin Press, 1983.

"By the Turtles of Tasman" (1911)

This unusual tale of two brothers first appeared in the *San Francisco Call Monthly Magazine* in November 1911 and was included in the collection *The Turtles of Tasman* (1916). As in "The House of Pride," this tale involves two brothers of vastly different temperaments, one cold and reserved and one warm and open hearted.

SYNOPSIS

Frederick Travers, a wealthy Californian and self-made man, is expecting a visit from his brother, Tom Travers, a world roamer and adventurer, a "harum scarum," indeed a prodigal son (*Stories*, 2,065). Frederick has received a letter from Tom's daughter, Bronislawa Plaskoweitzkaia Travers (Polly), telling him that Tom is—unbeknownst to him—dying. The brothers are a study in contrasts. Frederick, "a seriously groomed man," believes in "law, order, and restraint." His face is that "of one used to power and who had used power with wisdom and discretion. Clean living had made the healthy skin, and the lines graved in it were honest lines. Hard and devoted work had left its wholesome handiwork, that was all" (2,064). His long history of public service in the form of waterworks, highways, ferries, and other developments destine him to be the next governor. Tom is the older brother:

> Alike they looked, of the unmistakable same stock, their features reminiscent of a common origin; and there resemblance ceased. Tom was three inches taller, and well-greyed was the long, Viking moustache. His was the same eagle-like nose as his brother's, save that it was more eagle-like, while the blue eyes were pronouncedly so. The lines of the face were deeper, the cheek-bones higher, the hollows larger, the weather-beat darker. It was a volcanic face. There had been fire there, and the fire still lingered. Around the corners of the eyes were more laughter-wrinkles and in the eyes themselves a promise of deadlier seriousness than the younger brother possessed. Frederick was bourgeois in his carriage, but in Tom's was a certain careless ease and distinction. It was the same pioneer blood of Isaac Travers in both men, but it had been retorted in widely different crucibles. (2,069)

Soon Frederick's formerly well-ordered home is filled with young people come to see Polly, whom he detests as foreign and overly demonstrative, preferring the behavior of his quiet and genteel daughter, Mary, and then by adventure-trail friends of Tom's. Cigarettes and liquor consume the guests, to Frederick's strong disapproval. And yet for his brother's sake he tolerates them.

But even though his brother is dying, Frederick finds himself filled with resentment of him and jealousy of his friendships and exciting life:

> There was an unfairness about it that perplexed Frederick, until he found solace in dwelling upon the failure Tom had made of life. Then it was, in quiet intervals, that he got some comfort and stiffened his own pride by showing Tom over the estate.
>
> "You have done well, Fred," Tom would say. "You have done very well."

He said it often, and often he drowsed in the big smooth-running machine.

> "Everything orderly and sanitary and spick and span—not a blade of grass out of place," was Polly's comment. "How do you ever manage it? I should not like to be a blade of grass on your land," she concluded, with a little shivery shudder.
>
> "You have worked hard," Tom said.
>
> "Yes, I have worked hard," Frederick affirmed. "It was worth it."
>
> He was going to say more, but the strange flash in the girl's eyes brought him to an uncomfortable pause. He felt that she measured him, challenged him. (2,075)

Sure enough, not long after this, Polly directly challenges him: "'You seem to value life in terms of profit and loss,' she said. 'I wonder if you have ever known love.'" Her remarks make a deep impression on Frederick: "The shaft went home. He had not kissed his woman. His marriage had been one of policy. . . . He had never had time to love. He had worked hard. He had been president of the chamber of commerce, mayor of the city, state senator, but he had missed love." His lack is reinforced when he notices Polly and her father's mutual affection: "At chance moments he had come upon Polly, openly and shamelessly in her father's arms, and he had noted the warmth and tenderness in their eyes. Again he knew that he had missed love. Wanton as was the display, not even in private did he and Mary so behave. Normal, formal, and colourless, she was what was to be expected of a loveless marriage. He even puzzled to decide whether the feeling he felt for her was love. Was he himself loveless as well?" (2,075) Depressed, he feels that "his hands had grasped ashes," but then he wonders "Well, what did Tom possess?" (2,076) Once "he, too, had dreamed of amazing adventure in far places and desired to go out on the shining ways. And he had planned to go; yet he had known only work and duty" (2,086). After Tom has a visit from Captain Carlsen, who enters swearing, "'By the turtles of Tasman! When I heard you was in California, Captain Tom, I just had to come and shake hands.'" Frederick, hearing of their adventures, continues to question himself:

> The thought of all his property seemed to put a dry and gritty taste in his mouth. Property! Now that he looked at it, one thousand dollars was like any other thousand dollars; and one day (of his days) was like any other day. . . . A man could sleep in only one bed at a time—Tom had said that. He shuddered as he strove to estimate how many beds he owned, how many blankets he had bought. And all the beds and blankets would not buy one man to come from the end of the earth, and grip his hand, and cry, "By the turtles of Tasman!"

He tells Polly a bit about his feelings about his life and Tom's, and she answers: "'It couldn't have been otherwise. Father bought it. He never drove bargains. It was a royal thing, and he paid for it royally. You grudged the price, don't you see. You saved your arteries and your money and kept your feet dry'" (2,086).

In the end, Tom dies, having slowly faded away, and when a last wayfarer comes to see him, Frederick hears him repeat the oath, and then repeats it himself: "'By the turtles of Tasman, he was a man,' Frederick repeated; nor did he stumble over the unaccustomed oath" (2,088).

COMMENTARY

Several elements in the story reinforce its theme of opposites: the brothers' radically different personalities, responsibility versus adventure, foreignness versus traditional American values, profligate versus Puritan, love versus sterility. These conflicts probably reflect London's own competing identities at the time, adventurer or rancher? It also accords with his practice of showing two different points of view in many of his stories; often, the more conventional point of view is challenged by otherness, as in "The House of Pride," "The Red One," or "The Water Baby." Finally, something Charmian London often complained about was her husband's habit of inviting all kinds of people to the ranch and holding long, drunken dinner parties each night, after which he and his guests would sit up telling stories of their adventures. London

was ever the host and ever gregarious, while she would have appreciated a break from all the commotion of guests.

CHARACTERS

Frederick Travers A millionaire businessman whose contributions to his region include a waterworks, railroad, ferries, and highways, Frederick is in line to be the next governor of California. He took to heart the Puritan teachings of his parents, unlike his adventuring brother, who roams the world and sends IOUs to his more responsible brother. Frederick realizes in the course of the story that while he owns much property, he has missed life's most important experience, love.

Tom Travers Tom might be described as Frederick's ne'er-do-well brother; instead of working hard all his life building public works and a fortune, he has lived just on the edge of lawlessness in his wanderings around the world, smuggling opium, guns, and other contraband in dozens of exotic places. He returns home at the behest of his daughter, Polly, to die, though he does not know it.

Mary Travers The polite, well-bred but colorless daughter of Frederick Travers. Much like her father, she has been sheltered all of her life and has experienced little of it. She is impressed with her cousin Polly's flair for beauty and apparel.

Bronislawa Plaskoweitzkaia Travers (Polly) The daughter of Tom Travers and a woman from Buenos Aires, she is warm, sexually attractive, and forthright where Mary is quiet and dull. She challenges Frederick throughout the story, unnerving him with her insouciance and "wild" nature.

Captain Carlsen "Captain Carlsen was a giant hulk of a man, with gimlet eyes of palest blue, a slash-scarred mouth that a blazing red beard could not quite hide, and a grip in his hand that made Frederick squirm" (2,079). He is a friend of Tom's; they were together in the South Seas and survived terrifying adventures. Tom borrows $1,000 from Frederick and gives it to Carlsen.

unnamed South Seas and Yukon Adventurers
When Tom is staying at his brother's home, dozens of former friends from all corners of the Earth come to visit him, regaling Frederick and Mary with wild tales of adventure: from shipwreck and sharks to "the head-decorated palisade that surrounded the grass palace wherein dwelt the Malay queen with her royal consort, a shipwrecked Chinese Eurasian; of the intrigue for the pearl of Desay; of mad feasts and dances in the barbaric night, and quick dangers and sudden deaths; . . . of the coming of the plague; of the beating of tom-toms and the exorcising of the devil-devil doctors; of the flight over the man-trapped, wild-pig runs of the mountain bush-men; and of the final rescue by Tasman, he who was hatcheted only last year and whose head reposed in some Melanesian stronghold—and all breathing of the warmth and abandon and savagery of the burning islands of the sun" (2,085).

The Call of the Wild (1903)

A title search on amazon.com for *The Call of the Wild* reveals that it exists in hundreds of editions, translated into nearly every language in the world. There are arty hardbacks, paperback versions, electronic texts, cassettes, CDs, MP3 player versions, Kindle versions, films, television shows, audiobooks, editions with thesauruses, student guides, teacher lesson plans, illustrated "classics," comic books, graphic novels, casebooks, annotated versions, abridgments, editions including *White Fang* or *The Sea-Wolf,* a version with *Black Beauty,* a vocabulary-building version, even an edition sponsored by Chick-fil-a. And these are samples of only English editions; on the international scene it has earned its place as America's best candidate for a world novel. "If you like dogs, you will like this book," notes an anonymous reviewer of *The Call of the Wild* in 1903 (Wilcox, 149). This is as true today as it was in London's time. And yet another early reviewer, J. Stewart Doubleday, wrote in 1903: "It must be patent to all, we think, that the man who can, through the simple story of a dog, set us thought-wandering over illimitable ways, is

a man of language to be respectfully classed and reckoned with. There is nothing local or narrow about Jack London. . . . His voice is the voice of a man in the presence of the multitude, and he utters the word that is as bread to him. . . . [He is] the stalwart youthful leader of the promising far West. In his own field he is master; and more than this we ought not to exact of any man" (Wilcox, 151).

In a letter of March 10, 1903, London responds to an offer by GEORGE BRETT at MACMILLAN for *The Call of the Wild.* Explaining that he had already sold the serial rights to the SATURDAY EVENING POST, which first published the story, London agreed to receive only $2,000 as an outright sale and no royalties; he later received $700 from the *Saturday Evening Post.* Thus, for a book that has sold tens of millions of copies, London received only $2,700. In the same letter, he confesses that he did not like the title *The Call of the Wild,* chosen by the *Post,* but preferred *The Sleeping Wolf* or *The Wolf,* though he did not like them much either. He also explains the composition of the book: "The whole history of this story has been very rapid. On my return from England I sat down to write it into a 4,000 word yarn, but it got away from me & I was forced to expand it to its present length" (*Letters,* 351–352).

"To this day Jack London is the most widely read American writer in the world," E. L. Doctorow observes, in large part because of *The Call of the Wild* (Doctorow, 1). Earle Labor sees it as "America's greatest world novel" (Labor and Reesman, 133). Alfred Kazin calls Buck "London's greatest invention" (Kazin, 88). Buck's story is enjoyed by nearly all ages as an adventure with as universal a hero as any storyteller has ever conceived. Today, the title phrase is a household word. One sees it in ads from *Sports Illustrated* to *Vogue,* as well as in endless headlines and captions in the travel section. That it is almost always used without attribution indicates its ubiquity. The novel appears on thousands of syllabi every year and is often one of a handful of books incoming college students have in common. It has inspired everyone from rock bands to poets to the unfortunate Christopher McCandless, the subject of Jon Krakauer's *Into the Wild.*

Critics such as James C. Walcutt have seen *The Call of the Wild* as an example of Adamic innocence

The Call of the Wild 47

VII THE SOUNDING *of the* CALL

HEN BUCK earned sixteen hundred dollars in five minutes for John Thornton, he made it possible for his master to pay off certain debts and to journey with his partners into the East after a fabled lost mine, the history of which was as old as the history of the country. Many men had sought it; few had found it; and more than a few there were who had never returned from the quest. This lost mine was steeped in tragedy and shrouded in mystery. No one knew of the first man. The oldest tradition stopped before it got back to him. From the beginning there had

Marginalia art by Paul Bransom from 1926 Macmillan reprint of *The Call of the Wild (Huntington Library)*

or redemption. Charles N. Watson, Jr., points out that it shares with *Huckleberry Finn* "the perennial American dream of escape and freedom associated with the natural world," which London believed was a better world (Watson, 40). It is read as autobiographical. Andrew Sinclair reads the book as London's record "of his own childish fears of cold, deprivation, and solitude, as well as his compulsion to be always free and roving, on the hunt to gratify every desire" (Sinclair, 93).

Jacqueline Tavernier-Courbin describes London losing himself "in a world of beauty and purity" in contrast to his own impoverished background and steadily deteriorating marriage. She characterizes it as a "naturalistic romance," a blended genre emblematic of London's conflicts among various sides of himself, especially INDIVIDUALISM and SOCIALISM. In *The Call of the Wild,* London imagines an arena ruled over by the neutral god of Nature, where survival is fair because the god is

truly impartial (Tavernier-Courbin, 8–9). According to Joseph C. Sciambra, *The Call of the Wild* is a Darwinian working out of "the conflict of the yearning for freedom and power with the desire to be part of the strong group. Within the wolf pack, Buck finds the ideal situation. There are no weaklings in a wolf pack; there is no love, no kindness. Only the fittest survive" (Sciambra, 59). In *The Call of the Wild: A Naturalistic Romance,* Tavernier-Courbin argues that *The Call of the Wild* is "one of the world's most romantic novels," in that "[i]ts naturalistic, mythical, and archetypal characteristics, far from being at odds with romanticism, are an intrinsic part of it. But it is also romantic in other ways. Like much of London's work, it is romantic because of its emphasis on love, beauty, justice, and because of its appeal to a complete range of emotions, from pity and anger to admiration and envy. It is also romantic because it dramatizes a human dream of adventure, freedom, and personal fulfillment" (Tavernier-Courbin, 99). Tavernier-Courbin is especially helpful in understanding the influences on London's work, especially from ÉMILE ZOLA. Similarly, Franklin Walker reads it as a spiritual autobiography. James Dickey praises its sense of the connection between "the creative powers of the individual writer and the unconscious drive to breed and to survive, found in the natural world" (Dickey, 7). Jonathan Auerbach traces in *The Call of the Wild* the development of the writer's maturing conception of himself and his craft (Auerbach, 25).

SYNOPSIS

The story begins at Judge Miller's "big house in the sun-kissed SANTA CLARA VALLEY," back from the road, hidden by trees, surrounded by a "wide cool veranda" on four sides. A long gravel drive winds through spreading lawns "under the interlacing boughs of tall poplars," while in the rear are arranged "great stables, where a dozen grooms and boys held forth, rows of vine-clad servants' cottages, an endless and orderly array of outhouses, long grape arbors, green pastures, orchards, and berry patches" (16). Buck, half-St. Bernard and half-SCOTCH SHEPHERD, is a prized house dog who lords it over the lesser dogs and who thinks that he also rules the humans. "And over this great demesne Buck ruled": neither house nor kennel dog, Buck has the run of the place, "for he was king,—king over all creeping, crawling, flying things of Judge Miller's place, humans included" (note the language of Genesis). As a king, a "sated aristocrat," and "country gentleman" (16–18), Buck's estimation of himself is high, but he is mistaken about everyone seeing him this way.

Manuel, one of the gardener's helpers, kidnaps Buck and sells him as a KLONDIKE sled dog. The economics of the "yellow metal" that "men, groping in the Arctic darkness" have unearthed also generates the economics of Manuel: "Manuel had one besetting sin. He loved to play Chinese lottery. Also in his gambling, he had one besetting weakness—faith in a system; and this made his damnation certain. For to play a system requires money, while the wages of a gardener's helper do not lap over the needs of a wife and numerous progeny" (19).

Buck is handed over to a saloon keeper and then sold. He is, to his great surprise, severely manhandled by the men who buy him and choked senseless with a rope before he is placed in a crate and then into a wagon, bound for a train north. En route to the NORTHLAND, he is deprived of food and water and then brutally beaten by the man in the red sweater: "That club was a revelation. It was his introduction to the reign of primitive law. . . . The facts of life took on a fiercer aspect; and while he faced that aspect uncowed, he faced it with all the latent cunning of his nature aroused" (32–33). The meeting with the man in the red sweater and the painful encounter with his club subdue Buck, but he is not broken. Upon arrival in his New World, Buck is sold. His first owners, François and Perrault, are Canadian government agents who carry the mail between SKAGWAY and DAWSON. Buck has to learn the new language they speak: "Perrault was a French-Canadian, and swarthy; but François was a French-Canadian half-breed, and twice as swarthy. They were a new kind of men" (37). As the *Narwhal* steams north, at the end of the chapter, Buck is greeted with his first taste of the Northland, a fall of fresh white snow, which he has never seen before, an emblem of the

WHITE SILENCE he will face. Tavernier-Courbin finds that "Despite its literal and symbolic coldness, despite its awesome power and immensity, despite its lack of forgiveness for errors and weaknesses," London's trope of the White Silence, "the vast, still, and frozen Northland wilderness, is a symbol of freedom and purity. While the minds and bodies of survivors rot slowly in the putrid slums, the White Silence provides a moral and physical school of endurance over which presides a harsh but just God" (Tavernier-Courbin, 45–46). Such an impartial justice on a naturalistic level of survival is the antidote to the capitalist-slave system that makes Buck its prisoner.

After Buck faces the "nightmare" of DYEA BEACH, with its teeming men and dogs, he witnesses the death of Curly, whose friendly approach to another dog results in her being killed. The attacker, Spitz, is a huge white husky who gives no mercy. Buck surmises: "So that was the way. No fair play. Once down, that was the end of you" (45). Spitz, the leader, and Dave, the "wheel dog," help the men teach Buck the ways of the sled. He resents having the sled harness placed upon him, "such as he had seen the grooms put on the horses at home," but though his "dignity [is] made sore by thus being a draught animal, he was too wise to rebel" (46). Each dog is portrayed as a character type: Spitz, the lead dog, Dave, the hard worker, Billee, the timid, Sol-leks, the "Angry One." The other dogs each serve to teach Buck lessons about his own survival. They also reflect the Darwinian adaptation Buck increasingly exhibits. As his education progresses, Buck must interpret his surroundings. By adapting, Buck engages in self-discovery, as when his first theft of food marks him "as fit to survive in the hostile Northland environment," dispensing with civilized morality: "His development (or retrogression) was rapid" (59).

As time goes by, Buck becomes more and more aware of the sense of an "other" self, of "the old life within him." On the cold and still nights, he joins the other dogs and "pointed his nose at a star and howled long and wolflike, it was his ancestors, dead and dust, pointing nose at a star and howling down through the centuries and through him, . . . what to them was the meaning of the stillness, and the cold, and dark" (62). The dogs sing their "defiance of life" at the aurora borealis, "with long-drawn wailings and half-sobs, and was more the pleading of life, the articulate travail of existence, . . . one of the first songs of the younger world in a day when songs were sad" (84). Yet the narrator ironically comments, "Thus, as token of what a puppet thing life is, the ancient song surged through him and he came into his own again; and he came because men had found a yellow gold in the North, and because Manuel was a gardener's helper whose wages did not lap over the needs of his wife and divers small copies of himself" (62–63).

The title of "The Dominant Primordial Beast," Dan Dyer points out, "refers not only to Buck but to Jack London himself," using the words of a promotional booklet MACMILLAN issued that described how London's "sturdy ancestral stock" enabled him "to prove his mastery over environment" (Dyer, xxxi). Buck challenges Spitz for leadership, and the dogs fight, though they join in the heady chase of the snowshoe rabbit. In Buck's fight with Spitz, Buck wins through "imagination" as well as strength, using both experience of other fights and his "head" in planning his attack. At the end of the chapter, "The dark circle became a dot on the moon-flooded snow as Spitz disappeared from view. Buck stood and looked on, the successful champion, the dominant primordial beast who had made his kill and found it good" (99). Buck takes from Spitz the role of the leader, even borrowing language from the Creator himself in Genesis I. Yet, the title of the next chapter, "Who Has Won to Mastership," suggests that Buck is still deluded by his role as a "master" among fellow slaves. He must break free of man entirely.

Despite the team's excellent performance under Buck's leadership, they are suddenly sold to a "Scotch half-breed" mail carrier. Buck forms no bond with this new master, who seems only interested in working the dogs as hard as he can. Dave, though dying, refuses to be left behind when he falters in the traces and desperately tries to keep up his work. Dave is shot out of mercy, and his death casts a pall over things. Buck feels torn between his desire to be the leader under the sway of the men and to realize his own identity. Dave's absurd resis-

tance and desire to work to his dying breath, to be the perfect slave, cannot be lost upon Buck. Buck seeks to look beyond civilization with its slavery to a more radical self.

Though he does not flee them, he feels apprehensive about his next masters, the disorderly Hal, Charles, and Mercedes. The men are effeminate and ineffectual, like the antiheroes of "In a Far Country," and the woman is spoiled and hysterical. She insists she be treated with "gentlemanly chivalry" and places all their lives in danger to satisfy her wants, including underfeeding the dogs nearly to starvation after spoiling them by overfeeding. The dogs begin to die off, and the party bicker among themselves, especially the "pretty and soft" Mercedes, who, when told to get off and walk so the sled can carry enough food for the dogs "wept and importuned Heaven" (144). Of an original team of 14, only five dogs are still alive when Hal, Charles, and Mercedes arrive at John Thornton's camp. When they prepare to depart, Thornton warns them that the ice over which they are traveling is melting and that they may fall through it. Hal dismisses his warning. The other dogs begin to move, but Buck refuses. When Hal begins to beat him, Thornton intervenes, knocking a knife from Hal's hand and cutting Buck free of the traces. Hal curses Thornton and starts the sled again, but before they have gone a short distance, the ice breaks open, swallowing humans and dogs alike.

Buck recovers his strength and joins Thornton's camp. He gets along well with Thornton's easygoing dogs. With Thornton he finds "love, genuine passionate love," for the first time. Their relationship is different from the distant relations he had with the Judge, but it is a reenactment of that subservient relationship after all, no matter how beloved he is or how ideal a master Thornton is. For Buck, "in spite of this great love he bore John Thornton, which seemed to bespeak the soft civilizing influence, the strain of the primitive, which the Northland had aroused in him, remained alive and active" (166). He increasingly feels "the eternity behind him," which "throbbed through him in a mighty rhythm to which he swayed as the tides and seasons swayed" (168). This birth imagery signals that Buck is about to undergo a final transformation into his true self. Ironically, the past is the source of his future.

Buck begins to stay away from Thornton for longer periods of time, meeting the wolf pack and hunting with them. In return, Thornton enforces tests of love upon Buck. Buck defends his master from a desperado and saves his life. Thornton demands Buck jump off a cliff, stopping him at the last moment. He then places a huge bet on Buck's pulling a one-ton load on a sled. That London says Buck "earned" the $1,600 for his master is, as Auerbach notes, "a bit troubling," pointing to the delusion of thinking that a slave will ever be anything more than a thing to his master. But with Thornton and his party, who toil for treasure in the East, Buck still works for his master (197). In this, says Auerbach, he has not yet "lost touch with civilization" (Auerbach, 237–239). But Thornton, the love of Buck's life, must be killed off in order for Buck to be fully realized, and Buck must shed the remnants of his internal image as a slave in order to be free, no matter what.

In the last chapter Buck alternates between his newfound identity as "a thing of the wild, come in from the wild to sit by John Thornton's fire" (210) and Thornton's companion. With his new wolf brothers, Buck hunts and kills, culminating in the death struggle of the great moose. When he returns after many weeks to camp, he finds the YEEHATS celebrating their massacre and robbery of Thornton and his dogs, and he retaliates as "the Fiend incarnate": "At times, when he paused to contemplate the carcasses of the Yeehats, he forgot the pain of [Thornton's death]; and at such times he was aware of a great pride in himself,—a pride greater than any he had yet experienced. He had killed man, the noblest game of all, and he had killed in the face of the law of club and fang" (223). This passage marks Buck's final escape from slavery, paradoxically the most grievous and most liberating event of his life, the death of his "father," echoing London's conflicted psychological search for a father in the Klondike fiction.

At the end, Buck has become himself, an individual within the COMMUNITY of the pack: "When the long winter nights come on and the wolves follow their meat into the lower valleys, he may be seen running at the head of the pack through the pale moonlight or glimmering borealis, leaping gigantic above his fellows, his great throat a-bellow as he sings a song of the younger world, which is the song of the pack" (231). Thornton could no longer be Buck's God, nor could any human master, but only the just if harshly impartial god of NATURALISM Tavernier-Courbin describes. Buck has found himself through his place in nature, which transcends civilization.

COMMENTARY

London's observations of the poor in London's East End in *The People of the Abyss* helped inspire both his naturalistic survival themes and also his romantic visions of release and escape from industrial civilization in *The Call of the Wild*, as he advocated emigration by Britons to the wild spaces of the North American West. As a socialist, he despised capitalist greed, reflected in the novel. It can also be seen as a forecast of the modern alienated hero. Like *Huckleberry Finn*, at its core it is a fight for survival against the restrictions of an enslaving "civilization." Like that novel, it derives in part from the slave narrative.

Such characteristically American genres as "New World" discovery narratives, the frontier adventure, the trickster tale, the animal fable, and the captivity narrative helped shape *The Call of the Wild*. But it is most clearly related to the slave narrative, the genre of personal narratives by African Americans who escaped slavery. It may seem odd that London, so often a proponent of ANGLO-SAXON supremacy would write a slave narrative, but it is consistent with London's personality and environment and has roots in his childhood. Not only did he feel enslaved by poverty and see as meaningless the drudgery of the working class wage slaves or work-beasts as a form of slavery, but he was in part raised by an African-American foster mother, Mrs. VIRGINIA PRENTISS, an escaped slave from Tennessee who told him of her exploits. And as a reader of MARK TWAIN and Harriet Beecher Stowe, he was drawn to slaves' stories of individual and communal heroism in their quest for a new identity. Slavery in fact is a repeated feature in his fiction.

London often created heroes of a common denominator who struggle against powerful forces that would obliterate them if unchecked—child laborers, racial others, slaves, worn-down boxers, hobos, mutinous sailors, and so on—though not usually as "common" as a dog. His choice of a canine point of view allowed London to explore in both a naturalistic and mythic narrative the most fundamental issues of human individuality and community, without resorting to a hero of any race or culture. Hence, the novella's near-universal popularity among its millions of readers each year.

Besides the search for identity and freedom, the novel contains other important themes. Indeed, one of the key themes of *The Call of the Wild* is ATAVISM, or an individual's (in this case, Buck's) recovery of the instincts of his wild ancestors. For Buck, this involves repeated visions of his primitive past, which usually occur late at night when he is lying alongside a campfire. He imagines the men around him as primitive men, clothed in furs and wary of the prehistoric dark around them, and then he has visions of himself as a primitive, wild creature, hunting his prey in the primeval forests. Each of these visions brings him closer to his destiny, which is the return to his ancestors' ways and becoming a wild animal himself. When Buck enters the Northland, he must learn many lessons in order to survive, and he learns them well. All of the old rules—such as not fighting, not stealing food—from Judge Miller's place are abandoned. But the novel suggests that this is not merely a matter of *learning* the ways of the wild; rather, Buck *recovers* his primitive instincts and the racial memory of his wild ancestors, which are buried when dogs become civilized creatures. London constantly reminds us that Buck is "retrogressing," as the novel puts it, into a wilder way of life that all dogs once shared": "He was older than the days he had seen and the breaths he had drawn. . . . He linked the past with the present, and the eternity behind him throbbed through him in a mighty rhythm to which he swayed as the tides and seasons swayed" (168). Critics also call what London does with Buck anthropomorphism, or giving human qualities to animals. Buck does not speak, but London does give the dog human thoughts and emotions. It's a nice bit of irony that he begins the story with "Buck

did not read the newspapers," as though suggesting he could if he wanted to (1).

Another theme that is often invoked is the theme of individualism; FRIEDRICH NIETZSCHE is cited as the most important influence on the book. However, this is a mistake. For one thing, London did not read much Nietzsche until 1906. Also, he later renounced Nietzsche and parodies him in the character of Wolf Larsen in *The Sea-Wolf*, but, more important, in London's works neither animals nor people survive well on their own. Buck does find out who he is and becomes his own individual and his story is inspiring to anyone engaged in struggle and self-determination. But Buck exists first within the sled team and next in the wolf pack; he is far from alone. (The idea of entering the wild alone was the mistake made by Chris McCandless, the young man whose doomed attempt to live alone in the wilderness of Alaska is related in Jon Krakauer's *Into the Wild*.)

Furthermore, as suggested earlier, as London's primitivism can function as a rhetorical device meant to inspire his readers to share his political views (as in, for example, "South of the Slot"), in this case he was thinking of the corruption and worship of money of the age and also the evils of the capitalist system. Although London's nature and adventure stories have often been seen as irrelevant to political beliefs, most often his work can be understood only through an appreciation of the way in which these two elements of his writing are related. In the class struggle London described elsewhere, as in *The Iron Heel*, there are similar fights for self-determination; in *The Valley of the Moon*, nature itself is an opponent of the meanness of strike-torn OAKLAND.

There is a pronounced Darwinian theme. London remarked in a 1912 interview with George Wharton James that he had "always been impressed with the awful plasticity of life" and therefore could "never lay enough stress upon the marvelous power and influence of environment" (quoted in Labor, "Introduction," xv). For London, success or failure was not whether one was a strong individual, but whether or not one could adapt to a changing environment, demonstrating London's allegiance to DARWIN and not Nietzsche; in contrast to Buck's evolutionary fitness and ADAPTATION, the two cowardly cabinmates of "In a Far Country" fail to adapt at all to the Northland, and as a result they die. In *The Call of the Wild*, Buck is said to be able to "adjust himself to changing conditions" after he is kidnapped and taken into the Northland, where he "unconsciously . . . accommodated himself to the new mode of life" (60).

The most insightful reading of *The Call of the Wild*, Earle Labor's exploration of its mythic elements, considers as critical this unconscious life. Labor describes what happens to Buck in the final chapter as an "apotheosis." He emphasizes the eerie, primordial quality of the landscape into which Thornton and his party have journeyed, a "journey into the East after a fabled lost mine, the history of which was as old as the history of the country" (193). As Labor notes, "From the opening paragraph of this chapter it is evident that the place toward which the group is moving is extraordinary: 'Many men had sought it; few had ever found it; and more than a few there were who had never returned from the quest. This lost mine was steeped in tragedy and shrouded in mystery. No one knew of the first man. The oldest tradition stopped before it got back to him'" (Labor, "Jack London's Mondo Cane," 193). Labor relates this description to Joseph Campbell's words in *The Hero With a Thousand Faces*: "[The 'call of adventure'] signifies that destiny has summoned the hero and transferred his spiritual center of gravity from within the pale of society to a zone unknown. This fateful region of both treasure and danger may be variously represented: as a distant land, a forest, a kingdom underground, beneath the waves, or above the sky, a secret island, lofty mountaintop, or profound dream state; but it is always a place of strangely fluid and polymorphous beings, unimaginable torments, superhuman deeds and impossible delight," and, Labor adds, a sort of *Ur-welt*, or primeval world (Campbell, 58):

> To Buck it was boundless delight, this hunting, fishing, and indefinite wandering through strange places. For weeks at a time they would hold on steadily, day after day; and for weeks upon end they would camp, here and there, the

dogs loafing and the men burning holes through frozen muck and gravel and washing countless pans of dirt by the heat of the fire. Sometimes they went hungry, sometimes they feasted riotously, all according to the abundance of game and the fortune of hunting. . . . The months came and went, and back and forth they twisted through the uncharted vastness, where no men were and yet where men had been if the Lost Cabin were true. They went across divides in summer blizzards, shivered under the midnight sun on naked mountains between the timber line and the eternal snows, dropped into summer valleys amid swarming gnats and flies, and in the shadows of glaciers picked strawberries and flowers as ripe and fair as any the Southland could boast. In the fall of the year they penetrated a weird lake country, sad and silent, where wild fowl had been, but where then there was no life nor sign of life—only the blowing of chill winds, the forming of ice in sheltered places, and the melancholy rippling of waves on lonely beaches. . . . Spring came on once more, and at the end of all their wandering they found, not the Lost Cabin, but a shallow placer in a broad valley where the gold showed like yellow butter across the bottom of the washing pan. They sought no farther. Each day they worked earned them thousands of dollars in clean dust and nuggets, and they worked every day. The gold was sacked in moosehide bags, fifty pounds to the bag, and piled like so much firewood outside the spruce-bough lodge. Like giants they toiled, days flashing on the heels of days like dreams as they heaped the treasure up. (195–196)

As Labor explains, "This 'fateful region of both treasure and danger' is a far cry from Judge Miller's ranch and even from the raw frontier of the Klondike gold rush: enveloped in the atmosphere of the dream world, it is the timeless landscape of myth." He mentions CARL JUNG's formulation of a world that "derives its existence from the hinterland of man's mind—that suggests the abyss separating us from pre-human ages, or evokes a super-human world of contrasting light and darkness. It is a primordial experience which surpasses man's understanding" (Jung, 156–157). In other words, adds Labor, "the world into which Buck moves at the end of the story is a world of the 'collective unconscious,' the primordial world which modern man has blocked off with the inhibiting barriers of reason and social convention but a nonetheless real world to which he would return, in dreams, to find his soul." When he is released by the death of Thornton, Buck loses his last tie to the conventional world. He achieves "the ultimate freedom for which men unconsciously yearn." Buck "is no longer a dog—not even a superdog—but a projection of the reader's essential mythic *self*, a dynamic symbol of libido, *elan vital*, the life force" (Labor, "Jack London's Mondo Cane," 210–213).

CHARACTERS

Buck The protagonist of the tale, Buck, is part St. Bernard, part "Scotch shepherd." At the beginning of the story, Buck is a domesticated dog who lives in the home of Judge Miller in California. After being kidnapped and taken to ALASKA to become a sled dog, Buck's wild nature is reawakened, and he slowly returns to the ways of his ancestors and joins a wolf pack in the far North as its leader, becoming a legend among the Natives.

John Thornton The man who rescues Buck from Hal's cruelty. He is by far the most admirable human character in the story, kindly but strong. Buck loves him dearly but must leave him in order to become his fully realized animal self.

Judge Miller Quiet and sedate, he is Buck's original owner, and they live on his prosperous estate in Santa Clara, California. He admires Buck but is not especially demonstrative with him. Judge Miller is based on the father of two of London's Klondike friends, Louis and Marshall Bond; their dog Jack was the inspiration for Buck, and Judge Miller's place is based on Judge Bond's.

Manuel The gardener's helper on Judge Miller's estate who kidnaps and sells Buck to fund his gambling habit and his large family.

man in the red sweater Wielding his club, he disciplines all dogs that will be sold for sledding. Ruthless in his repeated beatings of Buck, he maintains composure and control, not beating out of anger but in order to toughen the dogs and teach them their place. Buck never forgets the law of the club.

François A French-Canadian sled driver who carries mail. He is particularly knowledgeable about dogs, and he is also very strict with them.

Perrault A French-Canadian like François, who works for him, and an agent of the Canadian government. He is admired by Buck for his fearlessness in blazing trails and crossing dangerous ice.

Spitz Spitz, a strong and vicious husky, is the lead dog on Buck's first dogsled team. He recognizes Buck as a rival and lays in wait to attack him. Buck kills him in a fight for leadership.

Curly A pleasant-natured Newfoundland, Curly is a member of Buck's first dogsled team. She is killed by Spitz when she makes a friendly advance toward him; from her death Buck learns that he will have to fight for survival and never allow himself to be vulnerable like Curly.

Dave Another one of Buck's first companions, he is the "wheel dog" and an extraordinarily hard worker. He helps teach Buck how to pull the sled and takes pride in his work. However, he eventually weakens and is shot out of mercy. From his death, Buck receives an inkling of why work alone will not satisfy him.

Sol-leks Called "the Angry One," Sol-leks is blind in one eye and will attack any dog who approaches him on that side.

Billee A member of the dog team who is good-natured and considerate: he shows Buck how to make a bed in the snow. He is killed by Hal.

Joe Billee's brother. Unlike Billee, Joe is always snarling and defensive.

Pike   Another member of the team, often referred to as "the malingerer." He rarely gets up on time, and he will steal food and generally undermine the expedition. When Buck becomes leader, he transforms Pike into a helpful member of the team.

Dub   Dog team member who is an awkward blunderer and gets blamed for Buck's stealing food.

Dolly   A member of Buck's mail run team, Dolly goes mad after being bitten by wild huskies, tries to attack Buck, and is killed by François.

Hal   Hal is a young man who buys Buck and his team once they have used up their usefulness to the government's mail runs. He seeks gold in the Klondike, but he is too lazy and incompetent to survive in the Northland. He also betrays a lack of understanding about how to manage dogs, and he mistreats them cruelly.

Charles   Hal's brother-in-law, a weak figure who follows Hal around, does what he is told, and is henpecked by his wife.

Mercedes   Sister of Hal, wife of Charles. She is foolish in her handling of the dogs and, because she is so spoiled and self-centered, spends most of her time crying and complaining. Like her companions, she is a creature of civilization and unfit to survive in the Northland.

Pete and Hans   Partners of Thornton.

"Black" Burton   An incorrigible troublemaker who starts a bar fight, causing Thornton to step in.

Matthewson   A miner who bets Thornton that Buck cannot pull a ton of weight.

Jim O'Brien   A man who loans Thornton the money to make the bet against Matthewson.

Yeehats   Fictional name for the group of Natives who raid John Thornton's place and kill him and his dogs. When Buck returns, he kills most of them. From then on, they tell tales of a gigantic dog pos-

sessed of great power who roams the forest at the head of a wolf pack.

Skeet   An Irish setter who belongs to Thornton. She nurses Buck through his recovery.

Nig   A huge black dog who belongs to Thornton, with a friendly nature.

lone wolf   A wolf, the "wild brother" Buck meets in the forest. Suspicious at first, the lone wolf helps adopt Buck into the wolf pack.

FURTHER READING

Anon. "A 'Nature' Story—*The Call of the Wild* by Jack London." *Literary World* 34 (September 1903): 229. Reprinted in Earl J. Wilcox, ed. *The Call of the Wild by Jack London: A Casebook with Text, Background Sources, Reviews, Critical Essays, and Bibliography.* Chicago, Ill.: Nelson-Hall, 1980, 149.

Auerbach, Jonathan. *Male Call: Becoming Jack London.* Durham, N.C.: Duke University Press, 1996.

Berton, Pierre. *Klondike Fever: The Life and Death of The Last Great Gold Rush.* New York: Alfred A. Knopf, 1958.

The Call of the Wild: Annotated and Illustrated. Edited by Dan Dyer. Norman: University of Oklahoma Press, 1997.

Campbell, Joseph. *The Hero with a Thousand Faces.* New York: Meridien, 1956, 40–171 *passim.*

Dickey, James. *Introduction to "The Call of the Wild," "White Fang," and Other Stories,* by Jack London. Edited by Andrew Sinclair. New York: Penguin, 1981, 7–16.

Doctorow, E. L. Review of *The Letters of Jack London, New York Times Book Review,* December 11, 1988.

Doubleday, J. Stewart. "*The Call of the Wild.*" Review. *Reader* 2 (September 1903): 408–409. Reprinted in Earl J. Wilcox, ed. *The Call of the Wild by Jack London: A Casebook with Text, Background Sources, Reviews, Critical Essays, and Bibliography.* Chicago, Ill.: Nelson-Hall, 1980, 150–151.

Giles, James R. "Assaulting the Yeehats: Violence and Space in *The Call of the Wild.*" In *Twisted from the Ordinary: Essays on American Literary Naturalism.* Edited by Mary E. Papke. Knoxville: University of Tennessee Press, 2003, 188–201.

Hopkins, Lisa. "Jack London's Evolutionary Hierarchies: Dogs, Wolves, and Men." In *Evolution and Eugenics in American Literature and Culture, 1880–1940.* Edited by Lois Cuddy and Claire M. Roche. Lewisburg, Pa.: Bucknell University Press, 2003, 89–101.

Jung, C. G. *Modern Man in Search of a Soul.* New York: Harvest, 1933.

Kazin, Alfred. *On Native Grounds.* New York: Doubleday and Co., 1942.

Labor, Earle. "Jack London's Mondo Cane: The Call of the Wild and White Fang." *Jack London Newsletter* 1 (September–December 1967): 2–13. Reprinted in Earl J. Wilcox, ed. *The Call of the Wild by Jack London: A Casebook with Text, Background Sources, Reviews, Critical Essays, and Bibliography.* Chicago, Ill.: Nelson-Hall, 1980, 202–216.

Labor, Earle, and Jeanne Campbell Reesman. *Jack London, Revised Edition.* New York: Macmillan (Twayne U.S. Authors Series), 1994.

Reesman, Jeanne Campbell. *Jack London's Racial Lives.* Athens: University of Georgia Press, 2009.

Sciambra, Joseph C. "From Herbert Spencer to Alfred Schultz: Jack London, His Library, and the Rise of Radical Racialism in Turn of the Century America." M.A. Thesis, Sonoma State University, 1977.

Sinclair, Andrew. *Jack: A Biography of Jack London.* New York: Harper & Row, 1977.

Tavernier-Courbin, Jacqueline. *The Call of the Wild: A Naturalistic Romance.* New York: Twayne, 1994.

———. "*The Call of the Wild* and *The Jungle*: Jack London's and Upton Sinclair's Animal and Human Jungles." In *The Cambridge Companion to American Realism and Naturalism: Howells to London.* Edited by Donald Pizer. Cambridge: Cambridge University Press, 1995, 236–262.

Walcutt, Charles Child. *Jack London.* Minneapolis: University of Minnesota Press, 1967.

Walker, Franklin. *Jack London and the Klondike: The Genesis of an American Writer.* San Marino, Calif.: Huntington Library, 1966.

Watson, Charles N., Jr. *The Novels of Jack London: A Reappraisal.* Madison: University of Wisconsin Press, 1983.

Wilcox, Earl J., ed. *The Call of the Wild by Jack London: A Casebook with Text, Background Sources, Reviews, Critical Essays, and Bibliography.* Chicago, Ill.: Nelson-Hall, 1980.

"The Chinago" (1909)

Included in the collection *When God Laughs and Other Stories* (1911), "The Chinago" was first published in the United States in *Harper's Monthly Magazine* 11 (July 1909). It relates the last meditations of a Chinese coolie, called a "Chinago" in TAHITI, who is unjustly condemned to death by an indifferent plantation system. One of London's most powerful anticolonialist stories, it reflects his sense of outrage at the plight of bound plantation workers in the South Pacific, and it reverses key stereotypes of Asians and Europeans prevalent at the time.

SYNOPSIS

The story opens with Ah Cho, the protagonist, listening uncomprehendingly to the French plantation bosses who are staging his trial for murder. He knows that he is innocent and marvels at the stupidity of the Frenchmen: "It was just so much gabble to Ah Cho, and he marvelled at the stupidity of the Frenchmen who took so long to find out the murderer of Chung Ga, and who did not find him at all. The five hundred coolies on the plantation knew that Ah San had done the killing, and here was Ah San not even arrested. It was true that all the coolies had agreed secretly not to testify against one another; but then, it was so simple, the Frenchmen should have been able to discover that Ah San was the man. They were very stupid, these Frenchmen" (1,405). Ah San has murdered another plantation worker, Chung Ga, but Ah Cho has been wrongfully blamed. He believes he has nothing to be afraid of, since he is innocent. London reiterates that "Ah Cho did not understand everything" and "Ah Cho did not understand all this" (1,406), indicating his linguistic and racial alienation from his masters. Having worked three of his five years of contract labor, he looks forward to returning home. His foreman, Karl Schemmer, has worked him cruelly, "for he was a brute, a brutish brute. But he earned his salary. He got the last particle of strength out of the five hundred slaves; for slaves they were until their term of years was up." Schemmer extracts "the strength from those five hundred sweating bodies and . . . transmute[s] it into bales of fluffy cotton ready for export." The narrator identifies his "dominant, iron-clad, primeval brutishness" as what enables him "to effect the transmutation." He is also "assisted by a thick leather belt, three inches wide and a yard in length, with which he always rode and which, on occasion, could come down on the naked back of a stooping coolie with a report like a pistol-shot" (1,407).

Ah Cho muses that "There was no understanding these white devils. Ah Cho pondered their inscrutableness. . . . There was no telling what went on at the back of their minds. . . . Their minds all moved in mysterious ways there was no getting at. They grew angry without apparent cause, and their anger was always dangerous. They were like wild beasts at such times. . . . They were not temperate as Chinagos were temperate; they were gluttons, eating prodigiously and drinking more prodigiously. A Chinago never knew when an act would please them or arouse a storm of wrath" (1,408). But when he realizes that he is about to be sentenced to death as Ah Chow, due to a recording error, Ah Cho protests, "'But I tell you, I am Ah Cho. I don't want my head cut off'" (1,412). The gendarme Cruchot contemplates his options and decides to go ahead with it. Ah Cho protests to Schemmer, but meets the same answer: "'Who can tell one Chinago from another?'" Cruchot replies, "'All right, go ahead with it. He is only a Chinago'" (1416).

At the moment of death, feeling the guillotine's edge "for one great fleeting instant," Ah Cho "remembered Cruchot and what Cruchot had said. But Cruchot was wrong. The knife did not tickle. That much he knew before he ceased to know" (1,417).

COMMENTARY

In "The Chinago," the barrier of language acts to condemn to death the innocent Chinese plantation worker. King Hendricks calls "The Chinago" "the greatest story of London's career," with its "building of an atmosphere, the telling of a narrative, and the development of irony" (Hendricks, 24). For Thomas R. Tietze and Gary Riedl, "The Chi-

nago" shows the absurd results of reliance upon an absolute text. Fatal misunderstandings occur: "The Chinago" shows how inscrutable the West must be from an Asian perspective.

This story's first and last sentences address knowledge: "Ah Cho did not understand French" (*Stories*, 1,405) and "That much he knew before he ceased to know" (1,417). It thus presents understanding as limited by cultural and personal ignorance. Knowledge in this tale is either wrong (despite the central motif of the trial as a way to find out truth), misinterpreted, or deliberately covered up. In addition to English, Riedl and Tietze point out, in the story seven other languages appear, from the court proceedings in "unceasing, explosive French" (1,405) to the various dialects spoken by the workers. Misinterpretation and confusion instead of understanding mean that after three weeks in prison, since Ah Chow's marks are still unhealed, he, not Ah Cho, is the one marked to die, while Ah Cho receives only 20 years in the penal colony on New Caledonia. But through another series of interpretive mistakes, Ah Cho is again mistaken for Ah Chow and taken out to the guillotine. London's insistence on having linguistic confusion twice condemn Ah Cho makes his irony inescapable. Such problems, he believed, could be avoided and mutual understanding enhanced if Asians and Americans would learn each other's languages, a point he insisted upon in a 1915 lecture in HONOLULU, "The Language of the Tribe."

CHARACTERS

Ah Cho The protagonist of the story, a Chinese peasant bound out to plantation labor in Tahiti. He is resigned to his fate, but he believes because he is innocent and the French do not know it, that they are stupid. He does not realize how expendable he is to them. "Ah Cho was twenty-two years old. He was happy and good-natured, and it was easy for him to smile. While his body was slim in the Asiatic way, his face was rotund. It was round, like the moon, and it irradiated a gentle complacence and a sweet kindliness of spirit that was unusual among his countrymen. Nor did his looks belie him. He never caused trouble, never took part in wrangling.

He did not gamble. His soul was not harsh enough for the soul that must belong to a gambler. He was content with little things and simple pleasures. The hush and quiet in the cool of the day after the blazing toil in the cotton field was to him an infinite satisfaction. He could sit for hours gazing at a solitary flower and philosophizing about the mysteries and riddles of being" (1,407).

Ah Chow Another coolie charged with murder; because his name is like Ah Cho's, he escapes when an error is made. At first, all five coolies are convicted, and Ah Chow is to have his head cut off. The reason he is to suffer the worst punishment is that his wounds from a beating by his plantation master have not healed, thus in some superstitious way indicating his guilt.

Chung Ga The fieldworker who is murdered by Ah San. His murder is blamed on Ah Cho.

Ah San The killer of Chung Ga, who is not even arrested for his crime, though all the coolies know he is guilty.

Karl Schemmer The brutal and stupid GERMAN master of the plantation on which Ah Cho labors; he does not want to be inconvenienced by a new trial once he finds out Ah Cho is innocent and orders his execution. He builds the guillotine Ah Cho is executed on.

Cruchot A gendarme who "had seen twenty years of service in the colonies, from Nigeria and Senegal to the South Seas, and those twenty years had not perceptibly brightened his dull mind. He was as slow-witted and stupid as in his peasant days in the south of FRANCE. He knew discipline and fear of authority, and from God down to the sergeant of gendarmes the only difference to him was the measure of slavish obedience which he rendered. In point of fact, the sergeant bulked bigger in his mind than God, except on Sundays when God's mouthpieces had their say. God was usually very remote, while the sergeant was ordinarily very close at hand" (1,410). Cruchot goes along with Schemmer's execution of Ah Cho even though he

knows he is innocent; he also (wrongly) tells Ah Cho the knife will not hurt. To add to his bungling, he places Ah Cho faceup on the block of the guillotine.

FURTHER READING

Hendricks, King. "Jack London: Master Craftsman of the Short Story." Thirty-third Faculty Honor Lecture. Logan: Utah State University Press, 1966.

Reesman, Jeanne Campbell. *Jack London's Racial Lives*. Athens: University of Georgia Press, 2009, chapter 4.

Riedl, Gary, and Thomas R. Tietze. "Misinterpreting the Unreadable: Jack London's 'The Chinago' and 'The Whale Tooth.'" *Studies in Short Fiction* 34, no. 4 (Fall 1997): 507–518.

Tietze, Thomas R., and Gary Riedl. "'Saints in Slime': The Ironic Use of Racism in Jack London's South Sea Tales." In *Thalia: Studies in Literary Humor* 12, nos. 1–2 (1992): 59–66.

"Chun Ah Chun" (1910)

First published, after being turned down by a number of magazines, in *Woman's Magazine* 21 (Spring 1910), "Chun Ah Chun" is an ironic tale of a wealthy CHINESE businessman who makes his home in HAWAI'I. It is loosely based on the real-life Chun Ah Fong, a legendary HONOLULU figure in his day who was called Hawai'i's Chinese Merchant Prince. An immigrant who worked his way into a fortune, he married a HAOLE woman, Julia Fayerweather, and raised "American" children.

SYNOPSIS

From an "undersized" and unimpressive youth immigrating to Hawai'i from China, Chun Ah Chun works hard and gains great wealth, marrying an American woman and siring a large family. If "[t]he average tourist, casually glimpsing him on the streets of Honolulu, would have concluded that he was a good-natured little Chinese, probably the proprietor of a prosperous laundry or tailorshop," the casual observer would not know that he was enormously wealthy (*Stories*, 1,455). But the observer should look closer, as London's narrative does, and recognize something else in Ah Chun:

> Ah Chun had shrewd little eyes, black and beady and so very little that they were like gimlet-holes. But they were wide apart, and they sheltered under a forehead that was patently the forehead of a thinker. For Ah Chun had his problems, and had had them all his life.—Not that he ever worried over them. He was essentially a philosopher, and whether as coolie, or multi-millionnaire and master of many men, his poise of soul was the same. He lived always in the high equanimity of spiritual repose, undeterred by good fortune, unruffled by ill fortune. All things went well with him, whether they were blows from the overseer in the cane field or a slump in the price of sugar when he owned those cane fields himself. Thus, from the steadfast rock of his sure content he mastered problems such as are given to few men to consider, much less to a Chinese peasant. (1,455)

Though as a peasant he was "born to labor in the fields all his days like a beast," he was also "fated to escape from the fields like the prince in a fairy tale" (1,455). As in some other stories, most notably "Mauki," London demonstrates how surface appearances can deceive, especially when connected with racial stereotypes.

The key to Ah Chun's success is his power of observation: "He perceived little details that not one man in a thousand ever noticed. Three years he worked in the field, at the end of which time he knew more about cane-growing than the overseers or even the superintendent, while the superintendent would have been astounded at the knowledge the wizened little coolie possessed of the reduction processes in the mill." However Ah Chun does not only study how sugar is processed: "He studied to find out how men came to be owners of sugar mills and plantations" (1,456). He invests his savings once his labor term is up in a small import business, while he works as a cook, becoming the highest-paid chef in Honolulu. With boom times in Hawai'i, he invests further in land and traders. He marries Stella Allendale, a mixed ANGLO-SAXON and Hawaiian woman with ties to royalty: "Thus,

his children by Mrs. Ah Chun were one thirty-second Polynesian, one-sixteenth Italian, one-sixteenth Portuguese, one-half Chinese, and eleven thirty-seconds English and American." Ah Chun's family is "wonderful in many ways. First, there was its size. There were fifteen sons and daughters, mostly daughters. The sons had come first, three of them, and then had followed, in unswerving sequence, a round dozen of girls. The blend of the races was excellent. Not alone fruitful did it prove, for the progeny, without exception, was healthy and without blemish. But the most amazing thing about the family was its beauty" (1,457).

And yet, though Ah Chun has "furnished the groundwork upon which had been traced the blended patterns of the races," Ah Chun's daughters lack suitors among the haole elite of Honolulu (1,458). They begin to spell the family name A'Chun, to makes it less Asian, just as the Ah Fong family spelled their name "Afong." While he prefers Chinese customs, the children are all totally Americanized. He feels himself drifting apart from his family. With his "philosopher's soul" (1,460), he feels he has no place "amongst this marvelous seed of his loins," and he starts to plan to return to China: "He did not understand his children. Their conversation was of things that did not interest him and about which he knew nothing. The culture of the West had passed him by. He was Asiatic to the last fibre, which meant that he was heathen. Their Christianity was to him so much nonsense. . . . Their souls were inaccessible to him, and by the same token he knew that his soul was inaccessible to them" (1,461).

Soon Ah Chun discovers that large dowries solve the problem of the marriages of his daughters, and, after they are all married off and living their haole American lives, which he finds he does not wish to share—as opposed to cannot share—he sells his possessions and retires to Macao. He is particularly tired of their arguing over money. When he is refused a room en route at a posh hotel in Hong Kong, he simply buys the hotel. Ah Chun defeats his exile on his own terms with his sense of identity intact and his inner peace. He eschews a purely Chinese identity just as he avoided an "American" identity—by choosing to live in Macao, a place of racial mixing like Honolulu, rather than China, and thus he finds his own home. He writes wise letters to his daughters urging them to stop fighting over money, with "admirable texts and precepts" to help his family "to live in unity and harmony" (*Stories*, 1,466).

COMMENTARY

Because the sons of the white families in Honolulu reject Chun Ah Chun's mixed-race daughters as potential wives, and yet Chun Ah Chun still manages, with enough dowries, to marry them off to the finest families and retire a contented man, London expresses in this story what Jessica Greening Loudermilk refers to as a lesson in "the fluidity of identity." The "unqualified success" of the racial blending of Ah Chun's children reflects a new concept of race, as does his own hybridity. Loudermilk quotes this passage:

> As beauties, the Ah Chun girls were something new. Nothing like them had been seen before. They resembled nothing so much as they resembled one another, and yet each girl was sharply individual. There was no mistaking one for another. . . . Maud, who was blue-eyed and yellow-haired, would remind one instantly of Henrietta, an olive brunette with large, languishing dark eyes and hair that was blue-black. The hint of resemblance that ran through them all, reconciling every differentiation, was Ah Chun's contribution. He had furnished the groundwork upon which had been traced the blended patterns of the races. He had furnished the slim-boned Chinese frame upon which had been builded the delicacies and subtleties of Saxon, Latin, and Polynesian flesh. (1,458) (Loudermilk, 48–49).

For himself, Chun Ah Chun beats the haoles at their own game, which satisfies him greatly.

CHARACTERS

Chun Ah Chun Born a peasant in China, he immigrates to Hawai'i and becomes first a field contract worker and then, in a gradual rise, a wealthy merchant and trader. After he becomes successful he turns to real estate: "So he bought land. He bought land from merchants who needed ready cash, from impecunious natives, from riotous traders' sons, from widows and orphans and the lepers deported to MOLOKAI; and, somehow, as the years went by, the pieces of land he had bought proved to be needed for warehouses, or office buildings, or hotels. He leased, and rented, sold and bought, and resold again" (1,456–1,457). He also becomes Chinese consul. Once he marries off his mixed-blood daughters to the elite of Honolulu, he retires to philosophical contemplation. In the end, back in the East smoking his pipe, he concludes that "it is a very funny world" (1,466).

Ah Yung An early business partner of Ah Chun: the firm they found "ultimately became the great one of 'Ah Chun & Ah Yung,' which handled anything from India silks and ginseng to guano islands and blackbird brigs" (1,456).

Stella Allendale (Mama Achun) Ah Chun's wife, she is a mixed "ANGLO-SAXON" and POLYNESIAN woman with ties to the royal family; to marry her Ah Chun must become a Hawaiian subject. Her great-grandmother is the famous Princess Paahao and her great-grandfather was a Captain Blunt, "an English adventurer who took service under Kamahameha I and was made a tabu chief himself" (1,457). She also has Portuguese and Italian blood.

Maud and Clara Ah Chun
Daughters of Ah Chun; Maud is "blue-eyed and yellow-haired" (1,458).

Henrietta Ah Chun Oldest daughter of Ah Chun who is "an olive brunette with large, languishing black eyes and hair that was blue-black" (1,457).

Harold Ah Chun Son of Ah Chung who attends Harvard and Oxford.

Albert and Charles Ah Chun Sons of Ah Chun who attend Yale University.

FURTHER READING

Dye, Bob. *Merchant Prince of the Sandalwood Mountains, Afong and the Chinese in Hawaii.* Honolulu: University of Hawaii Press, 1997.

Loudermilk, Jessica Greening. *Ka Aina Ka Pono: Jack London, Hawai'i, and Race.* M.A. thesis, University of Texas at San Antonio, 2006.

McBride, Christopher Mark. *The Colonizer Abroad: American Writers on Foreign Soil, 1846–1912.* New York: Routledge, 2004.

Reesman, Jeanne Campbell. *Jack London's Racial Lives.* Athens: University of Georgia Press, 2009, chapter 4.

———. *Jack London: A Study of the Short Fiction.* New York: Macmillan (Twayne Studies in Short Fiction Series), 1999.

The Cruise of the **Snark** (1911)

Perhaps no yacht had ever been so aptly named, for London's was called the *Snark* after LEWIS CARROLL's nonsense poem "The Hunting of the Snark." The poem uncannily predicts the *Snark*'s trickiness. The 42-foot *Snark* was certainly a "Boojum," as it is called in the poem. But she sailed for two years through sometimes dangerous seas, and she brought the crew in contact with peoples and places that few Americans had seen or would know what to make of if they had. London sent back dozens of works—stories, novels, travel narratives, and photographs—such as readers had rarely encountered. *The Cruise of the* Snark is a nonfiction travel narrative composed of stories he wrote for magazines such as WOMAN'S HOME COMPANION and COSMOPOLITAN. It features numerous photographs he made as well as his accounts of people and places from HAWAI'I to the SOLOMON ISLANDS.

The Londons got the idea of the *Snark* voyage while reading CAPTAIN JOSHUA SLOCUM's account of his solo sail around the world. As London explains in the opening pages of the book, his motivation is first what he calls "I LIKE." He sees the challenge as success in ADAPTATION:

> When I have done some such thing I am exalted. I glow all over. I am aware of a pride in myself that is mine, and mine alone. It is organic. Every fibre of me is thrilling with it. It is a mere matter of satisfaction at adjustment

to environment. It is success. Life that lives is successful, and success is the breath of its nostrils. . . . The trip around the world means big moments of living. (*Cruise,* 5)

For him such "moments of living" and the thrill of adapting to them could counterbalance the arbitrariness of life: "It is good to ride the tempest and feel godlike" (*Cruise,* 6–7).

The five-ton iron keel of the *Snark* was to have been laid on April 18, 1906, but that was the very day of the SAN FRANCISCO EARTHQUAKE, which struck as far north as Santa Rosa, near the Londons' ranch; they could see the fires in San Francisco from the top of Sonoma Mountain. Perhaps this was an omen. By the time the *Snark* was ready, far behind schedule and over budget in spring 1907, its shoddy materials and craftsmanship due to the huge boom in construction did not auger

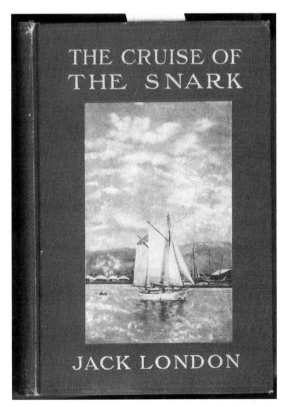

The cover of the first edition of *The Cruise of the* Snark (1911) *(Huntington Library)*

Elderly plantation worker on Ewa Plantation, Oahu, Hawa'i, 1907 *(Huntington Library)*

ing in a trough. "Captain" Eames knew nothing of navigation so London taught himself. The boat was refitted in Hawai'i and Eames was fired. The *Snark* made a supposedly impossible south by southeast run to the MARQUESAS, and the crew enjoyed the Society Islands. But when they reached the southwest Pacific, especially the Solomon Islands, they were unprepared for what they would find. There were spear and gun battles between islanders and white BLACKBIRDERS, or labor "recruiters," evidence of CANNIBALISM, and the stupidity and cruelty of white colonizers. But it was the tropical diseases they encountered in the Solomon Islands that finished them, after all of the voyaging and observing, evading storms and reefs from Hawai'i through the Marquesas, TAHITI, Raiatea, BORA BORA, SAMOA, Suva, FIJI, the PAUMOTUS, NEW HEBRIDES, the Gilberts, LORD HOWE ATOLL, and the Solomons.

London wrote his MACMILLAN editor GEORGE BRETT, on October 25, 1908, from PENDUFFRYN PLANTATION on GUADALCANAL, "Just dropping you

well for its durability. London had specified that the wood used be free of butts, but it was full of them. Nonetheless, early on the morning of April 23, 1907, London hoisted his college friend Jimmy Hopper's UNIVERSITY OF CALIFORNIA blue and gold sweater up the mast and they set sail for Hawai'i. The crew included London, CHARMIAN LONDON, Charmian's uncle ROSCOE EAMES as captain, BERT STOLZ as mate, MARTIN JOHNSON as cook, and the Londons' servant Paul Tochigi as cabin boy. (In Hawai'i Tochigi was replaced by YOSHIMATSU NAKATA.)

The voyage, originally planned for seven years, was cut short when London and the crew were overcome by tropical diseases, especially the dreaded Solomon Island sores, or yaws, which London treated with corrosive sublimate of mercury, almost surely a factor in his death eight years later from kidney failure. But from the beginning it was a challenge. In fact, the entire boat nearly went to pieces en route to its first port in Hawai'i. The *Snark* would not heave to avoid being swamped nor would it come about, leaving it vulnerable to capsiz-

We Two (1906). Portrait of Jack and Charmian London by Annie Brigman *(Huntington Library)*

a line from the Solomon Islands." But his light-hearted tone would abruptly change: "[T]he *Snark* is a hospital ship. There was never a time when some of us were not sick, and most of the time most of us were sick. Fever was the principal affliction, from which none of us escaped. One of my native sailors, a Tahitian, nearly died of it, and incidentally was crazy for a while. The cook, a Japanese, from sheer funk over the general sickness and over the fear of being eaten by the natives, went crazy and left us at Meringe Lagoon, on Ysabel Island, where he remained over two months before he could get away. I don't know whether I told you or not of the book I had been thinking of writing, some time ago, namely, *Around the World With Two Gasoline Engines and a Wife*. I am now contemplating another book: *Around The World in the Hospital Ship* Snark" (*Letters*, 754).

SYNOPSIS

Chapters 1–8

If in chapter 1 London exults at his zest for life, by chapter 2, "The Inconceivable and Monstrous," realities strike home. He details the boat's many ills. It is simply a miracle they ever reached HONOLULU. Only days out, they realized how much the boat had been damaged when two lumber scows in the OAKLAND harbor had dragged their anchors and laid up against the sides of the *Snark*, flattening her rail on one side and causing it to bulge out two inches on the other; this meant that she would not steer as she should. Soon, every system on board had failed: She wouldn't heave to; she wouldn't come about; the deck leaked; the four watertight compartments below all leaked; the sides and bottom leaked; the gasoline leaked out through the bulkheads; much of the food spoiled and had to be thrown overboard; the 70-horsepower engine fell off its block and had to be lashed to the deck, useless; the coal, delivered in rotten potato sacks, went washing through the scuppers into the ocean; the head became inoperable; the lifeboat was found to leak; and the launch engine would not start.

Chapter 3, "Adventure," returns to the months before the *Snark*'s sailing, when London was inundated with letters from would-be adventurers. The

one he selected was Johnson, the son of a jeweler from Independence, Kansas. Johnson later became a world adventurer on his own. London was so taken with all the letters and telegrams he received that he remarks, "Some day, when I have made a lot of money, I'm going to build a big ship, with room in it for a thousand volunteers. They will have to do all the work of navigating that boat around the world, or they'll stay at home. I believe that they'll work the boat around the world, for I know that Adventure is not dead. I know Adventure is not dead because I have had a long and intimate correspondence with Adventure" (*Cruise*, 46). Eventually the seasickness lifted, and the crew began to solve problems and enjoy the voyage. London soon returned to his usual 1,000 words a day regimen, writing several works including the second version of "To Build a Fire." He also began *Martin Eden*.

Chapter 4 relate London's unhappy discovery that Eames was incompetent and records his struggle to learn navigation himself, which he mastered in time to get the boat to Hawai'i:

> Proud? I was a worker of miracles. I forgot how easily I had taught myself from the printed page. I forgot that all the work (and a tremendous work, too) had been done by the masterminds before me, the astronomers and mathematicians, who had discovered and elaborated the whole science of navigation and made the tables in the "Epitome." I remembered only the everlasting miracle of it—that I had listened to the voices of the stars and been told my place upon the highway of the sea. Charmian did not know, Martin did not know, Tochigi, the cabin-boy, did not know. But I told them. I was God's messenger. I stood between them and infinity. I translated the high celestial speech into terms of their ordinary understanding. We were heaven-directed, and it was I who could read the sign-post of the sky!—I! I! (*Cruise*, 55–56)

Chapter 5, "The First Landfall," records their arrival in Hawai'i; they were met with great fanfare since reports had gone out that they were lost at sea. Stumbling ashore, he says,

We were like awakened Rip Van Winkles, and it seemed to us that we were dreaming. On one side the azure sea lapped across the horizon into the azure sky; on the other side the sea lifted itself into great breakers of emerald that fell in a snowy smother upon a white coral beach. Beyond the beach, green plantations of sugar-cane undulated gently upward to steeper slopes, which, in turn, became jagged volcanic crests, drenched with tropic showers and capped by stupendous masses of trade-wind clouds. At any rate, it was a most beautiful dream. (*Cruise*, 67–68)

In Hawai'i the *Snark* went in for extensive repairs. Eames was fired, and a new captain and cabin boy were signed on.

The five months the Londons spent in Hawai'i proved to be happier than they had dreamed. Wherever they went, they were entertained, even by Hawaiian royalty. They stayed in a cottage at Pearl Lochs and in a spacious tent-cabin on Waikiki, near the site of the original Outrigger Club (now occupied by the Outrigger Waikiki Hotel). They visited Maui, the BIG ISLAND, and MOLOKAI. On Maui they rode over the Von Tempsky ranch on HALEAKALA, and on the Big Island they were guests of the Baldings at Wainaku, where they tried riding bundles of sugarcane down steep flumes. London learned SURFING; his article "A Royal Sport" (*Cruise*, chapter 6) popularized the Hawaiian sport on the West Coast of the United States. He was asked to join the Outrigger Canoe Club.

London was struck not only with the natural beauty and the soothing environment of Hawai'i, but also with its MYTHOLOGIES, peoples, and politics. He remarked that Americans on the mainland "don't know what they've got!" (Charmian London, *Our Hawaii*, ix). But he came to believe Hawai'i represented the chance for an ideal community quite different from the Anglo-American vision, one of diverse peoples in a progressive and cosmopolitan environment. Yet he also came to see that Hawai'i had not (yet) developed this way. London became involved in the Hands-Around-the-Pacific Club (and later in the PAN-PACIFIC UNION)—an antiwar movement for world brotherhood and sisterhood founded by ALEXANDER HUME FORD (1868–1945), a young entrepreneur who settled in Hawai'i in 1907. A week and a day after the *Snark* reached Pearl Harbor, Ford greeted London at the Royal Hawaiian Hotel. The two became friends, and it was Ford who introduced London to SURFING. For London, surfing was "a royal sport for the natural kings of the earth," the surfer as a "brown Mercury" (*Cruise*, 75). London kept practicing in "the wonderful sun of Hawaii" and received a terrible sunburn. But his description of the "royal" Hawaiian surfer is telling: The local surfer is a "Kanaka—and more, he is a man, a member of the kingly species that has mastered matter and the brutes and lorded it over creation" (*Cruise*, 77–78). His great admiration for Hawaiian Natives is expressed clearly in this chapter.

The Londons' July 1907 visit to the LEPER COLONY on MOLOKAI's Kalauapapa peninsula was also one of their most meaningful times in Hawai'i, and they visited it again in 1915 (*Cruise*, chapter 7). Molokai too had a transforming effect on London's writings about the Pacific, addressing so dramatically definitions of identity, race, health v. disease, white v. native, rebels and outsiders v. the establishment. At the turn of the century, LEPROSY (now known as Hansen's Disease) was believed to be not only extremely contagious, but beyond the pale of society. Molokai had once been a site of rape, murder, and drunkenness before the arrival of the Belgian priest FATHER DAMIEN, who turned it into a model community. Lucius E. Pinkham, president of the Board of Health, later the territorial governor, wanted to dispel distorted notions about Molokai and the lepers. He asked London to make a visit to the leper colony and write about it for the world, which London did, raising the ire of the Honolulu establishment who did not want leprosy associated with their new tourist businesses.

"Leprosy is terrible," London writes, "there is no getting away from that"; but, he points out, worse sights can been seen in any major city in the United States (*Cruise*, 105). He relates the Fourth of July parade, the costumes, the bands, and the horsemanship contests he and Charmian witnessed. Describing a donkey race, "I tried to check myself. I assured myself that I was witnessing one of the horrors of Molokai, and that it was shameful for me, under such circumstances, to be so light-hearted and light-headed. But it was no use. . . . And all the while nearly a thousand lepers were laughing uproariously at the fun. Anybody in my place would have joined with them in having a good time" (*Cruise*, 92–93). London's warm and humane descriptions of the lepers helped change world opinion. He focuses not on the physical effects of the disease but upon the everyday lives of the lepers and upon certain individuals. His photographs are especially moving.

Chapters 9–17

The *Snark* set sail for the South Seas from Hilo on October 7, 1907. For the next two months, they never encountered another ship. London depended upon his engine to get them there, but of course all the engines broke down again, leaving the *Snark* to depend only on her sails and on London's optimism. They began to run low on water, and they encountered terrible storms. At last they made port in TAIOHAE Bay on the Marquesan island of NUKU HIVA.

In the Marquesas, they expected the idyllic TYPEE VALLEY that HERMAN MELVILLE wrote of in his novel *Typee*, which inspired London to make the voyage, but he was disappointed. The Marquesas had fallen victim to the diseases of white intruders; nearly all were dying of tuberculosis and elephantiasis. London wrote: "There are more races than there are persons, but it is a wreckage of races at best. Life faints and stumbles and gasps itself away . . . asthma, phthisis, and tuberculosis flourish as luxuriantly as the vegetation. Everywhere, from the few grass huts, arises the racking cough or exhausted groan of wasted lungs." Tommo, the protagonist of *Typee,* confesses that "'Had a glimpse of the gardens of paradise been revealed to me I could scarcely have been more ravished with the sight,'" but Melville, says London, "saw a garden. We saw a wilderness" (*Cruise*, 165–167). As Charmian put it, "we were too late" (Charmian London, *Log*, 47).

The Londons rented the house in Taiohae that ROBERT LOUIS STEVENSON had also used when he visited Nuku Hiva on the *Casco.* The *Snark* party

recovered from their long voyage. On December 10 they rode "ferocious little stallions" up an ancient road and into the thick jungle of Typee Valley: "On every side were the vestiges of a one-time dense population. Wherever the eye could penetrate the thick growth, glimpses were caught of stone walls and of stone foundations, six to eight feet in height, built solidly throughout, and many yards in width and depth," the foundations of *pae-paes* described by Tommo (stone platforms upon which families lived). Sadly, however, "the houses and the people were gone, and huge trees sank their roots through the platforms and towered over the under-running jungle. . . . Once or twice, as we ascended the valley, we saw magnificent *pae-paes* bearing on their general surface pitiful little straw huts, the proportions being similar to a voting booth perched on the broad foundation of the pyramid of Cheops" (*Cruise*, 161–163). He asks,

> Where were the hundred groves of the breadfruit tree he saw? . . . Where was the Ti of Mehevi, the bachelors' hall, the palace where women were taboo, and where he ruled with his lesser chieftains, keeping the half-dozen dusty and torpid ancients to remind them of the valorous past? From the swift stream no sounds arose of maids and matrons pounding tapa. And where was that hut that old Narheyo eternally builded? In vain I looked for him perched ninety feet from the ground in some tall cocoanut, taking his morning smoke. (*Cruise*, 167)

Only a "few dozen wretched creatures" were left from a population Melville estimated at 2,000. The reason? "Not alone were the Typeans physically magnificent; they were pure. Their air did not contain all the bacilli and germs and microbes of disease that fill our own air. And when the white men imported in their ships these various microorganisms of disease, the Typeans crumbled and went down before them" (*Cruise*, 167–170). London is led to wonder: "When one considers the situation, one is almost driven to the conclusion that the white race flourishes on impurity and corruption" (*Cruise*, 170–171). A crew member Johnson was similarly struck: "Better had it been had the natives never seen the missionaries. What happened in the

Marquesas has happened in many other South Sea islands, and no doubt is happening to-day. My conscience smote me. To think, the very pennies I had given in Sunday School for foreign missions had contributed to the calamitous end of the inhabitants of this beautiful garden-spot!" (Johnson, 164).

Chapter 11, set in Papeete, Tahiti, focuses on an American known as the NATURE MAN, whose name was Ernest Darling and whom London had met years ago in California. Critic Rod Edmond sees the Nature Man as an emblem of European regeneration in contrast to the degeneration of Typee (Edmond, 208). Darling does at first glance seem to be the prototype of the healthy beachcomber who, though white, could adapt to the Tropics and thrive. As a young man, Darling was frequently ill, and it was not until he ran away and lived in the forest that he recovered. Darling headed to Tahiti, where he went about in a red loincloth preaching SOCIALISM and vegetarianism to the islanders. He built a terraced farm above the harbor. He wrote his own version of the Ten Commandments in phonetic spelling: "Thous shalt not eet meet" and "Vizit troppikle cuntriz." The Londons admired Darling's "Return-to-Nature life," as Charmian called it. However, alarmed at his socialism (he flew a red flag in front of his shack visible in much of Papeete), the French authorities seized Darling's farm planted with papayas, avocados, breadfruit, mangoes, bananas, coconuts, and other bounty, and they blocked the road to his farm. Even here in fabled Tahiti the dream of crossing the beach was doomed.

Recalling their departure, London writes, "And I shall see you always as I saw you that last day, when the *Snark* poked her nose once more through the passage in the smoking reef, outward bound, and I waved good-bye to those on shore. Not least in goodwill and affection was the wave I gave to the golden sun-god in the scarlet loin-cloth, standing upright in his tiny outrigger canoe" (*Cruise,* 197).

In BORA BORA London, always the generous host himself, fondly relates the great hospitality of Bora Bora; it was his favorite stop on the entire voyage. Visiting his new pilot TEHEI (the inspiration for Otoo in "The Heathen") and his wife Bihaura, he and his party were feasted "in the high seat of abundance," with raw fish marinated in lime juice, roast chicken, suckling pig, bananas, yams, poi, cocoanut milk, and coffee. Sleeping in happy comfort in their host's house, London muses,

> [O]f all the entertainment I have received in this world at the hands of all sorts of races in all sorts of places, I have never received entertainment that equalled this at the hands of this brown-skinned couple of Tahaa. I do not refer to the presents, the free-handed generousness, the high abundance, but to the fineness of courtesy and consideration and tact, and to the sympathy that was real sympathy in that it was understanding. . . . Perhaps the most delightful feature of it was that it was due to no training, to no complex social ideals, but that it was the untutored and spontaneous outpouring from their hearts. (*Cruise,* 209–210)

Bora Bora was the closest to paradise that the *Snark* found. But as they sailed farther west, the climate started to change.

London writes that "If I were a king, the worst punishment I could inflict on my enemies would be to banish them to the Solomons. On second thought, king or no king, I don't think I'd have the heart to do it" (*Cruise,* 283). In appearance, the MELANESIANS were darker and wilder-looking than the lighter-skinned POLYNESIANS of Hawai'i and Tahiti, who were more acceptable racially and culturally to the Americans. It is surprising London felt that way about a place in which he lingered for five months, the same amount of time spent in Hawai'i. The crew lived at PENDUFFRYN PLANTATION on GUADALCANAL and made short forays to the neighboring islands. One of the Penduffryn partners who was their host, GEORGE DARBISHIRE, and his associates were overrun, murdered, and eaten by workers in 1914.

In the Solomons, the social climate seemed to befit the disease-ridden physical environment. Most terrifying was the attack by islanders on MALAITA. The Londons went along on a BLACK-BIRDING, or labor-recruiting ship, the *MINOTA,* and were besieged when they ran aground near an island. Headlines around the world claimed that they had been captured by cannibals, but this was averted when a local MISSIONARY and Captain Keller of the nearby *Eugénie* came and quelled the riot. (Sadly, the *Snark* herself was eventually sold to a company that converted her into a blackbirder.) London recorded in a 1916 letter that one day when he was sunning on Waikiki Beach, "a stranger introduce[d] himself as the person who settled the estate of Captain Keller," who "came to his death by having his head chopped off and smoke-cured by . . . cannibal headhunters" (*Letters,* 1,599). The islanders were indeed savage, but London also describes the degraded whites, with their laziness, alcoholism, and stupidity.

However, one feature of Solomon Island life won his admiration, and that was the use of BÊCHE-DE-MER ENGLISH. He devotes all of chapter 16 to it, including a sermon preached by a Native man:

> "Bimeby God big fella marster belong white man He make 'm one fella man and put 'm along garden belong Him. He call 'm this fella man Adam. . . . He speak, 'This fella garden he belong you.' And He look 'm this fella Adam he walk about too much. Him fella Adam all the same sick; he no savvee kai-kai; he walk about all the time. And God He no savvee. . . .
>
> "Bimeby God He scratch 'm head belong Him too much, and speak: 'Me fella me savvee, him fella Adam him want 'm Mary.' So He make Adam he go asleep, He take one fella bone belong him, and He make 'm one fella Mary along bone. He call him this fella Mary, Eve. He give 'm this fella Eve along Adam, and He speak along him fella Adam: 'Close up altogether along this fella garden belong you two fella. One fella tree he tambo [taboo] along you altogether. This fella tree belong apple.'"
> (*Cruise,* 305)

In January 1909, London issued a statement to the press, "A Brief Explanation," from his hospital bed in Sydney. He had left the *Snark* at anchor in the Solomons and had gone to Australia by steamer to go into the hospital for multiple tropical ailments. He agreed to a series of lectures across the continent. But he soon realized he wasn't up to it. He worried especially about the peeling of the hands: "The biggest specialist in Australia in

this branch, confesses that not only has he never observed anything like it, but that not a line has been written about it by other observers." He wryly notes, "There are many boats and many voyages, only one set of toe-nails but I have only one body; and, . . . I have prescribed myself my own climate and environment, where always before my nervous equilibrium has been maintained. . . . There is nothing more for me to say except this, namely, a request to all my friends. Please forego congratulating us upon our abandonment of the voyage. We are heart-broken." What was wrong with London's hands was probably the result of exposure to mercury, and after the *Snark* voyage his health began to deteriorate. It was a high price to pay for adventure, but he did not regret a day of it.

COMMENTARY

In *The Cruise of the* **Snark**, one finds not only London's highly entertaining account of his adventures but numerous elements common in South Seas writing. There are descriptions of the long days at sea, spectacular sunsets, their first glimpse of the Southern Cross. They encounter flying fish, sharks, and an albatross who lands on deck. In Hawai'i, they found "paradise" spoiled by an exploitive plantation labor system; searching for Typee, they find only the ruin and death of a culture. In Nature Man, they recognize the figure of the beachcomber; in Bora Bora, they encounter Native hospitality. But in the Solomons, they witness slave-trading, signs of cannibalism, and an even more destructive colonization by whites. London's racial attitudes were considerably transformed by the voyage, but still he could not overcome his disgust at the Solomons. However, this is partly because he had come to realize that as a white man he was unfit to survive in the tropics. Thus, as a constant theme in the book, in every chapter anxieties about disease versus bodily wholeness appear, and it takes on the feel of a physical and psychological memoir. As Edmond notes, "The idea of European immunity from the diseased Pacific, which the stories explore so uneasily, had completely broken down" (Edmond, 221). As he also remarks, "London's counter-discourse of health, incorporating as it does a myth of colonization, is almost simultaneously undermined by the Pacific taking its revenge on the colonizer" (Edmond, 209). A loss of health meant to him a loss of "authority."

London's self-preoccupation is partly revealed by reading Charmian's *Log of the* Snark and Johnson's *Through the South Seas with Jack London,* which describe things more as travel books would, with details of the places and peoples that are part of a general survey of the location. They are descriptive and alert, and both are occasionally romantic, but they never use the intense psychological metaphors London uses. Charmian writes upon day-to-day operations of the ship, interspersed with descriptions of the sea, her souvenir-hunting, and the daily lives of the islanders. Johnson is more captivated with the anthropology of the islanders they encounter, but unlike London he remained throughout most of his subsequent exploring and filmmaking happy with stereotypes instead of characters. For himself, London is the subject and most important character in the book. Its subject is not just the South Seas, but the development of an authorial identity to relate it.

FURTHER READING

Edmond, Rod. *Representing the South Pacific: Colonial Discourse from Cook to Gauguin.* Cambridge: Cambridge University Press, 1997.

Ellis, Juniper. "'A Wreckage of Races' in Jack London's South Pacific." *Arizona Quarterly* 57, no. iii (2001): 57–75.

Ford, Alexander Hume. "Jack London." *Mid-Pacific Magazine* 9 (1916): 327.

Johnson, Martin. *Through the South Seas with Jack London.* New York: Dodd, Mead, 1913. Reprinted Cedar Springs, Mich.: Wolf House Books, 1967.

Kersten, Holger. "The Erosion of the Ideal of the Heroic Explorer: Jack London's *The Cruise of the* Snark." In *Narratives of Exploration and Discovery: Essays in Honour of Konrad Gross.* Edited by Wolfgang Kloss. Trier, Germany: Wissenschaftlicher Verlag Trier, 2005, 85–97.

London, Charmian. *Our Hawaii.* New York: Macmillan, 1917.

———. *The Log of the* Snark. New York: Macmillan, 1915.

London, Jack. "A Brief Explanation: [of abandoning the Snark voyage]," photocopy of autographed typescript, Henry E. Huntington Library, JL 21258.

———. *Jack London's Tales of Cannibals and Headhunters: Nine South Seas Stories by America's Master of Adventure.* Edited by Gary Riedl and Thomas R. Tietze. Albuquerque: University of New Mexico Press, 2006.

———. *The Letters of Jack London.* Edited by Earle Labor, Robert C. Leitz, III, and I. Milo Shepard. 3 vols. Stanford: Stanford University Press, 1988.

Marovitz, Sanford E. "London in Melville's Wake: Two Sons of the Sun in Polynesia." In *The Call: The Magazine of the Jack London Society* 14, no. ii (Fall–Winter 2003): 3–7, 10.

McBride, Christopher Mark. *The Colonizer Abroad: American Writers on Foreign Soil, 1846–1912.* New York: Routledge, 2004.

Melville, Herman. *Typee, or, a Peep at Polynesian Life.* London: J. Murray, 1846. Reprinted Oxford and New York: Oxford University Press, 1996, Introduction by Ruth Blair.

Moreland, David A. "The Author as Hero: Jack London's *The Cruise of the* Snark." In *Jack London Newsletter* 15, no. 1 (1982): 57–75.

Phillips, Lawrence. "The Canker of Empire: Colonialism, Autobiography and the Representation of Illness: Jack London and Robert Louis Stevenson in the Marquesas." In *Postcolonial Theory and Criticism.* Edited by Laura Chrisman and Benita Parry. Cambridge, England: Brewer, 1999, 115–132.

Reesman, Jeanne Campbell. *Jack London's Racial Lives.* Athens: University of Georgia Press, 2009, chapter 4.

Slocum, Joshua. *Sailing Alone Around the World.* New York: Century, 1900.

A Daughter of the Snows (1902)

More or less everyone, including London, agrees that London's first novel was a failure. Charles N. Watson, Jr., faults it for its stylistic irregularities, its lack of a "sense of economy and pace," and its stereotypes (Watson, 21–22). At first, in the late summer of 1900, London happily wrote about his new novel to his writer friend CLOUDESLEY JOHNS, but a few months later confessed, "Well, I am on the home stretch of the novel, and it is a failure" (*Letters*, 203, 240). MCCLURE, PHILLIPS AND CO. agreed to pay London an advance against royalties of $125 per month for five months beginning August 1, 1900, but advanced him over $1,500 by the time he finished in March 1901. They sold the rights to J. B. Lippincott Company, which published it in October 1902. Looking back, London sighed, "Lord, Lord. How I squandered into it enough stuff for a dozen novels" (Charmian London, *Book of Jack London* I: 384). Earle Labor and Jeanne Reesman have termed the book "a potpourri of [London's] pet ideas on SOCIAL DARWINISM, ANGLO-SAXON supremacy, environmentalism, and joy-through-fitness. So preoccupied is the author with ideology that he confuses fiction with essay. . . . [T]he simple truth is that he was a born sprinter who never acquired the artistic stamina of the long-distance runner. The faults in this book were chronic ones he would commit again in later books, with their long episodic plots, strained dialogue, and characters as ideological caricatures" (Labor and Reesman, 37–38).

ANNA STRUNSKY WALLING and BESS LONDON are possible as models for Frona, Anna for her independence and intellect and Bess for being an Anglo-Saxon mother-woman, as London called her. Features of both women are evident in Frona. Yet the names *Flora* (London's mother) and *Frona* are too similar to ignore, especially as FLORA LONDON was a struggler in life whose energy was in part fueled by her racial fantasies and prejudices. Frona is also a lot like Jack London, always on her soapbox. For Joseph Sciambra, Frona is a Spencerian "valkyrie" (Sciambra, 17). Watson sees her as a "dime-novel" character such as Calamity Jane or Hurricane Nell, but also compares her to FRANK NORRIS's western women in *Blix* (1899) and *A Man's Woman* (1900) (Watson, 28). Today the novel can be taught in a class on the American NEW WOMAN or as a fin de siècle race novel. Yet overshadowing Frona's potential as a proto-feminist protagonist is her obsessive need to satisfy her father, so that she becomes not a New Woman but remains an ideal daughter, for in the end she

chooses her father over Corliss. Most important, Frona's humanity and believability as a character are limited by her RACIALISM.

SYNOPSIS

Chapters 1–10

In chapter 2, Frona emerges after her perilous journey from SKAGWAY over the CHILKOOT PASS:

> She came out of the wood of glistening birch, and with the first fires of the sun blazoning her unbound hair raced lightly across the dew-dripping meadow. . . . The flush of the morning was in her cheek, and its fire in her eyes, and she was aglow with youth and love. For she had nursed at the breast of nature,—in forfeit of a mother,—and she loved the old trees and the creeping green things with a passionate love; and the dim murmur of growing life was a gladness to her ears, and the damp earth-smells were sweet to her nostrils. (24)

But things have changed in the KLONDIKE in her absence. It is no longer "the flush of the morning." Though she recognizes Neepoosa, an old squaw, Frona realizes that while she had been friends with the NATIVES who live near her father's camp, now there are "wild-eyed Sticks from over the Passes, fierce Chilcats, and Queen Charlotte Islanders. And the looks they cast upon her were black and frowning" (26). In chapter 3, she recalls her trek over the Chilkoot Pass and the hardy SCANDINAVIANS ahead of her who set the pace: "They were huge strapping blond-haired giants, each striding along with a hundred pounds on his back. . . . Their faces were as laughing suns, and the joy of life was in them. The toil seemed child's play and slipped from them lightly" (32). And yet when they wade out into a fast-moving river to retrieve the body of a dead man, five of the six of them drown. So much for her Vikings. Frona next comes upon a man abandoned by his partners because he couldn't keep up. Instead of helping him, she tells him he is unfit: "'My friend,' and Frona knew she was speaking for the race, 'you are strong as they. You can work just as hard as they; pack as much. But you are weak of heart. This is no place for the weak of heart. . . . Therefore the country has no use for you. The north wants strong men,—strong of soul, not body. The body does not count. So go back to the States. We do not want you here'" (38). The reader may wonder if this means that the Scandinavians lacked heart, but they voluntarily went out to retrieve a dead man.

In chapter 4, Frona arrives in Happy Camp and stumbles exhausted into the tent of Vance Corliss, and they spend the night together—strictly as trailmates. He is mostly silent, and he mistakes her for a dance-hall girl, as many have been passing through. But she surprises him with her knowledge and frank manner. Meeting up with her associate Del Bishop, she parts from Corliss by inviting him to see her in DAWSON. Chapter 5 presents her reunion with her father, Jacob Welse, "a giant trader in a country without commerce, a ripened product of the nineteenth century flourishing in a society as primitive as that of the Mediterranean vandals. A captain of industry and a splendid monopolist, he dominated the most independent aggregate of men ever drawn together from the ends of the earth. An economic missionary, a commercial St. Paul, he preached the doctrines of expediency and force." As London describes him the dualities multiply: "Believing in the natural rights of man, a child himself of democracy, he bent all men to his absolutism. Government of Jacob Welse, for Jacob Welse and the people, by Jacob Welse, was his unwritten gospel. . . . At his ukase, the population ebbed and flowed over a hundred thousand miles of territory, and cities sprang up or disappeared at his bidding" (55). After numerous calls from men he is working with to help avert a famine in Dawson due to the great influx of would-be miners, he welcomes Frona home.

Corliss's thoughts return to Frona; he is "a product of a sheltered life" and feels drawn to her "vitality" (75). In chapter 8, as they get to know each other, they argue about race, Corliss making fun of Frona's devotion to Anglo-Saxons and racialism; however, "Though they quarreled and disagreed on innumerable things, deep down, underlying all, there was a permanent unity" (88). Chapter 9 concerns Corliss and Frona meeting Lucile on the trail outside Dawson; Lucile is a dance-hall girl (and woman of low repute). While Frona is sympathetic

to her and walks with her back into town, when Corliss appears he chastises Frona for consorting with her; in response Frona nearly strikes him with her whip.

Chapters 11–20

Chapter 11 takes place in the Opera House, where Corliss apologizes to Lucile and defends a stranger, Gregory St. Vincent, from a brawl. In chapter 12, St. Vincent spins his false history about being captured by the barbaric "Chow Chuen" or "Deer Men" of the coast of eastern Siberia; though he begins as their slave, he becomes "a man of importance" whose advice, medicine, and surgery make him welcome in the tribe. Frona thinks him "[a] brave man, . . . a splendid type of the race" (130). The next morning, she is still smitten with his "healthful, optimistic spirit" which "corresponded well to her idealized natural man and favorite racial type" (133). Perhaps Corliss decides to cater to Frona's racial ideas to win her back, for it is just after this in chapter 14 that he speaks of his own "Viking" ancestry and quotes Norse heroic poetry. He proposes to her, but she angrily refuses, claiming her independence. Yet she always tries to please her father, a trait of hers at odds with both her destiny as a mother of the Anglo-Saxon race and her freedom. In chapter 17, her father tells her, "'When they said your boat was coming, death rose and walked on the one hand of me, and on the other life everlasting. Made or marred; made or marred,—the words rang through my brain till they maddened me. Would the Welse remain the Welse? Would the blood persist? Would the young shoot rise straight and tall and strong, green with sap and fresh and vigorous?'" (176). Apparently, she remained undefiled by the world. Welse is concerned about the love triangle developing among Frona, Corliss, and St. Vincent. Lucile comes to Frona and asks her to forgo marriage with St. Vincent, since he is not worthy of her, while he is worthy of Lucile.

Chapters 21–30

After some diversions including a big gold strike and a production of Henrik Ibsen's *A Doll's House*, events build toward several dramatic climaxes. Frona and Corliss are tested when they set out in chapter 25 to rescue some men stranded by the breakup of the YUKON ice. Wrecked, they fight off their panicked comrade Tommy and barely survive. On shore, they stumble upon a cabin in which an ad hoc court of miners is trying St. Vincent for murder. Frona and Corliss are joined by Jacob Welse, the Baron Courbertin, and Del Bishop, who step in to defend St. Vincent.

It is revealed that St. Vincent's story of his enslavement by the Deer Men came from a journal of a Russian missionary priest, Father Yakontsk, who actually was enslaved in eastern Siberia, which Bishop, with the Baron's help, has had translated. Yet Frona, Welse, the Baron, and their party still try to save St. Vincent because St. Vincent is one of them. Jacob Welse believes in taking the accused to a court of the Queen's government, that miners' meetings such as this one are outdated. Welse has sized St. Vincent up as a coward who could not have committed a murder. The situation rapidly deteriorates. Their attempt to rescue St. Vincent is momentarily interrupted by a hammer thrown at Jacob Welse by the "judge," miner Bill Brown. When St. Vincent tries to run, he is captured by Pierre La Flitche. St. Vincent is rushed by "the hanging committee" and finally overpowered by Tim Dugan, "a stalwart Celt." St. Vincent buries his teeth in Dugan's arm. Frona talks him into releasing Dugan and tells him that even though he is to die, "'At least you can be a man. It is all that remains'" (320). St. Vincent suddenly confesses what really happened. He is no murderer, but worse in the NORTHLAND CODE: He is a coward who abandoned his trailmate. St. Vincent lay hidden in his cot and did nothing to stop the murder of his partner John Borg, even though he had a revolver. Borg manages to get the gun on his own and kills his Native wife Bella, then struggles with the Native intruder. More shots are fired; the intruder escapes; Borg dies. The crowd does not believe St. Vincent, but they do believe a boatman who suddenly arrives with the injured Native, Gow, who gets to tell his story. La Flitche, who understands some of the "dim-remembered words" of the "Stick talk of the Upper White" (328), acts as Gow's mouthpiece to tell his story in Gow's last words. La Flitche relates:

"This man make true talk. He come from White River, way up. He cannot understand. He surprised very much, so many white men. He never think so many white men in the world. He die soon. His name Gow.

"Long time ago, three year, this man John Borg go to this man Gow's country. He hunt, he bring plenty meat to the camp, wherefore White River Sticks like him. Gow have one squaw, Pisk-ku. Bime-by John Borg make preparation to go 'way. He go to Gow, and he say, 'Give me your squaw. We trade. For her I give you many things.' But Gow say no. Pisk-ku good squaw. No woman sew moccasin like she. She tan moose-skin the best, and make the softest leather. He like Pisk-ku. Then John Borg say he don't care; he want Pisk-ku. Then they have a skookum big fight, and Pisk-ku go 'way with John Borg. She no want to go 'way, but she go anyway. Borg call her 'Bella,' and give her plenty good things, but she like Gow all the time." La Flitche pointed to the scar which ran down the forehead and past the eye of the Indian. "John Borg he do that."

"Long time Gow pretty near die. Then he get well, but his head sick. He don't know nobody. Don't know his father, his mother, or anything. Just like a little baby. Just like that. Then one day, quick, click! something snap, and his head get well all at once. He know his father and mother, he remember Pisk-ku, he remember everything. His father say John Borg go down river. Then Gow go down river. Spring-time, ice very bad. He very much afraid, so many white men, and when he come to this place he travel by night. Nobody see him 'tall, but he see everybody. He like a cat, see in the dark. Somehow, he come straight to John Borg's cabin. He do not know how this was, except that the work he had to do was good work."

St. Vincent pressed Frona's hand, but she shook her fingers clear and withdrew a step.

"He see Pisk-ku feed the dogs, and he have talk with her. That night he come and she open the door. Then you know that which was done. St. Vincent do nothing, Borg kill Bella. Gow kill Borg. Borg kill Gow, for Gow die pretty quick. Borg have strong arm. Gow sick inside, all smashed up. Gow no care; Pisk-ku dead." (329–330)

Oddly, given the book's racialism, Gow's speech resonates with the values of justice, masculinity, and protecting one's race, while Frona's paragon of white superiority is a sniveling coward.

In the last chapter, Frona tells St. Vincent off: "'Because you broke the faith of food and blanket. Because you broke salt with a man, and then watched that man fight unequally for life without lifting your hand. Why, I had rather you had died in defending him; the memory of you would have been good. Yes, I had rather you had killed him yourself. At least, it would have shown there was blood in your body'" (333). Frona asks Corliss to take her to Dawson. Once there, she may accompany her father on international business. She leaves Corliss guessing. Frona's coy final scene seems to lead him on, but it also indicates her choice of father over mate.

COMMENTARY

Russ Kingman has praised London for "ahead of his time liberating women when he introduced the independent, well-educated heroine, Frona Welse, . . . unconventional and free, . . . durable and different." Yet here and throughout his career, "London would be accused of poor female character portrayal." The fundamental problem, in Frona's character, he rightly asserts, is in her "blatant Anglo-Saxon chauvinism" (Kingman, 103–104). *A Daughter of the Snows* was written during the Progressive Era and reflects its notion of the New Woman, a figure also prominently featured in the work of such writers as Henry James, Kate Chopin, Charlotte Perkins Gilman, Edith Wharton, and Sarah Orne Jewett. But Frona does not make a believable New Woman (she barely makes a believable character of any kind). She does not become independent of her father, and her rabid racial views make her a curiosity of the past, not a harbinger of the future. *A Daughter of the Snows* perfectly illustrates how a high level of racialism inevitably brings about artistic failure. Despite her description as a "ripened child of the age, and

[who] fairly understood the physical world and the workings thereof," with "a love for the world, and a deep respect," Frona's fantasies about her own racial glory make her ridiculous. For the most part the narrator does not object to her ideas, nor does she change. However the book subtly casts doubts about Frona's character and London's intentions. Frona's ideal "race man," Gregory St. Vincent, is shown to be a coward and a fraud. St. Vincent's self-destruction critiques the very things Frona holds dear: racialism, education, travel, and social pretension—as well as "adventure." But the reader is unsure how to read such an opposition. Like *Adventure,* this novel is constantly at odds with itself, and one is never sure of London's intentions. Is it a romance or not? Does it promote women's rights or not? Is it satiric or not? It is at once too abstract and too personal—too abstract in its racial pronouncements and too personal in its valorizing of Frona, surely a figure of London's mother, about whom he had very mixed feelings. Flora was an ardent racist and forbade her son to play with neighboring families of Greeks, Portuguese, and Italians. London admired her fiery spirit but suffered from her ignoring him. Perhaps the novel functioned psychologically for London to displace the mother with a strong father figure, which helps explain why Jacob retains his "right" to Frona in the end. It is interesting that Jacob Welse is supposed to be Irish and Welsh (even giving him a surname that says "Welsh"), when in Frona's eyes he is supposed to be an Anglo-Saxon (and Frona's mother is first called Irish and then later Saxon). If the book aims to promote ideas of Anglo-Saxon supremacy, then why are these key characters not Anglo-Saxon? *A Daughter of the Snows* raises many more such questions that trouble the reader—and cause it to fail as a novel.

CHARACTERS

Frona Welse Daughter of Jacob Welse, the fabulously successful entrepreneur of Dawson, Frona was raised by him as a free spirit in the wilderness. She is educated in the States but returns to Dawson after her long absence. She is a staunch believer in Anglo-Saxon superiority and of the right of the whites to conquer the Northland. She is romanced by two men but in the end seems to choose to remain with her father.

Jacob Welse   Frona's father, Jacob, has become immensely wealthy since he arrived in the Klondike. He is a fantasy figure of a father such as London would have wished for himself; his Welsh ancestry echoes London's mother's own and his background John London's: "The trapper father had come of the sturdy Welsh stock which trickled into early Ohio out of the jostling East, and the mother was a nomadic daughter of the Irish emigrant settlers of Ontario. From both sides came the Wanderlust of the blood, the fever to be moving, to be pushing on to the edge of things. In the first year of his life, ere he had learned the way of his legs, Jacob Welse had wandered a-horse through a thousand miles of wilderness, and wintered in a hunting-lodge on the head-waters of the Red River of the North" (*Daughter*, 56).

Vance Corliss   A mining engineer, he is Frona's suitor who first meets her in a tent on the trail. Corliss is somewhat reserved and even priggish in his suit, but he adopts Frona's racialist rhetoric in order to woo her. At the end he is left uncertain, as she declares she will be traveling with her father instead of settling down.

Gregory St. Vincent   St. Vincent enters the story when he is rescued from a barroom brawl by Corliss. A writer-adventurer, he works for the Amalgamated Press Association. He impresses Frona with tales of his exploits in Siberia, only to be revealed as a coward and liar in the end. St. Vincent lies still and does nothing, even though he has a loaded gun, when his partner John Borg is killed by Gow, a Native whom Borg has robbed of his squaw.

Del Bishop   A pocket-miner who meets Frona when she returns to the Northland; he journeys with her over the Chilkoot Pass. Bishop warns everyone about St. Vincent and is the one who eventually exposes him.

Mr. Thurston, First Officer   On the steamer that brings Frona home to Dawson. He says he cannot spare a boat for her, but then sees her log-house home on shore and understands her haste to be home. He admires Frona: "'Jove!' he muttered, doffing his cap gallantly. 'There is a *woman!*'" (12).

Whitehall Boatman   A "Whitehall" is a kind of dingy often used as a water taxi; the boatman is nearly crushed by two large canoes. The steamer's first officer accuses him of being a pirate for charging 20 dollars to land Frona. The entire DYEA scene reflects its chaotic nature as men and boats collide in their eagerness to get to the gold fields.

French Louis   French Louis appears early in the novel with his backpack and silk kerchief instead of a hat. He owns "'three Eldorado claims in a block,'" Frona is told, worth 10 million dollars (19).

Swiftwater Bill   Another "Eldorado King" who appears early in the novel.

Matt McCarthy   A miner Frona recognizes in Skagway, who has struck it rich. He eagerly greets her: "'Thin it's yer ownself afther all? The little motherless darlin', with the gold hair I combed the knots out iv many's the time? The little witch that run barefoot an' barelegged over all the place?'" (20).

Neepoosa   An elderly squaw who recognizes Frona when she returns home and calls her by her Native name Tenas Hee-Hee, which means "Little Laughter."

Muskim   An old Native man who greets Frona upon her return; he complains of the changes in his tribe: "'The women . . . have found favor, in the eyes of thy white men, and they look no more upon the young men of their own blood. Wherefore the tribe does not increase, nor do the little children longer clutter the way of our feet. It is so. The bellies are fuller with the white man's grub; but also are they fuller with the white man's bad whiskey. . . . So these are bad days, Tenas Hee-Hee, and they behold old Muskim go down in sorrow to the grave'" (29–30). London often uses older Native men to lament the changes that occurred after the whites' arrival in the Northland.

ferryman Frona shames the ferryman at the lakes on top of the Chilkoot Pass to take her through the rapids; afterward, she compliments him on his bravery, and he is impressed with her pluckiness.

police captain Jacob Welse warns him that with all the prospectors flooding into Dawson there will be food shortages, so they must be prepared "before it is too late." The captain agrees to "take five thousand men out of Dawson" to prevent the famine (61).

Mr. Smith A clerk of Jacob Welse's who announces warehouse orders and the arrival of Captain McGregor.

Captain McGregor A ship captain who works for Jacob Welse; Welse sends him with 300 men to take care of the thousand or so who will need work downcountry; they will chop cordwood under McGregor's management.

John Melton Melton calls on Jacob Welse to complain about a freight bill, but Welse tells him he'll do his own freighting to help the citizens of Dawson.

Dave Harney Another caller on Jacob Welse, a "Yankee" who tries to borrow money from Welse. He makes money in Dawson by selling sugar.

Mrs. Schoville The wife of the Gold Commissioner, she hosts a party at which Vance Corliss meets up again with Frona and is the force behind the production of *A Doll's House*. She is very impressed with St. Vincent's tales of his adventures.

Miss Mortimer A guest at Mrs. Schoville's party whom Corliss talks to "on the decadence of the French symbolists" (79).

Carthey "Carthey, a little Texan who went to work for [Corliss] for a while, opened or closed every second sentence, on an average, with the mild expletive, 'By damn!' It was also his invariable way of expressing surprise, disappointment, con-

sternation, or all the rest of the tribe of sudden emotions. By pitch and stress and intonation, the protean oath was made to perform every function of ordinary speech" (93).

Lucile A dance-hall girl, Lucile receives sympathy from Frona when Frona finds her weeping outside town, but disdain from Corliss; they have an argument about Frona's being seen with her. Corliss explains that his revulsion toward her is not from prejudice but because she cleaned out a miner at poker and he killed himself. She is romanced by St. Vincent but decides to marry Colonel Trethaway.

Bash One of Jacob Welse's Natives, Bash delivers a note from Frona to Corliss demanding to see him the day after they encounter Lucile.

Colonel Trethaway He comments on the women of the saloon and later gets into the barroom brawl that ensues when a man is jostled by another, the man in the yellow wolf-skin hat. Marries Lucile.

Tommy McPherson A Scotch-Canadian miner who accompanies Frona and Corliss when they try to save some people caught in the spring breakup of the STEWART RIVER. Tommy loses his wits and nearly causes the death of his companions on the river.

Baron Coubertin A visitor to Dawson who helps rescue people stranded on the river breakup and becomes involved in the miners' trial of St. Vincent.

How-ha Native woman who brings Frona a note from Lucile, asking to see her. How-ha does not approve of Lucile.

Jake Cornell Cornell has wrecked his sled with his wife Blanche and is helped by Corliss and the others.

Captain Alexander A captain of the North-West Mounted Police asked to marry Trethaway and Lucile.

Scandinavian A witness against St. Vincent in the miners' meeting.

Pierre La Flitch Part French, part Native man who acts as a witness against St. Vincent at the miners' meeting.

Bill Brown Acts as judge at the miners' trial of St. Vincent.

Tim Dugan Dugan tackles St. Vincent when he flees the miners' meeting and is bitten for his trouble.

John Borg Partner of St. Vincent's who is killed by Gow, a Native whom Borg has robbed of his squaw.

Pis-ku/Bella Gow's squaw who is taken away by John Borg. Pis-ku helps Gow murder Borg.

FURTHER READING

Furer, Andrew. "'Zone-Conquerors' and 'White Devils': The Contradictions of Race in the Works of Jack London." In *Rereading Jack London.* Edited by Leonard Cassuto and Jeanne Campbell Reesman. Stanford: Stanford University Press, 1996, 158–171.

Kingman, Russ. *A Pictorial Life of Jack London.* New York: Crown, 1979.

Labor, Earle, and Jeanne Campbell Reesman. *Jack London, Revised Edition.* New York: Macmillan (Twayne U.S. Authors Series), 1994.

London, Jack. *The Letters of Jack London.* Edited by Earle Labor, Robert C. Leitz, III, and I. Milo Shepard. 3 vols. Stanford: Stanford University Press, 1988.

Reesman, Jeanne Campbell. *Jack London's Racial Lives.* Athens: University of Georgia Press, 2009.

Sciambra, Joseph C. "From Herbert Spencer to Alfred Schultz: Jack London, His Library, and the Rise of Radical Racialism in Turn of the Century America." M.A. thesis, Sonoma State University, 1977.

Walker, Franklin. *Jack London and the Klondike: The Genesis of an American Writer.* San Marino, Calif.: The Huntington Library, 1966.

Watson, Charles N., Jr. *The Novels of Jack London: A Reappraisal.* Madison: University of Wisconsin Press, 1983.

"The Death of Ligoun" (1902)

Never published in serial form, this story first appeared in the collection *Children of the Frost* (1902), London's most compelling collection of stories on the NATIVES of the NORTHLAND. As in two others in the book, in this tale the death of a prominent chief is related by an eyewitness.

SYNOPSIS

Palitlum, a Chilcat, is being regaled with brandy and cajoled into telling the story of the death of a famous chief to a white interlocutor. Palitlum speaks of his boyhood and the fame of Ligoun, who was a great warrior and chief. Ligoun travels to Boston and observes the peaceful society there; he returns to the Northwest bound to make peace among the many warring tribes. He gives a great potlatch and spreads his influence. However, a rival chief, Niblack of the Skoots, gives an even greater "summit meeting" of all the chiefs, the Chilcat, Sitkas, Stickeens, Wrangels, Hoonahs, Sundowns, Tahkos, Awks, Naass, Tongas, Kakes, Siwashes, Cassiars, Teslin, and Sticks. (Such detailed tribal identities demonstrate London's research into his subject.) At Niblack's potlatch, as the chiefs sit in a circle and drink kvass (a cheap beer made by the Russian method), Opitsah, the Knife, chief of the Sticks, spits his kvass upon the ground, by custom insulting the greatest chief there, Ligoun. He rises and dances around Ligoun with his knife, stabbing him twice in the forehead. But Ligoun moves with great dignity and lack of haste toward Niblack, whom he must kill to save face. The group erupts into violence against each other based on different feuds; many are killed, and everyone tries to kill Ligoun. Palitlum kills Opitsah, and Ligoun kills Niblack. At the end of the story, the narrator tries to buy the knife of Ligoun from Palitlum, but even though he offers 10 bottles of brandy, Palitlum refuses: "'I am Palitlum, the Drinker, but I was once Olo, the Ever-Hungry, who bore up Ligoun with his youth!'" (*Stories,* 763).

COMMENTARY

The story has the feel of a folktale and its primary actors are all Natives. However, London modernizes the tale with his frame structure. The story is told by a Native to a white "Boston man"; London often uses this device to convey insights into the tragedy of indigenous people undergoing colonization. Adding a further irony, the story-teller Palitlum is goaded into telling his story by the white man's three-star brandy. Alcohol was one of the most devastating products of civilization for the Natives; the story also references the labor the whites are getting from them: "Palitlum, and the brothers of Palitlum, dig the gold for thee and net the fish" (*Stories*, 757). Most of the stories of *Children of the Frost* relate the sad decline of the Natives' bodies and lives as the whites take over.

CHARACTERS

unnamed narrator   Called "Boston man" and "Hair-face" by Palitlum, he seeks the story of the death of Ligoun, who had journeyed once to Boston: perhaps he knew him there. He trades a bottle of three-star brandy to Palitlum for his tale.

Palitlum   Though his original name was Olo, the Ever-Hungry, he is a Chilcat Indian who has been rechristened Palitlum, "the Drinker." As a young man, he witnesses the massacre at the potlatch of Niblack and the death of Ligoun; he kills Opitsah and Skulpin to avenge Ligoun. He is the second narrator in the frame structure.

Ligoun   Once a mighty warrior, Ligoun of the Thlinket tribe journeys to Boston and witnesses the lives most there live in peace. He returns to the Northwest determined to make peace among the many tribes. He holds a great potlatch, but when another chief, Niblack, holds one even bigger, the potlatch erupts into violence when Ligoun is menaced by a young chief of the Sticks, Opitsah, the Knife. Ligoun is killed by him and the other chiefs but kills Niblack.

Chief Niblack   Head of the Skoot tribe, he holds a potlatch to rival Ligoun's, but a melee erupts when Opitsah tries to kill Ligoun. Niblack is killed by Ligoun just before his own death.

Opitsah   Young chief of the Stick Indians, he tries to kill Ligoun; he is slain by Palitlum. He dances around Ligoun and taunts him, wanting to kill him only for the fame it will bring him.

Lamuk and Klok-Kutz   A Kake Native who has a grudge against the Stickeen, and so kills Klok-Kutz, a Stickeen.

Katchahook   Recalling a quarrel with the Naass River people and the Tongas, he shoots the chief of the Tongas.

Goolzug and Kadishan   One a fish-eater and one a meat-eater, they "closed together for the honor of their tribes" and "rage madly about" trying to kill each other at Niblack's potlatch (762).

Skulpin   A Sitka Native, he is killed by a knife thrown in the potlatch struggle; because he drags Palitlum down with him, Palitlum kills him.

"Demetrios Contos" (1905)

First published in *The Youth's Companion* on April 27, 1905, this autobiographically based story was included in *Tales of the Fish Patrol* (1905), tales based on London's teenage exploits first as an oyster pirate in SAN FRANCISCO BAY and later a member of the FISH PATROL who captured them. One evening, quite drunk, London decided to drown himself by jumping off a pier at Benicia. He sobered up in the cold waters of the bay and changed his mind. He was rescued by a passing Greek fisherman.

SYNOPSIS

The narrator and Charley Le Grant are members of the Fish Patrol in San Francisco Bay and its environs. They are particularly resented by the local community of GREEK fishermen: "We confiscated illegal traps and nets, the materials of which had cost them considerable sums and the making of which required weeks of labor. We prevented them from catching fish at many times and seasons, which was equivalent to preventing them from making as good a living as they might have made had we not been in existence. And when we captured them, they were brought into the courts of law, where heavy cash fines were collected from them. As a result, they hated us vindictively. As the dog is the natural enemy of the cat, the snake of man, so were we of the fish patrol the natural enemies of the fishermen" (*Stories*, 874). Demetrios Contos is, next to another Greek called Big Alec, the "largest, bravest, and most influential man among the Greeks" (*Stories*, 874). Contos acquires a new boat that is faster than any other on the bay or rivers. He sends a challenge to the Fish Patrol in Benicia that he will come on Sunday and right in front of them set out his salmon nets. This he does, catching a big salmon, and when Charley and the narrator give chase, he easily eludes them. They are made sport of by the other fishermen on the pier. The same thing happens the next Sunday. The narrator and Charley come up with a plan; Charley will walk away and secretly get on a horse to ride for Contos's home in Vallejo while the narrator takes the boat out after him. Contos has trouble with his centerboard and so heads homeward; meanwhile, the treacherous currents and riptides of the Carquinez and Vallejo Straits that pour into San Pablo Bay test the narrator's skills, though he is thrilled to be handling the boat so expertly in such dangerous seas. However, he hits a submerged pile and staves in his bow; he is caught in the sail rigging and goes down with the boat. Drowning, he struggles in the whitecaps and freezing water. He is rescued by Contos. Over his protestations to let Contos go, Charley testifies against him, and Contos receives a fine of $100. However, Charley immediately pays the fine and tells the narrator he will need to pay his half. Contos warmly shakes Charley's hand. The three become good friends, and Contos stops taking illegal fish.

COMMENTARY

This story and the others in the collection reflect London's knowledge not only of sailing in the tricky waters of the bay, but also his sense of the multinational community of fishermen, in this case the Greeks. He emphasizes the rules that have evolved on both sides: "Of course, he could have drawn his revolver and fired at Demetrios; but we had long since found it contrary to our natures to shoot at a fleeing man guilty of only a petty offence. Also a sort of tacit agreement seemed to have been reached between the patrolmen and the fishermen. If we did not shoot while they ran away, they, in turn, did not fight if we once laid hands on them. Thus Demetrios Contos ran away from us, and we did no more than try our best to overtake him; and, in turn, if our boat proved faster than his, or was sailed better, he would, we knew, make no resistance when we caught up with him" (*Stories*, 877). This odd camaraderie between lawbreakers and patrolmen illustrates the common bond they share with boats and sailing, a sort of code that transcends the law when it can.

CHARACTERS

Unnamed Narrator A young man new to the Fish Patrol who learns its lessons from Charley Le Grant. He narrates all the Fish Patrol stories.

Charley Le Grant An older man who trains the narrator in the art of sailing and in the duties of the Fish Patrol. Like the narrator, he loves sailing for itself and also the adventures they share together.

Demetrios Contos Greek fisherman who builds a special salmon boat that can outrun the Fish Patrol. He is shown as breaking the law but in the end exhibits warm good nature and friendliness to his pursuers.

Judge Sentences Contos to pay a fine of $100 for illegal fishing.

"The Devil's Dice Box" (1898)

London's first KLONDIKE story remained unpublished until 1976 when it appeared in the SATURDAY EVENING POST 248 (December 1976). Both *McClure's* and *Munsey's* magazines rejected the story when London submitted it in 1898, which seems odd since the GOLD RUSH was still going on then and the story would have been timely. Despite its publication record, it is an important story, for in several ways it forecasts the major themes and image patterns of later Klondike tales. London made a cryptic note in his notebook next to the story: "To be changed." Undoubtedly, he is referring to the name of the character he calls "the Innuit Kid" who dies in this story; in his original version he had "Malemute Kid," but this character was to live on in seven stories in *The Son of the Wolf.*

SYNOPSIS

The unnamed narrator of the story explains that while trailing a moose, he finds a NATIVE woman dead on the ice, on whom he finds a birch-bark manuscript, chewed leather, and gold. She clearly starved to death. He withholds the location the manuscript names because he plans to go there one day "and come back very rich." The manuscript tells of seven men and a woman staying together during the short days of December when a stranger from the east arrives with over 100 pounds of gold on his sled. They are curious about the gold and about how someone could get to their location, the STEWART RIVER, from that direction. The stranger will not give them any information. After resting, the stranger prepares to depart on CHRISTMAS DAY; however, his brother arrives and they square off against each other: "Never did Christmas day look down on [a] stranger scene. It was high noon, and the upper rim of the sun, barely showing above the southern horizon, cast a blood-red streak athwart the heavens. On the other hand a SUN DOG blazed, while the air was filled with scintillating particles of frost. A great silence prevailed" (117–118). The newly arrived brother kills his brother and rides off, leaving the corpse on the ground. The seven men, led by the Innuit Kid and his wife, the Native woman Lucy, place the corpse on the roof to keep it away from the dogs, then determine to set out after the brother and his party, who are surely heading to the gold strike. Gold fever strikes them all, which the narrator calls "the Madness."

They struggle for three terrible months on the trail in pursuit of the others, having to kill and eat nearly all their dogs and abandoning one of their party, Charley, to die. Tired and worn to the point of contemplating suicide, they persist at their horrific journey, with the thermometer at 74 degrees below zero: "Our faces were frozen a purplish-black and covered all over with great scabs, while we were in continual agony from our feet. Constant snow shoeing had developed large running sores on the soles" (*Stories,* 122). They reach the Rockies and enter a gorge to find themselves "on a large plateau, above which towered lofty peaks, dismal and repellent in their white splendor" (*Stories,* 123). In the very center of the plateau, they find a gigantic hole 1,000 feet deep and 300 feet across. Skirting the edge, they look for the one descent they can make at the site of an avalanche. Dogs, sleds, and men from both parties tumble down together. Several of the men and dogs are killed. The survivors hole up in a small cabin where they find over $50,000 in gold nuggets and the skeleton of a man clutching a birch-bark with writing upon it. They learn that the writer was left by his comrades 20 years ago to die alone. They find another note that they realize is from their visitor from the East, mocking the dead man and signed "Griffith Benson." Eating "straight dog," they fruitlessly hunt for game as they feverishly take out gold. When the brother's team steals one of the Ralington party's dogs, a melee breaks out and all are killed save Lucy and Ralington. He is dying, but she kills two moose and prepares to depart once he is gone. She is the dead woman the narrator finds on the trail, and she carries the last words of Ralington.

COMMENTARY

This story establishes several major themes and image patterns that would reappear in other Klondike stories. London's reading in GREEK MYTHOLOGY had taught him that the SUN, personified by Apollo, represents the eye of Heaven that judges the deeds of men. Accordingly, the position of the sun is often referenced in the Klondike stories; it appears just as an unjust deed is about to be committed. London also refers to the god as "Old SOL," the Roman version. Sol/Apollo's number is seven and his feast day

December 25. He witnesses the oaths and actions of men for all the gods, stressing personal responsibility and justice. Tacitus described him as the revealer of the crimes of men. Apollo rules that murder demands expiation; he particularly takes an interest in how men bury or fail to bury the dead. London also uses sun dogs in a number of stories; these are a rare occurrence (though more common in Arctic latitudes) in which two mock suns appear on either side of the sun, an effect of the atmosphere caused by refraction and reflection of light through ice and snow crystals. Romans saw them as harbingers of important events; an obvious example was the cross Constantine is supposed to have seen in the sky. Perhaps for London, they hint at the clear oppositions of right and wrong in the story. Finally, as another detail of the story suggests, Greeks and Romans feared the East, which they never fully conquered.

Using this mythic structure as a guide, it is clear that the men who lust more for gold than they care about their fellow men (and dogs) are doomed by their lack of BROTHERHOOD; they foolishly pit themselves against COMMUNITY, nature, and JUSTICE as demanded by the gods, and so they perish. The story's epigraph is a poem written by London with a Miltonian reference to Mammon:

> We worshipped at alien altars; we bowed our
>   heads in the dust;
> Our law was might is the mightiest; our creed
>   was unholy lust;
> Our law and our creed we followed—strange is
>   the tale to tell—
> For our law and our creed we followed into the
>   pit of hell.
>   —"The Mammon Worshippers"

The story's central image of a dice box as a yawning pit of hell is the site of the Fall, an abyss of gold and skeletons; brother murders brother and leaves the dead scattered about. This was a dice box in which everyone loses.

CHARACTERS

unnamed narrator Trailing a wounded moose and far from his camp, he comes across a Native woman who has died on the trail; on her he discovers a birch-bark manuscript that tells of the terrible fate of two gold-hunting parties. He does not seem to learn from what he reads, because he wishes to repeat their experiences and look for the gold himself.

James Ralington Author of the birch-bark manuscript found by the narrator. He dies alone in a cabin and warns others in his last words to stay away from the cursed place.

Innuit Kid The most experienced of his party, he is the model for the later hero of many of London's Klondike tales, the Malemute Kid, who is half-Native and half-white. He is seasoned and capable, but nevertheless succumbs to the gold fever that infects his trail mates.

Lucy Indian woman educated by missionaries who is the Innuit Kid's wife. She is the only survivor of the disaster at the Devil's Dice Box, but she does not make it home, dying of starvation and cold.

Randolf Brothers/Abe and John Randolph Oddly, Randolf/Randolph is spelled two ways in the story; they are prominent Kentuckians who are in the Klondike to prospect for gold.

two sailors Members of Ralington's party.

Charley Member of Ralington's party who is left on the trail to die, since they cannot carry him as they rush onward toward the treasure.

man from the East/Griffith Benson He arrives at Ralington's camp with 100 pounds in gold and refuses to say where he found it. He is murdered by his own brother before he can depart.

strangers including the man from the East's brother The second set of prospectors who lead the way to the Devil's Dice Box and its cursed treasure. All of them die.

"The Devils of Fuatino"
(1911)

First published as "The Goat Man of Fuatino" in the SATURDAY EVENING POST 184 (June 29, 1911), it is one of the David Grief stories of *A Son of the Sun* (1912) and one of the most significant in its racial attitudes.

SYNOPSIS

David Grief arrives at the fictitious Raiatean island of Fuatino, known as the "love-island" for its romantic legends: "'Look here, young man,' Captain Glass rumbled threateningly at his mate. 'Are you romantic? Because if you are, on board you stay. Fuatino's the island of romantic insanity. Everybody's in love with somebody. They live on love. It's in the milk of the cocoanuts, or the air, or the sea. The history of the island for the last ten thousand years is nothing but love affairs. I know. I've talked with the old men. And if I catch you starting down the beach hand in hand—'" (1,920). But instead of love, Grief and Captain Glass find the island overrun with French pirates and many of its inhabitants murdered. They are joined by Mauriri, the "Goat Man," who nimbly swims to their schooner, the *Rattler,* and easily heaves himself over the rail. He tells Grief of the pirates and asks for his help. The pirates have taken Captain Dupuy's ship the *Valetta* and murdered him and most of his crew; they have also kidnapped women from the neighboring island of Huahine as well the daughter of Queen Mataara of Fuatino, Naumoo. Grief, Mauriri, a crewman, Brown, and a few others climb to the Big Rock overlooking the harbor. They shoot at the pirates and drop dynamite on their ship, blowing it to pieces. The pirates steal the *Rattler,* and, after a fruitless parlay with Grief, come to a standoff in which they are all killed along with the captive Naumoo. Order is restored on Fuatino, despite the tragedy of so many deaths of its denizens. Grief and his party nearly starve waiting out the pirates, and they dare sharks to gain water and food. Grief tricks the pirate leader into thinking they are well supplied. When the final battle occurs, Mataara and

Captain Glass are saved. Grief asks Mataara, "'How is it with you, Sister?'" to which she replies, "'Naumoo is gone, and Motauri, Brother, but Fuatino is ours again. This day is young. Word shall be sent to all my people in the high places with the goats. And to-night, and as never before, we shall feast and rejoice in the Big House'" (*Stories,* 1,940–1,941).

COMMENTARY

David Grief is a white rover and businessman in the South Seas who is London's fantasy figure of a white man who can master the Tropics. He starts out in the volume almost ridiculously perfect; in stories such as "The Proud Goat of Aloysius Pankburn," Grief, like a tribal chief, beats another white man out of his ALCOHOLISM. "A Little Account With Swithin Hall" portrays Grief as a model of fairness and justice as he settles his debts. But by "The Devils of Fuatino," Grief's role changes from self-righteous white boss to comrade on the side of indigenous resistance to whites. He helps save— note the "helps"—the Raiatean island occupied by white "robbers and pigs" (1,926). In their suspenseful standoff with the pirates, Grief and the islanders, including Mauriri, withstand attack after attack, eventually routing the pirates with their sharpshooting and explosives. The Goat-Man's body and bravery, not Grief's, is central, and value is not so much placed on individual heroics but the restoration of COMMUNITY. When the Raiateans attack the pirates, we are told that they "singled out the blond heads and the brown" to aim at from their cliffside perches, as Grief watches approvingly (1,940). This is a distinctive moment, to say the least, when London has nonwhite characters single out Caucasian heads to aim at as a white man looks on and then shoots at them too. Interestingly, the manuscript of "The Devils of Fuatino" shows several penciled changes that heighten the racial dimension of the story, such as repeated additions of the word "darkness" to refer to the islanders or the term "white savage" to apply to their opponents.

CHARACTERS

David Grief   Grief is identified with the sun, a motif going back to KLONDIKE tales, where SOL, a version of Apollo, was the Eye of Heaven looking down in judgment on the deeds of human beings. In "The Proud Goat of Aloysius Pankburn," he is contrasted with a lesser white man, Griffith, sick from the sun, whiskey, and fever: "'Nothing's too mean and low for me now,'" he says, "'and I can understand why the niggers eat each other, and take heads, and such things. I could do it myself'" (1,890). Grief, on the other hand, is a true "son of the sun":

> He had been born to the sun. One he was in ten thousand in the matter of sun-resistance. The invisible and high-velocity light waves failed to bore into him. Other white men were pervious. The sun drove through their skins, ripping and smashing tissues and nerves, till they became sick in mind and body, tossed most of the Decalogue overboard, descended to beastliness, drank themselves into quick graves, or survived so savagely that war vessels were sometimes sent to curb their license. (*Stories*, 1,894–1,895)

Like a tall-tale hero, Grief arrived in the South Seas in a hurricane. His yacht wrecked, he stayed behind in TAHITI to make his fortune. He becomes a boyish rover, but hidden beneath his good humor, eternal youth, and brown physique is a sharp businessman and advocate of island peoples.

Taute   A POLYNESIAN lookout on Grief's ship the *Rattler*; he tells Grief that in Raiatea it is called the "Dayborn." He sights land that turns out to be the island of Fuatino.

Captain Glass   Skipper of Grief's favorite ship, the *Rattler*, a "yacht-like schooner of ninety tons with so swift a pair of heels that she had made herself famous, in the old days, opium-smuggling from San Diego to Puget Sound, raiding the seal-rookeries of Bering Sea, and running arms in the Far East" (1,918). He comes down with fever and is unable to help Grief with the ship or the pirates.

Pilsach   A German trader on Fuatino who abandoned Captain Glass and married a native woman: When Captain Glass seeks him, he finds "him in a straw house in the bush, barelegged, a white savage, all mixed up with flowers and things and playing a guitar. Looked like a bally ass. Told me to send his things ashore. I told him I'd see him damned first. And that's all. You'll see her to-morrow. They've got three kiddies now—wonderful little rascals. I've a phonograph down below for him, and about a million records" (*Stories*, 1,920). Pilsach is killed by the French pirates.

Notutu   Pilsach's wife who captures her man with a wreath of white flowers.

Mauriri   Called "the Goat Man" and a "sea-faun," Mauriri is David Grief's blood brother and, in the native custom, has exchanged names with him. He calls Grief "Big Brother" and together they defend Fuatino from French pirates. He is a man with "[b]road brown shoulders and a magnificent chest, with an unearthly grace and agility." His enchantment includes "long elfin locks, and . . . a face with roguish black eyes, lined with the marks of wildwood's laughter" (*Stories*, 1,920).

Brown   Mate of the *Rattler*, he is impressed with "the faun-likeness" of Mauriri like the magical beings he has read about in books. He is thrilled to visit the legendary isle of Fuatino. He assists Grief and Mauriri in attacking the pirates.

Mataara   Queen of Fuatino who weeps for the destruction of her people and prays for Grief's return; her daughter, Naumoo, is kidnapped by the pirates, and her lover, Motauri, is killed by them along with many others. "It was as if the place had been struck with the plague, was Grief's thought, as he finally approached the Big House. All was desolation and disarray. . . . In the doorway, crouched and rocking back and forth, sat Mataara, the old queen. She wept afresh at sight of him, divided between the tale of her woe and regret that no follower was left to dispense to him her hospitality. . . . 'My people have fled and are starving with the goats. And there is no one to open for you even a drinking cocoanut. O Brother, your white brothers be devils.'" But Grief says they are no brothers of his, but "robbers and pigs" (1,926).

the "Hare-Lip" Formerly a cook at a French hotel in Papeete, he becomes the cook of the pirates' ship, the *Valetta*, and is forced to kill Captain Dupuy, its former skipper, and his crew. He throws himself on Grief's feet and begs for help. He joins Grief and Mauriri on the rocky heights to shoot at the pirates.

Raoul Van Asveld Signed on in Tahiti by Captain Dupuy, he serves as mate on the *Valetta*. He is the ringleader of the French pirates. He poisons half the crew of the *Valetta* and has Captain Dupuy killed. Hare-Lip tells Grief that he is "'the chief devil, . . . and his eyes are blue like yours. He is a terrible man. See! He holds Naumoo that we may not shoot him'" (1,931).

Carl Lepsius Hired by Captain Dupuy of the *Valetta* as supercargo; with Van Asweld a pirate.

Mautau A Raiatean man who dares the tiger sharks of the lagoon to help Grief collect water for their position on the Big Rock.

Tehaa A Raiatean man who joins Grief and the others on the Big Rock. He is instructed by Grief to prepare all of their food when Van Asveld arrives at a parlay.

Naumoo Daughter of Queen Mataara, she is kidnapped by Van Asveld and used as a shield when he is fired upon by Grief and Mauriri. She is killed when Grief dynamites the *Rattler*, which the pirates have seized.

"The Dream of Debs" (1909)

First appearing in the *International Socialist Review* 9 (January 1909), the dystopian fantasy "The Dream of Debs" was included in the collection *The Strength of the Strong* (1914). It is one of London's most overtly socialist stories. And yet it employs features of futuristic science fiction and NATURALISM, as well as a disturbing tone of dark humor.

SYNOPSIS

The narrator, Mr. Corf, is a wealthy San Franciscan. On the morning of May 1, at some time projected into the 1930s, he awakes to a strange quiet on the streets. Summoning a servant, he learns that there is a general strike of all the unions and working class. He is dismayed that the creamery has not delivered cream for his coffee, nor has the bakery sent round his morning French rolls. And his problems intensify as the strike unfolds. He and his friends at his club debate what to do, but soon food shortages and lawlessness are rampant—but not among the working class, only the upper class and the slum dwellers. With some other men from the club he gathers what food and candles he can, but an attempt to journey to the countryside and butcher a cow turns into a grotesque misadventure when they are first beaten by the I.L.W. union guards, then robbed by vagabonds. Things turn even darker when he joins up with some others on horseback to escape to the countryside south of the city. They witness murder and destruction on a scale none of them had ever imagined, as people turn atavistic in the fight for survival. Only when he is nearly dead from starvation and exposure does he return to a working class home he once had a meal in and finds out the strike is over. He reflects: "It was worse than a war. A general strike is a cruel and immoral thing, and the brain of man should be capable of running industry in a more rational way. . . . Brown never came back, but the rest of the servants are with me. I hadn't the heart to discharge them—poor creatures, they were pretty hard-pressed when they deserted with the food and silver. And now I can't discharge them. They have all been unionized by the I.L.W. The tyranny of organized labour is getting beyond human endurance. Something must be done" (*Stories*, 1,277–1,278).

COMMENTARY

Like most DYSTOPIAN FICTION, the story has a nightmarish and dreamlike quality, coupled with a naturalistic sense of the physical aspects of survival. It is a comment on both the blindness and cruelty of CAPITALISM toward workers, and it also discloses the capitalists' history of manipulation of labor. And there is the eerie fact that the narrator recalls that while in college he wrote a pamphlet that the strike seems to emulate, called "The Dream of Debs": "For a generation the general strike had been the dream of organized labour, which dream had arisen originally in the mind of Debs, one of the great labour leaders of thirty years before. . . . I had treated the idea very cavalierly and academically as a dream and nothing more. Time and the world had rolled on, Gompers was gone, the American Federation of Labour was gone, and gone was Debs with all his wild revolutionary ideas; but the dream had persisted, and here it was at last realized in fact" (*Stories*, 1,262). The narrator is referring to two of the great labor leaders of London's day, EUGENE V. DEBS and Samuel Gompers, as well as to the American Federation of Labor, one of the first federations of labor unions in the United States. London's acronym I.L.W. is supposed to suggest the I.W.W., or International Workers of the World. These references add verisimilitude. The fact that the story occurs on May Day, or May 1, is a nod to International Workers' Day, which celebrates the achievements of the labor movement, including the eight-hour day, as declared in 1910 by the Second International (1889–1916), an organization of socialist and labor parties formed in Paris on July 14, 1889.

CHARACTERS

Mr. Corf   Narrator of the story, he is a wealthy man used to his privileges and can scarcely believe that the strike occurs. He struggles to survive, even trying to butcher a cow and a calf himself. He recalls that he once envisioned such a strike, but never thought it would actually happen.

Brown   A servant of Corf's who brings him his last morning paper and coffee without cream.

Mr. Hammed   Butler to Mr. Corf, he is unable to acquire food because he cannot drive. He continues to work loyally for Mr. Corf.

Mr. Harrison   Former chauffeur of Mr. Corf who goes on strike with the Teamsters Union.

Miss Chickering   Lady whom Corf assists in buying candles. Though she says to him, "'Oh, Mr. Corf!' she hailed. 'It's dreadfully awful, isn't it?'", he sees from "her sparkling eyes" that "she was enjoying it hugely. Quite an adventure it was, getting those candles" (*Stories*, 1,263).

General Folsom   Commander of the army post at the Presidio, he calls in 3,000 troops to guard banks, the Mint, the post office, and public buildings. "Nursing his capacious paunch in a window-seat in the smoking-room was defending himself against half-a-dozen excited gentlemen who were demanding that he should do something. 'What can I do more than I have done?' he was saying. 'There are no orders from Washington. . . . There is no disorder whatever. The strikers are keeping the peace perfectly. You can't expect me to shoot them down as they walk along the streets with wives and children all in their best bib and tucker'" (*Stories*, 1,264).

Jimmy Wombold   Club man who declares, "'I'd like to know what's happening on Wall Street'"; the narrator confides that "'I could imagine his anxiety, for I knew that he was deep in the big Consolidated-Western deal'" (*Stories*, 1,264).

Atkinson   Club man who wants to borrow the narrator's car and then another man's boat to try to reach his wife, who is stranded in Northern California.

Rollinson   Owner of the "the *Lurlette*[,] . . . a two-hundred-ton, ocean-going schooner-yacht" at anchor in Sausalito; the men cannot use it because, as Rollinson says, "'You couldn't get a longshoreman to land the machine on board, even if I could get the Lurlette over, which I can't, for the crew are members of the Coast Seamen's Union, and they're on strike along with the rest'" (*Stories*, 1,265).

Halstead   Club man who suggests getting Rollinson's yacht across the bay.

Bertie Messener   Enormously rich, this blasé young man has spent his life as a world traveler, sportsman, and athlete and so disdains his more sedentary fellow club men. He lectures them on how the strike is only the result of their unfair labor practices and business manipulations; he frames the situation as a naturalistic power struggle in which the other side now has the advantage.

Garfield "'One of the traction millionaires,'" he argues with Messener and boasts, "'and we'll play all right! . . . We'll show this dirt where its place is—the beasts! Wait till the Government takes a hand'" (*Stories*, 1,266).

Hanover Called "little Hanover" by the narrator, he is a club member who keeps objecting to the strike: "'It's not right, I tell you.'" Messener replies: "Labour is doing nothing wrong in going out on this general strike. It is violating no law of God nor man. . . . It's a dirty little sordid scrap, that's all the whole thing is. You've got labour down and gouged it, and now labour's got you down and is gouging you, that's all, and you're squealing'" (*Stories*, 1,266).

Brentwood Club member who accuses Messener of profiting from labor gouging, to which Messener responds that people like Brentwood did the dirty work for him. He accompanies Halstead and the narrator on the ill-fated expedition to butcher a cow; the narrator recalls, "'Brentwood, I remember, was a perfect brute, snarling and snapping and threatening that murder would be done if we did not get our proper share'" (*Stories*, 1,271).

Rider Club member who crosses the bay from Oakland in his launch to bring news of food shortages.

little girl She guards her cows and when she sees the party from San Francisco trying to steal the cow, she runs for the I.L.W. guards who arrive armed and beat the perpetrators: "The little girl danced up and down in anger, the tears streaming down her cheeks, crying: 'Give it to 'em! Give it to 'em! That guy with the specs—he did it! Mash his face for him! Mash his face!'" This man is the narrator.

Hanover, Collins, and Dakon Three men who accompany the narrator on Dakon's horses for a trip to the country south of the city toward Menlo Park and Stanford. All three are killed or disappear, and three of the four horses are caught and killed by scavengers.

workman's wife The narrator trades her a large silver pitcher for a meal early in the story; at its conclusion she happily feeds him and gives him the news: "'Why, you poor man,' she said, 'haven't you heard? The strike was called off this afternoon. Of course we'll give you something to eat.' She bustled around, opening a tin of breakfast bacon and preparing to fry it" (*Stories*, 1,277).

"The Enemy of All the World" (1908)

This naturalistic study of how child abuse leads to a life of crime was first published in *Red Book* 11 (October 1908). It was then included in *The Strength of the Strong* (1914). It reflects both the general fears of "foreign" anarchism at the turn of the last century (the anarchist, Gluck, has a GERMAN name), as well as London's own experiences as a child and his concern about a future of violence and unrest. It makes an interesting contrast with another story of CHILD LABOR, "The Apostate," in which the protagonist escapes.

SYNOPSIS

Set in the 1930s, the story relates the early life of an Emil Gluck and his subsequent career as an ANARCHIST bomber. His parents having died, he was raised by a neglectful aunt. Though he is a "sensitive, shrinking boy," she, a "vain, shallow, and heartless woman," does not want the boy; she even leaves him on the street with a broken leg and kicks him there on the ground for troubling her (*Stories*, 1,247). As the narrator explains, "No kind word was spoken to him, no soothing hand laid upon his brow, no single touch or act of loving tenderness—naught but the reproaches and harshness of Ann Bartell, and the continually reiterated information that he was not wanted. And it can well be understood, in such environment, how there was generated in the lonely, neglected boy much of the bitterness and hostility for his kind that later was to express itself in deeds so frightful as to terrify the world" (*Stories*, 1,248).

Against many odds, Gluck attends college at Bowdoin and then follows his professor to the UNIVERSITY OF CALIFORNIA for graduate work. He becomes a chemistry instructor there and attains worldwide prominence for a book called *Sex and Progress*, but it is "'played up . . . yellow,'" sensationalized for its ideas on trial marriages; he is besieged by reporters and photographers (*Stories*, 1,250). He is fired by the university. Another publication of his is seen by the press as advocating revolution: "Persecuted, maligned, and misunderstood, the forlorn and lonely man made no attempt at retaliation" (*Stories*, 1,251). He unsuccessfully romances a young woman and is beaten by her boyfriend. Still, he does not understand his bad luck. The woman is murdered, and he is arrested and sent to prison. Yet, when he is released because the real murderer is caught, he is again notorious.

A series of murders of policemen, newspapermen, and other "enemies" ensues, culminating in the now-avowed anarchist's assassination of the King and Queen of Portugal and the destruction of nearly all U.S. army and navy bases, ships, and storehouses. Having become a working man after his firing, he learned from electroplating a means of exploding bombs at long distance using a wireless device. Finally, he is caught and confesses that he wished he had done more damage. He is executed but not before the French government tries to buy his secret from him. He was, in the conclusion, "one of the world's most unfortunate geniuses, a man of tremendous intellect, but whose mighty powers, instead of making toward good, were so twisted and warped that he became the most amazing of criminals" (*Stories*, 1,260).

COMMENTARY

This is a frame story "Culled from Mr. A. G. Burnside's 'Eccentricitics of Crime,' by kind permission of the publishers, Messrs. Holiday and Whitsund"

(1260). An unnamed narrator who uses the pronoun "we" relates a narrative worthy of ÉMILE ZOLA—how a criminal is formed by forces beyond his control, reflecting London's NATURALISM, especially his sense of how the effects of childhood abuse could warp a human being into a monster. Oddly, "gluck" is the German word for "luck," but here the protagonist starts out unlucky, luckily finds a means of revenge against the world, and then, once again, unluckily, is caught on a small technicality. Autobiographical details include the portrait of an unloving mother, a general sense of childhood deprivation, and a burning desire to succeed. Like London, Gluck is "a remarkable student. Application such as his would have taken him far; but he did not need application. A glance at a text meant mastery for him. The result was that he did an immense amount of collateral reading and acquired more in half a year than did the average student in half-a-dozen years. In 1909, barely fourteen years of age, he was ready—'more than ready' the headmaster of the academy said—to enter Yale or Harvard" (*Stories*, 1,249). London crammed at Belmont Academy, doing two years college preparation in a few months, but unlike Gluck he was able to rise above his early formation and become successful in writing. It is worth remembering, however, that he did advocate armed revolution by socialists and admired the famous anarchist, EMMA GOLDMAN, and that he was sometimes hounded by the press. Still, the story is much less about him than it is a warning that criminals are made, not born.

CHARACTERS

narrator The narrator tells of Gluck's early background to help explain his violent attacks upon society: "This side of his story has never been told before, and from his confession and from the great mass of evidence and the documents and records of the time we are able . . . to discern the factors and pressures that moulded him into the human monster he became and that drove him onward and downward along the fearful path he trod" (*Stories*, 1,247).

Silas Bannerman Detective who finally arrests Gluck for his crimes, having long suspected him.

Emil Gluck Abused as a child, vilified by a yellow press, and persecuted by the police, Gluck is the picture of a criminal made by social forces around him; as the narrator remarks, "While the deeds of Emil Gluck were all that was abominable, we cannot but feel, to a certain extent, pity for the unfortunate, malformed, and maltreated genius" (*Stories*, 1,247).

Mrs. Ann Bartell Gluck's aunt, who unwillingly takes him in and treats him cruelly: "[I]n her breast was no kindly feeling for the sensitive, shrinking boy. . . . Young Emil Gluck was not wanted, and Ann Bartell could be trusted to impress this fact sufficiently upon him" (*Stories*, 1,248).

Elizabeth Shepstone Neighborhood woman who finds Gluck with a broken leg and has him placed on a shutter, calls the doctor, and carries him to Mrs. Bartell's house.

Professor Bradlough A professor and Gluck's only friend; Gluck studies with him at Bowdoin and follows him for graduate work at the University of California, Berkeley.

policeman Carew Testifies against Gluck that he rarely leaves his electroplating shop, only in the early morning hours.

Irene Tackley Young woman Gluck tries to romance in a soda shop across the street from his electroplating business. She complains to her boyfriend, who beats Gluck.

William Sherbourne Tackley's boyfriend, he is "a gross and stolid creature, a heavy-jawed man of the working class who had become a successful building-contractor in a small way" (*Stories*, 1,252).

Captain Shehan Oakland policeman who perjures himself in testifying against Gluck for the murder of Irene Tackley.

Tim Haswell A robber who is the actual murderer of Irene Tackley; he is killed in a gunfight in Piedmont Heights and confesses before he dies.

Bert Danniker Haswell's accomplice in the murder of Irene Tackley, he confesses before he dies of tuberculosis in Folsom Prison.

John Hartwell Citizen who accuses Gluck of the murder of Tackley despite the confessions of Danniker and Haswell. He is killed by Gluck.

policeman Phillipps Helps frame Gluck for Tackley's murder and is shot in the leg by an unknown assailant.

king and queen of Portugal Assassinated by Gluck on their wedding day, causing a widespread riot and massacre.

crown prince of Germany Gluck assassinates him and blows up the German navy, inciting the German-American War, with 800,000 casualties.

George Brown An operator employed by the Wood's System of Wireless Telegraphy.

"The Eternity of Forms"
(1911)

Included in *The Turtles of Tasman* (1916), this fanciful story was first published in *Red Book* 16 (March 1911). Like OSCAR WILDE's *The Picture of Dorian Gray*, it tells of a guilty man's hallucinations.

SYNOPSIS

Two unmarried brothers, Sedley and James Crayden, live together and enjoy long talks into the night on all manner of learned subjects. They continue to debate the existence of a metaphysical or spiritual realm and life after death. Without realizing what he is doing, Sedley becomes so incensed with James's beliefs that he kills him with a poker. He is haunted ever after by the apparition of James sitting at his desk and writing; only by occupying his desk chair forever is he rid of the delusion. Of course, it is he who is writing jagged and rambling jottings in his journal about what he sees. His servants despair of his recovery, and he dies in his chair, victim of his hallucination.

COMMENTARY

In this strange story, the frame device is doubled, with a prefacing newspaper account and a servant's statement, followed by the excerpts from Sedley Crayden's manuscript. A fantastic tale comparable to Henry James's ghost story "The Jolly Corner," the tale references London's own internal debate concerning materialism versus metaphysics, which preoccupied him throughout his life. Ironically, the more Sedley argues against "the eternity of forms," the more he is obsessed with the "form" of his dead brother.

CHARACTERS

Rudolph Heckler Narrator and "confidential servant and valet" of Sedley Crayden's who excerpts his manuscript and makes it available to the world (*Stories*, 1,751).

Sedley Crayden Protagonist of the story who kills his brother and is haunted not only by his argument about the spiritual world but specifically by the apparition of his brother taking his place at his desk and writing "his" journal.

James Crayden Brother of the protagonist who is killed by him in an argument over the existence of life after death.

"The Feathers of the Sun" (1912)

One of the David Grief stories of *A Son of the Sun* in which Grief helps South Sea islanders to rid themselves of a white tyrant, "The Feathers of the Sun" first appeared in SATURDAY EVENING POST 184 (March 9, 1912).

SYNOPSIS

David Grief arrives at the island of Fitu-Iva to find his trader, Ieremia, and the entire island upset because a scurrilous white man, Cornelius Deasy, calling himself "the Feathers of the Sun," has become chancellor of the exchequer and manipulated the King, Tulifau, into introducing paper money; meanwhile Deasy collects all the gold and silver on the island. To raise more money, he harshly fines traders and other ships that happen into his port. He arrests Grief and issues orders that his ship be seized. However, Grief organizes an islandwide council at which Deasy is exposed; in punishment he is beaten with a dead pig and run off the island.

COMMENTARY

Fitu-Iva is called the "last independent POLYNESIAN stronghold in the South Seas" because of its isolation, the warlike nature of its inhabitants, and the fact that it escaped a European protectorate when "Japan, France, Great Britain, Germany, and the United States discovered its desirableness simultaneously. It was like gamins scrambling for a penny. They got in one another's way" (*Stories*, 2,044). London combines a good deal of what he observed in the Society Islands and in FIJI on his two-year Pacific cruise on the SNARK in this story, and it is remarkable in part because it contains so many "nationalities." For example, the opening description of young people dancing on the graves in front of the church (*himine* house, or "hymn" house) is based on what he saw in BORA BORA and recorded in chapter 12 of *The Cruise of the* Snark: ". . . on the village green, by forgotten graves on the beach, found the youths and maidens dancing, flower-garlanded and flower-bedecked, with strange phosphorescent flowers in their hair that pulsed and dimmed and glowed in the moonlight. Farther along the beach we came upon a huge grass house, oval-shaped seventy feet in length, where the elders of the village were singing himines. They, too, were flower- garlanded and jolly, and they welcomed us into the fold as little lost sheep straying along from outer darkness" (*Cruise*, 215–216). The mention of a "Broom Road" is a reference to that road on NUKU HIVA in TAIOHAE; "Fululea" or "Feathers of the Sun" is Fijian; Levuka is a town on the southeast coast of the Fijian island of Ovalau; Deasy and Smee are IRISH, Grief ANGLO-SAXON,

Peter Gee CHINESE, Ieremia Samoan. We learn that the people of Fitu-Iva fight like Maoris. Perhaps using all of these different cultures indicates that London saw the story as a sort of parable or fable about the white presence in the South Seas.

With its slapstick humor and folktale details, it can certainly be read as a comic fable, despite the serious theme of the predations of whites. There are such images as the fat chiefs lolling around under avocado trees, the henpecked husbands (Ieremia and Tulifau), the exaggeration of Deasy's fines and punishments against Grief—which Grief first thinks is a joke, the image of the split silk shirt on the king, the backsliding preacher, and finally the hilarity of beating the bad guy with a dead pig—an insult in any language, but one particularly meaningful in Polynesia. Grief wins by guile and by public laughter that shames "the Feathers of the Sun" into woeful submission.

CHARACTERS

David Grief   Grief is London's South Seas action hero, a rover and businessman who appears in all the stories of *A Son of the Sun*. Though he is an ANGLO-SAXON by heredity, unlike other white men he thrives in the Tropics. In most of the stories, like this one, he helps right wrongs mostly brought on by whites invading the islands. He is a physical as well as a moral model.

Cornelius Deasy   An unscrupulous and drunken Irishman who has spent his days as a beachcomber in FIJI. He arrives on Fitu-Iva and charms the king with gin and a scheme to introduce paper money. Calling himself Fululea, Fijian for "the Feathers of the Sun," he bilks the king, the chiefs, the traders, and the common villagers out of their gold and silver and causes an islandwide food shortage.

Tui Tulifau   Tulifau "was a kingly king, a royal figure of a man, standing six feet and a half, and, without being excessively fat, weighing three hundred and twenty pounds. But this was not unusual for Polynesian 'chief stock'" (*Stories*, 2,044). He is called a "sympathetic monarch," but he is easily manipulated by Deasy, turning into a drunk and receiving beatings from his wife.

Sepeli   Wife of Tui Tulifau, she is a large and commanding Polynesian woman who beats her husband with her huge fist. Grief conspires with her to defeat Deasy.

Uiliami   Brother of Queen Sepeli, he works for Deasy and arrests Grief, but at the council he speaks for the army and relates how discontented they are with Deasy, paper money, and lack of food and pay.

Willie Smee   Supercargo (an officer on a merchant ship in charge of the cargo and business affairs) aboard Grief's ship the *Cantani*, he goes ashore to visit a woman, Taitua, but Grief warns him that if Tui Tulifau spies the fine white silk shirt he is wearing, he will take it from him, which he does. The king is so fat he splits the shirt open in several places. London may have borrowed his name from Captain Hook's pirate sidekick in J. M. Barrie's play *Peter Pan*; in the play he is a fairly genial pirate who is treated as a comic character.

mate   Mate of the *Cantani*, he explains to Grief why Smee is so eager to get to shore—it is to see a woman, Taitua. Willie tells him he's only jealous.

Peter Gee   Chinese pearl and shell trader who is arrested, fined, and imprisoned by Deasy. Gee also appears in the story "A Goboto Night," in which Grief saves him from the attack of a racist Australian.

five thousand inhabitants of Fitu-Iva   One of the folktale elements of this story is that *all* of the island's inhabitants arrive for the council. They are all alarmed at what Deasy has wrought and bring news of how it has affected them: "In turn, the talking man of the windward coast, the talking man of the leeward coast, and the talking man of the mountain villages, each backed by his group of lesser talking men and chiefs, arose and made oration. . . . They grumbled about the paper money. Affairs were not prosperous. No more copra was being smoked. . . . Prices were going up and commodities were getting scarce. It cost three times the ordinary price to buy a fowl, and then it was tough and like to die of old age if not immediately sold." In addition, there are strange "signs and omens": a plague of rats, small apples, avocado trees that won't bear fruit, mangoes with no flavor, plantains eaten by worms, no fish in the lagoon, the flight of the wild goats to inaccessible summits: "There were rumblings in the mountains, night-walking of spirits; a woman of Punta-Puna had been struck speechless, and a five-legged she-goat had been born in the village of Eiho. And that all was due to the strange money of Fulualea was the firm conviction of the elders in the village councils assembled" (*Stories*, 2,057).

council of chiefs   Generally as drunk as Tulifau, his chiefs are convened to hear the council debate the paper money and food shortages and also the fate of David Grief.

Captain Boig   Captain of the *Cantani*, he recoils from the smell on Deasy when he begs to be let aboard ship after his ignominious encounter with the dead pig. Grief arranges to take him to Yap.

"Finis" (1907)

"Finis" tells of the desperate plan of a starving man in the YUKON to kill a passerby and steal his sled, dogs, and food. This he finally manages to do, fighting against 60 degree below zero cold and advancing scurvy, but it is too late for him. A relatively early story, "Finis" did not appear in book form until it was included in *The Turtles of Tasman* (1916); it first appeared as "Morganson's Finish" in *Success* 10 (May 1907).

SYNOPSIS

A Yukon traveler down on his luck is trying to survive on scanty rations outside the town of Minto, but he is rapidly freezing, suffering from scurvy, and starving. He coldly resolves to murder a passerby on a sled and steal the sled, its dogs, and its contents. He journeys into town for a drink but has no money to buy food. He manages to kill a moose and thinks he will sell the meat in Minto, but WOLVES clean out his poorly made cache. Declining all of the time, he lays in wait on the trail for passersby but is frustrated by his advancing weakness: "On the first day after his last flour had gone it snowed. It was always warm when the snow fell, and he sat out the whole eight hours of daylight on the bank, without movement, terribly hungry and terribly patient, for all the world like a monstrous spider waiting for its prey. But the prey did not come, and he hobbled back to the tent through the darkness, drank quarts of spruce tea and hot water, and went to bed" (*Stories*, 1,175). He goes to Minto a second time and meets Jack Thompson and his comrade Oleson and lays in wait for them the next day, which is CHRISTMAS DAY. He does manage to kill them with his last bullets, but when he approaches their sled he finds no money but instead vengeful dogs who defend their masters. He is badly bitten by the lead dog, and he dies along with his prey on the ice.

COMMENTARY

A naturalistic narrative of degeneration, "Finis" emphasizes the physical details of Morganson's decline and the logistics of how he manages to survive for so long, starving, on the snow and ice of the Yukon, but it does not question nor even deliberate the immorality of his plan; his death after he has achieved his goal of killing men to steal from them is his only judgment. We know how many biscuits, how much frostbite, how progressively bad the scurvy and weakness are, which fingers are frozen, how many feet he has to crawl, but we are not given a judgment of Morganson by the narrator. The overriding question is fitness; as in "To Build a Fire" the protagonist is unfit to survive in the Yukon, and it seems to go without out saying that he is both physically and morally unfit. Yet it is a moral parable: The mention of Christmas Day as the day on which he shoots Jack Thompson and Oleson indicates the overall judgment of the figure of SOL, the Roman god of the sun whose feast day was December 25, upon his deed; in many KLONDIKE stories London uses the GREEK and Roman MYTHOLOGY of the SUN as the eye of Heaven and judge of the acts of men. The story also relates interesting details on survival in the Yukon: packing a sled, knowing that when it snows it gets warmer, making spruce tea for scurvy, building a cache for meat, shooting a bobbing and fast-moving target of game (or men) from a distance. But none of this trail-craft helps Morganson, who dies like his human prey alone on the snow, the dogs howling about him.

CHARACTERS

Morganson A Yukon traveler who is down and out; starving, freezing, and suffering from scurvy and frostbite, he resolves to kill the occupants of a passing sled and steal their belongings: "Out of the chaos of his fortunes he had finally achieved a way. But it was not a pretty way. His face had become stern and wolfish, and the thin lips were drawn very tightly" (*Stories*, 1,171). He is finally able to do this, but the dogs belonging to his two victims attack him, and he bleeds to death on the snow. Several times he is compared to a ravening wolf himself.

barkeeper In his saloon in Minto, he offers the woeful-looking and frostbitten Morganson free drinks out of pity. Looking Morganson over, he comments, "'Kind of all in, I'd say,' the other laughed sympathetically. 'No dogs, no money, and the scurvy. I'd try spruce tea if I was you'" (*Stories*, 1,171).

Jack Thompson One of the two men Morganson meets in the Minto saloon whom he kills on the trail: "'Jack Thompson,' the barkeeper said. 'Made two millions on Bonanza and Sulphur, and got more coming'" (*Stories*, 1,180). Morganson repeatedly notices his black beard pointed at the sky after he kills him.

Oleson Trail-mate of Jack Thompson; he is also killed by a long rifle shot by Morganson. He is "a fair-haired, ruddy-faced giant" (*Stories*, 1,180).

"The *Francis Spaight*" (1908)

Composed in 1908, this story, subtitled "A True Tale Retold," was sent by London to a dozen magazines for initial publication, but he retired the story until it was included in *When God Laughs and Other Stories* (1911). It is certainly a peculiar enough yarn to have caused magazine editors trepidation, though it was based on a true story. In December 1835, a young cabin boy Patrick O'Brien and later three others were cannibalized aboard a ship called the *Francis Spaight* sailing to its home port of Limerick, Ireland, from St. John's, Newfoundland, with a cargo of timber. The ship was upended by strong gales. After 16 days of cold, hunger, and thirst, the captain of the ship, Thomas Gorman, decided that one of the crew should be killed to keep the rest alive. Lots were drawn, and Patrick O'Brien drew the shortest lot. They cut his wrists, but he was so dehydrated the blood would not flow. Eventually, the cook cut the boy's throat. Eleven surviving crew members were rescued by a passing ship, and no charges were brought against them.

SYNOPSIS

The *Francis Spaight* is bringing timber home from Newfoundland when she is swamped in a violent snowstorm and gale on the North Atlantic. The freezing survivors huddle in the upended poop of the ship, finding that their water and food are far below in the fore hold. Starving, they start to turn upon the cabin boys, one in particular, O'Brien, but the captain proposes the drawing of straws to determine who will be killed and eaten. In a rigged drawing, O'Brien is chosen, but when the cook, Gorman, tries to open a vein in the dehydrated boy there is no blood. In the cacophony of the screaming sailors and shrieking O'Brien, he is murdered by Gorman, who then insists on putting his body overboard. Just then, they all sight an approaching sail, and they are rescued. Gorman goes into the arms of the rescuers laughing hysterically—the one most affected by their mutual sin.

COMMENTARY

The first paragraph of the story, like so many of London's carefully crafted openings of stories, deserves close reading:

The *Francis Spaight* was running before it solely under a mizzentopsail, when the thing happened. It was not due to carelessness so much as to the lack of discipline of the crew and to the fact that they were indifferent seamen at best. The man at the wheel in particular, a Limerick man, had had no experience with salt water beyond that of rafting timber on the Shannon between the Quebec vessels and the shore. He was afraid of the huge seas that rose out of the murk astern and bore down upon him, and he was more given to cowering away from their threatened impact than he was to meeting their blows with the wheel and checking the ship's rush to broach to. (*Stories*, 1,483)

An overall mood of indefiniteness and indecision presents itself: the ship is running before "it"; it is using a middling amount of sail; what happens is only called "the thing"; there is carelessness, inexperience, and lack of discipline; the man who is supposed to be most in charge—the man at the wheel—cowers in fear. Such ambiguity of causation seems appropriate to survivors who would not like to tell their tale, and it builds a sense of uncertainty and fear. As the story ends without comment on the survivors' state of mind, the reader is left to wonder how this horrific experience will have changed them.

CHARACTERS

Michael Behane   "The man at the wheel in particular, a Limerick man, had had no experience with salt water beyond that of rafting timber on the Shannon between the Quebec vessels and the shore" (*Stories*, 1,483), we are told in the first paragraph; later it is Behane to whom O'Brien fruitlessly appeals to save the boys.

O'Brien   Though he and Mahoney are the brave ones who take up observation on the freezing deck of the doomed ship, "The boy, O'Brien, was specially maltreated. Though there were three other boys, it was O'Brien who came in for most of the abuse. . . . [H]is was a stronger and more dominant spirit than those of the other boys, and that he stood up more for his rights, resenting the petty injustices that were meted out to all the boys by the men" (*Stories*, 1,485).

captain   Losing his mate in the swamping of the ship, the captain is "now scarcely less helpless than his men." Beyond cursing them, "he did nothing" (*Stories*, 1,484). But it is he who brings up the plan of drawing straws to see who will be eaten.

mate and crew   "The men were out of hand, helpless and hopeless, stupid in their bewilderment and fear, and resolute only in that they would not obey orders. Some wailed, others clung silently in the weather shrouds, and still others muttered prayers or shrieked vile imprecations; and neither captain nor mate could get them to bear a hand at the pumps or at setting patches of sails to bring the vessel up to the wind and sea. . . . When she went over, the mate was caught and drowned in the after-cabin, as were two sailors who had sought refuge in the forecastle" (*Stories*, 1,483–1,484).

Mahoney   A "Belfast man" (*Stories*, 1,484), Mahoney takes over the operation of the ship after she is swamped and helps O'Brien take watches: "Mahoney was the only man who spoke in favor of the boys, declaring that it was the fair thing for all to share alike" (*Stories*, 1,486).

Sullivan   "Sullivan and the captain insisted on the drawing of lots being confined to the boys. There were high words, in the midst of which Sullivan turned upon O'Brien, snarling:—'Twould be a good deed to put you out of the way. You deserve it. 'Twould be the right way to serve you, an' serve you we will'" (*Stories*, 1,486).

Johnny Sheehan   Young crewman who does not draw the fatal short stick. He weeps when O'Brien does, yet screams for his blood later on.

George Burns   Another crewman spared by drawing the longer stick.

John Gorman   The cook, he is the one charged with slitting O'Brien's arm. He initially refuses but after the lottery is persuaded against his will. When O'Brien does not bleed, Gorman is forced to murder him, but has O'Brien's body tossed overboard just as a sailing ship approaches.

The Game (1905)

BOXING was one of Jack London's favorite sports. He began early, boxing with friends, and his interest never waned. He got his start in newspaper journalism by covering boxing matches in the Bay Area, and later he covered the two world heavyweight matches between JACK JOHNSON and TOMMY BURNS (1908) and between Johnson and JAMES JEFFRIES, "the Great White Hope." He wrote some of the first boxing stories ever published, such as "The Mexican" and "A Piece of Steak." But according to his biographer Russ Kingman, "His favorite sparring partner was his wife CHARMIAN LONDON. They boxed nearly every day. They boxed at home, all the way to the SOLOMON ISLANDS on the *Snark,* from Sydney, Australia, to Ecuador on the *Tymeric,* and from Baltimore to Seattle on the *DIRIGO.*" According to Kingman, "It was on the *Snark* that they had the most fun. In the morning they put on their bathing suits, boxed for a full hour, threw buckets of salt water on one another, and went below to dress for a day of work and sailing. This constant boxing with Charmian gave Jack an excellent defense, for he couldn't strike back as with a man. However, he would box any man, in deadly earnest or for a few rounds of sparring" (Kingman, 224–225). *The Game* was first serialized in *Metropolitan Magazine* (April–May 1905), then published in a handsome black-and-ochre pen-and-ink illustrated book by MACMILLAN (1905). As Kingman notes, the novel made headlines when critics claimed the story was unrealistic, that a fighter could not be killed by hitting his head on the canvas. London told them that he had seen this actually happen in the West Oakland Athletic Club. Jimmy Britt, then lightweight champion of the world, favorably reviewed *The Game* for the EXAMINER (SAN FRANCISCO) and stated that London really knew "the game." Rumor had it that veteran fighter Gene Tunney decided to retire after reading it, and that he gave the book to Rocky Marciano to encourage his retirement. Yet London himself claimed, "I would rather be heavyweight champion of the world—which I can never be—than King of England, or President of the United States, or Kaiser of Germany" (quoted in Kingman, 225).

SYNOPSIS

In *The Game,* a young man of 20, Joe Fleming, works as a sailmaker supporting his mother and siblings. He also enters prizefighting to earn extra income. On the eve of his marriage to Genevieve Pritchard, a beautiful and idealistic young woman who works in a candy shop, Joe is to fight his last time, having promised her to give up "the game," which, while she hates and fears it, he enjoys as a manly and "clean" sport, and one also challenging—and atavistic. Joe, perhaps trying for one last time to help Genevieve understand what he loves about fighting, asks her to witness the fight, which she agrees to do, only to see her lover beaten to death before the howling crowd.

In chapter 1, Joe and Genevieve shop for carpets for their newly rented home, eagerly anticipating their upcoming marriage. The chapter focuses on their differences on prizefighting. Genevieve

Pen-and-ink drawing by Henry Hutt and T. C. Lawrence on the inside back cover of *The Game,* Macmillan, 1905 *(Huntington Library)*

fears and detests it as a rival, and Joe agrees to give it up after one last fight. He vainly tries to explain its appeal to him: "'All I know, Genevieve, is that you feel good in the ring when you've got the man where you want him, . . . an' all the house is shouting an' tearin' itself loose, an' you know you're the best man, an' that you played m' fair an' won out because you're the best man. I tell you—'" (21–22). But he is suddenly silenced, "alarmed by his own volubility and by Genevieve's look of alarm." While "his inward vision" takes in his tottering opponent, the lights, the shouting—and he feels "swept out and away from her on this tide of life that was beyond her comprehension, menacing, irresistible, making her love pitiful and weak" (22), she sees only how thinking of fighting changes him before her: "The fresh boyish face was gone, the tenderness of the eyes, the sweetness of the mouth with its curves and pictured corners. It was a man's face she saw, a face of steel, tense and immobile; a mouth of steel, the lips like the jaws of a trap; eyes of steel, dilated, intent, and the light in them and the glitter were the light and glitter of steel. . . . This face she did not know at all" (22–23). Yet she is aware of her pride in him: "His masculinity, the masculinity of the fighting male, made its inevitable appeal to her, a female, moulded by all her heredity to seek out the strong man for mate, and to lean against the wall of his strength." She is also aware that "for her sake, for Love's own sake, he had surrendered to her, abandoned all that portion of his life" (23–24). For his part, because she agrees to watch the fight, he is filled with pride and amazement.

Chapter 2 opens with a description of the young couple as "working-class aristocrats." As the narrator explains, "In an environment made up largely of sordidness and wretchedness they had kept themselves unsullied and wholesome. Theirs was a self-respect, a regard for the niceties and clean things of life, which had held them aloof from their kind" (45). As a girl, Genevieve lost both parents and was taken in by the Silversteins, who run a candy store. She keeps to herself as the years pass: "'That stuck-up doll-face,' was the way the girls of the neighbourhood described her; and though she earned their enmity by her beauty and aloof-

ness, she nonetheless commanded their respect. 'Peaches and cream,' she was called by the young men— . . . while they stood in awe of Genevieve, in a dimly religious way, as a something mysteriously beautiful and unapproachable" (49). The narrator expands on her seemingly contradictory gentility and womanliness: "Withal, she was sheerly feminine, tender and soft and clinging, with the smouldering passion of the mate and the motherliness of the woman. But this side of her nature had lain dormant through the years, waiting for the mate to appear" (50–51). When he does appear in the store one day and orders an ice cream soda, they are smitten with each other. However, Genevieve finds out from Mrs. Silverstein that Joe is a prizefighter, to her dismay. But in chapter 3 she dresses as a boy and enters the stands for the fight. Though she is at first stifled by the noise and smoke, at the same time, "Her blood was touched, as by fire, with romance, adventure—the unknown, the mysterious, the terrible—as she penetrated this haunt of men where women came not. And there were other thrills. It was the only time in her life she had dared the rash thing. For the first time she was overstepping the bounds laid down by that harshest of tyrants, the Mrs. Grundy of the working class. She felt fear, and for herself, though the moment before she had been thinking only of Joe" (111). Joe installs her safely in a dressing room with a peep-hole so she can see the next fight in privacy.

Chapter 4 begins with Genevieve's vision of Joe entering the ring: "His bath robe fell away from him, and he stepped forth to the centre of the ring, naked save for the low canvas shoes and a narrow hip-cloth of white. Genevieve's eyes dropped. She sat alone, with none to see, but her face was burning with shame at sight of the beautiful nakedness of her lover. But she looked again, guiltily, for the joy that was hers in beholding what she knew must be sinful to behold. . . . But it was delicious sin, and she did not deny her eyes" (111). She then sees his swarthy, bestial opponent, John Ponta, enter the ring. Against her lover's beauty, Ponta seems apelike, brutal, menacing. The crowd favors Joe, and Ponta glares at them: "He was like an animal in the circle of its enemies, and he turned and glared at them with malignant eyes" (119).

In chapters 5 and 6, the fight is on; it begins with Joe forced to a crouch to protect himself from Ponta's bruising barrage of blows. Joe ducks and nimbly avoids Ponta's next onslaught and catches him unguarded and strikes hard blows to his stomach. They each land strikes to the jaw, and Joe goes down for a count of nine seconds. The fighters clinch and break, clinch and break, neither getting in the knockout blow. In the sixth round, Joe again avoids Ponta's rushes, and they each land blows. But in the next rounds, the fight dramatically changes, first as Joe takes the offensive. Ponta is punished over and over, but then just at the moment of victory Joe's foot slips on the canvas and Ponta crashes into him, knocking him out. His limp body is brought into the dressing room where Genevieve is hiding. Joe is dead—the entire back of his skull smashed. In her horror and grief, Genevieve thinks, "This, then, was the end of it all—of the carpets, and furniture, and the little rented house; of the meetings and walking out, the thrilling nights of starshine, the deliciousness of surrender, the loving and the being loved." And yet her main feeling is of being "stunned by the awful facts of this Game she did not understand—the grip it laid on men's souls, its irony and faithlessness, its risks and hazards and fierce insurgences of the blood, making woman pitiful, not the be-all and end-all of man, but his toy and his pastime; to woman his mothering and caretaking, his moods and his moments, but to the Game his days and nights of striving, the tribute of his head and hand, his most patient toil and wildest effort, all the strain and the stress of his being—to the Game, his heart's desire" (179).

COMMENTARY

Underneath a seemingly straightforward story of lost love and a doomed hero, London interweaves a number of issues from the psychological to the Darwinian. Both Genevieve and Joe are in a sense at war with themselves: they both simultaneously struggle against both propriety and primitivism. Just as Genevieve is thrilled to buck "Mrs. Grundy" and attend a prizefight, so Joe is not at one with his feelings; after promising never to fight again after the upcoming match, he reflects, "And yet, in the very moment of promising her, he knew vaguely, deep down, that he could never abandon the Game; that somewhere, sometime, in the future, he must go back to it" (78). These internal "primitive" desires reflect London's interest in ATAVISM and Darwinism, even as his portrayal of the death of a young god, as in "The Night-Born," points to the novel's mythic dimensions. It interrogates gender roles, especially in its portrayal of real manliness as "cleanliness," but a cleanliness London associated with the primitive, what he called the abysmal brute who is defined as a sort of ur-white man:

> "Look at me. I tell you I have to live clean to be in condition like this. I live cleaner than she does, or her old man, or anybody you know— baths, rub-downs, exercise, regular hours, good food and no makin' a pig of myself, no drinking, no smoking, nothing that'll hurt me. Why, I live cleaner than you, Genevieve—"
>
> "Honest, I do," he hastened to add at sight of her shocked face. "I don't mean water an' soap, but look there." His hand closed reverently but firmly on her arm. "Soft, you're all soft, all over. Not like mine." (26–27)

Yet unlike some of London's other white heroes, Joe is not described as ANGLO-SAXON, though this is of course implied. Instead, Joe and Genevieve strike one primarily as immigrants into American respectability who have to use any means they can to get there; this places them on the same plane as the Silversteins, who are Jewish immigrants from central Europe and who take Genevieve in at the beginning as they comfort her at the end. She is useful to them as a Gentile to run the shop on the Sabbath, but they are also genuinely fond of her and are intended to represent a stable (and successful) family. Such themes complicate the primary plot of the book.

CHARACTERS

Joe Fleming Joe is an Adonis of a young man of the working class. His beautiful and clean-living physique and mind find themselves drawn to the prize ring for extra income on top of his wages as a sailmaker; he supports his mother and siblings and plans to marry Genevieve Pritchard after his last fight. He dies instead, leaving her to ponder the hold "the game" of fighting had on him.

Genevieve Pritchard   "If ever a girl of the working class had led the sheltered life, it was Genevieve. In the midst of roughness and brutality, she had shunned all that was rough and brutal. She saw but what she chose to see, and she chose always to see the best, avoiding coarseness and uncouthness without effort, as a matter of instinct" (46). Genevieve was orphaned as a girl and taken in by a kindly Jewish couple who run a candy store. There, she shields herself from her class and from men in general. But she falls in love with Joe Fleming, a prizefighter, and she detests this part of his life: "She revolted instinctively against this Game which drew him away from her, robbed her of part of him. It was a rival she did not understand. Nor could she understand its seductions. . . . [S]he grappled in the dark with an intangible adversary about which she knew nothing" (30).

Mr. and Mrs. Silverstein   The proprietors of the candy store in which Genevieve works and also her foster parents. Genevieve tells Joe Mrs. Silverstein does not approve of boxing, to which Joe responds, "'Mrs. Silverstein is a dub, and a softy, and a knocker,' he said good-humoredly" (26). When Mrs. Silverstein loudly protests to her husband about Genevieve's going out with a prizefighter, he defends Joe as a good man and the sole support of his six brothers and sisters, and he defends the sport itself.

Mr. Clausen   Head of the rug department at the store Joe and Genevieve visit at the beginning of the novel: "'Think I was never coming back, Joe?' queried the head of the department, a pink-and-white-faced man, whose austere side-whiskers were belied by genial little eyes" (32). Clausen is a fan of Joe's boxing career and worries that his impending marriage will spook him in the coming fight.

Lottie Fleming   Joe's sister, who helps him disguise Genevieve as a man so she can attend Joe's final boxing match. She is affectionate to them both.

John Ponta   Joe's formidable opponent in the fight, described as an atavism: "She knew terror as she looked at him. Here was the fighter—the beast with a streak for a forehead, with beady eyes under lowering and bushy brows, flat-nosed, thick-lipped, sullen-mouthed. He was heavy-jawed, bull-necked, and the short, straight hair of the head seemed to her frightened eyes the stiff bristles on a hog's back. Here were coarseness and brutishness—a thing savage, primordial, ferocious. He was swarthy to blackness, and his body was covered with a hairy growth that matted like a dog's on his chest and shoulders" (117–18).

FURTHER READING

Emmert, Scott. "The Familiar Uncommon Spectator: Jack London's Female Watchers in *The Game* and *The Abysmal Brute*." *Aethlon: The Journal of Sport Literature* 22, no. 1 (Fall 2004): 137–146.

Kingman, Russ. *A Pictorial Life of Jack London.* New York: Crown, 1979.

London, Jack. *Sporting Blood: Selections from Jack London's Greatest Sports Writing.* Edited by Howard Lachtman. Novato, Calif.: Presidio Press, 1981.

Mitchell, J. Lawrence. "Jack London and Boxing," *American Literary Realism* 36, no. 3 (Spring 2004): 225–243.

Shillingsburg, Miriam J. "Jack London's Boxing Stories: Parables for Youth." *Eureka Studies in Teaching Short Fiction* 5, no. 1 (Fall 2004): 7–15.

"Getting into Print" (1903)

Published in *The Editor,* London's advice to would-be published writers begins with reminiscences about his early challenges as a writer: "I had many liabilities and no assets, no income, several mouths to feed, and for landlady a poor widow whose imperative necessities demanded that I should pay my rent with some degree of regularity" (London, *No Mentor,* 54–55). London confides his early ignorance of how to write to editors, how to know which published which kind of work, or anyone to ask for advice: "So I sat down and wrote in order to get an experience of my own." London says he "wrote everything—short stories, articles, anecdotes, jokes, essays, sonnets, ballads, villanelles, trolets, songs, light plays in iambic tetrameter, and heavy tragedies in blank verse. These various creations I stuck into envelopes, enclosed return postage, and dropped into the mail. . . . All my manuscripts came back. . . . the process seemed like the working of a soulless machine. . . . [S]ome cunning arrangement of cogs and cranks at the other end . . . had transferred the manuscript to another envelope, taken the stamps from the inside and pasted them outside, and added the rejection slip" (55).

After analyzing his experiences, especially after his eventual success in the magazines, he offers writers several pieces of advice:

Don't quit your job in order to write unless there is none dependent upon you.

Don't dash off a six-thousand word story before breakfast.

Don't write too much. Concentrate your sweat on one story rather than dissipate it over a dozen.

Don't loaf and invite inspiration: light out after it with a club, and if you don't get it you will nonetheless get something that looks remarkably like it.

Set yourself a "stint," and see that you do that "stint" every day.

Study the tricks of the writers who have arrived. They have mastered the tools with which you are cutting your fingers.

Keep a notebook. Travel with it, eat with it, sleep with it. Slap into it every stray thought that flutters up into your brain. Cheap paper is less perishable than gray matter, and lead pencil markings endure longer than memory.

And work. Find out about this earth, this universe. (56–57)

FURTHER READING

London, Jack. "Getting Into Print." Reprinted in *No Mentor but Myself: A Collection of Articles, Essays,* *Reviews, and Letters, by Jack London, on Writing and Writers.* New York: Kennikat Press, 1979. Reprinted in expanded edition as *No Mentor But Myself: Jack London on Writers and Writing.* Edited by Dale L. Walker and Jeanne Campbell Reesman. Stanford, Calif.: Stanford University Press, 1999.

"A Goboto Night" (1911)

First published in the SATURDAY EVENING POST 184 (September 30, 1907), it appeared in *A Son of the Sun,* one of the David Grief stories in which Grief rights racial wrongs in the South Seas. Grief defends a CHINESE man, Peter Gee, abused by a young Australian racist who hates "Chink blood" (*Stories,* 2,008). After the Australian is straightened out by a beating from Grief, he has to sign an oath that "'I must always remember that one man is as good as another, save and except when he thinks he is better'" (*Stories,* 2,018).

SYNOPSIS

One of the Florida Islands, "Goboto" refers most likely to the actual island of Gavutu in the SOLOMON ISLAND chain, which London would have known about from his SNARK voyage. There, London imagines a port in which "the traders come off their schooners and the planters drift in from far, wild coasts, and one and all they assume shoes, white duck trousers, and various other appearances of civilization. At Goboto, mail is received, bills are paid, and newspapers, rarely more than five weeks old, are accessible; for the little island, . . . serves as the distributing point for the whole wide-scattered group." However, it is also a place "heated, unhealthy, and lurid, and for its size it asserts the distinction of more cases of acute ALCOHOLISM than any other spot in the world" (*Stories,* 2,006). The "mecca of sprees," Goboto is a place the soap company that controls its trade finds it hard to staff: "It is a very hard job at Goboto. That is why the pay is twice that on other stations, and that is why the company selects only courageous and intrepid men for this particular station. They last no more than a year or so, when the wreckage of them is shipped back to Australia, or the remains of them are buried in the sand across on the windward side of the islet" (*Stories,* 2,007). And yet, playing at being "gentlemen," the traders enforce a dress code on their visitors.

One night, hosts and visitors sit down to their evening meal and hear David Grief's anchor chain go down. They are "Seven of them, with glimmering eyes and steady legs, [who] had capped a day of Scotch with swivel-sticked cocktails and sat down to dinner. . . . At first wine was served by the black servants to those that drank it, though all quickly shifted back to Scotch and soda, pickling their food as they ate it, ere it went into their calcined, pickled stomachs" (*Stories,* 2,008). The men, joined by Grief, play cards, bridge, and other games to pass the evening, but as the drink and the bets wear on, an Australian, Deacon, becomes more and more belligerent toward Peter Gee, a Chinese pearl merchant, finally drunkenly challenging him to a game of casino. Grief enters the game and beats Deacon miserably. He tells Deacon he is to be put on a boat for the remote island of Karo-Karo. He then reads him a list of rules and subdues him into submitting to the "gentleman's" code, especially of racial tolerance and BROTHERHOOD.

COMMENTARY

Peter Gee illustrates the complex nature of London's racial breakthrough on the *Snark* voyage. He had elsewhere written disparagingly of the Chinese, but here he presents a multilayered character whose interests, economic and social, are defended, although he has to make him half-white and exceptional for a "Eurasian." But one should note that the white blood is not Gee's better half, though he has mastered its tongue better than white native speakers: "Peter Gee was that rare creature, a good as well as clever Eurasian. In fact, it was the stolid integrity of the Chinese blood that toned the recklessness and licentiousness of the English blood which had run in his father's veins. Also, he was better educated than any man there, spoke better English as well as several other tongues, and knew and lived more of their own ideals of gentlemanness than they did themselves.

And, finally, he was a gentle soul. Violence he deprecated, though he had killed men in his time. Turbulence he abhorred. He always avoided it as he would the plague" (*Stories,* 2,009). "A Goboto Night" fits well with the other David Grief stories in that it shows both his heroism but also his sense of his relativism in the achievements of racial "Others," as well as the context of indignity and injustice of racism, especially to talented individuals like Peter Gee.

CHARACTERS

David Grief   London's fantasy figure of a South Seas rover; Grief is ANGLO-SAXON but tans dark brown. Unlike other whites in the South Seas, he is able so to pass and able to survive its challenges and prosper as a businessman—notably not a MISSIONARY, capitalist, or colonialist. In many of the stories of *A Son of the Sun* he helps oppressed racial "Others" in their struggles.

Jerry McMurtrey   Manager at Goboto and host of the dinner.

Eddy Little and Jack Andrews   Clerks assigned by the soap company to Goboto and present at the dinner.

Captain Stapler   Master of the "recruiting" ketch *Merry,* a slaver, and guest of McMurtrey at dinner and an active participant in the gambling that follows.

Darby Shryleton   Planter from Tito-Ito who comes to dinner on Goboto.

Peter Gee   A dinner guest of McMurtrey's, he is "A half-caste Chinese pearl-buyer who ranged from Ceylon to the Paumotus" (*Stories,* 2,008). David Grief defends him from a beating by a drunken, racist Australian, Alfred Deacon.

Alfred Deacon   A visitor to Goboto who stopped off from the last steamer and torments Peter Gee. In the gambling, he challenges Grief and loses, after which Grief punishes him by having him recant his racism toward Gee.

Captain Donovan Skipper of the *Gunga*, bound for Karo-Karo, which refers to a port in Sumatra. He takes Deacon aboard in Grief's attempt to reform him.

"The God of His Fathers" (1901)

This story, first published in *McClure's Magazine* 17 (May 1901), both laments and extols the arrival of white men into the YUKON, particularly their effect upon the NATIVES of the region.

SYNOPSIS

Hay Stockard, his wife, child, and partner, Bill, are camped near a Native village ruled by the half-breed Baptiste the Red. Baptiste tells Stockard of his history, how he is the offspring of a British father and the daughter of a chief, how he tried to marry a white woman but was refused by the church, and how that woman and later their daughter met their deaths. Baptiste blames the church and the whites in general for his sad experiences. Now he has turned savage in his quest to obliterate the white men's belief in their god; whenever one appears in his camp, he forces him to recant his faith. As he explains, "'We ask to be let alone. We do not want your kind. If we permit you to sit by our fires, after you will come your church, your priests, and your gods. And know this, for each white man who comes to my village, him will I make deny his god'" (*Stories*, 385).

Sturges Owen, a MISSIONARY, arrives and at first refuses to deny GOD. Stockard warns him:

"If you think it your duty to strive with the heathen, well and good; but do exercise some wit in the way you go about it. This man, Red Baptiste, is no Indian. He comes of our common stock, is as bull-necked as I ever dared be, and as wild a fanatic the one way as you are the other. When you two come together, hell 'll be to pay, and I don't care to be mixed up in it. Understand? So take my advice and go away. If you go down-stream, you 'll fall in with the Rus-

sians. There's bound to be Greek priests among them, and they 'll see you safe through to Bering Sea,—that's where the Yukon empties,—and from there it won't be hard to get back to civilization. Take my word for it and get out of here as fast as God'll let you." (*Stories*, 388)

But after a bloody battle with the Natives in which Stockard, his wife, and child are killed, Owen reveals himself as a coward and recants. The story ends with Owen on his way out of the camp: "that he might carry to the Russians the message of Baptiste the Red, in whose country there was no god" (*Stories*, 394).

COMMENTARY

Baptiste the Red is one of London's more dramatic villains, and yet the reader is invited to sympathize with his vain attempt to preserve his Native culture and people against the intrusions of white men. The whites are coming into the Yukon from all directions: RUSSIANS, Americans, and Europeans, and Baptiste knows what this means for the future of his people. Hay Stockard is a heroic figure, just as the missionary Sturges Owen is a coward. Women mentioned in the story—white and Native—are tragic figures who pay with their lives for their relationships with white men, a common pattern in the KLONDIKE stories. Throughout the story, London uses Biblical imagery and references (to St. Paul, to Cain and Abel), but the primary image pattern is the color red, especially how the midnight SUN stains the sky: "The sun hurried round to the north, sinking closer to the horizon. The heavens in that quarter grew red and bloody. The shadows lengthened, the light dimmed, and in the sombre recesses of the forest life slowly died away" (*Stories*, 392). As in other Klondike stories, here the sun as the eye of heaven witnesses the foul deeds of men.

CHARACTERS

Baptiste the Red Chief of his tribe, Baptiste is the half-breed son of an Englishman and the daughter of a chief. Because he has been so betrayed by whites and especially by their church, he makes it his mission to force anyone coming into his camp to deny the white man's god, whom he calls a "bad god."

Hay Stockard Stockard has come into the Yukon to mine for gold and has taken a Native woman as his mate, who bears him a son. She and the child are murdered by Baptiste, who also murders Stockard after Stockard's valiant defense of his family and Sturges Owen.

Stockard's Indian mate A woman of the Teslin Indians, she is killed by Baptiste along with her child. Just before this, she and Stockard are married by Owen, an act meaningless to her.

Bill Bill is Stockard's partner who helps him defend against the Native attack.

Sturges Owen A missionary and a coward, his initial refusal to disown his God and his determination to convert the Natives is replaced by his cowardly recantation. He alone survives the battle with the Natives.

"Goliah" (1910)

Included in *Revolution and Other Essays* (1910), this is the only short story to be included in either of London's two collections of socialist analysis (the other is *War of the Classes*). A DYSTOPIAN narrative of a world dictator set in 1924, "Goliah" may be read as a socialist analysis of fascism. Like London's novel *The Iron Heel*, it warns of a future in which people are kept happy by a ruthless madman, so that they fail to notice such things as his extermination of the racially "unfit." However, since Goliah calls himself a utopian socialist and brings the capitalist establishment to its knees, it is also a satire of how SOCIALISM as an ideology can be abused.

SYNOPSIS

A man whose real name is Percival Stultz calls himself "Goliah," an echo of "Goliath," the Philistine giant slain by King David. He calls all the businessmen, politicians, and scientists of the world to embrace his "enlightened" social ideals, but only the scientists meet with him; when the others refuse, they are murdered. Focusing at first on San Francisco and then the United States before he conquers the rest of the world, Goliah engages in terrorism against society with bombings and assassinations. As he grows in power, this mysterious figure uses weapons of mass destruction unheard of in his day, like another Connecticut Yankee. Addressing the world at large in letters, he succeeds in bringing down government, labor, commerce—indeed, nearly every part of human civilization—before he is done. His announced ideal is a peaceful world of productive rationality; with his laborsaving devices he ensures a life of leisure and contentment, with no war or class oppression. He claims to be a "superman, a scientific superman" (*Stories*, 1,220), and he provides food and shelter to all, and, with universal disarmament and without the struggle for material gain, the world seems to become a utopia: "And with food and shelter automatic, the incentive of material gain passes away from the world forever. With food and shelter automatic, the higher incentives will universally obtain—the spiritual, aesthetic, and intellectual incentives that will tend to develop and make beautiful and noble body, mind, and spirit. Then all the world will be dominated by happiness and laughter. It will be the reign of universal laughter" (*Stories*, 1,205).

However, that laughter masks a grim reality. Goliah's world peace is bought with a high price. For example, he kidnaps and forces into slavery Africans and Asians on Palgrave Island. He removes "all hereditary inefficients," who are "segregated and denied marriage" (*Stories*, 1,218). An "incurable" remnant is confined in asylums. He manages all this by using his machine, the "Energon," which is a power source fueled by the light of the SUN. In his palace, Asgard, he erects a statue of himself with the Ozymandias-like legend, "ALL WILL BE JOY-SMITHS, AND THEIR TASK SHALL BE TO BEAT OUT LAUGHTER FROM THE RINGING ANVIL OF LIFE" (*Stories*, 1,221). Ironically, the story is actually narrated by a naïve young student writing a school essay in a future still under Goliah's control; such a narrator helps expose the foolish naïveté of Goliah's subjects.

COMMENTARY

"Goliah" reflects a number of London's preoccupations, from his knowledge of the BIBLE, of GREEK and Roman myths (especially of the sun), Norse MYTHOLOGY, and medieval literature (the name "Percival" refers to the knight of Camelot who forgot to ask the meaning of the Grail symbols and so helps lose the kingdom); to the very topical subjects of labor unrest and reform, the bombings and assassinations of anarchism in London's day; to competing notions of socialism. There is also the theme of a dark future, which London imagined in several works such as "The Unparalleled Invasion" that were written around this time. It may also be that Goliah himself is a satire of some of London's more extreme positions; for instance, London signed his letters "Yours for the Revolution," while Goliah signs his "Yours for the reconstruction of society" (Stories, 1,202). Like London, Goliah defines himself as a materialist and professes no "unscientific sentimentality about the value of human life" (Stories, 1,202). Goliah actually sounds a good deal like Wolf Larsen of The Sea-Wolf:

> "In this theory of mine, lives are but pawns; I deal with quantities of lives. . . . The game is big. There are fifteen hundred million human lives to-day on the planet. What is your single life against them? It is as naught, in my theory. And remember that mine is the power. Remember that I am a scientist, and that one life, or one million of lives, mean nothing to me as arrayed against the countless billions of billions of the lives of the generations to come. It is for their laughter that I seek to reconstruct society now; and against them your own meagre little life is a paltry thing indeed" (Stories, 1,204–1,205).

London also seems to be satirizing his early views on RACIALISM. Finally, the story evokes such later autobiographies of dictators such as Adolf Hitler's Mein Kampf in its satire of the world master; before

long, Goliah signs his letters "'Mine is the power. I am the will of God. The whole world shall be in vassalage to me, but it shall be a vassalage of peace. I am Goliah'" (Stories, 1,208).

CHARACTERS

Percival Stultz (Goliah) Stultz/Goliah is a German-American scientist who invents a machine called the Energon and uses it to conquer the world. As he explains in one of his many letters to leaders of government and industry, "the proposition that the majority of the people are not pioneers, that they are weighted down by the inertia of the established; that the government that is representative of them represents only their feebleness, and futility, and brutishness; that this blind thing called government is not the serf of their wills, but that they are the serfs of it; in short, speaking always of the great mass, that they do not make government, but that government makes them, and that government is and has been a stupid and awful monster, misbegotten of the glimmerings of intelligence that come from the inertia-crushed mass." Thus, he has determined "'. . . to step in and become captain of this world-ship for a while. I have the intelligence and the wide vision of the skilled expert. Also, I have the power. I shall be obeyed. The men of all the world shall perform my bidding and make governments so that they shall become laughter-producers" (Stories, 1,202). Goliah exterminates those whom he sees as unfit or enslaves them, but he does make good on his promise of worldwide peace and prosperity for those he deems racially fit. He has to kill thousands, however, before he achieves his goal.

Walter Bassett The story opens with Bassett, "the greatest captain of industry west of the Rockies, and . . . one of the small group that controlled the nation in everything but name" (Stories, 1,201), receiving a letter he thinks is from a crank, but it is from Goliah. He heeds Goliah's call to come aboard his yacht when it arrives in San Francisco; though he implores his fellow captains of industry, they refuse Goliah's invitation and are murdered.

"Good-by, Jack" (1909)

First appearing in *Redbook* 13 (June 1909), this story is among London's other stories of LEPROSY in HAWAI'I and his article "The Lepers of Molokai" (included in *The Cruise of the* Snark) that infuriated London's friends among the KAMĀINA elite of HONOLULU who were working to build the islands' tourism. It pairs well with another story along similar lines—a white man contracts the disease—"The Sheriff of Kona."

SYNOPSIS

Yale graduate Jack Kersdale, a millionaire sugar king, coffee planter, rubber pioneer, cattle rancher, and promoter of other businesses, enjoys his life as a club member, yachtsman, and eligible bachelor in Honolulu. He is a member of the elite "Missionary Crowd," wealthy descendants of New England MISSIONARIES who have profited greatly from business in Hawai'i: "The missionary who came to give the bread of life" by converting the Hawaiians to CHRISTIANITY "remained to gobble up the whole heathen feast" (*Stories*, 1,474). Kersdale feels quite complacent about leprosy, certain that as a white man he will never be infected, and supportive of the banishment of lepers to the colony on MOLO-KAI. However, he witnesses the deportation of the lepers, including his girlfriend, Lucy Mokunui, "the epitome of Polynesian charms, an artist as well, and well beloved of men—" (*Stories*, 1,480). He did not know of her disease, and as he watches her board the ship he fears that he will be next.

COMMENTARY

The story opens, "Hawaii is a queer place" (*Stories*, 1,474), and the first-person narrator proceeds to tell a queer tale, a case of the unexpected that confronts a hypocrite: "Jack Kersdale, the man I wanted to tell about; he came of missionary stock. That is, on his grandmother's side. His grandfather was old Benjamin Kersdale, a Yankee trader, who got his start for a million in the old days by selling cheap whiskey and square-face gin. There's another queer thing. The old missionaries and old traders were mortal enemies. You see, their interests conflicted. But their children made it up by

intermarrying and dividing the islands between them" (*Stories*, 1,474). Kersdale is a promoter of Hawai'i and an authority on leprosy; he enthusiastically supports the sending of lepers to Molokai. However, he is one of the wealthy white characters London invents to attack in his Hawaiian stories, such as Percival Ford of "The House of Pride." As in that story, pride motivates Kersdale into carelessness about other people, but in contrast to Ford's victory over his Hawaiian half-brother, Kersdale is punished for his hubris in the end. "'And I never knew. I never knew'" (*Stories*, 1,482).

CHARACTERS

narrator Friend of Jack Kersdale's, who witnesses the departure of Lucy Mokunui and Jack's reaction to her diagnosis of leprosy. He muses on the mutability of life and wonders if just anyone could be stricken with a terrible disease without warning.

Jack Kersdale Kersdale, a descendant of traders and missionaries in Hawai'i, lives an idyllic life until he realizes he has been exposed to leprosy. Ironically, according to the narrator, "leprosy was one of his hobbies. He was an ardent defender of the settlement at Molokai, where all the island lepers were segregated. There was much talk and feeling among the natives, fanned by the demagogues, concerning the cruelties of Molokai, where men and women, not alone banished from friends and family, were compelled to live in perpetual imprisonment until they died. . . . 'I tell you they are happy there,' Kersdale insisted. . . . 'The horrors of Molokai are all poppycock. I can take you through any hospital or any slum in any of the great cities of the world and show you a thousand times worse horrors'" (*Stories*, 1,476–1,477).

Lucy Mokunui "The Hawaiian nightingale" (*Stories*, 1,479), she is a singer and a "magnificent creature" (*Stories*, 1,480) of a woman. Deported to Molokai as a leper, she calls out to Jack Kersdale to say good-by. He then realizes he has been exposed to leprosy.

Mr. McVeigh Superintendant of the settlement on Molokai, he manages the transfer of the newly diagnosed lepers to the ship that will take them to Molokai. He is based on the real McVeigh, whom London visited on Molokai and at whose behest he wrote his article about the lepers there.

Dr. Georges Physician to the lepers of Molokai; he assures the narrator of the lepers' happiness at their settlement.

Lucy's mother "An old woman . . . who was rocking back and forth and gazing at the steamer rail out of tear-blinded eyes" (*Stories*, 1,481).

Martin Jack Kersdale's driver, whom he begs to hurry to Doctor Harvey's so he can be tested for leprosy.

"The Heathen" (1909)

First appearing in *London Magazine*, 23, no. 2 (September 1909), "The Heathen" is a moving story of a cross-racial friendship, but one that reflects the conflicts in London's South Seas work when it comes to race.

SYNOPSIS

The narrator, Charley, is aboard the overcrowded trading ship *Petite Jeanne* when a huge hurricane strikes. Everyone goes overboard, and the ship sinks. Charley, a Bora Boran named Otoo, and Captain Oudouse struggle to float on hatch covers as the seas rage about them. Charley observes Otoo trying to join the captain on his hatch cover, but "Whenever a fling of the sea threw him closer, the Frenchman, hanging on with his hands, kicked out at him with both feet. Also, at the moment of delivering each kick, he called the KANAKA a black heathen. 'For two centimes I'd come over there and drown you, you white beast!' I yelled" (*Stories*, 1,507). Charley beckons Otoo to share with him, saving his life; when they finally approach land, Otoo drags Charley ashore and saves his life. In the South Seas ritual of friendship, ". . . we had performed the ceremony of exchanging names. In the South Seas, such a ceremony binds two men closer together

than blood-brothership. The initiative had been mine, and Otoo was rapturously delighted when I suggested it" (*Stories*, 1,508). When Otoo calls him "master," Charley responds, "'Why do you "master" me?' I demanded, with a show of hurt feelings. 'We have exchanged names. To you I am Otoo. To me you are Charley. And between you and me, forever and forever, you shall be Charley and I shall be Otoo. It is the way of the custom. And when we die, if it does happen that we live again, somewhere beyond the stars and the sky, still shall you be Charley to me and I Otoo to you'" (*Stories*, 1,509). Otoo and Charley return to TAHITI and are friends and partners for 17 years. Otoo's admiration for Charley helps Charley lead a more responsible life and eventually become rich. However, when they are trading in the SOLOMON ISLANDS at a place called Savo, known for its sharks, Charley's canoe capsizes and the other passengers, Solomon Islanders, are eaten by sharks. As Charley weakly swims to the ship, Otoo plunges into the water to save his brother and is eaten by a shark. The story concludes, "We met in the maw of a hurricane and parted in the maw of a shark, with seventeen intervening years of comradeship the like of which I dare to assert have never befallen two men, the one brown and the other white. If Jehovah be from his high place watching every sparrow fall, not least in His Kingdom shall be Otoo, the one heathen of BORA BORA. And if there be no place for him in that Kingdom, then will I have none of it" (*Stories*, 1,518).

COMMENTARY

This story is a good example of the inconsistencies inherent in many of London's treatments of race. London, like Charley, admired POLYNESIANS but was repulsed by the darker denizens of the Solomon Islands, then called MELANESIANS. Though he praises Ah Choon as a "white" Chinese, he calls Captain Oudouse a "white beast" (*Stories*, 1,507). Despite his friendship for Otoo, Charley calls the islanders "niggers" and "wooly heads" (*Stories*, 1,512).

CHARACTERS

narrator A pearl buyer named Charley, and Otoo become brothers by saving each other from the perilous seas after the *Petite Jeanne* sinks. "He was brother and father and mother as well. And this I know—I lived a straighter and better man because of Otoo. . . . I had to live straight in Otoo's eyes. Because of him I dared not tarnish myself. He made me his ideal, compounding me, I fear, chiefly out of his own love and worship and there were times when I stood close to the steep pitch of hell, and would have taken the plunge had not the thought of Otoo restrained me. His pride in me entered into me, until it became one of the major rules in my personal code to do nothing that would diminish that pride of his" (*Stories*, 1,509).

Ah Choon   The narrator calls Ah Choon "the whitest Chinese I have ever known" (*Stories*, 1,501). Ah Choon dies when the *Petite Jeanne* sinks.

Captain Oudouse   A Frenchman, he and the narrator quarrel over how to prepare the ship for the hurricane. Oudouse kicks Otoo away from his floating hatch cover and is cursed at by Charley, who saves Otoo. Captain Oudouse dies at sea.

Otoo   Otoo is the "Heathen," the title character. A Bora Boran, he and Charley save each other when their ship goes down. They become brothers, and Otoo later dies saving Charley's life. The narrator admires Otoo: "And that was how Otoo and I first came together. He was no fighter. He was all sweetness and gentleness, a love creature, though he stood nearly six feet tall and was muscled like a gladiator. He was no fighter, but he was also no coward. He had the heart of a lion; and in the years that followed I have seen him run risks that I would never dream of taking. What I mean is that while he was no fighter, and while he always avoided precipitating a row, he never ran away from trouble when it started" (*Stories*, 1,507).

"The Hobo and the Fairy" (1911)

First published in the SATURDAY EVENING POST 183 (February 11, 1911), this unusual tale of

redemption reflects London's hoboing experiences and also his life in SONOMA VALLEY, with its grapevines, blackberry bushes, madrono trees, bees, meadowlarks, and quail. It also points to his love of his oldest daughter, JOAN MILLER LONDON, and perhaps his desire for children with CHARMIAN KITTREDGE LONDON; the couple suffered the death of their newborn in the summer of 1910.

SYNOPSIS

Ross Shanklin, a hobo and convict, has passed out from drinking in a field on a farm. Joan, a little girl eight or so years old, emerges from a small bungalow with her parasol. She discovers Shanklin and shields him from the sun with her parasol. When he awakens, they talk, mainly about whether the world is a good or a bad place because of human nature. Having been treated cruelly all his adult life, he is shocked by her beauty and innocence; he tells her he thought at first she was a fairy. Joan's mother, who also displays no fear of him, comes to retrieve her daughter. Because of his experiences with them, Shanklin decides to give up his alcoholic hoboing and secures a job at a horse ranch.

COMMENTARY

The descriptions of nature and of the nature of the little girl, Joan (namesake of London's eldest daughter), make the story touching and even a bit magical. Her beauty and purity match not only the beauty and purity of Sonoma Valley but also Shanklin's memories of his horse-ranching days as a boy: "'Hosses ain't like men. They're better. They're clean—clean all the way through and back again'" (*Stories*, 1,780).

CHARACTERS

Ross Shanklin   As he lies passed out in the grass, Shanklin is described by the narrator as a wreck:

> . . . the straggling, unkempt hair was matted with the foxtails and burrs of the dry grass on which it lay. He was not a pretty sight. His mouth was open, disclosing a gap in the upper row where several teeth at some time had

been knocked out. He breathed stertorously, at times grunting and moaning with the pain of his sleep. Also, he was very restless, tossing his arms about, making jerky, half-convulsive movements, and at times rolling his head from side to side in the burrs. This restlessness seemed occasioned partly by some internal discomfort, and partly by the sun that streamed down on his face and by the flies that buzzed and lighted and crawled upon the nose and cheeks and eyelids. There was no other place for them to crawl, for the rest of the face was covered with matted beard, slightly grizzled, but greatly dirt-stained and weather-discolored. (*Stories*, 1,771)

As a teenager, Shanklin, who dreamed of being a Texas cowboy, was unfairly sentenced to 14 years in prison for horse-stealing, and there he suffered "hell," learned "every infamy of human cruelty," and comes out "crippled in body for life" (*Stories*, 1,773–1,774). He is momentarily redeemed by his contact with Joan, the "fairy."

Joan A beautiful, innocent, and sweet little blond girl who encounters Shanklin in a field near her farmhouse. Her untutored remarks to him about there being good in all people lead him to desire reform. She calls herself "the good Samaritan" and lectures Shanklin on good and bad habits; she listens as he finally relaxes and tells her about his love of horses.

mother She too is unafraid of Shanklin and has raised her daughter to be fearless and to live a healthy life. She is "a woman, clad in a soft, clinging gown, come through the gate from the bungalow. She was a slender, graceful woman, and to his charmed eyes she seemed rather to float along than walk like ordinary flesh and blood" (*Stories*, 1,781).

farmer "Keen-eyed and middle-aged" (*Stories*, 1,782), the farmer observes Shanklin approach his porch; when Shanklin tells him "'I know hosses'" (*Stories*, 1,782), he agrees to hire him to work on his ranch, even though Shanklin does not appear very promising.

"The House of Mapuhi" (1909)

First published in *MCCLURE's* 32 (January 1909), "The House of Mapuhi" reads like a fable of survival after a gigantic hurricane levels an island full of terrified inhabitants.

SYNOPSIS

On the atoll of Hikueru, a young man, Mapuhi, finds an enormous pearl: "It was large as a pigeon egg, a perfect sphere, of a whiteness that reflected opalescent lights from all colors about it. It was alive. . . . It was without flaw or blemish. The purity of it seemed almost to melt into the atmosphere out of his hand. In the shade it was softly luminous, gleaming like a tender moon" (*Stories*, 1,386). Mapuhi tries to sell it to Alexandre Raoul, the local supercargo, or manager of a cargo owner's trade. Mapuhi demands a house: "'It must have a roof of galvanized iron and an octagon-drop-clock. It must be six fathoms long with a porch all around. A big room must be in the centre, with a round table in the middle of it and the octagon-drop-clock on the wall. There must be four bedrooms, two on each side of the big room, and in each bedroom must be an iron bed, two chairs, and a washstand. And back of the house must be a kitchen, a good kitchen, with pots and pans and a stove. And you must build the house on my island, which is Fakarava'" (*Stories*, 1,386). His wife also demands a sewing machine. However, calculating the costs, Raoul refuses. The pearl is stolen by Toriki, to whom Mapuhi owes money, then sold to Levy. However, a gigantic hurricane kills most of the islanders and levels every structure; in the storm Mapuhi's mother is blown to another island, where she finds Levy dead and regains the pearl. Though she is an old woman, she survives for weeks on the island then, in a makeshift canoe, battles sharks and strong currents to return home. When she does, she tells Mapuhi to sell the pearl to Raoul and build her house.

COMMENTARY

The story presents dramatic descriptions of a hurricane:

It was a horrible, monstrous thing, a screaming fury, a wall that smote and passed on but that continued to smite and pass on—a wall without end. It seemed to him that he had become light and ethereal; that it was he that was in motion; that he was being driven with inconceivable velocity through unending solidness. The wind was no longer air in motion. It had become substantial as water or quicksilver. He had a feeling that he could reach into it and tear it out in chunks as one might do with the meat in the carcass of a steer; that he could seize hold of the wind and hang on to it as a man might hang on to the face of a cliff.

The wind strangled him. He could not face it and breathe, for it rushed in through his mouth and nostrils, distending his lungs like bladders. At such moments it seemed to him that his body was being packed and swollen with solid earth. Only by pressing his lips to the trunk of the tree could he breathe. Also, the ceaseless impact of the wind exhausted him. Body and brain became wearied. He no longer observed, no longer thought, and was but semiconscious. (*Stories*, 1,396)

The story is characterized both by a strong sense of NATURALISM and by a mythic journey of salvation. Biblical imagery appears in the cataclysm that uproots churches and snatches people at random, in the idea of building a house upon a firm foundation, and also in the motif of the Pearl of Great Price.

CHARACTERS

Alexandre Raoul Raoul tries to buy Mapuhi's pearl at the beginning, but loses out to Toriki. After Mapuhi's mother retrieves the pearl, Mapuhi plans to sell it to Raoul for 5,000 francs and build his mother a house. He is ". . . a young man garbed in the tropic white that marks the European. The golden strain of Polynesia betrayed itself in the sun-gilt of his fair skin and cast up golden sheens and lights through the glimmering blue of his eyes. Raoul he was, Alexandre Raoul, youngest son of Marie Raoul, the wealthy quarter-caste, who owned and managed half a dozen trading schooners similar to the *Aorai*" (*Stories*, 1,385).

Huru-Huru Described as "a tall native" whose "chest and shoulders were magnificent, but the stump of a right arm, beyond the flesh of which the age-whitened bone projected several inches, attested the encounter with a shark that had put an end to his diving days and made him a fawner and an intriguer for small favors" (*Stories*, 1,385). He tells Alec about Mapuhi's pearl.

Mapuhi Mapuhi finds an enormous pearl and demands of Raoul a house, a clock, and a sewing machine. The pearl is stolen from him by Toriki and then sold to Levy. It is his mother who retrieves the pearl and returns to her island so Mapuhi can build her house.

Tefara Mapuhi's wife, who berates him for losing his pearl and demands a sewing machine.

Nauri Mapuhi's mother, who calls him a fool for losing his pearl. Paumotan-born, she is nearly 60 years old but survives being blown out to sea onto a nearby island. She finds Levy dead and takes the pearl back from him. She survives on coconuts and tins of salmon, then, with no rescue in sight, she repairs an outrigger canoe and returns to Hikueru, swimming through sharks and against powerful currents. Upon her arrival, she has to persuade her family she is not a ghost. She instructs Mapuhi to sell his pearl to Raoul, and she looks forward to her house and octagon drop-clock.

Ngakura Mapuhi's daughter, who makes fun of him too. She breaks her arm in the storm and is terrified when Nauri returns, for she assumes she is a ghost.

Toriki Owner and supercargo of the *Orohena*, he is a "half-caste trader" (*Stories*, 1,388) owed money by Mapuhi for trade goods advanced the year before; he steals Mapuhi's pearl and sells it to Levy.

Levy A German Jew "with massive asymmetrical features" and a wide girth who buys the pearl from Toriki for 25,000 francs. He is found dead by Nauri, who reclaims Mapuhi's pearl.

Captain Lynch Described as a "doughty patri-arch" (*Stories*, 1,394), he is witness to the sale of the pearl to Levy who is astonished by the severity of the storm. He provides rope to Raoul and some women to tie themselves to trees when the storm hits. He is blown out to sea with the coconut tree he clings to.

Mormon missionary and gendarme These men count the survivors of the hurricane; from 1,200 islanders they count only 300 left.

"The House of Pride" (1910)

One of London's most pointed attacks on white racism in HAWAI'I, this story first appeared in *Pacific Monthly* 24 (December 1910). It is the first Hawaiian story London wrote and gives its name to the volume that contains it. In it, London directly attacks colonialism as he offers a memorable por-trayal of a nonwhite hero and a scathing portrait of a white master. Several of the stories in this collec-tion ignited protest: The white elite of HONOLULU, many of them MISSIONARY descendants, feared that radical working-class politics and the men-tion of leprosy would taint Hawai'i's growing tour-ist business. They also reacted to the "didactic" nature of these stories, specifically their attacks on colonialism.

SYNOPSIS

This is the tale of how missionary descendant Percival Ford betrays his illegitimate half-brother, Joe Garland, forcing him to leave Hawai'i, when he finds out the secret of Joe's birth from a Hawaiian woman and his father, missionary Isaac Ford, whom Percival reveres. Despite the fact that Joe has always looked out for him and defended him, Ford cruelly banishes Joe to the mainland. Ford's friend, appropriately a doctor, sees his spiritual disease. Chastising him, he can hardly believe that while everyone else knows the real history of Ford's outwardly pious father, Isaac Ford, and his out-of-wedlock son, Ford still pretends ignorance:

"You are pure New England stock. Joe Garland is half Kanaka. Your blood is thin. His is warm. Life is one thing to you, another thing to him. He laughs and sings and dances through life, genial, unselfish, childlike, everybody's friend. You go through life like a perambulating prayer-wheel, a friend of nobody but the righteous, and the righteous are those who agree with you as to what is right. . . . You live like an anchorite. Joe Garland lives like a good fellow. Who has extracted the most from life? We are paid to live, you know." (*Stories*, 1,346)

The doctor knows that Ford's problem lies beyond merely his ancestry and his physical frame, but in his prideful spirit, fueled by raw malice. However, ignoring the doctor's pleas, Ford will not be swayed, and in the end leans back in his chair to enjoy his lemonade and savor his victory over Joe.

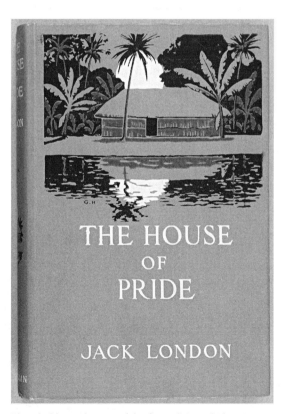

The clothbound cover of the first edition of *The House of Pride* (1908) *(Huntington Library)*

COMMENTARY

The story was completed in early July 1907, only six weeks after London arrived in Hawai'i, but according to his Magazine Sales Record, it was turned down by nearly 20 magazines over three years. Neither of his usual overseas agencies, James B. Pinker or William Heinemann & Co., could sell the story at all. Such difficulty getting published was very unusual for London at that point in his career. Something about this story put off the editors. The problem most likely lay in its attack on racism and critique of American colonial exploitation in Hawai'i, a stance not at all popular and puzzling to many of London's fans. Here, as in the subsequent Hawaiian stories, London presents Hawaiian characters not as nostalgic noble savages from an exotic past, but as modern people with identities and communities confused by colonization.

Yet Ford's true feeling toward his brother is not racism but unconscious envy. Ford believes he upholds the strongest religious, racial, and familial standards, but his lack of self-awareness surfaces everywhere, as in his sexual anxieties. His obsession with his father—the symbol of his racial ancestry—blinds him to reality.

The racial tropes in this story begin with the denial of humanity to the racial "other," coupled with rejection of the scapegoat family member. While Ford fixates on the "crime" of miscegenation, the reader instead sees only Ford's own crime of denying his brother. The doctor asks Ford, "'Who the devil gave it to you to be judge and jury? Does landlordism give you control of the immortal souls of those that toil for you?'" (*Stories*, 1,346). But for Ford, learning of his father's "unruly blood" is "like learning suddenly that his father had been a leper and that his own blood might bear the taint of that dread disease. Isaac Ford, the austere soldier of the Lord—the old hypocrite! What difference between him and any beach-comber? The house of pride that Percival Ford had built was tumbling about his ears" (*Stories*, 1,353–1,354).

Why does Garland agree to be banished? If he shows Christlike patience with his brother and agrees out of misplaced respect for him to follow his wishes, he somehow will rise above his situation and remain himself, free of his evil twin. With the name "Garland," London runs the risk of stereotyping Garland as a noble savage or as a merely romantic character. But if Garland is romanticized he is also realistic; he alone is no match for the power of CAPITALISM and colonialism. The story is also realistic psychologically in its Freudian dissection of Ford's disturbed mind and the effects of his identity crisis on Garland. Finally, however, in Darwinian evolutionary terms, Garland has succeeded where Ford has failed; Ford will never, one is sure, pass on his genes, for he will not adapt to the reality around him, as Garland has probably already done.

CHARACTERS

Percival Ford   Percival's rejection symbolizes his rejection of humanity itself:

> Percival Ford was no more a woman's man than he was a man's man. A glance at him told the reason. . . . [H]e lacked vitality. His was a negative organism. No blood with a ferment in it could have nourished and shaped that long and narrow face, those thin lips, lean cheeks, and the small, sharp eyes. The thatch of hair, dust-colored, straight and sparse, advertised the niggard soil, as did the nose, thin, delicately modeled, and just hinting the suggestion of a beak. His meagre blood had denied him much of life, and permitted him to be an extremist in one thing only, which thing was righteousness. (*Stories*, 1,346)

Joe Garland   Percival Ford calls Joe "'dissolute and idle. He has always been a wastrel, a profligate'" (*Stories*, 1,348), but the doctor calls him a creature of love and loyalty. He is the son of Isaac Ford and Eliza Kunilio.

Dr. Kennedy   The doctor tries to counsel Ford against further persecution of Joe Garland and reminds him of Joe's having helped him out as a boy when he was attacked by other boys and also points to his sunny and appealing nature. He also informs Ford that Joe is his half-brother.

John   Ford's clerk who confirms, reluctantly, what the doctor has told Ford about Joe's ancestry; he confides that "'We always thought that that was why you had it in for him'" (*Stories*, 1,353).

FURTHER READING

Berkove, Lawrence I. "Jack London's 'Second Thoughts': The Short Fiction of His Late Period." In *Jack London: One Hundred Years a Writer.* Edited by Sara S. Hodson and Jeanne Campbell Reesman. San Marino, Calif.: Huntington Library Press, 2002, 60–76.

Riedl, Gary, and Thomas R. Tietze. "Fathers and Sons in Jack London's 'The House of Pride.'" In *Jack London: One Hundred Years a Writer.* Edited by Sara S. Hodson and Jeanne Campbell Reesman. San Marino, Calif.: Huntington Library Press, 2002, 44–59.

"How I Became a Socialist" (1905)

Included in his collection of social writings *War of the Classes*, the title of "How I Became a Socialist" may have been inspired by William Morris's essay with that title published in the journal *Justice* in 1894.

SYNOPSIS

London opens his essay with the remark that "It is quite fair to say that I became a Socialist in a fashion somewhat similar to the way in which the Teutonic pagans became Christians—it was hammered into me. Not only was I not looking for SOCIALISM at the time of my conversion, but I was fighting it. I was very young and callow, did not know much of anything, and though I had never even heard of a school called INDIVIDUALISM, I sang the paean of the strong with all my heart" (*War of the Classes*, 267). Optimistic because he is healthy and strong and used to both work and the outdoor life, as a youth he gave little thought to "the unfortunates, the sick, and ailing, and old, and maimed," (270) preferring to play the man's game of individualistic

Jack London and his dog, Brown Wolf, relaxing together *(Huntington Library)*

achievement. As "one of Nature's strong-armed noblemen," he views the "dignity of labor . . . [as] the most impressive thing in the world." And he confesses, "I was as faithful a wage slave as ever capitalist exploited" (271). Though he later realized he was "dominated by the orthodox bourgeois ethics" (272), he resolves to go hoboing. In so doing, he encounters "all sorts of men, many of whom had once been as good as myself and just as *blond-beastly*; sailor-men, soldier-men, labor-men, all wrenched and distorted and twisted out of shape by toil and hardship and accident, and cast adrift by their masters like so many old horses" (273). Begging for food, jumping freight trains, and shivering with them in city parks, he listens to their life histories and realizes that he too can be a victim of the "Social Pit" (274). He resolves to escape: "*I shall climb out of the Pit, but not by the muscles of my body shall I climb out I shall do no more hard work, and may God strike me dead if I do another day's hard work with my body more than I absolutely have to do*" (275). However, when he is apprehended and thrown into the ERIE COUNTY PENITENTIARY for vagrancy, he realizes that he is at heart a socialist, and he returns to CALIFORNIA to "open the books": "Since that day I have opened many books, but no economic argument, no lucid demonstration of the logic and inevitableness of Socialism affects me as profoundly and convincingly as I was affected on the day when I first saw the walls of the Social Pit rise around me and felt myself slipping down, down, into the shambles at the bottom" (278).

COMMENTARY

This essay furnishes biographical interest as well as a clearer understanding of the nature of London's socialism. His prison experience—which came about because he camped out at Niagara Falls to see the sunrise—was one of his most formative; he later noted that he saw things there that he could never tell. The realization of how the lower classes are victimized by CAPITALISM and that one day his body would give out helped propel him to become instead a writer, what he called a "vender of brains."

"The Hussy" (1916)

First published in COSMOPOLITAN 62 (December 1916), "The Hussy" was the first of 11 stories London wrote in his last year, after a hiatus from short fiction between 1912 and 1915. It was the first London story published after his death on November 22, 1916. It reflects London's experiences when he and Charmian took a break from the SNARK voyage in spring 1909, traveling on the tramp collier *Tymeric* out of Australia. They visited both Guayaquil and Quito, Ecuador.

SYNOPSIS

The narrator tells of meeting a man named Julian Jones at the Australian Building at the Panama Pacific Exposition, where there is an exhibit of facsimiles of record nuggets "discovered in the gold fields of the Antipodes" (*Stories*, 2,279). Jones is a railroad engineer with experience in South America; he scoffs that the nuggets on display are small compared to what he has seen. The narrator is introduced to his wife, Sarah, and the three walk to the lagoon, where Jones tells his tale.

Jones says he has seen a nugget bigger than the whole exhibit put together. He explains that he went to Ecuador on a tramp collier out of Australia after hearing of high wages on the American railroad running from Guayaquil over the Andes to Quito. Guayaquil was a scene of disease and death, as the yellow fever ravaged the populace and killed the famous American cartoonist Thomas Nast, who was U.S. Consul General in Ecuador. But though "'bubonic plague and small-pox were raging, while dysentery and pneumonia were reducing the population,'" the railroad "'was raging worst of all. I mean that. For them that insisted in riding on it, it was more dangerous than all the other diseases put together'" (*Stories*, 2,282). The trip over the mountains is so tricky that the train only runs in daylight. He adds that that the country was in a "Kill the Gringos" frame of mind, especially when there was a train accident.

Jones meets Vahna, a woman whom Sarah calls "the hussy!" (*Stories*, 2,284). Jones had taken a locomotive to Amato, 30 miles from Quito, with

Seth Manners being broken in as fireman, when a Native girl shows up on the track; Jones and Manners manage to stop the locomotive just 20 feet from her. A tall, slender girl wrapped in ocelot skins, her eyes shut and weeping, she behaves mysteriously. Jones manages to get her on board and to Quito. Seth tells him he saved her life and "'now she belongs to you. Custom of the country'" (*Stories*, 2,287).

Jones brings her to his home, and to pay for her keep she gives him a large nugget worth $500. Jones gets word that his aunt had died and left him a farm, and he prepares to pull out "for God's country" (*Stories*, 2,290), but Vahna, interpreted by Paloma, Jones's cook, tells him that if he will stay she will show him a gigantic gold nugget, a secret of her tribe. He follows Vahna into the Andes. There he sits down on a big rock—which turns out to be the nugget. With a hatchet he cuts into it. It is solid gold, coated with a paint or lacquer, a boulder 10 feet long and five through, tapering on the ends like an egg. He puts a chip in his pocket. Suddenly there appears on the mountain an old man and some 30 Natives. "'No, no,'" Vahna cries. "'This is death. Good-by, amigo—'" (*Stories*, 2,292), after which Jones is knocked out. When he revives, he finds Vahna spread-eagled on top of the nugget: "'I couldn't lift a hand, being held down, and being too weak besides,'" Jones says. "'And—well, anyway, that stone knife did for her, and me they didn't even do the honour of killing there on top their sacred peak. They chucked me off of it like so much carrion'" (*Stories*, 2,293). He survives the fall by landing in a snowdrift. It takes him two years to understand what happened.

Back in Nebraska, as he sits dully on the porch of Sarah's father's farmhouse, she puts the gold chip in his hand, found in a torn lining of a trunk he had brought out of Ecuador, and "'all of a sudden there was a snap inside my head as if something had broken'" (*Stories*, 2,293), and he remembers all that had happened.

He hasn't figured out how to get back to the nugget but has figured out what it was: It was all the gold the Incas had hid away from Pizarro and his "'gang of robbers and cutthroats,'" (*Stories*, 2,295), smelted together by the surviving Indi-

ans, disguised in plain sight on the mountain. The narrator agrees to finance a return journey to the mountain, and Jones promises to call at the hotel next morning—but he does not. The narrator is told that Mr. and Mrs. Jones had departed with their baggage for Nebraska.

COMMENTARY

"The Hussy" is a fantasy of gold, sex, and adventure told with a mythic set of images: the girl wrapped in ocelot skins, the ritualized sacrifice, the historical mystery of the nugget itself. London would go on after "The Hussy" to pen "The Red One," which relates an even more fantastic and mythologized tale of an explorer on GUADALCANAL who finds a gigantic red sphere which he assumes fell from the heavens.

CHARACTERS

narrator The narrator resembles Jack London himself; we know this because Jones tells him, "'Of course I've heard of you, seen your picture in the papers, and all that, and, though I say it that shouldn't, I want to say that I didn't care a rap about those articles you wrote on Mexico'" (*Stories*, 2,280). After hearing Jones's tale, he offers to finance a return expedition.

Julian Jones Jones is a railroad engineer who worked in South America. He tells the narrator a fantastic tale of a beautiful Native maiden and a gigantic gold nugget. The narrator notes that "he stood something like six feet four inches in height. His hair, a wispy, sandy yellow, seemed as dimmed and faded as his eyes. It may have been the sun which had washed out his colouring; at least his face bore the evidence of a prodigious and ardent sun-burn which had long since faded to yellow. As his eyes turned from the exhibit and focused on mine I noted a queer look in them as of one who vainly tries to recall some fact of supreme importance" (*Stories*, 2,279).

Sarah Jones Jones's wife seems obsessed with the danger presented by the Native woman, "the hussy," whom she hates and fears for her effect on her husband. The narrator notes that "It was patent that she had never heard of me, and she surveyed me bleakly with shrewd black eyes, set close together and as beady and restless as a bird's" (*Stories*, 2,281). She is described as thin-lipped and unsmiling, and when she speaks she "snaps," "hisses," or "complains."

Vahna The mysterious woman who stops the train by standing on the tracks. Jones describes her strange appearance: "'slim and slender, you know the kind, with black hair, remarkably long hanging, down loose behind her, as she stood there no more afraid than nothing, her arms spread out to stop the engine. She was wearing a slimpsy sort of garment wrapped around her that wasn't cloth but ocelot skins, soft and dappled, and silky. It was all she had on—'" (*Stories*, 2,286).

Seth Manners Jones's fireman on the Ecuadorian train. He explains to Jones that having saved Vahna's life she is his responsibility.

Paloma Jones's cook, who can converse with Vahna and who demands that Jones take care of her, even saying she'll leave too if Vahna has to leave. But she fears what Vahna will bring after her: seeing Vahna's anxiety, Jones relates, "'I tried to worm it out of Paloma what was worrying the girl, but all the old woman did was to look solemn and shake her head like all the devils in hell was liable to precipitate a visit on us'" (*Stories*, 2,288).

Indian boy Possibly Vahna's brother or relation, as he resembles her. He brings Jones a nugget for payment in helping Vahna.

old Indian man Vahna's second visitor, "'He was a lean, tall, white-headed old Indian, with a beak on him like an eagle. He walked right in without knocking. Vahna gave a little cry that was half like a yelp and half like a gasp, and flumped down on her knees before me, pleading to me with deer's eyes and to him with the eyes of a deer about to be killed that don't want to be killed. Then, for a minute that seemed as long as a life-time, she and the old fellow glared at each other'" (*Stories*, 2,289). He tries to persuade her to return to her people, but she refuses.

"A Hyperborean Brew" (1901)

First published in the *Metropolitan* magazine 14 (July 1901), this story is one of a pair with "A Relic of the Pliocene," which also features Thomas Stevens. Its full title is "A Hyperborean Brew: The Story of a Scheming White Man Among the Strange People Who Live on the Rim of the Arctic Sea."

SYNOPSIS

After many travels, Thomas Stevens and his NATIVE companion Moosu arrive famished at the Native camp at Tattarat. Finding the Natives uncongenial, Stevens sets about a plan to get their food from them. Using flour, sugar, and molasses, he makes a still and brews "hooch," or liquor, and manages to get them all to drink it. They gladly trade their goods for more and more. Stevens hides a great cache of meat against his departure. The shaman, jealous of Stevens, creates his own hooch, but it lacks a kick, and he is attacked by the rest of the tribe. Moosu begins to wrest power away from Stevens, the new chief, and demands to marry several women. Through a series of tricks, Stevens defeats him and, with Moosu tied to the sled and receiving blows from Stevens's whip, takes his "brother," who must forever call Stevens master, out of the village and on the open trail.

COMMENTARY

Like "The Master of Mystery," this story is a trickster tale probably based on Native legend. It features one of London's cleverest and most unscrupulous protagonists, Thomas Stevens, who uses his wiles to get his way with the Natives. There is a hint of white superiority in Stevens's treatment of his companion, Moosu, and of the Natives in general, but it is a lighthearted story—at least from Stevens's point of view.

CHARACTERS

narrator The narrator is unnamed. He is acquainted with Stevens's reputation as a traveler and storyteller and he listens to Stevens's tale while drinking and gambling in John O'Brien's DAWSON saloon.

Thomas Stevens   The narrator begins the story with a description of Stevens: "Thomas Stevens's veracity may have been indeterminate as x, and his imagination the imagination of ordinary men increased to the nth power, but this, at least, must be said: never did he deliver himself of word nor deed that could be branded as a lie outright. . . . He may have played with probability, and verged on the extremest edge of possibility, but in his tales the machinery never creaked. That he knew the Northland like a book, not a soul can deny. That he was a great traveller, and had set foot on countless unknown trails, many evidences affirm" (*Stories,* 498). Stevens manages to fool a Native tribe into saving him by making "hooc," or liquor, and getting them drunk.

Moosu   Stevens describes him as "'. . . an Indian from over on the edge of the Chippewyan country'" who had "'picked up a smattering of the Scriptures'"; though he had "'never seen applied Christianity, . . . his head was crammed with miracles, battles, and dispensations, and what not he didn't understand. Otherwise he was a good sort, and a handy man on trail or over a fire'" (*Stories,* 499). Moosu helps Stevens make his hooch and gain power over the tribe at Tattarat but grabs power himself. He is defeated (and rescued) by Stevens.

Tummasook   Chief of the village who hoards tea in his igloo. He is overthrown by Stevens and then by Moosu.

Ipsukuk   A poor Native woman who hoards flour, sugar, and molasses.

Tukeliketa   She is the "'daughter of a big hunter and wealthy man. A likely girl. Indeed, a very nice girl'" (*Stories,* 500) according to Moosu, who marries her.

Neewak the Shaman   The village shaman is jealous of Stevens's secrets and learns to make hooch himself, but his is not potent.

Angeit   Native who stays loyal to Stevens and helps him overthrow Moosu.

Kluktu   Youngest daughter of the chief, whom Stevens tries unsuccessfully to marry; Moosu, having declared polygamy, marries her instead.

FURTHER READING

Berkove, Lawrence I. "Thomas Stevens: London's Comic Agent of Evolutionary Criticism." In *Thalia: Studies in Literary Humor* (Special issue on the humor of Jack London) 12, nos. 1, 2 (1992).

"If Japan Awakens China" (1909)

This essay, which pairs well with "The Yellow Peril," appeared in *Sunset* magazine in December 1909; it is included in *Jack London Reports* (1970). It reflects his experiences covering the RUSSO-JAPANESE WAR in 1904 and, later, his greater understanding of the world's peoples following his voyage of the SNARK.

SYNOPSIS

In this brief essay, London warns his readers that Westerners do not understand the JAPANESE mind and vice versa: "It is a weakness of man to believe that all the rest of mankind is moulded in his own image, and it is a weakness of the white race to believe that the Japanese think as we think, are moved to action as we are moved and have points of view similar to our own" (*Jack London Reports,* 358). He identifies the work of Lafcadio Hearn in Japan as the best insights into the Japanese produced by a white man, but notes that Hearn died feeling he had only barely penetrated the surface. He also uses the example of a white woman of his acquaintance who claimed that the Japanese have no souls: "In this she was wrong. The Japanese are just as much possessed of soul as she and the rest of her race. And far be it from me to infer that the Japanese soul is in the smallest way inferior to the Western soul. It may even be superior" (360). The point is that they do not know us, nor we them. He warns the West about the distinct possibility that Japan would conquer CHINA and "awaken" the Chinese to industrial greatness and competition with the West. He particularly notes how adept the Japanese are at using Western technology for their own ends. Pointing to the example of how the Russians were defeated in 1904, he predicts an Asian "race-adventure" that will have enormous consequences for the world (361).

COMMENTARY

This essay along with "The Yellow Peril" is often cited as evidence of London's anti-Asian feelings, but even a cursory reading of it draws the opposite interpretation: London is not demeaning the Japanese and Chinese but pointing out to his English-speaking audience that they had better be prepared for the economic and military rise of Asia in the 20th century, which proved largely correct.

"In a Far Country" (1899)

Appearing first in the OVERLAND MONTHLY 33 (June 1899), this early story powerfully employs motifs and themes drawn from YUKON lore but also from the BIBLE, Shakespeare's *The Tempest,* and GREEK and Roman MYTHOLOGY, especially the presence of the SUN as the eye of heaven. Its characters, who are too lazy to break camp for the winter, remain behind their fellows. It is not long before they are literally at each others' throats.

SYNOPSIS

The story opens with a warning to all those who seek to enter the wild:

> When a man journeys into a far country, he must be prepared to forget many of the things he has learned, and to acquire such customs as are inherent with existence in the new land; he must abandon the old ideals and the old gods, and oftentimes he must reverse the very codes by which his conduct has hitherto been shaped. To those who have the protean faculty of adaptability, the novelty of such change may even be a source of pleasure; but to those who happen to be hardened to the ruts in which they were created, the pressure of the altered environ-

ment is unbearable, and they chafe in body and in spirit under the new restrictions which they do not understand. This chafing is bound to act and react, producing divers evils and leading to various misfortunes. It were better for the man who cannot fit himself to the new groove to return to his own country; if he delay too long, he will surely die. (*Stories,* 209)

This lofty perspective, with its echo of the story of the prodigal son (Luke 15:11–32), who journeys "into a far country" with his inheritance, only to squander it, reflects a wisdom that the two protagonists of this story sadly lack. As the narrator continues, "For the courtesies of ordinary life," a man who wishes to survive in the NORTHLAND "must substitute unselfishness, forbearance, and tolerance. Thus, and thus only, can he gain that pearl of great price,—true comradeship. He must not say 'Thank you'; he must mean it without opening his mouth, and prove it by responding in kind. In short, he must substitute the deed for the word, the spirit for the letter" (*Stories,* 209).

Carter Weatherbee, formerly a clerk, organizes a party of men to take him to DAWSON via the Edmonton trail, which means traveling for a great distance in canoes as well as dogsleds on a trail never used anymore due to its length and hardships. The party is joined by Percy Cuthfert, a wealthy and idle young man. In camp and on trail, these two become "shirks and chronic grumblers" (*Stories,* 210). By the time the party enters the Little Peel River near the Arctic Sea, the sun has "already passed its northern solstice and was leading the winter south" (*Stories,* 211), and, realizing how short their time is, Jacques Baptiste, their voyageur, has to beat them to make them work. The party comes across an abandoned cabin marked by two graves, a foreshadowing of what is to come. Their guide, Merritt Sloper, announces that they are only 300 miles from the YUKON RIVER, which they can drift down for the 700 more miles to Dawson. The two "Incapables," Weatherbee and Cuthfert, as the narrator calls them, decide to hole up in the cabin for winter rather than struggle along to Dawson. Their comrades are not sorry to leave them behind.

After the others depart, at first they get along well enough, and they have plenty of food and fuel. But because they are moral degenerates, because Weatherbee is an unimaginative fool, because Cuthfert is merely a sentimental dilettante, because each thinks only of himself, but mainly because each lacks the Darwinian survival mechanism of ADAPTABILITY, they are doomed. They quickly devolve, eventually committing all of the Seven Deadly Sins against each other. First, pride appears in their arrogance and their class separation. Next is lust and greed, when they consume with sensual promiscuity their supply of sugar, mixing it with water to put on their flapjacks, and also in their giving up bathing and "and, for that matter, common decency" (*Stories*, 216). Sloth overtakes them as they slip into lethargy and resentment:

> As the sugar-pile and other little luxuries dwindled, they began to be afraid they were not getting their proper shares, and in order that they might not be robbed, they fell to gorging themselves. The luxuries suffered in this gluttonous contest, as did also the men. In the absence of fresh vegetables and exercise, their blood became impoverished, and a loathsome, purplish rash crept over their bodies. Yet they refused to heed the warning. Next, their muscles and joints began to swell, the flesh turning black, while their mouths, gums, and lips took on the color of rich cream. Instead of being drawn together by their misery, each gloated over the other's symptoms as the scurvy took its course. (*Stories*, 216)

Jealousy and envy appear when they divide their sugar supply and hide their shares from one another, obsessed with suspicion. The last of the sins, anger, surfaces when they succumb to their fears of the unknown, deep in the Arctic darkness, and in a nightmarish scene of murderous delusion, set upon one another and kill each other. Clinched together in struggle, Weatherbee severs Cuthfert's spine with an ax just after Cuthfert shoots him with a pistol. The last lines of the story point toward both their judgment and their "brotherhood" in death: "Well, he would have company. If Gabriel ever broke the silence of the North, they would stand together, hand in hand, before the great White Throne. And God would judge them, God would judge them! Then Percy Cuthfert closed his eyes and dropped off to sleep" (*Stories*, 223).

COMMENTARY

Among London's tales of BROTHERHOOD on the NORTHLAND trail, this story, like "To Build a Fire," serves as an obverse lesson of what happens when there is no brotherhood. Weatherbee and Cuthfert do not learn one of the most important lessons in life, that survival is not primarily a matter of physical but of spiritual fitness. Throughout the story the sun appears as a judge of these men. They are seized with fear when the sun stays below the horizon the first time: "To all this was added a new trouble,—the Fear of the North. This Fear was the joint child of the Great Cold and the Great Silence, and was born in the darkness of December, when the sun dipped below the southern horizon for good. It affected them according to their natures" (*Stories*, 216). Without the sun, Weatherbee falls prey to "the grosser superstitions," while Cuthfert becomes obsessed with the lack of wind to indicate the coming of spring. Their spirits are "crushed" by "the perfect cessation of wind and motion, the immensity of the snow-covered wilderness, the height of the sky and the depth of the silence" (*Stories*, 217). Cuthfert broods: "There was no sun. This was the Universe, dead and cold and dark, and he its only citizen. Weatherbee? At such moments Weatherbee did not count. He was a Caliban, a monstrous phantom, fettered to him for untold ages, the penalty of some forgotten crime" (*Stories*, 218). When at last the sun barely peeps over the horizon at noon, they momentarily feel better: "There were tears in their eyes as they sought each other. A strange softening came over them. They felt irresistibly drawn toward each other. The sun was coming back again" (*Stories*, 220). But its quick disappearance maddens them anew, and Cuthfert plots to kill Weatherbee with his pistol. As they struggle with pistol and ax and knife, they think of the sun but around them is only the immense darkness with its whispers of the dead.

CHARACTERS

Carter Weatherbee Upon hearing news of gold in the Arctic, Weatherbee "threw up his snug clerkship, turned the half of his savings over to his wife, and with the remainder bought an outfit. There was no romance in his nature,—the bondage of commerce had crushed all that; he was simply tired of the ceaseless grind" (*Stories*, 210). Like his "partner," Cuthfert, he is lazy and selfish and unfit for survival in the Northland. Weatherbee is shot to death by Cuthfert.

Percy Cuthfert He too joins the party exploring for gold: "He was an ordinary man, with a bank account as deep as his culture, which is saying a good deal. He had no reason to embark on such a venture,—no reason in the world, save that he suffered from an abnormal development of sentimentality. He mistook this for the true spirit of romance and adventure. Many another man has done the like, and made as fatal a mistake" (*Stories*, 210). Cuthfert's spine is severed by an ax-wielding Weatherbee.

Merritt Sloper Based on a man of that name London knew in the Klondike, Sloper is a small, wiry man weakened by fever: "The fresh young muscles of either Weatherbee or Cuthfert were equal to ten times the endeavor of his; yet he could walk them into the earth in a day's journey. And all this day he had whipped his stronger comrades into venturing a thousand miles of the stiffest hardship man can conceive. He was the incarnation of the unrest of his race, and the old Teutonic stubbornness, dashed with the quick grasp and action of the Yankee, held the flesh in the bondage of the spirit" (*Stories*, 213). Sloper accurately predicts the fate of the two "Incapables," whom he compares to the Kilkenny cats "who fought till neither hide, nor hair, nor yowl, was left" (*Stories*, 214).

Jacques Baptiste A French-Canadian voyageur with a NATIVE mother, he is startled by Weatherbee's plan to take the Edmonton trail but agrees to guide him anyway. Jacques Baptiste curses Weatherbee and Cuthfert for their laziness.

"The Inevitable White Man"
(1910)

First appearing in the Bristol (England) *Observer*, May 14, 1910, this grisly tale was inspired by his five months in the SOLOMON ISLANDS while on the *Snark* voyage. As in some other stories, such as "'Yah! Yah! Yah!,'" written just before it, he portrays the whites who trade and colonize in the South Seas as depraved but smugly sure of their superiority to the islanders they oppress. Captain Woodward is based on a real labor recruiter the Londons sailed with in the Solomons, Captain Jansen of the MINOTA; they were attacked and nearly overrun by angry islanders on MALAITA. His name also suggests one of London's sources for his views on RACIALISM, a book by Dr. Charles E. Woodruff, a surgeon with the U.S. Army, called *The Effects of Tropical Light on White Men* (1905).

SYNOPSIS

Three men, bartender Charley Roberts, labor recruiter Captain Woodward of the steamer *Savaii*, and an unnamed narrator talk over drinks in Charley's bar in Apia, SAMOA. (Labor recruiters, called BLACKBIRDERS, either recruited volunteers from islands they visited or sometimes simply kidnapped young men and boys and forced them into labor on plantations.) The men discuss the struggles of whites to "manage" the blacks in the Southwest Pacific, what used to be called MELANESIA, primarily the Solomon Islands. Captain Woodward states that whites and blacks will never understand each other, to which Roberts replies, "'Half the trouble is the stupidity of the whites,'" which he says while "pausing to take a swig from his glass and to curse the Samoan bar-boy in affectionate terms. 'If the white man would lay himself out a bit to understand the workings of the black man's mind, most of the messes would be avoided'" (*Stories*, 1,555). Captain Woodward scoffs at those who think they understand the blacks:

> "I've seen a few who claimed they understood niggers," Captain Woodward retorted, "and I always took notice that they were the first to

be kai-kai'd (eaten). Look at the missionaries in New Guinea and the New Hebrides—the martyr isle of Erromanga and all the rest. Look at the Austrian expedition that was cut to pieces in the Solomons, in the bush of GUADALCANAL. And look at the traders themselves, with a score of years' experience, making their brag that no nigger would ever get them, and whose heads to this day are ornamenting the rafters of the canoe houses. (*Stories,* 1,557–1,558)

He then relates a harrowing tale of being attacked by islanders at Malu on MALAITA; he is saved by a man called John Saxtorph, monumentally stupid and inept as a sailor, according to Woodward, but a crack shot. When the ship under his command is overrun by islanders, Saxtorph shoots all of them without one miss from his perch in the rigging. At the end of the story the point is made again that the white man wins by a stupidity that makes him "inevitable."

COMMENTARY

This story seems on the surface to be totally racist, complete with the word "nigger," but this has to be qualified. The practice of labor recruiting was exploitive and managed by brutally stupid and criminal men, to be sure, but for the most part it was voluntary, as it was in Captain Woodward's practice. Thus the attack on Malaita was not provoked by recruiting; the Malaitans were after ammunition and heads. By 21st-century standards, no matter how fierce or cannibalistic, a culture would not be described as merely barbaric, but in London's day readers were less sensitized to race and these particular tribes were bloodthirsty and constantly at war with each other as well as with the white intruders. Finally, the story states that the white race wins by stupidity, and win or not, stupidity was not something London admired. The tone is ambiguous, especially as the narrator reserves comment.

CHARACTERS

narrator   Unnamed in the story, he discusses the "farming of the world" by Euro-Americans and why they are able to do so with Charley Roberts and Captain Woodward. He hears Woodward's story of

an attack by islanders on Malaita that nearly killed him and of the whites' vengeance.

Captain Woodward   "The black will never understand the white, nor the white the black, as long as black is black and white is white." With these words Captain Woodward opens the story. The narrator describes him as "short and squat, elderly, burned by forty years of tropic sun, and with the most beautiful liquid brown eyes I ever saw in a man." He speaks "from a vast experience," made plain by the "crisscross of scars on his bald pate bespoke a tomahawk intimacy with the black, and of equal intimacy was the advertisement, front and rear, on the right side of his neck, where an arrow had at one time entered and been pulled clean through" (*Stories,* 1,557).

Charley Roberts   Bartender at Apia who listens with the narrator to Captain Woodward's story. He mixes drinks called "Abu Hameds" and trades opinions about blacks and whites with the other men.

John Saxtorph   A small, sandy-haired, undistinguished man whom Captain Woodward takes aboard as a sailor; as he describes him, "'He was certainly the most stupid man I ever saw, but he was as inevitable as death. There was only one thing that chap could do, and that was shoot'" (*Stories,* 1,559). Though he is useless as a sailor, Saxtorph's sharpshooting saves Captain Woodward from a violent attack by islanders at Malu on Malaita.

FURTHER READING

Moreland, David A. "Violence in the South Sea Fiction of Jack London." In *Jack London Newsletter* 16 (January–April 1983): 1–35.

Woodruff, Charles E. *The Effects of Tropical Light on White Men.* New York: Rebman Co., 1905.

"In the Forests of the North" (1902)

First appearing in *Pearson's Magazine* 14 (September 1902), this fanciful tale of a man who tries to "go native" by living among NATIVES, has the feel of an Edgar Rice Burroughs's jungle yarn.

SYNOPSIS

A man named Avery Van Brunt journeys into the NORTHLAND to rescue a friend, John Fairfax, whom he believes is lost in the wilderness. He discovers him living with Natives and married to a Native woman. When he is "found," Fairfax does not wish to return to civilization. As he explains:

> "At least they're honest folk and live according to their lights. And then they are amazingly simple. No complexity about them, no thousand and one subtle ramifications to every single emotion they experience. They love, fear, hate, are angered, or made happy, in common, ordinary, and unmistakable terms. . . . If a woman likes you, she'll not be backward in telling you so. If she hates you, she'll tell you so, and then, if you feel inclined, you can beat her, but the thing is, she knows precisely what you mean, and you know precisely what she means. No mistakes, no misunderstandings. It has its charm, after civilization's fitful fever. Comprehend?"
>
> "No, it's a pretty good life," he continued, after a pause; "good enough for me, and I intend to stay with it." (*Stories*, 659)

But Van Brunt sees it only as "beastly" and urges his friend to reconsider, especially to rejoin his white fiancé back in the States. But in trying to escape, the entire party of whites and Fairfax's wife are killed by the outraged Native village—because he is abandoning her.

COMMENTARY

Like most of the other stories of *Children of the Frost*, this tale both valorizes and condescends to the Natives. Though the Natives succeed in getting revenge on the whites, the fact that they kill one of their own—Fairfax's wife—points toward a general theme in the KLONDIKE stories of white predations on them and the particular hardships borne by their women who marry white men. As Fairfax explains to his wife, who calls out to him, "'My man! My man! My man!,'" with "the ruthless ten-

derness of the Eternal Woman, the Mate-Woman, looking out at him from her eyes,"

> "Thom," he said gravely, in English, "you were born in the Northland forest, and you have eaten fish and meat, and fought with frost and famine, and lived simply all the days of your life. And there are many things, indeed not simple, which you do not know and cannot come to understand. You do not know what it is to long for the flesh-pots afar, you cannot understand what it is to yearn for a fair woman's face. And the woman is fair, Thom, the woman is nobly fair. You have been woman to this man, and you have been your all, but your all is very little, very simple. Too little and too simple, and he is an alien man. Him you have never known, you can never know. It is so ordained. You held him in your arms, but you never held his heart." (*Stories*, 662–663)

CHARACTERS

Avery Van Brunt Avery Van Brunt, "or, in full distinction, Professor A. Van Brunt of the Geological Survey," is second in command of an expedition up the Thelon River. He comes upon an unrecorded village, where he stops with his party of "eight men, two of them French-Canadian voyageurs, and the remainder strapping Crees from Manitoba-way. He, alone, was fullblooded Saxon, and his blood was pounding fiercely through his veins to the traditions of his race" (*Stories*, 656). Van Brunt finds there his friend, John Fairfax.

John Fairfax Fairfax has spent five years in a lonely village in the "Barrens" near the Arctic Circle and has taken an ESKIMO wife. As he explains to Van Brunt, "'I came in from Edmonton after muskox, and like Pike and the rest of them, had my mischances, only I lost my party and outfit. Starvation, hardship, the regular tale, you know, sole survivor and all that, till I crawled into Tantlatch's, here, on hand and knee'" (*Stories*, 658). Fairfax decides to return to the States, but he is prevented and killed by the Natives who have taken him in.

Thom Fairfax's Native wife, she is killed in the melee that breaks out when Fairfax and Van Brunt try to escape. As she listens to Van Brunt try to persuade Fairfax to leave, she crouches by her husband's side, "motionless as a bronze statue, only her eyes flashing from face to face in ceaseless search. And Avery Van Brunt, as he talked on and on, felt a nervousness under the dumb gaze. . . . [H]e would become suddenly conscious of the black eyes burning into him, and would stumble and flounder till he could catch the gait and go again" (*Stories,* 661).

Tantlatch   Chief of the village, he is the father of Thom and an old man, weary with the struggle of survival. However, he is able to summon his warriors and defend the honor of his daughter by trying to force Fairfax to stay.

Chugungatte   Tantlach's shaman, like him a weary old man who does not wish to be stirred to battle, but who also wishes to defend the honor of the tribe.

Keen   He is present when Tantlatch receives Fairfax in his igloo. He is "a young man and chief favorite in the tribe. . . . quick and alert of movement, and his black eyes flashed from face to face in ceaseless scrutiny and challenge" (*Stories,* 664). Once betrothed to Thom, Keen argues to let the white men leave. Keen kills Fairfax and Thom with one arrow, as Thom throws herself upon her husband to try to save him.

The Iron Heel (1908)

Joseph Blotner calls *The Iron Heel* "the first apocalyptic novel of the century" (*Modern American Political Novel,* 150–151). It purports to be a copy of the "Everhard manuscript," written and then hidden by Avis Everhard, widow of Ernest Everhard, leader of the failed "Second Revolt" against the oligarchy he calls "the Iron Heel," and edited seven centuries later by a historian, Anthony Meredith, in the year 2600 or 419 B.O.M. (Brotherhood of Man), when a socialist world government has at last been established. Meredith supplies an introduction and series of (often lengthy) footnotes written from the perspective of a scholar. Avis's document covers a 20-year period from 1912 to 1932 when the capitalist oligarchy destroys all opposition and cements its terrible power.

SYNOPSIS

Chapters 1–12
Meredith's foreword and notes criticize Avis's historical shortsightedness and overly heroic portrait of her husband, but he praises its REALISM and psychological insights as it portrays the years of revolution and oppression from 1912 to 1932. He explains that it was found hidden after seven centuries.

Avis first writes of her privileged childhood as the daughter of a university scientist, John Cunningham; relates her marriage to the socialist revolutionary Ernest Everhard; describes the fall of democracy in the United States and the world; and tells of her years in the underground resistance from the First Revolt through the years leading to the Second Revolt.

She first meets Ernest Everhard at a dinner party hosted by her father. This "working-class philosopher" (6), as she calls him, does not impress her, due to his silence and ill-fitting suit, but his magnificent physique and bold stare intrigue her. He has been invited as a representative of his class, and when asked to speak to the clergy and other guests assembled, he bluntly begins, "'You know nothing, and worse than nothing, about the WORKING CLASS. Your sociology is as vicious and worthless as is your method of thinking.'" Avis is startled by him: "It was not so much what he said as how he said it. I roused at the first sound of his voice. It was as bold as his eyes. It was a clarion-call that thrilled me. And the whole table was aroused, shaken alive from monotony and drowsiness" (7–8). Ernest proceeds to argue the merits of science over metaphysics, SOCIALISM over CAPITALISM:

Battle royal raged, and the ministers grew red-faced and excited, especially at the moments when Ernest called them romantic philosophers, shadow-projectors, and similar things. And always he checked them back to facts. 'The fact, man, the irrefragable fact!' he would proclaim triumphantly, when he had brought one of them a cropper. He bristled with facts. He tripped them up with facts, ambuscaded them with facts, bombarded them with broadsides of facts. (15)

Quoting HERBERT SPENCER and DAVID STARR JORDAN, Ernest offers his test of truth formulated by Jordan: "'Will it work? Will you trust your life to it?'" (17). He concludes:

> "It is the capitalist class that pays you, that feeds you, that puts the very clothes on your backs that you are wearing to-night. And in return you preach to your employers the brands of metaphysics that are especially acceptable to them; and the especially acceptable brands are acceptable because they do not menace the established order of society." (19–20)

As to their role in the affairs of the working class, Ernest tells them, "'do not come down to the working class and serve as false leaders. You cannot honestly be in the two camps at once'" (21). Thus, chapter 1 sets up the relationship that will grow between Ernest and Avis but also lays out the broad philosophical conflicts in the world of the novel. It introduces Ernest as a powerful foe of capitalism and an articulate spokesman for his class.

Avis's father continues his new interest in philosophy and economics and hosts these dinners to debate ideas. Avis finds herself quickly falling in love with Ernest, whom she sees as intellectually "swashbuckling" (26), and she reads his books. However, when he comes for tea with Bishop Morehouse, she is angered by his arguments against the BOURGEOISIE. He does persuade Bishop Morehouse to rethink the church's complacency in the face of CHILD LABOR and other ills. When the Bishop says that men ought to coexist peacefully, Ernest replies that he is more interested in what men naturally are, which is selfish; thus, class conflict is inevitable. Noting a one-armed peddler named Jackson passing by, Ernest points out to Avis that he lost an arm in her father's factory, Sierra Mills. He was discharged, and the company successfully blocked his compensation. Bishop Morehouse is convinced by Ernest's arguments to protest labor injustice, but Ernest warns him that

he will be fired for doing so. Avis vows to investigate "Jackson's arm."

Avis talks to Jackson himself, foremen, the factory superintendent, and Jackson's lawyer. What she finds proves Ernest's thesis: The company, in order to reap larger dividends for its stockholders, suppressed the injury claims and has cowed all witnesses into submission. She confesses to Ernest that she is ashamed of her class and its practices. Avis begins to think of him as a Christ figure of redemption for the "lowly and oppressed" (61), as she also notes the powerful effect he has had upon not only her, but her father and Bishop Morehouse, who now is exhausted and thoroughly disheartened by Ernest's taking him through "hell" to show him the lives of the poor. Avis meets Colonel Ingram at a church reception, the Sierra Mills lawyer who defeated Jackson's suit, and he bolts after he hears her mention Jackson's name. Avis writes a story for the newspapers, but they refuse to print it. She interviews the two main stockholders in her father's company and their wives and their smug sense of privilege converts her to Ernest's point of view.

Ernest speaks to the Philomath Club, a private organization of the wealthy that likes to present the latest discoveries in science and learning. Two hundred industrialists hear Ernest speak of his life among the working class and his yearning to escape, as well as his notion that paradise lay with the people of the upper classes. However, he explains, he learned from the keen intellects of socialists he met and from the example of those broken by the capitalist establishment that there was a struggle to overthrow an "irrational society" (78). He warns them: "'We are going to take your governments, your palaces, and all your purpled ease away from you, and in that day you shall work for your bread even as the peasant in the field or the starved and runty clerk in your metropolises. Here are our hands. They are strong hands!'" (83). As a "throaty rumble" of anger fills the room, Ernest continues: "'You have failed in your management. You have made a shambles of civilization.'" The revolution will happen, concludes Ernest: "'Stop it if you can'" (86–87). Colonel Van Gilbert, who is presiding, springs to his feet and denounces Ernest: "The confusion and babel was indescribable. Never had Mrs. Pertonwaithe's spacious walls beheld such a spectacle. These, then, were the cool captains of industry and lords of society, these snarling, growling savages in evening clothes" (89). Mr. Wickson coolly responds to Ernest,

"We have no words to waste on you. When you reach out your vaunted strong hands for our palaces and purpled ease, we will show you what strength is. In roar of shell and shrapnel and in whine of machine-guns will our answer be couched. We will grind you revolutionists down under our heel, and we shall walk upon your faces. The world is ours, we are its lords, and ours it shall remain. As for the host of labor, it has been in the dirt since history began, and I read history aright. And in the dirt it shall remain so long as I and mine and those that come after us have the power" (96).

Ernest starts to believe that there is much behind Wickson's words, a conspiracy against labor. He learns that Cunningham has been reprimanded for association with socialists by his university president. When Bishop Morehouse makes a public address urging the wealthy to share with the poor and explains how he is picking up prostitutes and taking them to shelter in his home, he is thought to be insane and is led from the stage by two other speakers. At a dinner at Cunningham's, Ernest lectures a group of small to mid-size business owners on their naïveté: they protest the trusts but believe in getting large profits for themselves. Ernest explains the fundamental flaws of capitalism (using KARL MARX's doctrine of surplus value) and argues for the evolutionary necessity of socialism. Yet, he also foresees the possibility that the plutocracy or oligarchy, which he calls "the Iron Heel," will rise up and take over the nation and the world.

The summer of 1912 brings strikebreaking, the suppression of the *Appeal to Reason* and other socialist newspapers, a Wall Street crash, and Cunningham's being fired from the university and finding that his book is suppressed. At the same time, the Iron Heel works to destroy the middle class.

There are payoffs of labor leaders, foreclosures of farms, mysterious disappearances, assassinations, beatings, and riots, led by the Iron Heel's Mercenaries. Ernest prepares to run for Congress, but he realizes the violence is not going to stop. Cunningham is warned by Wickson to desist from pursuing socialist ideas; when he refuses, he finds that his company stock has disappeared and his house is foreclosed upon by a mortgage that he did not have. The marriage of Ernest and Avis is further saddened by the reappearance of Bishop Morehouse, who has sold all he has and busies himself hiding out from the authorities and feeding the poor. But even his meager existence at the fringes of society is ended when he is recommitted to the insane asylum. As Ernest observes, "'Christ told the rich young man to sell all he had,' Ernest said bitterly. 'The Bishop obeyed Christ's injunction and got locked up in a madhouse. Times have changed since Christ's day. A rich man to-day who gives all he has to the poor is crazy. There is no discussion. Society has spoken'" (203).

Chapters 13–25

Ernest is elected to Congress, but the Iron Heel grows in power, its organization based in monopoly trusts that bankrupt smaller businesses and reduce farmers to serfdom. Democratic concerns such as William Randolph Hearst's newspaper syndicate collapse. The oligarchy maintains power through its Mercenaries and preferred labor class in essential industries like steel and rail, privileged by receiving decent wages, housing, and education. The revolutionaries stage a general strike: "The United States was paralyzed. No one knew what was happening. There were no newspapers, no letters, no despatches. Every community was as completely isolated as though ten thousand miles of primeval wilderness stretched between it and the rest of the world" (212). But the Iron Heel begins to treat revolutionaries and average workers with greater brutality. Though there is the socialist electoral breakthrough when 50 socialist Congressmen are elected and join with the Grange Party (of farmers), when they attempt to take their seats, they are nearly all prevented from doing so. The Iron Heel arranges to have a man named Pervaise blow up a bomb when Ernest introduces a bill, and they manage to cast the blame on the socialists.

On the international scene, the United States prepares to go to war with GERMANY, which Ernest believes is a result of lobbying by war profiteers. In response, socialists in both countries launch a general strike leading to peace and an alliance between Germany and the United States. JAPAN conquers East Asia and creates its own empire, while India gains independence. Canada, Mexico, and Cuba form their own oligarchies aligned with the United States. Germany, Italy, FRANCE, Australia, and New Zealand overthrow their governments and form cooperative commonwealths under socialist governments following the end of the war between Germany and the United States. Yet these positive changes do not withstand the Iron Heel.

Soon the Iron Heel begins confiscating farmland from indebted farmers, and their secret agents start a riot in Sacramento designed to show their strength in suppressing it with their private soldiers, who kill 11,000 residents. The Militia Law is put into effect; Kowalt and Asmunsen are courtmartialed and executed for refusing to serve. Agents of the Iron Heel murder the officers of the Kansas militia. Next, the strike of three-quarters of a million coal miners is crushed. The ruler Alfred Pocock I initiates slavery using striking workers. An internal passport system is introduced on the urging of Pocock to track and restrict the free movement of citizens across the United States.

Ernest helps form labor "fighting groups" to combat the Iron Heel. But revolutionary leaders are caught and convicted and sent to jails throughout the United States; Ernest is sent to Alcatraz. Avis is released from prison and returns to San Francisco. She hides in the GLEN ELLEN Refuge, one of many hideouts for the revolutionaries. She creates a new identity as "Mary Holmes" and infiltrates the ranks of the Iron Heel. Despite this victory, she learns that her father has disappeared. Ernest is released from jail by revolutionaries, and he and Avis both are spies inside the Iron Heel.

The Chicago Commune is formed, but a riot instigated by the Iron Heel results in the deaths of hundreds of thousands of Mercenaries and rebels including Bishop Morehouse. Chapter 23, called "The People of the Abyss" after London's 1903 sociological study of the poor of LONDON, ENGLAND, is a dramatic set piece showing the gruesome details of the battle and its defeat. Avis describes the riot as

> a fascinating spectacle of dread. It surged past my vision in concrete waves of wrath, snarling and growling, carnivorous, drunk with whiskey from pillaged warehouses, drunk with hatred, drunk with lust for blood—men, women, and children, in rags and tatters, dim ferocious intelligences with all the godlike blotted from their features and all the fiendlike stamped in, apes and tigers, anaemic consumptives and great hairy beasts of burden, wan faces from which vampire society had sucked the juice of life, bloated forms swollen with physical grossness and corruption, withered hags and death's-heads bearded like patriarchs, festering youth and festering age, faces of fiends, crooked, twisted, misshapen monsters blasted with the ravages of disease and all the horrors of chronic innutrition—the refuse and the scum of life, a raging, screaming, screeching, demoniacal horde. (326–327)

She can understand their fury, however: "The people of the abyss had nothing to lose but the misery and pain of living. And to gain?—nothing, save one final, awful glut of vengeance. And as I looked the thought came to me that in that rushing stream of human lava were men, comrades and heroes, whose mission had been to rouse the abysmal beast and to keep the enemy occupied in coping with it." Avis realizes that she has lost the fear of death and feels exalted by the Cause: ". . . the Cause would be here to-morrow, the same Cause, ever fresh and ever burning" (327). However, the Chicago ghetto is destroyed and repopulated with workers from other cities. In the spring of 1918, the First Revolt is planned but it is quickly put down by the Iron Heel. Avis attends a meeting of the 'Frisco Reds. Ernest and Avis witness the revolutionary tribunals that convict enemies and traitors to the movement.

By 1932, the Iron Heel, having destroyed nearly all opposition, begins the construction of its wonder city of Asgard. Ernest is soon thereafter executed. Avis again flees to WAKE ROBIN LODGE in CALIFORNIA and writes the Everhard Manuscript, hiding it in an oak tree before being captured by the Mercenaries and presumably executed. The Second Revolt does take place but ultimately fails. From here on, the manuscript itself ceases, and only isolated events separated by decades or centuries are provided by Meredith's footnotes. As he explains, between the years 2180 and 2200 the Iron Heel is finally overthrown. The Socialist Brotherhood of Man is established.

COMMENTARY

Motivated by his commitment to socialism, his experiences in the slums of the East End of LONDON in 1902 (described in *The People of the Abyss* [1903]), the SAN FRANCISCO EARTHQUAKE of 1906, and his reading of W. H. Ghent's *Our Benevolent Feudalism* (1902), which described a coming modern state ruled by feudal overlords, even his home at Wake Robin Lodge in GLEN ELLEN (where Avis hides out and deposits her manuscript), London also poured into *The Iron Heel* all his best socialist speeches and essays, with the result that the book is overloaded with Ernest's words, powerful though they are. As president of the INTERCOLLEGIATE SOCIALIST SOCIETY, London had spent much of the year prior to this novel's composition touring the country and lecturing. At Yale on January 26, 1906, he told the audience, "We will be content with nothing less than all power, with the possession of the whole world. We Socialists will wrest power from the present rulers. By war, if necessary. Stop us if you can" (quoted in Carolyn Johnston, xiii). This is what Everhard tells the upper-class Philomath Club.

The events London describes before 1906 are all based in fact. He covers the railroad trusts, the Militia Act, CHILD LABOR, strikebreaking, false tribunals, private police forces, THEODORE ROOSEVELT's presidency, European wars opposed by socialists, Herbert Spencer and David Starr Jordan, powerful industry figures Hearst and John D. Rockefeller, and important socialist figures including Austin Lewis and E. Untermann. Yet despite its topicality and its futuristic vision, it was a failure as a book: sales were poor, reviews bad, and social-

ists rejected it. Despite its weaknesses, it remains one of the most important DYSTOPIAN novels of the century, comparable in many respects to the works of GEORGE ORWELL and Aldous Huxley, who were influenced by it.

The main problems with the novel lie in its characterizations. Ernest is a somewhat embarrassing fantasy figure of Jack London, and he never ceases in haranguing his various audiences with his ideological pieties. He feels superiority to the average worker, betraying a sense of London's radical INDIVIDUALISM, there despite his socialism. Ernest is just too much larger than life: his body splendid, his logic irrefutable, his words heroic. At the same time Avis's sentimental hero-worship of her husband becomes cloying:

> Once, the feeling strong upon me that my little world and all the world was turning over, I thought of Ernest as the cause of it; and also I thought, "We were so happy and peaceful before he came!" And the next moment I was aware that the thought was a treason against truth, and Ernest rose before me transfigured, the apostle of truth, with shining brows and the fearlessness of one of God's own angels, battling for the truth and the right, and battling for the succor of the poor and lonely and oppressed. And then there arose before me another figure, the Christ! He, too, had taken the part of the lowly and oppressed, and against all the established power of priest and pharisee. And I remembered his end upon the cross, and my heart contracted with a pang as I thought of Ernest. Was he, too, destined for a cross?—he, with his clarion call and war-noted voice, and all the fine man's vigor of him! (60–61)

Yet the book was commended by EUGENE V. DEBS, Leon Trotsky, and Anatole France. Philip Foner calls it "probably the most amazingly prophetic work of the twentieth century" (97), while Maxwell Geismar finds it "a key work—perhaps a classic work—of American radicalism" (163).

In *The Iron Heel*, London foresaw the rise of socialism and fascism and modern European and Asian wars, but it is mainly an attack on American capitalism. True that he underestimated the power of the rising U.S. middle class and was wrong that the trusts would never be broken, and he did not foresee the New Deal of the 1930s. Yet through the writings of Avis and Meredith, and in Ernest's many speeches, he demonstrated his belief in historical MATERIALISM as taught by Marxism, which predicted an inevitable battle between capital and labor, on the long road from the feudalism of the past to the socialism of the future. The SOCIALIST LABOR PARTY never caught on in the United States, and London feared that if it did it would be destroyed by the establishment. Though this never occurred, the novel reflects the violent means capitalists and industrialists used against striking workers and labor organizers in his day.

The novel's competing themes—it is at once an adventure story, a political dystopia, a biography of Ernest, an autobiography of Avis, and the object of study by the future Anthony Meredith—both weaken and enrich it. Its narrative device of using the words of Avis to convey those of Ernest, framed by the future perspective of the scholar Meredith is confusing at times but deepens the tragic plight of Avis and her revolutionary comrades.

London interweaves socialist sources with more traditional ones, including primarily the BIBLE but also OSCAR WILDE and other poets. He draws the name Asgard for the Iron Heel's city from the home of fallen heroes in Norse MYTHOLOGY, imparting a significant racist cast to the oligarchy, while Ardis, the Brotherhood of Man city in which Meredith lives, is drawn from Celtic tradition; it is a variant of "Arden," the magical and beautiful forest of Shakespeare's *As You Like It*.

But the primary image pattern in the novel is that of blood, which is first introduced by Ernest in chapter 2:

> "With the introduction of machinery and the factory system in the latter part of the eighteenth century, the great mass of the working people was separated from the land. The old system of labor was broken down. The working people were driven from their villages and herded in factory towns. The mothers and children were put to work at the new machines.

Family life ceased. The conditions were frightful. It is a tale of blood" (34).

In another description, Ernest speaks of "'Children, six and seven years of age, working every night at twelve-hour shifts? They never see the blessed sunshine. They die like flies. The dividends are paid out of their blood'" (36–37). Finally, he tells Avis that because of her father's labor practices "'the gown you wear is stained with blood. The food you eat is a bloody stew. The blood of little children and of strong men is dripping from your very roof-beams. I can close my eyes, now, and hear it drip, drop, drip, drop, all about me'" (39). In chapter 4 and throughout the book, the imagery is continued:

> It seemed monstrous, impossible, that our whole society was based upon blood. And yet there was Jackson. I could not get away from him. Constantly my thought swung back to him as the compass to the Pole. He had been monstrously treated. His blood had not been paid for in order that a larger dividend might be paid. And I knew a score of happy complacent families that had received those dividends and by that much had profited by Jackson's blood. If one man could be so monstrously treated and society move on its way unheeding, might not many men be so monstrously treated? I remembered Ernest's women of Chicago who toiled for ninety cents a week, and the child slaves of the Southern cotton mills he had described. And I could see their wan white hands, from which the blood had been pressed, at work upon the cloth out of which had been made my gown. And then I thought of the Sierra Mills and the dividends that had been paid, and I saw the blood of Jackson upon my gown as well. Jackson I could not escape. Always my meditations led me back to him. (59–60)

In conclusion, one theme of *The Iron Heel* that generally goes without remarking is the importance of education. For nearly every character, educational level is mentioned, with the idea that the better the education—and London mainly means science and economics—the better the man or woman. James Smith, though a factory foreman, has a sympathetic view of Jackson because he finished high school; Ernest's lifework is based on his education in history and science. Avis becomes educated by him, as do her father and Bishop Morehouse. From Meredith comes the framing idea that ultimately reason will prevail. But despite Meredith's happy life, the future doesn't answer the question of human nature Ernest poses when he says that men are all selfish. What could possibly have changed this? Centuries of war? Government reform? Broader education? *The Iron Heel* would suggest not: It was bloody revolution that finally prevailed.

CHARACTERS

Anthony Meredith A historian of the future world of the Brotherhood of Man, a socialist world in which history is analyzed through the lens of socialism and revolution, which has brought about universal peace. He writes from a city called Ardis in the year 2600, or 419 B.O.M. His foreword and extensive notes interestingly contrast his "larger" view of the eventual triumph of world socialism with the bloody efforts of Ernest Everhard and his comrades in the revolts against the capitalist oligarchy in the first third of the 20th century. His dry and often condescending comments provide an alternate frame by which to view the apocalyptic events of the "Everhard manuscript," and to some extent London satirizes his detachment.

Avis Everhard Author of the "Everhard manuscript," she was raised in the bourgeois class as the daughter of a noted professor at the University of California. Though she at first resists Ernest Everhard's ideas, she falls passionately in love with both him and his principles, and she becomes his wife. She works side by side with her husband and other revolutionaries to bring about the "Second Revolt," which she believes, wrongly, will succeed. She records her story and hides the manuscript under a tree at Wake Robin Lodge in Glen Ellen, California. She is presumably executed by the oligarchy.

Ernest Everhard Formerly a hostler, Everhard is described as a "natural aristocrat" by Avis when she first meets him, but it is less his class (which is beneath hers) than his physical appearance that draws her interest:

> In the first place, his clothes did not fit him. He wore a ready-made suit of dark cloth that was ill adjusted to his body. In fact, no ready-made suit of clothes ever could fit his body. And on this night, as always, the cloth bulged with his muscles, while the coat between the shoulders, what of the heavy shoulder-development, was a maze of wrinkles. His neck was the neck of a prize-fighter, thick and strong. So this was the social philosopher and ex-horseshoer my father had discovered, was my thought. And he certainly looked it with those bulging muscles and that bull-throat. Immediately I classified him—a sort of prodigy, I thought, a Blind Tom of the working class. (4–5)

Early in the novel, when Avis meets him, Ernest is presented as a young working-class genius who is a leader in the local socialist organizations, a soapbox orator, and a student at the university studying biology. He is also writing a book called *Philosophy and Revolution*. He becomes Avis's husband—her "eagle"—and the leader of the failed Second Revolt. He is executed by the oligarchy.

John Cunningham Avis's father and a physicist at the University of California. He seems to enjoy watching Ernest use science to upset the metaphysics of the clergyman at his dinner table. He later becomes more closely attached to socialism and pays with his job, home, and probably his life, as he disappears late in the novel.

Bishop Morehouse Avis describes him as "a favorite of mine, a sweet and serious man of middle age, Christ-like in appearance and goodness, and a scholar as well" (5). The Bishop is impressed with Ernest: "'A strong young man,' he said; 'and very much alive, very much alive. But he is too sure, too sure'" (26). Bishop Morehouse speaks out against the wealthy who do not help the poor; for this he is hounded out of the church and institutionalized. He dies in the Chicago Commune riot.

Dr. Hammerfield   The first dinner guest in the novel's opening scene to be challenged by Ernest, who questions his notion of sincerity. Ernest argues against his metaphysics and infuriates him with his logic. Later Hammerfield declines to meet Ernest again and calls him "'an insolent young puppy, made bumptious by a little and very inadequate learning'" (26). When the Iron Heel takes over Hammerfield is amply rewarded for his support, along with his friend Dr. Ballingford.

Jackson   In trying to save a valuable machine from being destroyed, Jackson reaches into its whirling cogs to retrieve a piece of flint and his arm is chewed off. He sues the company, Sierra Mills, but loses because no one will testify for him. When Avis meets him she describes him as "the meek and lowly man he had been described. . . . I fancied I caught the first note of a nascent bitterness in him when he said: 'They might a-given me a job as watchman, anyway'" (43).

Joseph Hurd   A "weak and inefficient-looking man, the lawyer" (46), Avis notes of the man who defended Jackson. He "whines" that he had no choice; he had to allow the Mills to win because he has a wife and children and also complains that against the company he had no chance. He begs Avis for his life much later when he is captured by the revolutionaries.

Peter Donnelly   Donnelly is one of the foremen who testified at Jackson's trial. When Avis meets him and asks him why he lied, he responds, "'Because I've a good wife an' three of the sweetest children ye ever laid eyes on, that's why.'" When she presses him, he confesses, "'In other words, because it wouldn't a-ben healthy'" (49–50). Avis later meets him again when he joins the 'Frisco Reds. She and Ernest hide out near his ranch. His son joins the Mercenaries.

Timothy Donnelly   A member of the Mercenaries, he commands them to murder 800 striking weavers. He is captured by Anna Roylston and handed over to the 'Frisco Reds.

Henry Dallas   Henry Dallas is the Mills superintendent whom Avis describes as "a vulpine-faced creature who regarded me insolently and refused to talk. Not a word could I get from him concerning the trial and his testimony" (51). He is killed by Peter Donnelly during the revolution.

James Smith   Avis meets this foreman at Sierra Mills who is quite direct about his view of Jackson's arm case: he is "a hard-faced man, . . . mentally superior to the average of his kind. He agreed with Peter Donnelly that Jackson should have got damages, and he went farther and called the action heartless and cold-blooded that had turned the worker adrift after he had been made helpless by the accident. Also, he explained that there were many accidents in the mills, and that the company's policy was to fight to the bitter end all consequent damage suits" (51).

Colonel Ingram   The powerful corporate lawyer who defends Sierra Mills against Jackson's claim of compensation for his injury.

Percy Layton   "He was a graduate of the university, had gone in for journalism, and was then serving his apprenticeship as reporter on the most influential of the three newspapers. He smiled when I asked him the reason the newspapers suppressed all mention of Jackson or his case. 'Editorial policy,' he said. 'We have nothing to do with that. It's up to the editors'" (64). Layton is another tool for the capitalists against labor.

Mr. Philip Wickson and Mr. Pertonwaithe   Avis interviews these "two men who held most of the stock in the Sierra Mills. But I could not shake them as I had shaken the mechanics in their employ. I discovered that they had an ethic superior to that of the rest of society. It was what I may call the aristocratic ethic or the master ethic. They talked in large ways of policy, and they identified policy and right. And to me they talked in fatherly ways, patronizing my youth and inexperience. They were the most hopeless of all I had encountered in my quest. They believed absolutely that their conduct was right" (66). Mr. Wickson addresses Ernest at the Philomath's meeting to warn him of the power of the capitalist establishment. His son, also called Phillip Wickson, also acts as an agent within the Iron Heel.

Mrs. Wickson and Mrs. Pertonwaithe Wives of the largest stockholders in Avis's father's mills, "They were society women. Their homes were palaces. They had many homes scattered over the country, in the mountains, on lakes, and by the sea. They were tended by armies of servants, and their social activities were bewildering. They patronized the university and the churches, and the pastors especially bowed at their knees in meek subservience." These women, Avis realizes, "were powers. . . . They aped their husbands, and talked in the same large ways about policy, and the duties and responsibilities of the rich. They were swayed by the same ethic that dominated their husbands—the ethic of their class; and they uttered glib phrases that their own ears did not understand" (66).

Miss Brentwood Wealthy philanthropist who finances the Philomath Club and brings in Ernest Everhard as a speaker because she believes him to be the usual sort of reformer.

Colonel Van Gilbert Presides at the meeting of the Philomath Club, he is a "great corporation lawyer" and "immensely wealthy," taking for his smallest fee $100,000: "He as a master of law. The law was a puppet with which he played. He moulded it like clay, twisted and distorted it like a Chinese puzzle into any design he chose" (76). He introduces Ernest to the Club in a derogatory manner.

Bishop Dickinson Present on the stage the night Bishop Morehouse makes his entreaty for the rich to help the poor, following Christ's model, he angrily stalks offstage when he hears his fellow bishop's "insanity."

H. H. Jones Head of the ethical department at the University of California, he also objects to Bishop Morehouse's speech.

Mrs. W. W. Hurd A great charity organizer who is present on stage at the conference when Bishop Morehouse speaks.

Philip Ward A great philanthropist present at Bishop Morehouse's speech, he helps Jones get Morehouse off the stage.

Owen Proprietor of Silverberg, Owen & Company—a large grocery firm with several branch stores. Owen protests the trusts, but Ernest points out how his store put smaller ones out of business.

Kowalt and Washburn Partners of the big drug firm of Kowalt & Washburn. They too protest the trusts. They are executed for refusing to serve in the militia.

Asmunsen Owner of a large granite quarry in Contra Costa County.

Calvin Formerly the owner of a profitable dairy business, forced out by the railroad's unfair tariffs.

Simpson A revolutionary comrade of Ernest and Avis.

Hartman A member of the revolutionary party, Hartman witnesses the terrible riot in Chicago with Avis and Ernest.

Garthwaite He joins the revolutionaries and helps save Avis during the Chicago riot.

Anna Roylston An important leader of the revolutionaries, she earns the sobriquet "the Red Virgin."

O'Connor O'Connor, leader of the Association of Machinists, refuses to give Ernest assurances that they will agree to another general strike, leading to the beginning of the defection of the major unions.

Pervaise A prison inmate who agrees to a deal from the Iron Heel to throw a bomb in Congress during Ernest's introduction of his bill on unemployment relief in return for freedom. The act is blamed on the socialists, prompting soldiers to storm Congress and arrest all socialist congressmen. (Later, he is struck with heart disease and confesses to a priest on his deathbed of the truth behind the Congress bomb plot.)

Lora Peterson and Kate Bierce   Young revolutionaries whom Avis meets while she is hiding out awaiting Ernest's release from prison.

John Carlson   Revolutionary whom Avis meets while in hiding; he kills a spy within their organization: "'I fixed him,' was Carlson's unimaginative way of describing the affair. 'I fixed him,' he repeated, while a sombre light burnt in his eyes, and his huge, toil-distorted hands opened and closed eloquently. 'He made no noise. I hid him, and tonight I will go back and bury him deep'" (277).

FURTHER READING

Barley, Tony. "Prediction, Programme and Fantasy in Jack London's *The Iron Heel*." In *Anticipations: Essays on Early Science Fiction and Its Precursors.* Edited by David Seed. Syracuse, N.Y.: Syracuse University Press, 1995, 153–171.

Beauchamp, Gorman. "Jack London's Utopian Dystopia and Dystopian Utopia." In *America as Utopia.* Edited by Kenneth M. Roemer. New York: Franklin, 1981, 91–107.

Blotner, Joseph. *The Modern American Political Novel, 1900–1960.* Austin: University of Texas Press, 1966.

Foner, Philip S., ed. *Jack London: American Rebel—A Collection of His Social Writings Together with an Extensive Study of the Man and His Times.* New York: Citadel Press, 1947.

France, Anatole. Preface to *The Iron Heel.* In *Critical Essays on Jack London.* Edited and translated by Jacqueline Tavernier-Courbin. Boston: Prentice Hall, 1983, 35–37.

Geismar, Maxwell. *Rebels and Ancestors: The American Novel, 1890–1915.* Boston, Mass.: Houghton Mifflin, 1953.

Ghent, W. J. *Our Benevolent Feudalism.* New York: Macmillan, 1902.

Johnston, Carolyn. *Jack London—An American Radical?* Westport, Conn.: Greenwood, 1984.

Shor, Fran. "*The Iron Heel*'s Marginal(ized) Utopia." In *Extrapolation: A Journal of Science Fiction and Fantasy* 35, no. 3 (Fall 1994): 211–229.

———. "Power, Gender, and Ideological Discourse in *The Iron Heel.*" In *Rereading Jack London.* Edited by Leonard Cassuto and Jeanne Campbell Reesman. Stanford: Stanford University Press, 1996, 75–91.

Tambling, Victor R. S. "Jack London and George Orwell: A Literary Kinship." In *George Orwell.* Edited by Courtney T. Wemyss and Alexej Ugrinsky. Westport, Conn.: Greenwood Press, 1987, 171–175.

Ward, Susan. "Ideology for the Masses: Jack London's *The Iron Heel.*" In *Critical Essays on Jack London.* Edited by Jacqueline Tavernier-Courbin. Boston: Prentice Hall, 1983, 166–179.

Whalen-Bridge, John. "Dual Perspective in *The Iron Heel.*" In *Thalia: Studies in Literary Humor* 12, nos. 1–2 (1992): 67–76.

———. "How to Read a Revolutionary Novel: *The Iron Heel.*" In *Jack London Journal* 5 (1998): 38–63.

Jack Johnson fight coverage (1908–1910)

In the 1908 and 1910 world heavyweight boxing matches, which pitted JACK JOHNSON against first TOMMY BURNS in Sydney, Australia, and then JIM JEFFRIES in Reno, Nevada, London was a press correspondent and wrote detailed fight stories. Johnson easily beat his opponents and was the first black heavyweight champion. The fights were front-page news all over the world, especially because of the racial dimension; Jeffries was called the "Great White Hope," while Johnson was viewed by whites with great trepidation. London's exposure to Johnson influenced some of his short stories including "The Mexican" and "A Piece of Steak."

The Sydney, Australia, fight was Johnson's biggest break yet. Canadian fighter Burns had refused to fight a black man, but when the promoters offered him enough money, he agreed. Burns would get $30,000, win or lose (Johnson received $5,000 when he won). The fight took place on December 26, 1908, and the stadium was filled with a crowd of 5,000 spectators with 30,000 more outside. The *Australian Star* spoke of "race war" (quoted in Richard Broome, 74–75, 352–353).

With the odds 7–4 in favor of Burns, the fight was Johnson's from the outset. Johnson weighed 220 pounds and was 6′2″; he could run 100 yards in 11 seconds and high-jump nearly six feet. Burns was only 5′7″ and weighed 175 pounds, so he depended upon his "innate" racial abilities (Jakoubek, 45). This was a mistake. He was not prepared for a fighter in top condition who did not subscribe to myths of white superiority. Johnson teased him again and again, avoiding the knockout he could have had, further humiliating Burns. According to London, Johnson kept telling Burns where to try next, pointing to his stomach. By the second round, Burns's right eye and mouth were injured but the fight went on. Burns called Johnson a "cur" and a "big dog," growling "Come on and fight, nigger. Fight like a white man." But Burns's "mouth-fighting" only pleased Johnson, and he out-mouthed Burns as he outboxed him. London notes how Johnson made up an "English" accent against Burns's Canadian accent, so that "Tommy" sounded like "Tahmy": "Poor little Tahmy, who told you you were a fighter?", "Good boy, Tahmy," and "Poor, poor Tahmy. Who taught you to hit? Your mother? You a woman?" By the 13th round, spectators yelled for the fight to be stopped; in the 14th, Burns was struck with a hard right knock, and he collapsed after eight seconds. The fight was over (Roberts, 63–64). To calls of "Stop the fight!" London answers, "There was no fight. . . . A golden smile tells the story, and that golden smile was Johnson's (London in *Reports*, 260). But the rest of the press responded with stories about how "white beauty" had faced a black "primordial ape": "He was still beauty by contrast—beautiful but to be beaten; clean sunlight fighting darkness and losing" (quoted in Broome, 356). Burns was the hero; Johnson could not even be served in restaurants and hotels.

At the time of the 1908 fight, London happened to be in Australia, a place U.S. newspapers could usually not afford to send correspondents. London's stories were syndicated in hundreds of newspapers around the world (*see Letters*, 876). The headline to London's story the day after the fight in the *Australian Star* read: "The Great Glove Fight. Boxing Championship of the World. Johnson's Smile. Burns Hopelessly Out-Classed. Vivid Description. . . . Black Versus White. By Jack London, Author of 'The Call of the Wild' and other works." As the New York *Herald* ran the story on December 27, "Jack London Says Johnson Made Noise Like a Lullaby with His Fists as He Tucked Burns in His Little Crib in Sleepy Hollow, with a Laugh. Plucky, but Absolutely Helpless, the White Man Seemed to Be the Victim of a Playful Ethiopian Who Did Just as He Would. NEGRO'S GOLDEN SMILE A TAUNT FOR HIS OPPONENT ALL THE TIME. Smashed to the Floor in the First Round, the Canadian Fighter Was Going Uphill Ever After and Never Had the Ghost of a Chance for Victory. SHOULD HAVE ENDED IN THIRTEENTH ROUND." London wrote: "There is no use in minimizing Johnson's victory in order to soothe Burns's feelings. . . . Personally I was with Burns all the way. He is a white man, and so am I. Naturally, I wanted to see the white man win. Put the case to Johnson and ask him if he were the spectator at a fight between a white man and a black man which he would like to see win. Johnson's black skin will dictate a parallel to the one dictated by my white skin." But just because "a white man wishes a white man to win, this should not prevent him from giving absolute credit to the best man who did win, even when that man was black. All hail to Johnson. His victory was unqualified." Johnson displayed "bigness, coolness, quickness, cleverness, and vast physical superiority." Alas, says London, "Men are not born equal and neither are pugilists" (*Reports* 258–259). London concludes, "Jack Johnson, here's my hand too. I wanted to see the other fellow win, but you were the best man. Shake" (259–260).

In conclusion, London adds, "When he smiled a dazzling flash of gold filled the wide aperture between his open lips, and he smiled all the time. He had not a trouble in the world, . . . as inaccessible as Mont Blanc" (London in *Reports*, 262). He asks, "But one thing remains. Jeffries must emerge from his alfalfa farm and remove that smile from Johnson's face. 'Jeff, it's up to you.'" (London in *Reports*, 264). This closing line has been quoted as evidence of London's racism, but it is quoted out of context. London ironically compares Mont Blanc (Johnson) with an alfalfa field (Jeffries). His exit line is a jab at Jeffries.

In 1910 the winner was to get 75 percent of the $101,000 and the loser 25 percent. As was correctly predicted, violence followed the fight. Blacks were lynched, and mobs black and white ran riot. Later, the fight films were suppressed by a bill passed in Congress out of fears that there would be more mayhem. This match was the most wide-ranging public racial spectacle of the day—and its significance was not lost on London. For one thing, London was positioned by the press as a white icon. The St. Louis, Missouri, *Republic* claimed (June 12, 1910): London is "the most famous of living authors"; the model of the strenuous life, "no living man better understands the physical supermen of which Jeffries is the Caucasian perfect prototype." For the *Republic*, London was the pride of the ANGLO-SAXON race:

The creator of Wolf Larsen and Martin Eden has lived his life among men who have beaten down mountains, curbed torrents, felled forests, fought flames, conquered the frozen glaciers of Alaska, wrested wealth from the bowels of the earth and health from the oxygen of the vacant spaces of the world. He sold newspapers as a boy, tramped with tramps, sailed with sailors to the Arctic and Antarctic seas, lived among the modern cave men, the men who have torn solid granite out of the path of progress, and he knows the psychology, physiology, and physique of his muscle men. No living man is better fitted to tell the titanic tale of the tremendous contest between the mightiest men of muscle the white race has given to the prize ring and the avatar of the sons of Ham, who will try in his person to avenge, as far as one man in one fight may, the numberless humiliations which the supermen of the white race have put upon the Negro.

The *Republic* goes on (incorrectly) to claim that London had "often boxed with the great champion of the ring himself," had attended every fight in the last 15 years, and was said to be "a personal friend of James J. Jeffries." This sort of stuff explains why the Syracuse, New York, *Herald* would joke that "Nothing now can happen to the big fight—unless Jack London should suddenly be taken ill, necessitating its postponement" (June 30, 1910). And yet London, despite his reverence for Jeffries, not only took Johnson's side but ate and drank in his camp, praising his wit, singing, and hospitality. Jeffries brushed London off.

On July 4, the fight was on. London opens his story:

Once again has Johnson sent down to defeat the chosen representative of the white race, and this time the greatest of them all. And, as of old, it was play for Johnson. From the opening to the closing round he never ceased his witty sallies, his exchanges of repartee with his opponent's seconds and with the spectators. And, for that matter, Johnson had a funny thing to say to Jeffries in every round. The golden smile was as much in evidence as ever, and neither did it freeze on his face nor did it vanish. It came and went throughout the fight spontaneously, naturally. (London in *Reports,* 293)

Johnson confidently "played and fought a white man in a white man's country, before a white man's crowd," and he answered taunts with "Chesterfieldian grace" (London in *Reports*, 294). Here again is the focus upon Johnson's winning speech and "naturally" occurring smile, even before describing his boxing moves. When he does turn to the fighting, he sees that Jeffries had no chance. Johnson entered the ring at 2:30 P.M.,

airy, happy, and smiling, greeting friends and acquaintances here, there, and everywhere in the audience, cool as ice . . . with never a signal flown of hesitancy nor timidity. Yet he was keyed up, keenly observant of all that was going on, even hearing much of the confused babble of tongues about him—hearing, ay, and understanding too. There is nothing heavy or primitive about this man Johnson. He is alive and quivering, every nerve fiber in his body and brain, withal that it is hidden, so artfully, or naturally, under that poise of facetious calm of his. He is a marvel of sensitiveness, sensibility and perceptibility. He has a perfect mechanism of mind and body. His mind works like a chain lightning and his body obeys with equal swiftness. (London in *Reports*, 295)

In contrast to the strategically maneuvering Johnson, "'Primordial Jeffries' . . . sat down in his corner. . . . The man of iron, the grizzly giant was grim and serious. The man of summer temperament smiled and smiled. That is the story of the whole fight" (London in *Reports*, 296).

London's coverage is almost entirely focused on Johnson. Johnson is the victor in each round, for he "held his own in the clinches, . . . unhurt and . . . smiling all the way" (London in *Reports*, 299). Jeffries is knocked out by a left punch he never believed Johnson possessed. London comments:

> Even so, it is to be doubted if the old Jeff could have put away this amazing Negro from Texas, this black man with the unfailing smile, this king of fighters and monologists. . . . Johnson is a wonder. No one understands him, this man who smiles. Well, the story of the fight is the story of smile. If ever a man won by nothing more fatiguing than a smile, Johnson won today. And now where is the champion who will make Johnson extend himself, who will glaze those bright eyes, remove that smile and silence that golden repartee? (London in *Reports*, 300–301)

London seems to be mocking his earlier conclusion to the 1908 Johnson-Burns coverage, when he called Jeffries to come off the alfalfa farm and bring down Johnson/Mont Blanc. His qualifier *And now* is the key—there really wasn't anyone left to beat Johnson.

FURTHER READING

Broome, Richard. "The Australian Reaction to Jack Johnson, Black Pugilist, 1907–09." In *Sport in History: The Making of Modern Sporting History.* Edited by Richard Cashman and Michael McKernan. Brisbane St. Lucia, Australia: University of Queensland Press, 1979.

Fradella, Sal. *Jack Johnson.* Boston: Branden Publishing Co., 1990.

Jakoubek, Robert. *Jack Johnson.* New York: Chelsea House, 1990.

London, Jack. *Jack London Reports: War Correspondence, Sports Articles, and Miscellaneous Writings.* Edited by King Hendricks and Irving Shepard. Garden City, N.Y.: Doubleday & Co., 1970.

Reesman, Jeanne Campbell. *Jack London's Racial Lives.* Athens: University of Georgia Press, 2009.

Roberts, Randy. *Papa Jack: Jack Johnson and the Era of White Hopes.* New York: Free Press, 1983.

Streible, Dan. "Race and the Reception of Jack Johnson Fight Films." In *The Birth of Whiteness: Race and the Emergence of U.S. Cinema.* Edited by Daniel Bernardi. New Brunswick, N.J.: Rutgers University Press, 1996.

John Barleycorn (1913)

What exactly is the book *John Barleycorn*? Titled with a slang term for whiskey, it has been called autobiography, memoir, confession, temperance tract, sociological study, and a novel. It is all that—and more. *John Barleycorn* tells the tale of a battle between a struggling hero and a dangerous foe, alcohol, which the narrator pictures as a death's head, "the Noseless One," but its outcome is modern and realistic in that it ends with a sense of defeat at the hands of the enemy. It may be categorized as a Künstlerroman, or the story of the development of an artist, for while it is a compelling account of the author's struggle with alcohol, it also narrates the development of the author as a man and artist in search of stable identity. The author who relates his inability to escape from his alcohol also successfully writes the book, using himself as an example of why Prohibition should be passed.

John Barleycorn is one of the most revealing of London's books, a courageous and painful act of self-examination. It further cemented his position as one of the leading American writers in the world. It has never been out of print, and it has been translated into dozens of languages. It is still a staple of Alcoholics Anonymous. London's personal and professional credo included as its highest value sincerity, and that value motivates the telling of *John Barleycorn.* Yet the book is anything but a simple revelation—it is layered with many ironies—and some sincere denial.

By 1912, London was the highest-paid writer in America, having begun writing as a poverty-stricken youth in the ghettos of OAKLAND, CALIFORNIA, and having struggled through the life of CHILD LABOR, sailor, coal shoveler, laundryman, hobo, and gold prospector. As he tells us in chapter 25, "Some are born to fortune, and some have fortune thrust upon them. But in my case I was clubbed into fortune, and bitter necessity wielded the club" (237–238). Turning to writing after abandoning the life of the WORK-BEAST, as he called it, and after failing to take a job at the post office, London worked steadily at his chosen craft until by 1903 he had become world famous for *The Call of the Wild.*

In 1912, London was producing his steady 1,000 words a day, running his BEAUTY RANCH in SONOMA VALLEY, and recovering from illnesses contracted on the two-year *SNARK* voyage of 1908–09. His infant daughter, JOY, died in 1910. In 1909, he had published *Martin Eden,* and in 1911 he published the first of the Sonoma novels, *Burning Daylight.* Both of these works demonstrate a turn inward and a growing process of self-criticism; in the latter a good woman (modeled on his second wife, CHARMIAN KITTREDGE LONDON) saves the hero from drink and the worship of money, and all three Sonoma novels imagine a healthy return to the land. In 1912, London read SIGMUND FREUD, whose theory of the unconscious and id seemed to confirm his psychological and ALCOHOLIC struggles as somehow out of his control and in the control of his unconscious. He also published his first collection of Hawaiian stories, *The House of Pride,* in 1912. He entertained constantly at the ranch; as he told people, from bums to old friends from all walks of life who arrived unannounced at the ranch, "the latch string is always out." With all the pressure on

him, he overworked and to compensate he drank more and more heavily. In fact, 1912 brought a real crisis in his drinking.

On Christmas Eve, 1911, the Londons boarded a train in Oakland, bound for New York City. They arrived on January 2, 1912, where London was to meet with his new publisher, CENTURY COMPANY, having abandoned his long relationship with MACMILLAN (but a relationship that would soon be mended). London was drinking heavily, staying out all night, and generally treating Charmian very badly. There were rumors of chorus girls and other women around him. Charmian's diaries relate her shock at his behavior. On January 6 she writes, "Very cold. Beastly cold, with cutting wind. Sick [and] miserable. . . . Wish I were anywhere than in New York. Dismal place for a woman!" On January 25, she confides, "Mate in bad shape, poisoned." A few days later, "Everything so broken. . . . Hope it will come out all right. It must—only I don't feel spirited enough to fight." The low point came when London came home with a shaved head on February 29. Charmian writes that she "cried for a couple of hours. Awful shock. He laughed. I was a sight." Charmian took scissors and sheared off eight inches of her own hair, and she refused to look at her husband until a stubble grew back. The couple had to attend a ceremony at the new memorial to EDGAR ALLAN POE in the Baltimore graveyard where he was buried, but Charmian refused to go to dinner with her husband afterward. "[G]o to bed early on bathroom floor. Sleep poorly." A photograph taken of them at the Poe memorial shows Jack with a hat that seems too large for him (as it sits on his ears) and a sheepish grin; Charmian is pale and tight-lipped. London claimed his shaving his head was a trick of sailors to ward off lice, but it may also have been a gesture of self-abnegation. On the next day, March 1, the couple prepared for sailing on the *DIRIGO* on March 2; the *Dirigo* was a steel-hulled four-masted sailing ship bound around CAPE HORN for Seattle. Charmian writes: "Go aboard Dirigo. Don't want to look at Jack. He's awful. He drinks pretty steadily all morning. Throws up some of it. Well, this is the lucky last-drink day." A few days later, she observes, "Men are so strange. I actually believe has forgotten the past two months, or, that he never realized what they were meaning to me" (Huntington Library).

Once he sobered up, in an intense attempt to salvage their marriage (and perhaps his life), they agreed that if he would stop drinking they would try to conceive another child. The painful confrontation within his marriage and his terrible bout in New York and Baltimore are what he leaves out of *John Barleycorn* but were almost certainly the spur to write the book; he says his views on women's suffrage were his reason. He believed that women voters would vote in Prohibition, but the book is more a testament to his unsparing examination of himself as a drinker. In four years, he would be dead, and this seems to have been the point when he realized his own mortality.

The voyage of the *Dirigo*—Jack drinking only tea—was a very happy and productive time for the Londons. Jack had signed on as third mate, Charmian as stewardess, and their servant YOSHIMATSU NAKATA as assistant steward. After not having written for two months, a very long lapse for him, he wrote the story "The Captain of the Susan Drew," the story of a tragic transformation of an ailing man, and he made notes for *John Barleycorn*. As Russ Kingman points out, "with Seattle in sight he completed the most extensive project of the cruise" (Kingman, 237), *The Valley of the Moon*, another story of male transformation by a strong female pregnant with his child. However, at the end of the novel, one is not so sure that the man, Billy Saxon, has really changed at all. Charmian did become pregnant again on the cruise, but miscarried again.

The voyage would last five months and so would London's sobriety; when they reached California he informed Charmian that he would continue to drink, but "responsibly," something that was hard for him at his stage of alcoholism. By all accounts, he lived up to his word, however, and never descended into the pit of suicidal drinking that he had encountered in Baltimore. But still he drank seven cocktails a day or more, until he became too ill in his last year to drink at all. He never stopped writing, though he was dying of kidney disease in his last year of 1915–16; amazingly, he wrote some of his finest short stories, the genre to which he

returned after a four-year hiatus, the Hawaiian and South Pacific stories of his last summer. His kidney problems that would become fatal (London died of uremic poisoning) arose largely from his tropical illnesses but more so from the treatment he liberally used on himself for yaws, or SOLOMON ISLAND sores: corrosive sublimate of mercury. Never one to do things moderately, he used a lot of mercury, and there can be little doubt that this destroyed his kidneys.

In London's day, the word "alcoholic" carried a terrible stigma, as alcohol addiction was thought to be a flaw in one's character and not a disease itself. London's heavy protein diet and his drinking did not help health matters, and, after reading *John Barleycorn*, one surmises that he was a thoroughgoing alcoholic, despite what he says at the end about being able to control it—this after a vision of himself as a skull-face in a mirror and a dialogue with this "Noseless One" about the inevitability of alcohol's deadly grip on him. Yet the reader's role is not to judge the author, but to discover what his "alcoholic memoirs" tell us about his creative life as an artist.

John Barleycorn forms a logical argument that begins with a clear rationale and ends with obfuscation. The narrator (whom most call "London," but the two are not necessarily identical) struggles in his fight against death, the "Noseless One," with an appeal to the books that have formed his intellectual life. Though we seem to move from an issue of choice (voting) to a realization of the lack of choice (addiction), the book's conclusion is ambivalent. Is it an assertion of philosophical pessimism accompanied by a false innocence, or is it a genuine belief that the integrity of the self will overcome challenges? In any case, while ambivalent, it reflects a terrible honesty.

In a way, the narrative of *John Barleycorn* resembles a "rake's progress," as in Henry Fielding's *Tom Jones* or William Makepeace Thackeray's *Barry Lyndon*. It also falls into the European tradition of philosophical novels (it is worth pointing out here that London is regarded as a socialist philosopher in Europe), such as Goethe's *The Sorrows of Young Werther*, Mary Shelley's *Frankenstein*, or Marcel Proust's *Remembrance of Things Past*. John

Barleycorn is an instance of romantic self-revelation that reveals more than it set out to; it manages thus to be both romantic and naturalistic. London's objective rendering of events in the book foretells Ernest Hemingway's spare self-recollections, but it takes the struggle to a symbolic, even spiritual, level. It also compares with the turn-of-the-century confessions of former drinkers now on the temperance bandwagon. Finally, it is an invaluable biographical source.

According to Kingman, when *John Barleycorn* was serialized in the SATURDAY EVENING POST beginning in March 1911, "it was a sensation" (Kingman, 241). The Women's Christian Temperance Union used excerpts from it in their campaign. In April, Thomas T. Horton of the U.S.S. *Wyoming* wrote to London that "We are all reading your *John Barleycorn* on board this battle-wagon and I guess all the other crews of the fleet are doing the same" (quoted in Kingman, 241). Hobart Bosworth's film *John Barleycorn* (1914) was a huge success and played all over the country; a headline in the *Rochester Union* said, "JOHN BARLEYCORN DECLARED TO BE THE MOST POWERFUL TEMPERANCE ARGUMENT EVER BROUGHT FORTH" (quoted in Kingman, 242). London was nominated to be president of the United States by the Prohibition Party. But there was a flip side: Having earlier claimed it was a word-for-word autobiography, London did not like the press calling him a drunkard and so equivocated on whether or not it was all factual: "I shall not go so far as to say that *John Barleycorn* is the story of my life, but I will go so far to say that it is a true story of that part of my life" (quoted in Kingman, 242). Yet in a later letter to Howard H. Russell, general superintendent of the Anti-Saloon League of America, London stated: "*John Barleycorn* is frankly and truthfully autobiographical. There is no poetic license in it. It is a straight, true narrative of my personal experiences, and is toned down, not up" (*Letters*, 1,484). Readers are divided on whether to see London as the actual narrator or whether he constructed yet another persona.

With such confusions of narrative identity, it is fitting that a key theme in the book is London's realization of the tension between his personal and artistic goals and the popular image he had to maintain to sell books, some written for discerning readers but some written for mass consumption. London needed to present himself as both an icon of masculinity (which means saloons) and as a normal man (the word "normal" is repeated throughout the book) brought down by an evil force: "My body is a strong body," he says in chapter 31, "It has survived where weaklings died like flies. And yet these things which I am relating happened to my body and to me. I am a fact. My drinking is a fact. My drinking is a thing that has happened, and is no theory nor speculation; and, as I see it, but lays the emphasis on the power of John Barleycorn" (274–275).

The rehearsal of his engagements with alcohol begins with his youthful encounters with John Barleycorn by accident, then progresses as he becomes a teenager into something needed to belong to the rough society of sailors and oystermen he fell among. As *John Barleycorn* relates, he had his first drinking experience at a wedding of an Italian family on a farm near his own parents' farm. As a teen, he drank so heavily while an oyster pirate and later FISH PATROL member on SAN FRANCISCO BAY, that one night he attempted suicide by jumping off a pier. He was rescued freezing cold, sober, and very much wanting to live, by a passing Greek fisherman. He had evolved into a social drinker—indeed, most of the book is about how he is trying to manage his drinking or avoid it altogether. He protests that he hates the taste of liquor but explains how becoming a man for him had involved the places men gathered, saloons. Alcohol helped him achieve masculinity, but it poisoned his later life when he should have been at the height of his powers. Claiming he preferred candy, he drinks more and more. He details his descent into slavery to alcohol: first, reneging (temporarily) on his debt to his former nurse, Mrs. VIRGINIA PRENTISS, who loaned him money for his first boat; his realization from observing the men around him that drink spares the dull and conventional and instead "takes the good fellows," the "livest, keenest ones," and the "venturous, more individual" because they seek the company of other men in saloons (126–127); his near-suicide and drowning while drunk; his introduction to the nihilism of what he called the WHITE LOGIC of John Barleycorn; his growing after the disastrous and nearly deadly drunk he went on with the Hancock Fire Brigade on election day (politicians would hand out free liquor in exchange for votes)—again a near-death experience due to drinking. London powerfully relates his sense that alcohol, while promising a good time, would actually take all pleasure away from otherwise pleasurable experiences, as with his aborted explorations of the Bonin Islands and JAPAN while on the sealing ship SOPHIA SUTHERLAND in 1895, when he stayed ashore with his mates and drank instead of exploring the landscape, as he had planned. John Barleycorn also sends a call to the adventure path, promising to warm with its fellowship the cold feet and drudgery of work, but he learns that it lies. Back at home, he abandons his wage slavery of backbreaking unskilled labor and hits the road as a hobo. But he decided to cut that short when he was arrested in New York and put in ERIE COUNTY PENITENTIARY on charges of vagrancy. Heading home, he took the entrance exams for the UNIVERSITY OF CALIFORNIA, but embarks on a "real drunk" after the exams: "The call was imperative. There was no uncertainty about it. . . . For the first time in my life I consciously, deliberately desired to get drunk." The "intellect has its *Katzenjammers*" (213).

London says he never wanted drinking to interfere with his work, but before that eventually did occur it interfered with his relationships. Even when he conquered his LONG SICKNESS or depression of 1905, citing his salvation as "THE PEOPLE," that is, his socialist beliefs as expressed in *Martin Eden* and *The Iron Heel,* he also seems to have begun using alcohol to separate himself from people who distracted him or bored him, though he always kept up a lively round of acquaintance. He says he drank to make other people more interesting, for "the sparkle of human intercourse [had] paled." He says he has started to see the "cogs" behind the entertainments people enjoy. He notes that he has read "too many books" and that others failed to see the truths that he did, naturalistic, materialist truths: "I swear I was not pessimistic. I was merely bored. I had seen the same show too often. . . . I knew too much about box-office

receipts. . . . It doesn't pay to go behind the scenes and see the angel-voiced tenor beat his wife" (260).

Now he must deliberately grasp at illusions: "I knew the illusions were right, and I exalted the illusions," he states in chapter 31. "'But the bugs will jump,'" the Noseless One replies. "'You'll get yours in the end, but in the meantime, laugh. It's a pretty dark world. I can illuminate it for you'" (281). London finds he is unable to resist daytime drinking, desiring to drink to attain more "happiness" than he has—a happiness he unhappily celebrates and recognizes even as he wants more.

Suddenly, very suddenly in the book, he is a pessimist and a constant drinker. Chapter 35 begins, "But the freight has to be paid. John Barleycorn began to collect, and he collected not so much from the body as from the mind. The old long sickness, which had been purely an intellectual sickness, recrudesced. The old ghosts, long laid, lifted their heads again." As he explains, "Alcohol tells truth, but its truth is not normal. What is normal is healthful. What is healthful tends toward life. Normal truth is a different order, and a lesser order, of truth" (303–305). The Noseless One comes to London as he rides happily on his ranch—he is its prey and devotee. London has an interesting exchange with an old farmer in this chapter about the meaning of life, but again he faces the Noseless One as the harbinger of his own death. In a passage both beautiful and tragic, he tells us,

> Wander with me through one mood of the myriad moods of sadness into which one is plunged by John Barleycorn. I ride out over my beautiful ranch. Between my legs is a beautiful horse. The air is wine. The grapes on a score of rolling hills are red with autumn flame. Across Sonoma Mountain wisps of sea fog are stealing. The afternoon sun smoulders in the drowsy sky. I have everything to make me glad I am alive. I am filled with dreams and mysteries. I am all sun and air and sparkle. I am vitalised, organic. I move, I have the power of movement, I command movement of the live thing I bestride. I am possessed with the pomps of being, and know proud passions and inspirations. I have ten thousand august connotations. I am a king

in the kingdom of sense, and trample the face of the uncomplaining dust. (312–313)

And yet, he continues,

[W]ith jaundiced eye I gaze upon all the beauty and wonder about me, and with jaundiced brain consider the pitiful figure I cut in this world that endured so long without me and that will again endure without me. . . . Never again can I swing dizzily aloft and trust all the proud quick that is I to a single rope-clutch in the driving blackness of storm. Never again can I run with the sled-dogs along the endless miles of Arctic trail.

I am aware that within this disintegrating body which has been dying since I was born I carry a skeleton, that under the rind of flesh which is called my face is a bony, noseless death's head. All of which does not shudder me. To be afraid is to be healthy. Fear of death makes for life. But the curse of the White Logic is that it does not make one afraid. The world-sickness of the White Logic makes one grin jocosely into the face of the Noseless One and to sneer at all the phantasmagoria of living. (313)

Despite this dark night of the soul, in chapter 38 he tells us that he has not been destroyed by alcohol, though he has been "scorched," and, "like such a survivor of the old red War who cries out, 'Let there be no more war!'" his book is a cry against alcohol abuse: "It is for the healthy, normal boys, now born or being born, for whom I write." London praises women as the "true conservators of the race," for the men are "the wastrels, the adventure-lovers and gamblers, but in the end it is by their women that they are saved. . . . The women know. They have paid an incalculable price of sweat and tears for man's use of alcohol" (336). (Oddly, this chapter also includes a mention of burning witches!) The very last chapter informs us that London will continue to drink but now "responsibly," having presumably conquered the demon of addiction: "The White Logic now lies decently buried alongside the Long Sickness. Neither will afflict me again. It is many a year since I laid the Long Sickness away; his sleep is sound. And just as sound is the sleep of the White Logic. And yet, in conclu-

sion, I can well say that I wish my forefathers had banished John Barleycorn before my time. I regret that John Barleycorn flourished everywhere in the system of society in which I was born, else I should not have made his acquaintance, and I was long trained in his acquaintance" (343).

In keeping with this contradictory ending, *John Barleycorn* contains not only a narrative of descent but also some positive themes that transcend his personal story: a critique of American notions of masculinity and social responsibility; the desire for freedom from wage slavery and "money-grubbing" in favor of "comradeship"; the need of humans for adventure and escape; and the yearning for imaginative fulfillment.

First, John Barleycorn is a memoir, but it is also a criticism (in the vein of London's SOCIALISM) of American society at the turn of the century. London attacks the easy tolerance most people had for heavy drinking and the ubiquity of alcohol as a means to social intercourse among men. He describes it as a ritual of manhood (*see* especially chapter 6). He calls John Barleycorn a "well" for boys to fall in—a destructive and unnecessary part of their development. Several times in the book he says he himself had no boyhood.

Second, London tells how drinking drew him away from wage slavery and money-grubbing, even freeing him from class boundaries. He sought comradeship as a high value and also notes how alcohol works to help forge business relationships (many saloon-keepers were unofficial banks for their patrons, making loans and keeping tabs). For someone who grew up realizing that his body was merely a machine that was paid a pittance to do men's work (as described in "The Apostate"), the revelation of the Noseless One that "'Is this flesh yours you? Or is it an extraneous something possessed by you? Your body—what is it? A machine for converting stimuli into reactions. . . . Then you are in your consciousness these experiences," may not have come as a surprise (327). If alcohol kept the lower classes from achieving, it also gave London a means to interact with other men and eventually work his way out of the lower class into a position where (at least he believed) he "owned" his own body—and more importantly, his imagination.

The connection between writing and drinking is well established in American literature (see books by Tom Dardis and John W. Crowley). For many writers, addiction and artistry seemed to go hand in hand. And alcohol London saw as a ticket to the adventure path and away from the considerable hazards of the factories of the day. It was conjoined with "adventure, fancy-filled with tales of buccaneers and sea-rovers," and "imagination-maddened by the stuff, . . . It was life raw and naked, wild and free." He adds, "Wherever life ran free and great, there men drank. Romance and adventure seemed always to go down the street locked arm in arm with John Barleycorn. To know the two, I must know the third" (44). But such adventure could also lead to the squalid life of the hobo and the convict, as related in *The Road*.

Most important, John Barleycorn seemed to free up London's imagination, though he came to realize it also freed up the darker side of imagination. Moving from avoidance of alcohol when working to an absolute need for it to *start* working, London details the interactions of liquor with his creativity. But in the last chapter he seems to feel that his desire for the "illusions" is so powerful a rebuttal to the White Logic that it may just prevail:

> And I laugh my defiance; for now, and for the moment, I know the White Logic to be the arch-impostor of them all, whispering his whispers of death. And he is guilty of his own unmasking, with his own genial chemistry turning the tables on himself, with his own maggots biting alive the old illusions, resurrecting and making to sound again the old voice from beyond of my youth, telling me again that still are mine the possibilities and powers which life and the books had taught me did not exist. (331)

Did alcohol play a decisive role in London's literary oeuvre, that is, did it profoundly affect much of his writing? The answer is mostly no. He did most of his work before he became severely troubled by alcohol, and some of his very best work, the late Pacific tales, were written after he had had to stop drinking that last summer of 1916. But this fact speaks for itself; would London have been a better writer if he had been sober? In the end, we can conclude that while this question remains unanswered, London's drinking did directly give us *John Barleycorn*, one of his most significant works and one in which the agonies of the creative spirit are laid bare. If alcohol could scorch "the joy-fields of art" (115), as he memorably put it, it could also make possible the startling self-revelation of one who thought long and deeply about his companion, John Barleycorn.

FURTHER READING

Baskett, Sam S. "Jack London: 'In the Midst of It All.'" In *Jack London: One Hundred Years a Writer.* Edited by Sara S. Hodson and Jeanne Campbell Reesman. San Marino, Calif.: Huntington Library, 2002, 123–146.

Crowley, John W. *The White Logic: Alcoholism and Gender in American Modernist Fiction.* Amherst: University of Massachusetts Press, 1994.

Dardis, Tom. *The Thirsty Muse: Alcohol and the American Writer.* Boston, Mass.: Houghton Mifflin, 1991.

DeCaire, John. "The Boy's Books of Despair." *Southwest Review* 88, nos. 2–3 (2003): 277–290.

Hornung, Alfred. "Evolution and Expansion in Jack London's Personal Accounts: *The Road* and *John Barleycorn*." In *An American Empire: Expansionist Cultures and Policies, 1881–1917.* Edited by Serge Ricard. Aix-en-Provence: Université de Provence, 1990, 197–213.

Kingman, Russ. *A Pictorial Life of Jack London.* New York: Crown, 1979.

London, Charmian Kittredge. *Diary*, January–March 1912. Used by permission of the Jack London Collection at the Huntington Library, San Marino, California.

Okun, Peter T. "John Barleycorn's Body." *Arizona Quarterly: A Journal of American Literature, Culture, and Theory* 52, no. 2 (Summer 1996): 63–86.

"The Jokers of New Gibbon" (1911)

First published in the *Saturday Evening Post* 184 (11 November 1911), this story was included in *A*

Son of the Sun. Its opening finds London's South Seas white hero, David Grief, on a ship called the *Wonder,* with Wallenstein, the German resident agent from Bougainville in the SOLOMON ISLANDS.

SYNOPSIS

Wallenstein remarks on what Grief has accomplished on the "devil island" of New Gibbon (Solomon Islands) with its chief, old Koho, "a black Napoleon, a head-hunting, man-eating Tallyrand" (*Stories,* 1942). Wallenstein remembers that Koho once hanged one of his wives by one arm out in the sun for two days and nights and had three more women staked out up to their necks in running water, their bones broken and joints crushed: "The process was supposed to make them tender for the eating" (*Stories,* 1942). This was actually a practice in FIJI London read about in missionary accounts; New Gibbon is a fictional island.

As they journey to Grief's New Gibbon plantation where he is harvesting copra (or dried cocoanut kernels from which oil would be extracted), run by a Scotsman named McTavish, the two men discuss the work of McTavish, the "Troublemender," Grief had assigned to pacify New Gibbon. McTavish imported bushmen from MALAITA, burned villages, captured Koho's son, and laid down the rate of head-exchange: for each head of his own people he promised to take ten of Koho's. Peace with the elderly Koho was made. Thus he recommended himself to David Grief. Koho realizes that to save his people he must submit (*Stories,* 1,944).

New Gibbon, populated by warring tribes, is supposedly under British and German control, but is in reality a zone of wildness and lawlessness, visited by traders and slavers (called BLACKBIRDERS), its cocoanut plantation abandoned after several managers and contract laborers have lost their heads. As Worth, the manager of New Gibbon, pulls the tooth of a New Georgia worker, Koho, carrying a Snider rifle, "indescribably filthy. . . . grinning like a shrewd little ape" approaches (*Stories,* 1,945). He cannot shake hands since it is against his *tambo* (or taboo), as Grief introduces him to Wallenstein: "Koho was a conservative. His fathers before him had worn no clothes, and neither did he, not even

a g-string. The many perforations in his nose and lips and ears told of decorative passions long since dead. The holes on both ear-lobes had been torn out, but their size was attested by the strips of withered flesh that hung down and swept his shoulders. He cared now only for utility, and in one of the half dozen minor holes in his right ear he carried a short clay pipe" (*Stories,* 1,946).

Soon after Koho leaves to try to get drinks from the supercargo, Denby, on the *Wonder,* Grief observes, "'How are the mighty fallen. . . . To think that he used to be Koho, the fiercest red-handed murderer in the Solomons, who defied all his life the two greatest world powers'" (*Stories,* 1,947). Denby plays a practical joke on Koho by fooling him into thinking a bottle of essence of mustard is a bottle of rum. After drinking it, Koho's mouth and throat burn, but his face remains composed. Then, "It dawned on him that a trick had been played, and into his eyes came an expression of hatred and malignancy so primitive, so abysmal, that it sent chills up and down Denby's spine" (*Stories,* 1,949). With dignity, he gets up and leaves.

Next Wallenstein plays a joke on Koho, making him think a bottle of horse liniment he is using to clean his gun is a bottle of Scotch. He hears Koho splutter and cough and a few minutes later hears a rifle shot and learns that the boathouses and barracks are on fire. Grief finds the cook, a child, and a young assistant manager murdered by Koho. The next day, against the smoke signals and drums of war in the bush, or interior, Grief tells the others to stay close and wait for McTavish, whom Grief will send up on another ship, the *Wanda,* with a score of Malaita bushmen. Denby and Wallenstein confess their roles in Koho's rebellion and remain behind to try to straighten things up.

Grief sails to the island of GUADALCANAL; a few weeks later he sees the *Wanda* at anchor in the harbor at Guvutu. McTavish has just returned from New Gibbon: "He was a cold flame of a man, small as Koho, and as dried up, with a mahogany complexion and small, expressionless blue eyes that were more like gimlet-points than the eyes of a Scotchman" (*Stories,* 1,953). He relates his tale to Grief: "'Tis a thing to be condemned, a damned shame, this joking with heathen niggers,'"

McTavish says, "'Also, 'tis very expensive'" (*Stories,* 1,954). McTavish tells Grief what happened on the plantation on New Gibbon: "'All the years of our work have gone for naught. 'Tis back where we started, where the missionaries started, where the Germans started—and where they finished. Not a stone stands on another at the landing pier. The houses are black ashes. Every tree is hacked down, and the wild pigs are rooting out the yams and sweet potatoes. . . . Not one is left to tell the tale'" (*Stories,* 1,454). He shows Grief the heads of Denby, Wallenstein, and Worth, dumped from a bag onto the floor. "'I suppose they'll have regular funerals over them,'" says McTavish, "'and put them in the ground. But in my way of thinking they'd make excellent curios. Any respectable museum would pay a hundred quid apiece'" (*Stories,* 1,954). At this Grief turns pale.

COMMENTARY

This darkly comic story has the feel of a tall tale passed around by South Seas traders, as well as the trickster elements of the indigenous folktale. In fact, in more ways than one, it could be described as "black comedy." Though it seems at first to dwell on the foolishness and gullibility of Koho, he repays the whites who tease him with a savage revenge: their heads. As in "The Feathers of the Sun," "The Jokers of New Gibbon" punishes the white men who try to demonstrate their superiority to islanders.

The story also demonstrates London's deft use of the BÊCHE-DE-MER ENGLISH dialect of the Southwest Pacific:

> "Don't shake hands with him, Wallenstein," Grief warned. "Tambo, you know." Then to Koho, "My word, you get 'm too much fat stop along you. Bime by you marry along new fella Mary, eh?"
>
> "Too old fella me," Koho answered, with a weary shake of the head. "Me no like 'm Mary. Me no like 'm kai-kai (food). Close up me die along altogether." He stole a significant glance at Worth, whose head was tilted back to a long glass. "Me like 'm rum."
>
> Grief shook his head.
>
> "Tambo along black fella. . . ."
>
> "Me fella sick."

> "You fella big liar," Grief laughed. "Rum tambo, all the time tambo. Now, Koho, we have big fella talk along this big fella marster." (*Stories,* 1,947)

It is this conversation that sets in motion the events that lead to Koho's being tricked and to his revenge.

The real black comedy of the story lies in its surprise ending. The unwholesome, drunken "savage" Koho has taken his bloody revenge, which shows how vulnerable and stupid the whites are, how their condescending to the "niggers" has blinded them from their opponents' power. But the final joke is that a white man, Grief's trader, the Scotsman McTavish, reveals his plan to Grief to sell the heads as curios—a stereotype of the thrifty Scot?

CHARACTERS

David Grief London's fantasy South Seas white man, Grief is a self-made adventurer and millionaire who cruises the South Seas, often finding himself in the position of settling disputes between whites and native islanders. He has managed New Gibbon into peace, though it is a "devil island." He hears the story of what happened to the whites there when they tried to shame the chief, Koho. By contrast to them, Grief's moral code would not have allowed him to tease Koho the way they do, but he does make fun of him in his first conversation with him in the story, so Grief shares in a sense of white privilege and superiority.

Wallenstein German resident commissioner at Bougainville, in the Solomon Islands. He accompanies Grief to his plantation and helps him doctor the workers. He tricks the chief, Koho, into drinking liniment he is using to oil his gun. He is beheaded by Koho.

Koho Chief of New Gibbon, known for his brutal ways, "the big chief devil of them all" (*Stories,* 1,942), according to Wallenstein. Grief notes that he is not entirely "pacified," though "'he comes in once in awhile and eats out of the hand'" (*Stories,* 1,942). Koho is tricked by Denby and Wallenstein and kills them along with Worth.

Denby Supercargo of the *Wonder*, Denby is sympathetic to Koho's thirst for rum and his symptoms of old age, and when Koho comes aboard he kindly offers him medicines, which Koho refuses. For some perverse reason, he decides to play a joke on Koho and tricks him into drinking essence of mustard instead of rum. He pays with his head.

Worth Manager of New Gibbon, he tries to extract teeth from sick workers. Worth is frightened of Koho and wants to leave when he appears, showing a good deal more sense than Wallenstein and Denby. He confiscates Koho's Snider rifle. Worth is the one who gives the alarm when Koho begins his revenge. He is beheaded by Koho.

McTavish Wallenstein calls him a "the Trouble-Mender"; for his service on New Gibbon Grief calls him "worth it" and a "wizard" who is starting a plantation for Grief (*Stories*, 1,943). McTavish witnesses the beheadings of Denby, Wallenstein, and Worth, and he brings the heads with him when he meets David Grief again. He plans to sell his friends' heads!

Captain Ward As he sits with Grief, Worth, and some sick workers from New Georgia, he speaks of seeing a man remove teeth as a second mate on a "lime-juicer." He witnesses Grief and Wallenstein struggle to pull teeth from a worker.

"Just Meat" (1907)

First published in COSMOPOLITAN 42 (March 1907), "Just Meat" was included in *When God Laughs*. It is the ironic tale of two "partners" who end up killing each other, neither having the chance to enjoy their booty. It compares well with "In a Far Country" and its two "Incapables."

SYNOPSIS

Two thieves carry out their plan to rob a diamond merchant. As Jim anxiously watches the house to be burgled across the street, a policeman passes. When he is gone, Jim whistles for his partner Matt. Matt emerges and says he has a "fat" haul of "goods" (*Stories*, 1,188). He tells Jim that he had to strangle the homeowner and shows no remorse; rather, he berates Jim: "'I've got to run all the risks. I put my head in the trap while you stay on the street'" (*Stories*, 1,189). Matt empties his pockets of diamonds of all sizes from huge to tiny and a pearl necklace. Matt hides the treasure in paper bags and stores them under his pillow. He and Jim each claim that they want to be "square" with one another, especially after they learn from the newspapers that their victim had robbed his partner and was about to leave the country with millions of dollars in diamonds, more than Matt and Jim have imagined. But every time either leaves their rooms, the other imagines stealing all of the jewels, or "jools," as they say. Matt leaves to buy food, and when he returns, serves a porterhouse steak. Jim poisons Matt's coffee, and Matt poisons Jim's steak. Each tries to avert death by drinking mustard and water, but each dies an agonizing death. The story concludes with Matt's attempt to reach the door:

> He tried to soliloquize, to be facetious, to have his last grim laugh at life, but his lips made only incoherent sounds. . . . And in the midst of the paroxysm, with his body and all the parts of it flying apart and writhing and twisting back again into knots, he clung to the chair and shoved it before him across the floor. The last shreds of his will were leaving him when he gained the door. He turned the key and shot back one bolt. He fumbled for the second bolt, but failed. Then he leaned his weight against the door and slid down gently to the floor. (*Stories*, 1,200)

COMMENTARY

The story's central metaphor is that of meat, a porterhouse, and the bodies of two thieves: Just as they celebrate their robbery and dine on a one-inch-thick steak, they reveal themselves in a naturalistic sense as only "meat." They debate the existence of an afterlife, but they live only by the rules of earthly power and survival—including murder. Like the two "Incapables" of "In a Far Country," they murder what they love: themselves.

"What do you think about the next life anyway, Matt?" he asked a little later, while secretly he wondered why the other had not yet touched his coffee.

"Ain't no next life," Matt answered, pausing from the steak to take his first sip of coffee. "Nor heaven nor hell, nor nothin'. You get all that's comin' right here in this life."

"An' afterward?" Jim queried out of his morbid curiosity, for he knew that he looked upon a man that was soon to die. "An' afterward?" he repeated.

"Did you ever see a man two weeks dead?" the other asked.

Jim shook his head.

"Well, I have. He was like this beefsteak you an' me is eatin'. It was once steer cavortin' over the landscape. But now it's just meat. That's all, just meat. An' that's what you an' me an' all people come to—meat." (*Stories*, 1,196–1,197)

Later, when Jim realizes Matt has poisoned him, his very muscles or "meat" are what is affected:

He felt a disruptive influence at work in the flesh of him, and in all his muscles there was a seeming that they were about to begin to twitch. He sat back suddenly, and as suddenly leaned forward with his elbows on the table. A tremor ran dimly through the muscles of his body. It was like the first rustling of leaves before the oncoming of wind. He clenched his teeth. It came again, a spasmodic tensing of his muscles. He knew panic at the revolt within his being. His muscles no longer recognized his mastery over them. . . . This was revolution within himself, this was anarchy; and the terror of impotence rushed up in him as his flesh gripped and seemed to seize him in a clutch, chills running up and down his back and sweat starting on his brow. (*Stories*, 1,197–1,198)

The alternative to the naturalistic idea of life as merely a matter of feeding meat (oneself) would

be BROTHERHOOD, as London shows so often in the KLONDIKE stories. But among these thieves there is no honor, much less brotherhood. This story is a slice of life outside the bounds of decency, and it is as unsparing in its melodramatic gore as it is in its NATURALISM—and yet, almost in a dark comic sense, there is a restoration of order at the end, as the evil do not live to enjoy their spoils.

CHARACTERS

Jim Jim, the thief who waits outside as his partner strangles and robs a diamond dealer, is first described as "a shadow of a man sliding noiselessly and without undue movement through the semidarkness. Also he was very alert, like a wild animal in the jungle, keenly perceptive and receptive. The movement of another in the darkness about him would need to have been more shadowy than he to have escaped him" (*Stories*, 1,186). He poisons his partner's coffee and is poisoned by him.

Matt Matt seems the more practical of the two. He does not wonder about the afterlife and does not mind killing; he also organizes the jewels and discusses fair separation of them, but he too is a frightening character: "He was in every way a contrast to the other. No city had bred him. He was heavy-muscled and hairy, gorilla-like in strength and aspect. For him there was no unseen world" (*Stories*, 1,190). His most revealing description shows him threatening Jim:

"Look here, Jim," he snarled. "You've got to play square. If you do me dirt, I'll fix you. Understand? I'd eat you, Jim. You know that. I'd bite right into your throat an' eat you like that much beefsteak."

His sunburned skin was black with the surge of blood in it, and his tobacco-stained teeth were exposed by the snarling lips. Jim shivered and involuntarily cowered. There was death in the man he looked at. Only the night before that black-faced man had killed another with his hands, and it had not hurt his sleep. And in his own heart Jim was aware of a sneaking guilt, of a train of thought that merited all that was threatened. (*Stories*, 1,193)

"Keesh, the Son of Keesh" (1902)

First published in *Ainslee's Magazine* in January 1902, this tale has a sequel, "The Story of Keesh" (1904), which tells of the bear-hunting exploits of the father of the protagonist in "Keesh, the Son of Keesh."

SYNOPSIS

Keesh, chief of the Thlunget, makes an offer to Gnob, chief of the Tana-naw, for the hand of his daughter Su-Su. But Gnob refuses, saying that Keesh has been corrupted by his contact with the whites at the local mission, and has converted to CHRISTIANITY. Among other things, this means that Keesh will no longer kill for his tribe. He is denounced by Su-Su's brothers. In the words of Gnob and the brothers there is the larger story of the effect the whites have had on the NATIVES, from forcing them to work to stealing Native brides. Gnob forecasts a day of reckoning when the Natives will fight the whites to the death. Madwan, the shaman, tries to get Keesh to kill a slave boy to show that he is still part of the tribe, but Keesh refuses. When Keesh confronts Su-Su, who had been much in love with him, she angrily refuses him because he has departed from the tribal ways with his Christianity. She tells him than unless he shows that he has not changed and brings her three heads, she will not marry him. Keesh retreats to the mission, and in the meantime Su-Su finds another suitor. When Keesh hears of this, he does bring her her three heads, plus one more: her new suitor, her two brothers, and her father. And then he pulls out the big Russian knife she has given him and takes her head too.

COMMENTARY

The irony in this story is grim. From being a Christian convert, Keesh becomes a murderer of his own people. The tribe wants Keesh to behave as one of them, and they get what they wanted. London wrote many stories, especially in *Children of the Frost,* in which this one is included, that show the brutal effects of the white intrusion into the Native lands of the Northwest, especially their enslaving the Native men and taking Native women as brides. London elevates the speech of the Natives by using King James English, ennobling them and their way of life. The events of the story play out against the larger background of the fate of Natives beset by whites, and Gnob eloquently states this in his speeches to Keesh.

CHARACTERS

Keesh Chief of the Thlunget and a mighty hunter and warrior, Keesh asks for the hand of the Tana-naw woman Su-Su, but is rejected by her and her family because he has converted to Christianity. Keesh obtains bloody revenge on the Tana-naw and rejects his Christian faith. When the pastor at the mission asks Keesh if he is going hunting at the end of the story, he replies, "'No; I go to hell'" (*Stories,* 571).

Gnob Chief of the Tana-naw and father of Su-Su; he denies Keesh his daughter's hand because he has been consorting with whites and has become a Christian: "'O they lay hands upon all they behold, these white men, and they go everywhere and behold all things. And ever do more follow in their steps, so that if nothing be done they will come to possess all the land and there will be no room for the tribes of the Raven. Wherefore it is meet that we fight with them till none are left'" (*Stories,* 567). He denies Keesh because Keesh will not fight and kill with his people.

Su-Su Daughter of Gnob and Keesh's intended, Su-Su was once in love with Keesh but scorns him because he has been influenced by white ways. She demands he show that he is still part of the tribe by bringing her heads, which he does, but they are her family and new suitor; she is also beheaded by Keesh.

Madwan Madwan is "the shaman, high-priest of the tribe and maker of medicine" (*Stories,* 564). He counsels Gnob against Keesh because Keesh has become a Christian. He tries to get Keesh to demonstrate his fidelity to Native ways by killing a slave boy.

Kitz-noo A slave boy whom Madwan presents to Keesh with a demand that he kill him to show he is no Christian. But Keesh refuses to take an innocent life.

Macklewrath A trader living near the Tana-naw with a Tana-naw wife. He does not believe Natives can really be converted to Christianity and objects to efforts to do so.

Makamuk Brother of Su-Su and son of Gnob; he denounces Keesh and the practice of Native women marrying white men, which he observes when he passes by the white trader Macklewrath's cabin and sees his Indian wife. He and his brother are killed by Keesh.

Nossabok Favorite brother of Su-Su, he laments the state of the tribe under the whites: "'And I saw Indians with the sweat running into their eyes and their knees shaking with weariness—I say, I saw Indians groaning under the logs for the store which the Trader Macklewrath is to build. And with my eyes I saw them chopping wood to keep the Shaman Brown's Big House warm through the frost of the long nights. This be squaw work. Never shall the Tana-naw do the like. We shall be blood brothers to men, not squaws; and the Thlunget be squaws'" (*Stories*, 568–569). He and his brother are killed by Keesh.

Reverend Jackson Brown The pastor at the mission is very proud of his conversion of Keesh and other Natives and boasts about it to Macklewrath. However, he is disproven by Keesh's actions.

Nee-Koo Su-Su's new suitor, he is described as "'a nervy young hunter who had bid brilliantly for her by old Gnob's fire'" (*Stories*, 571). He is presented to Su-Su as one of the four heads Keesh has collected.

The Kempton-Wace Letters (1903)

This unusual epistolary novel, published anonymously in 1903, features a debate carried out in letters between the fictional characters Herbert Wace of California and Dane Kempton of LONDON, ENGLAND. Herbert Wace's part was written by London; Wace is a proponent of MATERIALISM and evolutionary theory. ANNA STRUNSKY wrote the part of Dane Kempton, a defender of the power of romantic love. Wace, a young relative of Kempton's, does not believe in love but in what he thinks of as biological and practical mating.

Wace is a young sociology professor who believes in logic and EVOLUTION only. Kempton's faith is in poetry and romantic idealism. In the first of the letters, Kempton congratulates young Wace on his engagement to be married, only to receive the cool reply that marriage is a mere institution to perpetuate the species.

During the two years of working on the book, London and Strunsky would grow closer and closer, provoking the jealousy of London's wife, BESS LONDON, with their intimacy. As the project progressed, their passions developed. By October 1901, London was writing to Strunsky, whom he much admired for her beauty, socialist ideas, and intellectual accomplishments as a Stanford University graduate and member of the intelligentsia in the BAY AREA, as "Dear You." By January 1902, he wrote to her as "Dear, Dear You." In the summer of 1902, he declared his love, "I am sick with love for you and need of you" (*Letters*, 297–298). He threw caution to the winds, and their friendship began to approach scandal. London received a call from the American Press Association to report the effects of the peace in South Africa after the ending of the Boer War. He accepted readily. When, having arrived in London, he found that the assignment to South Africa was cancelled, he stayed in London to dress and live as a homeless AWOL American sailor, to photograph and write about the slums and the homeless of London instead in *The People of the Abyss* (1903). When Bess filed for divorce in 1904, she named Strunsky as correspondent, not realizing that their affair had ended when he was in London and that Jack was now in love with CHARMIAN KITTREDGE [LONDON], who became his second wife when the divorce was final in 1905. What happened to the love affair of Jack and Anna? Why did they not marry? Charmian was friendly with Anna after the marriage, but always kept an eye on her when she visited Jack, for she knew of their great passion for each other.

SYNOPSIS

When Wace replies to Kempton's warm letter of congratulations on his engagement, he merely says that nearly everyone marries at some time. He dispassionately describes his decision to enter the "institution" of marriage as biologically based for "the perpetuation of the species." He worries over the disruption of his "dear little system of living," and relates that the couple is postponing the actual wedding until he has completed his doctorate in social science. He "cannot view with equanimity" this new and "disturbing element in my life-work," yet he describes his fiancé, Hester Stebbins, as a scientist (but also, curiously, a poet) who is as practical and as little possessed with romantic illusions as himself (7).

Kempton writes back with a severe tone:

It is because you know not what you do that I cannot forgive you. Could you know that your letter with its catalogue of advantages and arrangements must offend me as much as it belies (let us hope) you and the woman of your love, I would pardon the affront of it upon us all, and ascribe the unseemly want of warmth to reserve or to the sadness which grips the heart when joy is too palpitant. But something warns me that you are unaware of the chill your words breathe, and that is a lapse which it is impossible to meet with indulgence. (11)

He further scolds Wace with Wace's sister's words (the sister lives with Kempton): "'He does not love her.'" He demands, "Tell me, do you still read your Wordsworth on your knees?" (13).

Wace in turn describes Kempton as a priest "of a dying faith," and defends his materialistic view of life. Kempton's "prayers are futile, your altars crumbling. . . . Poetry is empty these days, empty and worthless and dead" (19). Lyrics will not

. . . put this very miserable earth of ours to rights. . . . The old world is dead, dead and buried along with its heroes and Helens and

knights and ladies and tournaments and pageants. You cannot sing of the truth and wonder of to-day in terms of yesterday. And no one will listen to your singing till you sing of to-day in terms of to-day. This is the day of the common man. Do you glorify the common man? This is the day of the machine. When have you sung of the machine? The crusades are here again, not the Crusades of Christ, but the Crusades of the machine. . . . We are crusading to-day, not for the remission of sins, but for the abolition of sinning, of economic and industrial sinning. The crusade to Christ's sepulchre was paltry compared with the splendour and might of our crusade to-day toward manhood. (19–20)

He concludes: "We have no poets these days, and perforce we are singing with our hands. The walking delegate is a greater singer and a finer singer than you, Dane Kempton. The cold, analytical economist, delving in the dynamics of society, is more the prophet than you. The carpenter at his bench, the blacksmith by his forge, the boilermaker clanging and clattering, are all warbling more sweetly than you" (21).

Thus are the terms of the debate opened, and the many letters back and forth which follow debate the virtues and faults of ROMANTICISM versus materialism. Kempton reiterates the need for men and women to be true to their natures—meaning both the practical and the romantic—and says that anyway, "To shut out glory is not to be practical." A man who tries to do so will live a life "of too much strain, too little warmth, too much self-complacence." He sees Wace's position as that of a very young, untried man, and predicts that inevitably, "her soul will escape yours" (29). Love is something not of "the financiers," but of "the blood" (30). He contrasts Wace to his sister Barbara, who fell in love against all advice with a man named Earl who was a poverty-stricken cripple. But Wace can only continue to argue that "Love is a disorder of mind and body . . . a phase of the function of reproduction, and it occurs solely in man" as mere "emotional excitement" (97). Wace quotes a French proverb that "The first sigh of love is the last of wisdom," and insists that "only the individual who escapes love can be rational" (140). Kempton counters that perhaps "Nature tricks her creatures and the race lives on, and I, overcivilized, decadent dreamer that I am, rejoice that the past binds us, am proud of a history so old and so significant and of a heritage so marvellous. . . . You are suffering from, what has been well called, the sadness of science" (125). He believes that "We live most when we love most," for love is not a means to an end but an end in itself. It becomes clear that their debate is not really only on the role of love in human life, but more generally the nature of the imagination, and much of their discussion is as applicable to what makes great literature as it is to what makes great love.

The book concludes with letters of Hester Stebbins to Kempton explaining that because she does not feel Wace really loves her, she is breaking off the engagement for "a youth here who loves me. If Herbert's face could shine like that for one hour, I believe I would be happier than I have ever been." For Herbert, she prays that one day "knowledge of love [will] come to the man over whom the love of my girlhood was spilled. Do you ask what is left me, dear friend? Work and tears and the intact dream. Believe me, I am not pitiable" (256).

COMMENTARY

Judging from what Wace has to say about human life and love, it is clear that the British philosopher and social scientist HERBERT SPENCER's grandiose racial abstractions and notions of evolution leading inexorably to the dominance of the ANGLO-SAXON race inappropriately influenced London's choice of mate. If he had followed his heart he would have married Anna. London and Strunsky participated in the activities of the Bay Area socialists; theirs became an affair of two intellectuals and more. It seems that one Wednesday afternoon in late March 1900, London planned to propose marriage to her, as they rested from a bicycle trip into the Berkeley hills. But Anna's reserve put him off. Raised as a genteel young woman, she had little experience in love, and, believing it was proper to remain a bit coy with suitors, she told him she loved him but that she had to leave for the Russian Revolution for her writing in the near future. Embarrassed

and frustrated, a day or two later he impulsively proposed to Bess Maddern, a friend who had also been his math tutor when he was cramming to pass the entrance exams at Berkeley. They were married three days later. He declared that they would raise "seven sturdy Saxon sons, and seven beautiful daughters." But he kept up his friendship with Strunsky, actually proposing in 1902 when he was in London writing *The People of the Abyss,* but too late. She had discovered that Bess was pregnant for the second time, and in a letter to him she broke things off for good (though her memoir and subsequent letters to London strongly suggest she harbored romantic feelings for him for much of her adult life).

The authors spent intense months working on this novel. Perhaps seeking to rationalize his own loveless marriage of mere "breeding" potential, London self-consciously has Wace argue that marriage is only a biological device to ensure Spencer's "race maintenance," while Strunsky's character stresses the primacy of love in marriage. Wace characterizes love as a primitive instinct, breeding as an intellectual duty. Jacqueline Tavernier-Courbin explains that Wace desires "to better the fate of humanity in tangible terms. . . . [with] a human elite to apply to itself the same selection process applied to the scientific breeding of animals." Wace's "laws of development" meant that through natural potential men may rise from obscurity to prominence, an argument for London's newfound identity as a writer at the time. The hyper-intellectual Wace also paraphrases Spencer's notion of women as obedient mothers of the race, which must have amused Strunsky, who wryly wondered in a letter to Charmian why they spent nearly two years writing the book "trying to convert each other to positions which, at bottom, we must both have held?" (Tavernier-Courbin, "To Love," 265; Walling, Letter to Charmian London). As Tavernier-Courbin also observes, "London could probably have written Anna's side of the argument far more convincingly than she did," and with her own coolness, she could have written his as well ("To Love," 266). Such confusion paradoxically rings true: London was always constructing and opposing one self or identity to another.

London told Bess that procreation was his purpose, that he was not in love with her. Presumably she was lonely, given that her former fiancé had only recently died, and she agreed. Perhaps she thought she could change him. Ironically, Anna later married, also not for love: she married a wealthy socialist, William English Walling for his politics. Theirs was not a happy union.

More than anyone close to him ever was to be again, Anna seems to have understood the conflicts in London's thinking on RACIALISM versus SOCIALISM as features of his psychology and upbringing, separate from his ultimate values. She believed that they would evolve over time to resemble her own liberal views. As she wrote in an obituary published in *The Masses* in 1917,

> He was youth, adventure, romance. He was a poet and a social revolutionist. He had a genius for friendship. He loved greatly and was greatly beloved. But how fix in words that quality of personality that made him different from everyone else in the world? How convey an idea of his magnetism and of the poetic quality of his nature? He is the outgrowth of the struggle and the suffering of the Old Order, and he is the strength and the virtue of all its terrible and criminal vices.

London, she muses, "rose out of the Abyss . . . to become as large as the race and to be identified with the forces that shape the future of mankind." She calls him "an idealist without any illusions" and "an individualist who was consecrated to the cause of mankind. As long as he lived he would strip the veils from truth and be a living protest against all the evils and injustices of society." She contrasts the ideas "he flaunted" when young with those of his mature development. In the beginning, she recalls, "He believed in the inferiority of certain races and talked of the Anglo-Saxon people as the salt of the earth. He inclined to believe in the biological inferiority of woman to man." London "held that love is only a trap set by nature for the individual. One must not marry for love but for certain qualities discerned by the mind. This he argued in *The Kempton-Wace Letters* brilliantly and passionately; so passionately as to again make one

suspect that he was not as certain of his position as he claimed to be." Later, she recalls, London "became the most mellow of thinkers, as passionately promulgating his new ideas as he had then assailed them. He now believed in romantic love, he had helped in the agitation for woman suffrage and was jubilant over its success in California." London developed into "an absolute internationalist and anti-militarist" and laughed at himself when he recalled "how in the Russian-Japanese War he had been on the Russian side although all Socialists wanted Russia beaten for the sake of the revolutionary movement. The Russians were white men and the Japanese were not" (Walling, *Memoirs*, 13–14).

The novel remains a fascinating glimpse not only into the two authors' lives, but also a complex discussion of the central question raised every day in every culture on Earth: What is the meaning of human love?

CHARACTERS

Dane Kempton   An older man and resident of LONDON, ENGLAND, Kempton corresponds with a young relative about his engagement. Kempton is a romantic idealist who argues for the irrationality of love and for the freedom of the spirit and imagination.

Herbert Wace   A young economist and sociology graduate student at the UNIVERSITY OF CALIFORNIA who is engaged to be married, but who views his marriage as merely a biological necessity and says that he does not believe in love, only in material reality. He does not expect that his "practical" fiancé will tire of his theories.

Hester Stebbins   Wace's fiancée, she is a young scientist known for her own materialistic view of life, but she is also a poet, and, as Kempton predicts, she chooses to marry someone else who shows that he really loves her.

FURTHER READING

Boylan, James. *Revolutionary Lives: Anna Strunsky and William English Walling.* Amherst: University of Massachusetts Press, 1998.

Tavernier-Courbin, Jacqueline. "Jack London and Anna Strunsky: Lovers at Cross-Purposes." In *Jack London: One Hundred Years a Writer.* Edited by Sara S. Hodson and Jeanne Campbell Reesman. San Marino, Calif.: Huntington Library Press, 2002, 21–43.

———. "To Love or Not To Love? Jack London and Anna Strunsky's *The Kempton-Wace Letters.*" *Symbiosis* 1, no. 2 (1997): 255–274.

Walling, Anna Strunsky. Letter to Charmian Kittredge, London, January 17, 1919; quoted in Charmian Kittredge London. *The Book of Jack London.* 2 vols. New York: Century, 1921, I: 323–324.

———. "Memoirs of Jack London." *The Masses* 9 (July 1917): 13–17.

"Koolau the Leper" (1909)

First published in the *Pacific Monthly* 22 (December 1909), this provocative tale of Hawaiian resistance to British and American occupiers was one of the first tales of HAWAI'I London wrote when he visited the Islands on the *SNARK* voyage. It is based on the true story of a well-respected ranch foreman (and crack rifleman) on the island of KAUAI who contracted LEPROSY and was sentenced to be deported to the leper colony at Kalaupapa on the island of MOLOKAI. He was told his wife and son, who were not ill, could accompany him as his *kokuas,* or helpers, but at the last moment this permission was denied. Koolau KALUAIKOOLAU, his wife Piilani, and their son fled to the nearly impenetrable valleys on the north side of the island, the Na Pali coast. They hid out in Kalalau Valley, but were pursued by the sheriff of Kauai, LOUIS STOLZ, and his posse, and then they were shelled by the U.S. Navy. However, they managed to elude capture. Koolau shot and killed Stolz and other pursuers. After many months of hiding out, Koolau finally died of leprosy, as did his son, who had contracted it. Piilani buried them with all the proper rituals and several months later dared to emerge. She was not prosecuted. She told her tale to a MISSIONARY, Glen Sheldon, and the Hawaiian transcript he made was later translated and published by Hawaiian scholar Frances Frazier. London himself actually heard the story from BERT STOLZ, a crewman aboard the *SNARK* and the son of Sheriff Stolz. It is thus a bit surprising that the story London wrote is entirely sympathetic to Koolau. The story infuriated London's well-to-do HAOLE (white) Honolulu friends, among them LORRIN THURSTON, editor of the *Honolulu Advertiser,* who denounced London for mentioning leprosy and Hawaiian resistance at a time that the powerful classes of Hawai'i were trying to develop a tourist industry.

Another version of the Koolau story is told by W. S. Merwin in his epic poem *Folding Cliffs* (1998).

SYNOPSIS

The story begins in Kalalau Valley on Kauai where Koolau and his group of lepers are hiding out from the authorities who want to send them to the leper colony on Molokai. As they sit together, he tells them, "'Because we are sick they take away our liberty. We have obeyed the law. We have done no wrong. And yet they would put us in prison. Molokai is a prison. That you know. Niuli, there, his sister was sent to Molokai seven years ago. He has not seen her since. Nor will he ever see her. She must stay there until she dies. This is not her will. It is not Niuli's will. It is the will of the white men who rule the land. And who are these white men?'" Koolau's words immediately connect the problem of their shared disease with the problem of their shared Hawaiianness at the hands of white colonizers:

"We know. We have it from our fathers and our fathers' fathers. They came like lambs, speaking softly. Well might they speak softly, for we were many and strong, and all the islands were ours. As I say, they spoke softly. They were of two kinds. The one kind asked our permission, our gracious permission, to preach to us the word of God. The other kind asked our permission, our gracious permission, to trade with us. That was the beginning. To-day all the islands are theirs, all the land, all the cattle—everything is theirs. They that preached the word of God and they that preached the word of Rum have foregathered and become great chiefs. They live like kings in houses of many rooms, with multitudes of servants to care for them. They who had nothing have everything, and if you, or I, or any Kanaka be hungry, they sneer and say, 'Well, why don't you work? There are the plantations.'" (*Stories*, 1,441)

As Koolau speaks, the narrator describes the sharp contrast between the beauties of the valley—flowers, vines, moonlight—and the horror of the deformities of the lepers: "The moonlight bathed the scene in silver. It was a night of peace, though those who sat about him and listened had all the seeming of battle-wrecks. Their faces were leonine. Here a space yawned in a face where should have been a nose, and there an arm-stump showed where a hand had rotted off. They were men and women beyond the pale, the thirty of them, for upon them had been placed the mark of the beast" (*Stories*, 1,441–1,442). The valley is "a flower-throttled gorge, with beetling cliffs and crags, from which floated the blattings of wild goats. On three sides the grim walls rose, festooned in fantastic draperies of tropic vegetation and pierced by cave-entrances" (*Stories*, 1,442). The narrator describes the fourth side of the valley where "the earth fell away into a tremendous abyss, and, far below, could be seen the summits of lesser peaks and crags, at whose bases foamed and rumbled the Pacific surge." As he notes, in good weather a boat might be able to land on the rocky beach at the entrance to Kalalau Valley. He also notes, "And a cool-headed mountaineer might climb from the beach to the head of Kalalau Valley, to this pocket among the peaks where Koolau ruled; but such a mountaineer must be very cool of head, and he must know the wild-goat trails as well. The marvel was that the mass of human wreckage that constituted Koolau's people should have been able to drag its helpless misery over the giddy goat-trails to this inaccessible spot" (*Stories*, 1,442). The lepers sit and listen to Koolau, "flower-garlanded, in the perfumed, luminous night, and their lips made uncouth noises and their throats rasped approval of Koolau's speech." The narrator describes them as "grotesque caricatures of everything human. . . . Their hands, when they

possessed them, were like harpy-claws. Their faces were the misfits and slips, crushed and bruised by some mad god at play in the machinery of life. Here and there were features which the mad god had smeared half away, and one woman wept scalding tears from twin pits of horror, where her eyes once had been" (*Stories*, 1,442).

As the lepers await attack from either side, they hear their leader's words: "'What did these preachers of the word of God and the word of Rum give us for the land? Have you received one dollar, as much as one dollar, any one of you, for the land? Yet it is theirs, and in return they tell us we can go to work on the land, their land, and that what we produce by our toil shall be theirs. Yet in the old days we did not have to work. Also, when we are sick, they take away our freedom'" (*Stories*, 1,443). When Kiloliana asks who brought the sickness, Koolau explains that it was the foreign cheap labor from CHINA. Kapalei arises and asks Koolau not to make trouble, to make sure they are left alone. But, he says, he will use his nearly fingerless hands to fight the authorities if they pursue Koolau and his group. The lepers try to celebrate the night, as Koolau tells them, "'Life is short, and the days are filled with pain. . . . Let us drink and dance and be happy as we can'" (*Stories*, 1,444). Calabashes are filled with ti-plant liquor and the woman "who wept scalding tears from open eye-pits was indeed a woman apulse with life as she plucked the strings of an ukulele and lifted her voice in a barbaric love-call such as might have come from the dark forest-depths of the primeval world. The air tingled with her cry, softly imperious and seductive" (*Stories*, 1,444).

On the day the sheriff's posse attempts to attack Koolau from behind, the sheriff and all five deputies are shot at long range by Koolau, but not without warning them first to approach no closer. More pursuers come, but, not knowing how treacherous the valley is, they fall to their deaths, as Koolau and his men watch: "Side by side they lay among the morning-glories, with the yellow blossoms of the hau dropping upon them from overhead, watching the motes of men toil upward, till the thing happened, and three of them, slipping, rolling, sliding, dashed over a cliff-lip and fell sheer half a thousand feet" (*Stories*, 1,448). Next, the U.S. Navy begins to shell the lepers in their caves from far down below in the sea: "It was as if all the gods had caught the envelope of the sky in their hands and were ripping it apart as a woman rips apart a sheet of cotton cloth" (*Stories*, 1,448). Many of the lepers are killed or run away. Koolau thinks of

> . . . a fleeting prod of pride. With war guns and rifles, police and soldiers, they came for him, and he was only one man, a crippled wreck of a man at that. They offered a thousand dollars for him, dead or alive. In all his life he had never possessed that much money. The thought was a bitter one. . . . [B]ecause he had caught the sickness, he was worth a thousand dollars—but not to himself. It was his worthless carcass, rotten with disease or dead from a bursting shell, that was worth all that money. (*Stories*, 1,450)

When Koolau and his fellows are again attacked from the rear by an army captain and his soldiers, everyone surrenders but Koolau, who shoots the captain and several of his men:

> For six weeks they hunted him from pocket to pocket, over the volcanic peaks and along the goat trails. When he hid in the lantana jungle, they formed lines of beaters, and through lantana jungle and guava scrub they drove him like a rabbit. But ever he turned and doubled and eluded. There was no cornering him. When pressed too closely, his sure rifle held them back and they carried their wounded down the goat trails to the beach (*Stories*, 1,453).

Two years later, Koolau, still unbroken, crawls into a thicket: "Free he had lived, and free he was dying. A slight drizzle of rain began to fall, and he drew a ragged blanket about the distorted wreck of his limbs" (*Stories*, 1,453). He lifts "his monstrous hands" and gazes at them in wonder: "But how? Why? Why should the wholeness of that wild youth of his change to this? Then he remembered, and once again, and for a moment, he was Koolau, the leper. His eyelids fluttered wearily down and the drip of the rain ceased in his ears. A prolonged trembling set up in his body. This, too, ceased. He half-lifted his head, but it fell back. Then his eyes

opened, and did not close. His last thought was of his Mauser, and he pressed it against his chest with his folded, fingerless hands" (*Stories*, 1,454).

COMMENTARY

There are major differences between Piilani's version and London's. He eliminates Piilani and her son, as well as her belief that their salvation from the authorities was due to their Christian faith. He adds a rebel band of lepers but has Koolau die alone. Most important, London adds his specific critique of the whites' gobbling up all the land as well as their sometimes cruel policies toward lepers and their families. As though to support Koolau's heroism on a mythic level, his eloquent speech is phrased in King James English and is full of Biblical references, the "mark of the beast," lions and lambs, and linguistic markers. King James English is a frequent device of London's in rendering noble the speech of nonwhite indigenous peoples. The story demonstrates London's growing realization of race-based wage slavery in Hawai'i, as successive waves of workers were tried out by British and American colonizers, first Hawaiians, then Chinese, JAPANESE, Filipino, and other groups. He combines a sense of lost paradise before WAGE SLAVERY with a very modern sense of indigenous resistance. The story offers another instance of his ability to pair a heroic individual with a group; Koolau fights not just for himself but for his whole group of lepers and in a larger sense for all indigenous Hawaiians.

CHARACTERS

Koolau   Koolau is a foreman on a Kauai ranch when he is diagnosed with leprosy. He refuses to surrender and be sent to the leper colony on Molokai. He leads a band of lepers who hide out in Kalalau Valley on the north coast of the island. Many of them surrender, leaving him alone to withstand the attacks of guns, cannons, and shells. Koolau dies triumphant, his fingerless hands clutched upon the trigger of his rifle.

Kiloliana   He is a follower of Koolau, "a lean and wiry man with a face so like a laughing faun's that one might expect to see the cloven hoofs under him. They were cloven, it was true, but the cleavages were great ulcers and livid putrefactions. Yet this was Kiloliana, the most daring climber of them all, the man who knew every goat-trail and who had led Koolau and his wretched followers into the recesses of Kalalau" (*Stories*, 1,443).

Kapalei A follower of Koolau's: "Once he had been a judge. He had gone to college at Punahou. He had sat at meat with lords and chiefs and the high representatives of alien powers who protected the interests of traders and missionaries. Such had been Kapalei. But now, as Koolau had said, he was a hunted rat, a creature outside the law, sunk so deep in the mire of human horror that he was above the law as well as beneath it. His face was featureless, save for gaping orifices and for the lidless eyes that burned under hairless brows" (*Stories*, 1,443).

army captain and his men The captain leads his men into Kalalau Valley and converses with Koolau, urging him to surrender; though his remaining people do surrender, Koolau is defiant, and shoots the captain and some of his soldiers.

sheriff and his men Koolau warns the sheriff and his men to approach no closer as they trail him over a sharp ridge; when they ignore his command, Koolau shoots and kills them.

FURTHER READING

Kaluaikoolau, Piilani. *The True Story of Kaluaikoolau: As Told by His Wife, Piilani.* Translated by Frances N. Frazier. Honolulu: University of Hawai'i Press, 2001.
London, Charmian Kittredge. *Our Hawaii.* New York: Macmillan, 1917.
Merwin, W. S. *Folding Cliffs: A Narrative.* New York: Knopf, 1998.

"The Law of Life" (1901)

First published in *McClure's Magazine* 16 (March 1901), this story is an almost perfect illustration of literary NATURALISM especially as influenced by DARWIN. It was included in *Children of the Frost*. It is one of the most-often anthologized of London's stories.

SYNOPSIS

Koskoosh is the chief of an ESKIMO tribe. Now an old man who is blind and lame, he cannot accompany his tribe as they prepare to leave their camp; it is their custom to leave the helpless behind because they would be a burden on the rest. Their tribe is very old and has survived by such practices of putting the group first. His son leaves him a pile of sticks to feed the fire beside him for as long as he can. As Koskoosh waits alone for death, he thinks of the time he left his own father in the snow. He also remembers having seen a old moose killed by WOLVES when it straggled behind the rest of the herd. Koskoosh's memory of the moose, who fights off the wolves until it is overpowered and on the bloody snow, foreshadows his own death. But unlike the moose, which fights to the very end, Koskoosh remains calm in the face of the inevitable. Koskoosh recalls how the Great Famine ravaged his tribe, against which they were all helpless. He reflects on the eternal cycle of life and death, on how even the most vigorous animal or warrior will fall prey to old age:

> It was the way of life, and it was just. He had been born close to the earth, close to the earth had he lived, and the law thereof was not new to him. It was the law of all flesh. Nature was not kindly to the flesh. She had no concern for that concrete thing called the individual. Her interest lay in the species, the race. This was the deepest abstraction old Koskoosh's barbaric mind was capable of, but he grasped it firmly. He saw it exemplified in all life. The rise of the sap, the bursting greenness of the willow bud, the fall of the yellow leaf—in this alone was told the whole history. But one task did Nature set the individual. Did he not perform it, he died. Did he perform it, it was all the same, he died. Nature did not care; there were plenty who were obedient, and it was only the obedience in this matter, not the obedient, which lived and lived always. (*Stories*, 446–447)

The only thing NATURE requires is procreation; having accomplished this, Koskoosh has in the eyes of nature outlived his usefulness. When he feels the cold muzzle of a wolf against his cheek and hears the pack closing in on him, at first he tries to fight them off, then resigns himself to his fate.

COMMENTARY

The moose who desperately fights against the pursuing wolves is an analogue of Koskoosh, and he recognizes the parallel:

> He strained his ears, his restless brain for the moment stilled. Not a stir, nothing. He alone took breath in the midst of the great silence. It was very lonely. Hark! What was that? A chill passed over his body. The familiar, long-drawn howl broke the void, and it was close at hand. Then on his darkened eyes was projected the vision of the moose—the old bull moose—the torn flanks and bloody sides, the riddled mane, and the great branching horns, down low and tossing to the last. (*Stories*, 450)

The image both connects Koskoosh to the natural world around him and at the same time enobles him, two seemingly contradictory effects. But as in many London stories, the individual is not apart from the group nor is he apart from nature, and Koskoosh is only following the rules all men live by, whether civilized or not.

Leaving a sick member of the family to die alone in a harsh environment may seem cruel to the more civilized peoples of the world, but to the NATIVE tribe of Koskoosh, hardened by times of great famine and constant struggle with the elements, such custom is seen as an act of survival by the larger group, whose younger members must survive to propagate the race. Perhaps to modern readers their choice reflects NATURALISM, but to them it was simply natural.

A second kind of naturalism, not man against the elements but man against himself, appears in Koskoosh's memory of how in times of plenty they let meat spoil "and the dogs were fat and worthless with overeating—times when they let the game go unkilled, and the women were fertile, and the lodges were cluttered with sprawling men-children and women-children." However, it was also at these times when "the men became high-stomached, and revived ancient quarrels, and crossed the divides to the south to kill the Pellys, and to the west that they might sit by the dead fires of the Tananas" (*Stories*, 448). In this case, the brute within man, another frequent theme of the naturalistic work, is discovered as a type of ATAVISM.

CHARACTERS

old Koskoosh Koskoosh is an elder of his tribe once respected and admired. However, he has gotten old and feeble, and he is blind. He is left behind as the tribe pulls out for the season, and as he sits feeling the frostbite creep up on him along with a pack of wolves, he meditates on the meaning of "the law of life."

Sit-cum-to-ha She is Koskoosh's granddaughter, but she seems to have no interest in Koskoosh's situation, no tenderness to spare him. She is first seen beating the sled dogs into submission, which emphasizes both the rigors of life on the trail and also the hard facts of survival: "Camp must be broken. The long trail waited while the short day refused to linger. Life called her, and the duties of life, not death. And he was very close to death now" (*Stories*, 445).

Koskoosh's son He approaches his father to say good-bye before he leaves, asking him, "'Is it well with you?'", to which Koskoosh replied, "'It is well. I am as a last year's leaf, clinging lightly to the stem. The first breath that blows, and I fall. My voice is become like an old woman's. My eyes no longer show me the way of my feet, and my feet are heavy, and I am tired. It is well'" (*Stories*, 446).

Zing-ha A companion of Koskoosh's youth, Zing-ha and Koskoosh follow the wounded moose; he is quick to read the signs of its battle with wolves: he says it is "'an old one who cannot keep up with the herd. The wolves have cut him out from his brothers, and they will never leave him.' And it was so. It was their way. By day and by night, never resting, snarling on his heels, snapping at his nose, they would stay by him to the end. How Zing-ha and he felt the blood-lust quicken! The finish would be a sight to see!" (*Stories*, 448).

FURTHER READING

Brandt, Kenneth K. "London's Fiction Technique and His Use of Schopenhauer as the 'Motif under the Motif' in 'The Law of Life.'" In *Eureka Studies in Teaching Short Fiction* 5, no. 1 (Fall 2004): 54–66.

Fellers, Carla. "Reading London: Searching 'The Law of Life' for Stylistic Principle." In *Eureka Studies in Teaching Short Fiction* 5, no. 1 (Fall 2004): 26–33.

McKenna, John J. "Jack London's 'The Law of Life': A 21st Century Prophesy." In *Eureka Studies in Teaching Short Fiction* 5, no. 1 (Fall 2004): 20–25.

Monteiro, George. "Fear and Desire in Jack London's 'Law of Life.'" In *Estudios Anglo-Americanos* 27–28 (2003): 91–94.

"The League of the Old Men" (1902)

"The League of the Old Men" appears with the other tales sympathetic to NATIVES in *The Children of the Frost*, but it was first published in *Brandur Magazine* 1 (October 4, 1902). Set in the YUKON in DAWSON, the story allows old Imber, who is on trial for murdering dozens of whites, to tell his side of things, and the reader ends up sympathetic to his cause. London later said that he thought this was his best short story: "The voices of millions are in the voice of old Imber, and the tears and sorrows of millions are in his throat as he tells the story; his story epitomizes the whole vast tragedy of the contact of the Indian and white man" ("My Best Short Story," in *The Grand Magazine* [London, England, August 1906], quoted in Walker, 222). One of the things that set London apart from other writers portraying NATIVE subjects is the fact that he has his Natives speak eloquently in their own voices.

SYNOPSIS

Their tribe having been decimated by the growing number of whites entering their lands, with their sharp trading practices, stealing of men and women, and diseases, an elderly group of Native men have turned into terrorists to try to repay the whites for ruining their time-honored way of life. After dozens of murders, their leader, old Imber, turns himself in and is tried in Dawson. At his trial, Imber, chief of the Whitefish people, relates through an interpreter to a shocked courtroom his deeds and, more important, his reasons:

> And then began the story, the epic of a bronze patriot which might well itself be wrought into bronze for the generations unborn. . . .
>
> "I am Imber of the Whitefish people. . . . My father was Otsbaok, a strong man. The land was warm with sunshine and gladness when I was a boy. The people did not hunger after strange things, nor hearken to new voices, and the ways of their fathers were their ways. The women found favor in the eyes of the young men, and the young men looked upon them with content. Babes hung at the breasts of the women, and they were heavy-hipped with increase of the tribe. Men were men in those days. In peace and plenty, and in war and famine, they were men." (*Stories*, 816)

There were plenty of fish in the sea and game in the forest. Their DOGS were WOLVES, "'warm with thick hides and hard to the frost and storm,'" like their masters. The Whitefish defended their lands against Native tribes: "'For we were men, we Whitefish, and our fathers and our fathers' fathers had fought against the Pellys and determined the bounds of the land.'" However, with the coming of the whites and their weak and hairless dogs from the SOUTHLAND, who, though unsuited to the frost, mated with the wolves, Imber tells how slowly the Natives' animals grew weak: "'big-headed, thick-jawed, and short-haired, and helpless'" (*Stories*, 817). More and more white men come, taking with them the best of the Natives' hunters, maidens, and dogs, trading nothing of real value in return:

> "It be true, we ate flour, and salt pork, and drank tea which was a great delight; only, when we could not get tea, it was very bad and we became short of speech and quick of anger. So

we grew to hunger for the things the white men brought in trade. Trade! trade! all the time was it trade! One winter we sold our meat for clocks that would not go, and watches with broken guts, and files worn smooth, and pistols without cartridges and worthless. And then came famine, and we were without meat, and two score died ere the break of spring." (*Stories*, 818)

Imber has journeyed to Dawson to turn himself in; having killed many, he is ready to die. He is spotted by two young people who think he must be insane. But a mounted trooper passes by and hears what is going on; he takes him to the police and then to his trial. Exhausted and alone, Imber waits to hear his confession read by a former tribesman of his, now working for the whites, Howkan. Imber is amazed that when he gave Howkan his story, Howkan was able to make marks on paper and then read the confession out loud in court. As he reads Imber recalls other murders and they are copied into the court proceedings; with each one the audience gasps in recognition of someone they knew. Then Imber turns to his reasons for the murders; above Howkan's objections, he explains. As the tribe's resources are pillaged by the whites and the Natives begin to succumb to the "devil" white men's diseases:

[T]he white men come as the breath of death; all their ways lead to death, their nostrils are filled with it; and yet they do not die. Theirs the whiskey, and tobacco, and short-haired dogs; theirs the many sicknesses, the smallpox and measles, the coughing and mouth-bleeding; theirs the white skin, and softness to the frost and storm. . . . And yet they grow fat on their many ills, and prosper, and lay a heavy hand over all the world and tread mightily upon its peoples.

"As I say, the meat in the forest became less and less. It be true, the white man's gun is most excellent and kills a long way off; but of what worth the gun, when there is no meat to kill? . . . [N]ow the hunter may take the trail ten days and not one moose gladden his eyes, while the caribou uncountable come no more at all." (*Stories*, 819)

Imber concludes, "'There are no Whitefish now. Of the old men I am the last. The young men and young women are gone away, some to live with the Pellys, some with the Salmons, and more with the white men. I am very old, and very tired, and . . . I am come seeking the Law" (*Stories*, 822).

COMMENTARY

London clearly stands on the side of Imber and sees his situation as tragic, even calling him "a bronze patriot." There is also more than an undercurrent of admiration for the whites, especially as ANGLO-SAXONS. He writes a series of eloquent speeches for Imber and draws the reader's anger at what has happened to him and his people and also sympathy. But the story does not end with old Imber's poignant words. Instead, it ends with the thoughts of the "square-browed judge" who "likewise dreamed." In the judge's imagination, "all his race rose up before him in a mighty phantasmagoria—his steel-shod, mail-clad race, the lawgiver and world-maker among the families of men. He saw it dawn red-flickering across the dark forests and sullen seas; he saw it blaze, bloody and red, to full and triumphant noon; and down the shaded slope he saw the blood-red sands dropping into night" (*Stories*, 822). One notes that in the story's first paragraph there is mention of the Anglo-Saxon, and here in the judge's mind is an Anglo-Saxon fantasy of world-conquering, the very thing Imber has been struggling against. The judge's thoughts connect the law of the Yukon with the law of nature, "the Law, pitiless and potent, ever unswerving and ever ordaining, greater than the motes of men who fulfilled it or were crushed by it, even as it was greater than he, his heart speaking for softness" (*Stories*, 822).

When he wrote this story London was still under the sway of the RACIALISM of HERBERT SPENCER, who, along with a number of others, predicted the eventual triumph of the white race above all others, as ordained by EVOLUTION. Later, London would reject the premise that the races must engage in competition, though evolution does demonstrate such struggle against a rival group. In his essay "The Human Drift," London broadens his vision to include a sense of how throughout time all groups have had the same impulse to settle new places. But the most important thing about the ending of "The League of the Old Men" is precisely the false sentimentality; the judge imagines his ancestors victorious, as Imber imagined his, but the judge also indulges himself in feeling sorry for Imber. It is hard to know how to read this; certainly London intended for the reader to sympathize with Imber, but the judge's sympathy seems forced, given his jarring visions of Anglo-Saxon forebears and his failure even to consider the merits of Imber's "confession." Thus, like "The Chicago," it is a profoundly ironic story.

CHARACTERS

Imber   Chief of the Whitefish people, Imber and his few remaining men become random murderers of whites in revenge for everything the whites have taken away from them: lands, men, brides, dogs, blankets. By this time the tribe has nearly wasted away. Imber tells the story of his reasons for his acts in a packed courtroom in Dawson, where he is on trial for his life.

little Dickensen   A failed prospector working as a clerk in a brokerage house, he is the first to spot Imber emerging from the Yukon River to turn himself in. A "romantic little chap," he "forever afterward prided himself upon his swiftness of discernment" (*Stories*, 810).

Emily Travis   She chats with Dickensen on the street; she is "dainty and delicate and rare, and whether in London or KLONDIKE she gowned herself as befitted the daughter of a millionaire mining engineer" (*Stories*, 810). Imber stares at her, marveling at her delicacy, when she calls Jimmy, a "white" Native, to her side.

Jimmy   He is "a big, hulking Indian clad in approved white-man style, with an Eldorado king's sombrero on his head. He talked with Imber, haltingly, with throaty spasms. Jimmy was a Sitkan, possessed of no more than a passing knowledge of the interior dialects" (*Stories*, 811); however, he identifies Imber as Whitefish and explains that Imber wishes to turn himself in.

mounted trooper   Imber responds admiringly to the trooper, who is "a stalwart young fellow, broad-shouldered, deep-chested, legs cleanly built and stretched wide apart, and tall though Imber was, he towered above him by half a head. His eyes were cool, and gray, and steady, and he carried himself with the peculiar confidence of power that is bred of blood and tradition" (*Stories*, 812).

Howkan   A former member of the Whitefish people and Imber's sister's son, "Howkan had fallen among the mission folk and been taught by them to read and write" (*Stories*, 814). It is Howkan who takes Imber's confession and reads it in court. Howkan tries to prevent Imber from giving his reasons and listing the grievances of the Natives, but Imber silences him and tells his story.

FURTHER READING

Walker, Franklin. *Jack London and the Klondike: The Genesis of an American Writer* (1966). Reprinted in 2005. San Marino, Calif.: Huntington Library.

"Like Argus of the Ancient Times" (1917)

Included in the posthumous collection *The Red One*, this story first appeared in *Hearst's Magazine* (March 1917). Though it is a very late story, one of London's last four, it recounts in greater detail more about London's actual KLONDIKE experiences than any other of his tales. Its hero is based on an old man London met in the Klondike named John Tarwater, a former mail carrier in Santa Rosa, CALIFORNIA. London met him at Sheep Camp after climbing the CHILKOOT PASS above Dyea Canyon in August 1897 on the long journey to DAWSON. In this story, Tarwater treks from DYEA BEACH to Dawson, a sort of alter ego to London, but he also encounters another alter ego in the young prospector Liverpool, who defends Tarwater against other members of their party and gives him the hope to follow his dream of gold. Thus, in a psychological and autobiographical story, London places different versions of Jack London in dialogue with each other. (London tentatively titled his manuscript draft of an autobiography *Jack Liverpool.*)

SYNOPSIS

In the summer of 1897, there is much trouble in the Tarwater family. Grandfather Tarwater is getting "itchy feet," as he calls it, for the Klondike. Tarwater prospected in the California gold rush of 1849, selling his land in Michigan for his adventure. After years of mining in the Sierras he settled in SONOMA COUNTY. Now, at 60 years old, he decides to hunt gold once again in Patagonia. His family are all opposed. After all, he is too old. Giving up Patagonia, he deeds his 10 acres to his family and takes a wagon and horses so he can get a job as a contract mail deliverer. The family further doubts his sanity. Then, he decides to prospect in the Klondike "'and pick up enough gold to buy back the Tarwater lands'" (*Stories*, 2,439), for which notion he is called an "old fool." His son William explains the high cost of the land and the expenses of travel and outfitting in the Klondike and notes how the papers warn that only the youngest and most hardy will be able to withstand the NORTHLAND.

Undeterred, Tarwater leaves one morning, sells his remaining belongings, and with almost nothing to his name takes the train to San Francisco—he is Klondike-bound. Nearly two weeks later, he lands in the chaos and confusion of men and dogs and supplies trying to get beached at Dyea near SKAGWAY, ALASKA. He has few supplies, but he heads for the Chilkoot Pass along with the others. He finds a man in the river and rescues him; the man, Anson, introduces him to his partners, and Tarwater joins them, washing dishes, collecting wood, repairing supplies, and loading sleds. When Liverpool hears a man named Charles's argument that they get rid of the old man, Liverpool curses them: "'Hell's fire and corruption! . . . The old codger goes down the Yukon with us, stack on that, my hearty! . . . Hard? You don't know what hard is unless I show you! . . . I'll bust the whole outfit to hell and gone if any of you try to side-track him! . . . Just try to side-track him, that is all, and you'll think the Day of Judgment and all God's blastingness has hit the camp in one chunk!'" (*Stories*, 2,448). On the long

and terrible trail to Dawson, they pass Crater Lake, Long Lake, Deep Lake, Lake Lindeman, Lake Bennett, Lake Le Barge, and the rapids of many rivers: "There was no rest. Across the lake, a mile above a roaring torrent, they located a patch of spruce and built their saw-pit. Here, by hand, with an inadequate whipsaw, they sawed the spruce-trunks into lumber. They worked night and day. Thrice, on the night-shift, underneath in the saw-pit, Old Tarwater fainted. By day he cooked as well, and, in the between whiles, helped Anson in the building of the boat beside the torrent as the green planks came down" (*Stories*, 2,448–2,449).

By the time winter settles in Tarwater is ill with cough and chills. Liverpool offers him money for his passage home on a steamer, but Tarwater refuses. Charles tries to turn him over to the mounted police as unfit to enter Canada (all men had to be fit and carry one ton of supplies), but again he is defended by Liverpool. Over the winter he works chopping wood in Dawson and trapping game. While trying to trap a bobcat who has carried away the trap, he is lost in a heavy snowfall. Despite his warm clothes and his kill of a moose, he is in a precarious state. What are the chances that anyone will find him? Soon his scurvy worsens and he falls into a trancelike state "unaware of what was day-dream and what was sleep-dream in the content of his unconsciousness. And here, in the unforgettable crypts of man's unwritten history, unthinkable and unrealizable, like passages of nightmare or impossible adventures of lunacy, he encountered the monsters created of man's first morality that ever since have vexed him into the spinning of fantasies to elude them or do battle with them." In his delirium, "in the dusk of Death's fluttery wings," he slowly sinks into unconsciousness: "But the waking hours grew less, becoming semi-waking or half-dreaming hours as the process of hibernation worked their way with him. Slowly the sparkle point of consciousness and identity that was John Tarwater sank, deeper and deeper, into the profounds of his being that had been compounded ere man was man, and while he was becoming man, when he, first of all animals, regarded himself with an introspective eye and laid the beginnings of morality in foundations of nightmare peopled by the monsters of his own ethic-thwarted desires" (*Stories*, 2,455–2,456). Then, just at the point of no return, he is startled to hear an injured moose stumble into his camp; he kills the moose and realizes that since it came from the east there must be men in the east chasing it. He packs up all the moose-meat he can carry and heads eastward like "an Argus rejuvenated" (*Stories*, 2,457); he finds a camp and begins to recover, doing his same menial tasks for the men there. But on his own, he finds gold: "The sun smoldered on dully glistening yellow. He shook the handful of moss, and coarse nuggets, like gravel, fell to the ground. It was the Golden Fleece ready for the shearing" (*Stories*, 2,459).

Triumphant, Tarwater sells his holdings for $500,000 and heads home to California. He enjoys the properties that are now his and the obsequiousness of his family, who now "fulsomely [eat] out of the gnarled old hand that had half a million dollars to disburse" (*Stories*, 2,460). Tarwater Valley and Tarwater Mountain are once again his, despite the lack of faith of his family.

COMMENTARY

Like Argus of the ancient times,
We leave this modern Greece,
Tum-tum, tum-tum, tum-tum, tum-gum,
To shear the Golden Fleece.

The fact that this is one of London's last stories and that it tells of the struggle of an old man to prove himself to his family suggests that London saw himself in Tarwater, both because of the illnesses at the time that were fast aging him and also his final sense of his achievement; it is fitting that the story returns to the scene of his early success as a writer using the materials he absorbed from his Klondike experiences.

The title of the story implicitly compares Tarwater with several ancient GREEK myths. The ancient city of Argos was part of a kingdom with Mycenae and Tiryns in the Peloponnese region of Greece. One Argus was king of Argos and fought in the Trojan War with Agammemnon of Mycenae. He was the son of Zeus and the nymph Niobe. Another Argus was the builder of Jason's *Argonaut* (surely Tarwater's quest likewise for gold is

an argosy). Argus was the name of one of the sons of Jason and Medea. Argus was the name of Odysseus's dog, who was the only one besides Telemachos to recognize him on his return to Ithaca; this points to Tarwater's triumphal return home all but unrecognizable to his family. Odysseus as related by HOMER was one of London's most common heroic patterns. Another reference is to *Argus Panoptes*, the guardian of the heifer-nymph Io, a primordial giant whose epithet, "all-seeing," arose because his entire body was covered with a hundred eyes; he was the ideal guard because while some of his eyes might be sleeping, others were always open. Argus was set by the jealous Hera to watch Io, a lover of Zeus, whom Hera had transformed into a heifer. To free Io, Zeus had Argus slain by Hermes, who, disguised as a shepherd, first put all of Argus's eyes asleep with his poetry. According to Ovid Hera had the hundred eyes of Argus preserved forever in the peacock's tail. The many eyes of Argus the guardian are paralleled by the visions Tarwater has as he nears the limits of his endurance, which lead him to his treasure.

The earlier Klondike stories are characterized by a set of Homeric myths and archetypes, and in this late story London returned to classical sources. Since "Argus" refers to so many mythological characters, it lends the story its own sense of timeless struggle against all odds, whether old age, the gods, the family, the elements, the self. In its motif of a quest for gold it looks back to Jason's golden fleece, but unlike all the other Arguses (except Odysseus's dog), this argonaut prevails and finds instead of tragedy a new life. By the time he wrote this story, London had read CARL JUNG's *Psychology of the Unconscious* (1916) with its idea of racial memory as Tarwater experiences in his visions.

In addition, there are the names or "epithets" applied to Tarwater by others in the story, which is a Homeric device. For example, when he at last finds a camp and his life is saved when he has been trapped by snowstorm and starvation in the wilderness, the narrator describes how he "tottered down the hill to them, still singing; and when he ceased from lack of breath they called him variously: Santa Claus, Old Christmas, Whiskers, the

Last of the Mohicans, and Father Christmas. And when he stood among them he stood very still, without speech, while great tears welled out of his eyes. He cried silently, a long time, till, as if suddenly bethinking himself, he sat down in the snow with much creaking and crackling of his joints, and from this low vantage point toppled sidewise and fainted calmly and easily away" (2,457). These names, especially the three that refer to Christmas, connect with the classical imagery (as is also the case in other Klondike stories) in that London uses CHRISTMAS DAY and images related to it as the feast day of SOL, when the gods would look down to judge the deeds of men. Surely Tarwater has been judged righteous! At the end of the story, the biblical reference to the parable of the prodigal son is neatly turned into the parable of the prodigal grandfather: "Tarwater arrived home a true prodigal grandfather for whom the fatted calf was killed and ready" (2,459–2,466). However, unlike the great love and gratitude the father has for his son in the parable, to Tarwater's family it is all money. No matter. Tarwater has returned his own prodigal self to himself, having suffered through the great physical and spiritual trials of his adventure. More than anything else, he has found himself, something London was pursuing more and more in his last year. The story's visionary quality and mythic structures speak to the importance of the quest back into his past for him and a vision of a future of redemption.

CHARACTERS

John Tarwater   Tarwater more than proves his readiness for the trail, as much as it costs him physically: "a striking figure on a trail unusually replete with striking figures." Along with "thousands of men, each back-tripping half a ton of outfit, retracing every mile of the trail twenty times, all came to know him and to hail him as 'Father Christmas.'" None of his party complain of his work, if they do complain it's because of his constantly whistling the tune, "Like Argus of the Ancient Times." At times, his joints stiffen with rheumatism and he moves slowly, "and seemed to creak and crackle," but "he kept on moving. Last into the blankets at night, he was first out in the morning, so that the

other three had hot coffee before their one before-breakfast pack. And, between breakfast and dinner and between dinner and supper, he always managed to back-trip for several packs himself" (Stories, 2,448). Though an old man whose family thinks he is mad, Tarwater prevails in his treasure search and returns home a new man.

Mary   John Tarwater's daughter; he is so old that she herself is a grandmother. She tries to dissuade her father from the Klondike with newspaper accounts of the hardships: "'It's worse than the north pole. And they've left their dead a-plenty there themselves. Look at their pictures. You're forty years older 'n the oldest of them'" (Stories, 2,440).

William Tarwater   A son of John Tarwater's who thinks his father has become insane with his wild plans of gold-mining. He advises his father of the expense involved, but Tarwater will not listen to him.

Harris Topping   He is a "day labourer, husband of Annie Tarwater, and father of her nine children" (Stories, 2,439). He also thinks old Tarwater is crazy.

Anson   Soon after his arrival in the Northland, Tarwater observes "a little man weighing no more than a hundred, staggering along a foot-log under all of a hundred pounds of flour strapped on his back. Also, he beheld the little man stumble off the log and fall face-downward in a quiet eddy where the water was two feet deep and proceed quietly to drown" (Stories, 2,441). Tarwater rescues him and joins his group for Dawson.

Liverpool   Liverpool is a stand-in for Jack London. He is a sailor who manages the crossing of lakes and rivers to get to Dawson. The others in his party must have his final approval to allow Tarwater to join them: "'What kind of a party might he be?' Tarwater inquired. 'He's a rough-neck sailor, and he's got a quick, bad temper.' 'Some turbulent,' Anson contributed. 'And the way he can cuss is simply God-awful,' Big Bill testified. 'But he's square,' Big Bill added" (*Stories*, 2,444). London is having a bit of fun with this caricature of himself. Liverpool demands that Tarwater stay with the outfit after all he has done to reach Dawson.

Charles Crayton   The business manager of Anson's party, he invites Tarwater to work for them by cooking, loading, and tending camp. Charles is initially skeptical of allowing Tarwater to join his group, when their food might run low with an extra man, but acquiesces when Tarwater tells him "'I'm seventy, and ain't starved to death never yet'" (*Stories*, 2,444). Crayton unsuccessfully tries to persuade Liverpool and the others to abandon Tarwater.

Big Bill   Member of Anson's party who is impressed with Tarwater's cooking: "'My goodness, the first cheerful and hearty-like camp since we hit the beach,' Big Bill remarked as he knocked out his pipe and began pulling off his shoes for bed" (*Stories*, 2,443).

The Little Lady of the Big House (1916)

Published in London's last year, first in CosmopolITAN (April 1915–January 1916), *The Little Lady of the Big House* presented him with one of his greatest challenges as a novelist. How to write a tragic romance, an agrarian novel, and a record of his successes and failures as a rancher and author—and also as a husband? The novel cannot be said to be successful as a whole, given its numerous ambitions, but it provides a fascinating insight into London's estimation of himself and his working and home life as he neared his end. Few are the novels that feature such searing self-analysis and even condemnation of their creators. Perhaps it is best viewed as having two very different (if not completely conscious) goals: to write a novel to appease his wife for her severe disappointment in him during the time just before it was written and to try to write a modern novel that would not sentimentalize love and sex and marriage but would place it within a materialistic, even Darwinian frame.

The book was panned by reviewers in its day for its sexual imagery and its frank portrayal of adultery. However, readers today find it antiquated in its combination of sexual imagery (like that that of Paula astride the gigantic stallion in the lake) and Victorian fussiness and sentimentality, but the main complaint is its unlikable characters and the fact that they won't stop talking about themselves. Perhaps it was, like much of London's work, ahead of its time: too modern for his readers and not modern enough for ours.

London said of this novel: "It is all sex from start to finish—in which no sexual adventure is actually achieved or comes within a million miles of being achieved, and in which, nevertheless, is all the guts of sex, coupled with strength" (*Letters*, 1,135). Perhaps he was trying to sell his publisher on the book, but nevertheless *The Little Lady of the Big House* might be compared to modernist novels of sex and not romance, survival against existential despair, and power as it corrupts the successful (a theme London's friend Upton Sinclair treated in his 1927 novel *Oil*, made into the naturalist film by Paul Thomas Anderson, *There Will Be Blood* [2007]). Though Dick Forrest is not technically a capitalist, as a rancher, in his mind a man of the land, Forrest is the very emblem of the amoral and spiritually empty business tycoon of the early 20th century who would also be parodied in Theodore Dreiser, Sinclair Lewis, and F. Scott Fitzgerald's works.

SYNOPSIS

Chapters 1–10
The first half of the novel centers on Dick Forrest, and the reader quickly becomes aware that Dick Forrest is centered on Dick Forrest. Awakening at the beginning to the throaty bellows of his favorite horse, Mountain Lad, Dick asserts his own male dominance by pressing various buttons for light, temperature, and servants, an ironic juxtaposition. He rides out in the morning to survey the fecundity of his ranch and give orders to his foremen, but his hyperefficiency contrasts with the natural scenes he encounters. Dick loves his wife dearly

but disdains women in general and children in particular. He advises his hog foreman, Crellin, not to let his daughter attend college at Stanford because she will only marry and throw away her education. Dick compares women with his mare Fotherington Princess, happening by with a manure-spreader; she is a "normal female," evolved by man through generations of breeding. He complains that there is no biological sanction for the way modern women behave about "suffrage and career." Woman should be "first, the mother, second the mate of man." Crellin wonders to himself why Forrest gives such advice when he has no child. Dick contemplates the birth of five children on the ranch from the "least hopeful" and rash farm families, admitting to himself that his farm experiment with people, animals, crops, and land "works out splendidly on paper, with decently wide margins for human nature. And there I admit is the doubt and the danger—the human nature" (286–287). Typical of Dick, he assigns humanity to the margins.

Dick enjoys playing hide-and-seek with Paula's young female relatives who visit the ranch, dragon to their princesses, which makes one question Dick's sexuality and emotional maturity and the odd tone of violence against women. Such tension is echoed when Paula's repeated visits to Dick in his office find her ignored or in Dick's dinner-table tirades. Dick admires the stallion's notion of "love": "Mountain Lad doesn't moon about the loved one. He doesn't moon at all. He incarnates love, and rears right up in meeting and tells them so" (275). In chapter 9, Paula rides Mountain Lad into the lake, as if to challenge Dick's control of the incredible stallion's power.

Paula, clad only in a thin white tunic, climbs upon Mountain Lad, the huge black stallion that is her husband's pride and joy, and rides him down into the swimming lake on the ranch in full view of all visitors. Evan Graham, a visitor to the ranch, finds the vision of her magical, and Dick describes her as "the boy girl, the child that never grew up, the grittiest puff of rose-dust that was ever woman" (106), but he worries that she nearly broke the neck of $35,000 worth of HORSE. As if in response, the following chapter portrays a stag party interrupted by Paula in a dinner gown; Evan muses on the form beneath the gown: "[She] seemed to glint an impression of . . . jewel-like steel. She seemed strength in the most delicate terms and fabrics" (111–112). That night Evan dreams of "the processes of evolution that could produce from primeval mire and dust the glowing, glorious flesh and spirit of woman" (133).

Chapters 11–20

Dick and Paula entertain their many guests, and Evan grows more and more attracted to Paula. The adults seem like children, playing counting games, singing games, practical jokes (like pretending to drown). Dick proudly shows his friend his entire ranch, especially his prize livestock. Evan, a writer, starts his book but is distracted by thoughts of Paula. Paula desperately clings to her husband, but his response to the growing situation is to disappear into his work. Evan and Paula grow closer as they ride horses and spout poetry and philosophy. Paula complains that she is tired of having Dick explain everything scientifically while she yearns for mystery and romance.

Chapters 21–31

Evan can stand the tension no longer and tells himself he should leave. Instead, he boldly takes Paula in his arms and kisses her. She runs away. Dick and Paula talk around the situation, but the tension between them is growing too. While they are squirrel-hunting, Mountain Lad rushes some mares, nearly injuring Dick and Paula. As they rest on the grassy hillside afterward, Paula's eyes are shut as Dick picks the squirrels off one-by-one as they emerge from their dens. Paula is connected with the earth; Dick is killing what emerges from it. Each is hoping in this scene to talk about their situation, but neither can.

Paula and Evan discuss their affair, and he urges her to be the one to decide. This is also what Dick asks of her; she tells each of them she can love both of them but they tell her she cannot. "'It will work out,' she assured him gravely. 'It will have to work out somehow. Dick says all things work out. All is change'" (305). Dick scorns the women guests as "cats" who will find out Paula's secret (308). Soon after this Dick rescues a woman about to be raped by one of his foremen, not because he "climbed over another man's fence but because [he was] guilty of causing a circumstance that is an impairment to ranch efficiency" (316–317). Hearing this, Paula assumes Dick would also look upon her loss as a question of ranch efficiency, seeing him as "a philosopher who would not lift a hand to hold her" (348–349).

Their marriage is a fundamentally conflicted one. When Dick sings Mountain Lad's song, "Hear me! I am Eros. I stamp upon the hills," Paula asks to hear instead the "Song of Red Cloud, the Acorn Planter," an agrarian, peaceable figure. She wants to see Dick as both a modern man and as the idealized planter, not just "a male human that finds Trojan adventures in sieges of statistics" (85–86). Despite their love, they do not know each other; for example, they often visit each other's private quarters when the resident is not there. Perhaps when they met, they were free spirits, but somehow marriage has stultified their natural feelings. The rigid rancher Dick was actually running a Paris coffee house and Paula was painting in the Quartier Latin. Now they find themselves trapped in the roles of traditional marriage, hosting endless drunken dinner parties. In particular, Paula becomes fed up with Dick's philosophical ramblings and arguments with guests. She tells Evan: "'Words, words, words—and I want to know what to do, what to do with myself, what to do with you, what to do with Dick'" (259).

Among other things to annoy Paula is the tendency of Dick's men friends to discuss the shortcomings of women as "conservative," "half-sex," and "half-soul" (263). They tease the young poet Leo for his admiration of Paula. With their faith in OSCAR WILDE and George Bernard Shaw's cynicism, they belittle Leo and Paula's arguments for beauty and idealism. However, perhaps they are right; Leo points to the Forrests' marriage as an example of true love.

Paula revels in the "madness of it, the hell of it and joy of it" of her affair; for his part, Evan abandons "priest and code" for "other wisdoms and decisions," thinking that it will all be settled "somehow as human affairs are, and that someone would be hurt," but "life was hurt" (254). Evan seems to manipulate Paula through their scenes together

and does not seem to realize that his "modern" view of life and love does not account for her situation; in this he resembles Dick. Prince Charming starts to show his concealed willfulness and selfishness.

Paula finds it impossible to free herself either from her loveless marriage to Dick or her affair with Evan, and part of her struggle is her notion of what a woman should be, taught to her by her society and her husband. She has failed as mother, and perhaps feels that she must fend for herself. Though the three in the love triangle are described as "straight-talkers" (309), they are not able to discuss the situation. Paula and Evan look to Dick as "the one who acted, did things, no matter what there were. . . . Well, Dick could solve it. He could solve anything" (310). In the meantime, Paula is experiencing the fullness of "living, living, living" on the top of the "wave of her life" (312), enjoying her position as one sought after by two such worthy hunters. She is thrilled by her newfound sense of being fought over.

Paula rushes around serving her guests, drinking, laughing, pretending to be satisfied. She urges Dick and Evan to be "good fellows together," singing and citing poetry to them of the Viking past. They talk of famous battles, and, emboldened, she aggressively argues her ideas. She has had her Darwinian moment:

> They were right. It was a game. The race was to the swift, the battle to the strong. They had run such races, fought such battles. Then why not she? And as she continued to look, that self-query became reiterant. . . . Men were men, and they were two such men. She felt a burn of jealousy against those unknown women who must have been, and her heart hardened. They had taken their fun where they found it—Kipling's line ran through her head.
>
> Pity? Why should she pity, any more than she should be pitied? The whole thing was too big, too natural, for pity. They were taking a hand in a big game, and all could not be winners. Playing with the fancy, she wandered on to a consideration of the outcome. Always she had avoided such consideration, but the tiny highball had given her daring. It came to her

that she saw doom ahead, doom vague and formless but terrible. (324–325)

Paula is aware that Dick has had other women before her and resents the freedom of men to have sex where they find it. Paula wishes to experience a freer life, but her tragedy is that she has only male models to follow. She senses doom but follows her affair with Evan anyway. "Let come what would," she thinks, "She had never lived before, and it was worth it, no matter what the inevitable payment must be made ·in the end. Love?—had she ever really loved Dick?" (326).

And then another crisis occurs: Dick sees Paula and Evan kissing on the terrace. After a visit to Paula's chambers, he plans to kill himself in a staged hunting accident. But first he goes to his rooms and reviews insurance papers and his will. However, Paula enters and confesses her affair to him. Dick professes his love, but she pulls away from him and confronts him with his lack of attention to her. She says she is confused, not knowing whether to stay with him or go away with Evan. The most important issue for her is who she really loves, but second is who really loves her. Dick tells her it is her decision. Wryly, she urges him to avoid "hunting accidents."

She returns to his room one more time to talk, but she finds him working at business, seemingly the last straw for her. Silently she leaves and calls him to tell him he is her choice. But before he can appreciate his sense of relief, he hears the report of her rifle and rushes to her chambers: "'She beat me to it. She beat me to it'" (382). She "'had the grit. She had the grit,'" he repeats (386). As Paula breathes her last breaths, she asks each man, Dick and Evan, to sing to her. She tells them both of her love and apologizes to Dick that "'there were no babies'" (341). As she dies, the men hear in the background the cries of Mountain Lad and Fotherington Princess.

The novel ends with Paula wounding herself mortally with a rifle—the reader is not told explicitly whether it is suicide, as her lover Graham believes, or an accident, as she tells her husband—and convincing a doctor to inject her with an overdose of morphine. As she drifts off, she says good-bye to both of her lovers: "Two bonnie, bonnie men. Good-by, bonnie men. Good-by, Red Cloud. . . . Stretch the skin tight, first. You know I don't like to be hurt'" (392).

COMMENTARY

Fraud everywhere, from affairs to social games to diving contests to Jong Keena hand games, disguises, hoaxes, practical jokes, hide-and-seek, suicide ruses. Yet Clarice Stasz, a biographer of London, sees this novel as a "frank borrowing" from his life with his second wife CHARMIAN KITTREDGE LONDON and a "psychologically valid" record of events in their lives in the winter of 1912–13 (Stasz, *Dreamers*, 257). London's ALCOHOLISM and depression had gotten out of hand on their visit to New York City, and he mistreated Charmian terribly; their wounds were (mostly) healed on the voyage home around CAPE HORN on the *DIRIGO*, but again in 1913 their marriage suffered, and Charmian nearly had an affair with two handsome young visitors to the BEAUTY RANCH that year. After much soul-searching, the couple reconciled, and *The Little Lady of the Big House* is one result; Charmian recalled that they wept over it when Jack read his ending to her. It certainly does seem to reflect London's anxious soul-searching at this time in his life, as a man, husband, and author whose body was beginning to fail him. The love triangle in the story parallels certain events at the Londons' ranch. Like Charmian, Paula is an insomniac and has no children. Like Dick, London could be extremely overbearing—and drunk with his guests to the exclusion of Charmian. Graham offers Paula a gentleness that Dick cannot. Dick's main problem is his obsession with success at everything; he cannot merely run his large ranch—he places it above his attentions to his wife. He imagines himself as a great stallion lording it over the valley. London too could be entirely self-absorbed. But he paid a price and seems to have learned from it. Dick may raise the livestock and crops to win prizes, but he has, in the biblical sense, neglected his vineyards where it most counts. Just before he began *The Little Lady of the Big House*, London had completed another self-revelation, *John Barleycorn*, which is even more unsparing of himself than this novel.

Stasz argues that, as in *John Barleycorn*, in this novel there is "expressed for all to see the detailed dynamics of a situation that almost destroyed their marriage." They were proud that they had averted destruction, and they felt their bond strengthened by the test of affection. London wrote this book, Stasz believes, as a "tone poem of love for the woman who stood by him through the LONG SICKNESS, the trials of the South Seas, the WHITE LOGIC, and more." Yet it is so self-revelatory that it "cuts to the quick of masculine values, digs at their worth," by questioning the entire back-to-the-land Jeffersonian myth, that "the American pioneer hero's dream" of "relentless male achievement, even in the idyllic setting of agrarian reform, is not alone the answer to a man's needs." London realized that his dreams of "conquer[ing] the earth" paled beside his encounter with "the darker feminine side." The chance of Charmian's adultery forced him to reevaluate his entire "self-concept." This was nothing short of a "conversion experience." Followed soon upon by the burning of WOLF HOUSE, it helped London (like Dick) discover that his scientific approach to life was empty; though Dick likes to measure things and "considers and values only those objects amenable to easy measurement," he finds that this is not enough to build a life around (Stasz, *Dreamers*, 260, 284–285).

In an essay devoted to the ironic possibilities of this novel, Jeanne Campbell Reesman argues that the book intends to present Dick Forrest with a sense of irony and, at times, even contempt and blames him completely for the death of his marriage and his wife. London writes Dick as a self-parody: "In this dark and difficult last novel, London brings together through painful irony his analysis of the position of women in modern American society by means of a ruthless examination of his own difficulties as a husband and lover" (33). Surprisingly, the Sonoma novels all seem as if they were written by an advocate for women's rights, what we today would call a feminist. London's views on women were ahead of his time. As early as *A Daughter of the Snows* or *The Sea-Wolf*, he was interested in women who initially appear weak but who demonstrate extraordinary strength, especially in transforming their men. *The Little Lady of the Big House*

is a disappointing work in many ways, but it is best read from a feminist point of view, which reveals its irony.

The novel exists in the tradition of unhappy and even suicidal women who are destroyed by their love relationships: in Tolstoy's *Anna Karenina*, Flaubert's *Madame Bovary*, Chopin's *The Awakening*, and Wharton's *The House of Mirth*. In these novels, a heroine finds she cannot overcome the restrictions of patriarchy and chooses what she thinks is the only way out of an impossible situation. In addition, it is influenced by novels in which male protagonists are challenged by the Feminine, such as Hawthorne's Arthur Dimmesdale in *The Scarlet Letter*, Miles Coverdale in *The Blithedale Romance*, and Young Goodman Brown; James's Ralph Touchett (*The Portrait of a Lady*), Merton Densher (*The Wings of the Dove*), and John Marcher ("The Beast in the Jungle"). Though these men do not resemble Dick in his furious displays of masculinity, like him they have in their interactions with women opportunities for spiritual growth which they squander.

Self-satire and ridiculous male display are everywhere in this novel, from the offensive names the Forrests give their Chinese servants to Dick's excruciating imitations of the stallion Mountain Lad's "love song." But the strongest attack is upon Dick's neglect of his relationship with his wife in favor of all his other interests. He is an efficient, intelligent man who runs his farm like a machine in a factory and thinks of the animals and everything else there as cogs in his engine of success. Realizing how far the affair of Paula has progressed, first Dick, then Paula, decide to kill themselves. The fact that Paula "beats" Dick to it and sacrifices herself reflects her adoption of Dick's hypermasculinity. Paula has no model but her husband, and he proves to be a fatal one; she does what she knows *he* would do instead of what she would do, a double tragedy.

CHARACTERS

Dick Forrest   Dick Forrest, owner of a huge ranch in SONOMA VALLEY, California, is a driven success at everything he tackles, or at least he believes so. The son of a wealthy man reared in the city, he uses his inheritance to return to the land and build his 250,000-acre ranch. He is known for everything from his football exploits in college, his adventures as a young man, his gold and silver prospecting, and his great success at stock-breeding:

> Five feet, ten inches in height, weighing a clean-muscled one hundred and eighty pounds, Dick Forrest was anything but insignificant for a forty year old man. The eyes were gray, large, over-arched by bone of brow, and lashes and brows were dark. . . . The jaws were strong without massiveness, the nose, large-nostriled, was straight enough and prominent enough without being too straight or prominent, the chin square without harshness and uncleft, and the mouth girlish and sweet to a degree that did not hide the firmness to which the lips could set on due provocation. . . .
>
> Laughter lurked in the mouth corners and eye-corners, and there were cheek lines about the mouth that would seem to have been formed by laughter. Equally strong, however, every line of the face that meant blended things carried a notice of surety. Dick Forrest was sure—sure, when his hand reached out for any object on his desk, that the hand would straightly attain the object without a fumble or a miss of a fraction of an inch. (37–38)

Dick is obsessed with his work. He lives by the rules of his own system but is not able to see how his success is causing failure in his most important relationship. His selfishness leads his wife to suicide.

Paula Forrest Symbolic of the Jungian anima or force of life, Paula worships beauty and love, which connects her with other London characters such as Ruth Morse in *Martin Eden,* Maud Brewster in *The Sea-Wolf,* or Lucy in "The Night-Born." Paula is an accomplished artist, musician, and athlete who, though she is devoted to Dick, feels restless in her marriage because he pays so little attention to her.

Evan Graham Dick describes Evan to Paula before his arrival: "'He's a man, all man. He delivers the goods. You know the type—clean, big, strong, simple; been everywhere, seen everything, knows

most of a lot of things, straight, square, looks you in the eyes—well, in short, a man's man'" (94). Dick recalls his friend as "hardbitten" (95) and as of yet uncaught by a woman, with "'good wind and fast legs'" (96). Evan is a blonder, taller, thinner version of Dick minus the self-aggrandizement, with full red lips, graceful brow, and straighter nose. He is a true Prince Charming for Paula. Evan is visiting the ranch for a chance to work on his writing, but he falls in love with Paula and abandons writing for riding in the hills and picnicking with her.

Oh My Oh My is based on London's manservant Yoshimatsu Nakata; like Oh My, Nakata was the first person London saw each morning. Dick has breakfasted and is dressed—in bed by Oh My. As Nakata also recalled of London, Oh My notes how Dick wakes up with a smile on his face every morning. The Forrests name their servants with nicknames.

Oh Joy, Ah Me, Oh Well, Oh Hell, Oh Dear, Oh Ho Other Asian servants at the Forrest Ranch. Oh Dear is Paula's maid.

Thayer A buyer of sheep from Idaho who is staying in the Big House. He is thrilled at the quality of Dick's livestock.

Hanley A ranch worker with whom Dick talks about a new dam he is building; he asks Hanley for figures on what it will cost to haul gravel and crush rocks.

Mr. Dawson Dick's crop-manager with whom Dick discusses weather, rat-catching, and the delivery of some tractors.

Mr. Hennessy The veterinarian on the Forrest Ranch; he breaks horses for Paula to ride and discusses the various horsemen on the ranch. He and Dick decide to fire two men.

Crellin Hog foreman whose daughter wishes to attend Stanford University. London himself made it a practice to send any ranch workers' children to college who so desired. Yet Dick tries to talk Crellin out of it, as he believes education is wasted on women.

Mendenhall   He is Dick's horse-manager as well as pasture expert, "and who was reputed to know, not only every blade of grass on the ranch, but the length of every blade of grass and its age from seed-germination as well" (23). They discuss irrigation on the ranch.

Thompson   A "greasy little man" (25), he is the machinist who repairs Dick's refrigerator, a great luxury at the time. Dick tells him how to fix the dynamo and the milking machines.

Naismith   A guest at the ranch, "a youngish man of thirty, with glasses" (26), he is a writer for *Breeders' Gazette*. Of Dick he remarks, "'Forrest's the real wooz. He's the brains that picks brains. He could run an army, a government, or even a three-ring circus'" (93).

Bert Wainwright   Another young guest at the ranch who challenges Naismith to billiards. Bert is a great favorite of the ladies.

Rita Wainwright   Bert's sister, she is one of the young girls Dick watches sing and dance and plays hide-and-seek with.

Ernestine Desten   Paula's half-sister and a long-time guest at the ranch. Ernestine plays the piano. She is described as "a small but robust blonde of eighteen" (29) who jumps into a pillow fight with Dick. His regard of her verges on the lewd: "Her breasts heaved from the exertion, and he marked the pulsating of the shimmering cherry-colored silk with delight as he flung his glance around to the other two girls similarly breathing" (30–31).

Lute Desten   Another of Paula's sisters, she teases Dick for spying on the girls: "'[R]un along, little boy. Run along'" (28). She also leads the rush on Dick with seat cushions, and he threatens to spank her.

Mr. Blake   Dick's secretary. Dick maintains a heavy "correspondence that included learned soci-

eties and every sort of breeding and agricultural organization and that would have compelled the average petty business man, unaided, to sit up till midnight to accomplish" (35).

Pittman   Pittman is Dick's "show-manager" (35), one of a steady stream of managers and foremen Dick meets with each day. Dick holds all his employees to his discipline and time-saving: "As Dick Forrest had taught them, the minutes spent with him were not minutes of cogitation" (35).

Bonbright   Dick's assistant secretary who transcribes Dick's plans in shorthand; Dick uses Bonbright's notes to remind his other employees of exactly what he wants to do.

Paulson   Dick's head plowman, he complains to Dawson about Dick's "genius" and the way he drives his men.

Wardman   Dick's sheep-manager who takes Thayer to look over Dick's Shropshire rams. He works with Bonbright on following Dick's orders.

Messrs.   Crockett,   Davidson,   and   Slocum   Attorneys, or Board of Guardians, who read young Dick his father's will and counsel him against his plan to go traveling the world. They also refuse to give him much of his money until he is 21.

Tim Hagan   A friend of Dick's who fights with him and hits the road with him. They depart from the Ferry Building and ride trains as hobos. Dick arranges with Tim to have his father, a policeman, pick Dick up and earn a $30,000 reward. Tim is killed in a train accident while hoboing with Dick.

Mrs.   Summerstone   Woman hired by the Board of Guardians to look after the 13-year-old heir "Young Dick" after his father's death. She is shocked when Dick returns after a three-year absence and she does not recognize him now that he has become a man hardened by his adventures.

John Chisum   Owner of the Jingle-bob Ranch in New Mexico where Dick learns horsemanship.

Ah Sing Chinese cook in Dick's Nob Hill mansion; he is Dick's confidant in his dealings with his guardians.

Professors Carey and Barsdale Professors at the UNIVERSITY OF CALIFORNIA whom Dick pays to coach him for admission.

Aaron Hancock A philosopher who visits the ranch and debates the existence of GOD with Dick; he is modeled on London's tramp-philosopher friend Frank Strawn-Hamilton.

Terrence McFane Another philosopher and guest at the ranch; Paula describes him as "'an epicurean anarchist, if you know what that means. He wouldn't kill a flea'" (115). Dick is constantly bailing him out of trouble.

Leo (Theo Malken) A poet visiting the ranch. He is disowned by his wealthy parents and spends his time with his verse. After years of starving tutoring immigrant Jews, he is taken up by the Forrests and housed at the ranch.

Dar Hyal A Hindu revolutionist who is a political refugee from India in danger of being deported. He is an advocate of terrorism and mass action and is basically hiding out at the ranch.

Eddie Mason Guest at the ranch who plays ragtime on the piano surrounded by girls. He joins with the others in asking Dick to sing his "Acorn Song."

Mrs. Mason Guest at the ranch who asks Paula to play the piano.

Wombold "Young Mr. Wombold, Graham gleaned, was an hereditary large land-owner in the vicinity of Wickenberg who prided himself on not yielding to the trend of the times by becoming an absentee landlord" (118); Wombold argues that JAPANESE coolies should be imported to do farm labor in California.

Adolph Weil, Jeremy Braxton, Edwin O'Hay, Chauncey Bishop New visitors to the ranch who come to consult Dick about various business interests: Weil, a lawyer who is concerned with a water rights suit; Braxton, Dick's general superintendant of the Harvest Group he runs in Mexico; O'Hay, "a red-headed Irish musical and dramatic critic" (165); and Bishop, a fraternity brother of Dick's and editor of the *San Francisco Dispatch*. Braxton is killed by a mob of Mexicans who try to rob him in the mountains.

Martha Tully, Mr. Gulhuss, Mr. Deacon, Captain Lester Lunch guests at the ranch who represent various interests of Dick's: Mrs. Tully is a society matron who is Paula's aunt; Gulhuss is state veterinarian; Lester is captain of a Pacific mail ship; and Deacon is a portrait painter.

Donald Ware A pianist visiting the ranch whose playing transports Paula, causing Graham to feel jealous.

Colonel Stoddard Business manager for Dick on the Harvest project in Mexico; he debates financing the project with Dick.

Mr. Winters An agricultural college graduate visiting the ranch for an article to be published in the *Pacific Rural Press* and a protégé of Dick's.

Smith Ranch foreman who is fired by Dick for attacking a woman; he is sent "down the hill" for inconveniencing Dick (317).

Froelig A sculptor friend of Dick's, he is modeled on Finn Froelich, a sculptor friend of London's who created many decorations for the ranch and a famous bust of London.

Xavier Martinez A famous California painter and friend of Dick's; he is modeled on the real Martinez, a close friend of London's.

Lottie Mason, Miss Maxwell, Mrs. Watson Mason is a "tall, striking brunette of twenty-five, undeniably beautiful, undeniably daring" (347); Dick once cheated with her on Paula, but he did not actually have sex with her. Maxwell and Watson are other women visitors.

Callahan A ranch employee who fetches the doctor at the end of the novel.

Dr. Robinson Arrives after Paula shoots herself and administers morphine to her.

FURTHER READING

Bender, Bert. "Jack London and 'the Sex Problem.'" In *Jack London: One Hundred Years a Writer*. Edited by Sara S. Hodson and Jeanne Campbell Reesman. San Marino, Calif.: Huntington Library 2002, 147–188.

Campbell, Donna. "'The (American) Muse's Tragedy': Jack London, Edith Wharton, and *The Little Lady of the Big House*." In *Jack London: One Hundred Years a Writer*. Edited by Sara S. Hodson and Jeanne Campbell Reesman. San Marino, Calif.: Huntington Library, 2002, 189–216.

Fine, David. "Jack London's Sonoma Valley: Finding the Way Home." In *San Francisco in Fiction: Essays in a Regional Literature*. Edited by David Fine and Paul Skenazy. Albuquerque: University of New Mexico Press, 1995, 56–72.

Furer, Andrew J. "Jack London's New Woman: A Little Lady with a Big Stick." *Studies in American Fiction* 22, no. 2 (Autumn 1994): 185–214.

Labor, Earle. "From 'All Gold Canyon' to *The Acorn-Planter*: Jack London's Agarian Vision." In *Western American Literature* 11 (1976): 83–101.

Reesman, Jeanne Campbell. "Irony and Feminism in *The Little Lady of the Big House*." In *Thalia: Studies in Literary Humor* 12, nos. 1–2 (1992): 33–46.

Stasz, Clarice. *American Dreamers: Charmian and Jack London*. New York: St. Martin's, 1988.

———. *Jack London's Women*. Amherst: University of Massachusetts Press, 2001.

Watson, Charles N., Jr. *The Novels of Jack London: A Reappraisal*. Madison: University of Wisconsin Press, 1983.

"Li Wan, the Fair" (1902)

First published in ATLANTIC MONTHLY (August 1902) and included in *Children of the Frost*, "Li-Wan, the Fair" is one of several KLONDIKE sto-ries in which London explores the painful effects of race on half-white, half-NATIVE children in the Northwest.

SYNOPSIS

Li Wan is a young woman of mixed white and Native parentage, a fact of which she is unaware until she and her husband visit a white settlement to sell their furs. At the beginning of the story, she bravely fights off their wolf-dogs for the moose meat she cooks for her husband. But she is troubled with strange thoughts of being different from the other Native women and dreams of yellow-haired men. She recalls being beaten by her mother for talking about such visions. When she first sees the white settlement and hears the word "cabin," she feels that "it seemed at last that all things were coming clear. Now! now! she thought. A sudden moisture swept into her eyes, and the tears trickled down her cheeks. The mystery was unlocking, but the faintness was overpowering her. If only she could hold herself long enough!" Fainting, she calls out "'Daddy! Daddy!'" (*Stories*, 595). After looking with puzzlement at the miners who are toiling away, even digging under the town's streets, Li Wan sees a white woman "fair of skin and rosy as a child," graced with lustrous black hair. She hears the woman singing and suddenly is "smitten with a vision" of her mother (*Stories*, 597). When her husband, Canim, is asleep, she sneaks back to where she saw the woman. This woman is Evelyn Van Wyck, a wealthy society woman who, as a widow, went North to prospect with her partner, Myrtle Giddings; Mrs. Van Wyck "cultivated the primitive with refined abandon" (*Stories*, 598). Li Wan enters their cabin and cries out, "'O Woman, thou art sister of mine!'" but as she speaks in her own tongue the white women cannot understand. Mrs. Van Wyck wants to buy Li Wan's "ragged and trail-worn" furs for her collection, but is disturbed by Li Wan's excited weeping and trembling. But she gains control of herself and points around the cabin, saying "table" and "stove"; the women think she is there to show off the little mission education she once had. Mrs. Van Wyck tries to get her to trade her jacket for Mrs. Van Wyck's wrapper, and in showing it to her she accidentally exposes a breast. Li Wan "uttered a loud cry, and ripped and tore at her skin-shirt until her own breast showed firm and white as Evelyn Van Wyck's. Mrs. Van Wyck realizes she is a "half-breed" and pities her (*Stories*, 601). Suddenly Canim appears and retrieves his wife, telling her he will teach her to forget her dreams.

COMMENTARY

"Li Wan, the Fair" is a poignant but strained tale of racial confusion and nostalgia, compounded by the harsh treatment Li Wan receives from her husband and contextualized by the entire social problem of being "other." This story, along with one written three weeks earlier, "Nam-Bok the Unveracious," caused *McClure's Magazine* to drop London's contract as the stories were found to be unsuitable for *McClure's* readers. The story does have a certain sensational feel to it, but its overall tone is tragic; Li Wan wants to be who she really is but realizes that she will never be able to rejoin her white half brothers and sisters.

CHARACTERS

Li Wan   Li Wan is the wife of Canim and humbly serves him. When they journey to DAWSON, she meets two white women and realizes that she too is part white; her dreams have spoken strange words to her and now she hears them in waking life. She is dragged away from her heritage by Canim at the end of the story.

Canim the Canoe   "He was a large Indian fully six feet in height, deep-cheated and heavy-muscled, and his eyes were keener and vested with greater mental vigor than the average of his kind. The lines of will had marked his face deeply, and this, coupled with a sternness and primitiveness, advertised a native indomitability, unswerving of purpose, and prone, when thwarted, to sullen cruelty" (*Stories*, 590).

Mrs. Evelyn Van Wyck   Mrs. Van Wyck is an unusually adventurous women from the States who has left behind her life as a wealthy socialite after her husband's death. She prospects for gold and collects Native artifacts.

Miss Myrtle Giddings   Miss Giddings is Mrs. Van Wyck's partner but is a little less brave than her friend. When Li Wan appears in their doorway, Miss Giddings, "with a leap that would have done credit to a cave-woman," jumps behind the table. Unlike her partner, she is scornful of Li Wan.

"Love of Life" (1905)

First published in *McClure's Magazine* 26 (December 1905), this gripping narrative of desperate survival is one of London's most memorable KLONDIKE stories. Vladimir Lenin had his wife read it to him on his deathbed, as he struggled at the end of his life.

SYNOPSIS

"'I say, Bill, I've sprained my ankle'" (*Stories*, 923). So the protagonist tells his partner as they struggle across a stream, loaded down with heavy packs among the rocks. But Bill ignores his pleas and walks ahead:

> Bill staggered on through the milky water. He did not look around. The man watched him go, and though his face was expressionless as ever, his eyes were like the eyes of a wounded deer. . . . His lips trembled a little, so that the rough thatch of brown hair which covered them was visibly agitated. His tongue even strayed out to moisten them. "Bill!" he cried out. It was the pleading cry of a strong man in distress, but Bill's head did not turn. The man watched him go, limping grotesquely and lurching forward with stammering gait up the slow slope toward the soft sky-line of the low-lying hill. He watched him go till he passed over the crest and disappeared. Then he turned his gaze and slowly took in the circle of the world that remained to him now that Bill was gone (*Stories*, 923).

Abandoned by his partner, the protagonist endures a terrible journey, first limping, then crawling, then merely pulling himself ahead with his arms for mile upon mile. He thinks hopelessly of reaching

Coronation Bay far away, which he has seen on a Hudson Bay Company chart. He finds himself in a strange no-man's-land: "Again his gaze completed the circle of the world about him. It was not a heartening spectacle. Everywhere was soft sky-line. The hills were all low-lying. There were no trees, no shrubs, no grasses—naught but a tremendous and terrible desolation that sent fear swiftly dawning into his eyes" (*Stories*, 923). Continually calling to Bill, he lurches forward towards a fir forest where he thinks Bill will be waiting for him. Yet he knows better: "But hard as he strove with his body, he strove equally hard with his mind, trying to think that Bill had not deserted him, that Bill would surely wait for him at the cache. He was compelled to think this thought, or else there would not be any use to strive, and he would have lain down and died" (*Stories*, 925).

But die he does not, creeping his way along, chewing berries and milk grass, which sicken him, occasionally catching a small bird, and a few minnows, but slowly starving; he feels "a hope greater than knowledge and defying experience" (*Stories*, 925). In heavy fog and under an unseen sun, he even crawls in his sleep, his feet bleeding from the sharp rocks. Delirious, he tries to shoot a bear and fails; he begins to hear the howls of WOLVES. He longs to "die and sleep": "It was only life that pained. There was no hurt in death. . . . Then why was he not content to die" (*Stories*, 933). Enduring snow and rain, he crawls along feeling the life slowly dying within him: "He, as a man, no longer strove. It was the life in him, unwilling to die, that drove him on. He did not suffer. His nerves had become blunted, numb, while his mind was filled with weird visions and delicious dreams" (*Stories*, 933).

Soon a wolf is on his trail. Peering out of his cave, he sees it: "Again came the snuffle and cough, and outlined between two jagged rocks not a score of feet away he made out the gray head of a wolf. The sharp ears were not pricked so sharply as he had seen them on other wolves; the eyes were bleared and bloodshot, the head seemed to droop limply and forlornly. The animal blinked continually in the sunshine. It seemed sick. As he looked it snuffled and coughed again" (*Stories*, 934). The wolf is sick, but it is as persistent as the protagonist.

It gets so close to him that he can see its yellowish brown tongue. He turns around as he crawls to see it licking the blood from his trail: "The patience of the wolf was terrible. The man's patience was no less terrible. For half a day he lay motionless, fighting off unconsciousness and waiting for the thing that was to feed upon him and upon which he wished to feed. Sometimes the languid sea rose over him and he dreamed long dreams; but ever through it all, waking and dreaming, he waited for the wheezing breath and the harsh caress of the tongue" (*Stories*, 937). Playing dead, the man lets the wolf approach and even sink his teeth into his hand; however, with his last strength the man strangles the wolf and then, fastening his teeth into the wolf's neck, drinks its blood: "It was not pleasant. It was like molten lead being forced into his stomach, and it was forced by his will alone" (*Stories*, 938). He is saved and at last sleeps. When he awakens, he sees that he is at Coronation Bay, where a whaling ship sits in the harbor. He is rescued, but it is months before he recovers from his experience. One wonders what sort of man he will be back in the city of San Francisco.

COMMENTARY

As in "In a Far Country," in this story the NORTHLAND CODE of BROTHERHOOD on THE TRAIL is broken by Bill, but his partner's (misguided) faith that Bill is waiting for him up ahead fuels his desperate fight for life, ironically illustrating the great importance of brotherhood to decent men like the protagonist. It is a brutal tale of competition between man and beast, testament to London's sense of the primacy of the will to live and the Darwinian imperative of survival and ADAPTATION to a threatening environment. The protagonist becomes like the wolf that pursues him, learning to wait as patiently as it does for a chance. He eventually kills and drinks the blood from the wolf. Though the men on the *Bedford* see him as just a "thing" when they encounter him, the story upholds his indomitable spirit of survival. The Northland maxim was never travel alone, and so there is a sense of justice in Bill's death. As in other Klondike stories, the SUN witnesses the false deeds of men: "Near the horizon the sun was smouldering dimly, almost obscured by formless mists and vapors, which gave an impression of mass and density without outline or tangibility" (*Stories*, 923).

CHARACTERS

unnamed protagonist A gold prospector who breaks his ankle as he and his partner cross a huge landscape to try to gain the Coppermine River. Though he is abandoned by his partner, Bill, his will to survive drags him across the rocks and streams and helps him kill a pursuing wolf. In addition, his knowledge of the plants, animals, and waters of the region, as well as his sense of direction to Coronation Bay, learned by studying maps, helps save him as well.

Bill Bill is the protagonist's partner who coldly abandons him when he breaks his ankle in a stream. The protagonist later finds that Bill has dropped his gold, and then he finds Bill, dead of exhaustion and starvation.

sailors and scientists Aboard the *Bedford*, the ship the protagonist spies in the harbor at Coronation Gulf. The ship is a whaler that has strayed to a bay on the Arctic Ocean near the mouth of the Coppermine River. When the protagonist creeps down the shore to the water, they see him and rescue him: "[T]hey saw something that was alive but which could hardly be called a man. It was blind, unconscious. It squirmed upon the ground like some monstrous worm. Most of its efforts were ineffectual, but it was persistent, and it writhed and twisted and went ahead perhaps a score of feet an hour" (*Stories*, 938). The men nurture him back to health and he remembers who he is. They put down his hoarding of food to his traumatic experience, and they predict he will be well once they reach SAN FRANCISCO BAY.

"The Madness of John Harned" (1909)

First published in England in *Lady's Realm* (May–October 1909), which may sound like a rather inappropriate magazine for a story of raw masculinity. "The Madness of John Harned" was inspired by a bullfight the Londons saw in Quito, Ecuador, on the SNARK voyage. It was included in *The Night-Born*.

SYNOPSIS

John Harned is a wealthy American visiting Ecuador. He has fallen in love with the entrancing Maria Valenzuela, with whom several Ecuadorians are also in love; she is an heiress mainly pursued by Luis Cervallos. The narrator, Manuel Jesus de Patino, describes her with images of Cleopatra and Circe: "Women like Maria Valenzuela are born once in a hundred years. They are of no country and no time," says Patino. "They are what you call universal. They are goddesses" (*Stories*, 1,647). Patino's discourse demonstrates London's command over dialect, as he narrates in English inflected with Spanish linguistic markers: "I am Ecuadoriano, true, but I am Spanish. I am Manuel Jesus de Patino. I own many haciendas, and ten thousand Indians are my slaves, though the law says they are free men who work by freedom of contract" (*Stories*, 1,648). He seems to be narrating his story to an Anglo audience, as he avers, "Yes, I believe in God. I am not pagan like many of you English" (*Stories*, 1,648).

At a bullfight, Harned gets into an argument with the Ecuadorians about the relative merits and demerits of bullfighting versus BOXING. He sees bullfighting as primitive and crude, and that is how the Ecuadorians view prizefighting. Patino is genuinely puzzled when Harned's argument over sports breaks out into violence. Harned's complaint against bullfighting is that the bulls, unlike boxers, have no choice: "'The bull was doomed from the first. The issue was not in doubt. Every one knew, before the bull entered the ring, that it was to die. To be a sporting proposition, the issue must be in doubt. It was one stupid bull who had never fought a man against five wise men who had fought many bulls. It would be possibly a little bit fair if it were one man against one bull'" (*Stories*, 1,651). As they watch good and bad bulls, Harned continues to criticize the sport, despite the casual flirting of Maria. But she is angered when he says the toreadors are not brave men, and when Cervallos smiles at Patino he thinks to himself, "it broke upon my mind surely the game he was playing. He and I were to be banderilleros. The big American bull was there in the box with us. We were to stick the darts in him till he became angry, and then there might be no marriage with Maria Valenzuela. It was a good sport. And the spirit of bull-fighters was in our blood" (*Stories*, 1,652). After more discussion, they watch the slow death of a bull who will neither conquer his opponents nor give up; it is eventually stabbed to death after many attempts. Harned calls such "'The cowardly sport of a cowardly people'" (*Stories*, 1,656), and compares them to the Spanish Inquisition.

But what really sends Harned mad are the screams of one of the picador's blindfolded horses that is gored by the next bull. Harned jumps to his feet and punches Cervallos "so that he fell like a dead man across the chairs and did not rise again" (*Stories*, 1,658). Cervallos's friend Castillo smites Harned with his cane, and then a huge fight erupts that includes the soldiers and occupants of the Presidente's box. By the end, many are killed by blows and gunshots. As Patino reports: "It was horrible to behold. The Americans and the English are a brutal race. They sneer at our bull-fighting, yet do they delight in the shedding of blood. More men were killed that day because of John Harned than were ever killed in all the history of the bull-ring of Quito, yes, and of Guayaquil and all Ecuador" (*Stories*, 1,658). Patino can only conclude that it was the horse who drove John Harned mad, but he also confides that "There is no understanding the Gringos. They are barbarians" (*Stories*, 1,659).

COMMENTARY

The story is a richly layered, complex tale of cultural difference that challenges each side's presuppositions about the other. It is a culturally relativistic look at differences between Latinos and Anglos, the main plot overlaid with intrigue and romance. London allows his relativism to expose the blindness of those who fail to understand other cultures and points of view, and what can become deadly consequences. His choice of an Ecuadorian narrator who finds the Gringos barbarians and

his balanced argument for bullfighting as against boxing shows his ability to see things from other cultural points of view and satirize American shortsightedness and prejudice.

CHARACTERS

John Harned   A wealthy American visiting Ecuador, John Harned is in love with Maria Valenzuela and attends a bullfight with her and her friends. He argues with all of them about the immorality of bullfighting and goes berserk when a horse is gored by one of the bulls.

Manuel Jesus de Patino   An Ecuadorian landowner who prides himself on his Spanish blood, he is the narrator of the story. He schemes to marry the wealthy Maria Valenzuela to his friend Luis Cervallos, with whom he has many business interests. Despite being a witness to the melee at the bullring, he does not understand what could have provoked the Gringo to such violence.

Maria Valenzuela   A haughty and beautiful heiress in Ecuador, she flirts with John Harned until he insults the toreadors at the bullring. She seems to egg him on to his violent anger.

Luis Cervallos   "Luis Cervallos is my friend, the best of Ecuadorianos. He owns three cacao plantations at Naranjito and Chobo. At Milagro is his big sugar plantation. He has large haciendas at Ambato and Latacunga, and down the coast is he interested in oil-wells. Also has he spent much money in planting rubber along the Guayas. He is modern, like the Yankee; and, like the Yankee, full of business. He has much money, but it is in many ventures, and ever he needs more money for new ventures and for the old ones" (*Stories*, 1,649). Patino hopes to arrange a marriage for Cervallos to Valenzuela.

El Presidente, General José Eliceo Salazar, General Joaquin Endara, General Urcisino Castillo, Colonel Jacinto Fierro, Captain Baltazar de Echeverria   Political and military leaders who occupy the box at the bullfight next to that of Luis Cervallos. This proximity shows Cervallos's social position. They join in the fight at the end of the story; presumably they are offended by Harned's criticisms of bullfighting.

Martin Eden (1909)

After *The Call of the Wild,* many regard *Martin Eden* as London's masterpiece. Despite its stylistic unevenness and philosophical conflicts, this autobiographical novel of a young sailor who becomes a successful writer continues to draw many readers in each generation. As Earle Labor and Jeanne Campbell Reesman have noted, reasons for its enduring popularity include the following: "it belongs to a fictional genre that never seems to lose its appeal for sensitive, youthful readers; it is archetypal both in theme and in structure; it articulates an especially potent cultural myth; and it is tremendously charged with London's personal vitality" (Labor and Reesman, *Jack London,* 76). It is part of a literary tradition called the bildungsroman, or novel of development, in which a young hero faces obstacles to full manhood and eventually prevails. Yet because Martin Eden does not prevail, the novel can be seen as a critique of the traditional hero myth. Perhaps it is better described as a Künstlerroman, or the novel of the development of the artist. *Martin Eden* partakes of many literary traditions. Like *The Call of the Wild,* it is both romantic and naturalistic. London thought it was an indictment of Nietzschean INDIVIDUALISM and an argument for SOCIALISM. There is also the pattern of the "Dark Fall," the fall from innocence into experience: as Labor and Reesman note, it is "about the price paid for the unhappy gift of knowledge." Martin is Adam before the Fall when he meets Ruth Morse: "As he emerges from the Edenic sea and enters her world, the modern capitalist world, he becomes for the first time in his life *self*-conscious, shamed by his social and intellectual nakedness" (Labor and Reesman, *Jack and London,* 79). As Martin turns to books to impress Ruth, the novel also furnishes a detailed catalogue of major thinkers who influenced London: Adam Smith, KARL MARX, CHARLES DARWIN, and HERBERT SPENCER. It is a

love story, the story of an artist, a story of disillusionment, the story of a psychological breakdown, a critique of capitalist society, and a naturalist narrative of descent in which no matter how hard Martin tries, he is doomed to failure by forces—both social and psychological—beyond his power to control.

SYNOPSIS

Chapters 1–15

Martin Eden is a husky sailor who saves a young gentleman, Arthur Morse, from an attack by hooligans; he is asked in return to visit the Morse home. The Morses are wealthy San Franciscans and pride themselves on their refinement and luxury. Martin feels hopelessly out of place in their home; in contrast to their polite conversation he is embarrassed about the crudity of his own speech. Nevertheless, Martin is very intelligent and tries to adapt himself to these surroundings. He has ventured all over the world, but he feels trapped by what he sees as the Morses' immense superiority to him. Nevertheless, he falls in love with Ruth Morse, a delicate blonde who is well educated, poised, and articulate. Martin has never been around a woman such as Ruth. In order to impress her, he stops drinking, smoking, and cursing; he begins to bathe regularly and brush his teeth; but most important he is determined to become educated and so spends countless hours in the library. Ruth admires his vitality and decides she will reform him by tutoring him in art and literature; they begin to meet regularly.

Martin is a fast learner. He reads philosophy, science, literature; however, what he reads eventually helps him to begin to sense the hollowness and hypocrisy of the Morses and their world, though his feelings for Ruth remain intense. Ruth finds herself falling in love with him. She urges him to find a steady job, such as the post office; however, he decides to take up writing. He rents a typewriter and writes everything from poetry to scientific essays in a frenzy of production; he sleeps only five hours per night and studies or writes when he is awake. But his stories come back rejected by editor after editor. He has to pawn his bicycle, his only suit, and his overcoat to buy stamps.

In the first scenes of the novel, Martin's discomfort at trying to join a higher class is first signaled through his observance of how easily Arthur navigates parlor and drawing room, contrasted with the sailor's gait Martin tries to manage indoors. His physical awkwardness is exacerbated by his "bronze" color and his breaking into a sweat: "[I]n the eyes there was an expression such as wild animals betray when they fear the trap" (2). Martin does not feel at home, and he never will, though he will be searching with all of his heart for it. Unlike Buck, who was also awkward at first, Martin will not fully adapt to his new world.

Martin is dazzled by the first appearance of Ruth, "a pale, ethereal creature, with wide, spiritual blue eyes and a wealth of golden hair" (4). But before he can properly enjoy the apparition, his mind is jolted by other, darker memories:

> Immediately, beside her, on either hand, ranged the women he had known. . . . He saw the weak and sickly faces of the girls of the factories, and the simpering, boisterous girls from the south of Market. There were women of the cattle camps, and swarthy cigarette-smoking women of Old Mexico. These, in turn, were crowded out by Japanese women, doll-like, stepping mincingly on wooden clogs; by Eurasians, delicate featured, stamped with degeneracy; by full-bodied South-Sea-Island women, flower-crowned and brown-skinned. All these were blotted out by a grotesque and terrible nightmare brood—frowsy, shuffling creatures from the pavements of Whitechapel, gin-bloated hags of the stews, and all the vast hell's following of harpies, vile-mouthed and filthy, that under the guise of monstrous female form prey upon sailors, the scrapings of the ports, the scum and slime of the human pit. (4–5)

Such a leap sexualizes Ruth and establishes Martin's masculinity, but it is also a sign of trouble to come: Martin cannot reconcile the racial, class, or gender binaries he confronts, and, like ALGERNON SWINBURNE, the poet Ruth talks about, he unconsciously fears the "nightmare" of the female.

Ruth is both fascinated and repelled by Martin, noting his scarred neck and face and his cheap suit.

We feel for Martin's awkwardness as the Morses examine him. As Maria De Guzmán and Debbie López observe, because Martin "has consorted with what Anglo culture classified as non-white (Eurasians, South Sea Islanders, Mexicans, Hawaiians, even the Portuguese)," like MELVILLE's Ahab "in the 'deadly scrimmage with the Spaniard afore the altar in Santa,' he has been indelibly marked as Other." Martin's scar is a mark of his own tragic dividedness, as well as what renders him both fascinating and repulsive to Ruth, "whose eyes and hands wander repeatedly to his neck" (De Guzmán and López, "Algebra of Twisted Figures," 100–101).

Ruth's instincts ring "clarion-voiced through her being, impelling her to hurdle caste and place and gain to this traveller from another world. . . . She was clean, and her cleanness revolted; but she was woman, and she was just beginning to learn the paradox of woman" (9). Ruth's conflicting loyalties could have cast her into one of the many novels of the NEW WOMAN of her day; to appreciate her position it helps to remember that she suffers for it, not unlike New Women heroines.

Martin realizes the immediate social barrier is his manner of speech, which will of course be the very thing he develops in himself as a writer. He realizes that "He wasn't of their tribe, and he couldn't talk their lingo. . . . He couldn't fake being their kind. The masquerade would fail, and besides, masquerade was foreign to his nature. There was no room in him for sham or artifice. Whatever happened, he must be real." Martin believes that in time he will be able to speak like them: "Upon that he was resolved. But in the meantime, talk he must, and it must be his own talk, toned down, of course, so as to be comprehensible to them and so as not to shock them too much." He is aware that "each roughness of speech was an insult to her ear, each rough phase of his life an insult to her soul" (19).

Hoping to find evidence that he could be meant for a destiny among the upper reaches of society, Martin studies himself intently in the mirror:

> He wondered if there was soul in those steel-gray eyes that were often quite blue of color and that were strong with the briny airs of the sun-washed deep. He wondered, also, how his

eyes looked to her. . . . Well, they were honest eyes, he concluded, and in them was neither smallness nor meanness. The brown sunburn of his face surprised him. He had not dreamed he was so black. He rolled up his shirt-sleeve and compared the white underside of the arm with his face. Yes, he was a white man, after all. But the arms were sunburned, too. He twisted his arm, rolled the biceps over with his other hand, and gazed underneath where he was least touched by the sun. It was very white. He laughed at his bronzed face in the glass at the thought that it was once as white as the underside of his arm. (35)

He thinks, "What would she think if she learned that he had never washed his teeth in all the days of his life? He resolved to get a tooth-brush and form the habit. He would begin at once, to-morrow. It was not by mere achievement that he could hope to win to her. He must make a personal reform in all things, even to tooth-washing and neck-gear, though a starched collar affected him as a renunciation of freedom" (35–36). This scene opposes Martin's soul-searching with his worry about his appearance, as though his own power of seeing is mocked by what he sees of himself when Ruth looks at him. Like Buck in the *Call of the Wild,* he wishes to control his own identity, rather than be controlled by someone else. The best route would be to concentrate on making art, not remaking himself as an object of show.

Chapters 16–31

Broke, Martin takes a job at a laundry and works 14 hours a day, too exhausted afterward even to read. London himself held this job, at Belmont Academy in the spring of 1897. By week's end Martin is unable to read or even leave his bed:

He was dead. His soul seemed dead. He was a beast, a work-beast. He saw no beauty in the sunshine sifting down through the green leaves, nor did the azure vault of the sky whisper as of old and hint of cosmic vastness and secrets trembling to disclosure. Life was intolerably dull and stupid, and its taste was bad in his mouth. A black screen was drawn across his mirror of inner vision, and fancy lay in a darkened sick-room where entered no ray of light. (15, 153)

He quits to return to writing, only to have rejection after rejection. Martin finds this a growing source of conflict between him and Ruth, who wants him to settle down into a normal job instead of writing. Martin's vision of being a writer is a very idealistic one, but he engages in writing for the very practical hope of attaining Ruth:

The creative spirit in him flamed up at the thought and urged that he recreate this beauty for a wider audience than Ruth. And then, in splendor and glory, came the great idea. He would write. He would be one of the eyes through which the world saw, one of the ears through which it heard, one of the hearts through which it felt. He would write—everything—poetry and prose, fiction and description, and plays like Shakespeare. There was career and the way to win to Ruth. The men of literature were the world's giants. (76)

Though he becomes a "Napoleon of the pen," Ruth misses what he is trying to do and, in the end, so does he.

Martin discovers Herbert Spencer and is thrilled by his interpretation of Darwinian EVOLUTION. Spencer teaches Martin that knowledge is the key to survival: "And here was the man Spencer, organizing all knowledge for him, reducing everything to unity, elaborating ultimate realities, and presenting to his startled gaze a universe so concrete of realization that it was like the model of a ship such as sailors make and put into glass bottles. There was no caprice, no chance. All was law. It was in obedience to law that the bird flew, and it was in obedience to the same law that fermenting slime had writhed and squirmed and put out legs and wings and become a bird" (108). This passage is indicative both of Martin's highest ideals and dreams and also of his limitations. The idea that through his writing, one can attain not only a woman but also mastery of an entire world of knowledge, is nothing less than an impossible dream, but Martin plunges into it. The image of the "slime" and alternatively of the "bird" whose wings represent freedom and the attainment of a soul further illustrate Martin's conflicts. Though Martin reads numerous philosophers, scientists, economists, and others before Spencer, after he encounters Spencer he reads virtually no one else. Writers and works he reads before Spencer include Thomas Bulfinch, Madame Helena Blavatsky, KARL MARX, Adam Smith, John Stuart Mill, Arthur Schopenhauer, Immanuel Kant, George John Romanes, August Bekel, and, in literature, KIPLING, Henley, Longfellow, Swinburne, the Brownings, TENNYSON, and others, not to mention works on other subjects from algebra to navigation. Post-Spencer, he gives up these and other interests in Latin, algebra, geometry, chemistry. For Martin, Spencer explains everything:

> Martin had ascended from pitch to pitch of intellectual living, and here he was at a higher pitch than ever. All the hidden things were laying their secrets bare. He was drunken with comprehension. At night, asleep, he lived with the gods in colossal nightmare; and awake, in the day, he went around like a somnambulist, with absent stare, gazing upon the world he had just discovered. At table he failed to hear the conversation about petty and ignoble things, his eager mind seeking out and following cause and effect in everything before him. In the meat on the platter he saw the shining sun and traced its energy back through all its transformations to its source a hundred million miles away, or traced its energy ahead to the moving muscles in his arms that enabled him to cut the meat, and to the brain wherewith he willed the muscles to move to cut the meat, until, with inward gaze, he saw the same sun shining in his brain. (108)

Like Wolf Larsen, Martin later wishes he had never opened the books. In the midst of his reading of Spencer, he recalls his childhood fight with a rival named Cheese-Face. Martin muses, "'And so you arise from the mud, Martin Eden,' he said solemnly. 'And you cleanse your eyes in a great brightness, and thrust your shoulders among the stars, doing what all life has done, letting the "ape and tiger die" and wresting highest heritage from all powers that be'" (138).

In chapter 19, Mrs. Morse sits down to talk to Ruth. Though Ruth admits Martin is not their "kind," and agrees with her mother that he "has not lived a clean life," Ruth defends Martin by saying that "[i]t has not been his fault" (164). Ruth claims he is her "protégé," then likens him to having a pet bulldog. (165). Ruth's mother says, "'there is one thing you must always carry in mind'—'Yes, mother.' Mrs. Morse's voice was low and sweet as she said, 'And that is the children. . . . Their heritage must be clean, and he is, I am afraid, not clean. Your father has told me of sailors' lives and—and you understand'" (166–167). From sex with nonwhite women, Martin has presumably been infected with disease and racially tainted. The word "pitch" ironically inverts its earlier usage in chapter 13, when Martin is said to ascend "from pitch to pitch of intellectual living" (108).

But Ruth doesn't listen: "tearing herself half out of his embrace, suddenly and exultantly she reached up and placed both hands upon Martin Eden's sunburnt neck. So exquisite was the pang of love and desire fulfilled that she uttered a low moan, relaxed her hands, and lay half-swooning in his arms" (179). Martin too privately engages in some private insight: "As he held Ruth in his arms and soothed her, he took great consolation in the thought that the Colonel's lady and Judy O'Grady were pretty much alike under their skins. It brought Ruth closer to him, made her possible. Her dear flesh was as anybody's flesh, as his flesh. There was no bar to their marriage" (182). If it were not for the ensuing complications of class identity, this meeting of minds and bodies might have worked, as it does with other seemingly mismatched couples such as Elam Harnish and Dede Mason of *Burning Daylight* (1910).

With his laundry job, Martin is able to afford a rented room, with a "Portuguese landlady, Maria Silva, a virago and a widow, hard working and harsher tempered, rearing her large brood of children somehow. . . . From detesting her and her foul tongue at first, Martin grew to admire her as he observed the brave fight she made" (192). Martin challenges Ruth for the first time, "'You worship at the shrine of the established,' he told her once, in a discussion they had over the Praps and Vanderwater. 'I grant that as authorities to quote they are most excellent—the two foremost literary critics in the United States. Every school teacher in the land looks up to Vanderwater as the Dean of American criticism. Yet I read his stuff, and it seems to me the perfection of the felicitous expression of the inane. Why, he is no more than a ponderous bromide.'" Ruth responds, "I think I am nearer the truth," she replied, "when I stand by the established, than you are, raging around like an iconoclastic South Sea Islander" (203). Unfortunately, Ruth was never appreciated his work. For example, when he excitedly reads to her:

> She listened closely while he read, and though he from time to time had seen only disapprobation in her face, at the close he asked:
> "But that character, that Wiki-Wiki, why do you make him talk so roughly? Surely it will offend your readers, and surely that is why the editors are justified in refusing your work."
> "Because the real Wiki-Wiki would have talked that way."
> "But it is not good taste."
> "It is life," he replied bluntly. "It is real. It is true. And I must write life as I see it." (297–298)

Chapters 32–46

Russ Brissenden, Martin's new poet friend, seems to be the only one who believes in his literary genius, though, as a socialist, he argues against Martin's individualism. Based on London's poet-friend GEORGE STERLING, Brissenden suffers from cynicism and disdain; he is a tuberculosis patient, and perhaps because he knows he may die soon, he rejects everything but his own ideals. Brissenden takes Martin to a socialist meeting, where Martin gives a speech *against* socialism. However, since he is the strongest speaker, a local reporter misinterprets him and publishes a story in which Martin is the leader of the revolutionaries. Ruth and her family are appalled; Martin is further depressed by the news soon thereafter of Brissenden's suicide.

In chapter 26, Martin has given up on literary success, haunted by the rejection slips and bills. Then he receives the news that a magazine called the *White Mouse* is offering him $40 for his story

"The Whirlpool" (220). Martin takes the Silva family out to celebrate the good news with a trip to the candy store. But when Martin is observed by Ruth in the company of the Silvas, she is furious:

> It was with this extraordinary procession trooping at his and Maria's heels into a confectioner's in quest of the biggest candy-cane ever made, that he encountered Ruth and her mother. Mrs. Morse was shocked. Even Ruth was hurt, for she had some regard for appearances, and her lover, cheek by jowl with Maria, at the head of that army of Portuguese ragamuffins, was not a pretty sight. But it was not that which hurt so much as what she took to be his lack of pride and self-respect. Further, and keenest of all, she read into the incident the impossibility of his living down his working-class origin. There was stigma enough in the fact of it, but shamelessly to flaunt it in the face of the world—her world—was going too far. Though her engagement to Martin had been kept secret, their long intimacy had not been unproductive of gossip; and in the shop, glancing covertly at her lover and his following, had been several of her acquaintances. She lacked the easy largeness of Martin and could not rise superior to her environment. (308)

Ruth breaks up with Martin.

Snubbed by his lover, and done with writing, Martin looks for other interests. Brissenden fascinated Martin as a model of the tragic poet, such as Keats, whose body and soul could not survive the world, but Brissenden's socialism was less revolutionary than simply snobbery toward the intellect of the BOURGEOISIE. Brissenden elected not to pass into any group, and to die alone, a suicide. So that even though London thought socialism could have cured Martin Brissenden is a poor model for this alternative.

Martin is soon lionized by the cultural elite, and Ruth comes back to him, begging his forgiveness and even offering to cohabit with him. But she is too late. Disillusioned with her and everything else, he tells her off. Soon afterward, he books passage on a steamship to the South Seas, dreaming of reestablishing himself in the MARQUESAS ISLANDS.

However, halfway there, he climbs through his porthole and drowns in the sea, no desire left to live in a corrupt world. Unable to write, Martin has had a vision of escape:

> How long he sat there he did not know, until, suddenly, across his sightless vision he saw form a long horizontal line of white. It was curious. But as he watched it grow in definiteness he saw that it was a coral reef smoking in the white Pacific surges. Next, in the line of breakers he made out a small canoe, an outrigger canoe. In the stern he saw a young bronzed god in scarlet hip-cloth dipping a flashing paddle. He recognized him. He was Moti, the youngest son of Tati, the chief, and this was Tahiti. . . . Then he saw himself, sitting forward in the canoe as he had often sat in the past, dipping a paddle that waited Moti's word to dig in like mad when the turquoise wall of the great breaker rose behind them. . . . [There] was a rush and rumble and long-echoing roar, and the canoe floated on the placid water of the lagoon. Moti laughed and shook the salt water from his eyes, and together they paddled. (346–347)

The "white line" symbolizes the barrier to Ruth's class Martin now understands. Martin calls up new companions, racially "Other," the bronzed Moti and his father Tati. But Martin is still looking to move up in terms of class, to live with the ruling class, but he now imagines a differently raced ruling class, more suitable to David Grief: "The South Seas were calling, and he knew that sooner or later he would answer the call" (351). Increasingly lonely and isolated, he is desperate:

> The cessation from writing and studying, the death of Brissenden, and the estrangement from Ruth had made a big hole in his life; and his life refused to be pinned down to good living in cafes and the smoking of Egyptian cigarettes. . . . He knew a valley and a bay in the Marquesas that he could buy for a thousand Chili dollars. . . . He would buy a schooner— one of those yacht-like, coppered crafts that sailed like witches—and go trading copra and pearling among the islands. . . . He would build

> a patriarchal grass house like Tati's, and have it and the valley and the schooner filled with dark-skinned servitors. He would entertain there the factor of Taiohae, captains of wandering traders, and all the best of the South Pacific riffraff. He would keep open house and entertain like a prince. And he would forget the books he had opened and the world that had proved an illusion. (355)

But Martin is already too sick. He has been poisoned by his desire for bourgeois whiteness, as it were, and has lost his real self, the source of his creativity and storytelling ability. London often uses whiteness as a negative value, as in the WHITE SILENCE and WHITE LOGIC, while he also uses the archetype of darkness to signify the unconscious, even feminine self, the (dark) place of creativity and the life force.

In the end, his long-sought but deadly whiteness blinds him to any sense of hope or of a future:

> Life was to him like strong, white light that hurts the tired eyes of a sick person. During every conscious moment life blazed in a raw glare around him and upon him. It hurt. It hurt intolerably. It was the first time in his life that Martin had travelled first class. On ships at sea he had always been in the forecastle, the steerage, or in the black depths of the coal-hold, passing coal. In those days, climbing up the iron ladders out the pit of stifling heat, he had often caught glimpses of the passengers, in cool white, doing nothing but enjoy themselves, under awnings spread to keep the sun and wind away from them, with subservient stewards taking care of their every want and whim, and it had seemed to him that the realm in which they moved and had their being was nothing else than paradise. Well, here he was, the great man on board, in the midmost centre of it, sitting at the captain's right hand, and yet vainly harking back to forecastle and stoke-hole in quest of the Paradise he had lost. He had found no new one, and now he could not find the old one. (407)

Finally squeezing through his porthole into the sea, Martin gives up control over his destiny:

His wilful hands and feet began to beat and churn about, spasmodically and feebly. But he had fooled them and the will to live that made them beat and churn. He was too deep down. They could never bring him to the surface. He seemed floating languidly in a sea of dreamy vision. Colors and radiances surrounded him and bathed him and pervaded him. What was that? It seemed a lighthouse; but it was inside his brain—a flashing, bright white light. It flashed swifter and swifter. There was a long rumble of sound, and it seemed to him that he was falling down a vast and interminable stairway. And somewhere at the bottom he fell into darkness. That much he knew. He had fallen into darkness. And at the instant he knew, he ceased to know. (411)

Martin, at last becoming whitened, sinks in the dark water a "white statue," the white bonita striking at him and slowly consuming his body (408–411). There are many ironies in the last chapters, the attaining of everything Martin has desired followed by his rejection of it all, the competing "meanings" of his suicide that will circulate after his death, and most of all the ironic imagery of whiteness and darkness as it relates to class. The concluding passage opposes the beckoning white light of a lighthouse with the "darkness" of the basement Martin figuratively falls into. What is ultimately lost for Martin is his fondest ability, the ability to learn, to "know," to express himself as an artist. In trying to pass into the upper-middle-class world, Martin destroys that which defines him. Instead of finding his position in society, finding his true voice or "perspective," as London described his own moment of self-discovery in the YUKON, Martin chooses oblivion, like the suicidal heroines, not heroes, of his day, Edna Pontellier or Lily Bart.

COMMENTARY

Martin Eden has been a favorite of literary critics, as it is both autobiographical and a novel of ideas, as has been discussed in many essays, including those by Sam S. Baskett, Joseph R. McElrath, Jr., María DeGuzmán and Debbie López, and Young Min Kim. Some of the major themes concern the nov-

el's autobiographical elements; its clash between individualism and socialism; its racial subtext; its use of metaphor; its mythic dimensions; and its reversal of the American Dream and American Adam.

Though Martin is certainly modeled on his creator, he exhibits important differences. London was the first to insist upon these. As he remarked,

Martin Eden lived only for himself, fought only for himself, and, if you please, died for himself. He fought for entrance into the bourgeois circles where he expected to find refinement, culture, high-living and high-thinking. He won his way into those circles and was appalled by the colossal, unlovely mediocrity of the bourgeoisie. He fought for a woman he loved and had idealized. He found that love had tricked him and failed him, and that he had loved his idealization more than the woman herself. These were the things he had found life worth in order to fight for. When they failed him, being a consistent Individualist, being unaware of the collective human need, there remained nothing for which to live and fight. And so he died. (*Letters*, 865)

Yet most readers see Martin as a replica of London, and Martin's suicide has helped advance the mistaken notion that London committed suicide. Readers do not connect to the book's ideas so much as they do to Martin personally, and they want his individualistic struggle to succeed. Indeed, the conflict between London's stated theme (socialism) and what most readers interpret the main character as (heroic individualism) is striking. The main problem in London's critique of Martin's individualism is that Martin is not "unaware of the needs of others." He is the most "socialistic" character in the book. He helps Maria Silva with her washing and her children and buys them a dairy farm. Though London argued that if Martin been a socialist he would not have died, most people read this novel as a tragic struggle of its sympathetic and heroic protagonist rather than a case study in politics. It has almost never been viewed as a socialist text even by socialist critics. If *Martin Eden* had been read as a socialist novel, Jonathan Harold

Spinner points out, it would have been as "one of the first novels that document the disintegration of the American success story, the final collapse of the Horatio Alger lesson, the great fall of the Gospel of Wealth myth," an "existential drama of the modern anti-hero" (Spinner, "Jack London's 'Martin Eden,'" 114). Though its appeal largely lies in its romanticism, Robert Barltrop also argues that it was a modernist book ahead of its time, an existential search that results in meaninglessness. He states that if it were rejected in its own day for its pessimism, it would have fit the temper of the times admirably post–World War I, alongside the novels of Hemingway and Fitzgerald. Barltrop finds such artistic prescience in London's fiction to be, ironically, one of the reasons much of his work has been traditionally "denied literary importance" (Barltrop, *Jack London: The Man*, 180).

Metaphor and myth are more prominent in this novel than a coherent political agenda. As Earle Labor and Jeanne Campbell Reesman observe, "Viewed symbolically, Martin's 'education' is a growth in consciousness: a breaking away from the primal rhythms of the unconscious—symbolized by the sea—into the fractured world of over-reason—culture, intellect, civilization, money." Martin's is the "universal sickness of a modern man caught in the Naturalistic trap" (Labor and Reesman, *Jack London*, 79). These authors use the works of CARL JUNG to explore the meaning of the sea as the ultimate symbol for the unconscious:

> The hero emerges from the sea at the outset and returns to the sea at the end. The ocean metaphor, usually set forth in nautical imagery, recurs throughout and serves to unify the novel. When Martin first enters the Morse home, he feels as if he were on the unsteady deck of a ship in rough seas; and one of the first sights his eyes focus on is an oil painting of a pilot schooner surging through a heavy sea against a stormy sunset sky; later in the evening, he likens himself to "a sailor, in a strange ship, on a dark night, groping about in the unfamiliar running rigging" (10). These images are prophetic as well as descriptive; during his nervous breakdown, he thinks of himself as "chartless

and rudderless" with no port to make, as drifting nowhere (349) (Labor and Reesman, *Jack London*, 78).

As suggested earlier, *Martin Eden* is also a tragic study of the myth of the American Dream, a rags-to-riches story in which the hero represents the values of a culture he also rejects. London's original title for the novel was "Success." As Labor and Reesman note, "Martin is . . . a member of . . . [an] American literary fraternity comprising Horatio Alger, Frank Algernon Cowperwood, and Jay Gatsby. Like Gatsby especially, Martin is destroyed by the delusions that an ideal goal may be attained through material means and that success is synonymous with happiness." Martin thinks of "work performed" when he berates Ruth for only coming back to him because he is now famous: "The joy was in becoming, not in being. And that is why, having arrived, Martin, like Gatsby, finds himself nowhere, and why, therefore, he has nothing left except to die" (Labor and Reesman, *Jack London*, 81).

CHARACTERS

Martin Eden   Martin Eden, a sailor, is described in the first sentence of the novel as "a young fellow who awkwardly removed his cap. He wore rough clothes that smacked of the sea, and he was manifestly out of place in the spacious hall in which he found himself. He did not know what to do with his cap, and was stuffing it into his coat pocket when the other took it from him. The act was done quietly and naturally, and the awkward young fellow appreciated it" (1). Martin's social awkwardness is soon followed by his intense desire to rise in class status as an author and attain his lady-love, Ruth Morse. His rise and fall are tragic; even as he attains his dream, he finds it bitter and rejects his glowing future for suicide.

Arthur Morse   Son of the Morse family and Ruth's brother, Arthur is rescued from some waterfront toughs by Martin and so gains access to the Morse home. Arthur is quite understanding about Martin's initial awkwardness in his home. Yet he also tries to draw out the "wild man" in Martin during dinner (20).

Ruth Morse Initially described as a sort of apparition, Ruth catches Martin's eye when they are introduced: "She was a pale, ethereal creature, with wide, spiritual blue eyes and a wealth of golden hair. He did not know how she was dressed, except that the dress was as wonderful as she. He likened her to a pale gold flower upon a slender stem. No, she was a spirit, a divinity, a goddess; such sublimated beauty was not of the earth. Or perhaps the books were right, and there were many such as she in the upper walks of life. She might well be sung by that chap, Swinburne" (4). She becomes his fiancé but breaks with him over his class allegiances and determination to write.

Mrs. Morse Ruth's mother and a grande dame of social convention; initially hoping that Martin will arouse some womanly spirit in her daughter, later she tries to talk Ruth out of a romance with Martin because he is stained by his contacts on the seven seas with racial "Others" and is thus not a suitable husband.

Mr. Morse Ruth's father, who indulges Martin in dinner-table debates; he does not seem to realize the romance that is taking place under his eyes. He questions his wife's plan to "'use this young sailor to wake [Ruth] up'" to the attentions of men (85).

Norman Morse Arthur and Ruth's brother, Norman sits opposite Martin at his first dinner in the Morse home. Martin observes how loving the parents and siblings are in the Morse family. He also observes Arthur and Norman to see which fork to pick up next and to check his manners throughout the meal. Norman explains trigonometry to Martin.

policeman He hears Martin talking out loud to himself on the way to the streetcar after dining at the Morses; the policeman thinks Martin is drunk.

Bernard Higginbotham Martin's brother-in-law and proprietor of Higginbotham's Cash Store. Bernard is repulsive to Martin: "What his sister had seen in this man was beyond him. The other affected him as so much vermin, and always aroused in him an impulse to crush him under his foot." His eyes are "weasel-like, and cruel" as well as "subservient, . . . smug, and oily," and he makes Martin's living with them a nightmare of peevish recriminations (29).

Gertrude Higginbotham Martin's beat-down sister and wife of Bernard, Gertrude is described as "a large, stout woman, always dressed slatternly and always tired from the burdens of her flesh, her work, and her husband" (30). Gertrude later repudiates Martin for embarrassing the Higginbothams with his speech to the socialists. She is a pitiable, abused figure of her class.

Alfred Higginbotham One of Gertrude and Bernard's "numerous progeny," Alfred is soothed by Martin when Gertrude spanks him while he is having a bath. Martin slips him a quarter and tells him to go buy some candy for himself and his brothers and sisters (39).

Jim A second boarder in the Higginbotham house; he has "a sick, faraway look in his eyes" and is a plumber's apprentice with a "weak chin and hedonistic temperament, coupled with a certain nervous stupidity" that "promised to take him nowhere in the race for bread and butter" (41). He is hungover from the previous night's drunk.

Lizzie Connolly Working-class girlfriend of Martin's, Lizzie is a factory girl who likes to go out with her friends and meet men. Martin finds himself no longer attracted to her after he meets Ruth; he later tries to rejoin her but cannot, as their interests are now so far apart.

library attendant He checks out books for Martin, newly a wide reader, and gives him advice on how to call upon a young lady. He "talks polite," unlike Martin, who wishes to learn (57).

Professor Hilton Hilton informs Martin of his marks on his high school entrance examinations, which he has failed save the exam on grammar. Ruth is very disappointed in Martin's failure.

Mr. Butler A self-made man, he is a good friend of Mr. Morse's and a frequent guest at his dinner table. Butler agrees with Morse that Spencer's agnosticism renders him unfit as a philosopher. Martin thinks of him as a "sordid dollar-chaser" (117).

Will Olney A young man included at the Morse dinners who does not like Ruth; he is described as a "young fellow" with a disagreeable sneer and "glasses and [a] mop of hair" (110). Olney tells Martin he is after "career not culture" (113).

Cheese-Face A waterfront hoodlum Martin recalls beating when he was young; the victory was a test of masculinity Martin recalls as he struggles to find acceptance as a writer.

Joe Dawson Hires Martin as a laundryman at the Shelly Hot Springs resort. He, like Martin, is a broke and beaten-down laborer, but Martin thinks only of the gulf between them, now that Martin has been exposed to "the books" (141). "'This is hell, ain't it?'" Joe observes of the laundry (149).

Maria Silva Martin's Portuguese landlady; she and he have in common their time in the South Seas and their adventurous spirit. Martin promises to buy her dreamed-of dairy farm when he strikes it big.

Mary, Teresa, Nick, and Joe Silva Children of Maria Silva. Martin helps them with their chores and buys them candy when he gets his first publication.

dinner guests at the Morse home One evening, Ruth's cousins Dorothy and Florence; university professors including Professor Caldwell, with whom Martin argues about biology and Spencer and Joseph Le Conte; "a young army officer just back from the Philippines, one-time school-mate of Ruth's; a young fellow named Melville, private secretary to Joseph Perkins, head of the San Francisco Trust Company; and finally of the men, a live bank cashier, Charles

Hapgood, a youngish man of thirty-five, graduate of Stanford University, member of the Nile Club and the Unity Club, and a conservative speaker for the Republican Party during campaigns—in short, a rising young man in every way. Among the women was one who painted portraits, another who was a professional musician, and still another who possessed the degree of Doctor of Sociology and who was locally famous for her social settlement work in the slums of San Francisco" whom Mrs. Morse invites to decorate her salon evenings (235).

Marian Eden and Hermann von Schmidt Martin's sister who is keeping company with a young German mechanic, Hermann von Schmidt. Hermann finds Martin's poetry about his sister "indecent" (261). Marian challenges him to give up writing and "go to work" (262).

Russ Brissenden A cynic and a consumptive, Brissenden is a well-born critic of the bourgeois class who befriends Martin and takes him to socialist meetings. Brissenden is a poet who believes his work is finer than the public's comprehension; he commits suicide out of despair.

Mr. Ford, Mr. Ends, Mr. White Mr. Ford is editor of the *Transcontinental*, Mr. Ends and Mr. White are his associates; Martin physically accosts them for payment for a story and receives it.

Kreis, Norton, and Hamilton Socialists to whom Brissenden introduces Martin so that they can debate Ernst Haeckel and other thinkers; Kreis is an idealist and socialist. Norton and Hamilton are other socialists Martin debates.

Judge Blount A frequent guest of the Morse's, Blount debates Martin about labor union politics; Martin accuses him of socialistic ideas and claims he himself is free of them.

cub reporter An inexperienced reporter who attends the socialist meeting at which Martin speaks; he misinterprets Martin's individualism for socialism and draws a portrait of him in the newspaper as a red agitator.

FURTHER READING

Barltrop, Robert. *Jack London: The Man, The Writer, The Rebel.* New York: Pluto Press, 1976.

Baskett, Sam S. "Jack London's Heart of Darkness." In *American Quarterly* 10 (Spring 1958): 66–77.

———. "Jack London: 'In the Midst of It All.'" In *Jack London: One Hundred Years a Writer.* Edited by Sara S. Hodson and Jeanne Campbell Reesman. San Marino, Calif.: Huntington Library Press, 2002, 123–146.

———. "*Martin Eden:* Jack London's Poem of the Mind." In *Modern Fiction Studies* 22 (Spring 1976): 23–26.

DeGuzmán, María, and Debbie López. "Algebra of Twisted Figures: Transvaluation in *Martin Eden.*" In *Jack London: One Hundred Years a Writer.* Edited by Sara S. Hodson and Jeanne Campbell Reesman. San Marino, Calif.: Huntington Library Press, 2002, 98–122.

Johnston, Carolyn. *Jack London—An American Radical?* Westport, Conn.: Greenwood, 1984.

Kim, Young Min. "A 'Patriarchal Grass House' of His Own: Jack London's *Martin Eden* and the Imperial Frontier." In *American Literary Realism* 34 (2001): 1–17.

Labor, Earle, and Jeanne Campbell Reesman. *Jack London: Revised Edition.* New York: Twayne, 1994.

McElrath, Joseph. "Jack London's *Martin Eden:* The Multiple Dimensions of a Literary Masterpiece." In *Jack London: One Hundred Years a Writer.* Edited by Sara S. Hodson and Jeanne Campbell Reesman. San Marino, Calif.: Huntington Library Press, 2002, 77–97.

Reesman, Jeanne Campbell. *Jack London's Racial Lives.* Athens: University of Georgia Press, 2009, chapter 6.

Spinner, Jonathan Harold. "Jack London's 'Martin Eden': The Development of the Existential Hero." In *Jack London: Essays in Criticism.* Edited by Ray Wilson Ownbey. New York: Peregrine Smith, 1978, 114–120.

Watson, Charles N., Jr. *The Novels of Jack London: A Reappraisal.* Madison: University of Wisconsin Press, 1983.

"The Master of Mystery"
(1902)

First published in *Out West* (September 1902), "The Master of Mystery" was included in *Children of the Frost,* its folktale motif appropriate to a volume of stories largely told from a NATIVE point of view.

SYNOPSIS

In a Thlinket village, there is much consternation because some especially thick and warm blankets belonging to Hooniah have been stolen. Rejecting the abilities of the local shaman, Scundoo, Hooniah brings in a much-feared visiting shaman, Klock-No-Tan, to solve the mystery. Klock-No-Tan fails to identify the thief, whereupon Scundoo plays a trick on everyone and is able to finger the wrongdoer, the skeptic Sime, by using a "charm" from the Raven Jelchs, which is really his having noted the thief's blackened hands from having stolen a cooking pot too. Sime restores the blankets, and Scundoo is vindicated in front of the tribe.

COMMENTARY

Probably based on a trickster folktale from the Native peoples of the Northwest, this story does not contain white men or women, nor does it contain any reference to the newcomers. In this sense, it is a "pure" example of London's attempt to tell a Native tale to nonnative audiences. Yet it contains his usual ingredients of wit and irony as Scundoo reclaims his place as tribal shaman. Perhaps London heard a version of the tale when he was in the KLONDIKE.

CHARACTERS

Di Ya A child said to be "the cause of it all," who is "soundly thrashed, first by Hooniah, his mother, and then by his father, Bawn, and was now whimpering and looking pessimistically out upon the world from the shelter of the big overturned canoe on the beach" (*Stories,* 621).

Hooniah When she turns around to scold her son Di Ya for overturning a pot, Hooniah sees that her special blankets are gone.

Bawn Husband to Hooniah, he opines that villagers have stolen the blankets through witchcraft since no guests are in the camp.

Scundoo Shaman who has promised his village a good south wind for sailing to a potlatch feast but who is in disgrace when the north wind springs up.

Ty-Kwan He sells Hooniah some special blankets taken from a dying Englishman; Hooniah cannot believe his cheap price but does not know the blankets' origin.

Klock-No-Tan A fearsome shaman Hooniah sends for to regain her blankets; she does not trust in the powers of their own shaman, Scundoo.

Sime A young member of the tribe who scoffs at the supposed powers of the shamans. He points out that if men were not evil, there would be no need for shamans. "'Bah! You children-afraid-of-the-dark!'" he says (*Stories*, 623). Sime steals the blankets of Hooniah to try to shame the shaman.

La-lah Scundoo suggests to Klock-No-Tan that La-lah has stolen the blankets, but he is mistaken. His goal is to make a fool of the visiting shaman. No one believes Klock-No-Tan.

"Mauki" (1908)

"Mauki" was finished on October 8, 1908, and published first in *Hampton's Magazine* 23 (December 1909). Earle Labor and Jeanne Reesman pointed out the irony London employs to "the immoral stupidities of the white race in its treatment of darker-skinned peoples," but few critics have looked at "Mauki" (Labor and Reesman, *Jack London*, 134). "Mauki" deserves close attention for its satire of racism in which the victor is a cruelly oppressed Malaitan boy and the villain a strongman German plantation manager. As noted by Thomas R. Tietze and Gary Riedl, two of the few critics to address "Mauki," it is quite deliberate in its racial trangressions: it "forced white middle-class magazine readers to sympathize with, and vicariously share the experiences of, [a] heroic non-white character." "Mauki" is a "horrific picture of white supremacy" turned by its protagonist into a "tale of revenge" and "a grimly inspirational tribute to indomitable independence" (Tietze and Riedl, "'*Saint in Slime*,'" 60–61). The events of the story support racial satire as well as heroism and the achievement of freedom not only for one's self but for one's people.

SYNOPSIS

On LORD HOWE ATOLL, the *SNARK* crew stayed at the home of a local white trader. London heard of the crimes of their host's Malaitan cook, Mauki, which intrigued him, and so he met and talked with Mauki. Mauki was serving several sentences for committing various crimes, including murder, theft, and escape. The trader made a regular practice of beating him and other servants and showed off the graves of his three former wives, whom he also beat, just as he continued to beat his present three wives for not making copra fast enough. CHARMIAN KITTREDGE LONDON remarks on the disparity between this young cook's crimes—"murders, escapes in handcuffs, thefts of whaleboats—a history of bloodcurdling crimes and reprisals too long to go into," with his "mild" face and even "deceptive weak prettiness" (Charmian London, *Log of the* Snark, 445).

The story's opening description of Mauki is important because London carefully distinguishes between his appearance (to whites) and his inner reality (his *tambos*):

> He weighed one hundred and ten pounds. His hair was kinky and negroid, and he was black. He was peculiarly black. He was neither blue-black nor purple-black, but plum-black. His name was Mauki, and he was the son of a chief. He had three *tambos*. *Tambo* is Melanesian for *taboo*, and is first cousin to that Polynesian word. Mauki's three *tambos* were as follows: first, he must never shake hands with a woman, nor have a woman's hand touch him or any of his personal belongings; secondly, he must never eat clams nor any food from a fire in which clams had been cooked; thirdly, he must

never touch a crocodile, nor travel in a canoe that carried any part of a crocodile even if as large as a tooth.

Of a different black were his teeth, which were deep black, or, perhaps better, *lamp*-black. They had been made so in a single night, by his mother, who had compressed about them a powdered mineral which was dug from the landslide back of Port Adams. Port Adams is a salt-water village on Malaita, and Malaita is the most savage island in the Solomons—so savage that no traders nor planters have yet gained a foothold on it; while, from the time of the earliest bêche-de-mer fishers and sandalwood traders down to the latest labor recruiters equipped with automatic rifles and gasolene [sic] engines, scores of white adventurers have been passed out by tomahawks and soft-nosed Snider bullets. So Malaita remains to-day, in the twentieth century, the stamping ground of the labor recruiters, who farm its coasts for laborers who engage and contract themselves to toil on the plantations of the neighboring and more civilized islands for a wage of thirty dollars a year. (*Stories*, 1,532)

Mauki's nose, lips, and ears are pierced to hold such objects as a china teacup handle and other objects of trade, marking him as a strong village leader to his own people, but making him look only more "backward" to a white observer. By giving us an outside and inside view of Mauki, the narrator suggests that it is the inner life and not the surface that is important. To the white magazine reader, Mauki is the epitome of savagery, with his blackness extending all the way to his teeth: The word "black" is repeated in these two short opening paragraphs eight times. The casual observer or reader would not have the cultural information to note the meaning behind the black teeth—they were blackened deliberately by his mother to show his fierceness—and would not understand the importance of Mauki's *tambos* at all, because they are not visible, though they are the very key to Mauki's identity and the source of his power.

At the age of seven years, Mauki, a member of the "salt water men" (tribes living by the sea)

of MALAITA is stolen by the bushmen and carried away into the interior. He becomes the slave of Fanfoa, who is "head chief over a score of scattered bush-villages on the range-lips of Malaita, the smoke of which, on calm mornings, is about the only evidence the seafaring white men have of the teeming interior population. For the whites do not penetrate Malaita. They tried it once, in the days when the search was on for gold, but they always left their heads behind to grin from the smoky rafters of the bushmen's huts" (*Stories*, 1,533–1,534). Just as the unobservant viewer cannot penetrate Mauki's identity, the whites are not able to penetrate Malaita's secrets.

As the tale unfolds, Mauki is repeatedly an innocent victim who desires only to return home, while others around him are his exploiters. He is sold and resold, finally ending up a virtual slave for the Moongleam Soap Company (based on Lever Brothers, this company grows coconut trees for their kernels, which are dried into copra and used to make oil). The narrator calls him "a lamb led to the slaughter." Mauki is signed on for three years, but repeatedly escapes from several islands and is caught, with years added on every time to his contract as penalty. He is starved and overworked. But he learns BÊCHE-DE-MER ENGLISH, the South Seas patois, "with which he could talk with all white men, and with all recruits who otherwise would have talked in a thousand different dialects" (*Stories*, 1,536).

Ten years after his first being kidnapped by Fanfoa as a house boy, Mauki is fed up: "He hated work, and he was the son of a chief" (*Stories*, 1,536). He and several others steal a boat and flee, Mauki (the houseboy) having stolen the key to the boathouse while the whites drink away the afternoon. As someone who can learn from experience and continue to strive for his freedom, Mauki has been able to profit by being inside the white men's house, learning their language and their secrets and seeing behind things. He only has two more years to go, and he is in a good situation. He could patiently serve out two years. But his belief in himself and in freedom spur him to action. Another might have waited, maintaining the mind-set of an obedient slave.

He is once again apprehended. The Moong-leam Soap Company, finding him incorrigible, decides: "'We'll send him to Lord Howe,' said Mr. Haveby. 'Bunster is there, and we'll let them settle it between them. It will be a case, imagine, of Mauki getting Bunster, or Bunster getting Mauki, and good riddance in either event'" (Stories, 1,538). The narrator tells us that "Nobody ever comes to Lord Howe. . . . Thomas Cook & Son do not sell tickets to it, and tourists do not dream of its existence. Not even a white missionary has landed on its shore" (Stories, 1,539). Its history is particularly bloody, largely due to the psychopathic behavior of plantation manager Max Bunster, "a strapping big German, with something wrong in his brain. Semi-madness would be a charitable statement of his condition. He was a bully and a coward, and a thrice-bigger savage than any savage on the island" (Stories, 1,539). Mauki "had no idea of the sort of master he was to work for. He had had no warnings, and he had concluded as a matter of course that Bunster would be like other white men, a drinker of much whiskey, a ruler and a lawgiver who always kept his word and who never struck a boy undeserved." But, as we learn, "Bunster had the advantage. He knew all about Mauki, and gloated over the coming into possession of him." Mauki is to toil for eight and a half years, and, unlike his previous plantations, "[t]here was no escaping from Lord Howe. For better or worse, Bunster and he were tied together. Bunster weighed two hundred pounds. Mauki weighed one hundred and ten. Bunster was a degenerate brute. But Mauki was a primitive savage. While both had wills and ways of their own" (Stories, 1,540). From this description, it sounds like it will be "wills and ways of their own" that will decide the victor. A "degenerate," as it turns out, is not as good as a "primitive."

Bunster burns Mauki with cigars, rips his ornaments out of his nose and ears, beats him, kicks him down stairs—but his worst punishment is to strike Mauki with a mitten made of sharkskin, removing huge swaths of skin each time. He also uses this glove on other workers. The villagers have been unable to resist Bunster, but "Mauki was of a different breed, and, escape being impossible while Bunster lived, he was resolved to get the white man" (Stories, 1,541). More than anything, it is Bunster's pettiness with Mauki that seals his fate:

All other white men had respected his *tambos*, but not so Bunster. Mauki's weekly allowance of tobacco was two sticks. Bunster passed them to his woman and ordered Mauki to receive them from her hand. But this could not be, and Mauki went without his tobacco. In the same way he was made to miss many a meal, and to go hungry many a day. He was ordered to make chowder out of the big clams that grew in the lagoon. This he could not do, for clams were *tambo*. Six times in succession he refused to touch the clams, and six times he was knocked senseless. Bunster knew that the boy would die first, but called his refusal mutiny, and would have killed him had there been another cook to take his place. (Stories, 1,542)

This scene illustrates the depth of Mauki's belief in his *tambos* and hence himself: he is willing to suffer in order to uphold *tambos*.

When Bunster comes down with blackwater fever, "Mauki waited and watched, the while his skin grew intact once more. He ordered the boys to beach the cutter, scrub her bottom, and give her a general overhauling. They thought the order emanated from Bunster, and they obeyed." When Bunster begins to recover, and

lay convalescent and conscious, but weak as a baby, Mauki packed his few trinkets, including the china cup handle, into his trade box. Then he went over to the village and interviewed the king and his two prime ministers. "This fella Bunster, him good fella you like too much?" he asked. They explained in one voice that they liked the trader not at all. The ministers poured forth a recital of all the indignities and wrongs that had been heaped upon them. The king broke down and wept. Mauki interrupted rudely. "You savve me—me big fella marster my country. You no like 'm this fella white marster. Me no like 'm. Plenty good you put hundred cocoanut, two hundred cocoanut, three hundred cocoanut along cutter. Him finish, you go sleep 'm good fella. Altogether kanaka sleep 'm good fella. Bime by big fella noise along house, you no savve hear 'm that fella noise. You altogether sleep strong fella too much." In like manner Mauki interviewed the boat-boys. Then he ordered Bunster's wife to return to her family house. Had she refused, he would have been in a quandary, for his *tambo* would not have permitted him to lay hands on her. (*Stories*, 1,543)

Mauki uses negotiating skills from his position as a chief's son to persuade the islanders to help him. He takes the sharkskin mitten and carefully removes the white skin of his former master, the thing which oppressed him, and it is the rare reader who is not cheering him on:

> The house deserted, he entered the sleeping-room, where the trader lay in a doze. Mauki first removed the revolvers, then placed the ray fish mitten on his hand. Bunster's first warning was a stroke of the mitten that removed the skin the full length of his nose.
>
> "Good fella, eh?" Mauki grinned, between two strokes, one of which swept the forehead bare and the other of which cleaned off one side of his face. "Laugh, damn you, laugh."
>
> Mauki did his work thoroughly, and the kanakas, hiding in their houses, heard the "big fella noise" that Bunster made and continued to make for an hour or more.
>
> When Mauki was done, he carried the boat compass and all the rifles and ammunition down to the cutter, which he proceeded to ballast with cases of tobacco. It was while engaged in this that a hideous, skinless thing came out of the house and ran screaming down the beach till it fell in the sand and mowed and gibbered under the scorching sun. Mauki looked toward it and hesitated. Then he went over and removed the head, which he wrapped in a mat and stowed in the stern-locker of the cutter. (*Stories*, 1,543)

Mauki arrives at Port Adams "with a wealth of rifles and tobacco such as no one man had ever possessed before. But he did not stop there. He had taken a white man's head, and only the bush could shelter him. So back he went to the bush-villages, where he shot old Fanfoa and half a dozen of the chief men, and made himself the chief over all the villages." When Mauki's father dies, Mauki joins with his brother, who rules Port Adams, and unites the ancient enemies, the salt-water men and the bushmen: "the resulting combination was the strongest of the ten score fighting tribes of Malaita" (*Stories*, 1,544–1,545). He wisely makes peace with the Moongleam Soap Company, paying off his debt of $750 with gold.

COMMENTARY

It is important to note that Mauki not only exacts revenge, but he also uses his newfound power to benefit his people and his immediate neighbors; by satisfying the white man's justice by repaying his debt, he removes that threat to his people. This demonstrates the ethical power of his *tambos*. In the conclusion of the story, our eyes are once again directed both to outer appearances and inner realities, now successfully united in a leader: "Mauki no longer weighs one hundred and ten pounds. His stomach is three times its former girth, and he has four wives. He has many other things—rifles and revolvers, the handle of a china cup, and an excellent collection of bushmen's heads." His appearance and accoutrements now match his self-image. The narrator concludes, "more precious than the entire collection is another head, perfectly dried and cured, with sandy hair and a yellowish beard, which is kept wrapped in the finest of fibre lava-lavas. When Mauki goes to war with villages beyond his realm, he invariably gets out this head, and, alone in his grass palace, contemplates it long and solemnly. At such times the hush of death falls on the village, and not even a pickaninny dares make a noise. The head is esteemed the most powerful devil-devil on Malaita, and to the possession of it is ascribed all of Mauki's greatness" (*Stories* 1,545). Like Buck of *The Call of the Wild*, Mauki becomes his true self. He not only survives, and not only gets revenge upon his oppressor, but in the end his behavior reflects his inner tribal ethic, unspoiled by any outside force.

CHARACTERS

Mauki   Mauki is the son of a chief on the Solomon Island of Malaita. He is kidnapped and sold into slavery by a rival chief. Over the course of his childhood and young adulthood, he is sold several times, always attempting to escape his servitude. Though he and the other plantation workers have contracts, they are virtually slaves. Finally, he is sold to the Moongleam Soap Company, and after more attempts to run, sent to Lord Howe Atoll, where he eventually murders his cruel master and successfully returns home to assume the duties of chief.

Fanfoa   Chief of a bush tribe, Fanfoa enslaves Mauki as a child. When Mauki is 17, Fanfoa trades him for a case of tobacco to some white men "hiring" plantation workers. Fanfoa is shot and killed by Mauki when he returns from captivity.

Mr. Haveby   Manager of the Moongleam Soap Company on New Georgia, where Mauki works building roads. Haveby judges Mauki an incorrigible runaway and sends him to Lord Howe Atoll, ruled over by the brutal Max Bunster.

Max Bunster   A fearsome, half-deranged plantation manager who is Mauki's last master. Bunster beats his wives and his workers for sadistic pleasure; he especially enjoys torturing Mauki. When he falls ill with fever, Mauki skins him with the sharkskin mitten Bunster has used on him, then decapitates him and takes his head home as a powerful charm.

king and prime ministers   All the Native people of Lord Howe Atoll are frightened of Bunster, but Mauki enlists their aid in his escape and murder of Bunster.

boat-boys   Mauki gains the trust of the boat-boys on Lord Howe Atoll and with their assistance loads a boat with ammunition and tobacco for the journey home.

San Cristoval boy   On one of his escapes, Mauki and some fellow Malaitans also take with them a

boy from the island of San Cristoval. When they run out of food, they kill and eat him. Though this seems like a cruel trick, according to their notions of kinship and tribal loyalty it is a normative thing to do.

Mauki's brother   Mauki rules Port Adams with his brother; together they make peace with the bushmen and the Moongleam Soap Company and unite the salt-water men and bushmen into a strong confederation of fighting tribes.

FURTHER READING

Labor, Earle, and Jeanne Reesman. *Jack London: Revised Edition*. New York: Twayne, 1994.

London, Charmian. *The Log of the* Snark. New York: Macmillan, 1915.

Reesman, Jeanne Campbell. *Jack London's Racial Lives: A Critical Biography*. Athens: University of Georgia Press, 2009, chapter 4.

Tietze, Thomas R., and Gary Riedl. "'Saints in Slime': The Ironic Use of Racism in Jack London's South Sea Tales." In *Thalia: Studies in Literary Humor* 12, nos. 1–2 (1992): 59–66.

"The Mexican" (1911)

First published in the SATURDAY EVENING POST (August 19, 1911) and included in the collection *The Night-Born*, "The Mexican" is another of London's tales to relativize race by turning the tables on white racism through a heroic young Mexican prizefighter, Felipe Rivera, who, despite his small size, fights and defeats all of his white opponents—his goal is to earn enough money to buy guns for the MEXICAN REVOLUTION. The story was partly inspired by London's coverage of the JACK JOHNSON world heavyweight fights, when Johnson, an African-American fighter, trounced his white adversaries.

SYNOPSIS

"Nobody knew his history," the story begins (*Stories*, 1,983), this strange intense boy whom his fellow revolutionaries fear as "the breath of death," a "wild wolf," a "primitive" (*Stories*, 1,986–1,987)—

an appropriate beginning for a story of survival. One day, a skinny, underfed boy appears asking to work for the revolution. The junta members are afraid of him because he is so cold and seemingly unfeeling, while at the same times his eyes burn with rage. The activities of the junta include strategizing, spying, and writing letters to raise funds. Rivera cleans their office for them. When the junta finds itself without money, Rivera offers to raise $5,000 to buy guns, to their shock and disbelief. Secretly at night, Rivera begins to fight in the boxing ring. Because he spends time as a trainer, he learns to survive all kinds of blows, and though he is slight of build, he slowly becomes toughened and experienced.

Identifying with Rivera in the story means understanding why he fights: not for money, nor even to punish his gringo opponents, but for JUSTICE for the damage done to his family and his country. His memories of injustice, a childhood spent in slavery and the murder of his parents and his entire village on the RÍO BLANCO, are intercut with the present, especially in the ring:

> He saw the white-walled, water-power factories of Río Blanco. He saw the six thousand workers, starved and wan, and the little children, seven and eight years of age, who toiled long shifts for ten cents a day. He saw the perambulating corpses, the ghastly death's heads of men who labored in the dye-rooms. (*Stories*, 1,995–1,996)

The Río Blanco textile mill in the State of VERACRUZ was the site of a famous massacre of striking workers in January 7, 1907, in which dozens of workers were shot down by the guns of government soldiers, an act that stiffened opposition to dictator Porfirio Díaz and helped propel the outbreak of revolution in 1910. Rivera recalls that his father, "[b]ig, hearty Joaquin Fernandez," called the dye-rooms on this deathly river of whiteness "suicide holes." Fernandez was a writer and printer who worked for the revolution. (Felipe Rivera's real name is "Juan Fernandez.") He used to watch his father setting type in the "little printery, or scribbling endless hasty, nervous lines on the much-cluttered desk," carrying on midnight meetings.

Then came the strike, the lockouts, and eventually the "death-spitting rifles" of Díaz's soldiers—a horrific end of childhood: "He saw the flat cars, piled high with the bodies of the slain, consigned to Vera Cruz, food for the sharks of the bay. Again he crawled over the grisly heaps, seeking and finding, stripped and mangled, his father and mother. His mother he especially remembered—only her face projecting, her body burdened by the weight of dozens of bodies" (*Stories*, 1,996). "'His soul has been seared,'" May Sethby remarks; "'Light and laughter have been burned out of him. He is like one dead, and yet is fearfully alive'" (*Stories*, 1,985).

Rivera's desire for justice is contrasted with the values of the unscrupulous fight promoters and their main client, favorite of the fans and pride of the ANGLO-SAXONS, Danny Ward. The promoters are drunks with stereotypical IRISH names like "Michael Kelly" and "Spider Hagerty," but to Rivera, Ward is "the whitest Gringo of them all" (*Stories*, 1,994), a big, loud, crowd-pleasing fighter, never without his famous smile, interested in the purse and the pleasures it would bring. When Danny enters the ring, the roar of the crowd interrupts Rivera's memory of the village massacre: "The house was in a wild uproar for the popular hero who was bound to win. Everybody proclaimed him. . . . His face continually spread to an unending succession of smiles. . . . Never was there so genial a fighter. His face was a running advertisement of good feeling, of good fellowship. He knew everybody." But crossing the ring to Rivera's corner, he whispers to Rivera: "'You little Mexican rat,' hissed from between Danny's gaily smiling lips, 'I'll fetch the yellow outa you.'" (*Stories*, 1,997).

During the fight, starting to lose his confidence, again and again Danny has to return to his corner "smiling through all desperateness and extremity. 'The smile that won't come off!' somebody yelled; and the audience laughed loudly in its relief." On the other hand, Rivera's "Indian blood, as well as Spanish" allows him to sit back in a corner, "silent, immobile, only his black eyes passing from face to face and noting everything" (*Stories*, 1,992). Danny unleashes a "man-eating attack" on Rivera, but after two minutes "the whirling, blurring mix-up ceased suddenly. Rivera stood alone. Danny, the redoubtable Danny, lay on his back" (*Stories*, 1,999). Danny rises as the house yells at Rivera to take the licking that he is supposed to take. As Danny rallies for the last time in the 17th round, the crowd bellows its frustration at Rivera much as it did at Johnson: "'Why don't you fight?' it demanded wrathfully of Rivera. 'You're yellow! You're yellow!' 'Open up, you cur! Open up!' 'Kill 'm, Danny! Kill 'm. You sure got 'm! Kill 'm!'" Rivera catches Danny off guard and fells him with "a clean drive to the mouth" (*Stories*, 2,004). Rivera strikes the last blow just seconds before the police chief and the referee try to stop him. He demands a count and the victory:

> "Who wins?" Rivera demanded. Reluctantly, the referee caught his gloved hand and held it aloft.
>
> There were no congratulations for Rivera. He walked to his corner unattended, where his seconds had not yet placed his stool. He leaned backward on the ropes and looked his hatred at them, swept it on and about him until the whole ten thousand Gringos were included. His knees trembled under him, and he was sobbing from exhaustion. Before his eyes the hated faces swayed back and forth in the giddiness of nausea. Then he remembered they were the guns. The guns were his. The Revolution could go on. (*Stories*, 2,005)

Rivera's victory is booed, and Danny's sloppy defeat is mourned. In the end, the revolution triumphs, the sounds of the "death-spitting rifles" Rivera will buy drowning out Danny's insults and the "war-chant of wolves" from the crowd. Though he is once described as a "lamb led to the slaughter" (*Stories*, 1,994), Rivera manages to save the revolution without himself being sacrificed.

COMMENTARY

As in "Mauki," London sets up the reader to dislike and fear Felipe, using this time the point of view of the junta, then demolishes that point of view with the grotesque racial hatred toward Felipe from Anglo boxers and fight handlers, emotionally contrasting Rivera's flashbacks to the massacre of his family at the hands of Díaz's soldiers. The junta's fear and ignorance ironically parallels the inability of the whites to know Felipe Rivera. Thus, in this story, London gives us Parts I and II told from the junta's point of view; Part III from the white boxers and promoters; and Part IV from the hero's point of view. The tale critiques U.S. attitudes toward Mexicans and the Mexican Revolution, intercutting flashbacks of Rivera's past in Mexico, his visions of the future revolution, and his location in the brutal present of the Los Angeles BOXING ring. Thus the emotional flashbacks are counter-pointed by a spare, suspenseful, blow-by-blow, fight story.

In keeping with the varied point of view, the hero himself is, as Jeff Jaeckle has observed, "a living paradox: a collection of irreconcilable personality traits that culminate in a largely unknown but yet undeniably dominant character," existing within a "world of contradiction," in setting, diction, and narration: "Ultimately, these patterns of paradox echo naturalist concerns with knowledge, as characters and readers find themselves perpetually confronted with their own ignorance" (Jaeckle, "Patterns of Paradox, 2–3). Though Rivera walks into the junta office in Los Angeles and volunteers to work for the revolution, Paulino Vera and his comrades fear he would kill anyone who opposed him (*Stories*, 1,985). He may be "the Revolution incarnate, . . . the destroying angel moving through the still watches of the night" (*Stories*, 1,987). Instead of the zeal of "honest, ordinary revolutionists whose fiercest hatred of Díaz and his tyranny after all was only that of honest and ordinary patriots," this ragged boy strikes Vera and the others as menacing, "the unknown" (*Stories*, 1,984). "He has no heart. He is pitiless as steel, keen and cold as frost. He is like moonshine in a winter night when a man freezes to death on some lonely mountain top" (*Stories*, 1,986), one character observes. He is only a slender boy of 18, but he works harder than any man. All of these paradoxes add up to the story's overall questioning of stereotypes. As Jaeckle also notes, there is a high incidence of the words "know" and "no" in the story, and negation appears every 47 words on average in the 9,366 words of the story. A word referring to "knowledge" is often coupled with the negative, as in "Nobody knew his history." When we put together Rivera's internal reality with the narrator's disdain for the ignorance of Rivera's observers, we can appreciate London's multiple visions of racism and identity in this story.

Joe S. Bain has praised the story's "consistent and clear" representation of the Chicano, showing "Mexicans and Mexican Americans in the present and future, rather than the past, and . . . figures who are more fighters and participants in an ongoing social drama than romantic lovers or idle bystanders," a Mexican-American character who is not a victim but a hero. As he remarks, "No longer are Mexican Americans the amiable, contented ranch hands of an old California hacienda, as in [Helen Hunt Jackson's] *Ramona,* or the idle old men of a dying Mexican town, as are the Guadalajara residents in [FRANK NORRIS's] *The Octopus.* 'The Mexican's' Mexicans are Spanish-speaking people with a goal and a purpose," in contrast to Norris's old man Vacca, shaving candle wax onto the floor at Annixter's barn dance, the "silent Hispano, concentrating intensely on his carefully circumscribed role in a predominantly Anglo-Saxon society" (Bain, "Interchapter," 115–116).

CHARACTERS

Felipe Rivera "No one knew his history," begins the story, as the members of the junta Rivera has joined try to figure out what drives him; they call him their "'little mystery,' their 'big patriot,'" as he performs menial tasks to help them. Because he does not explain himself, the junta believe him to be a spy for the dictator Porfirio Díaz, and they fear him: "There was no smile on his lips, no geniality in his eyes. Big dashing Paulino Vera felt an inward shudder. Here was something forbidding, terrible, inscrutable. There was something venomous and snakelike in the boy's black eyes. They burned like cold fire, as with a vast, concentrated bitterness" (*Stories,* 1,983). At night, Rivera boxes to raise money for the revolution; his is a personal quarrel since Díaz's men assassinated his parents. His real name is Juan Fernandez, but when he fled the scene of the massacre he changed his name.

Paulino Vera "Big and dashing," Vera is a leader of the junta who fears Rivera as "the unknown" (*Stories,* 1,983). When he questions Rivera, all he will say is that he will work for free for the revolu-

tion. Vera and the other junta members describe him as "'a great and lonely spirit,'" "'not human,'" "'like one dead'" (*Stories,* 1,985). Vera persuades the others to let him work.

Arrelano and Ramos, May Sethby Junta members who suspect Rivera of being a spy. "[T]hey could not bring themselves to like him. They did not know him. His ways were not theirs. He gave no confidences. He repelled all probing. Youth that he was, they could never nerve themselves to dare to question him" (*Stories,* 1,985).

Michael Kelly Manager of the renowned white fighter Danny Ward, Kelly arranges a match between Ward and Rivera when another fighter cancels on Ward. He is shocked by Rivera's calm statement that he can beat Ward.

Danny Ward Popular champion whom Rivera unexpectedly defeats. When he enters the promoters' meeting "he breezed in like a gusty draught of geniality, good-nature, and all-conqueringness. Greetings flew about, a joke here, a retort there, a smile or a laugh for everybody. . . . He was a good actor, and he had found geniality a most valuable asset in the game of getting on in the world. But down underneath he was the deliberate, cold-blooded fighter and business man. The rest was a mask" (*Stories,* 1,991). Despite grinning at the crowd, Danny whispers vile racial slurs in Rivera's ear when they are clinched.

Kelly's secretary Kelly's secretary is "a distinctively sporty young man" who sneers at Rivera's claim to be able to win against Ward (*Stories,* 1,989).

Roberts Rivera's manager, "a tall, lean, slack-jointed individual" who mostly stays drunk. He assures Kelly that Rivera can "put up a fight. . . . I know Rivera. Nobody can get his goat. He ain't got a goat that I could ever discover. . . . He's a devil. . . . He'll make Ward sit up with a show of local talent that'll make the rest of you sit up" (*Stories,* 1,990).

Spider Hagerty Boxing promoter who is Rivera's chief second; he warns Rivera to be careful with Danny and make it last as long as he can so the newspapers will not question the fairness of prizefighting.

Joaquin Fernandez   Rivera remembers his father as "large, big-moustached and deep-chested, kindly above all men, who loved all men and whose heart was so large that there was love to overflowing still left for the mother and the little muchacho playing in the corner of the patio" (*Stories*, 1,995). Because he wrote pamphlets for the revolution, he and his wife are executed by the soldiers of Díaz.

Mrs. Fernandez   Rivera has happy memories of her cooking and caring for him, but seared into his mind is the image of her and her husband crushed by dozens of other bodies on a train to be taken to the sea and dumped.

Bill   The referee in the fight who cannot call a foul blow on Rivera when he knocks Danny Ward out because he does not foul; the crowd screams at him to do it anyway.

FURTHER READING

Bain, Joe S., III. "Interchapter: Jack London's 'The Mexican.'" In *Jack London Newsletter* 15, no. 2 (1982): 115–116.

Harvey, Anne-Marie. "Sons of the Sun: Making White, Middle-Class Manhood in Jack London's David Grief Stories and the *Saturday Evening Post*." In *American Studies* 39, no. 3 (1998): 37–68.

Jaeckle, Jeff. "Patterns of Paradox in Form and Content in 'The Mexican.'" In *The Call* 11, no. 1 (2001): 2–5.

Reesman, Jeanne Campbell. *Jack London's Racial Lives: A Critical Biography*. Athens: University of Georgia Press, 2009, chapter 5.

Mexican War correspondence (1914)

Though London expressed sympathy for the Mexican revolutionaries in speeches and articles in 1911, the seven articles he wrote for COLLIER'S WEEKLY three years later on the actual MEXICAN REVOLUTION, which he covered from VERACRUZ, were definitely not what his public expected from him as a socialist. In these articles, though he has sympathy for NATIVE peasants, whom he calls "peons" at the mercy of inept, ruthless leaders, his RACIALIST attacks upon the mestizo (what he called mixed-breed) leaders undid all his sympathy toward the peons. And his support for American oil interests in Mexico exasperated his socialist friends. But JOAN LONDON notes that during the revolution, Mexico presented to the United States "a picture of horror and chaos." The revolution developed "so swiftly and erratically" that observers could not keep up with it. Americans did not understand that "[b]ehind the revolution and driving it on was an outraged people whose activity boiled and seethed within the narrow confines set by a purely local perspective. They not only lacked any semblance of a class consciousness; they were not even aware that they were part of a nation." The Mexican urban working class had barely developed; the middle class remained weak and frightened; and the capitalist class was practically nonexistent "save as agents of foreign capital." The United States "saw nothing but violence, lawlessness, betrayal, intrigue and the criminal destruction of private property. . . . But others saw Mexico's fabulously rich oil wells and, watchfully noting events, bided their time until they might strike effectively and secure them" (Joan London, *Jack London and His Times*, 345–346). As Carolyn Johnston remarks, London tried to make sense of "this murky, complex revolution," his position resting on the idea that "the efficient, 'humane' Americans had accepted their white man's burden to uplift the 'inferior' peoples. . . . He failed to apply a Marxist analysis of the situation. His Social Darwinism and racism eclipsed his socialism." If the revolution had, in his mind, truly represented the general interests of the masses, he might have supported it. But in his eyes the revolution had failed, and thus Americans were obliged to intervene (Johnston, *Jack London—An American Radical?*, 156–157).

Collier's offered London $1,100 a week and expenses to go to Veracruz and cover the American invasion, though there really was little of "war" to cover. Beyond the shelling of the Naval Academy and raids by the Americans and some action between the Federals and the Constitutionalists, London had to seek out the details of life during wartime from the streets, the prisons, and the law courts of Veracruz. He helped rescue Americans and Constitutionalists from Tampico, and photographed prisoners in San Juan de Ulua prison and wrote his dispatches. But people wanted to read about the firebrand London's daring adventures in Mexico, not dry economic history and racialist theory, to which he turned when he ran out of action to report. None of London's articles expressed any real support for the revolution, which further angered socialists. (Kingman, *A Pictorial Life of Jack London*, 253–254).

In "With Funston's Men," May 23, 1914, his second dispatch, London contrasts the disorder of the Mexicans and the calm and orderly management of Veracruz by the Americans. Mexican officers "seem to have notions different from ours in the matter of prosecuting war." The efficient and technologically advanced U.S. troops seem effortlessly to restore order: "Our fighting ships are ten and fifteen million-dollar electrical, chemical, and mechanical laboratories, and they are manned by scientists and mechanicians" (London, *Reports*, 140–141). Against "our highly equipped, capably led young men," the Mexican troops—mostly Native—seem untrained and without properly trained officers, as they are "descendants of the millions of stupid ones who could not withstand the several hundred ragamuffins of Cortez and who passed stupidly from the harsh slavery of the Montezumas to the no less harsh slavery of the Spaniards and the later Mexicans" (London, *Reports*, 145).

London avers that given the nature of humankind, war is necessary, the stance he took on World War I, shared by many Americans, but criticized by the socialists:

> War is a silly thing for a rational, civilized man to contemplate. To settle matters of right and justice by means of introducing into human bodies foreign substances that tear them to pieces is no less silly than ducking elderly

A *soldadera,* or camp follower, during the Mexican Revolution, Veracruz, Mexico, 1914 *(Huntington Library)*

ladies of eccentric behavior to find out whether or not they are witches. But—and there you are—what is the rational man to do when those about him persist in settling matters at issue by violent means? (London, *Reports*, 145)

His "Americanness" intensified, however, when he interviewed refugees from the American mines and oil fields rescued by U.S. troops; they were angry, believing that American troops were the only way for Americans in Veracruz to get a "square deal" (London, *Reports*, 148). "Mexico's Army and Ours," May 30, 1914, London's third dispatch, is also his longest and the one most focused on abstract racial differences between Americans and Mexicans instead of what was transpiring around him. Here, he displays an odd blend of genuine sympathy for the oppressed Natives of Mexico and racialist abstractions such as the fear of "mongrels":

> Changes of government mean to the peon merely changes of the everlasting master. His harsh treatment and poorly rewarded toil are ever the same, unchanging as the sun and seasons. He has little to lose and less to gain. He is born to an unlovely place in life. It is the will of God, the law of existence.
>
> With rare exceptions he does not dream that there may be a social order wherein can be no masters of the sort he knows. (London, *Reports*, 154–155)

This is certainly a sympathetic insight, given the miseries of Mexico's Natives under several dictators, but the pseudoscientific racialist theories obscure the sense of the individual. But despite the RACIALISM he continues to express sympathy for the peon in the abstract:

> A peon seeks to gladden his existence by drinking a few cents' worth of half-spoiled pulque. The maggots of intoxication begin to crawl in his brain, and he is happy in that for a space he has forgotten in God knows what dim drunken imaginings. Then the long arm of his ruler reaches out through the medium of many minions, and the peon, sober with an aching head, finds himself in jail waiting the next draft to the army. . . .
>
> He does not know whom he fights for, for what, or why. He accepts it as the system of life. It is a very sad world, but it is the only world he knows. This is why, . . . in the midst of battle or afterward, he so frequently changes sides. He is not fighting for any principle, for any reward. It is a sad world, in which witless, humble men are just forced to fight, to kill, and to be killed. The merits of either banner are equal, or, rather, so far as he is concerned, there are no merits to either banner. (London, *Reports*, 157)

Perhaps most surprising in the dispatches is how London, a socialist, writes in support of American interests in Mexico's commercial possibilities:

> The Mexican peon residing in the United States at the present time—and there are many thousands of him—is far better treated than are his brothers south of the border. . . . Why not toss the old drugs overboard and consider the matter clear-eyed? [A] civilization introduced by America and Europe is being destroyed by the madness of a handful of rulers who do not know how to rule. . . . The big brother can police, organize, and manage Mexico. The so-called leaders of Mexico cannot. And the lives and happiness of a few million peons, as well as of many millions yet to be born, are at stake. (London, *Reports*, 159–160)

London's racialism once again stood directly in the way of logical analysis of Mexico's situation, which, minus the attacks on "breeds" and "mongrels," is actually one of the better ones published in the American press of the day.

FURTHER READING

Johnston, Carolyn. *Jack London—An American Radical?* Westport, Conn.: Greenwood, 1984.

Kingman, Russ. *A Pictorial Life of Jack London.* New York: Crown, 1979.

London, Jack. *Jack London Reports: War Correspondence, Sports Articles, and Miscellaneous Writings.* Edited by King Hendricks and Irving Shepard. Garden City, N.Y.: Doubleday & Co., 1970.

London, Joan. *Jack London and His Times.* New York: Doubleday, 1939. Reprinted with new introduction by the author. Seattle: University of Washington Press, 1968.

Reesman, Jeanne Campbell. *Jack London's Racial Lives: A Critical Biography.* Athens: University of Georgia Press, 2009, chapter 8.

"The Minions of Midas"
(1901)

First published in *Pearson's Magazine* (May 1901), "The Minions of Midas" is a suspenseful tale of extortion and terrorism resulting in multiple deaths. It is included in the collection *Moon-Face & Other Stories.*

SYNOPSIS

A street-railway baron, Eben Hale, receives several letters from an anarchist underground group of dis-affected laborers who, desiring no longer to be wage slaves to Hale and his like, attempt to extort $20 million from Hale: "We are members of that intel-lectual proletariat, the increasing numbers of which mark in red lettering the last days of the nine-teenth century. We have, from a thorough study of economics, decided to enter upon this business. It has many merits, chief among which may be noted that we can indulge in large and lucrative operations without capital. So far, we have been fairly successful, and we hope our dealings with you may be pleasant and satisfactory" (*Stories*, 435). As they further explain, "The great trusts and busi-ness combinations (with which you have your rat-ing) prevent us from rising to the place among you which our intellects qualify us to occupy. Why? Because we are without capital. We are of the unwashed, but with this difference: our brains are of the best, and we have no foolish ethical nor social scruples. As wage slaves, toiling early and late, and living abstemiously, we could not save in threescore years—nor in twenty times threescore years—a sum of money sufficient successfully to cope with the great aggregations of massed capital which now exist. Nevertheless, we have entered the arena. We now throw down the gage to the capital of the world. Whether it wishes to fight or not, it shall have to fight" (*Stories*, 436). Thus, they begin their correspondence with Hale, who at first laughs the letters off as the work of cranks.

They warn that if he refuses them, they will start murdering someone every day until he relents. This they perform, to Hale's mounting horror, even tak-ing the life of a young friend of his daughter's. In a series of letters all signed "Very Cordially," they relate the murders one after another. They point out that they will not harm Hale but will con-tinue killing. As Atsheller relates, "As you know, John, Mr. Hale was a man of iron. He refused to surrender. But, oh, John, it was terrible, nay, hor-rible—this awful something, this blind force in the dark. We could not fight, could not plan, could do nothing save hold our hands and wait. And week

by week, as certain as the rising of the sun, came the notification and death of some person, man or woman, innocent of evil, but just as much killed by us as though we had done it with our own hands. A word from Mr. Hale and the slaughter would have ceased" (*Stories*, 439). But Hale is too proud to relent. Only with his own death does his suffer-ing cease; Atsheller also kills himself because of the knowledge of what his boss had allowed to happen.

COMMENTARY

Interestingly, the Minions of Midas turn to CHARLES DARWIN's theory of EVOLUTION to explain their behavior: "We are the inevitable. We are the culmination of industrial and social wrong. We turn upon the society that has created us. We are the successful failures of the age, the scourges of a degraded civilization. We are the creatures of a perverse social selection. We meet force with force. Only the strong shall endure. We believe in the survival of the fittest. . . . And now the ques-tion has arisen: UNDER THE PRESENT SOCIAL ENVIRONMENT, WHICH OF US SHALL SUR-VIVE? We believe we are the fittest. You believe you are the fittest. We leave the eventuality to time and law" (*Stories*, 442). London often warned that one day the lower classes would rise up in revolt against the capitalists; this story, like *The Iron Heel*, poses a sensational picture of what such a revolt might look like. The story does not advocate what this group does, but neither does it advocate Hale's refusal to pay the ransom. In the end, the Minions of Midas do not get their $20 million from Hale, but there is little doubt that they will keep on until they get it somewhere else.

CHARACTERS

Wade Atsheller Secretary to Eben Hale and an adopted son and business partner, Atsheller writes a summary of the demands of the extortionist group the Minions of Midas and preserves their letters to Hale. When he realizes that he can do nothing to stop this group from murdering random people, he kills himself.

Eben Hale An enormously wealthy street-rail-way magnate, Hale is extorted for $20 million by an underground group that calls itself the Minions of Midas. They accuse Hale and all his cronies of building their fortunes on the backs of mistreated laborers; they threaten to kill at random unless he pays. This they do, and Hale finally takes his own life.

John John is the narrator of the story; he is a friend of Atsheller's and receives the entire story and correspondence from him before his death.

The Mutiny of the Elsinore (1914)

Inspired by the Londons' own adventures on their voyage around Cape Horn aboard the *DIRIGO* in 1912, this novel is one of London's most promising but least satisfying works. No matter that it contains dramatic and even melodramatic scenes on the high seas and that it continues to be read around the world: Among American critics it is barely discussed, the general sense seeming to be that critically it fails. First, the hero, playwright John Pathurst, is extremely unlikable due to his racialist ideas. Second, the love story element is implausible—would a woman like Margaret West fall in love with a man like Pathurst, so weak, depressed, grouchy? Human and narrative logic says no, yet they do fall in love, survive a mutiny, and sail off happily in the end. One wonders what life will be like for her with such a self-absorbed man, who, besides his racial ideas, seems to have firm ideas about the role of women. This novel thus asks foundational questions of morality, gender, community.

SYNOPSIS

Pathurst, a successful New York playwright, has decided to get away from his hectic life as a celebrity by taking passage on a commercial sailing ship from Baltimore to San Francisco. Although acclaimed, he is a bitter man, without faith in love or friendship. Yet, over the course of the sea voyage he falls in love with Margaret West, the captain's daughter, and helps her, officers, and crew defend against a mutiny. In fighting the mutineers, he imagines that his racialist ideas of white superiority will be proven (though they are not exactly as it turns out). This character's RACIALISM is the main weakness of the book, which would otherwise be a fairly exciting and suspenseful sea yarn.

Pathurst complains from the beginning: the weather, his cabin, the pilot, the crew. He is not "keen" on the voyage but undertook it because

> . . . there was nothing else I was keen on. For some time now life had lost its savour. . . . I had lost taste for my fellow-men and all their foolish, little, serious endeavours. For a far longer period I had been dissatisfied with women. I had endured them, but I had been too analytic of the faults of their primitiveness, of their almost ferocious devotion to the destiny of sex, to be enchanted with them. And I had come to be possessed by what seemed to me the futility of art—a pompous legerdemain, a consummate charlatanry that deceived not only its devotees but its practitioners. (13)

Pathurst says he suffers from "the world-weariness, intellectual, artistic, sensational" that can come to a young man (57), reflecting London. Note the idea that the artist might feel like a charlatan. He imagines running away:

> Really, I had been, and was, very sick. Mad thoughts of isolating myself entirely from the world had hounded me. I had even canvassed the idea of going to Molokai and devoting the rest of my years to the lepers—I, who was thirty years old, and healthy and strong, who had no particular tragedy, who had a bigger income than I knew how to spend, who by my own achievement had put my name on the lips of men and proved myself a power to be reckoned with—I was that mad that I had considered the lazar house for a destiny. (57)

Like many neurotics Pathurst views the others aboard *Elsinore* as a cast of characters at his command, everyone as a stereotype that fits his scheme of the world. He compares Captain West to a "king or emperor, as remote as the farthest fixed star, as neutral as a proposition of Euclid"; his "long, lean . . . face" betrays "a touch of race I as yet could only sense" (9). Like the captain, the white officers and mates "were potent. They were iron. They were perceivers, willers, and doers. They were as of another species compared with the sailors under them" (25). Margaret explains that the crew are "the worst type of men," but "we do our best with them" (30). In a gender reversal, Margaret soothes the fretful Pathurst, who sounds like the stereotypical hysterical woman onboard ship, frightened as he is by the scruffy, mixed-race crew. Her tone evidently appeals to him, as does her nose: he notes that their "noses were alike, just the hint-touch of the beak of prowess and race" (49). He decides that she is "a physical type of the best of the womanhood of old New England" (113) and can fulfill his needs.

But Pathurst is not soothed; he cannot take his eyes off the grotesque crewmen: "There was something wrong with all of them. Their bodies were twisted, their faces distorted, and almost without exception they were undersized" (49). Pathurst describes "a wretched muck of men," all "dead men raised out of coffins or sick men dragged from hospital beds. Sick they were—whiskey-poisoned. Starved they were, and weak from poor nutrition" (42–43). Pathurst sees, by contrast, his Asian steward, as "keen, . . . quick with intelligence" (35); with those over whom Pathurst exercises dominance he feels safe. He tells the second mate Mr. Mellaire that he thinks the voyage is doomed. Sure enough, mutiny ensues when a "gangster clique" takes over the forecastle (128). Yet Pathurst is sure that himself and the officers, all "blond Aryan[s]" (161) will prevail. While the mutinous sailors, as he observes, have bare feet "scaled with patches of tar and pitch" and "unbathed bodies" clothed "in the meanest of clothes, dingy, dirty, ragged, and sparse," in contrast, as he surveys the captain's dinner table, he fantasizes about "mastering and commanding, like our fathers before us, to the end of our type on the earth" (161). On deck he confides in Margaret: "'[M]y forebears were Vikings. I was seed of them in their own day. With them I have raided English coasts, dared the Pillars of Hercules, forayed the Mediterranean, and sat in the high place of government over the soft sun-warm peoples. I am Hengist and Horsa; I am of the ancient heroes, even legendary to them." She laughs, "'I don't know anything about it," but adds, "'It sounds like poetry. . . . I have heard it aforetime, when skin-clad men sang in fire-circles that pressed back the frost and night'" (241). (Do people ever talk this way?) However, Pathurst's imaginary and romantic view of war is contrasted with the cook's:

> "They make fool with me, I fix 'em," he said vindictively. "Mebbe they kill me, all right; but I kill some, too."
>
> He threw back his coat, and I saw, strapped to the left side of his body, in a canvas sheath, so that the handle was ready to hand, a meat knife of the heavy sort that butchers hack with. He drew it forth—it was fully two feet long—and, to demonstrate its razor-edge, sliced a sheet of newspaper into many ribbons.
>
> "Huh!" he laughed sardonically. "I am Chink, monkey, damn fool, eh?—no good, eh? all rotten damn to hell. I fix 'em, they make fool with me." (293)

"The Chink" sounds a good deal more prepared for the mutiny than Pathurst.

Eventually the officers, Margaret, and Pathurst, along with Wada, Louis, the steward, two Japanese sailmakers, and a few others are hiding in the aft quarters. Fighting breaks out and several on each side are killed. The captain's party has most of the food supplies, but since the mutineers have the tackle, the ship either drifts or sits becalmed. Pathurst consoles himself that

> Nevertheless, here we are, masters of matter, adventurers in the micro-organic, planet-weighers, sun-analysers, star-rovers, god-dreamers, equipped with the human wisdom of all the ages, and yet . . . we are a lot of primitive beasts, fighting bestially. . . . And over this menagerie of beasts Margaret and I, with our Asiatics under us, rule top-dog. We are all dogs—there is no getting away from it. And we, the fair-pigmented ones, by the seed of our ancestry rulers in the high place, shall remain top-dog over the rest of the dogs. (366–367)

Typical of Pathurst to sit and think such thoughts when much of the ANGLO-SAXON contingent has been eliminated. He later has a somewhat more accurate view of the situation: "On board this ship, driving now through the South Atlantic for the winter passage of Cape Horn, are all the elements of sea tragedy and horror. We are freighted with human dynamite that is liable at any moment to blow our tiny floating world to fragments" (172–173). But he and Margaret survive, and the couple make their honeymoon plans as they steer the ship to port all by themselves.

COMMENTARY

The Mutiny of the Elsinore is even worse than *Adventure* in its racialism. How could London, who wrote such sensitive portraits of racial "Others" and such sharp attacks on white racism in the South Seas, write this? Is it possible that, as in *A Daughter of the Snows* and *Adventure*, that it is to be read ironically, that is, as a satire? Pathurst looks like one of London's satiric caricatures of arrogant, close-minded, and ultimately self-destructive "inevitable white men," like Percival Ford of "The House of Pride," Bernie Arkwright of "The Terrible Solomons," or Dick Forrest of *The Little Lady of the Big House*. Pathurst also suggests an incarnation of London at his worst, pandering to the public with stereotypes and 18th-century pirate clichés. Perhaps we are not supposed to like Pathurst. Yet London probably wrote this novel because he needed money from a potboiler.

CHARACTERS

John Pathurst Pathurst is a New York playwright, who, though successful, is depressed and decides to take a few months off and sail aboard a ship around CAPE HORN. At the beginning of the novel, he is full of complaints about the cold weather in Baltimore as he waits at the pier to board the ship. A friend has given him a fox terrier puppy, Possum, but he finds it only an annoyance. (This dog is based on a real one the Londons acquired just before their departure on the *Dirigo* in 1912, bound for Seattle around Cape Horn.) Pathurst is inordinately proud and unpleasant. His most unattractive quality is his obsessive racism. He experiences a mutiny and falls in love with the captain's daughter. It is hard to say whether or not these experiences will improve his personality and outlook and give meaning to his life.

Wada Pathurst's Japanese servant. During the mutiny, Pathurst relies on his loyalty. Wada is an excellent source of information on the crew for Pathurst.

Driver Waits in the freezing cold in the cab with Pathurst and Wada at the beginning of the novel near a pier in Baltimore.

Boy Brings the pilot's suitcase and announces to the waiting Pathurst and Wada that the pilot is coming and that they will be taken aboard the *Elsinore* by tug.

Pilot Pilot of the harbor who escorts Pathurst to the *Elsinore:* "Anything more unlike a pilot I could not have imagined. Here was no blue-jacketed, weather-beaten son of the sea, but a soft-spoken gentleman, for all the world the type of successful business man one meets in all the clubs. He introduced himself immediately, and I invited him to share my freezing cab with Possum and the baggage" (6–7).

Harrison and Gray Agents through whom Pathurst books his cabin aboard the *Elsinore;* he asks them to get the captain's cabin for him, which they fail to do.

Captain West Pathurst greatly admires Captain West, whom he sees as the ideal of Anglo-Saxon leadership and accomplishment (but whom he calls the "Samurai"). Pathurst constantly stares at the captain: "I never grow tired of watching Captain West. In a way he bears a sort of resemblance to several of Washington's portraits. He is six feet of aristocratic thinness, and has a very definite, leisurely and stately grace of movement. His thinness is almost ascetic. In appearance and manner he is the perfect old-type New England gentleman" (187). He has a daughter, Margaret, whom he has trained at sea to be as fine a sailor as he is. He dies of a heart attack as they cross Cape Horn.

Margaret West The beautiful, brave daughter of Captain West. She is Pathurst's love interest, but she seems far superior to him. Nevertheless, she does become engaged to him in the end. When they are introduced she gazes directly at him, without a sign of coyness; she proves herself strong and sure aboard ship. She resembles other no-nonsense London heroines such as Joan Lackland.

Mr. Pike First mate of the *Elsinore.* When Pathurst first meets him, he observes his huge hands and stiff but powerful bearing: "He smiled a stiff, crack-faced smile that I knew must be painful, but did not offer to shake hands, turning immediately to call orders to half-a-dozen frozen-looking youths and aged men who shambled up from somewhere in the waist of the ship. Mr. Pike had been drinking. That was patent. His face was puffed and discoloured, and his large gray eyes were bitter and bloodshot" (14). Pathurst knows of Pike's long sailing history and admires him for it. They become close friends.

Mr. Mellaire Second mate of the *Elsinore.* Though he is a reserved and polite Southerner, he frightens Pathurst: "His features and expression were genial and gentle, and yet his mouth was the cruellest gash I had ever seen in a man's face. It was a gash. There is no other way of describing that harsh, thin-lipped, shapeless mouth that uttered gracious things so graciously. . . . Back into his blue eyes I looked. On the surface of them was a film of light, a gloss of gentle kindness and cordiality, but behind that gloss I knew resided neither sincerity nor mercy. Behind that gloss was something cold and terrible, that lurked and waited and watched—something catlike, something inimical and deadly" (19). Pathurst discovers that Mellaire's real name is Sidney Waltham: "He is one of the Walthams of Virginia, a black sheep, true, but a Waltham. Of this I am convinced, just as utterly as I am convinced that Mr. Pike will kill him if he learns who he is" (168). Later, during the mutiny, Pike corners Mellaire: "'I know you,' he said, in a strange, shaky voice, blended of age and passion. 'Eighteen years

ago you were dismasted off the Plate in the *Cyrus Thompson.* She foundered, after you were on your beam ends and lost your sticks. You were in the only boat that was saved. Eleven years ago, on the *Jason Harrison,* in San Francisco, Captain Somers was beaten to death by his second mate. This second mate was a survivor of the *Cyrus Thompson.* This second mate'd had his skull split by a crazy sea-cook. Your skull is split. This second mate's name was Sidney Waltham. And if you ain't Sidney Waltham'" (306). He and Mr. Pike destroy each other over this long-held grudge.

Shorty "One, a most vivid-faced youth of eighteen, smiled at me from a pair of remarkable Italian eyes. But he was a dwarf. So short was he that he was all sea-boots and sou'wester. And yet he was not entirely Italian. So certain was I that I asked the mate, who answered morosely: 'Him? Shorty? He's a dago half-breed. The other half's Jap or Malay'" (14).

Sundry Buyers He is "a bosun, . . . so decrepit that I thought he had been recently injured. His face was stolid and ox-like, and as he shuffled and dragged his brogans over the deck he paused every several steps to place both hands on his abdomen and execute a queer, pressing, lifting movement. Months were to pass, in which I saw him do this thousands of times, ere I learned that there was nothing the matter with him and that his action was purely a habit. His face reminded me of the Man with the Hoe, save that it was unthinkably and abysmally stupider" (15).

Nancy He is another bosun: "Nancy could not have been more than thirty, though he looked as if he had lived a very long time. He was toothless and sad and weary of movement. His eyes were slate-coloured and muddy, his shaven face was sickly yellow. Narrow-shouldered, sunken-chested, with cheeks cavernously hollow, he looked like a man in the last stages of consumption. Little life as Sundry Buyers showed, Nancy showed even less life. And these were bosuns!—bosuns of the fine American sailing-ship *Elsinore!* Never had any illusion of mine taken a more distressing cropper" (34).

Henry He is "a youth of sixteen, who approximated in the slightest what I had conceived all sailors to be like. He had come off a training ship, the mate told me, and this was his first voyage to sea. His face was keen-cut, alert, as were his bodily movements, and he wore sailor-appearing clothes with sailor-seeming grace. In fact, as I was to learn, he was to be the only sailor-seeming creature fore and aft" (15). He is shot while at the wheel of the ship during the mutiny.

Chinese steward He explains the eating arrangements to Pathurst on his first day aboard and other details about ship life and about the crew; he is "smooth-faced and brisk of movement, whose name I never learned, but whose age on the articles was fifty-six" (23). Pathurst admires his "keen, Asiatic face, quick with intelligence" (34).

Tony the Greek He is a suicidal crewman unable to work because of all of his injuries from suicide attempts. Before the *Elsinore*'s departure, a "dark-skinned Mediterranean of some sort" jumps overboard and tries to swim away carrying a large knife with which he repeatedly wounds himself. Tony is hauled aboard and tied to his bunk. When Pathurst tells Pike he'll bleed to death, Pike says that that is fine; if he doesn't, Pike will toss him overboard once they're at sea. "'Bughouse,' Mr. Pike grinned at me. 'I've seen some bughouse crews in my time, but this one's the limit'" (26). He jumps again once they are at sea but is retrieved and put back to work.

Various crew members: "One man, however, large and unmistakably Irish, was also unmistakably mad. He was talking and muttering to himself as he came out. A little, curved, lop-sided man [Mulligan], with his head on one side and with the shrewdest and wickedest of faces and pale blue eyes, addressed an obscene remark to the mad Irishman, calling him O'Sullivan. But O'Sullivan took no notice and muttered on. On the heels of the little lop-sided man appeared an overgrown dolt of a fat youth [Bob], followed by another youth so tall and emaciated of body that it seemed a marvel his flesh could hold his frame

together. Next, after this perambulating skeleton, came the weirdest creature I have ever beheld. He was a twisted oaf of a man [the Faun]. Face and body were twisted as with the pain of a thousand years of torture. His was the face of an ill-treated and feeble-minded faun. His large black eyes were bright, eager, and filled with pain; and they flashed questioningly from face to face and to everything about. They were so pitifully alert, those eyes, as if for ever astrain to catch the clue to some perplexing and threatening enigma. Not until afterwards did I learn the cause of this. He was stone deaf, having had his ear-drums destroyed in the boiler explosion which had wrecked the rest of him. . . . And still they came: one, pallid, furtive-eyed, that I instantly adjudged a drug fiend [Deacon]; another, a tiny, wizened old man, pinch-faced and wrinkled, with beady, malevolent blue eyes; a third, a small, well-fleshed man, who seemed to my eye the most normal and least unintelligent specimen that had yet appeared. But Mr. Pike's eye was better trained than mine" (34–35). O'Sullivan is murdered by Charles Davis, and various others of these crewmen meet a bad end.

Charles Davis Crewman whom Mr. Pike interrogates: "'What's the matter with YOU?' he snarled at the man. 'Nothing, sir,' the fellow answered, stopping immediately. 'What are you limping about?' 'I ain't limpin', sir,' the man answered respectfully, and, at a nod of dismissal from the mate, marched off jauntily along the deck with a hoodlum swing to the shoulders. 'He's a sailor all right,' the mate grumbled; 'but I'll bet you a pound of tobacco or a month's wages there's something wrong with him'" (35–36). Davis threatens to sue the officers for mistreatment. He murders O'Sullivan because he interrupted his sleep.

Murphy, Bert Rhine, and Twist Three crewmen who display insolence to Mr. Pike; he renames Murphy Nosey and Twist Kid. Of them Mr. Pike remarks, "'I know their kidney. They've done time, the three of them. They're just plain sweepings of hell—'" (39). They become ringleaders of the mutiny and control the forecastle.

Larry   Mr. Pike observes him with five or six others sprawled out over a hatch; when he roughly asks him why he isn't in the forecastle, Larry pleads that he was drunk last night. Pike hits him and he flies across the deck.

Tom Spink   He is an Englishman who is efficient at the ship's wheel.

Louis   He is a half-Chinese man who is the ship's cook. He plans to defend himself from mutineers with his machete.

Sam Lavroff   From New York, he is the ship's carpenter. He is "a self-conscious, embarrassed individual, with the face of a stupid boy and the body of a giant" (51). He disappears as the *Elsinore* rounds Cape Horn; the crew think the strange castaways have killed him.

The Maltese Cockney   A crewman Mr. Mellaire praises as "'the best sailor in his watch, a proper seaman'" (97).

Steve Roberts   An ex-cowboy working under Margaret's direction to rid Pathurst's cabin of bedbugs; he uses turpentine and white lead. The voyage is his first time at sea; while his demeanor suggests frankness and intelligence, his friends are the trio of Murphy, Bert, and Twist. He is shot by Pathurst in the mutiny.

Mulligan Jacobs   "The second sailor Miss West rejected, after silently watching him work for five minutes, was Mulligan Jacobs, the wisp of a man with curvature of the spine. . . . I was in the room when Mulligan Jacobs first came in to go to work, and I could not help observing the startled, avid glance he threw at my big shelves of books. He advanced on them in the way a robber might advance on a secret hoard of gold, and as a miser would fondle gold so Mulligan Jacobs fondled these book-titles with his eyes. And such eyes! All the bitterness and venom Mr. Pike had told me the man possessed was there in his eyes. They were small, pale-blue, and gimlet-pointed with fire. His eyelids were inflamed, and but served to ensan-guine the bitter and cold-blazing intensity of the pupils. The man was constitutionally a hater, and I was not long in learning that he hated all things except books" (102).

Arthur Deacon   "He is the pallid, furtive-eyed man whom I observed the first day when the men were routed out of the forecastle to man the windlass—the man I so instantly adjudged a drug-fiend. He certainly looks it" (108). Pathurst learns he has been a white slaver.

Bob   An overweight youth who joins the ship as a sailor.

O'Sullivan   An Irishman who is murdered by Charles Davis for snoring. O'Sullivan figures in numerous rivalries and fights aboard the *Elsinore*; he tries to murder another crewman himself for a pair of boots.

Christian Jespersen   A Dutch crewman who has died: As Mr. Mellaire explains, "'He got in O'Sullivan's way when O'Sullivan went after the boots. That's what saved Andy. Andy was more active. Jespersen couldn't get out of his own way, much less out of O'Sullivan's'" (113–114).

Andy Fay   "I followed Mr. Mellaire's gaze, and saw the burnt-out, aged little Scotchman squatted on a spare spar and sucking a pipe. One arm was in a sling and his head was bandaged. Beside him squatted Mulligan Jacobs. They were a pair. Both were blue-eyed, and both were malevolent-eyed. And they were equally emaciated. It was easy to see that they had discovered early in the voyage their kinship of bitterness" (114). It is interesting in several descriptions of crew in this novel that blue eyes are associated with the primitive.

Isaac B. Chantz   A Jewish sailor who is beaten in the brawl by O'Sullivan. As Mr. Mellaire says, "'Sheenies don't take to the sea as a rule. We've certainly got more than our share of them. Chantz isn't badly hurt, but you ought to hear him whimper'" (114).

Herman Lunkenheimer A crewman who is "a good-natured but simple-minded dolt of a German"; he receives "a severe beating from the three because he refused to wash some of Nosey Murphy's dirty garments" (127). He is under the control of the three sailors who control the forecastle, Murphy, Rhine, and Twist. His throat is cut by Bombini and Twist.

Ditman Olansen A Norwegian crewman: "A good seaman, Mr. Mellaire had told me, in whose watch he was; a good seaman, but 'crank-eyed.' When pressed for an explanation Mr. Mellaire had said that he was the sort of man who flew into blind rages, and that one never could tell what little thing would produce such a rage. As near as I could grasp it, Ditman Olansen was a Berserker type. Yet, as I watched him pulling in good time at the oar, his large, pale-blue eyes seemed almost bovine—the last man in the world, in my judgment, to have a Berserker fit" (137). He is speared by Wada during the mutiny.

Boney the Splinter "The lanky splinter of a youth in Mr. Mellaire's watch" (153) who brings Mr. Pike news of Davis's murder of O'Sullivan. He is washed overboard as the ship rounds the Horn.

Bill Quigley A crewman who is "one of a forecastle group of three that herded uniquely together, though the other two, Frank Fitzgibbon and Richard Oiler, were in the second mate's watch. The three had proved handy with their fists, and clannish; they had fought pitched forecastle battles with the gangster clique and won a sort of neutrality of independence for themselves. They were not exactly sailors—Mr. Mellaire sneeringly called them the 'bricklayers'—but they had successfully refused subservience to the gangster crowd" (207–208). He is shot and flung overboard by Mr. Pike.

Three men rescued by the _Elsinore_ One evening, the crew start speaking of ghosts on board, and it turns out there are three men floating on casks who come aboard; they instill unreasoning fear in the men: "But such men! I know my East Side and my East End, and I am accustomed to the faces of all the ruck of races, yet with these three men I was at fault. The Mediterranean had surely never bred such a breed; nor had Scandinavia. They were not blonds. They were not brunettes. Nor were they of the Brown, or Black, or Yellow. Their skin was white under a bronze of weather. Wet as was their hair, it was plainly a colourless, sandy hair. Yet their eyes were dark—and yet not dark. They were neither blue, nor gray, nor green, nor hazel. Nor were they black. They were topaz, pale topaz; and they gleamed and dreamed like the eyes of great cats. They regarded us like walkers in a dream, these pale-haired storm-waifs with pale, topaz eyes. They did not bow, they did not smile, in no way did they recognize our presence save that they looked at us and dreamed" (256–257). Margaret calls them "'Horn Gypsies'" (259). Tom Spink calls them "'warlocks'" (260). Others surmise that they are Finns.

Mike Cipriani and Guido Bombini Italian crewmen who join the mutiny. Cipriani is shot and thrown overboard by Mr. Pike, "still alive and clinging to the log-line, cut adrift by the steward to be eaten alive by great-beaked albatrosses, mollyhawks, and sooty-plumaged Cape hens" (366).

Buckwheat A boy who sides with the officers in the mutiny.

Uchino Second sailmaker who defends Henry during the mutiny.

Petro Marinkovich Crewman who is murdered by the forecastle gangsters before the _Elsinore_ rounds the Horn, "his life cut out of him with knives, his carcass left lying on deck to be found by us and be buried by us" (365).

"Nam-Bok the Unveracious" (1902)

First published in _Ainslee's Magazine_ (August 1902) and included in _Children of the Frost,_ this black-comic tale shows the unhappy results of its hero's sojourn among the white men of San Francisco—results that culminate in his being exiled from his tribe of ESKIMOS. They fear he is a ghost returned from the dead, and they do not believe his accounts of the machines among which the white men live and work. Even his own mother disowns poor Nam-Bok.

SYNOPSIS

Nam-Bok is an ESKIMO who was lost at sea in his canoe; he is rescued by a passing ship and taken to live among whites in San Francisco. While there, he witnesses many of the great technological feats of civilization. He has anticipated telling his tribe what he has seen:

> The fisherfolk applauded with their hands, and gathering about them their work, prepared to listen. The men were busy fashioning spears and carving on ivory, while the women scraped the fat from the hides of the hair seal and made them pliable or sewed muclucs with threads of sinew. Nam-Bok's eyes roved over the scene, but there was not the charm about it that his recollection had warranted him to expect. During the years of his wandering he had looked forward to just this scene, and now that it had come he was disappointed. It was a bare and meagre life, he deemed, and not to be compared to the one to which he had become used. Still, he would open their eyes a bit, and his own eyes sparkled at the thought. (*Stories*, 578)

This is before he tries and fails to eat his old diet of boiled seal. But he eagerly tells what he has seen: gigantic ships that move of their own power against the wind, with no paddles; men learning to steer not by the land but by the stars; gigantic homes and cities; trains, which he calls "iron monsters" (*Stories*, 583); the thousands of people living in one "village."

Having marveled at his tales, his tribe does not believe him and furthermore fears that he is a ghost. The headman, a tribal elder, and his own mother all agree to turn him adrift at the end of the story. As Opee-Kwan puts it,

"Thou wast bidarka-mate with me when we were boys. . . . Together we first chased the seal and drew the salmon from the traps. And thou didst drag me back to life, Nam-Bok, when the sea closed over me and I was sucked down to the black rocks. Together we hungered and bore the chill of the frost, and together we crawled beneath the one fur and lay close to each other. And because of these things, and the kindness in which I stood to thee, it grieves me sore that thou shouldst return such a remarkable liar. We cannot understand, and our heads be dizzy with the things thou hast spoken. It is not good, and there has been much talk in the council. Wherefore we send thee away, that our heads may remain clear and strong and be not troubled by the unaccountable things."

"These things thou speakest of be shadows," Koogah took up the strain. "From the shadow-world thou hast brought them, and to the shadow-world thou must return them. Thy bidarka be ready, and the tribespeople wait. They may not sleep until thou art gone." (*Stories*, 586)

COMMENTARY

In a bleakly ironic sense, this is a comic story, but on a deeper level it both interrogates the Western hero myth of leaving home, fighting against circumstances, and returning home to be welcomed as a hero, as it also explores a likely result of NATIVE exposure to the white man's world. Many Natives London either observed or heard about left their homelands to dwell among the whites, and few of them were better off for it. The departure of young men and women from the tribes decimated their populations, even as these young men and women fell prey to alcohol, guns, and other introductions of the whites in the Northwest. It also shows some elements of the Native trickster tales London heard in the YUKON, in which a trickster visits a tribe making outlandish promises only to be exposed as a liar. The trickster god of many Northwest Native groups was the Raven. While, unlike the true trickster god, Nam-Bok does not redeem his people, they feel redeemed when they send him away, cleansed of the poison he brings to them. From Nam-Bok's point of view, the story may also be read as a tragedy.

CHARACTERS

Nam-Bok   One day Nam-Bok's canoe drifts too far out to sea, and he cannot return to land. He is picked up by a steamer and taken to San Francisco, where he receives an education in civilization among the whites. When he returns to his village, he is rejected by one and all as a ghost and a liar.

Bask-Wah-Wan   Nam-Bok's mother, who recognizes him as he approaches in a canoe by the clumsy way he rows. She always said he would come back, and she welcomes him eagerly, but later she is persuaded that he is a ghost and she turns against him.

Koogah   Called "the Bone-Scratcher" for his bone carvings, Koogah witnesses the return of Nam-Bok; he is terribly frightened by what he assumes is an evil ghost. He falls to the ground in his excitement.

Opee-Kwan   Headman of the tribe, he shows bravery in confronting the "spirit" of Nam-Bok. He opines, "'Who may know concerning the things of mystery? . . . We are, and in a breath we are not. If the man may become shadow, may not the shadow become man? Nam-Bok was, but is not. This we know, but we do not know if this be Nam-Bok or the shadow of Nam-Bok'" (*Stories*, 576). Opee-Kwan is enraged by what he takes as Nam-Bok's lies about ships that travel under their own power and other machines of the white men.

"The Night-Born" (1911)

London got the idea for this mythic tale from a newspaper clipping quoting HENRY DAVID THOREAU's words about "night-born" gods that can lead humans into their spiritual selves. The newspaper story was about a young woman who ran away to live among NATIVES and who returned to tell her tale of riches and living in NATURE. It was first pub-

lished in *Everybody's Magazine* in July 1911 and was included in the collection that bears its name.

SYNOPSIS

A man of 47, Trefathan, an ALCOHOLIC who already looks 20 years older, tells his fellow club men in San Francisco of an event that took place many years before, when he was prospecting in the YUKON as a youth. Lost and alone, he encounters a white woman, Lucy, ruling over a tribe of Natives. She is utterly captivating:

> "That's what took me off my feet—her eyes—blue, not China blue, but deep blue, like the sea and sky all melted into one, and very wise. More than that, they had laughter in them—warm laughter, sun-warm and human, very human, and . . . shall I say feminine? They were. They were a woman's eyes, a proper woman's eyes. You know what that means. Can I say more? Also, in those blue eyes were, at the same time, a wild unrest, a wistful yearning, and a repose, an absolute repose, a sort of all-wise and philosophical calm." (*Stories*, 1,662)

Lucy tells Trefathan of how she escaped from a brutal husband and life of drudgery to the Yukon. Frontier-born of poor settlers, she had never known happiness: "'I never seen the glory of the world,'" she remarks (*Stories*, 1,663). Marrying young, she works for her husband as a cook in Juneau, but she is abused for her labors. One day, she chances across a quotation from Thoreau, and it is the spur she needs to make her escape. Holding her husband at gunpoint, she demands a divorce and leaves. She journeys north, survives a shipwreck, and finds a huge cache of gold. With this, she journeys to an inland Native village and over time becomes their leader. Now she wants a mate of her own kind, and so she offers herself to Trefathan. Trefathan, though he feels himself falling in love with her, lies to her that he is already married, a lie he has the rest of his life to regret. Lucy would have meant vitality, love, and love of life, but he had not the courage to confront his desires for these things. Trefathan ends his tale, "'It would have been better had I stayed. Look at me'" (*Stories*, 1,671).

COMMENTARY

Opening with the news of a young fighter ignobly killed in the ring, the general sense of the corruption of the city sets the stage for Trefathan's tale of his encounter with Lucy in the far NORTH-LAND, in the spring of his youth. Like H. Rider Haggard's "She-Who-Must-Be-Obeyed," Lucy is a magnificent white woman who has joined—as chief—a band of Natives, ruling over a new Eden among them. The story contrasts what it presents as the purity of nature—human and otherwise—as against the evils of civilization, the fat, alcoholic Trefathan himself the prime exhibit, in contrast to the "full-blooded, full-bodied woman, and royal ripe" whom he rejects (*Stories*, 1,662). The insights of CARL JUNG illuminate Trefathan's failure to grasp his anima-figure, or soulmate, to live a healthy and productive life far away from the stench of the city; London often uses women to stand for what is lacking in the spiritual lives of his male heroes. Accordingly, this story is full of female archetypes, such as the cloak of swan's down, Lucy's all-seeing eyes, and her sexual allure. But Trefathan is not prepared to confront or embrace her and goes away brokenhearted. The masculine in the story is symbolized by the words of the first paragraph: "The grotesque sordidness and rottenness of manhate and man-meanness" (*Stories*, 1,660). Like the SONOMA novels, "The Night-Born" is a sharp critique of conventional notions of masculinity, as against such values as youth, romance, and nature—and as against life itself, as we observe at the end of the story when Trefathan cannot help but lift his glass, drunk already, in a hollow toast to "the Night-Born."

CHARACTERS

Trefathan Trefathan at 47 has the body of a 70-year-old. He recalls an experience he had with a strange woman while prospecting for gold. Her femininity challenged and repelled him at the time, but he looks back with regret on what might have been. "'Well, look at me now,' Trefathan commanded angrily. 'That's what the Goldstead did to me—God knows how many millions, but nothing left in my soul. . . . nor in my veins. The good red

blood is gone. I am a jellyfish, a huge, gross mass of oscillating protoplasm, a—a . . .' But language failed him, and he drew solace from the long glass" (*Stories*, 1,661).

Bardwell Bardwell listens to Trefathan's story at the Alta-Inyo Club and supplies a quote that makes Trefathan recall the tale; it is from Thoreau's "The Cry of the Human" in *A Week on the Concord and Merrimac Rivers*. In speaking of his suspicions in the national project of "civilizing" the Natives, Thoreau muses that

> By the wary independence and aloofness of his dim forest life he preserves his intercourse with his native gods, and is admitted from time to time to a rare and peculiar society with Nature. He has glances of starry recognition to which our saloons are strangers. The steady illumination of his genius, dim only because distant, is like the faint but satisfying life of the stars compared with the dazzling but ineffectual and short-lived blaze of candles. The Society-Islanders had their day-born gods, but they were not supposed to be "of equal antiquity with the *atua fauau po*, or night-born gods" (Henry David Thoreau, *A Week on the Concord and Merrimack Rivers*).

Milner Another of Trefathan's interlocutors at the Alta-Inyo Club: "Like Trefathan, he was another mining engineer who had cleaned up a fortune in the Klondike" (*Stories*, 1,661).

Lucy Lucy ran away from her miserable life as a fry-cook married to a brute. She experienced numerous adventures, including shipwreck and the find of a cache of gold, and she becomes the chief of a tribe of Natives. She longs for a mate of her own kind and proposes to Trefathan. She is so goddesslike, however, than he is frightened away from her. Lucy, whose name means "light," is an archetype of the feminine who represents the soul.

FURTHER READING

Labor, Earle, and Jeanne Campbell Reesman. *Jack London: Revised Edition*. New York: Twayne, 1994, 111–117.

"An Odyssey of the North" (1900)

The publication of this story in the January 1900 issue of the ATLANTIC MONTHLY signaled a new era in American fiction-writing with its stark NATU-RALISM and also the real beginning of London's fame as a writer. Having placed a story in this prestigious magazine meant that he had made it and could expect to publish work of similar quality anywhere. It is a lengthy story; it was nearly a novella before London was asked to trim it considerably. It appears in London's first short story collection, *The Son of the Wolf*.

SYNOPSIS

The story opens with one of London's most poetic descriptions of what YUKON life on the trail was like:

> The sleds were singing their eternal lament to the creaking of the harnesses and the tinkling bells of the leaders; but the men and dogs were tired and made no sound. The trail was heavy with new-fallen snow, and they had come far, and the runners, burdened with flint-like quarters of frozen moose, clung tenaciously to the unpacked surface and held back with a stubbornness almost human. Darkness was coming on, but there was no camp to pitch that night. The snow fell gently through the pulseless air, not in flakes, but in tiny frost crystals of delicate design. (*Stories*, 211)

The story-within-a-story narrative is told from a detached third-person omniscient viewpoint, but despite this it is a sensational tale of love and death; within the narrator's story are the first-person narrations of the Malemute Kid and Naass. At the outset, a group composed of the Malemute Kid and two men named Bettles and Meyers have been traveling hard on the trail and are only 75 miles from DAWSON, when they find their home cabin now occupied by Stanley Prince of the Mounted Police and some French-Canadian voyageurs. The Malemute Kid has learned that one of Prince's men, called "He-of-the-Otter Skins," has traveled

in winter from the Bering Sea to trade otter skins for dogs. The Kid calls him "Mr. Ulysses" and "the Strange One."

He-of-the-Otter-Skins meets the Kid and, with a grubstake, promises he will return the Kid's loan with great riches "'beyond the dreams of avarice'" (*Stories*, 235). After a year passes, the Kid, He-of-the-Otter-Skins, and a man named Axel Gunderson, a rough Scandinavian of seven feet tall and 300 pounds, and his NATIVE wife meet—her name has traveled throughout the NORTHLAND, but we are not told why. He-of-the-Otter-Skins plans to take the Gundersons to a valley rich with gold veins off in the far wilderness. But the Malemute Kid refuses to join the expedition; he merely expects to be repaid his loan.

Some time after the party departs, He-of-the-Otter-Skins looms in the Kid's cabin door, half-frozen, starving, and raving. He seems to have been maddened by some terrible experience and can only talk of someone called Unga's hatred for him. We learn that his true name is Naass and that he is a chief at Akatan in the Aleutian Islands, "'beyond Chignik, beyond Kardalak, beyond Unimak. . . . in the midst of the sea on the edge of the world'" (*Stories*, 242). When Naass tells his tale, he relates his love for a girl of his tribe. Then, a ship arrived at Akatan commanded by a blond-haired white man, a giant: "'a man such as the gods have forgotten how to fashion . . . in the making of Axel Gunderson the gods had remembered their old-time cunning, and cast him after the manner of men who were born when the world was young.'" He seemed "'a Norse sea rover, on southern foray.'" Gunderson gives Naass guns, steel, ammunition, and tools, then steals Unga away with him to his ship: "'took her in his great arms, and when she tore at his yellow hair, [he] laughed with a sound like that of a big bull seal in the rut'" (*Stories*, 246).

Thus Naass begins his search for Unga, traveling east and asking about the strange ship and the men of the sea. He visits remote settlements and sealing grounds, all the way to Japan. A Russian man-of-war, with Gunderson and Unga aboard, takes Naass prisoner and to slavery in Russian salt mines. Naass manages to escape and return to the Yukon, where he joins the Queen's service under Prince.

When he learns that Gunderson has become rich from gold prospecting, he follows them through their homes in Europe, only to learn eventually that they have lost their wealth and returned to the gold country of the Yukon.

Naass next encounters them in Dawson, but because of his many trials he has changed and they do not recognize him. He offers to be their guide to remote gold country and leads them east to "the spot where the bones and the curses of men lie with the gold." They travel into the great mountains and into a deep valley, "the mouth of hell," Gunderson called it, at the bottom of which was a cabin and the bones of dead men (*Stories*, 251), as in "The Devil's Dice Box." They discover a great vein of gold and depart for Dawson. However, they have miscalculated the journey, and they begin to starve, even eating their moccasins. Gunderson dies on the trail, and Naass reveals his identity to Unga: "'I had thought she would be overjoyed at the sight of me,'" he says, but she sneers at the idea of returning with him to Akatan to "'live in the dirty huts, and eat of the fish and oil, and bring forth a spawn . . .'" She calls him a pig and a dog and "'laughed till the silence cracked, and went back to her dead.'" Naass kills her as she lies prostrate on her husband, and, as Naass says, "'they still lie up there in the snow.'" At the end of the story, "Naass drew yet closer to the fire. There was a great silence, and in each man's eyes many pictures came and went" (*Stories*, 257).

COMMENTARY

In this ironic and tragic story, London continues his practice of using Roman myths of old SOL, or the SUN, and he also recalls Homer's ODYSSEY, which gives the story its basic structure of four sections: the adventures of Telemachos, the journey homeward of Odysseus; the retelling of his great wanderings; and the return of Odysseus to Ithaca. Each story takes 10 years, but like Homer's epic the story is not told in chronological order. London's version begins with the Malemute Kid (Telemachos), then the journey home of Naass, whom the Kid calls "'Mr. Ulysses'" (*Stories*, 234); then Naass's narrative of his wanderings; and finally Naass back at the Kid's camp (Ithaca). As in other Klondike stories the central action—and sin—of this tale is breaking the NORTHLAND CODE of BROTHERHOOD, violating the GREEK notion of hospitality to strangers. Such epithets as "'He-of-the-Otter-Skins'" (*Stories*, 235) recall Homer's epithets such as Odysseus, "the man of many turns." The story also references Telemachos's dream in the Malemute Kid's dream; the way the Kid recognizes Naass as Telemachos recognized Odysseus; the kidnap of Helen from Menelaus by Paris of Troy; and themes of revenge, but also loyalty and brotherhood. The conclusions of both stories are a bit ambiguous; as Prince objects to Naass's murders of Axel and Unga, the Kid interjects, "'there are things greater than our wisdom, beyond our justice. The right and wrong of this we cannot say, and it is not answerable by humans'" (*Stories*, 258).

CHARACTERS

Malemute Kid The Malemute Kid, half-white, half-Native, is one of London's favorite Northland heroes and narrators. Like many of London's non-white or mixed-blood heroes, he operates by an internal moral code that makes him a stand-in for the author's moral point of view. He observes the deeds of many in the Yukon, old-timers and newcomers, and his point of view serves as a judgment upon their failings. He is also an important character in "The White Silence."

Bettles and Meyers They are the rather nondescript trailmates of the Malemute Kid at the beginning of the story, as they labor to reach their cabin outside Dawson. They witness the meeting of the Kid and Naass and learn of the Kid's staking Naass for gold.

Stanley Prince An officer in the Royal Canadian Mounted Police, Prince and his voyagers take over the Kid's cabin outside Dawson. Prince tells the Kid about Naass, "He-of-the-Otter-Skins," and encourages the Kid to hire him to prospect for him.

Naass At first called "He-of-the-Otter-Skins," Naass is a chief of his tribe who falls in love with a girl called Unga. However, Naass is captured by a white sea captain, Gunderson, who enslaves Naass and steals his bride. Gunderson and Unga both die on the trail.

Unga   Unga is a member of Naass's tribe who is his betrothed. She is kidnapped and raped by a white sea captain and evidently adapts to her situation. When Naass encounters her after Gunderson's death and reveals his identity, she scorns him and mourns her dead husband. She is killed by Naass.

Axel Gunderson   A blonde giant seven feet tall and weighing 300 pounds, Gunderson is a ship captain who kidnaps and rapes the Native woman Unga, as he sells her Native man into slavery in Russian salt mines. He dies on the trail with Unga—for his sins.

"On the Makaloa Mat" (1919)

"On the Makaloa Mat," the title story for the collection in which it appears, was published posthumously in COSMOPOLITAN 66 (March 1919). It sets a tone for the entire collection of London's last Hawaiian stories, written in the summer and fall of 1916, contrasting the new and old HAWAI'I, and mourning the disappearance of the old ways. Being "on the mat" in Hawai'i is an expression meaning that one belongs.

SYNOPSIS

The story opens as two sisters, Martha Scandwell and Bella Castner, one-quarter Hawaiians who married Caucasian men of the HONOLULU elite, sit reminiscing about the old days. They discuss Bella's failed marriage to George Castner; Bella also discloses the secret of a brief affair she had with a Hawaiian prince, Lilolilo. The narrator clearly admires these women. As he tells us, the women of Hawai'i "age well and nobly." As Martha sits in the garden in front of her home, he describes the setting as

> . . . a noble situation—noble as the ancient hau tree, the size of a house, where she sat

as if in a house, so spaciously and comfortably house-like was its shade furnished; noble as the lawn that stretched away landward its plush of green at an appraisement of two hundred dollars a front foot to a bungalow equally dignified, noble, and costly. Seaward, glimpsed through a fringe of hundred-foot coconut palms, was the ocean; beyond the reef a dark blue that grew indigo blue to the horizon, within the reef all the silken gamut of jade and emerald and tourmaline. (*Stories*, 2,319)

Martha's husband Roscoe Scandwell is a descendant of New England Puritans, while "Martha no less straight descended from the royal chief-stocks of Hawaii whose genealogies were chanted in *meles* a thousand years before written speech was acquired" (*Stories*, 2,320). Despite the HAOLE blood, Martha and her sister, like Martha's children, are a beautiful light brown color, for "in each of them one-fourth of them was the sun-warm, love-warm heart of Hawaii" (*Stories*, 2,321). In contrast, Bella's haole husband, George Castner, is cold and unloving. As Bella recalls,

> "George Castner was never a brute, a beast. Almost have I wished, often, that he had been. He never laid hand on me. He never raised hand to me. . . . But that house of his, of ours, at Nahala, was grey. All the colour of it was very cold, grey cold, with that cold grey husband of mine. . . . Grey like those portraits of Emerson we used to see at school. His skin was grey. Sun and weather and all hours in the saddle could never tan it. And he was as grey inside as out." (*Stories*, 2,323)

Martha gently prods her sister to talk more about her marriage. Castner worked as a ranch foreman while he used Bella's dowry to buy up land and water rights, but because he is so focused on building wealth and is so abstemious, she was reduced to constant toil and penury, though much later in life his investments paid off for her. When Bella would complain about their lowly way of life, Castner would counsel her to be patient. But she is miserable: "'And I was nineteen, and sun-warm Hawaiian, . . . and I knew nothing save my girlhood splendours at Kilohana and my Honolulu education at the Royal Chief School, and my grey husband at Nahala with his grey preachments and practices of sobriety and thrift'" (*Stories*, 2,324). Bella grows more and more discontented: "'But was it worth it? I starved. If only once, madly, he had crushed me in his arms! If only once he could have lingered with me five minutes from his own business or from his fidelity to his employers! Sometimes I could have screamed, or showered the eternal bowl of hot porridge into his face, or smashed the sewing machine upon the floor and danced a hula on it, just to make him burst out and lose his temper and be human, be a brute, be a man of some sort instead of a grey, frozen demi-god'" (*Stories*, 2,327–2,328). Castner's response is to check her pulse, examine her tongue, dose her with castor oil, and put her to bed.

When Castner is called to Honolulu on business, Bella gets a much-deserved vacation and meets up with her old friends, including the Princess Lihue: "'And they came, riding up from Kawaihae, where they had landed from the royal yacht, the whole glorious cavalcade of them, two by two, flower-garlanded, young and happy, gay, on Parker Ranch horses, thirty of them in the party, a hundred Parker Ranch cowboys and as many more of their own retainers—a royal progress.'" Princess Lihue, who is dying of tuberculosis, is accompanied by her brother, "'Prince Lilolilo, hailed everywhere as the next king'" (*Stories*, 2,331). On a riding trip across the island, Bella and Prince Lilolilo fall in love and have a brief affair: "'He was a prince, Martha. . . . He filled the eyes of any woman, yes, and of any man. Twenty-five he was, in all-glorious ripeness of man, great and princely in body as he was great and princely in spirit. . . . His glance chanced to light on me, alone there, perturbed, embarrassed. Oh, how I see him!—his head thrown back a little, with that high, bright, imperious, and utterly care-free poise that was so usual of him. Our eyes met.'" Bella wonders, "'Did he command? Did I obey? I do not know. I know only that I was good to look upon, crowned with fragrant *maile*, clad in Princess Naomi's wonderful *holoku* loaned me by Uncle John from his taboo room; and I know that I advanced alone to him

across the Mana lawn, and that he stepped forth from those about him to meet me half-way. We came to each other across the grass, unattended, as if we were coming to each other across our lives'" (*Stories*, 2,333). Bella is transported with joy: "'It was the very atmosphere of love. And Lilolilo was a lover. I was for ever crowned with *leis* (wreaths) by him, and he had his runners bring me *leis* all the way from the rose-gardens of Mana— you remember them; fifty miles across the lava and the ranges, dewy fresh as the moment they were plucked. . . . And at the *luaus* (feasts) the for ever never-ending luaus, I must be seated on Lilolilo's Makaloa mat, the Prince's mat, his alone and taboo to any lesser mortal save by his own condescension and desire'" (*Stories*, 2,336). But when the royal party reaches Hilo, the Prince tells her their affair is "*pau*," or finished, for she is a married woman. However, after this heart-break, Bella can no longer tolerate Castner, and she leaves him.

At the end of the story-within-the-story, just as Bella and Martha wipe their moistened eyes, Martha's husband Roscoe Scandwell appears, the antithesis of Castner. He, unlike most haoles in Hawai'i, is also "on the mat": "Roscoe Scandwell, himself well taught of Hawaiian love and loveways, erect, slender, dignified, between the two nobly proportioned women, an arm around each of their sumptuous waists, proceeded with them toward the house" (*Stories*, 2,340).

COMMENTARY

An important theme in this story is the idea that Hawaiianness is not restricted to native Hawaiians and that race does not determine everything. Martha, Bella, and Scandwell demonstrate successful racial crossing in which sharing two cultures benefits them, so that character, and not race, is what is important. It is significant that the Hawaiian wives descended from chiefesses manage to hang onto their property by marrying whites. Martha owns several lavish houses on different parts of the island, as well as numerous investments and land. Bella's son attends Yale, and her daughter shops for her wedding in Paris. This is also the case with one of the two uncles, one, Uncle John, a "'warm human, and, therefore, wiser than Uncle Robert and George Castner, who sought the thing, not the spirit, who kept records in ledgers rather than numbers of heart-beats breast to breast, who added columns of figures rather than remembered embraces and endearments of look and speech and touch'" (*Stories*, 2,327). Thus, even a Hawaiian can be as cold and unloving as the haole Castner. Second, Bella's loveless marriage symbolically reflects London's critique of the colonialism that was slowly taking over the Hawaiians' lives and property; her affair with Lilolilo is doomed, as he represents the dying out of the old Hawai'i, which, like the love between them, cannot be preserved. (We learn that he and the Princess both die young.) But in the end it is also a story of departure and farewell, like "Aloha Oe." Bella loses the love of her life, and Hawai'i is changing before their eyes. However there is a sense of hope in the marriage of the Scandwells and their mixed-race children and grandchildren. Scandwell, though pure white, has "become" Hawaiian. He appears just at the end of the story, as though to punctuate all the themes of Hawaiianness and belonging: "Erect, slender, grey-haired, of graceful military bearing, Roscoe Scandwell was a member of the 'Big Five,' which, by the interlocking of interests, determined the destinies of all Hawaii. Himself pure haole, New England born, he kissed Bella first, arms around, full-hearty, in the Hawaiian way. His alert eye told him that there had been a woman talk, and, despite the signs of all generousness of emotion, that all was well and placid in the twilight wisdom that was theirs" (*Stories*, 2,339–2,340). Also, Bella is free of Castner, perhaps representing a new reality for Hawaiians who have managed to fashion a life post-colonization.

CHARACTERS

Martha Scandwell Martha, like her sister, is descended from Hawaiian royalty. She is happily married to a haole, Roscoe Scandwell, and has many children and grandchildren. She is wealthy in her own right and proud of her Hawaiian heritage. She discovers her sister's secret affair with a Hawaiian prince as they talk together on the shady lawn of her Waikiki home.

Bella Castner "Very haole was Bella Castner, fair-skinned, fine-textured. Yet, as she returned, the high pose of head, the level-lidded gaze of her long brown eyes under royal arches of eyebrows, the softly set lines of her small mouth that fairly sang sweetness of kisses after sixty-eight years—all made her the very picture of a chiefess of old Hawaii full-bursting through her ampleness of haole blood. Taller she was than her sister Martha, if anything more queenly" (*Stories*, 2,325).

Roscoe Scandwell Scandwell, a descendent of New England Puritans, is the husband of Martha. Unlike George Castner, Bella's husband, he has successfully become Hawaiian in adopting the warmth and loving spirit of the Islands. He has made his own fortune, but his marriage to Martha brought him her sizeable inheritance as well. Yet one senses that he, unlike Castner, is not in business for money alone, but to improve life in the Islands.

George Castner Grey, cold, and stingy is Bella's husband—he cares only for making money using Bella's dowry and refuses to show any affection toward her. He dies shortly after Bella leaves him, after her affair with Lilolilo. He is an example of the failure to adapt to life in Hawai'i and, like Percival Ford of "The House of Pride," one of London's most negative portraits of whites in Hawai'i.

Uncle Robert Uncle Robert is the practical uncle who urges Bella to wed Castner; he too is interested in making alliances only for money's sake.

Uncle John Uncle John is also Bella's uncle; unlike his brother he is warm and loving; however, he too urges the 19-year-old Bella to marry Castner, whom they see as an up-and-coming businessman and thus a good match. Both uncles point out that if the Hawaiians do not want to lose their lands and holdings they must cooperate with the whites.

Lilolilo Proud, beautiful, and fickle, Prince Lilolilo becomes Bella's lover for a brief time. He showers her with love, flowers, fine gifts, and has her sit on his mat because she too is a royal. However, when they reach Hilo on their horseback tour of OAHU, he leaves her.

old woman retainer "Her voice trailed off, and the sisters sat in soft silence while an ancient crone, staff in hand, twisted, doubled, and shrunken under a hundred years of living, hobbled across the lawn to them. Her eyes, withered to scarcely more than peepholes, were sharp as a mongoose's, and at Bella's feet she first sank down, in pure Hawaiian mumbling and chanting a toothless *mele* of Bella and Bella's ancestry.... And while she chanted her *mele*, the old crone's shrewd fingers *lomied* or massaged Bella's silk-stockinged legs from ankle and calf to knee and thigh" (*Stories*, 2,328–2,329).

"The Pearls of Parlay" (1911)

"The Pearls of Parlay," first published in the SATUR-DAY EVENING POST on October 14, 1911, is the last of the David Grief stories of *A Son of the Sun*. It is a tragic tale of greed and loss in which NATURE in the form of two gigantic typhoons plays the decisive role, despite the machinations of greedy men.

SYNOPSIS

At the story's opening, Captain David Grief and a guest, Gregory Mulhall, are on deck as their schooner the *Malahini* enters the lagoon entrance of the atoll Hikihoho in the PAUMOTU ARCHIPELAGO, now called "Parlay" after its owner, old Parlay, a Frenchman who is a major pearl dealer. Parlay has announced that he will hold an auction; Grief comments that "'If he really sells, this will be the biggest year's output of pearls in the Paumotus'" (*Stories*, 2,024). Grief and the others who know him think of Parlay as "'mildly insane'" (*Stories*, 2,025). They speak of the death of his daughter 15 years ago as the cause of his madness afterward. The trader had married an island chiefess, and, when she died, he inherited her estate. Their daughter Armande is sent to a French convent to be educated. When she reached the age of 18, Parlay sent for her.

However, there is a terrible typhoon, and Parlay arrives in Papeete, TAHITI, to pick her up too late. Armande has committed suicide after a failed love affair with a French officer. Parlay gets his revenge by shooting the French lieutenant, throwing a glass of wine in the governor's face, fighting a duel with the port doctor, beating his servants, and wrecking the hospital; he is straitjacketed but escapes to his schooner and sails away for Hikihoho, where he remains, amassing a huge collection of pearls but never selling one.

In anticipation of the auction, several schooners arrive in the Hikihoho lagoon. However, as the buyers examine Parlay's pearls, another great typhoon descends upon them and with great difficulty the schooners depart.

A former member of Grief's crew, Tai Hotauri, who has joined the crew of Narii Herring, an unscrupulous pearl dealer who hates Parlay, manages to climb aboard Grief's schooner to report that Herring, "'an English Jew half-caste. . . .the nerviest and most conscienceless scoundrel in the Paumotus'" (*Stories*, 2,024), has tried to steal Parlay's pearls and that Parlay is up in a tree, Herring in another. Herring tries to bribe some islanders to kill Parlay, but fails. Parlay and Herring manage to get aboard Grief's ship in the middle of the storm, along with some KANAKAS. In the storm, many men aboard the *Malahini* are killed from being buffeted on the violently pitching ship. Parlay is found, ribs smashed and dying; his parting words are, "'My brave gentlemen. . . . Don't forget . . . the auction . . . at ten o'clock . . . in hell'" (*Stories*, 2,042). The engine of Grief's *Malahini* gives out and the schooner is beached. All the other pearl-buyers are gone, and nothing is left standing on the island. Captain Warfield and Grief see a man walking on the beach toward them, Herring, who coolly asks for some breakfast. We never find out whether nor not he stole Parlay's pearls.

The story, like "The House of Mapuhi" and "The Heathen," contains a fine description of the fury of a typhoon: "They did not need glasses to see. A flying film, strangely marked, seemed drawing over the surface of the lagoon. Abreast of it, along the atoll, travelling with equal speed, was a stiff bending of the cocoanut palms and a blur of flying leaves. The front of the wind on the water was a solid, sharply defined strip of dark-coloured, wind-vexed water. . . . The sea, white with fury, boiled in tiny, spitting wavelets. . . . It was impossible to face the wind and breathe. Mulhall, crouching with the others behind the shelter of the cabin, discovered this, and his lungs were filled in an instant with so great a volume of driven air which he could not expel that he nearly strangled ere he could turn his head away" (*Stories*, 2,035).

COMMENTARY

The David Grief stories generally present a troublesome situation on one island or another resulting from clashes between islanders and the colonizing and trading whites who have invaded their world. Grief, with his unbendable moral code, is a sort of eye of judgment to what he observes. In "The Pearls of Parlay" he is witness to the death of a despised pearl trader and the evil plans of a competitor to murder and rob him of his pearls. As negative a character as the half-deranged old man is (he is called a "'vile beast'" [*Stories*, 2,030] by one character), his enemy, Narii Herring, is worse. The story is quite sensationalistic: There is madness, murder, a failed love affair, suicide, two typhoons, treachery, and bravery. However, its overall message is unclear: Is it a cautionary tale about greed? A story in which the petty deeds of men are bested by the power of nature? Or a story that dramatizes deep-seated conflicts about life post-colonization in the South Seas? It is all of these things, but it is best described as a narrative of descent.

CHARACTERS

David Grief David Grief—bronzed, muscled, wealthy—is a sea-rover who journeys about the South Pacific on his schooners trading, settling disputes, and passing along tales with his companions. He often witnesses atrocities brought on by colonization, and he acts as a judge of men. He beats one man out of ALCOHOLISM, defeats white pirates who besiege an island, defends a CHINESE trader against a racist Australian. As a white man he is able to "pass" in the South Seas; unlike most whites in the South Seas his skin tans easily and his physique saves him from many a threat.

Gregory Mulhall An Englishman, Mulhall is a guest aboard Grief's schooner the *Malahini*. He gets more than he bargained for when they land on Parlay's atoll, but he is a stalwart companion who tries to save as many sailors as he can during the typhoon.

Hermann Hermann is the Dutch mate of the *Malahini*; he too is a strong arm in saving the ship from destruction in the storm.

Captain Warfield Captain Warfield is the brave skipper of the *Malahini*; he is especially incensed at Narii Herring's plot to kill Parlay and plans to beat him for it at the end of the story.

kanaka sailors *Kanaka* is a Hawaiian word meaning "man"; it is not pejorative. These are hardy and experienced NATIVE sailors who are extremely loyal to Grief.

Tai-Hotauri He is supercargo of the *Malahini* but leaves Grief and joins Herring's crew on his schooner; during the storm he is washed to sea and climbs aboard Grief's schooner. He brings news of Herring's plot to murder Parlay.

Parlay "And through the curious company moved Parlay himself, cackling and sneering, the withered wreck of what had once been a tall and powerful man. His eyes were deep sunken and feverish, his cheeks fallen in and cavernous. The hair of his head seemed to have come out in patches, and his mustache and imperial had shed in the same lopsided way. 'Jove!' Mulhall muttered under his breath. 'A long-legged Napoleon the Third, but burnt out, baked, and fire-crackled. And mangy! No wonder he crooks his head to one side. He's got to keep the balance'" (*Stories*, 2,029).

Narii Herring An unscrupulous competitor of Parlay's who covets his pearls; during the storm he tries to bribe some islanders to kill Parlay. He appears unscathed and smiling insolently at Grief and Warfield at the end of the story.

Armande Parlay The half-caste daughter of old Parlay, she is sent to France for her education.

When she returns through Tahiti, she is scorned as half-caste by the French there. She has a love affair with a French lieutenant and, when he leaves her, commits suicide.

Peter Gee A Chinese pearl buyer who also appears in "A Goboto Night," he is one of Grief's friends. He and his ship manage to escape the storm.

The People of the Abyss (1903)

Near the end of his life, London said that "'Of all my books on the long shelf, I love most "The People of the Abyss." No other book of mine took so much of my young heart and tears as that study of the economic degradation of the poor'" (quoted in Charmian London, *Book of Jack London*, I, 381). In 1902, on his way to cover the Boer War in South Africa, when London got to LONDON, ENGLAND, he found that the war was over and his assignment cancelled. London bought used workmen's clothing for 10 shillings in Petticoat Lane and disguised himself as a stranded and broke American seaman; he did have a small flat to which he could retreat to write, but he spent most of his time over the next several weeks living in the East End of London among the poor and homeless who roamed the streets. The result was one of the first sociological books ever written by an American, one that compares well with other such works as Jacob Riis's *How the Other Half Lives* (1890). This was also the first time London made photographs to accompany his writing, and they are among his most moving. When he returned to CALIFORNIA, his stepsister, ELIZA LONDON SHEPARD, pasted his photographs into a photo album, inaugurating Jack and CHARMIAN LONDON's practice of making photo albums from London's thousands of photographs throughout his life.

Though London had certainly known poverty himself and endured many hardships, nothing prepared him for what he saw in the slums of the East End, which he called the "City of Degradation." As he wrote to ANNA STRUNSKY on August 16, 1902,

"The whole thing, all the conditions of life, the intensity of it, everything is overwhelming. I never conceived of such a mass of misery in the world before" (*Letters*, 305). This from a man who had fought his way into being a sailor, criminal, hobo, and penitentiary inmate, and who often spoke of having himself escaped the "abyss" of poverty. The next week he wrote her that he is working hard to finish his book: "Am rushing, for I am made sick by this human hell-hole called London Town. I find it almost impossible to believe that some of the horrible things I have seen are really so" (*Letters*, 306).

London roamed the streets among the homeless, driven on all day and night by policemen, prevented from so much as resting on a bench; got in line to get his ticket for beds and meals for

Jack London, London, England, 1902 *(Huntington Library)*

the homeless at shelters; worked picking hops in Kent; visited people's filthy, overcrowded novels. He also spent much time in research on the economic conditions of Britain in general. The book is a mixture of sociological and economic analysis along socialist lines and a series of vignettes about individual people he met and talked with. The data he supplies include statistics on living space; access to food and shelter; crime; infant mortality; workers thrown out of their homes after they are injured and can no longer work; men and women debauched by drink and dissolution.

Affecting him most deeply was the plight of the very young and the very old, the young who were inevitably doomed and the old who had suffered so much. He meets "the Carter" and "the Carpenter," who are decent workmen now too old to compete with younger men and so cast out by the industrial system that used them for so many years. They scavenge for garbage in the streets:

> . . . Both kept their eyes upon the pavement as they walked and talked, and every now and then one or the other would stoop and pick something up, never missing the stride the while. I thought it was cigar and cigarette stumps they were collecting, and for some time took no notice. Then I did notice.
>
> *From the slimy sidewalk, they were picking up bits of orange peel, apple skin, and grape stems, and they were eating them. The pips of green gage plums they cracked between their teeth for the kernels inside. They picked up stray crumbs of bread the size of peas, apple cores so black and dirty one would not take them to be apple cores, and these things these two men took into their mouths, and chewed them, and swallowed them; and this, between six and seven o'clock in the evening of August 20, year of our Lord 1902, in the heart of the greatest, wealthiest, and most powerful empire the world has ever seen.* (78)

At the other end of the spectrum are the children, three-fourths of whom will die before they reach the age of five:

> There is one beautiful sight in the East End and only one, and it is the children dancing in the street when the organ-grinder goes his round. It is fascinating to watch them, the new-born the next generation, swaying and stepping, with pretty little mimicries and graceful inventions all their own, with muscles that move swiftly and easily, and bodies that leap airily, weaving rhythms never taught in dancing school. . . . A joyous life is romping in their blood. They delight in music, and motion, and color, and very often they betray a startling beauty of face and form under their filth and rags.
>
> But there is a Pied Piper of London Town who steals them all away. They disappear. One never sees them again, or anything that suggests them. You may look for them in vain amongst the generation of grown-ups. Here you will find stunted forms, ugly faces, and blunt and stolid minds. Grace, beauty, imagination, all the resiliency of mind and muscle, are gone. Sometimes, however, you may see a woman, not necessarily old, but twisted and deformed out of all womanhood, bloated and drunken, lift her draggled skirts and execute a few grotesque and lumbering steps upon the pavement. It is a hint that she was once one of those children who danced to the organ-grinder. (274–275)

London sees the beat-down denizens of the East End as living like little more than animals, and he recognizes that so-called "primitive" peoples like the American NATIVES live better lives—and so do most animals—compared to the inhabitants of the ghetto:

> It is rather hard to tell a tithe of what I saw. Much of it is untellable. But in a general way I may say that I saw a nightmare, a fearful slime that quickened the pavement with life, a mess of unmentionable obscenity . . . It was a menagerie of garmented bipeds that looked something like humans and more like beasts, and to complete the picture, brass-buttoned keepers kept order among them when they snarled too fiercely.

He believes that they possess "neither conscience nor sentiment" and he knows that "they will kill for a half-sovereign, without fear or favor, if they are given but half a chance." These miserable men

The courtyard of a Salvation Army barracks on a Sunday morning, filled with men holding tickets for a free breakfast, London, England, 1902 *(Huntington Library)*

and women "are a new species, a breed of city savages. The streets and houses, alleys and courts, are their hunting grounds. As valley and mountain are to the natural savage, street and building are valley and mountain to them. The slum is their jungle, and they live and prey in the jungle" (285).

Still, most of the descriptions in the book are sympathetic to their plight, since London blames the capitalist industrial system that put these people where they are. One of his most ironic chapters concerns the coronation of King Edward VII, his golden coach cheered mightily by the dirty crowds on either side of the street. The British Empire, not the British poor, is his target.

London has no remedy readily at hand to solve the problems of the poor of London's East End, though he does offer strong analysis of the prob-

lems all through the book. He does suggest that the English poor, who begat so many Americans, be emigrated to the American West as a place where they might find rejuvenation in a healthy environment. Thus it fits into the larger pattern in his work of the hope of return to NATURE through farming in the West, a Jeffersonian return to the land. But his book mainly stands not as a solution, but an unsparing account of the realities of life in poverty, directed not just at British readers, but, of course, also at Americans, who tolerated similar social conditions among their own poor in their large cities. Perhaps *The People of the Abyss* had such resonance for him because he himself had escaped a life of WAGE SLAVERY through his imagination. He was, at the time he wrote this book, on the verge of worldwide fame as the author of *The Call of the Wild*.

FURTHER READING

Dow, William. "Down and Out in London and Orwell." In *Symbiosis: A Journal of Anglo-American Literary Relations* 6, no. 1 (April 2002): 69–94.

Hitchcock, Peter. "Slumming." In *Passing: Identity and Interpretation in Sexuality, Race, and Religion.* Edited by Maria Carla Sánchez and Linda Schlossberg. New York: New York University Press, 2001, 160–186.

London, Charmian Kittredge. *The Book of Jack London.* 2 vols. New York: Century, 1921.

Peluso, Robert. "Gazing at Royalty: Jack London's *The People of the Abyss* and the Emergence of American Imperialism." In *Rereading Jack London.* Edited by Leonard Cassuto and Jeanne Campbell Reesman. Stanford, Calif.: Stanford University Press, 1996, 55–74.

Phillips, Lawrence. "Jack London and the East End: Socialism, Imperialism and the Bourgeois Ethnographer." In *A Mighty Mass of Brick and Stone: Victorian and Edwardian Representations of London.* Edited by Lawrence Phillips. Amsterdam, Netherlands: Rodopi, 2007, 213–234.

Reesman, Jeanne Campbell, Sara S. Hodson, and Philip Adam. *Jack London, Photographer.* Athens: University of Georgia Press, 2010.

Swafford, Kevin R. "Resounding the Abyss: The Politics of Narration in Jack London's *The People of the Abyss.*" In *Journal of Popular Culture* 39, no. 5 (October 2006): 838–860.

"A Piece of Steak" (1909)

First published in the SATURDAY EVENING POST 182 (November 1909), this sad tale of the bitter end of an old boxer's career was one of the first prizefight stories and helped establish the genre. It contains a reference to JACK JOHNSON, whom London covered as a reporter at the 1908 and 1910 world heavyweight fights.

SYNOPSIS

Tom King, an old and tired prizefighter, and his wife eat a supper of flour gravy and send the children to bed with no supper. Suffering from heart trouble

from being pounded for so many years in the ring, King can no longer put up much of a fight, though he had once been great: "Well, a man had only so many fights in him, to begin with. It was the iron law of the game. One man might have a hundred hard fights in him, another man only twenty; each, according to the make of him and the quality of his fibre, had a definite number, and, when he had fought them, he was done." Of course, as he recalls, "he had had more fights in him than most of them, and he had had far more than his share of the hard, gruelling [sic] fights—the kind that worked the heart and lungs to bursting, that took the elastic out of the arteries and made hard knots of muscle out of Youth's sleek suppleness, that wore out nerve and stamina and made brain and bones weary from excess of effort and endurance overwrought. . . . He was the last of the old guard. He had seen them all finished, and he had had a hand in finishing some of them" (*Stories,* 1,633). Longing for a piece of steak to eat and despite being out of shape, he decides to visit the BOXING arena and try for a match. He fights an opponent named Young Pronto Sandel, who starts out beating King badly. Hoping to wear down his youthful enemy, King tries every trick he remembers. He nearly knocks Sandel out, but after a few minutes' rest Sandel is back on his feet. King gives the fight every ounce of strength he has: "All that was left of him was a fighting intelligence that was dimmed and clouded from exhaustion. The blow that was aimed for the jaw struck no higher than the shoulder. He had willed the blow higher, but the tired muscles had not been able to obey." Weakened by the match, he falls against Sandel into a clinch, "holding on to him to save himself from sinking to the floor. King did not attempt to free himself. He had shot his bolt. He was gone. And Youth had been served. Even in the clinch he could feel Sandel growing stronger against him. When the referee thrust them apart, there, before his eyes, he saw Youth recuperate" (*Stories,* 1,643–1,644). King is knocked out and, weeping out of hunger and frustration, he walks the long miles home.

COMMENTARY

"A Piece of Steak" is a tragic story of youth v. age, in which youth triumphs and age almost starves to death. Like "The Law of Life," it offers the pitiless evolutionary perspective of life that is able to adapt and go on living upon the dying out of the older generation. It is a fine study in NATURALISM and may also be read symbolically as an socialist indictment of industrial labor practices that tossed out older workers when they became unfit in favor of an endless supply of young bodies.

CHARACTERS

Tom King A broken-down boxer, Tom King and his wife live in poverty. He is something of an "abysmal brute," as London used the term:

> He was a solid-bodied, stolid-looking man. . . . His rough clothes were old and slouchy. The . . . cotton shirt, a cheap, two-shilling affair, showed a frayed collar and ineradicable paint stains.
>
> But it was Tom King's face that advertised him unmistakably for what he was. It was the face of a typical prize-fighter; of one who had put in long years of service in the squared ring and, by that means, developed and emphasized all the marks of the fighting beast. It was distinctly a lowering countenance. . . . The lips were shapeless, and constituted a mouth harsh to excess, that was like a gash in his face. The jaw was aggressive, brutal, heavy. The eyes, slow of movement and heavy-lidded, were almost expressionless under the shaggy, indrawn brows. Sheer animal that he was, the eyes were the most animal-like feature about him. (*Stories*, 1,629–1,630).

Mrs. King She is "a thin, worn woman of the working-class, though signs of an earlier prettiness were not wanting in her face. The flour for the gravy she had borrowed from the neighbor across the hall" (*Stories*, 1,629).

secretary The secretary of the Gayety Theater is "a keen-eyed, shrewd-faced young man, who shook [Tom's] hand" (*Stories*, 1,634). When he asks after Tom's health, Tom lies and says he is fit.

heavyweight contenders Young Pronto Sandel, an Australian, is Tom's fight that night at the Gayety; to Tom he is "Youth unknown, but insatiable—crying out to mankind that with strength and skill it would match issues with the winner" (*Stories*, 1,635). More young heavyweights are on hand also eager for a fight with Tom King.

sportswriters Tom recognizes in the crowd two reporters, Morgan, of the *Sportsman*, and Corbett, of the *Referee*.

Sid Sullivan and Charley Bates They are "seconds," or assistants, to King during the fight. They carefully tape his hands and prepare him to fight.

"The Red One" (1918)

"The Red One," one of London's most unusual stories, was completed in May 1916 in Hawai'i. It was published posthumously in COSMOPOLITAN in October 1918. It is set on the then-dangerous island of GUADALCANAL, where London spent five months while on the SNARK cruise. It tells of the expedition of a lepidopterist, Bassett, who encounters the strange god of a tribe deep in the bush. After his companion on the trail is murdered by bushmen, he journeys alone, exhausted, through the jungle, scattered with abandoned villages and evidence of CANNIBALISM, lured by a haunting and magnificent sound. Stumbling with fever, he is rescued by a bushwoman Balatta, who later, at the risk of her life, leads him to his first glimpse of the Red One, a gigantic red sphere half-buried in a circular pit near their village. In her village he meets the shaman, Ngurn. They argue about the origin of the Red One. Bassett thinks it must have come from some faraway civilization in outer space, only to fall among savages. He plans his escape and hopes to tell the world of his discovery, but he grows too sick with fever to leave. Knowing that he is dying, he offers Ngurn his head in exchange for another look at the Red One. As he peers into the undulating, singing surface of the mysterious orb, the rational scientist beholds something undreamt of: the face of Medusa.

SYNOPSIS

At the beginning of the story, Bassett, sick with fever, wanders through the dark, damp jungle of Guadalcanal toward a strange sound he likens to the "trump of an archangel," an "enormous peal" that fills the mountain gorges like "the mighty cry of some Titan of the Elder World vexed with misery or wrath" (*Stories*, 2,296). He thinks of his companion, Sagawa, butchered by bushmen along the trail, of the flitting shadows of bushmen who pursue him, of the stinging flies that torment him—a long series of nightmares:

> But seared deepest of all in Bassett's brain, was the dank and noisome jungle. It actually stank with evil, and it was always twilight. Rarely did a shaft of sunlight penetrate its matted roof a hundred feet overhead. And beneath that roof was an aerial ooze of vegetation, a monstrous, parasitic dripping of decadent life-forms rooted in death and lived on death. And through all this he drifted, ever pursued by the flitting shadows of the anthropophagi, themselves ghosts of evil that dared not face him in battle but that knew, soon or late, that they would feed on him. Bassett remembered that at the time, in lucid moments, he had likened himself to a wounded bull pursued by plains' coyotes too cowardly to battle with him for the meat of him, yet certain of the inevitable end of him when they would be full gorged. As the bull's horns and stamping hoofs kept off the coyotes, so his shotgun kept off these Solomon Islanders, these twilight shades of bushmen of the island of Guadalcanal. (*Stories*, 2,300)

Bassett has entered the jungle to find a rare butterfly and kill it. Instead, he is struggling to survive. He reaches some grasslands and there meets a bushwoman Balatta, who takes pity on him. He thinks only of her filthiness and ugliness, but she brings him water and some roasted pig. She leads him to her village, where his gun makes a tremendous impression on the bushmen. He enters the "devil-devil" house of Ngurn, the aged shaman, and since he has studied their language he is able to talk with Ngurn. Ngurn desires Bassett's head,

and when Bassett points to his gun, tells him that if Bassett shoots him then someone else will get the head eventually. Bassett says he can have it when he is dead. They debate the meaning and origin of the Red One. Ngurn's father thought it came from the stars and called it, among its many other names, "the Star-Born" (*Stories*, 2,304), but Ngurn argues that it came from the earth. The Red One is the secret to this village's power. When Bassett threatens Balatta enough, and she leads him down into the huge circular pit, he sees a gigantic metallic orb surrounded by human sacrifices. Bassett can hardly believe what he has seen. Later, lying ill in Ngurn's hut, he considers the terrible irony of his find, that something he thinks of as "Time's greatest gift" (*Stories*, 2,315) to humanity is lost here among primitive savages. But as the months pass, he realizes he will never leave, and when the time comes he offers his head to Ngurn, who agrees to let him approach the Red One. He is brought to the Red One on a litter; he begs Ngurn to have it struck with a giant post:

> . . . the great carved log, drawn back through two-score feet of space, was released. The next moment he was lost in ecstasy at the abrupt and thunderous liberation of sound. But such thunder! Mellow it was with preciousness of all sounding metals. Archangels spoke in it; it was magnificently beautiful before all other sounds; it was invested with the intelligence of supermen of planets of other suns; it was the voice of God, seducing and commanding to be heard. And—the everlasting miracle of that interstellar metal! Bassett, with his own eyes, saw colour and colours transform into sound till the whole visible surface of the vast sphere was a-crawl and titillant and vaporous with what he could not tell was colour or was sound. In that moment the interstices of matter were his, and the interfusings and intermating transfusings of matter and force. (*Stories*, 2,317)

But Ngurn grows impatient, and Bassett at last bends over and stretches his neck:

> He knew, without seeing, when the razor-edged hatchet rose in the air behind him. And for that

instant, ere the end, there fell upon Bassett the shadow of the Unknown, a sense of impending marvel of the rending of walls before the unimaginable. Almost, when he knew the blow had started and just ere the edge of steel bit the flesh and nerves, it seemed that he gazed upon the serene face of the Medusa, Truth. (*Stories*, 2,317–2,318)

COMMENTARY

"The Red One" is one of London's most mythic stories, using numerous archetypes: the wise old man, the persona, shadow, and anima—all in painful self-recognition. Though he read CARL JUNG's *Psychology of the Unconscious* after he wrote "The Red One," it is one of his most suggestive psychological parables and powerfully reflects his interest in psychology. As Lawrence I. Berkove has noted, though the edition of Jung's *Psychology of the Unconscious* London read and remarked upon was not published in English until the early summer of 1916, 15 of Jung's other works were translated between 1907 and 1916, including two monographs (Berkove, "The Myth of Hope," 203).

The idea for the story came from GEORGE STERLING, and it was a science fiction plot: an explorer would encounter in some faraway wilderness a message from Mars or some other planet, but would be unable to convey the message to the world. But the theme is much deeper than that: Like "To Build a Fire" the story is about self-knowledge. Bassett sets out upon a scientific mission, but finds himself on a quest for identity and eternity as he is overcome by the awe-inspiring sphere that calls into symbolic confrontation with his entire belief-system, including the idea that alien intelligences created it.

CHARMIAN KITTREDGE LONDON believed "The Red One" revealed "more of [London] than he would be willing to admit" (Charmian London, *Book of Jack London*, 2: 336). As London found himself ailing, his story reflects both his own inner journey toward spiritual meaning and his ever-growing sense of the community of all humankind, through the collective unconscious. Critics are divided over what the story's final image suggests: Some, such as Berkove, see the image of Medusa as a horrifying statement of life's utter lack of meaning, while others, such as Jeanne Campbell, James Kirsch, and Earle Labor, see her as an allusion to the feminine unconscious and hence a positive—and much-needed—corrective to Bassett's hyper-rationality. All agree that one of the most important roles of myth in the story is to illustrate how all people are connected through myth.

CHARACTERS

Bassett A scientist who studies butterflies. He has come to the remote SOLOMON ISLANDS to Guadalcanal to capture and preserve a rare specimen. His party is dispersed, and he is led, weak with fever, to a village of bushmen, where he is befriended by a woman Balatta and the shaman Ngurn. Bassett dies with a vision of the awful depths of the Red One.

Sagawa Bassett's companion and guide on the trail. Sagawa is killed and presumably eaten by bushmen.

Balatta A bushwoman who likes Bassett, and, in exchange for his making love to her, shows him the Red One for the first time. Bassett views her as barely human; he notes that she wears a freshly severed pig's tail in her ear.

Ngurn As the village shaman, Ngurn's specialty is curing heads in his "devil-devil house." He and Bassett debate the origin of the Red One, and he allows Bassett to see it in exchange for his head. Ngurn is a wise old man who thinks that knowledge comes from within, not from the skies: "A memory was not a star, was Ngurn's contention" (*Stories*, 2,305). Bassett considers shooting himself in the head at the last moment: "But why cheat him? was Bassett's next thought. Head-hunting, cannibal beast of a human that was as much ape as human, nevertheless Old Ngurn had, according to his lights, played squarer than square. Ngurn was in himself a forerunner of ethics and contract, of consideration, and gentleness in man. No, Bassett decided; it would be a ghastly pity and an act of dishonour to cheat the old fellow at the last. His head was Ngurn's, and Ngurn's head to cure it would be" (*Stories*, 2,317).

Gngngn "The addle-headed young chief ruled by Ngurn" (*Stories*, 2,303–2,304), most likely Ngurn's son.

FURTHER READING

Berkove, Lawrence I. "The Myth of Hope in Jack London's 'The Red One.'" In *Rereading Jack London*. Edited by Leonard Cassuto and Jeanne Campbell Reesman. Stanford, Calif.: Stanford University Press, 1996, 204–216.

Campbell, Jeanne. "'Falling Stars': Myth in 'The Red One.'" *Jack London Newsletter* 11 (May–December 1978): 87–101.

Kirsch, James. "Jack London's Quest: 'The Red One.'" *Psychological Perspectives* 11 (Fall 1980): 137–154.

Labor, Earle, and Jeanne Campbell Reesman. *Jack London: Revised Edition*. New York: Twayne, 1994.

London, Charmian Kittredge. *The Book of Jack London*. 2 vols. New York: Century, 1921.

"Revolution" (1910)

In this essay, based on socialist speeches given by London across the country, which can be found in *Revolution and Other Essays* published by Macmillan in 1910, London sets out to explain the reasons for and the inevitability of worldwide socialist revolution against the capitalist BOURGEOIS class. It is packed with statistics—70 million socialists around the world, the wages of a Chicago garment worker, the 80,000 children toiling in textile mills—but is also a passionate plea to the ruling classes to take note of their cruel mismanagement of their workers' lives; it even ends with a comparison of the coming revolution to the coming of Christ.

London characterizes SOCIALISM's revolution as unique: "There has never been anything like this revolution in the history of the world. There is nothing analogous between it and the American Revolution or the French Revolution. It is unique, colossal. Other revolutions compare with it as asteroids compare with the sun. It is alone of its kind, the first world revolution in a world whose history is replete with revolutions. And not only this, for it is the first organized movement of men to become a world movement, limited only by the limits of the planet" (4). The name that revolutionists use for each other is "comrade," London emphasizes: "It knits men together as brothers, as men should be knit together who stand shoulder to shoulder under the red banner of revolt. This red banner, by the way, symbolizes the BROTHERHOOD of man, and does not symbolize the incendiarism that instantly connects itself with the red banner in the affrighted bourgeois mind." He notes how comradeship of the revolutionists "passes over geographical lines [and] transcends race prejudice," a truly international brotherhood (5). Thus, he supports the 1905 Russian Revolution, even the assassinations carried out by the revolution's "Fighting Organizations," something he also mentions in *The Iron Heel*.

Blame for class inequalities, CHILD LABOR, urban poverty, even starvation of unemployed workers, all lies squarely on the capitalists:

> The capitalist class has managed society, and its management has failed. And not only has it failed in its management, but it has failed deplorably, ignobly, horribly. The capitalist class had an opportunity such as was vouchsafed to no previous ruling class in the history of the world. It broke away from the rule of the old feudal aristocracy and made modern society. It mastered matter, organized the machinery of life, and made possible a wonderful era for mankind, wherein no creature should cry aloud because it had not enough to eat, and wherein for every child there would be opportunity for education, for intellectual and spiritual uplift . . . Here was the chance, God-given, and the capitalist class failed. It was blind and greedy. It prattled sweet ideals and dear moralities, rubbed its eyes not once, nor ceased one whit in its greediness, and smashed down in a failure as tremendous only as was the opportunity it had ignored. (14)

Thus the WORKING CLASS has no other option but resistance: they wish to put a stop to the abuses of the capitalist class, garner for themselves decent jobs and pay, and protect their children from entering the factories.

London spends a good part of the essay comparing the lives of CAVEMEN with modern workers: "The caveman, with his natural efficiency of I, got enough to eat most of the time, and no caveman went hungry all the time. Also, he lived a healthy, open-air life, loafed and rested himself, and found plenty of time in which to exercise his imagination and invent gods. That is to say, he did not have to work all his waking moments in order to get enough to eat." In contrast, he writes, today there are 10 million people living in poverty in the United States alone, and many of them are simply starving. When "they are segregated in slum ghettos by hundreds of thousands and by millions, their misery becomes beastliness. No caveman ever starved as chronically as they starve, ever slept as vilely as they sleep, ever festered with rottenness and disease as they fester, nor ever toiled as hard and for as long hours as they toil" (15–17). He then proceeds to give actual examples of various workers' plights he has gleaned from newspapers: one New York City mother strangles her children because she cannot stand to see them starve; a San Francisco man leaves a diary of his starvation behind before he commits suicide; six-year-old children toil for a few cents a day in Southern textile factories for 11-hour shifts. Analyzing the incredible industrial productivity brought about by machines, London asks why conditions are as they are, when natural resources and production are so rich. But the capitalist class, politicians, and the press seem blind to the crisis. At the end of the essay, London concludes with a warning:

> There is no question about it. The revolution is a fact. It is here now. Seven million revolutionists, organized, working day and night, are preaching the revolution—that passionate gospel, the Brotherhood of Man. Not only is it a coldblooded economic propaganda, but it is in essence a religious propaganda with a fervor in it of Paul and Christ. The capitalist class has been indicted. It has failed in its management and its management is to be taken away from it. Seven million men of the working-class say that they are going to get the rest of the working-class to join with them and take the management away. The revolution is here, now. Stop it who can. (38)

FURTHER READING

Raskin, Jonah, ed. *The Radical Jack London: Writings on War and Revolution.* Berkeley: University of California Press, 2008.

Zamen, Mark E. *Standing Room Only: Jack London's Controversial Career as a Public Speaker.* Foreword by Earle Labor. New York: Peter Lang, 1990.

The Road (1907)

The Road is a compendium of the hoboing experiences London had in 1893 when he left grueling jobs in a jute mill, railway power plant, and cannery and hit the road with a group called Kelly's Army and headed eastward to Washington, DC, where the Army planned to join with a larger group called Coxey's Industrial Army to march on Washington. These groups were formed in response to dire conditions for workingmen; the economic panic of the early 1890s meant that farmers faced hard times, including deflated prices for corn and cotton and mortgage foreclosures; every day the news was of business failures and labor turmoil. In 1892, Jacob S. Coxey managed to get a bill introduced in Congress that would set aside $500 million to build roads across the nation, providing employment for thousands, but his ideas met with resistance. He decided to organize a group of unemployed men and march them to the capital. On the West Coast, a group was formed by "General" Charles T. Kelly of San Francisco. This was just London's excuse to leave OAKLAND's grimy slums for adventure. After a time with "road kids" in Sacramento with a buddy of his, he learned about the world of riding the rails, begging, rolling drunks, and living by one's wits. London soon acquired the veneer of the experienced tramp, which they called a "profesh." He was first given the moniker Sailor Kid and later Frisco Kid. On April 17, he connected with Kelly's Army at Reno and rode trains and walked to Des Moines, Iowa. Acquiring boats, the army sailed down the Mississippi to Cairo, Illinois, where they could turn upriver on the Ohio River to Wheeling, West Virginia, from whence they would walk to Washington.

By the time they reached Hannibal, Missouri, London was sick of the life of the army and eager to be on his own to seek adventure and examine from his own point of view how society was put together. He visited the Chicago World's Fair and stayed with relatives; he met among them his cousin Ernest Everhard, whose name he would use for his hero of *The Iron Heel.* He rode into Niagara Falls in a boxcar and headed for the Falls. He could not tear himself away even to "batter" the homes nearby for his supper. He fell asleep, and the next morning was arrested for vagrancy and put into ERIE COUNTY PENITENTIARY for a month. Though the book is full of adventure and humorous situations on the road as London becomes a fully fledged tramp, the scenes he describes in the prison are the real heart of the story: What he saw there led him to embrace SOCIALISM as a means of fighting a system that incarcerates the poor, places them on chain gangs, starves them with meals of salty water as "soup" and dry bread, and the constant threat of rape and beatings by guards and inmates. A few minutes after his release, he jumped a train and headed for Pennsylvania, slowly working his way home. As Russ Kingman points out, this experience was life changing. His mere ideas about socialism gelled into hard and fast knowledge and spurred him when he returned to become an active party member:

> He had been imprisoned without due process in the United States of America, where a man was supposed to be innocent until proven guilty. It was a miracle that he didn't chuck all his ideals and turn to crime, but he had studied that route too well and knew where it led.
>
> On the road he listened to stories from laboring men who were fired when their muscles were no longer strong, and he saw men who were let go when they lost an arm or a leg in an unprotected machine. He met others who were well-educated but who couldn't find a place in society because they challenged the accepted concepts of their day. Few teaching positions were available for the men who sought to change things rather than accept the things that were. (Kingman, *Pictorial Life of Jack London,* 59).

Furthermore, Kingman notes, "When Jack left Oakland, he was still a believer in KIPLING's work ethic. He had believed the teachers and preachers who proclaimed the honor of work. Now he could see that hard labor was not as honorable as he had been told" (Kingman, *Pictorial Life of Jack London,* 59). As soon as his young muscles would lose their strength, he would be discarded by the system just like the other tramps. He believed the castaways he knew on the road to be men just as good as himself. Finally arriving in Oakland on a coal ship from Vancouver, he immediately resumed his studies at Oakland High School and determined to make something of himself.

As noted above, some of the most gripping sections of *The Road* portray what London saw in prison. For example,

> I remember a handsome young mulatto of about twenty who got the insane idea into his head that he should stand for his rights. . . . Eight hall-men took the conceit out of him in just about a minute and a half—for that was the length of time required to travel along his gallery to the end and down five flights of steel stairs. . . . The mulatto struck the pavement where I was standing watching it all. He regained his feet and stood upright for a moment. In that moment he threw his arms wide apart and omitted an awful scream of terror and pain and heartbreak. At the same instant, as in a transformation scene, the shreds of his stout prison clothes fell from him, leaving him wholly naked and streaming blood from every portion of the surface of his body. Then he collapsed in a heap, unconscious. He had learned his lesson, and every convict within those walls who heard him scream had learned a lesson. So had I learned mine. it is not a nice thing to see a man's heart broken in a minute and a half (108).

There are many scenes such as this, leading London several times to say that he cannot fully reveal what took place because it is unprintable and not even believable: "Our hall was a common stews, filled with the ruck and the filth, the scum and dregs, of society—hereditary ineffi-cients, degenerates, wrecks, lunatics, addled intel-ligences, epileptics, monsters, weaklings, in short, a very nightmare of humanity" (115). Out of this nightmare, London managed to emerge and write about it—as he wrote of so many of his own experi-ences—with both the sense of the terrible trials of the poor and a developing analytical sense of what was wrong with the entire system of life in America.

FURTHER READING

Hornung, Alfred. "Evolution and Expansion in Jack London's Personal Accounts: *The Road* and *John Barleycorn*." In *An American Empire: Expansionist Cultures and Policies, 1881–1917.* Edited by Serge Ricard. Aix-en-Provence: Université de Provence, 1990, 197–213.

Kingman, Russ. *A Pictorial Life of Jack London.* New York: Crown, 1979.

London, Jack. *Jack London on the Road: The Tramp Diary and Other Hobo Writings.* Edited by Richard Etulain. Logan: Utah State University Press, 1979.

Luebke, Steven R. "*The Road* as Autobiography." *Jack London Newsletter* 21, nos. 1–3 (January 1988): 99–105.

Raskin, Jonah, ed. *The Radical Jack London: Writings on War and Revolution.* Berkeley: University of California Press, 2008.

Russo-Japanese War correspondence (1904)

When London was asked in January 1904 to serve as the HEARST SYNDICATE's war correspondent, he leapt at the opportunity. Enjoying his fame as the author of *The Call of the Wild*, he turned his business affairs over to his stepsister, ELIZA LON-DON SHEPARD, and left his manuscript of *The Sea-Wolf* to his soon-to-be wife, CHARMIAN KITTREDGE [LONDON], and his poet friend GEORGE STERLING for copyediting. He traveled by steamer, train, junk, sampan, horseback, and foot to reach the battles on the frozen Korean peninsula during the RUSSO-JAPANESE WAR.

He left for Japan on January 7, 1904, with other correspondents, on the SS *Siberia* to YOKOHAMA. For London, this was the beginning of a lengthy and frustrating trip to try to get to the front lines. He continued to violate the Japanese Army's cen-sorship and slip away to the front lines, but most of the time he was caught and sent back to SEOUL, KOREA. Twice, he was arrested and nearly court-martialed. When it was all over, few correspon-dents, including London, saw much action.

Upon arrival in Tokyo, he learned that the Japa-nese Army was about to launch a surprise offensive in Korea, but that the army would not issue the correspondents travel permits; on January 28 he left his comrades in Tokyo and headed out on his own on a train. He traveled on to Nagasaki and Moji. On February 8, the same day the Japanese navy started the war by torpedoing Russian ships at Port Arthur (today known as Dairen), he chartered a small boat and crew to sail up Korea's Yellow Sea coast to Chemulpo (today Incheon), Korea. "The wildest and most gorgeous thing ever!" he wrote to Charmian. "If you could see me just now, captain of a junk with a crew of three Koreans who speak neither English or Japanese and with five Japanese guests (strayed travelers) who speak neither Eng-lish nor Korean—that is, all but one, which last knows a couple of dozen English words. And with this polyglot following I am bound on a voyage of several hundred miles along the Korean coast to Chemulpo" (*Letters*, 410). For six long days, he and the crew fought the freezing storms and finally made landfall.

COLLIER'S correspondent Robert L. Dunn, who made Chemulpo a few days earlier, recorded his impressions of London's arrival:

Jack London is one of the grittiest men that it has been my good fortune to meet. He is just as heroic as any of the characters in his novels. He is a man who will stay with you through thick and thin. He doesn't know the meaning of fear and is willing to risk his life. . . . I did not recognize him. He was a physical wreck. His ears were frozen; his fingers were frozen; his feet were frozen. He said that he didn't mind his condition so long as he got to the front. He said his physical collapse counted for nothing. He had been sent to the front to do newspaper work and he wanted to do it. London was absolutely down and out, to use the slang expression. He had to undergo medical treatment for several days. As soon as he was able to move about he and I started for the front. (Dunn, "JACK LONDON KNOWS NOT FEAR," 1)

Another correspondent, F. A. McKenzie of London's *Daily Mail,* recalled that Jack London came to them "with the halo of adventure around his head. . . . On the days of our trip north whatever came (and we had our share of the very rough), his open, frank face never lost its laugh. He had to learn riding, and before many days his flesh was raw with saddle soreness. Then he laughed the more, even though his teeth were clenched, only insisting that we should ride harder, and himself hardest of all" (McKenzie, *From Tokyo to Tiflis,* 64).

London joined the Japanese army and marched with it, nearly 200 miles to the north, to Ping Yang (today Pyongyang), where the Russians were waiting. In Seoul he bought the former Russian ambassador's horse. He also bought pack animals and hired an interpreter and two *mapus* (grooms). A Korean youth named Manyoungi would serve as London's body servant and after the war would accompany London home to CALIFORNIA. London and the army reached Ping Yang on March 5, making London one of the first correspondents to reach that far north into the war zone. His first dispatch, wired on March 2, describes the first clash between Japanese and Russian land forces, focusing on a cavalry encounter with a detachment of Cossacks:

The Russians are boldly and fiercely pushing forward their advance south of the Yalu. . . . There has been no attempt by the Japanese as yet to dislodge the daring advance guard of the Russians. . . . The country between Anju and Ping Yang is very mountainous, and campaign-

ing there will be conducted under the greatest difficulties. But as the Japanese are in force here, a collision cannot be long deferred. How far behind the Russian advance is the main body of the invading army is not known here, but fleeing Koreans declare the invaders are in great force. . . . Ping Yang is in a state of panic so far as the natives are concerned. (*Jack London Reports,* 38–39).

At Sunan, he tried for the front lines, but was returned to SEOUL, where he spent his time investigating the area and its inhabitants. From there, he sent dispatches that resembled "human interest" pieces instead of his hoped-for battle coverage. One evening, on stage at the Seoul YMCA, dressed in a coat and top hat, he gave a command performance reading of *The Call of the Wild* for Japanese officers. In late April, he departed Seoul for Wiju (modern-day Uiju, North Korea). Then, from Antung, Manchuria, during the first week of May, he witnessed parts of the BATTLE OF THE YALU RIVER. According to London's reportage, the Russians were "sluggish" in battle, while "[t]he Japanese [understood] the utility of things" (*Jack London Reports,* 116). His biggest story was dated June 4: "JACK LONDON'S GRAPHIC STORY OF THE JAPS DRIVIING THE RUSSIANS ACROSS THE YALU RIVER, First Pen Picture Presented by Any Correspondent Eyewitness of the Remarkable Bravery and Skillful Tactics of the Victorious Japanese Army at Antung." The Japanese suffered 900 casualties while inflicting 4,000 casualties on the Russians, taking over 500 prisoners, and capturing guns and ammunition.

London became the most famous correspondent of the war, sending back hundreds of photos and several dispatches to the EXAMINER (SAN FRANCISCO). And yet the dispatch on the Yalu River battle was his only real scoop of battlefield reporting, and even then he could not actually see the entire battle.

London did appreciate his work in KOREA. He felt frustrated by the requirements of Japanese army officers and government officials, and he resented missing much of the battlefield action. In Moji, he was arrested for the first time. As he wrote in one dispatch,

Even before the taking of photographs was absolutely forbidden I once had the temerity to take a snap of an army farrier and his bellows. "Here at last was something that was not a military secret," I had thought in my innocence. Fifteen minutes' ride away I was stopped by a soldier who could not speak English. I showed my credentials and on my arm the official insignia of my position in the Japanese army. But it was no use. . . . After much delay an officer was brought to me. He was a captain, and his English was excellent—a great deal purer and better than my own. "You have taken a photograph of an army blacksmith," he said accusingly and reproachfully. With a sinking heart I nodded my head to acknowledge my guilt. "You must give it up," he said. . . . I came to war expecting to get thrills. My only thrills have been of indignation and irritation. (*Jack London Reports,* 120).

The situation was allayed when Japanese journalists, whom he called "brothers in craft," banded together to persuade a judge to return London's camera. Camaraderie with them was an index of how the professions of writer and photographer overcame barriers and provided shared identity.

Led by the Hearst papers, new technologies meant front-page newspaper layouts became larger and more dramatic. London was perfect material for such visual drama. Sidebars sketching him at work with his camera accompanied his war dispatches. The *Examiner* ran large studio portraits of him and a biography of his earlier personal adventures on its January 7, 1904, front page. His Korean photos and stories appeared in full-page layouts complete with cartoons; these stories most often ran across the full horizontal space of the top fold of the newspaper. On April 4, the *Examiner* headline read, "STRAIGHT FROM THE SEAT OF WAR: Glimpses of the Japanese Army." On February 7, 1904, the *New York American* ran on its front page a story headlined "JACK LONDON FREE! HE WAS NOT A SPY!" after London's arrest and release in Moji. The *Chicago Examiner* placed on its March 3, 1904, front page the banner headline "KOREANS FLEE IN TERROR FROM

RUSSIANS," with several subtitles to London's story, such as "Famous Author Tells of Daring Advance of Cossacks on Anju and Failure of Japanese to Try to Check Their Onward March" and "Foremost of America's Younger Writers, Author of 'A Daughter of the Snows,' 'Children of the Abyss [sic],' 'Kempton-Wace Letters,' 'The Call of the Wild,' 'The Son of the Wolf,' 'The Sea-Wolf,' and other stories" and more, before presenting the actual dispatch. This reminds us how important London's position was as an American author in the newspapers, an author as a representative of the values of his country. After his return home he continued to be celebrated as someone who should be consulted about the Yellow Peril. Yet in fact, London's own treatment of this sensational topic in two well-known essays he published after his war correspondence, "The Yellow Peril" and "If Japan Awakens China," is actually quite nuanced and should not be counted as yellow journalism; in both essays, he argues for the equality of the Western and Asian "souls" and advocates better understanding between Orient and Occident to be achieved mainly through learning each other's languages.

But because he could not visit many battles and was censored in what he could document, he turned to photographic and journalistic subjects behind the lines. Most of London's dispatches and photographs are about the lives of the villagers and soldiers, from Korean village *yangbans* (chiefs) to peasants serving as *mapus* or laboring on roads for the Japanese army, to high-ranking Japanese officers to their footsore but determined soldiers, there were also the Russian prisoners of war. In Korea, London completed his first portrait series, one of elderly Korean village men and another of beggar children. London's war portraits are HUMAN DOCUMENTS, like those in *The People of the Abyss.* Eventually London would fill nearly 20 albums with photographs of these human documents; only for the cruise of the SNARK did he make a larger batch of photographs.

By summer 1904, tired of censorship and his lack of battle material, London requested that Hearst bring him home. But before this could occur, he was arrested again—this time for striking a *mapu* for stealing from him. To avoid a Japanese court-martial, London appealed to the correspondent Richard Harding Davis, who cabled his friend from Cuban days, President THEODORE ROOSEVELT. Roosevelt then intervened through the U.S. Ministry in Tokyo. Whether London was expelled from or left Korea voluntarily, by July 1, he had passed through Yokohama and returned to California.

London underestimated what he accomplished in photography and war-reporting. His language is polished and effective, while maintaining an easy, journalistic style that conceals the careful narrative structure of each dispatch. He effectively employs dialogue and dramatic scenes. His subjects are developed at times like characters. As in so much of his work, he is intensely interested in problems of language and communication. He looks for the big picture as well as the telling detail. He gives us the details that support everyday life in the field, horses, how wagons are loaded, how soldier's packs are assembled, how food is obtained from villagers. But he is also quite visual and cinematic in his prose. He moves from a minute description of a soldier's kit to the panorama of wagon trains going across the frozen mud roads, placing that one soldier with his gear within the larger picture. The people London observes stay with the reader: Korean peasants displaced by the war trudge with families and belongings down frozen, muddy roads. Common soldiers of the Japanese forces limp under heavy packs. Army surgeons work on their injured feet. He seems to experience emotional connection with them: "And the troops stream by, the horses fight—*mapus*, cook, and interpreter are squabbling 4 feet away from me. And the frost is in the air. I must close my doors and light my candles. A Korean family of refugees— their household goods on their backs, just went by," he writes (*Letters*, 418).

FURTHER READING

Dunn, Robert L. "JACK LONDON KNOWS NOT FEAR." *Examiner* (San Francisco), June 26, 1904, 1.

Jack London Reports: War Correspondence, Sports Articles, and Miscellaneous Writings. Edited by King Hendricks and Irving Shepard. Garden City, N.Y.: Doubleday & Co., 1970.

McKenzie, F. A. *From Tokyo to Tiflis: Uncensored Letters from the War*. London: Hurst and Blackett, 1905.

Reesman, Jeanne Campbell. *Jack London's Racial Lives*. Athens: University of Georgia Press, 2009.

Reesman, Jeanne Campbell, Sara S. Hodson, and Philip Adam. *Jack London, Photographer*. Athens: University of Georgia Press, 2010.

Sweeney, Michael S. "'Delays and Vexation': Jack London and the Russo-Japanese War." In *Journalism and Mass Communication Quarterly* 75, no. 3 (Autumn 1998): 548–558.

Tsujii, Eiji. "Jack London and the Yellow Peril." In *Jack London Newsletter* 9, no. 2 (May–August 1976): 96–98.

———. "Jack London Items in the Japanese Press of 1904." In *Jack London Newsletter* 8, no. 2 (1975): 55–58.

"Samuel" (1913)

London had a good deal of trouble placing this unusual story written in SCOTS-IRISH dialect; he wrote it in 1909 but it was not published until it appeared in *Bookman* 37 (May 1913). He had submitted it to so many of magazines, including those he most often published in—WOMAN'S HOME COMPANION, *Century*, SATURDAY EVENING POST, COSMOPOLITAN, *McClure's*, and so on, for a total of 15 rejections. Instead of comprehending the story's tragic and mythic elements, editors found it peculiar and unlike the popular author's usual tales. Perhaps they objected to its theological implications in Margaret Henan's battle with the church. When in 1914, Ethan A. Cross, a professor of literature at Colorado State College at Greely, asked London's permission to include the story in a textbook anthology called *The Short Story: A Technical and Literary Study* (1914), London felt vindicated: "I am convinced that the publication of 'Samuel' in your book will be of distinct advantage to me. . . . 'Samuel' was hawked about by me to every big magazine in the U.S., and was invariable refused." He let *Bookman* have it "for a song" ($100). He wonders, "Personally, how can you account for the averseness of the American magazine editors regarding stories such as 'Samuel'? I have always found this so with practically all of my best short stories" (*Letters*, 1,308). Cross's analysis called the story "a true impression of life" (*Letters*, 1,309 n. 1).

SYNOPSIS

A woman living on Island McGill off the coast of Northern Ireland, Margaret Henan is past 70 but still vigorous and keen-witted. She has borne 12 children, eight of whom have survived. We meet her through the eyes of the narrator, an American visitor; he first observes her hauling 100-pound sacks of grain:

> Six times she went between the cart and the stable, each time with a full sack on her back, and beyond passing the time of day with me she took no notice of my presence. Then, the cart empty, she fumbled for matches and lighted a short clay pipe, pressing down the burning surface of the tobacco with a calloused and apparently nerveless thumb. The hands were noteworthy. They were large-knuckled, sinewy and malformed by labour, rimed with callouses, the nails blunt and broken, and with here and there cuts and bruises, healed and healing, such as are common to the hands of hard-working men. On the back were huge, upstanding veins, eloquent of age and toil."
> (*Stories*, 1,611)

But the most striking feature of this woman the narrator observes is her eyes: "The sunken cheeks and pinched nose told little of the quality of the life that flickered behind those clear blue eyes of hers. Despite the minutiae of wrinkle-work that somehow failed to weazen them, her eyes were clear as a girl's—clear, out-looking, and far-seeing, and with an open and unblinking steadfastness of gaze that was disconcerting. The remarkable thing was the distance between them. It is a lucky man or woman who has the width of an eye between, but with Margaret Henan the width between her eyes was fully that of an eye and a half" (*Stories*, 1,612). He remarks to her that she is very old to be working so hard, and in response,

She looked at me with that strange, unblinking gaze, and she thought and spoke with the slow deliberateness that characterized everything about her, as if well aware of an eternity that was hers and in which there was no need for haste. Again I was impressed by the enormous certitude of her. . . . No more in her spiritual life than in carrying the hundredweights of grain was there a possibility of a misstep or an overbalancing. The feeling produced in me was uncanny. Here was a human soul that, save for the most glimmering of contacts, was beyond the humanness of me. And the more I learned of Margaret Henan in the weeks that followed the more mysteriously remote she became. She was as alien as a far-journeyer from some other star, and no hint could she nor all the country-side give me of what forms of living, what heats of feeling, or rules of philosophic contemplation actuated her in all that she had been and was. (*Stories*, 1,612)

When the narrator learns Margaret's strange story from other villagers—that she continued to name her boy children "Samuel" even though each Samuel died—he decides to ask her about it himself. For her strange choice she is shunned by the other villagers as a sort of witch, but the narrator finds her to be nearly a saint.

He first learns from the villagers the basics of her story. When her son Samuel died, Margaret had another and another, calling each by the same name. The same fate befalls them. Once again, late in life, she delivers another Samuel. He is a mentally retarded boy and because of his incessant braying and moaning, his father goes crazy and kills him and himself. Margaret lives on, keeping to herself. The narrator is fascinated by "the marvel of it, the miraculous wonder of that woman's heroic spirit" (*Stories*, 1,623). He is also impressed with her defiance of the church; her battle against it, which her neighbor Mrs. Ross terms her "'wucked-headed an' vucious stubbornness'" (*Stories*, 1,617). When her favorite brother, Samuel Dundee, committed suicide, it was discovered that his marriage is illegal because the minister never registered his new church with the church in Dublin. This

Samuel married Agnes Hewitt and then took up his duties as a skipper of a sailing vessel. When the problem of the legality of the marriages arises, all the couples are remarried, except the Dundees; Samuel is away for years on his ship and misses the birth of his first child. The child's legitimacy in question, and Samuel declared lost, Agnes drowns herself and the child in the loch. But the ship was not lost, and when Samuel returns, he kills himself and dies blaspheming: "And, in the face of all this, Margaret Henan named her first child Samuel" (*Stories*, 1,620). The first Samuel dies of the croup. The next Samuel drowns at age three. The third Samuel is lost at sea off CAPE HORN; the fourth is the "idiot" killed by her husband.

As they chat by her kitchen door one long afternoon, he asks her why? Why keep giving a name that carries such bad luck? Why is she so persistent even in the face of condemnation by the church, risking her soul for her obsession? She answers, "'Do a wee but of a name change the plans o' God? Do the world run by hut or muss, an' be God a weak, shully-shallyun' creature thot ud alter the fate an' destiny o' thungs because the worm Margaret Henan seen fut tull name her bairn Samuel?'" (*Stories*, 1,627). Furthermore, she explains that she simply likes the name: "'I *like*— thot uz the first word an' the last. An' behind thot *like* no mon can go an' find the *why* o' ut. I *like* Samuel, an' I like ut wull. Ut uz a sweet name, an' there be a rollun' wonder un the sound o' ut thot passes understanding'" (*Stories*, 1,628). The narrator is left to wonder:

> Was she a martyr to Truth? Did she have it in her to worship at so abstract a shrine? Had she conceived Abstract Truth to be the one high goal of human endeavour on that day of long ago when she named her first-born Samuel? Or was hers the stubborn obstinacy of the ox? the fixity of purpose of the balky horse? the stolidity of the self-willed peasant-mind? Was it whim or fancy?—the one streak of lunacy in what was otherwise an eminently rational mind? . . . Was hers a steady, enlightened opposition to superstition? or—and a subtler thought—was she mastered by some vaster, profounder super-

stition, a fetish-worship of which the Alpha and the Omega was the cryptic *Samuel*? (*Stories*, 1,626–1,627)

COMMENTARY

Because of the heavy use of the Hebrides dialect, "Samuel" is a bit difficult to read, but it is well worth the effort in its archetypal portrait of an indomitable old woman—a parallel to CARL JUNG's "Great Mother"—against her family, village, and church. The story is based on a yarn told to him by Captain MacIlwaine of the coal steamer *Tymeric*, which the Londons boarded in Sydney in April 1909 for Guayaquil, Ecuador, on their way home from the SNARK voyage. MacIlwaine, from whom London learned the dialect he would use in the story as well as the story itself, was a native of a small island off the coast of Northern Ireland who also gave London the idea for his story "The Sea Farmer." In its remarkable portrait of Margaret and its numerous religious allusions, the story is not just a strange yarn but a complex statement on the nature of God and man, and how humans misconstrue what it means to participate in the Divine. Margaret stays true to her own beliefs and defies the church; much of her speech contains biblical allusions, however, and her name is that of St. Margaret, the patron saint of childbirth, while the name Samuel is Hebrew for "His name is God."

CHARACTERS

narrator An American visiting Island McGill, the narrator first heard of the place from "the skipper of a Glasgow tramp" when he is aboard as a passenger from Colombo to Rangoon; from the captain he receives a letter of introduction to Mrs. Ross on the island who can offer bed and board. After he meets Margaret Henan, he asks various villagers about her, until he finally asks her himself, "Why?"

Margaret Henan Regarded as a witch and enemy of the church by her neighbors, Margaret is past 70 but still strong and still determined that she was right to name her boys "Samuel" even though they all died. Her battle is not with the village, however; it is with the church that killed her brother and his family, and it is with God Himself.

Mrs. Ross At first Mrs. Ross does not want to talk about Margaret, being close-mouthed like most of Island McGill. Yet from her he learns that Margaret had once been one of the island belles; she was the daughter of a well-off farmer who married another, Tom Henan. Mrs. Ross tells the narrator the story of "the Samuels" and expresses her strong disapproval of Margaret, whom she thinks is insane.

Clara Ross Mrs. Ross's daughter, it is Clara who first mentions the several Samuels and piques the narrator's interest in Margaret; Clara snickers at the crazy old woman's behavior. Clara also tells him about Margaret's brother Samuel and his tragedy.

Gavin McNab Bosun of the *Starry Grace* and an Island McGill man, he tells the narrator about the terrible shipwreck that claimed the life of the third Samuel.

FURTHER READING

Bedwell, Laura. "Jack London's 'Samuel' and the Abstract Shrine of Truth." In *Studies in American Naturalism* 2, no. 2 (Winter 2007): 150–165.

Labor, Earle. "The Archetypal Woman as a 'Martyr to Truth': Jack London's 'Samuel.'" In *American Literary Realism* 24, no. 2 (Winter 1992): 23–32.

The Scarlet Plague (1912)

This DYSTOPIAN novella tells of a terrible plague that has struck the world, wiping out most of its inhabitants. Inspired by EDGAR ALLAN POE's "The Masque of the Red Death," London replicates the symptoms of the Red Death with its terrifying scarlet rash, convulsions, and death within minutes:

> The heart began to beat faster and the heat of the body to increase. Then came the scarlet rash, spreading like wildfire over the face and body. . . . Usually, they had convulsions at the time of the appearance of the rash. But these convulsions did not last long and were not very severe. If one lived through them, he became perfectly quiet, and only did he feel a numbness swiftly creeping up his body from the feet. The heels became numb first, then the legs, and hips, and when the numbness reached as high as his heart he died. They did not rave or sleep. Their minds always remained cool and calm up to the moment their heart numbed and stopped. And another strange thing was the rapidity of decomposition. No sooner was a person dead than the body seemed to fall to pieces, to fly apart, to melt away even as you looked at it. That was one of the reasons the plague spread so rapidly. All the billions of germs in a corpse were so immediately released. (73–75)

Like his story of germ warfare, "The Unparalleled Invasion," this tale points to an apocalyptic future. As Poe's Prince Prospero tried to hide with his guests from the Red Death, so the scientists at the UNIVERSITY OF CALIFORNIA barricade themselves in the chemistry building, along with an English professor, James Howard Smith; all but Smith perish. He escapes along with a few other people unaffected by the disease.

SYNOPSIS

In the year 2073, a boy and his grandfather, who is Smith but whom they call Granser, clad in animal skins, are walking through deep woods. Having fought off a bear, they come to a fire on the beach, where several other boys sit watching their sheep. Granser asks for a crab, but they tease him with empty shells until he cries. Finally, they relent and ask him to tell his story about the past and the scarlet plague.

As he relates, in the summer of 2013 rumors began that a new plague was killing people in New York. Those infected developed a scarlet rash, had convulsions, then became numb and died. The entire process took at most an hour, but sometimes as little as 10 minutes. Bacteriologists perished even as they tried to find a vaccine. Millions died. The plague finally reached San Francisco, and mayhem broke out there. The wealthy tried to flee the city while the poor murdered them and looted the city. Smith muses:

> "'The fleeting systems lapse like foam,'" he mumbled what was evidently a quotation. "That's it—foam, and fleeting. All man's toil upon the planet was just so much foam. He domesticated the serviceable animals, destroyed the hostile ones, and cleared the land of its wild vegetation. And then he passed, and the flood of primordial life rolled back again, sweeping his handiwork away—the weeds and the forest inundated his fields, the beasts of prey swept over his flocks, and now there are wolves on the Cliff House beach." He was appalled by the thought. "Where four million people disported themselves, the wild wolves roam to-day, and the savage progeny of our loins, with prehistoric weapons, defend themselves against the fanged despoilers. Think of it! And all because of the Scarlet Death—" (33–34)

Smith wandered through the desolate city and countryside in search of others. He lived alone in the Grand Canyon for three years, then set out to see if anyone else was alive. At Lake Temescal in CALIFORNIA, he does find others, a brutish, dark, hairy man called the Chauffeur:

> "He was a violent, unjust man. Why the plague germs spared him I can never understand. It would seem, in spite of our old metaphysical notions about absolute justice, that there is no justice in the universe. Why did he live?—an iniquitous, moral monster, a blot on the face of nature, a cruel, relentless, bestial cheat as well. All he could talk about was motor-cars, machinery, gasoline, and garages—and especially, and with huge delight, of his mean pilferings and sordid swindlings of the persons who had employed him in the days before the coming of the plague" (145).

Smith finds it ironic that this ATAVISM has survived. But he blames the economically totalitarian society of 2013: "In the midst of our civilization, down in our slums and labor-ghettos, we had bred a race of barbarians, of savages; and now, in the time of our calamity, they turned upon us like the wild beasts they were and destroyed us"(105–106). The Chauffeur has enslaved a woman from high society and beats her into doing work and having sex; Smith is astonished to recognize Vesta Van Warden: "the young wife of John Van Warden, clad in rags, with marred and scarred and toil-calloused hands, bending over the campfire and doing scullion work—she, Vesta, who had been born to the purple greatest baronage of wealth the world has ever known. John Van Warden, her husband, worth one billion, eight hundred millions and President of the Board of Industrial Magnates, had been the ruler of America" (146–147). When Smith ineffectually tries to protect Vesta from the Chauffer, the Chauffeur sneers at him:

> "Halter-broke and bridle-wise," the Chauffeur gloated, while she performed that dreadful, menial task. "A trifle balky at times, Professor, a trifle balky; but a clout alongside the jaw makes her as meek and gentle as a lamb."
>
> And another time he said: "We've got to start all over and replenish the earth and multiply. You're handicapped, Professor. You ain't got no wife, and we're up against a regular Garden-of-Eden proposition. But I ain't proud. I'll tell you what, Professor." He pointed at their little infant, barely a year old. "There's your wife, though you'll have to wait till she grows up. It's rich, ain't it? We're all equals here, and I'm the biggest toad in the splash." (159)

Smith meets others and begins a family which includes the boys to whom he is telling his story. There is no means of communicating across the country or to other nations. Society has been set back to a nomad existence. The boys do not believe most of their grandfather's story. They fight among themselves and with him in a language that is only partly English. Finally, they rise, leaving the grandfather to straggle along behind into the wilderness.

COMMENTARY

The Scarlet Plague was strangely prophetic; in 1918, two years after London died, the Spanish Influenza pandemic that killed between 50 and 100 million worldwide began. The novella addresses many of

London's most characteristic themes. His portrait of the totalitarian society of 2013 with its vast underclass is a socialist critique like *The Iron Heel*. His sense of the atavism that lurks in men just under the surface appears in many other works. There is a hint that the technologies of germ warfare may have been responsible for the plague. Finally, there is a sense in which NATURE, brutal though it can be, also offers an alternative to the 2013 urban world. In Part I, Smith reflects on the availability of crabs: "But there weren't many crabs in those days," the old man wandered on. "They were fished out, and they were great delicacies. The open season was only a month long, too. And now crabs are accessible the whole year around. Think of it—catching all the crabs you want, any time you want, in the surf of the Cliff House beach!" (31–32). For such a darkly pessimistic story, *The Scarlet Plague* does offer a sense of hope at the end. Granser tells his grandsons that one day false doctors like their local shaman will be replaced by real doctors; the steam engine will be reinvented; the alphabet reconstituted—but also that gunpowder will one day be rediscovered. This possibility causes him to doubt: "Just as the old civilization passed, so will the new. It may take fifty thousand years to build, but it will pass. All things pass. Only remain cosmic force and matter, ever in flux, ever acting and reacting and realizing the eternal types—the priest, the soldier, and the king. . . . It were just as well that I destroyed those cave-stored books" (179). This sense of cosmic time and flux is both frightening and somehow reassuring. Granser does have some hope for his grandchildren, or he would not spend so much time telling them history. And in a final vision of Nature, London leaves a sense of beauty:

> Edwin stopped suddenly and looked back. Hare-Lip and Hoo-Hoo and the dogs and the goats passed on. Edwin was looking at a small herd of wild horses which had come down on the hard sand. There were at least twenty of them, young colts and yearlings and mares, led by a beautiful stallion which stood in the foam at the edge of the surf, with arched neck and bright wild eyes, sniffing the salt air from off the sea (180–181).

And, after all, it was a literature professor who survived.

CHARACTERS

James Howard Smith, "Granser" Formerly a literature professor at the University of California, Smith flees the mass death and chaos of San Francisco to travel about the West looking for other survivors of the Scarlet Plague. He does come upon some, but they are for the most part complete brutes. Still, he survives to father children who give him grandchildren and lives to tell his tale.

Edwin, Hoo-Hoo, Hare-lip Smith's grandchildren, who know very little of the past and are mere savages. When they tease him with the shellfish, they display "only the cruel humor of the savage. To them the incident was excruciatingly funny, and they burst into loud laughter. Hoo-Hoo danced up and down, while Edwin rolled gleefully on the ground. The boy with the goats came running to join in the fun" (25).

Bill, the Chauffeur Bill is an atavism, or primitive throwback, a brutish, stupid man who gloats over his rape and kidnapping of his "wife," Vesta Van Warden, in the new savage world. He rules over a strong tribe of followers and becomes a legend of domination and cruelty. Smith is rightly frightened of him and does not try to save Van Warden from him.

Vesta Van Warden Widow of a fabulously rich San Franciscan magnate, she is the epitome of the upper-class, refined female; how terrible the irony that she is the slave of the Chauffeur.

Jones, Harrison, Cardiff, Hale, Wainwright, and their wives Fellow survivors who have formed the Santa Rosa Tribe in the Contra Costa Hills near the Straits of Carquinez. Smith joins them and marries a woman named Bertha and has a family.

Bertha "The wives of Cardiff and Wainwright were ordinary women, accustomed to toil, with strong constitutions just the type for the wild new life which they were compelled to live. In addition were two adult idiots from the feeble-minded home at Eldredge, and five or six young children and infants born after the formation of the Santa Rosa Tribe. Also, there was Bertha. She was a good woman, Hare-lip, in spite of the sneers of your father. Her I took for wife. She was the mother of your father, Edwin, and of yours, Hoo-Hoo. And it was our daughter, Vera, who married your father, Hare-Lip—your father, Sandow, who was the oldest son of Vesta Van Warden and the Chauffeur" (166).

Cross-Eyes A self-proclaimed doctor or shaman whom Smith despises. Responding to the dark superstitions of the savages around him, he engages in "selling charms against sickness, giving good hunting, exchanging promises of fair weather for good meat and skins, sending the death stick, performing a thousand abominations" (173).

The Sea-Wolf

The Sea-Wolf (1904), one of London's most popular novels and one continuously in print, was inspired by an event on the foggy night of November 30, 1901, when the ferry *Sausalito* hit the ferry *San Rafael* in SAN FRANCISCO BAY, in what was then the worst ferryboat collision in the history of the bay. Navigating in an era when skippers relied on the sound of foghorns, bells on buoys, sirens on piers, echoes of whistles and compasses, with, of course, instinct, the *Sausalito* never saw the *San Rafael* before she hit her amidships, her prow piercing the dining room of the smaller, older *San Rafael*. The side-wheel steamer sank in 20 minutes. Three people died as a result of the collision, and an old horse named Dick, who was used to move baggage carts, refused to leave and went down with the ferry. The two captains lashed their vessels together long enough to get the *San Rafael*'s passengers onto the *Sausalito*. This wreck London used as the basis of the sinking of the *Martinez* at the beginning of *The Sea-Wolf*, published by MACMILLAN at the height of his early fame in 1904. Its details derive from

several sources, especially London's time as an able seaman in 1893 aboard the SOPHIA SUTHERLAND, a sealing schooner that hunted in the North Pacific, and a famous sea captain of the day, CAPTAIN ALEXANDER MACLEAN.

SYNOPSIS

Chapters 1–10
Aboard the *Martinez* is the young and wealthy Humphrey Van Weyden, a literary critic, reading his latest essay in ATLANTIC MONTHLY and thinking of "how comfortable it was, this division of labor," as the sailors toil on the decks of the *Martinez* so that he can spend his time enjoying his intellectual life (2). However, when the collision occurs and the *Martinez* begins to sink, he is surrounded by a "screaming bedlam" of terror. The screaming of the women is the worst:

> I realized I was becoming hysterical myself; for these were women of my own kind, like my mother and sisters, . . . [but] the sounds they made reminded me of the squealing of pigs under the knife of the butcher, and I was struck with horror at the vividness of the analogy. These women, capable of the most sublime emotions, of the tenderest sympathies, were open-mouthed and screaming. They wanted to live, they were helpless, like rats in a trap, and they screamed. (7)

Van Weyden, half-drowned, is picked up by the outbound sealing schooner *Ghost*. He is hauled aboard and revived, only to find that this rescue is really the beginning of a long struggle for survival. The novel's central character emerges in Wolf Larsen, a ruthless ship captain and, surprisingly, a philosopher. Van Weyden's soft, weak muscles are put to the test as he is forced to join Larsen's brutish crew, and his gentility and morality are challenged by Larsen's deterministic MATERIALISM and nihilism. To Larsen, the question of the meaning of life can be measured in one word, "'Bosh!'" Life, he says, is mere "'piggishness'" (97), there is no such thing as human justice and no man's achievements can outlast death. Van Weyden is also threatened by the cook, Thomas Mugridge. Over time, as he grows stronger, he finds himself admiring Larsen's strength, both his piercing intellect and muscular body.

The first hint of the brutality that is to come occurs just after Van Weyden's rescue, when Larsen stands over and vilely curses a dying mate for robbing him of a crewman. Van Weyden is shocked at what he hears and sees: "[Larsen] continued to grin with a sardonic humor, with a cynical mockery and defiance. He was master of the situation" (21). Larsen refuses Van Weyden's request to be put onto a San Francisco-bound passing ship. As the sailors prepare to bury the mate at sea, Larsen asks Van Weyden if he is a preacher; when he learns that he is a literary critic, he grabs his hand and says, "'Dead men's hands have kept it soft. Good for little else than dish-washing and scullion work.'" A sailor, Johansen, is made mate, and the cabin-boy George Leach is made boat-puller, while Van Weyden is Larsen's new cabin-boy. When Leach balks, Van Weyden again witnesses Larsen's violence and prodigious strength, when one blow from him "crumples" Leach. The *Ghost* encounters heavy seas, and a gigantic wave nearly washes Van Weyden—now called "Hump" by the others—overboard, but he only injures his knee. As he tries to sleep amid the drunken uproar of the seal hunters' steerage, he begins fully to realize what life aboard the ship will be like. Though he is moved to a small cabin of his own, he continues to be mocked and assaulted by the cook and others.

When Van Weyden discovers Larsen's large library in his cabin, he is shocked: "It was patent that this terrible man was no ignorant clod, such as one would inevitably suppose him to be from his exhibitions of brutality. At once he became an enigma. One side or the other of his nature was perfectly comprehensible; but both sides together were bewildering" (48). Later, when Van Weyden tells Larsen that the cook has robbed him, Larsen laughs. When Van Weyden protests that he sees something finer, something "immortal" in Larsen's gaze, Larsen replies, "'Consider yourself and me. What does your boasted immortality amount to when your life runs foul of mine? You would like to go back to the land, which is a favorable place for your kind of piggishness. It is a whim of mine to keep you aboard this ship, where my piggishness

flourishes. And keep you I will. . . . I could kill you now, with a blow of my fist, for you are a miserable weakling. But if we are immortal, what is the reason for this?'" (50)

Only the strong survive, Van Weyden realizes. Louis, one of the seal hunters, warns Van Weyden that the *Ghost* is doomed. When a young sailor, Harrison, is nearly killed on orders from Larsen, Van Weyden protests, and they again argue about the value of life. Lying awake on the forecastle one evening, Van Weyden is startled to hear Larsen reciting some lines from RUDYARD KIPLING's poem "L'Envoi," and they again debate philosophy. In these early chapters, until the arrival of Maud Brewster, this is the consistent pattern: violence bookended by philosophical discussion. Van Weyden drifts to sleep hearing Larsen sing "The Song of the Trade Winds" by John Masefield. Appalled as he is by Larsen's materialism, Van Weyden also recognizes his yearning to believe in something. In a game of cards, Larsen wins Van Weyden's stolen money from Mugridge and refuses to part with it. He explains, "'Might is right, and that is all there is to it. Weakness is wrong. Which is a very poor way of saying that it is good for oneself to be strong, and evil for oneself to be weak—or better yet, it is pleasurable to be strong, because of the profits; painful to be weak, because of the penalties'" (52).

Chapters 11–20
Van Weyden finds himself in better condition, his muscles hardening and his knee and arm healing. Against the backdrop of increasingly violent confrontations among rival sailors and hunters, and between Larsen and the men, Van Weyden happens upon Larsen reading the BIBLE, quoting aloud several passages in Ecclesiastes. Larsen closes the book, and turns to Van Weyden:

"The Preacher who was king over Israel in Jerusalem thought as I think. You call me a pessimist. Is not this pessimism of the blackest?—'All is vanity and vexation of spirit,' 'There is no profit under the sun,' 'There is one event unto all,' to the fool and the wise, the clean and the unclean, the sinner and the saint, and that event is death, and an evil thing, he says. For the Preacher loved life, and did not want to die, saying, 'For a living dog is better than a dead lion.' He preferred the vanity and vexation to the silence and unmovableness of the grave. And so I." (106–107)

Van Weyden introduces Larsen to Omar Khayyam, and, though he appreciates Khayyam, as if to demonstrate the futility of meaning in life, Larsen seizes Van Weyden by the throat and nearly strangles him, all the while accusing him of an unreasonable fear of death and urging him to learn to "'To live! To live!'" (109). When Van Weyden comes to, he is offered a seat and a drink, and their debate begins anew.

But soon the violence that has been building among the men breaks out into a terrible beating of Johnson by Larsen and Johansen, the sailors and hunters beating Mugridge nearly senseless, and a fight between Johansen and Latimer. Van Weyden is sickened by it all. After all, he and Larsen had been discussing *Hamlet* when Larsen springs upon Johnson. Van Weyden generously tries to comfort the cook. When Johansen goes missing, Larsen and Van Weyden climb down into the forecastle to look for him. Larsen engages in a tremendous fight in the dark, closed space with the sailors, who are led by Leach and Johnson. Latimer helps him escape.

The men mutter mutiny but also continue to squabble among themselves. Van Weyden visits Larsen's cabin to dress his wounds, and he admires Larsen's SCANDINAVIAN body with its fair skin and muscles hard as iron: "I remember his putting his hand up to feel of the wound on his head, and my watching the biceps move like a living thing under its white sheath. It was the biceps that had nearly crushed out my life once, that I had seen strike so many killing blows. I could not take my eyes from him. I stood motionless, a roll of antiseptic cotton in my hand unwinding and spilling itself down to the floor" (142). Van Weyden is promoted to mate with a salary and a "Mister" in front of his last name.

When the ship lays to at Wainwright Island to take on water, Larsen threatens to kill Leach and Johnson. Kelly and Harrison escape to the island's interior. The mood aboard the *Ghost* becomes even more grim. Yet when they reach Japan and the seal

herd and begin to take seals, tempers subside a bit. Though still afraid of Larsen's "destructive criticism" (156), Van Weyden realizes that Larsen has taught him the lessons of reality and helped make him a stronger man. Interestingly, this thought connects naturalistically with Van Weyden's musing on how the violent death and skinning of the seals is meant to create beauty in women by supplying them with furs: "It was wanton slaughter, and all for woman's sake. . . . and the men, like butchers plying their trade, naked and red of arm and hand, hard at work with ripping and flensing-knives, removing the skins from the pretty sea-creatures they had killed" (155). With a similar logic, as the *Ghost* runs before a terrific storm and Larsen attempts to save his men who had drifted off in their boats, Larsen sacrifices Kelly's life to get back his boat. Larsen helps Leach, Nilson, and Smoke be resaved by a passing ship; finally, the *Ghost*, short four sailors (Henderson, Holyoak, Williams, and Kelly), again takes off after the seals.

When the ship is near the coast of JAPAN, Leach and Johnson steal a boat and sail for YOKOHAMA. While searching for them, the shipmates see a small boat drifting with four men and a woman in it, obviously lost from their ship. She is Maud Brewster. Van Weyden, who escorts her below, is both fascinated by and frightened of her beauty. In chapter 19, Van Weyden learns from Larsen, who plans to keep the four men and make sailors of them rather than putting their party ashore in Yokohama, that they were lost when their ship hit a gale and went down. They also come upon Johnson and Leach. Van Weyden begs Larsen not to lay hands on them, and, strangely, Larsen agrees, with the odd request that Van Weyden not kill Larsen. However, Larsen keeps his promise only literally, letting the two bedraggled men bail and paddle frantically to catch the schooner; just as they get close, Larsen shoots ahead and abandons them again and again, until finally for good. Van Weyden is horrified, but his thoughts turn mainly to protecting Brewster. When she recovers, she asks Larsen to take her to Yokohama, but he taunts her for her lack of strength and her upper social class. At supper, she and Van Weyden recognize each other: not only has he favorably reviewed her poetry, but she is the "first lady of American poetry" and he is "the dean of American letters." Critics have rightly viewed their seaborne reunion as improbable.

Chapters 21–30

Larsen becomes jealous of the relationship Brewster is forming with Van Weyden, and as Van Weyden notes, "It fell to Thomas Mugridge to be the victim" (200). Because he has been sending the men "messes and concoctions of the vilest order" out of his galley, Larsen has him tied to a long rope and thrown behind the ship. When Oofty-Oofty, who holds the line, cries out that he sees a shark, the men haul Mugridge back in, but not before the shark bites off his foot. Rolling about on the deck trying to recover, he buries his own teeth in Larsen's ankle. Larsen, who is explaining to the horrified Brewster that this is just "man-play" (204), easily pulls him off and gives him to Van Weyden to patch up. Brewster criticizes Van Weyden for not preventing this, but he responds, "'You must remember, Miss Brewster, that you are a new inhabitant of this little world, and that you do not yet understand the laws which operate within it. You bring with you certain fine conceptions of humanity, manhood, conduct, and such things; but here you will find them misconceptions'" (207). They debate the virtues of "moral courage" over violence; Van Weyden sounds like Larsen in trying to reeducate Brewster about reality, though they recognize in each other a capacity for moral and ethical courage. Van Weyden explains to Brewster the true nature of Larsen: "'[T]his man is a monster. He is without conscience. Nothing is sacred to him, nothing is too terrible for him to do.'" Van Weyden adds, "'It is the best we can do if we wish to live. The battle is not always to the strong. We have not the strength with which to fight this man; we must dissimulate, and win, if win we can, by craft. If you will be advised by me, this is what you will do. . . . We must stand together, without appearing to do so, in secret alliance. . . . We must provoke no scenes with this man, nor cross his will'" (208). Van Weyden realizes that he is in love with her, especially as he observes Larsen's frightening advances toward her.

Nearing the limit of their fishing waters, the *Ghost* is pursued by the *Macedonia*, captained by Larsen's hated brother Death Larsen. Brewster tries to coax Larsen to stop his violent ways. But Larsen sends out boats to attack the *Macedonia*'s boats, and the sailors and hunters skirmish before the *Ghost* gives up. Larsen relishes the damage he has done to his brother. Thoroughly revived by his victory, Larsen attempts to rape Brewster, but Van Weyden defends her and fights Larsen. Van Weyden draws his knife, but before he can strike, Larsen collapses with his hands over his eyes, moaning with a violent headache (in the end he will die blind, of a brain tumor). Van Weyden and Brewster load a boat, lower it, and set their course for Japan.

In the boat, as Van Weyden gazes longingly at Brewster as she combs her hair, he feels the "love of man and woman, I had always held, was a sublimated something related to spirit, a spiritual bond that linked and drew their souls together. The bonds of the flesh had little part in my cosmos of love. But I was learning the sweet lesson for myself that the soul transmuted itself, expressed itself, through the flesh; that the sight and sense and touch of the loved one's hair was as much breath and voice and essence of the spirit as the light that shone from the eyes and the thoughts that fell from the lips" (259–260). They take turns steering and sleeping, feeling unafraid of their fate. They survive winds and storms and finally land on an island, which they name Endeavour Island. Though without matches they set about trying to make a fire—which Van Weyden finally manages—and to lay in seal meat and build huts. A difficult test is to club the seals, but Van Weyden again manages to do it. He feels a surge of animal pride: "I shall never forget, in that moment, how instantly conscious I became of my manhood. The primitive deeps of my nature stirred. I felt myself masculine, the protector of the weak, the fighting male. And, best of all, I felt myself the protector of my loved one" (291).

Chapter 31–end

Reverting to first names, Maud and Humphrey enjoy their days and nights on the island, but separate at night to the two sealskin huts they build.

However, after several weeks, the *Ghost* appears offshore. Humphrey creeps aboard with his knife and a gun, but when he encounters Larsen, he cannot act: "'Hump,' he said slowly, 'you can't do it. You are not exactly afraid. You are impotent. Your conventional morality is stronger than you. You are the slave to the opinions which have credence among the people you have known and have read about. Their code has been drummed into your head from the time you lisped, and in spite of your philosophy, and of what I have taught you, it won't let you kill an unarmed, unresisting man.' 'I know it,' I said hoarsely" (302–303). Larsen is very ill after being attacked by his brother and left marooned on his disabled ship. Larsen begins to succumb to the pain and blindness of the brain tumor and soon dies blind and helpless, but not before he tries to cut the lanyards or rigging of the ship, tries to set his mattress on fire, and tries to strangle Humphrey. They place him in irons but he dies soon after, his last word being Bosh (354). The lovers manage to repair the ship and sail it away, to be rescued by a passing ship. In the end, they each demonstrate their true natures as moral and capable individuals who reject Larsen's crass individualism for the higher ideals of society. The ending, in which they playfully tease each other about sneaking a kiss—Oh!—before the rescue ship comes, is fraught with tensions between the very raw adventure in which they have been engaged, including the ways it has changed them, and their realization that they must now return to the sentimental Victorian parlors of San Francisco.

COMMENTARY

The Sea-Wolf, finished in the fall of 1903, was London's third novel; it was written during a great period of production after the Klondike. *Children of the Frost* (1902) and *The Faith of Men* (1904) were collections of short stories; an instant world classic was *The Call of the Wild* (1903); *The People of the Abyss* (1903) was London's socialist exposé of the lives of the British poor; a provocative study of modern love was coauthored with ANNA STRUNSKY as *The Kempton-Wace Letters* (1903). *The Sea-Wolf* is an adventure tale but also a philosophical novel, as it puts into play turn-of-the-century cul-

tural conflicts such as NATURALISM and ROMANTICISM, INDIVIDUALISM versus SOCIALISM, gender roles including ANDROGYNY, ethics versus biology, and the conscious/unconscious opposition of modern psychology. It questions models of traditional ethics as well as newer perspectives like EVOLUTION. London includes his responses to late 19th- and early 20th-century philosophers and scientists such as FRIEDRICH NIETZSCHE and CHARLES DARWIN. London also explores new definitions of sexuality and gender, drawing on analysis of the modern male personality such as that of SIGMUND FREUD.

In January 1904, London left for KOREA to cover the RUSSO-JAPANESE WAR for the *EXAMINER* (SAN FRANCISCO). His marriage to BESS MADDERN LONDON was rapidly deteriorating, and he welcomed the excuse to leave the country. He left his manuscript of *The Sea-Wolf* with his new love and soon-to-be second wife, CHARMIAN KITTREDGE, and his friend, the poet GEORGE STERLING, to see through page proofs and serialization in *Century Magazine* from January through November 1904. It was published in book form by MACMILLAN in October 1904.

There are actually five different versions of *The Sea-Wolf*, beginning with London's manuscript, which was charred during the 1906 SAN FRANCISCO EARTHQUAKE and fire and is now a conservator's curiosity at the HUNTINGTON LIBRARY in San Marino, California. In order to secure copyright, Macmillan brought out a paper-bound edition based on the manuscript (a copy of which is in the University of Virginia library). In its version, *Century* made a number of changes, mostly eliminating profanity and depictions of brutality, and when Macmillan brought out its book edition (now with three copyrights, which would come back to haunt London later in legal battles), London heavily revised the page proofs and paid for the changes, trying to return the manuscript to its pre–*Century Magazine* form. In his Riverside Edition of *The Sea-Wolf* (1964), Matthew Bruccoli notes that there are "thousands of differences between the serial and book versions" (1), and that he finds it impossible to determine which were deletions ordered by the magazine's censors and which were added by London in the summer of 1904. But using London's corrected typescripts, galleys, and marked copy of the book, he was able to restore 16 changes London made. He also reinstates London's experimental present-tense style in chapters 6 through 14, which was changed to the past tense by *Century*. As Bruccoli notes, "In its book form *The Sea-Wolf* begins as a memoir and becomes a diary, but in the serial it is narrated as a completed story in the past. This change in the design of the book is not the result of carelessness, but a deliberate effect introduced by the author to produce a sense of immediacy"(2).

Despite the censorship, London cleverly managed to insert some erotic elements that the censors would miss, as with the comic erecting of the mast in chapter 37:

> I called to her, and the mast moved easily and accurately. Straight toward the square hole of the step the square butt descended; . . . Square fitted into square. The mast was stepped.
>
> I raised a shout, and she ran down to see. In the yellow lantern light we peered at what we had accomplished. We looked at each other, and our hands felt their way and clasped. The eyes of both us, I think, were moist with the joy of success.
>
> "It was done so easily after all," I remarked. "All the work was in the preparation."
>
> "And all the wonder in the completion," Maud added. "I can scarcely bring myself to realize that that great mast is really up and in; that you have lifted it from the water, swung it through the air, and deposited it here where it belongs." (349–350)

The Sea-Wolf remains popular and critically acclaimed, having never gone out of print. It has also been the inspiration for many FILM ADAPTATIONS. (Hobart Bosworth's 1913 film *The Sea-Wolf* was the first full-length U.S. feature film.) While early reviewers did complain of its "excess of brutality" (*New York Times*), they also praised its characterization of Wolf Larsen and its "irresistible" suspense (*Argonaut*). Larsen is one of London's most memorable characters—a heroic villain with echoes of Shakespeare's Hamlet, JOHN MILTON's Satan, HERMAN MELVILLE's Ahab, Nietzsche's

Übermensch, and Robert Browning's Caliban. He is heroic because he questions the terms upon which life is lived, and villainous because he bends these terms only to benefit himself, and even then has no satisfaction, like the Misfit in Flannery O'Connor's "A Good Man Is Hard to Find."

Opposed to Wolf is an idealistic young couple who must develop the strength and maturity to best him. It is extremely improbable that the "dean of American letters" and the "first lady of American poetry" are thrown together by chance on the high seas, but what they symbolize is important: They are representatives of enlightened social ethics. They may accept ideas like Darwinian evolution and DETERMINISM (and we must remember they are the novel's breeding pair who adapt to survive), but they have more than just the material world to draw on. Though some readers complain that the characters seem merely to stand for ideas, and that they spend an inordinate amount of time in philosophical discussion, the novel's exploration of the transforming values of the modern era make it one of London's most significant works, a drama of ideas that turns abstract philosophical and literary ideas into scenes of intensely physical survival. In this sense it predicts *Martin Eden.* London believed Larsen, like Martin Eden, was a warning against the individualism of Nietzsche, but neither was generally read that way. He wrote to Mary Austin: "In the very beginning of my writing career, I attacked Nietzsche and his super-man idea. This was in *The Sea-Wolf.* Lots of people read *The Sea-Wolf,* no one discovered that it was an attack upon the superman idea" (*Letters,* 1,513). The problem is that despite the virtues of Van Weyden and Brewster, the larger-than-life Larsen steals every scene.

Larsen is both a romantic and a naturalistic figure. Like the lone romantic hero, he is sensitive, intelligent, arrogant, uninhibited as to social mores, and ultimately pathological—he is thus also an early version of the alienated 20th-century man who lacks purpose and direction (except for his fight with death, his brother, Captain Death Larsen). With no meaningful relationships, Wolf revels in cruelty and nihilism, though he is not satisfied. How can he be, with only himself as a reason for living? As Charmian London describes him:

"The superman is anti-social in his tendencies, and in these days of our complex society and sociology he cannot be successful in his hostile aloofness" (Charmian London, *Book of Jack London*, 2: 57). Larsen has not learned, as Conway Zirkle observes, that "strength was increased by cooperation, by union" (331). The atavistic individual, the lone wolf, is doomed to extinction.

From the point of view of its other hero, Humphrey Van Weyden, *The Sea-Wolf* is a bildungsroman with themes of initiation and of death and rebirth. Humphrey must complement his intellectual and moral strengths with new physical strengths and a much-expanded sense of reality. In both a socialist and a Darwinian sense, the importance of "the group," with its evolutionary imperatives for survival evolving into social virtues such as altruism, cooperation, even self-sacrifice, is justified in *The Sea-Wolf* as providing the foundation of real power. "Sissy" Van Weyden may have to grow his muscles, but his innate adaptability, intelligence, optimism, willingness to work with a partner, and capacity to love mark him as evolutionarily fit. Larsen is drawn toward Death, but Van Weyden matures to look forward to the future with his mate; as he becomes a whole man, Larsen declines, the two courses converging when he saves Maud Brewster from Larsen when he attempts to rape her. From this point on Larsen's power slips away as the couple ensure their survival.

Van Weyden's development, like Larsen's decline, reflects the ideas of Freud in the sense that, as Thomas R. Tietze has pointed out, the novel follows a full-grown man—who has been raised by women and supported by his father's money—coming into conflict with a father-figure, a "self-made individuality." Van Weyden has never seen raw masculinity, but London delineates a classic Oedipal struggle which Humphrey successfully completes. As Tietze frames it:

Here we have the infant drawn from a liquid environment (following screams of women on the sinking ferry) rubbed into life by an effeminate male, hurting himself when "a puff of wind" throws him down, learning to walk all over again, and defeating a bully by sitting opposite him and whetting the blade of his phallic knife until the other retreats in fear. (Is it too obvious a symbol that Hump has obtained his knife by trading some milk for it?) (Tietze, "Reply to 'Yuletide on Endeavor Island'")

Van Weyden certainly seems to experience his emergence onto the deck as his birth:

I seemed swinging in a mighty rhythm. . . . My rhythm grew shorter and shorter. . . . I could scarcely catch my breath, so fiercely was I impelled through the heavens. The gong thundered more frequently and more furiously. I grew to await it with a nameless dread. Then it seemed as though I were being dragged over rasping sands, white and hot in the sun. . . . I gasped, caught my breath painfully, and opened my eyes. Two men were kneeling beside me, working over me. My mighty rhythm was the lift and forward plunge of a ship on the sea. The terrific gong was a frying-pan, hanging on the wall, that rattled and clattered with each leap of the ship. The rasping, scorching sands were a man's hard hands chafing my naked chest. . . . (*Sea-Wolf*, 12)

Van Weyden's adolescence is shown by his admiration of Larsen's physique, who displays himself naked to Van Weyden and invites him to touch his muscles. "Now," observes Tietze, "whether the intrusion is 'believable' or not, Hump's psychological development *requires* the miraculous introduction of Maud" (13). Significantly, she first appears dressed as a boy. In the rape scene, Van Weyden uses his knife and "slays" the "father." As Sam Baskett has pointed out, Humphrey expresses the need for psychic androgyny—explaining Brewster's place in the novel. As Baskett notes, at the time of the composition of *The Sea-Wolf*, London was writing in letters to Charmian Kittredge and Anna Strunsky about his own need for an ideal mate who would help him express "the woman in me" (Baskett, "Sea-Change in *The Sea-Wolf*," 9). Though AMBROSE BIERCE rejected the love element altogether, "with its absurd suppressions and impossible proprieties" (quoted in Foner, *Jack*

London, American Rebel, 61), the Darwinian and Freudian contexts make clear why Brewster must enter the story.

CHARACTERS

Humphrey Van Weyden Humphrey is a young literary gentleman of San Francisco who has had some widespread recognition, publishing reviews in the *Atlantic Monthly* and earning the title "dean of American letters." This title suggests London is comparing him to William Dean Howells (1837–1920), who was actually called this and who was an extremely influential editor of the *Atlantic Monthly.* Howells championed diverse literary figures including Henrik Ibsen, ÉMILE ZOLA, Leo Tolstoy, Hamlin Garland, STEPHEN CRANE, Emily Dickinson, Mary E. Wilkins Freeman, Paul Laurence Dunbar, Sarah Orne Jewett, Charles W. Chesnutt, Abraham Cahan, and FRANK NORRIS, helping establish their literary reputations, if not Jack London's. Despite his diverse interests, Howells's notion of REALISM was at odds with London's NATURALISM. But from a mere critic of life Van Weyden grows into a man; in his conflicts with Wolf Larsen and the other men aboard the *Ghost,* by the time his potential mate, Maud Brewster, arrives, he has shed his effeminacy and strengthened his body and spirit so that he is able to defeat Larsen and win Maud Brewster.

Wolf Larsen Captain of the *Ghost* and the antagonist to Humphrey Van Weyden. A Dane, Larsen has been at sea most of his life, and what he has learned there he has fashioned into his own philosophy of determinism and materialism. Though he loves ideas and rough adventure—even sadism—he is a very well-read man with whom Van Weyden debates literature, theology, philosophy, evolution, and morality. Wolf's violent anger causes him to act the way he does, but it symbolically kills him in the form of a brain tumor. Despite his cruel nature and unspeakable acts, Wolf is allowed by London to deliver some stinging indictments of Western society and to enjoy some moments in which he feels fully alive. He aptly criticizes Van Weyden's social class and his lack of masculinity. However, he is an extreme character who embodies the harshest individualistic implications of Nietzsche and Spencer.

Maud Brewster Though poet Maud Brewster is first described by Humphrey Van Weyden as as delicate as fine Dresden china, Maud, like Humphrey, finds sources of strength and capability within her in her ordeal on the *Ghost,* and she proves an able and brave mate to Humphrey as they escape to Endeavour Island and refit the *Ghost* to take them home. Though she at first represents the best of bourgeois Victorian culture in her refinement (her best-known poem is called "A Kiss Endured"), she becomes an idealized woman whose bravery and strength, in addition to her poetic talent, present her as the New Woman of her era.

Dying mate At the beginning of Van Weyden's time aboard the *Ghost,* he witnesses the death and sea burial of an unnamed mate who had weakened himself with debauchery in San Francisco before sailing. Larsen curses him instead of mourns him. Van Weyden is soon given the man's job.

Death Larsen Wolf Larsen's brother and captain of the steamer *Macedonia.* Death hunts his brother over some unspecified conflict between them; their hatred for each other is legendary. Death eventually catches up with the *Ghost,* and defeats Wolf, leaving his him marooned on Endeavour Island with his disabled ship; all the while Wolf's death draws closer to him.

Thomas Mugridge Mugridge is the ship's cook, an ignorant, dirty, and debased Cockney who becomes Van Weyden's tormentor. He is called "cooky" by Larsen and "the doctor" or "Tommy" by the men. He makes Van Weyden call him "Mister Mugridge." He torments Van Weyden until Van Weyden fights back. But because Mugridge is so often the butt of jokes onboard, Van Weyden does not need revenge. Beaten by Larsen and his fellow men, Mugridge is also injured by events during a storm. He is finally thrown overboard on a rope and dragged behind the ship; he has his foot amputated by a shark and barely survives.

Harrison A "clumsy-looking country boy" and a boat-puller (61). Harrison is ordered by Johansen to climb the halyards and climb to the end of a crossbeam to free a sail. He falls and is nearly killed, which Van Weyden blames on Larsen's disregard for human life.

Henderson A sailor lost in the storm.

Holyoak Sailor rescued in the storm by a passing ship; he is later brought back aboard the *Ghost* by Larsen.

Jock Horner Jock Horner is quiet and easygoing, soft-spoken and polite, but he kills his boat-steerer. Horner is seen by Van Weyden as an example of the innate brutishness of the men.

Johnson Sailor whose name Larsen deliberately mispronounces as "Yonson," and an antagonist of Larsen's who teams up with another sailor, Leach, to attempt a mutiny. Johnson is a "man of the heavy Scandinavian type" who pulls Van Weyden from the sea and massages him into consciousness. He gives Humphrey his clothes. Van Weyden at first admires his "straightforwardness and manliness" as he is taunted by Larsen as a "squarehead," but later views him as dangerous (13). Johnson tries to desert at Yokohama, but when the *Ghost* comes upon him and Leach, they are left adrift in a small boat by Larsen.

Johansen The sailor whom Larsen orders to sew the body of the dead mate in a sail for burial; he was promoted to mate in his place. Johansen helps Larsen give Johnson a terrible beating. He is murdered by Leach and presumably thrown overboard, as his body is never found.

Kelly A sailor who is lost in the storm along with Henderson, Holyoak, and Williams.

Kerfoot A seal hunter who fights with Latimer, "vociferating, bellowing, waving his arms, and curs-

ing like a fiend, and all because of a disagreement with another hunter as to whether a seal pup knew instinctively how to swim" (41).

Latimer A hunter described as a "Yankee-looking fellow with shrewd, narrow-slitted eyes" (41). Latimer is involved in many fights in the novel, and he is described as excessively violent. However, it is he who pulls Larsen to safety after the fight in the forecastle.

Black The hunter Latimer's boat-steerer, who helps catch Mugridge to cast him off at the end of a rope.

George Leach Leach helps Johnson lead a mutiny. Though he is young, he has a criminal background. Van Weyden replaces him as cabin boy. He violently hates Larsen and is beaten repeatedly by him. Leach is lost during the storm but is found on a passing ship. When he plans to desert at Yokohama, he and Johnson are left to drift at sea by Larsen.

Louis Louis, who warns and advises Van Weyden, is a sailor and "a rotund and jovial-faced Nova Scotia Irishman." He tells Van Weyden, "'Ah, my boy,' he shook his head ominously at me, ''tis the worst schooner ye could iv selected, nor were ye drunk at the time as was I. 'Tis sealin' is the sailor's paradise—on other ships than this. The mate was the first, but mark me words, there'll be more dead men before the trip is done with. Hist, now, between you an' meself and the stanchion there, this Wolf Larsen is a regular devil, an' the *Ghost*'ll be a hell-ship like she's always ben since he had hold iv her'" (56).

Matt McCarthy Leach's father. Leach asks Van Weyden to contact him in San Francisco if he is killed by Larsen, which he is.

Mr. Haskins A fellow-survivor of the boat Maud Brewster arrives in; he tells her of Larsen's murder of Leach and Johnson.

Nilson A sailor, lost in the storm but recovered from a passing ship.

Oofty-Oofty A KANAKA or POLYNESIAN sailor. He radiates a strange sort of calm throughout the novel but is also capable of violence; for example, he helps catch Mugridge and holds the rope as Mugridge is thrown overboard on a rope.

Parsons A sailor.

Smoke A sailor not afraid to speak up to Larsen.

Standish A hunter who quarrels with Larsen about losing Harrison, his boat-puller.

Williams A sailor lost in the storm.

FURTHER READING

Baskett, Sam S. "Sea-Change in *The Sea-Wolf*." In *American Literary Realism, 1870–1910* 24, no. 2 (winter 1992): 5–22.

Bender, Bert. "Jack London in the Tradition of American Sea Fiction." In *American Neptune* 46 (summer 1986): 188–199.

Derrick, Scott. "Making a Heterosexual Man: Gender, Sexuality, and Narrative in the Fiction of Jack London." In *Rereading Jack London*. Edited by Leonard Cassuto and Jeanne Campbell Reesman. Stanford, Calif.: Stanford University Press, 1996, 110–129.

Dooley, Patrick K. "'The Strenuous Mood': William James's 'Energies in Men' and Jack London's *The Sea-Wolf*." In *American Literary Realism, 1870–1910* 34, no. 1 (fall 2001): 18–28.

Foner, Phillip S., ed. *Jack London, American Rebel: A Collection of His Social Writings Together with an Extensive Study of the Man and His Times.* New York: Citadel Press, 1947.

Heckerl, David K. "'Violent Movements of Business': The Moral Nihilist as Economic Man in Jack London's *The Sea-Wolf*." In *Twisted from the Ordinary: Essays on American Literary Naturalism.* Edited by Mary E. Papke. Knoxville: University of Tennessee Press, 2003, 202–216.

Kingman, Russ. *A Pictorial Life of Jack London.* New York: Crown, 1979.

Labor, Earle, and Jeanne Campbell Reesman. *Jack London.* Revised Edition. New York: Twayne, 1994, 58–63.

"Literary Notes: Jack London's Remarkable Book." Review of *The Sea-Wolf.* In *Argonaut* (San Francisco) 55 (14 November 1904): 311.

London, Charmian Kittredge. *The Book of Jack London.* 2 vols. New York: Century, 1921.

London, Jack. *The Letters of Jack London.* 3 vols. Edited by Earle Labor, Robert C. Leitz III, and I. Milo Shepard. Stanford, Calif.: Stanford University Press, 1988.

———. *The Sea-Wolf.* New York: Macmillan, 1904. (All references cited in text refer to this edition.)

———. *The Sea-Wolf.* Edited by Matthew J. Bruccoli. Riverside Editions. Boston: Houghton Mifflin, 1964.

Nolte, Carl. "Foggy Ferry Crash Remembered." *San Francisco Chronicle* (1 December 2001).

Oliveri, Vinnie. "Sex, Gender, and Death in *The Sea-Wolf*." In *Pacific Coast Philology* 38 (2003): 99–115.

Papa, James A., Jr. "Canvas and Steam: Historical Conflict in Jack London's *The Sea-Wolf*." In *Midwest Quarterly* 40, no. 3 (spring 1999): 1–7.

Qualtiere, Michael. "Nietzschean Psychology in London's *The Sea-Wolf*." In *Western American Literature* 16, no. 4 (winter 1982): 261–278.

"The Sea-Wolf." New York Times Saturday Review of Books and Art (12 November 1904), 768–769.

Tietze, Thomas. "A Reply to 'Yuletide on Endeavour Island.'" In *Jack London Foundation Newsletter* 6, no. 2 (April 1994): n.p.

Watson, Charles N., Jr. "Lucifer on the Quarter-Deck: *The Sea-Wolf*." In *The Novels of Jack London: A Reappraisal.* Madison: University of Wisconsin Press, 1983, 53–78.

Woodward, Robert H. "Jack London's Code of Primitivism." In *Folio* 18 (May 1953): 39–44.

Zirkle, Conway. *Evolution, Marxian Biology, and the Social Scene.* Philadelphia: University of Pennsylvania Press, 1959.

"The Seed of McCoy" (1909)

This strangely haunting story was first published in *Century* 77 (April 1909) and included in *South Sea Tales*. It compares well with "The Chinago" in its portrayal of a hero who is distinguished by the uncanny sense of inner peace in the face of adversity; it accomplishes this by using powerful Christian imagery.

SYNOPSIS

A ship called the *Pyrenees*, loaded with wheat, has caught fire in the hold as it tries to navigate the dangerous PAUMOTO ARCHIPELAGO. Near Pitcairn Island, home of the *Bounty* mutineers and their Tahitian wives, as the wheat smoulders and the decks grow hotter and hotter, an old man boards the vessel. He is the chief magistrate of Pitcairn and a great-grandson of McCoy of the *Bounty*. He agrees to pilot the ship to a safe harbor, but he will only get them to its entrance; the captain must steer it into the harbor. He brings food and a sense of calm to the terrified sailors, as he gazes upon them: "The glance from his liquid brown eyes swept over them like a benediction, soothing them, wrapping them about as in the mantle of a great peace. 'How long has she been afire, Captain?' he asked in a voice so gentle and unperturbed that it was as the cooing of a dove" (*Stories,* 1,358). The more frightened the men become in the days ahead, the more serene is McCoy; he promises them that if they will stick with him they will be saved. When the men talk of mutiny, he warns them about the terrible cost of the MUTINY OF THE *BOUNTY*: afterward, as they descended into anarchy on Pitcairn, "God had hidden His face" from them for the wickedness (*Stories,* 1,377–1,378). McCoy relates that after the first generation on Pitcairn was succeeded by the half-breed children, a new and peaceful POLYNE-SIAN society evolved, embodied in the Christ-like figure of McCoy himself. He does save the ship, and at the end he is eager to return home.

COMMENTARY

Despite his manly physique, still superb after he has grown old, McCoy shows feminine and child-like qualities that puzzle the sailors. It is interesting that one of London's most appealing heroes is both feminized and cross-racial, but this is in keeping with his questioning of race and gender in the South Seas stories and the later SONOMA novels such as *The Valley of the Moon*. There is a bounty of biblical imagery in the South Seas stories, in part due to London's research in MISSIONARY accounts, but in that London did not believe in GOD it sometimes puzzles his readers. Nothing is as heavily Christian as "The Seed of McCoy," save the portions of his never published "Christ Novel" that appear in *The Star Rover* in fragments. McCoy is presented as a symbol of Christ, and the story is loaded with references to faith in Him and to the BIBLE. The fact that McCoy, as the pilot, tells the Captain that he can lead him but not take him home, echoes Christ's teachings. When he finds the men starving, he produces food. He asks for their faith, and against their will they give it to him. As the decks turn into burning hell, McCoy calmly tries landing after landing. He manages to calm the sailors, even though they have "hell-fire hot beneath their feet" (*Stories,* 1,375). His voice is repeatedly described as "dove-like." He tells Captain Davenport "'I'll stay with you, Captain'" (*Stories,* 1,379). It is really his spirit that speaks to them, not merely the voice of a strange pilot: "McCoy spoke simply; but it was not what he spoke. It was his personality that spoke more eloquently than any word he could utter. It was an alchemy of soul occultly subtile [sic] and profoundly deep—a mysterious emanation of the spirit, seductive, sweetly humble, and terribly imperious. It was illumination in the dark crypts of their souls, a compulsion of purity and gentleness vastly greater than that which resided in the shining, death-spitting revolvers of the officers" (*Stories,* 1,376). When Captain Davenport is driven by fear and frustration, after they miss several possible landings, he starts to curse McCoy but stops: Though Davenport is not religious, "McCoy's presence was a rebuke to blasphemies" (*Stories,* 1,379). And this is just a small sampling of all the Christian allusions in the story.

CHARACTERS

McCoy   Chief magistrate of Pitcairn Island and *Bounty* mutineer descendant, McCoy appears out of nowhere to save a ship on fire. The words used to describe him all render him Christlike: peaceful, beneficent, gentle, soft, ineffable, benignant, placid. He counsels the Captain to head for Mangareva first, which they miss in a storm, but he guides them safely through the Paumotos to port at Fakarava.

Captain Davenport Captain of the *Pyrenees,* Davenport faces a life or death crisis when the wheat in the hold of the ship catches fire; though he first doubts that McCoy can help him, he later realizes what a miracle McCoy has wrought.

Mr. Konig First mate aboard the *Pyrenees,* he at first laughs harshly at McCoy's offer, but then introduces himself and asks whether McCoy is a *Bounty* descendant. He is angry when McCoy explains that there is no beach or anchorage at Pitcairn. The mate is also the one who refers to the burning ship's cabin as "'the anteroom of hell'" (*Stories,* 1,361).

"Shin Bones" (1918)

Completed at Waikiki in July 1916, only a few months before London died, and posthumously published as "In the Cave of the Dead" in COS-MOPOLITAN 65 (November 1918), "Shin Bones" is a nostalgic story in which present and past are brought together in a way that mourns the lost past and asserts the finality of death. It is included in London's last collection of Hawaiian tales, *On the Makaloa Mat.*

SYNOPSIS

A Hawaiian prince who has been educated at Oxford and believes himself a thoroughly modern man, Prince Akuli, tells his history to a white friend visiting his island while the two of them wait beside the prince's broken-down car on the side of the road. Descended from the *ali'i,* or Hawaiian royalty, Prince Akuli is the last in his family's line. He is merely a figurehead in the newly modernized HAWAI'I; he rides about in a limousine. He explains

some Hawaiian burial customs to his listener. His mother, Hiwilani, insists on maintaining the old ways, especially gathering and saving the bones of ancestors. Through sorcery she charms her servant, Ahuna, into revealing the location where he buried her mother and grandfather; Ahuna was supposed to protect the knowledge, but he accompanies Akuli to retrieve them. Hiwilana has bribed Akuli with the promise of an Oxford education. Now returned from his studies, he tells of gathering the bones from the secret burial cave in use for 800 years. While in the cave, Akuli desires the shinbone of an ancestor three centuries dead; there is a tragic love story attached to the legend of this ancestor, Keaho. Akuli collects the bone and also the shinbone of his ancestor's lover, Laulani, and keeps them as personal talismans:

> "To them, those poor pathetic bones, I owe more than to aught else. I became possessed of them in the period of my culminating adolescence. I know they changed the entire course of my life and trend of my mind. They gave to me a modesty and a humility in the world, from which my father's fortune has ever failed to seduce me.
>
> And often, when woman was nigh to winning to the empery of my mind over me, I sought Laulani's shin-bone. And often, when lusty manhood stung me into feeling over-proud and lusty, I consulted the spearhead remnant of Keola, one-time swift runner, and mighty wrestler and lover, and thief of the wife of a king. The contemplation of them has ever been of profound aid to me, and you might well say that I have founded my religion or practice of living upon them." (*Stories,* 2,394–2,395)

However, in the end, he also recognizes that his actions were futile:

> "I believe in no mystery stuff of old time nor of the kahunas. And yet, I saw in that cave things which I dare not name to you, and which I, since old Ahuna died, alone of the living know. I have no children. With me my long line ceases. This is the twentieth century, and we stink of gasolene. Nevertheless these other and

nameless things shall die with me. I shall never revisit the burial-place. Nor in all time to come will any man gaze upon it through living eyes unless the quakes of earth rend the mountains asunder and spew forth the secrets contained in the hearts of the mountains." (*Stories*, 2,394)

Akuli's father, Kanau, also collects bones, but he is thoroughly modernized in that he cares not for their meaning but for their worth; he sells what he finds to invest in sugar and bet on horses. Kanau has absorbed the very worst of English and American entrepreneurs, as, says critic Tanya Walsh, "he literally sells his heritage" (Walsh, "Historical Discourses," 198). Akuli rejects his father's views. Yet though he mourns modernity's effect on the past, he himself is not comfortable with Hawaiian tradition, as is apparent when he throws away the lei the old woman has made him as soon as she leaves.

COMMENTARY

As Walsh has pointed out, "'Shin Bones' reveals London's concern with history, how we know it, how we interpret it, and how we preserve it" (Walsh, "Historical Discourses," 193). In the story there are two primary historians, Prince Akuli and his mother. Due to his education, Akuli's historical perspective is Anglocentric. His mother's point of view is ethnocentric too, but anchored in Hawai'i's ancient past. As Walsh notes, ironically, "Akuli's historical discourse accomplishes quite the opposite of his Anglocentrism; it creates a void from which his 'Hawaiianness' emerges" (Walsh, "Historical Discourses," 195). At the same time, his mother's feverish insistence on saving her past is a result of seeing it progressively diminished by white settlement in Hawai'i. Finally, the unnamed HAOLE narrator has his point of view: He condemns the British colonization and American annexation of Hawai'i. His sense of the loss of Hawaiian identity is a tragic one. There is another perspective, that of the old Hawaiian woman who weaves a lei for Akuli; she recounts Akuli's history to the narrator. And finally there is Jack London's perspective, which appears in the obvious presence of his Hawaiian name, "Lakana," in the name of the fictional island "Lankanaii." Does he mean that the

story also speaks to him personally? He was fascinated with Hawaiian lore but must also have been looking inward that last summer as his body entered into the final stages of kidney disease. And we can see the influence of his reading of CARL JUNG on the story—it contains archetypes, myth, allusions to the collective unconscious. On a more factual level, the description of the side of the island where the caves are as an "Iron-Bound Coast" suggests Na Pali Coast of the island of KAUAI, where the remote Kalalau Valley is located—the valley in which Koolau the Leper hid out. There is even mention in "Shin Bones" of an old leper hiding in the foliage.

Names are important throughout the story. Akuli's recollection of the poet "Don Juan Byron" reflects his Anglocentric education. As Walsh says, "It is true that Lord Byron, the poet's cousin, commandeered a ship to Hawaii in 1825, but calling the poet 'Don Juan Byron' creates a literary parallel between the ironic hero of the epic poem and the failed, cynical protagonist of London's story: a Prince Squid (the English translation of Akuli) who is not really a prince" (Walsh, "Historical Discourses," 196). The narrator is careful to point this out more than once, perhaps alluding to the historical and psychic deeps the prince must traverse to find his history. There are other symbolic names and several literary allusions, especially to TENNYSON's "Idylls of the King" and its portrayal of Arthur, Lancelot, and Guinevere. But despite all the Western allusions, the story maintains a distinctly Hawaiian tone. As Walsh points out, London had obviously done his research on Hawaiian burial customs, which entailed complex rituals. Graves of the *ali'i* were secret, known only to the person responsible for the burial. Hawaiians believed that each individual possessed *mana*, or power; *ali'i* possessed the most *mana*, which remains in the bones of the deceased and can be harnessed by the one who had them. Bones were venerated and guarded, sometimes even deified: "In the nineteenth century, King Kalakaua started the bone-hunting craze" still going on at the time that the story is set, 1916. "Relatives would take the bones as keepsakes, as Hiwilani does, to discover their own history" (Walsh, "Historical Discourses," 197). This is why Hiwilani desires these sacred bones.

Like "The House of Pride" and "Koolau the Leper," "Shin Bones" contains a not-so-subtle critique of how Hawai'i was forever changed by colonization. As Walsh puts it, "All of the history of Hawai'i figures prominently in the weave of London's 'Shin Bones.' Behind the behavior of Prince Akuli, Hiwilani, and Kanau is the British and American influence and its varying effects on each individual: Hiwilani longs for her lost heritage; Kanau is completely absorbed by the white hegemony. Prince Akuli faces the nightmare of history and the nightmare of the future as well, for he is a modern man" (Walsh, "Historical Discourses," 199).

CHARACTERS

narrator The narrator is an American white man who knew Akuli when they both served in the Black Watch regiment of the British army in South Africa. He listens intently to Akuli's tale of the ancient past and the bones that it preserved; though he occasionally finds the contrast between the modern prince and the past amusing, he experiences a sense of tragedy as well. The dialogic structure of the story, with a white listener and a Hawaiian storyteller, also appears in "The Water Baby," where the white man's name is "Lakana."

Prince Akuli Prince Akuli has no real legal right to his title, the monarchy having been deposed by the Americans, but he is descended from one of the most sacred and noble Polynesian bloodlines, all the way back to demigods from SAMOA in the far past, but he has become modern from his education at Oxford: "And so, out of all incests and lusts of the primitive cultures and beast-man's gropings toward the stature of manhood, out of all red murders, and brute battlings, and matings with the younger brothers of the demigods, world-polished, Oxford-accented, twentieth century to the tick of the second, comes Prince Akuli, Prince Squid, pure-veined Polynesian, a living bridge across the thousand centuries, comrade, friend, and fellow-traveller out of his wrecked seven-thousand-dollar limousine, marooned with me in a begonia paradise fourteen hundred feet above the sea" (*Stories*, 2,378).

Hiwilani As Prince Akuli says of his mother, "'In her last years Hiwilani went back to the old ways, and to the old beliefs—in secret, of course. And, believe me, she was some collector herself. You should have seen her bones. She had them all about her bedroom, in big jars, and they constituted most all her relatives, except a half-dozen or so that Kanau beat her out of by getting to them first. The way the pair of them used to quarrel about those bones was awe-inspiring.'" Akuli says "'it gave me the creeps, when I was a boy, to go into that big, for-ever-twilight room of hers, and know that . . . in all the jars were the preserved bone-remnants of the shadowy dust of the ancestors whose seed had come down and been incorporated in the living, breathing me'" (*Stories*, 2,375). In going native, Hiwilani also sleeps on mats on the hard floor. She bribes Akuli and Ahuna to retrieve her dead mother and grandfather's bones.

Kanau Husband of Hiwilani who competes with her for bones; but unlike her, he is merely interested in money to finance his life of leisure, and when he can get bones he coldly sells them to the highest bidder.

Ahuna "'Old Ahuna was one of the real old ones with the hall-mark on him and branded into him of faithful born-slave service. He knew more about my mother's family, and my father's, than did both of them put together. And he knew, what no living other knew, the burial-place of centuries, where were hid the bones of most of her ancestors and of Kanau's. Kanau couldn't worm it out of the old fellow, who looked upon Kanau as an apostate,'" says Akuli (*Stories*, 2,379–2,380). Yet through some sorcery, Hiwilani charms Ahuna into revealing the secret of where he buried her mother and grandfather's bones.

old Hawaiian woman By the side of the road where Akuli and the narrator talk, an old woman makes a lei in honor of the prince: "The ancient crone was making a dearest-loved *lei* of the fruit of the *hala* which is the screw-pine or pandanus of the South Pacific" (*Stories*, 2,376). Though he does not let on, he abhors the lei and throws it away when she is gone.

FURTHER READING

Walsh, Tanya. "Historical Discourses in Jack London's 'Shin Bones.'" In *Rereading Jack London*. Edited by Leonard Cassuto and Jeanne Campbell Reesman. Stanford, Calif.: Stanford University Press, 1996, 192–204.

"The Son of the Wolf" (1899)

"The Son of the Wolf," first published in OVERLAND MONTHLY 33 (April 1899), was one of London's first major publications. It contains elements that would go on to characterize many of his KLONDIKE stories: the clash of cultures between NATIVES and whites, the threat of great change to Native ways because of the newcomers, interracial marriages, and the all-important TOTEM of WOLVES. London would soon take up the nickname "Wolf," using it to sign letters to his friend GEORGE STERLING; Sterling's nickname was "Greek."

SYNOPSIS

A frontiersman and prospector in the YUKON, "in the old days, before the country was stampeded and staked by a tidal-wave" of newcomers, "Scruff" MacKenzie "bore the earmarks of a frontier birth and a frontier life. His face was stamped with twenty-five years of incessant struggle with Nature in her wildest moods,—the last two, the wildest and hardest of all, having been spent in groping for the gold which lies in the shadow of the Arctic Circle" (*Stories*, 195). He comes to desire a wife. He arrives in the village of Chief Thling-Tinneh of the Upper Tanana Sticks, a tribe known for killing any whites who wandered near them, mingles with the Natives, and throws a potlatch, joining in their games and sports. He approaches them with a combination of "humility, familiarity, sang-froid, and insolence" (*Stories*, 196). MacKenzie shows off his marksmanship, aware that he must best the men of the tribe for the hand of the chief's daughter, Zarinksa. The camp rings with his exploits, such

as killing a moose at 600 yards. But when he asks the chief for the hand of his daughter, Zarinska, the warriors mutter; MacKenzie in return offers the chief lavish gifts for his daughter. However, the chief refuses his suit, saying "'O White Man, whom we have named Moose-Killer, also known as the Wolf, and the Son of the Wolf! We know thou comest of a mighty race; we are proud to have thee our potlatch-guest; but the king-salmon does not mate with the dog-salmon, nor the Raven with the Wolf'" (*Stories*, 199). MacKenzie objects that he has seen many daughters of the Raven in the camps of the Wolf. When a messenger enters to say that the people will have no part of this marriage, MacKenzie throws him into the snow. He warns the chief that if he is attacked or even killed many of his men will die too. The chief relents. When MacKenzie brings Zarinska to the center of the camp, he is cursed by the shaman. The shaman calls him a devil who has no right to marry into the tribe, whose totem is "Jelchs," the Raven. The shaman reviles him and all white men, calling upon the Native god, the "Fire-bringer," to punish him. At that moment a huge display of the aurora borealis appears. But the chief denounces the shaman as an evil fraud, urges the tribe to accept the Wolf. He placates two of her Native suitors. Nevertheless, the men are for war, and there is a battle. "Scruff" fights his attackers and two are killed, one, the Bear, by one of their own with a stray arrow, and the other, the shaman, by MacKenzie's knife, thrown full force at the shaman's neck when he draws a bow on MacKenzie. He is able to make peace with the remainder of the tribesmen. He carries off his bride and leaves Chief Thling-Tinneh a promise: "'Thling-Tinneh, I now give thee this rifle a second time. If, in the days to come, thou shouldst journey to the Country of the Yukon, know thou that there shall always be a place and much food by the fire of the Wolf. The night is now passing into the day. I go, but I may come again. And for the last time, remember the Law of the Wolf!'" (*Stories*, 208).

COMMENTARY

"The Son of the Wolf" is an odd combination of Anglo-Saxonism and respect for Native culture. It has the feel of a Native trickster tale, but its hero is a white man. While MacKenzie boasts and makes demands from the tribe, it is important to note that he first tries to secure his bride not by fighting for her, but by following the tribe's custom, offering gifts to her father, putting on a potlatch for the tribe, and demonstrating his strength—his worthiness as her mate. When this fails, he does fight, and he wins. Unlike most Klondike stories that involve Natives, this one does not mourn the ascendancy of the white man but glorifies it; again, not only can MacKenzie adapt to Native ways, but he can always call upon his superior weapons and his sense of power in his white totem, the Wolf. And present here too is the sad theme of tribes being decimated when their women marry white men and leave.

The story is characterized by its use of totems, as well as classical allusions; the Raven "Fire-bringer" god is called a "Prometheus" by the narrator. Though he thinks of his situation as like that of a knight and a lady of old, reflecting Western MYTHOLOGY, when he approaches the chief to ask for his daughter he claims the Raven himself told him to do so, showing his knowledge of the Natives' religion.

CHARACTERS

"Scruff" MacKenzie   "He was a sturdy traveler, and his wolf-dogs could work harder and travel farther on less grub than any other team in the Yukon. Three weeks later he strode into a hunting-camp of the Upper Tanana Sticks. They marveled at his temerity; for they had a bad name and had been known to kill white men for as trifling a thing as a sharp ax or a broken rifle. But he went among them single-handed, his bearing being a delicious composite of humility, familiarity, sangfroid, and insolence. It required a deft hand and deep knowledge of the barbaric mind effectually to handle such diverse weapons; but he was a pastmaster in the art, knowing when to conciliate and when to threaten with Jove-like wrath" (*Stories*, 196). When he desires a wife, he importunes Chief Thling-Tinneh for the hand of his daughter, Zarinska. To win her, he must prove his mettle and also respect the tribe's ways.

Chief Thling-Tinneh   The leader of the Upper Tanana Sticks, a tribe known for its fearlessness and ruthlessness when confronted by whites. He is persuaded, against his will, to hand over his daughter after MacKenzie kills two of his men.

Zarinska   The daughter of Chief Thling-Tinneh and the intended of MacKenzie: "In features, form, and poise, answering more nearly to the white man's type of beauty, she was almost an anomaly among her tribal sisters. He would possess her, make her his wife, and name her—ah, he would name her Gertrude! Having thus decided, he rolled over on his side and dropped off to sleep, a true son of his all-conquering race, a Samson among the Philistines" (*Stories*, 197).

Fox and Bear   Two young Native warriors who each desire the hand of Zarinska. They fight MacKenzie for her. Fox is merely bested and shamed by MacKenzie, but Bear is killed by an arrow the shaman intended for MacKenzie.

shaman   The shaman represents the religion and ancient traditions of the Sticks, but he is a figure doomed by modern progress. Even the chief thinks that his magic is fake. He is killed by MacKenzie when he tries to shoot him with an arrow.

"South of the Slot" (1909)

Included in the collection *The Strength of the Strong,* this story was first published in the SATURDAY EVENING POST 181 (May 1909). It is one of London's strongest socialist stories, but it is also a story of ATAVISM in which a sociology professor finds his inner self in the form of a burly WORKING CLASS man; thus, it offers a psychological interpretation as well as the fantasy idea of a doppelganger or alternate existence.

SYNOPSIS

Freddie Drummond, a widely respected sociology professor at the UNIVERSITY OF CALIFORNIA, sometimes goes slumming for his research on "the literature of progress" (*Stories*, 1,580). At first, the working class world feels alien to him, but slowly he adapts to it and eventually adopts a new persona,

"Big Bill" Totts, a leading labor leader (a reference to the actual labor leader "BIG BILL" HAYWOOD, head of the I.W.W.). Soon Drummond/Totts prefers the world of the working class. His knowledge of this world when he is part of it is everything compared to his superficial knowledge before his transformation:

> From doing the thing for the need's sake, he came to doing the thing for the thing's sake. He found himself regretting as the time drew near for him to go back to his lecture-room and his inhibition. And he often found himself waiting with anticipation for the dreamy time to pass when he could cross the Slot and cut loose and play the devil. He was not wicked, but as "Big" Bill Totts he did a myriad things that Freddie Drummond would never have been permitted to do. . . . Freddie Drummond and Bill Totts were two totally different creatures. The desires and tastes and impulses of each ran counter to the other's. Bill Totts could shirk at a job with clear conscience, while Freddie Drummond condemned shirking as vicious, criminal, and un-American, and devoted whole chapters to condemnation of the vice. Freddie Drummond did not care for dancing, but Bill Totts never missed the nights at the various dancing clubs. (*Stories,* 1,584)

Drummond was a rather shallow thinker in his previous life, as Totts becomes not just a thinker but a doer, living instead of talking abstractly of living.

The story opens with a description of "the slot," the iron cable-car track in the center of Market Street in San Francisco as a physical and symbolic metaphor for the division of the classes; to the north is the financial district, the theaters and hotels, the fancy department stores, while on the south side are the slums, factories, and laundries that make up the environment of the urban poor.

Drummond sometimes crosses over the barrier of the slot to do research for books such as his latest one, *The Unskilled Laborer.* Drummond works harder than any in his laborer guise as an employee of the Wilmax Cannery and is even beaten by his "fellows" for making them look lazy. Not surprisingly, he makes few friends; this is even more the

case as he does not use tobacco and beer, dresses neatly, and continues to try too hard. No one among the working class could care less that he is known as the author of such dry economic books as *Mass and Master, The Fallacy of the Inefficient, Women and Work,* and *Labor Tactics and Strategy.*

But when he adopts another persona altogether, Drummond became known as "Big Bill" Totts, who lives up to working class stereotypes: attacking scabs, joining the Longshoremen's Union, and of course drinking, eating, and chasing women with abandon. But Drummond soon feels that his dualistic game will have to stop, as he struggles to contain both personalities. He is both prompted to continue and to end the charade when he meets Mary Condon, a unionist and a tireless campaigner on behalf of her class. Perhaps out of fear of her, Drummond retreats to his class and proposes and wins another woman, Catherine Van Vorst, a college graduate whose wealthy father was once a philosophy professor. Yet once more he visits "south of the slot," encounters Condon, and kisses her passionately.

As the months of labor strife pass, Drummond tries to devote himself to Catherine. Only two weeks away from their wedding, she picks him up in a chauffeured automobile to eat at an elite club. But at the intersection of Kearny and Market Streets, where the slot runs, appears a mob of strikers, scabs, and policemen. Drummond suddenly reverts totally to Totts and leaps into the action, fighting the police and the scabs; he receives a bad head injury as Catherine faints out of shock. When she revives, Catherine sees Mary embrace and kiss Drummond/Totts. Without a glance back at her, they depart down the sidewalk laughing and talking, arm in arm, crossing Market with its slot, and disappear into the slums. Later, we are told, Totts and Condon married and went on to careers leading the International Glove Workers' Union No. 974.

COMMENTARY

"South of the Slot" compares well with *The People of the Abyss* as a piece of socialist writing typical of London. But here, instead of merely assuming a disguise to connect with the lives of the urban poor, a man actually discovers an alternate self. But this is no *Dr. Jekyll and Mr. Hyde:* The man's alter ego is a superior individual and working class hero. As such, the two sides of the personality reflect London's own sense of a writerly, even scholarly self and at the same time a vigorous fighting man—even an "abysmal brute," as London called him—for the socialist cause. Drummond's adaptability is a Darwinian feature of evolutionary fitness, and it also suggests the other stories of "reversion" or atavism of London's, such as "When the World Was Young." The hope suggested by the story is that people can change, can change classes and perspectives, if only they have the curiosity and care to try to do so. After all, London himself rose from the abyss of poverty to worldwide fame, though all along he held fast to his socialist ideas, at least until two years before his death, when he became disillusioned by the SOCIALIST PARTY. But as London would also portray, especially in the SONOMA novels, it is more than anything else the love of a woman that can change a man's values. From being duped by his notion of the working class into trying to become the perfect worker (as in "The Apostate"), the protagonist learns the absurdity of such a desire. Some readers, however, as they objected to the romance element in *The Sea-Wolf,* object to Mary Condon's role in the story, as her presence dilutes its socialist message. But not only in the Sonoma novels but in many other works such as the thoroughly socialist *The Iron Heel,* romantic love plays a part in the transformation of a man.

CHARACTERS

Freddie Drummond/"Big Bill" Totts Though he tries to do everything right, Drummond is well known if not well liked; nor is he happy. "For he was very young to be a Doctor of Sociology, only twenty-seven, and he looked younger. In appearance and atmosphere he was a strapping big college man, smooth-faced and easy-mannered, clean and simple and wholesome, with a known record of being a splendid athlete and an implied vast possession of cold culture of the inhibited sort" (*Stories,* 1,583). Drummond's slumming excursions "south of the slot" lead to his alter ego as labor leader "Big Bill" Totts.

Mary Condon A firebrand of an Irishwoman and an indefatigable fighter on behalf of her union, Mary resembles the working class woman Lizzie Connally in *Martin Eden.* Unlike Connally, Condon is able at the end of the story to claim her man, "Big Bill" Totts.

Catherine Van Vorst A young woman who represents the best of the elite class of San Francisco, Catherine is Drummond's fiancé, but she cruelly witnesses her replacement by Mary Condon at the end of the story, after a labor riot into which her fiancé jumps as "Big Bill" Totts. She resembles other London women such as Ruth Morse of *Martin Eden* and Vesta Van Warden of *The Scarlet Plague.*

FURTHER READING

Gair, Christopher. "Hegemony, Metaphor, and Structural Difference: The 'Strange Dualism' of 'South of the Slot.'" In *Arizona Quarterly* 49 (Spring 1993): 73–97.

Littell, Katherine M. "The 'Nietzschean' and the Individualist in Jack London's Socialist Writings." In *Jack London Newsletter* 15 (May–August 1982): 76–91.

The Star Rover (1915)

The Star Rover is based on the experiences of a former convict who had served time at SAN QUENTIN PRISON for robbing trains. London met this convict, ED. MORRELL, and heard his story of torture in prison, including the use of the straitjacket for weeks on end. After nearly dying in the jacket, Morrell claimed he mastered self-hypnosis or "astral projection" and, leaving his physical body to wander in time and space, visited his past lives. As in FRANK NORRIS's *The Octopus, The Star Rover* is an indictment of the predations of the Southern Pacific Railroad, but it more broadly attacks the CALIFORNIA prison system, penal reform being a long-standing interest of London's. Morrell wrote his own account of himself and his band of rancher-outlaws fighting the railroad monopoly—which routinely cheated farmers out of their land and charged impossible tariffs so it could obtain right-of-ways—called *The Twenty-Fifth Man* in 1924. Morrell was pardoned by the acting governor of California in 1909; he devoted his life after that to penal reform. He met London in 1912; as he recalled, "Jack London and I were very dear friends, and we had often talked about my experience in the dungeon, particularly those phases pertaining to the 'little death' in the strait-jacket . . . 'God, Ed. do you know what this means to me?' he often said. 'It has often been the ambition of my life to put across a staggering punch against the whole, damnable, rotten American Jail System. I want it to be my masterpiece'" (Morrell, *The Twenty-Fifth Man*, 367–368). Many of the prison episodes portrayed are factually corroborated by Morrell's book. As Earle Labor and Jeanne Campbell Reesman note, if *The Star Rover* is not London's masterpiece "it is not a dull book." Using Morrell's story as a basis, London added his own episodes of "soul-flight adventures, any one of which would have made a solid short story" (Labor and Reesman, *Jack London*, 74).

SYNOPSIS

Darrell Standing has been imprisoned in San Quentin for murder. Repeatedly tortured by the warden and placed in a straitjacket because he will not confess to an escape plot he had no part in, Standing learns to relive former lives by leaving his physical body through "astral projection." First, he is the French Count Guillaume Sainte-Marie, an actual Renaissance courtier and swordsman. Next, he is Jesse Fancher, a young boy killed in the infamous MOUNTAIN MEADOWS MASSACRE, a mass slaughter of the Fancher-Baker wagon train at Mountain Meadows, Utah Territory, by the local Mormon militia on September 11, 1857. The next incarnation is of a fourth-century Christian ascetic inhabiting a cave in the Egyptian desert; next is Adam Strang, a strongman newcomer to 16th-century KOREA; and then a huge and powerful Dane, Ragnar Lodbrog, captured in battle with the Roman army and subsequently an officer under Pontius Pilate who witnesses the crucifixion

of Christ. Last is DANIEL FOSS, a castaway for eight years on a remote island in the early 19th century.

Chapters 1–11

Chapter 1 opens, "All my life I have had an awareness of other times and places. I have been aware of other persons in me. Oh, and trust me, so have you, my reader that is to be. Read back into your childhood, and this sense of awareness I speak of will be remembered as an experience of your childhood." The dreams of childhood are based on fact, Standing argues:

> As a child, a wee child, you dreamed you fell great heights; you dreamed you flew through the air as things of the air fly; you were vexed by crawling spiders and many-legged creatures of the slime; you heard other voices, saw other faces nightmarishly familiar, and gazed upon sunrises and sunsets other than you know now, looking back, you ever looked upon.
>
> Very well. These child glimpses are of otherworldness, of other-lifeness, of things that you had never seen in this particular world of your particular life. Then whence? Other lives? Other worlds? Perhaps, when you have read all that I shall write, you will have received answers to the perplexities I have propounded to you, and that you yourself, ere you came to read me, propounded to yourself. (1–2)

Standing introduces himself as "neither fool nor lunatic" (3). He explains that he was a professor of agronomics at the UNIVERSITY OF CALIFORNIA; he murders a fellow professor but will not disclose why, as "it was purely a private matter" (2). Standing receives a life sentence and is sent to San Quentin, where he has spent eight years as the story opens, five in the darkness of solitary confinement. He claims that he has been "star-roving," leaving his body and traveling in time and space, something he learned from a fellow prisoner, Ed. Morrell.

However, he is transferred to Folsom Prison where he is to be hanged as an "incorrigible" prisoner for striking a guard at San Quentin. Standing has been the subject of a plot to blame him for a failed escape attempt by other prisoners. Standing and 39 other lifers confined to a dark dungeon are brought out into daylight and accused of planning the fictitious breakout; Standing is the only one not involved in the plot and the only one who thus does not confess. He is beaten into unconsciousness by Warden Atherton and Captain Jamie. At last, Standing is released from his five years of solitary but only to attend hearings of the Board of Directors to judge his punishment for striking a guard: "It is a cruel and unusual punishment, and no modern state would be guilty of such," comments Standing (29).

In chapter 5, Standing describes his life in solitary confinement, how he tried to construct chessboards behind his closed eyes, how he played with flies, and how he learned to communicate in a code of rapping with other prisoners, including Ed. Morrell and Jake Oppenheimer. Standing relates how as a child he knew the names of biblical sites when pictures were shown to him by a missionary, astonishing the missionary and his mother and father. Recalling this, Standing begins to self-hypnotize and revisit his strange memories of other lives. Through his memories, brief at first, he discovers "the tides of life [that] ran strong in me"; he determines not to allow Warden Atherton and Captain Jamie to kill him (52). Soon he is straitjacketed, and astral projection becomes essential to survive. When he survives 24 agonizing hours in the jacket, he emerges a different man; but he doesn't realize that later on, after months in the jacket, that will seem like nothing. The warden says he'll kill Standing in the jacket if he won't give up the dynamite. But from Morrell he learns to "die" in the jacket, to will oneself to die by relaxing the body as for sleep; then the spirit can separate from the "sleeping" body and wander free. He learns this just in time, for the Warden, furious with Standing, puts him into the jacket for 10 days.

Standing manages to practice Morrell's trick, and after slowly allowing his body to grow numb, feels his brain expand. He wanders the stars, and he lives the life of Count Guillaume de Sainte-Maure. He is served by an old man named Pons; a priest called Martinelli awaits him. When admitted, Martinelli warns the count not to marry Countess Phillipa, widow of Geoffroy, Duke of Aquitane, for the Pope has other marriage plans arranged for her.

The Count has to fight Italian and French swordsmen sent by the Pope; he kills many but is killed by one of the latter, Guy de Villehardouin. When Standing awakens from his trance, he laughs at the warden and guards and tells them to make his jacket tighter.

Chapters 12–22

Standing next revisits a former identity in a young boy, Jesse Fancher, part of a wagon train moving west from Arkansas. Jesse and his family are killed by Mormons and the Natives they hire in the Mountain Meadows Massacre. They are tracked by Lee, one of the Mormons. One of the settlers, Laban Wainwright, an old Indian fighter, curses the Mormons. Three scouts, Abel Milliken, Timothy Grant, and Will Aden, are attacked; Aden is killed. Jesse and Jed, his friend, are chosen to make a peace offer to the Natives and Mormons, which is refused. A man named Aaron Cochrane warns of an imminent attack. When it comes, many are killed, including Silas Dunlap, the Castleton baby, and more. The group also includes the Fairfax brothers, Robert Carr, Jed Dunham, the Chattox twins, and the Dunlap girls. In running after the Dunlaps, Jesse is killed.

Standing's next identity is Adam Strang, an Englishman of the 16th century who visits Pacific islands. Arriving via a shipwreck in Korea, he falls in love with a princess and becomes an important man under the emperor; however, the princess's fiancé eventually pursues and kills him. After this, Standing becomes Ragnar Lodbrog, a Danish slave who becomes a Roman freeman and witnesses the crucifixion of Christ. His next incarnation is Daniel Foss, shipwrecked for many years on a lonely island in the Pacific, after the wreck of the *Negociator* in 1809. At the end of his story, Standing relates many other reincarnations and the women he loved in them. But soon he is taken to his execution and hanged. Before he dies, he muses, "Here I close. I can only repeat myself. There is no death. Life is spirit, and spirit cannot die. Only the flesh dies and passes, ever a-crawl with the chemic ferment that informs it, ever plastic, ever crystallizing, only to melt into the flux and to crystallize into fresh and diverse forms that are ephemeral and that melt back into the flux. Spirit alone endures and continues to build upon itself through successive and endless incarnations as it works upward toward the light. What shall I be when I live again? I wonder. I wonder . . ." (329).

COMMENTARY

For a novel known for its fantastic elements, *The Star Rover* is based on a number of facts carefully collected by London over many years. He did not believe in astral projection, but he did champion Ed. Morrell's story as an indictment of the very real abuses in the California prison system, including the use of the straitjacket. As he wrote Roland Phillips, editor of COSMOPOLITAN, "It is the law to-day [in prison] that a man can be hanged by the neck until dead, for punching another man in the nose. . . . It is also legal in California to sentence a man to life-imprisonment in solitary. . . . I have really understood the severity of the use of the jacket" (*Letters*, 1,314–1,315). Perhaps this alludes to London's own experiences in the ERIE COUNTY PENITENTIARY when he was arrested for vagrancy as a youth, as detailed in *The Road*. He saw Morrell as a hero of the common man for his attacks on the Southern Pacific Railroad; there is also the inclusion of JAKE OPPENHEIMER, based on a real prisoner who went berserk one day at the mess in San Quentin and killed a guard. Because of this, the state law was changed so that any prisoner serving a life sentence who attacked another person with apparent intent to murder could be brought to trial, and, if convicted, could be sentenced to death, even though the person attacked was not killed. In fact, nearly all of the individuals mentioned in the novel are based on real people— the court of 16th-century Korea, the aristocrats of Renaissance France, the stranded sailor Daniel Foss, the participants and victims of the Mountain Meadows Massacre, and of course the story of Christ.

London had worked for many years on what he called his Christ novel and, though he never completed or published it, he used most of what he had of it in *The Star Rover*. It forms the longest of all the narrative lives of Darrell Standing. One of his primary sources was Ernest Renan's *Life of Jesus*, which was published in 1903 and is one of the more heavily annotated books in London's library.

The Star Rover has been virtually ignored by critics (but has rarely been out of print). It is somewhat difficult to assess, as JOAN LONDON observes, "Into this extraordinary and little-known book he flung with a prodigal hand riches which he had hoarded for years, and compressed into brilliant episodes notes originally intended for full-length books" (Joan London, *Jack London and His Times*, 362). But Joan also indicates the source of the book's difficulty; trying to handle so many narratives at once obscures a central theme. However, as Labor and Reesman remark, beyond its effectiveness as an attack on the prison system, it does have controlling themes if presented in many vignettes: mainly, "it is a dramatic tribute to humankind's historic capacity for suffering" (Labor and Reesman, *Jack London*, 74). It may also be seen as an instance of Darwinian ADAPTATION to circumstances: Standing survives by adapting using his IMAGINATION; the human race survives every setback through imagination as well, and, in the case of the Christ story, through faith. As Labor and Reesman observe, "Gone are his hard-nosed MATERIALISM and scientific rationalism; instead, we encounter a curious mixture of idealism, mysticism, and metempsychosis." As London wrote, "The key-note of the book is: THE SPIRIT TRIUMPHANT" (*Letters*, 1,315).

This was the time in London's life during which he realized that his body was fast deteriorating, and a year after *The Star Rover* was published he discovered the mythic and archetypal routes to self-understanding and fully integrated identity in the works of CARL JUNG. As Labor and Reesman add, a "naturalistic view as small comfort to a writer whose own once-splendid physique had begun to deteriorate from too many years of too little exercise and too many cigarettes, too much work and too little rest" (Labor and Reesman, *Jack London*, 75). As Standing says, "I have lived millions of years. I have possessed many bodies. . . . I am life. I am the unquenched spark ever flashing and astonishing the face of time, ever working my will and wreaking my passions on the cloddy aggregates of matter, called bodies, which I have transiently inhabited." Cut off his finger, Standing adds, "I live. The body is mutilated. I am not mutilated. The spirit that is I, is whole" (123). We may read this in two simultaneous but contradictory ways: The spirit endures, but this may also be a hopeless wish from a dying man instead of a faithful certainty. Standing adds, "but we know nothing of life noumenally, nothing of the nature of the intrinsic stuff of life. . . . I say, and as you, my reader, realize, I speak with authority—I say that matter is the only illusion" (122).

CHARACTERS

Darrell Standing   Narrator, a prisoner convicted of murder who is straitjacketed by the warden at San Quentin Prison. While so tortured, Standing experiences past selves, through "astral projection," learned from another prisoner, Ed. Morrell, London's real-life model for the hero. Standing becomes many heroes and mocks the warden's cruelty.

Warden Atherton and his guards   Standing's nemesis, Atherton, seems to enjoy torturing Standing; the guards are merely brutal: "Intelligent men are cruel. Stupid men are monstrously cruel. The guards and the men over me, from the warden down, were stupid monsters" (10). "Warden Atherton was a large man and a very powerful man. His hands flashed out to a grip on my shoulders. I was a straw in his strength. He lifted me clear of the floor and crashed me down in the chair" (25). Before Warden is through with him several heavy chairs are broken by Standing's body.

Cecil Winwood   "There was a poet in the prison, a convict, a weak-chinned, broad-browed degenerate poet. He was a forger. He was a coward. He was a snitcher. He was a stool—" (10). Winwood falsely claims he has dynamite to blow up the prison and claims he gave the dynamite to Standing to hide. Standing is blamed.

Long Bill Hodge   Of Winwood's plan to dope the guards and escape, he demands proof: "'Show me,' said Long Bill Hodge, a mountaineer doing life for train robbery, and whose whole soul for years had been bent on escaping in order to kill the compan-

ion in robbery who had turned state's evidence on him" (11). He is nearly beaten to death by guards.

Captain Jamie   A prisoner given the job of Captain of the Yard, he conspires with Winwood to blame Standing when no dynamite is found; he says Standing, who has been in solitary, is the mastermind.

Summerface   "Summerface was a strapping figure of a bucolic guard who hailed from Humboldt County. He was a simple-minded, good-natured dolt and not above earning an honest dollar by smuggling in tobacco for the convicts" (12).

Skysail Jack   His name suggesting Jack London, Skysail Jack warns the lifers that they will be punished and that they should tell the truth. Standing sees Skysail Jack after his five years in solitary; Jack has turned prematurely old, with white hair and caved-in chest, a "wreckage" of a man (28).

Luigi Polazzo   "A San Francisco hoodlum," he is a first-generation Italian who jeers at the guards but is beaten until he is "a gibbering imbecile" who is sent to "Bughouse Alley" in the prison (22–23).

Ignatius Irvine   A spy or "stool" sent to try to get something out of Standing about the dynamite; he is a drug addict who will do anything for drugs, but he is unmasked by Standing.

Thurston   The guard Standing punches in the nose; for this Standing is to be hung. As Standing notes, "He weighed one hundred and seventy pounds and was in good health. I weighed under ninety pounds, was blind as a bat from the long darkness, and had been so long pent in narrow walls that I was made dizzy by large open spaces. Really, mine was a well-defined case of incipient agoraphobia, as I quickly learned that day I escaped from solitary and punched the guard Thurston on the nose" (29–30).

Ed. Morrell   Based on the real Ed. Morrell, this man is a friend of Standing and Oppenheimer's in the dungeon. Like Oppenheimer, Standing says

Morrell has a fine mind and is moreover a "true comrade" (39). It is from Morrell that Standing learns "soul-flight."

Jake Oppenheimer Oppenheimer spent his "early years in a San Francisco slum," then joined a gang, an "initiation into all that was vicious when as a lad of fourteen he served as night messenger in the red-light district." Betrayed by his fellows, he becomes a hardened thief: "They called Jake Oppenheimer the 'Human Tiger.' . . . And yet I ever found in Jake Oppenheimer all the cardinal traits of right humanness. He was faithful and loyal. I know of the times he has taken punishment in preference to informing on a comrade. He was brave. He was patient. He was capable of self-sacrifice. . . . And justice, with him, was a passion. The prison killings done by him were due entirely to this extreme sense of justice. And he had a splendid mind. A lifetime in prison, ten years of it in solitary, had not dimmed his brain" (39).

Philadelphia Red Fellow prisoner who is also straitjacketed, he gives Standing advice on how to survive in the jacket: "'The only way is shut your face an' forget it. Yellin' an' hollerin' don't win you no money in this joint. An' the way to forget is to forget. Just get to rememberin' every girl you ever knew. That'll eat up hours for you. Mebbe you'll feel yourself gettin' woozy. Well, get woozy. You can't beat that for killin' time'" (57–58).

Doctor Jackson Prison physician who advises Atherton that the jacket alone will not kill a man. He is "a weak stick of a creature with a smattering of medicine" (61). He thinks Standing is a "'wooz'" who "'ought to have been dead long ago'" (75).

Al Hutchins Head trusty who tightens Standing's straitjacket too tight: "If ever a man deliberately committed murder, Al Hutchins did that morning in solitary at the warden's bidding. He robbed me of the little space I stole. And, having robbed me of that, my body was defenseless, so that with his foot in my back while he drew the lacing tight, he constricted me as no man had ever before succeeded in doing. So severe was this constriction

of my frail frame upon my vital organs that I felt, there and then, immediately, that death was upon me" (75).

Count Guillaume de Sainte-Marie He is a knight betrothed to the Duchess Philippa of Aquitaine, but his plans are challenged by the Pope, who sends numerous swordsmen after him. He is killed, ironically, by one of the least experienced of these.

Robert Lanfranc and Henry Bohemond, Fortini, and Felix Pasquini Lanfranc and Bohemond are friends of the Count Sainte-Marie who assist him in the swordfight with an Italian emissary of the Pope, Fortini. Fortini is a brilliant swordsman but is killed by the count. Felix Pasquini is a friend of Fortini's and nephew to Cardinal Pasquini. He too fights the count and is killed.

Guy de Villehardouin and Raoul de Goncourt The count thinks de Goncourt too noble to keep such company. He too is killed by the count. Villehardouin is a French provincial swordsman in service to the Pope; he picks a fight with the count and kills him.

Jesse Fancher and his party Jesse is killed in the Mountain Meadows Massacre. He is journeying west to California with his mother and father, but they are accosted by a stranger from Nephi who mistakes them for a group from Missouri who are enemies of the Mormons. They are led by Captain Hamilton. Others in their party include Laban Wainwright, Abel Milliken, Timothy Grant, Will Aden, Jed Dunham, Silas Dunlap, the Castletons, the Fairfax brothers, Robert Carr, the Chattox twins, and the Dunlap girls.

desert mystic The third of Standing's incarnations, he lives in a cave in the desert and longs for the City of God.

Adam Strang Strang's identity always awakens in a remote group of sandy islands ruled over by the chief, Raa Kook, and the priest, Abba Taak. But he departs on a Dutch merchantman with Captain Johannes Maartens and supercargo Hendrik Hamel. Along with the sailor Vandervoot they survive a wreck off Korea. They are discovered by the local *yang-ban,* or noble, Kwan Yung-jin, who imprisons them. They are visited by an emissary of the Lady Om, Kim, and freed. He takes them to her. For his strength, Strang is called Yi Yong-ik by the Koreans. They journey to Keijo, the capital, and meet the emperor. Because of his former life, Strang speaks to his captors in Korean, astonishing them. He wins a drinking contest with Taiwun, the emperor's brother. He is interviewed by Yusan, a Buddhist priest, then summoned to meet Lady Om, who enchants him as "the very flower of a woman" (187). Lady Om is the unhappy fiancé of Chong Mong-ju. Strang is caught up in the palace intrigue and plans to save her from a forced marriage. He wins her and is made a great landowner. When some of the Dutch sailors rob a royal tomb, they are all caught but one. Chong Mong-ju leads a coup in the palace and kills and tortures his enemies and the Dutch thieves. Lady Om and Strang become hunted and hide out as menial laborers. When they are accosted by Chong Mong-ju, Strang kills him and is killed by Chong's soldiers.

Ragnar Lodbrog A Dane and member of a Roman legion, he witnesses the persecution and crucifixion of Christ. As an infant tended to only by an old man, Lingaard, Lodbrog is born of a woman captured by the fearsome Tostig Lodbrog, his father. He is taught to fight and becomes one of the hardened men of the seas. He is captured by the rival tribe the Frisians and sold to Edwy of the Saxons, who enslaves him and gives him to Athel of the East Angles. He escapes to live among the Teutons but is captured by the Romans and made a galley-slave. Eventually he gains his freedom and journeys to Alexandria and Jerusalem. There he witnesses the events surrounding Christ's crucifixion and meets such figures as Pontius Pilate and his wife, and Caiaphas the high priest. He falls in love with a girl named Miriam, who, like Pilate's wife, becomes a follower of JESUS.

Daniel Foss Foss is a seaman aboard the *Negociator,* bound for the "Friendly Islands," or TAHITI.

With him when the ship starts to sink after crashing on rocks near the Cape of Good Hope are others who rush half-clad on deck to be swept away; Foss rummages through all their trunks in addition to his own for heavy clothes and boots. With the second mate, Aaron Northrup, he leaps aboard the longboat just leaving the ship; there he joins the mate, Walter Drake, the surgeon, Arnold Bentham, and Captain Nicoll. Also there are John Roberts, Arthur Haskins, Lish Dickerry, and a boy, Benny Hardwater. As the men begin to die and food runs short, the last three survivors, the captain, the surgeon, and Foss draw straws to see which of them will be eaten by the other two. The surgeon draws the short straw, but Foss stops him from killing himself. Everyone dies except Foss, who is marooned.

Ushu Ushu, the archer, is a caveman who lives with a woman, Igar, and her people. After this reincarnation, he recalls many other women he has loved and many other existences.

FURTHER READING

Gair, Christopher. "From Naturalism to Nature: Freedom and Constraint in *The Star Rover.*" In *Jack London Journal* 2 (1995): 118–132.

Gatti, Susan. "The Dark Laughter of Darrell Standing: Comedy and the Absurd in Jack London's *The Star Rover.*" In *Thalia: Studies in Literary Humor* 12, nos. 1–2 (1992): 25–32.

Kim, Tae Jin. "Jack London and Korea: The Korean Episode in *The Star Rover.*" In *The Journal of English Language and Literature* 38, no. 1 (spring 1992): 151–167.

Labor, Earle, and Jeanne Campbell Reesman. *Jack London: Revised Edition.* New York: Twayne, 1994.

London, Joan. *Jack London and His Times.* New York: Doubleday, 1939. Reprinted, with new introduction by the author. Seattle: University of Washington Press, 1968.

Morrell, Ed. *The Twenty-Fifth Man.* Montclair, N.J.: New Era, 1924.

Rivers, Kenneth. "Infinite Identities, Endless Environments: Jack London's *The Star Rover.*" In *Lamar Journal of the Humanities* 23, no. 2 (fall 1997): 21–33.

Tambling, Victor R. S. "A Nose for the King: Jack London's Version of a Korean Folk Story." In *Jack London Newsletter* 14, no. 2 (May 1981): 72–79.

Williams, James. "The Cell." In *Jack London Journal* 2 (1995): 133–155.

———. "On *Star Rover*." In *Jack London Journal* 2 (1995): 81–155.

"Story of a Typhoon Off the Coast of Japan" (1893)

In 1893, at the age of 17, Jack London followed the suggestion of his mother, FLORA WELLMAN LONDON, and submitted a story to the contest for young writers sponsored by the SAN FRANCISCO MORNING CALL. He won the princely sum of $25 and had his story, "Story of a Typhoon Off the Coast of Japan," published on November 12, 1893, based on his experiences aboard a sealing vessel, the SOPHIA SUTHERLAND. It was his very first attempt at story writing, and though it is so early, it clearly reflects the strengths that would later characterize London's work.

SYNOPSIS

The *Sophia Sutherland* is off Cape Jerimo, JAPAN, when the call comes at four bells in the morning watch to heave her to and for all hands to stand by the boats. As the schooner runs to leeward for protection, the whale boats set out with their rowers and hunters, their gear and shotguns. But the boat-steerer in the narrator's boat "shook his head ominously" as he sees the sunrise and "prophetically muttered, 'Red sun in the morning, sailor take warning'" (*Stories*, 1). The narrator describes the forbidding cliff face of Cape Jerimo, the whales "disporting themselves" under flocks of gulls, the seals breaching all around them. After a dozen seals are caught, the sailors see a red flag go up the mizzenmast of the ship, and they race on the wind to get back; the wind and whitecaps are building:

> The waves were holding high carnival, performing the strangest antics, as with wild glee they

danced along in fierce pursuit—now up, now down, here, there, and everywhere, until some great sea of liquid green with its milk-white crest of foam rose from the ocean's throbbing bosom and drove the others from view. But only for a moment, for again under new forms they reappeared. In the sun's path they wandered, where every ripple, great or small, every little spit or spray looked like molten silver, where the water lost its dark green color and became a dazzling, silvery flood, only to vanish and become a wild waste of sullen turbulence, each dark foreboding sea rising and breaking, then rolling on again. (*Stories*, 2)

They make it back, the last boat to come in. Black clouds obscure the sky as seas and winds grow stronger. Most of the sails are furled, but huge waves break over the decks, threatening the boats. After they are secured, the narrator goes below, where he notices the "green hand, the 'bricklayer,'" who is dying of tuberculosis (*Stories*, 3). In the forecastle, the sailors are surrounded by dark shadows, the roar of the wind, the loud crash of seas, the "creaking and moaning of the timbers, stanchions, and bulkheads" (*Stories*, 3). All hands are called on deck to take in more sail. Unable to heave to, the ship flies before the wind:

> She would almost stop, as though climbing a mountain, then rapidly rolling to right and left as she gained the summit of a huge sea, she steadied herself and paused for a moment as though affrighted at the yawning precipice before her. Like an avalanche, she shot forward and down as the sea astern struck her with the force of a thousand battering rams, burying her bow to the catheads in the milky foam at the bottom that came on deck in all directions—forward, astern, to right and left, through the hawse-pipes and over the rail. (*Stories*, 5)

The storm having passed, the ship puts on sail and heads westward, but the final image in the story is of the death of the bricklayer: "Below, a couple of men were sewing the 'bricklayer's' body in canvas preparatory to the sea burial. And so with the storm passed away the 'bricklayer's' soul" (*Stories*, 5).

COMMENTARY

London spent many months of 1893 aboard the *Sophia Sutherland* as an able seaman. Though he was a boy among hardened men, he held his own among them, used to defending himself on the tough waterfront of OAKLAND. The *Sophia Sutherland* cruised the Northern Pacific to hunt for seals. It visited HAWAI'I and Japan, London's first time abroad. In winning the story contest, he beat out students from Stanford University and the UNIVERSITY OF CALIFORNIA; one can guess that this was probably because his story smacked of adventure on the seas and presented an elemental contest for survival. His writing is terse, fast-moving, dramatic. He is already using symbolic elements such as the SUN with its "angry look" and clouds that seem "abashed and frightened and soon disappeared" in the face of a mounting storm (*Stories*, 1). His description of the phosphorescence in the sea is powerful and yet lyrical:

> A soft light emanated from the movement of the ocean. Each mighty sea, all phosphorescent and glowing with the tiny lights of myriads of animalculae, threatened to overwhelm us with a deluge of fire. Higher and higher, thinner and thinner, the crest grew as it began to curve and overtop preparatory to breaking, until with a roar it fell over the bulwarks, a mass of soft glowing light and tons of water which sent the sailors sprawling in all directions and left in each nook and cranny little specks of light that glowed and trembled till the next sea washed them away. (*Stories*, 4).

He also peppers the story with many sailing terms, adding verisimilitude.

The central events of the story are the gigantic typhoon and the death of the "bricklayer." The connection between them is powerful yet subtle. The suggestion that a bricklayer is not a man of the sea but a man who builds on the land adds irony to his death. London himself was the green hand aboard and, in a sense, through the death of the bricklayer, he records symbolically the "death" of his landlubber self and his rebirth into a true sailor, able to survive the storm, unlike the bricklayer who represents his former self.

CHARACTERS

narrator, "Jack"   When the storm is starting to take on its most violent aspect, the narrator describes how "the sleepy sailors tumbled out of their bunk and into their clothes, oil-skins, and sea-boots and up on deck. 'Tis when that order comes on cold, blustering nights that 'Jack' grimly mutters: 'Who would not sell a farm and go to sea? (*Stories*, 4).'" London probably means every sailor when he names him "Jack," since that was slang for a sailor, but it is interesting that he inserts his own name into the tale.

sailing-master and boat-steerer   Both men are fearful of a big typhoon, having read the signs in the skies and on the swelling seas. As experienced sailors, they know what is to come.

bricklayer   The bricklayer is a "green" or new hand—which London was—who dies of tuberculosis during the storm. London counterposes his death with the passing of the storm, creating a symbolic reading of the life and death of any man. There is also the naturalist sense that such a death may not seem of great consequence to sailors who have just saved their own lives.

"The Strength of the Strong" (1911)

In this unusual story, first published in *Hampton's Magazine* 26 (March 1911) and then giving its name to the book collection that came later, two seemingly unrelated themes are brought together: SOCIALISM and the ATAVISM of CAVEMEN.

SYNOPSIS

One peaceful night in their cave, Old Long Beard tells his grandchildren the story of how they once moved from the cave to the trees. As he relates, "'We were a very foolish crowd. We did not know the secret of strength. For, behold, each family lived by itself, and took care of itself. There were thirty families, but we got no strength from one another. We were in fear of each other all the time. No one ever paid visits.'" Each family builds in the top of its tree a grass house, arming themselves with piles of rocks in case they are visited by any one else. "'Also, we had our spears and arrows. We never walked under the trees of the other families, either'" (*Stories*, 1,567). Long Beard relates the kidnapping of his mother and Strong-Arm's wife by the fearsome Boo-oogh and explains that the tribe no longer does such things.

Long Beard was a member of the Fish-Eaters whose enemies were the Meat-Eaters who live nearby. When they are invaded by the Meat-Eaters, the Fish-Eaters do not know how to band together and so each family fights alone. Boo-oogh is killed, along with One-Eye and his family, Six-Fingers and his son, and others. Long Beard observes how effectively the Meat-Eaters work together. The Fish-Eaters follow their example and, as Long Beard puts it, "'we agreed to add our strength together and to be as one man'" (*Stories*, 1,569). But soon the old quarrels over women ensue, distracting the Fish-Eaters; they decide to kill anyone who steals a wife. However, the kidnappings continue; as Long Beard says, "it is not easy to make a tribe" (*Stories*, 1,570). The Fish-Eaters build a wall but realize they need a chief. Soon they have one, Dog-Tooth, who becomes corrupted and steals all the tribe's resources for himself and his retainers. As Long Beard recalls, "'But this was the strange thing: as the days went by we who were left worked harder and harder, and yet did we get less and less to eat'" (*Stories*, 1,574). Soon the Bug becomes the public relations voice of Dog-Tooth:

> "And there arose one who became a singer of songs for the king. Him they called the Bug, because he was small and ungainly of face and limb and excelled not in work or deed. He loved the fattest marrow bones, the choicest fish, the milk warm from the goats, the first corn that was ripe, and the snug place by the fire. And thus, becoming singer of songs to the king, he found a way to do nothing and be fat. And when the people grumbled more and more, and some threw stones at the king's grass house, the Bug sang a song of how good it was

to be a Fish-Eater. In his song he told that the Fish-Eaters were the chosen of God and the finest men God had made. He sang of the Meat-Eaters as pigs and crows, and sang how fine and good it was for the Fish-Eaters to fight and die doing God's work, which was the killing of Meat-Eaters. The words of his song were like fire in us, and we clamored to be led against the Meat-Eaters. And we forgot that we were hungry, and why we had grumbled, and were glad to be led by Tiger-Face over the divide, where we killed many Meat-Eaters and were content." (*Stories*, 1,574)

The Bug urges the others to give the leaders whatever they need for the good of the tribe. When one member, Split-Nose, defies him, the Bug sings "The Song of the Bees" about a robber wasp among bees and Split-Nose is killed. The only man left to rise up is Hair-Face, who also urges his fellows to unite against Dog-Tooth. But he is killed.

The tribe goes on losing strength, until one day the Meat-Eaters return and kill most of them, except the women, whom they take with them. Bug and Long Beard escape. Long Beard survives to kidnap a Meat-Eater woman and have a family, but he must hide in the high mountains. The Bug goes to live with the Meat-Eaters and becomes their singer of war songs. The story closes with Long Beard's hope that one day "'all the fools will be dead and then all live men will go forward. The strength of the strong will be theirs, and they will add their strength together, so that, of all the men in the world, not one will fight with another. There will be no guards nor watchers on the walls. And all the hunting animals will be killed, and, as Hair-Face said, all the hillsides will be pastured with goats and all the high mountain valleys will be planted with corn and fat roots. And all men will be brothers, and no man will lie idle in the sun and be fed by his fellows'" (*Stories*, 1,579).

COMMENTARY

Both a CAVEMAN tale and a socialist argument, "The Strength of the Strong" suggests that even in the dawn of humanity there were right and wrong ways to live. Old Long Beard's tribe, the Fish-Eaters, are destroyed first by their leaders who take everything themselves—mostly unopposed by the tribe, who cannot seem to band together to fight their common enemies. Eventually the tribe, weakened by the lack of resources, is overrun and destroyed by the Meat-Eaters. It is a cautionary tale applicable to conditions in London's day, when robber barons ruled the impoverished masses and only continued to do so because they were stronger and the common people were not united. Thus it implicitly calls for a socialist organization and an uprising. An interesting figure is "The Bug," an early prototype of the poet, who sings the praises of whomever is in power and also leads to the destruction of the Fish-Eaters. As an author himself, London critiques the role of "poets" in the 20th century whose work supports the power elite. Ironically, The Bug is one of the only two survivors of the Fish-Eaters; he throws in his lot with their conquerors, the Meat-Eaters.

CHARACTERS

old Long Beard As he tells his grandchildren his stories, "Long Beard laughed, too, the five-inch bodkin of bone, thrust midway through the cartilage of his nose, leaping and dancing and adding to his ferocious appearance. He did not exactly say the words recorded, but he made animal-like sounds with his mouth that meant the same thing" (*Stories*, 1,567).

Deer-Runner, Yellow-Head, and Afraid-of-the-Dark Grandsons of old Long Beard: "Skins of wild animals partly covered them. They were lean and meager of build, narrow-hipped and crooked-legged, and at the same time deep-chested, with heavy arms and enormous hands. There was much hair on their chests and shoulders, and on the outsides of their arms and legs. Their heads were matted with uncut hair, long locks of which often strayed before their eyes, beady and black and glittering like the eyes of birds. They were narrow between the eyes and broad between the cheeks, while their lower jaws were projecting and massive" (*Stories*, 1,566).

old Boo-oogh A very strong and fierce tree-man who steals old Long Beard's mother: "'It was said

he could pull a grown man's head right off. I never heard of him doing it, because no man would give him a chance'" (*Stories*, 1,567).

Strong-Arm A fisherman, he falls from a cliff, and Boo-oogh takes his wife because he is too injured to defend himself.

One-Eye and Six-Fingers Fish-Eaters killed by the Meat-Eaters when they first invade the valley in which the Fish-Eaters live.

Bug Bug is a rudimentary bard who, at Dog-Tooth's behest, sings a song of war against the Meat-Eaters. He is an effective propagandist for the ruling clique, urging the rest of the tribe to give the leaders whatever they need so they will be strong to defend the group.

Knuckle-Bone Fish-Eater who steals the wife of Three-Clams, in defiance of the new rule against this. He kills Three-Clams.

Three-Legs The member of the Fish-Eaters who first plants corn and takes up most of the free land of the tribe. He also invents trade.

Fith-Fith and Dog-Tooth and their associates When the chief, Fith-Fith dies, Dog-Tooth, his son, is made head of the Fish-Eaters. He is opposed by a prototype of the shaman, Twisted-Lip, also called Big-Fat because of his appetite. Big-Fat claims to know the will of the spirits and the secrets of the dead. Sea-Lion is Dog-Tooth's mouthpiece. Little-Belly is a tiny, thin man who learned to build a fish-trap; he sides with Dog-Tooth, like Pig-Jaw, who learns to keep goats. Sea-Lion invents money, further strengthening the chief. Broken-Rib is another tool of Dog-Tooth's. Tiger-Face is the head of Dog-Tooth's guards and his assassin.

Long Fang Looking to be a strong man too, Long Fang brews "firewater" but is killed for the recipe by minions of Dog-Tooth, along with his family.

Split-Nose He points out how the tribe has been weakened by the dictatorial class; he urges the rest to put their strength together and throw them off. But Bug sings "The Song of the Bees" which says Split-Nose is wicked, and the song maddens the Fish-Eaters with its "crooked words" (*Stories*, 1,577), and Split-Nose is stoned to death.

Hair-Face   Fish-Eater who urges his fellows to pool their strength to rise up against the useless class of chiefs that take all the resources. As he says of his vision of the future,

> "Where is the strength of the strong?" he asked. "We are the strong, all of us, and we are stronger than Dog-Tooth and Tiger-Face and Three-Legs and Pig-Jaw and all the rest who do nothing and eat much and weaken us by the hurt of their strength which is bad strength. Men who are slaves are not strong. . . . Let us add our strength and their strength together. Then will we be indeed strong. And then we will go out together, the Fish-Eaters and the Meat-Eaters, and we will kill the tigers and the lions and the wolves and the wild dogs, and we will pasture our goats on all the hillsides and plant our corn and fat roots in all the high mountain valleys." (*Stories*, 1,578)

"The Sun-Dog Trail" (1905)

First published in *Harper's Monthly Magazine* (December 1905), "The Sun-Dog Trail" is a KLON-DIKE story heavy with what Faulkner called "the human heart in conflict with itself." As Sitka Charley tells his mysterious adventure, he also suggests subtle ideas about how a story is to be interpreted at all.

SYNOPSIS

Sitka Charley and a companion, the narrator, sit smoking after a hard day on the trail. They notice some newspaper pictures pasted to the wall of the deserted cabin they have found. The first image is of a man shooting another man; the second is of Helen of Troy as the daughter of "Leda and the Swan"; the third is of a dying child. Sitka Charley cannot understand the present reality of the pictures since they have no narrative, no beginning nor end, but are just snapshots of various lives without connection and hence meaning. The two men try to construct a narrative to explain them, but fail. Sitka Charley then relates a strange adventure in which he participated seven years earlier, in 1897, which he titles "The Sun-Dog Trail."

In his story-within-a-story, he recalls that he was hired for a huge sum of money to take a beautiful but mysterious white woman to DAWSON. When they at last arrive on the YUKON RIVER before it freezes for the winter, they are joined by a young man; the woman pays Sitka Charley even more money to take them to Circle City, far to the north near the Arctic Circle. When they get there after an arduous journey, on Christmas Eve, they press on through CHRISTMAS DAY into the bitter cold beyond the settlement; along the way they nearly die of frostbite, starvation, and exhaustion. A one-eyed man conveys information to them they will not share with Sitka Charley, and they continue onward. Though Sitka Charley is alarmed, he has been paid the vast sum of $750 and does not desert them: "'They are my masters. I am their man. If they say, "Charley, come let us start for hell," I will harness the dogs'" (*Stories*, 977). As they go past the very last outposts on the barren waste of ice, Sitka Charley notes how the SUN "'looks at us for a moment over the hills to the south,'" and the "'northern lights flame in the sky, and the sun-dogs dance, and the air is filled with frost-dust'" (*Stories*, 978). They all begin to fail, having eaten even their sled harnesses. At last they come upon the man the couple have been tracking, a snarling, frost-blackened man who is himself dying, and the woman shoots him to death. Sitka Charley never finds out why, and he never asks, but takes them to ST. MICHAEL where they board a steamer. The narrator asks, "'But why did they kill the man?'" Sitka Charley replies:

> "I have thought much. I do not know. It is something that happened. It is a picture I remember. . . . They came into my life and

they went out of my life, and the picture is as I have said, without beginning, the end without understanding."

"You have painted many pictures in the telling," I said.

"Ay," he nodded his head. "But they were without beginning and without end."

"The last picture of all had an end," I said.

"Ay," he answered. "But what end?"

"It was a piece of life," I said.

"Ay," he answered. "It was a piece of life."
(*Stories*, 985)

Sitka Charley believes that only the SUN-DOGS— the twinned "suns" on either side of the real sun brought about by frost in the air—can know the truth of the act of vengeance he witnessed.

COMMENTARY

The imagery of the sun and specifically the Roman SOL and Christmas Day, originally Sol's day, as well as the mention of Sol's number, seven, permeate this strange tale, as is often the case in the Klondike stories, this time in the form of sun-dogs. There is the pervasive sense that while men do not understand the pictures they see—apropos of Plato's cave—the gods do. Like a Homeric narrator, Sitka Charley does not presume to know the meaning of things; he only narrates them as they happen and appeals to the gods (or to his audience?) for understanding. The story is both a retelling of Homeric myth, Roman sun worship, and a seemingly superhuman sense of justice, using myth and symbol, but it is also a story of the mystery of the NORTHLAND, with its weird regions and skies, with the unbelievable lengths men and women were put to as they tried to survive in its unforgiving environment. Was it love? Greed? Or something else that led to the murder? Certainly it was vengeance, and in a primitive code such as prevailed in such a primitive place, it was justice. Though Sitka Charley may not know all, he wisely admits that this is so. One final note: Sitka Charley appears throughout several Klondike stories as a wise interpreter of the deeds of humans, and he is one of London's many mixed-race heroes, being part NATIVE Sitka and part white. Though London repeatedly created such

mixed-breed protagonists, he also wrote elsewhere against "mongrels." The presence of Sitka Charley and others like him belie London's self-professed racialist beliefs.

CHARACTERS

Sikta Charley Sitka Charley is a favorite character of London's in the Klondike tales, in which he appears regularly. He is half-Native and half-white and the best of the trail guides. He often narrates the puzzling deeds of others and acts as a sort of judge on their behavior.

companion/narrator This unnamed individual is Sitka Charley's trail mate and tells the story Sitka Charley related to him about the murder of the man near the Arctic Circle by a mysterious man and woman.

unnamed white woman Described as lovely, she hires Sitka Charley for a huge sum of money to journey first to Dawson and then to and past Circle City. When she espies the man she is after, she shoots him dead.

unnamed young man Companion of the white woman and Sitka Charley on the punishing trek to the Arctic Circle. He witnesses the murder she commits and is delivered with her to a steamer at St. Michael at the mouth of the Yukon River.

unnamed man on the trail Nearly frozen to death, he is followed by the woman and her young companion to within the Arctic Circle; when he is found, the woman shoots him and kills him.

"The Tears of Ah Kim" (1918)

First published posthumously in COSMOPOLITAN 65 (July 1918) and included in the collection *On the Makaloa Mat*, London's last tales of HAWAI'I, this is a uniquely personal story of a CHINESE family of immigrants in HONOLULU. Its seriocomic tone makes it one of London's most engaging tales of immigrants in Hawai'i, and its hopeful ending shows modernity bringing needed changes to ancient ways. Thus, it stands out in a volume that generally mourns the coming of the modern.

SYNOPSIS

Ah Kim has tolerated the upbraiding and beatings from his mother all of his life, and though he is 50 years old he has never married. However, when he meets Li Faa, he falls in love, and she helps him fight for his freedom. Enduring more beatings, Ah Kim enlists Li Faa's aid in overcoming his mother. He tells Li Faa on their wedding night that when he finally was able to cry under one of her lashings, he finally broke her spell: "'I suddenly knew that my mother was nearing her end. There was no weight, no hurt, in her blows. I cried because I knew *she no longer had the strength enough to hurt me*'" (*Stories*, 2,354).

COMMENTARY

Though it is a comic tale of the ascendancy of youth and the modern ways of doing things over diehard traditionalists, "The Tears of Ah Kim" displays clearly London's newly developed interest in the ideas of CARL JUNG, whom he read in the summer of 1916 when this story was written. Joseph McClintock describes it as both "obscure" and "slapstick," but he also notes how it is "almost a programmatic presentation of specific symbols and themes discussed in [Jung's] *Psychology of the Unconscious*." It reflects both an Oedipus complex and the sacrifice of the mother by the individual who wishes to mature in favor of a sexual other; the mother's punishment for this inflicts guilt upon the son. Only through a kind of death can the son separate from the deathly mother and achieve a mature relationship with the sexual object (McClintock, *White Logic*, 339–340). However, the story also shows the agony Ah Kim feels, through his tears, when he realizes how feeble his mother is. His is not the only tragedy; life moves along its inevitable line toward death, and even in his marriage Ah Kim is aware of this.

The story is also a clever portrayal of class and race issues in Hawai'i. Ah Kim's mother despises "half-*pake*" or half-Chinese Li Faa; she wants him to marry a full *pake* woman. But, as Li Faa points out, "'That will do for China. I do not know China. This is Hawaii, and in Hawaii the customs of all foreigners change'" (*Stories*, 2,350). This comment illustrates London's ideal of Hawai'i as a place where old racial or cultural differences could be resolved.

CHARACTERS

Ah Kim   To the outside world of Honolulu's Chinatown, "No Chinese lad of tender and beatable years was Ah Kim. His was the store of Ah Kim Company, and his was the achievement of building it up through the long years from the shoestring of savings of a contract coolie labourer to a bank account in four figures and a credit that was gilt edged." As a middle-aged man, he is fat, short, and "moon-faced." He goes about in silk clothing and skullcap (*Stories*, 2,341). But he is regularly beaten by his mother. Despite her, Ah Kim is "bitten by the acid of modernity" (*Stories*, 2,349).

Mrs. Tai Fu   Ah Kim's mother, she beats him with a large stick for seeing the girl Li Faa, whom she regards as stuck-up and too Americanized and modernized. She wants Ah Kim to marry a traditional Chinese woman. In the end, she is defeated.

Li Faa   According to Mrs. Tai Fu, Li Faa is not Chinese enough:

> "All paké must my daughter-in-law be, even as you, my son, and as I, your mother. And she must wear trousers, my son, as all the women of our family before her. No woman, in she-devil skirts and corsets, can pay due reverence to our ancestors. Corsets and reverence do not go together. Such a one is this shameless Li Faa. She is impudent and independent, and will be neither obedient to her husband nor her husband's mother. This brazen-faced Li Faa would believe herself the source of life and the first ancestor, recognizing no ancestors before her. She laughs at our joss-sticks, and paper prayers,

and family gods, as I have been well told—" (*Stories*, 2,348).

On her side, Li Faa despises Ah Kim's mother with her immemorial Chinese ways. Li Faa is an early feminist, which further antagonizes Ah Kim's mother.

FURTHER READING

McClintock, James I. *White Logic: Jack London's Short Stories*. Grand Rapids, Mich.: Wolf House, 1975. Reprinted in 1997 as *Jack London's Strong Truths: A Study of the Short Stories*. East Lansing, Mich.: Michigan State University Press, 1997.

"The Terrible and the Tragic in Fiction" (1903)

Published in *The Critic* (June 1903) and included in London's *No Mentor but Myself*, this analysis of horror fiction should rank as one of the finest, though it is little known. Its analysis of EDGAR ALLAN POE alone makes it a significant literary essay. Like Poe in his essay "The Imp of the Perverse," London makes a case for why people like to read horror stories; the essay was written just before London wrote *The Sea-Wolf*, a tale of horror itself.

London begins by quoting several letters of Poe's to editors along with some from editors mostly expressing their distaste for his work. He also includes quotations from letters praising Poe by such contemporary figures such as Elizabeth Barrett Browning. Poe earned very little in his life from his writing, a fact London mourns. London feels that Poe's work was unfairly portrayed as "repulsive and unreadable." As London points out, "The public read Poe's stories, but Poe was not in touch with that public" (60). London identifies a strange paradox in Poe's career: Even as his work was attacked by editors, when it was published it was "read universally and discussed and remembered." The more conventionally popular writers of his day are now forgotten. London points out

the same problem for serious writers in his own day:

> No self-respecting editor with an eye to the subscription-list can be bribed or bullied into admitting a terrible or tragic story into his magazine; while the reading public, when it does chance upon such stories in one way or another . . . says it does not care for them. A person reads such a story, lays it down with a shudder, and says: "It makes my blood run cold. I never want to read anything like that again." Yet he or she will read something like that again, and again, and yet again, and return and read them all over again. The average man or woman, if asked, will agree that they have read "the terrible and horrible tales"; they "will shiver, express a dislike for such tales, and then proceed to discuss them with a keenness and understanding as remarkable as it is surprising. (61)

London surmises that people are "afraid that they do like to be afraid," and this explains the conundrum:

> Deep down in the race is fear. It came first into the world, and it was the dominant emotion in the primitive world. Today, for that matter, it remains the most firmly seated of the emotions. . . . What lures boys to haunted houses after dark? . . . What is it that grips a child, forcing it to listen to ghost stories which drive it into ecstasies of fear, and yet forces it to beg for more and more? . . . Or, again, what is it that sends the heart fluttering up and quickens the feet of the man or woman who goes alone down a dark hall or up a winding stair? Is it a stirring of the savage in them? (61)

London lists several writers who base their work on fear: Charles Dickens, W. W. Jacobs (author of "The Monkey's Paw"), AMBROSE BIERCE, William C. Morrow, ROBERT LOUIS STEVENSON. He further argues that the greatest works of literature in general recognize the important element of fear, especially great love stories.

"To Build a Fire" (1908)

"To Build a Fire," first published in *Century Magazine* 76 (August 1908) and included in the collection *Lost Face*, is London's best-known short story and is anthologized in hundreds of collections the world over. Readers rarely forget the story's ominous atmosphere of extreme cold, the futility of the man's attempts to save himself, having gone much too far into the terrible WHITE SILENCE of the NORTHLAND, and his lonely death under the uncaring heavens. The 1908 version is actually the second; in 1902 London wrote the first "To Build a Fire" for *Boy's Life Magazine*. The differences between this early version and the famous one he composed while trying to survive on the *SNARK* voyage are striking. In the 1902 version, the man has a name, "Tom Vincent," like a character out of boy's adventure books. He does have an accident in breaking through the ice but successfully builds a fire, ending up with only a case of

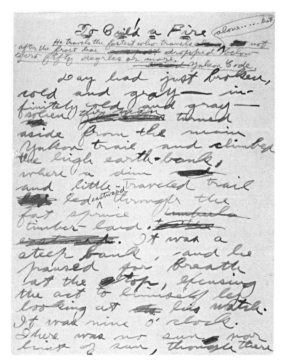

First manuscript page of "To Build a Fire," 1908 (*Huntington Library*)

frostbite, and there is no dog, an essential component of the later version. Those scholars fortunate enough to be able to examine the original manuscript of the 1908 version (housed with most of London's papers at the HUNTINGTON LIBRARY in San Marino, California) note that until the end of the first paragraph the man is once again called Tom Vincent, but London scratched through this with heavy strokes and simply substituted "the man." This change—and London rarely revised—is important because it allows the story a more universal resonance.

SYNOPSIS

An unnamed man is traveling across the YUKON TERRITORY on an extremely cold morning with a husky dog; it is actually 50 degrees below zero. As he is an inexperienced CHECHAQUO (or newcomer) to the Northland, he is not worried about the cold. He is mostly concerned with traveling a little-known path that he believes is a shortcut to his camp, where his companions await. He continually checks his watch, planning to arrive there at 6 P.M. How impressed they will be with him! No one believed he could make this trek. As it grows colder and his unprotected cheekbones start to freeze, he scorns the use of a nose-strap as something for weaker men. As he and the dog traverse a creek trail, he is aware that underneath there can be concealed springs; getting wet feet on such a cold day could be fatal. Thus, he forces the dog to walk in front of him.

He stops for lunch at noon and builds a fire. Back on the trail, he does fall through the ice with its deceptive covering of snow and soaks his feet. Cursing his bad luck, he stops to build a fire and dry his foot-gear; mainly he is angry at the delay. His feet and fingers are starting to go numb, but he starts the fire. He remembers the old-timer from Sulphur Creek (an experienced prospector, or *sourdough*) who had warned him that no man should travel in the KLONDIKE alone when the temperature is so many degrees below zero. Untying his frozen moccasins, before he can cut the strings on them, clumps of snow from a spruce tree above his fire fall and snuff out the flames. He should have made his fire in the open, but he was too lazy to wander very far for sticks. His pulling branches off the nearby tree is what led to the disaster.

Now quite aware of his predicament, he tries to build another fire, but as his fingers are already frozen stiff, he cannot manage the match. Panicked, he takes the entire bundle of seventy matches and strikes them all at once. The sulphur fumes choke him and he drops the matches in the snow. Next, he decides to kill the dog and puts his hands inside its warm body to restore his circulation, something he has heard about in Northland lore. However, when he calls to the dog, it senses the fear in his voice, something it has never heard before, as he usually speaks to it "with the sound of whip-lashes" (Stories, 1,307). The dog finally comes forward and the man grabs it in his arms. But he cannot kill it, since he is unable to pull out his knife or even choke the animal. He lets it go. The man realizes that death is approaching fast. He panics and runs along the trail, trying to restore his circulation. But his endurance gives out, and finally he falls and does not rise. He decides he should meet death with dignity, but he is slowly losing consciousness; whether with dignity or not, he is dying. He imagines his friends finding his body tomorrow. As the man feels himself falling off into a comfortable sleep, he again recalls the old-timer's advice and admits that he was right. The dog is puzzled by the man's stillness, but when it sniffs him it smells death. The dog turns and heads down the trail to the awaiting camp, "where were the other food-providers and fire-providers" (Stories, 1,315).

COMMENTARY

Day had broken cold and gray, exceedingly cold and gray, when the man turned aside from the main Yukon trail and climbed the high earthbank, where a dim and little-travelled trail led eastward through the fat spruce timberland. It was a steep bank, and he paused for breath at the top, excusing the act to himself by looking at his watch. It was nine o'clock. There was no sun nor hint of sun, though there was not a cloud in the sky. It was a clear day, and yet there seemed an intangible pall over the face of things, a subtle gloom that made the day

dark, and that was due to the absence of sun. This fact did not worry the man. He was used to the lack of sun. It had been days since he had seen the sun, and he knew that a few more days must pass before that cheerful orb, due south, would just peep above the sky-line and dip immediately from view. (Stories, 1,301)

Close analysis of this famous opening paragraph shows that it foreshadows the eventual outcome of the story. To begin with, the repetition of "cold and gray" in the first sentence reinforces the extreme conditions. We learn that he is, unwisely, on a little-traveled trail. What we observe next is critical. Climbing the earthbank, he is out of breath, but is not honest enough with himself to admit it; he pretends he needs to look at his watch. The watch itself is a small symbol of civilization, as and such it is ridiculously out of place in the barren waste. His civilized knowledge (what time it is) is clearly at odds with his environment, and the sun is gone months, not days, in winter. The lesson, which forecasts his end, is that in a survival situation to lie to yourself can be deadly.

The story contrasts the kind of knowledge the man possesses and the kind of knowledge he lacks. He thinks he represents objective knowledge of his environment and of himself, but he is wrong; he is not even a good observer of phenomena, much less an interpreter. The dog survives through instinctual knowledge—the cold tells it that it should not be out. The third kind of knowledge in the story is that of the old-timer's wisdom born of experience. The dog and old-timer's knowledge represent the experience of ADAPTATION, but the man thinks that nature should adapt to him and his schedule.

Often cited as a pure example of literary NATURALISM, "To Build a Fire" also contains metaphysical insights. The focus is not on merely survival or man against nature, but upon the relationships in the story: man and dog, man and old-timer, man and "the boys." Nature is thus redefined as human nature, and it is easy to see that the man is distant from himself:

But all this—the mysterious, far-reaching hairline trail, the absence of sun from the sky, the tremendous cold, and the strangeness and weirdness of it all—made no impression on the man. It was not because he was long used to it. He was a newcomer in the land, a chechaquo, and this was his first winter. The trouble with him was that he was without imagination. He was quick and alert in the things of life, but only in the things, and not in the significances. Fifty degrees below zero meant eighty-odd degrees of frost. Such fact impressed him as being cold and uncomfortable, and that was all. It did not lead him to meditate upon his frailty as a creature of temperature, and upon man's frailty in general, able only to live within certain narrow limits of heat and cold; and from there on it did not lead him to the conjectural field of immortality and man's place in the universe" (*Stories*, 1,301–1,302).

A bit later, as he starts to realize that he is getting frostbitten, the narrator remarks, "The cold of space smote the unprotected tip of the planet, and he, being on that unprotected tip, received the full force of the blow. The blood of his body recoiled before it. The blood was alive, like the dog, and like the dog it wanted to hide away and cover itself up from the fearful cold" (*Stories*, 1,308). As the man is "without imagination," he fails to understand what it means to feel the "cold of space."

In contrast to the great cold is the story's central image of the fire. There is a complex set of images throughout the story centering on fire: the old-timer's pipe, Sulphur Creek, sulphur matches, the "stars that leaped and danced" (*Stories*, 1,315) at the man's death (as the flame of his earlier fire also "danced"). As in the story of Prometheus, fire can be a symbol for knowledge, but this is precisely what the man lacks. The fire is supposed to mean life for the man, but even before he builds his first fire he is in a sense dead, since he is so disconnected from the world around him and so unaware of his relation to it. Had he built his fire, would he have continued that way? Other classical and literary images in the story are the "winged Mercury" (*Stories*, 1,313) and subtle allusions to the figure of Mammon in Milton's *Paradise Lost.* Of course the overall structure of a man setting out on a perilous journey goes back to the earliest hero-myths, but unlike Odysseus or the Red Cross Knight or Lancelot, this man is unprepared for what he will face and thus perishes.

The man is most unprepared when it comes to companionship and COMMUNITY. It is a mistake to read the lone wolf hero as London's ideal; in fact, the lone wolf, like Wolf Larsen in *The Sea-Wolf*, is doomed in London's works. Like a Kiplingesque hero of lone white man out to dominate new territory, or a Nietzschean superman, this protagonist neither sees himself in relation to the universe nor comprehends the value of ADAPTATION instead of attempting to conquer. He lives and dies alone, unable to learn from the dog or the old-timer. Without a trailmate, anyone attempting what he attempts is doomed, but he is too proud to learn that. He wanted to impress "the boys," but he dies imagining them finding his body and him, oddly, telling his story to awed listeners back home, a last, and too late, bid for membership in the human community.

CHARACTERS

the man   The protagonist is a lone white man, a CHECHAQUO, who sets out on a foolishly perilous journey across the frozen Northland. Instead of understanding the immensity of his situation, he likes to measure things: how many miles, how cold it is, what time of day it is, how many matches, how many twigs, how long he will be delayed. All of this is in ironic contrast to the timeless landscape around him and the inexorability of his fate.

the dog   The dog epitomizes instinctual knowledge. Unlike the man, it senses that it is too cold to travel, and it feels the "vague but menacing apprehension" around the pair (*Stories*, 1,303). As Earle Labor and King Hendricks have pointed out, the dog is a foil who exposes the protagonist as a "hollow man whose inner coldness correlates with the enveloping outer cold" and allows the "subtle counterpointing" between the dog's "natural wisdom" and the man's "foolish rationality" (Labor and Hendricks, "London's Twice-Told Tale," 335). This is one dog character who is not at all anthropomorphized, and there is no love between man and dog.

the old-timer   Before the protagonist leaves on his journey, the old-timer who lives at Sulphur Creek warns him, "Never travel alone." But the protagonist, unlike the old-timer, lacks imagination and experience and thus wisdom. This leads directly to his death.

FURTHER READING

Bowen, James K. "Jack London's 'To Build a Fire': Epistemology and the White Wilderness. In *Western American Literature* 5 (1971): 287–289.

Labor, Earle, and King Hendricks. "London's Twice-Told Tale." In *Studies in Short Fiction* 4 (1967): 334–347. Reprinted in *The Critical Response to Jack London*. Edited by Susan M. Nuernberg. Westport, Conn.: Greenwood Press, 1995, 9–16.

Reesman, Jeanne Campbell. *Jack London: A Study of the Short Fiction.* New York: Twayne, 1999.

———. "'Never Travel Alone': Naturalism, Jack London, and the White Silence." In *American Literary Realism* 29, no. 2 (winter 1997): 33–49.

Theisen, Kay M. "Realism as Represented in 'South of the Slot,' Naturalism as Represented in 'To Build a Fire': Critical Thinking and Pedagogy." In *Eureka Studies in Teaching Short Fiction* 5, no. 2 (Spring 2005): 99–107.

"Told in the Drooling Ward" (1914)

First appearing in *The Bookman* 39 (June 1914) and included in *The Turtles of Tasman*, "Told in the Drooling Ward" is one of London's most unusual stories. It is the humorous first-person narrative of a young mentally retarded man who narrates his escape with some fellows from the SONOMA STATE HOME. As the hospital grounds back up to London's ranch, Jack and CHARMIAN KITTREDGE LONDON frequently rode on its grounds and they appear in the story as the Endicotts. This is probably the first story ever narrated by a retarded person, and one of the earliest to treat the mentally retarded in literature. Note that terms such as "feebs" and "droolers" are not intended to be derogatory; these were terms used at the time by the inmates themselves.

SYNOPSIS

Twenty-eight-year-old Tom is a patient at the Sonoma State Hospital. At the outset of the story he is eager to make it clear that he is a "high-grade feeb" and not a "drooler." He sees himself as an assistant to the staff, regularly feeding the "low-grade droolers" in the ward. He has been an inmate for 25 years and is proud that he "do things," such as help care for his fellows and even play the drums and read music (*Stories*, 1,762). In the hospital, Tom explains, there are also "high grade epilecs" and "micros," with little heads no bigger than a fist, usually droolers, who live a long time; and "hydros," with big heads who don't drool, never grow up, and die young (*Stories*, 1,764). Unlike these pitiable cases, Tom has high ambitions, including marrying a nurse. He likes the Home, not the "outside." Once he was adopted and went to live on a ranch with a man named Peter Bopp and his wife. Mrs. Bopp was scared of Tom, and the Bopps made him sleep in a woodshed and rise at 4 A.M. to feed horses, milk cows, and deliver milk to neighbors. He is not allowed to play with the Bopp children and is taunted as "Looney Tom." One day, Mr. Bopp beats him with a strap for disobeying him. Tom runs away, back to the hospital.

The other escape in the story is when Tom joins some epilecs, Charley and Joe, in running away to a mountain gold mine. He carries his friend little Albert in his arms, a heavy chore. Soon the group grows hungry, hears strange noises at night, and eventually returns back home. Tom says the next time he runs away he won't take the epilecs with him but will just take little Albert. However, upon second thought, he says he won't be running away: "The drooling ward's a better snap than gold mines, and I hear there's a new nurse coming. Besides, little Albert's bigger than I am now, and I could never carry him over a mountain. And he's growing bigger every day. It's astonishing" (*Stories*, 1,770).

COMMENTARY

One of London's more unique experimental stories, with its lively and personable narrator and its wonderful sense of irony, "Told in the Drooling Ward" features a great comic narrative voice. Tom's perspective reveals his wide knowledge of the hospital's denizens, as it also reveals his innocence. It resembles other dramatic monologues, such as *Adventures of Huckleberry Finn* or Robert Browning's poems. As Don Graham has noted, it forecasts the Benjy section of *The Sound and the Fury* and the portrayal of Lenny in *Of Mice and Men*, as well as the "inverted world of the complete insane-asylum novel, Ken Kesey's *One Flew Over the Cuckoo's Nest*" (Graham, "Jack London's Tale," 429). It is "truly an anomaly in London's short fiction," for in no other story does he so successfully blend "three diverse elements: comedy, political commentary, and such familiar thematic matter as the search for gold" (Graham, "Jack London's Tale," 432–433). Its political commentary consists of Tom's observations about the system: "You bet we high-graders talk politics. We know all about it, and it's bad. An institution like this oughtn't to be run on politics. Look at Doctor Dalrymple. He's been here two years and learned a lot. Then politics will come along and throw him out and send a new doctor who don't know anything about feebs" (*Stories*, 1,764). Tom uses a conversational style as though he is engaged in a dialogue with the reader: "Me? I'm not a drooler. I'm the assistant"; "you see that house up there through the trees"; and "Feeb? Oh, that's feeble-minded. I thought you knew" (*Stories*, 1,762).

As narrated by Tom, life in the hospital provides a structured environment complete with a hierarchy. Tom occupies a spot near the top, but he feels looked down upon by the "high-grade epilecs" who live in their own "club house." As he relates, "They laugh at me, when they ain't busy throwing fits. But I don't care. I never have to be scared about falling down and busting my head. Sometimes they run around in circles trying to find a place to sit down quick, only they don't. Low-grade epilecs are disgusting, and high-grade epilecs put on airs. I'm glad I ain't an epilec. There ain't anything to them. They just talk big, that's all" (*Stories*, 1,763).

The trip to search for gold shows both Tom's falling under the sway of the high-grade epilecs and also falling prey to the values of the outside world. But on the actual trip he displays London's favorite heroic values of IMAGINATION, COMMUNITY, and JUS-TICE, especially in trying to carry and comfort little Albert, who is not little. When Tom returns home, he regains his place in the hospital community.

CHARACTERS

Tom   Tom is a talented storyteller; as he confides, "I know a lot" (*Stories*, 1,764). Tom's knowledge encompasses not only his fellow patients, but also the doctors and nurses at the hospital—in addition, he has informed judgment about the sorry state of the state hospital system (London did intend to criticize this system, just as he did the prison system in *The Star Rover*). He also possesses a moral sense. He explains that he isn't really a "feeb," but is fortunate that he happens to look like one and can live at the hospital: "My mouth is funny, I know that, and it lops down, and my teeth are bad. You can tell a feeb anywhere by looking at his mouth and teeth" (*Stories*, 1,764). He does not wish to enter the outside world—"I'd rather talk and be what I am" (*Stories*, 1,764)—but unwittingly he does. Tom also displays courage and adaptability, both critical for a London hero.

Little Albert   Albert is tended to by Tom, who is especially good at reading his face to see what he wants to eat: "He's a drooler, you know, and I can always tell the way he twists his left eye what's the matter with him" (*Stories*, 1,763).

Miss Jones and Miss Kelsey   Nurses in the hospital who rely on Tom to help with the feeding of 55 droolers in their ward. Miss Kelsey encourages Tom to write a book about his knowledge of the hospital.

Dr. Dalrymple   The attending physician in Tom's ward, he praises Tom's expertise in feeding droolers: "Dr. Dalrymple says I'm too smart to be in the Home, but I never let on" (*Stories*, 1,762). Dr. Dalrymple also says Tom has "the gift of language" (*Stories*, 1,763). Dr. Dalrymple is right, as this one brief but hilarious exchange shows when Tom runs into Charley and Joe, two epileptics: "'Hello,' Joe said. 'How's droolers?' 'Fine,' I said. 'Had any fits lately?'" (*Stories*, 1,767).

Mr. and Mrs. Bopp Tom is placed with the Bopps to work for them at their dairy farm 40 miles away, but they treat him cruelly and he escapes.

Doctor Mandeville Dr. Mandeville saves Tom from the Bopps: "I walked right into his office. He didn't know me. 'Hello,' he said, 'this ain't visiting day.' 'I ain't a visitor,' I said. 'I'm Tom. I belong here.' Then he whistled and showed he was surprised. I told him all about it, and showed him the marks of the strap halter, and he got madder and madder all the time and said he'd attend to Mr. Peter Bopp's case" (*Stories*, 1,765).

Mr. and Mrs. Endicott Tom identifies Mr. Endicott as "'the man who owns this ranch and writes books.'" Endicott wishes him well and reminds him to "'get back before dark.'" When Tom replies that "'But this is a real running away,'" the Endicotts laugh, and Endicott says, "'Good luck just the same. But watch out for the bears and mountain lions don't get you when it gets dark'" (*Stories*, 1,768). Endicott's good-natured warning provides the nudge that Tom needs to see how pointless his escape is and sends him and his friends back home to safety within their community.

Charley and Joe Two epileptic patients who get Tom to go with them in running away from the hospital to a supposed gold mine. Tom has a hard night managing them and little Albert: "I never had such an awful night. When Joe and Charley weren't throwing fits they were making believe, and in the darkness the shivers from the cold which I couldn't see seemed like fits, too. And I shivered so hard I thought I was getting fits myself. And little Albert, with nothing to eat, just drooled and drooled. I never seen him as bad as that before. Why, he twisted that left eye of his until it ought to have dropped out. . . . And Joe just lay and cussed and cussed, and Charley cried and wished he was back in the Home" (*Stories*, 1,769).

Doctor Wilson The latest in a succession of doctors who run the hospital; the number of them who come and go reflects the poor management of the hospital system by the politics of the state. He

is angry at Tom for running away, but relieved that he is back.

Miss Striker She is a nurse in the drooling ward who is so relieved Tom and his friends are back, she "just put her arms around me and cried, she was that happy I'd got back. I thought right there that mebbe I'd marry her. But only a month afterward she got married to the plumber that came up from the city to fix the gutter-pipes of the new hospital" (*Stories*, 1,770).

FURTHER READING

Graham, Don. "Jack London's Tale Told by a High-Grade Feeb." In *Studies in Short Fiction* 15, no. 4 (fall 1978): 429–433.

"The Unexpected" (1906)

"The Unexpected" is a grim tale of gold, greed, betrayal, and frontier justice; its protagonist is a strong woman who survives the near-murder of herself and her husband and brings sentence upon the wrongdoer. It first appeared in *McClure's Magazine* (August 1906) and was included in *Love of Life and Other Stories*. London based his tale on a story in the EXAMINER (SAN FRANCISCO) on October 14, 1900, in which there is "an account of the double-murder committed by Michael Dennin, and of his hanging by Mrs. Nelson and her husband, Hans" (*Letters*, 599). Under the headline "Woman Hangs a Man and the Law Upholds Her," the story tells how Dennin used a shotgun at point-blank range to kill two fellow prospectors at Latuya Bay, nearly 100 miles from SKAGWAY, ALASKA. The husband and wife held a makeshift trial, then hung him.

SYNOPSIS

The story opens with a statement similar to that about adaptability that opens "In a Far Country":

It is a simple matter to see the obvious, to do the expected. The tendency of the individual life is to be static rather than dynamic, and this tendency is made into a propulsion by civilization, where the obvious only is seen, and the unexpected rarely happens. When the unexpected does happen, however, and when it is of sufficiently grave import, the unfit perish. They do not see what is not obvious, are unable to do the unexpected, are incapable of adjusting their well-grooved lives to other and strange grooves. In short, when they come to the end of their own groove, they die. (*Stories*, 998)

Furthermore, civilization imposes human law upon environments until "it becomes machine-like in its regularity. The objectionable is eliminated, the inevitable is foreseen. One is not even made wet by the rain nor cold by the frost; while death, instead of stalking about grewsome [sic] and accidental, becomes a prearranged pageant, moving along a well-oiled groove to the family vault, where the hinges are kept from rusting and the dust from the air is swept continually away" (*Stories*, 998).

The heroine of "The Unexpected," Edith Whittlesey Nelson, grew up in rural England and emigrates to the United States as a lady's maid. She meets and marries Hans Nelson, then accompanies him to mine for gold and silver in Colorado, the Dakotas, Idaho, Oregon, and British Columbia. By mid-year 1898, the Nelsons are in the KLONDIKE prospecting with three other men. They journey in canoes paddled by Siwash NATIVES to Latuya Bay, Alaska, where they camp, cutting spruce trees and building a cabin. Edith cooks and keeps the camp as the men look for gold, which they find in a placer mine; they are able to dig out about $8,000 in dust—$1,600 each for the summer's work. Waiting for the right weather in which to depart, they spend their time preparing for the coming months of cold by making snowshoes, hunting and caching meat, talking, and playing cards.

There is no sense of friction or competition among the group. Edith is eminently responsible and composed; her husband is stolid and easygoing; Harkey is a laid-back Texan; and Michael Dennin, an IRISH braggart, is a big, powerful man seemingly good-natured, though occasionally prone to sudden bursts of anger over petty things. Dutchy,

a stereotypically dull-witted German character, is the butt of jokes.

Early one morning, Dennin suddenly enters the cabin with a shotgun and kills Dutchy and Harkey, but when he tries to reload, planning to kill Edith and Hans, Edith leaps on him, and Hans beats him unconscious. They tie him up. Sadly, they dig two graves in the frozen ground for Dutchy and Harkey, and, standing four-hour watches with the shotgun, guard Dennin for the many months of the winter, while they debate his punishment and fate. Hans begs to kill him, and Dennin eventually begs to die. Negook, headman of a nearby Native settlement, refuses to transport the killer by canoe to the nearest trading post. Edith, nearing her physical and emotional limits, reasons her way through to a solution: "It came to her that the law was nothing more than the judgment and will of any group of people. It mattered not how large a group of people. There were little groups, she reasoned, like Switzerland, and there were big groups like the United States" (*Stories*, 1,011). She relies on the long tradition of English law to reach her decision to try Dennin as an English court would. In the trial, she and Hans judge that Dennin must die for his crimes; Edith pronounces the sentence of hanging. After his sentencing, Dennin confesses that he had all along planned to kill them all for the gold. He planned to report the murders in Skagway as the work of Natives and depart for Ireland and his mother, whom he has not seen for 15 years, with the gold.

Edith and Hans stand Dennin on a barrel, place a noose about his neck, and throw the rope across an overhead branch. Throwing her weight against the barrel, Edith collapses. Hans finishes the job. She asks him, "'Take me to the cabin, Hans,'" and "With Hans's arm around her, supporting her weight and directing her helpless steps, she went off across the snow. But the Indians remained solemnly to watch the working of the white man's law that compelled a man to dance upon the air" (*Stories*, 1,016).

COMMENTARY

"The Unexpected" includes what one might expect from London in the sense that ADAPTATION is a key to survival; from DARWIN's sense of evolutionary fitness, London derives the character of Edith Nelson. Described as "clear-eyed" (*Stories,* 999) like many of London's heroines such as Margaret Henan of "Samuel" (and an allusion to the GREEK goddess Athena), Edith does not act out of revenge but out of an inherited sense of English justice, following long-established canons of procedure. She is able to realize that "The cabin epitomized the new world in which they must thenceforth live and move. The old cabin was gone forever. The horizon of life was totally new and unfamiliar. The unexpected had swept its wizardry over the face of things, changing the perspective, juggling values, and shuffling the real and the unreal into perplexing confusion" (*Stories,* 1,005). Edith holds out to let the authorities decide Dennin's fate, but when she realizes that this is impossible, she embodies the sense of English justice herself and follows its dictates.

CHARACTERS

Edith Whittlesey Nelson   "[T]here are those that make toward survival, the fit individuals who escape from the rule of the obvious and the expected and adjust their lives to no matter what strange grooves they may stray into, or into which they may be forced. Such an individual was Edith Whittlesey." Though she "was born in a rural district of England, where life proceeds by rule of thumb and the unexpected is so very unexpected that when it happens it is looked upon as an immorality," somehow she has learned the lessons of adaptability and endurance (*Stories,* 998).

Hans Nelson   Hans is married to Edith, who patiently follows him on his mostly unsuccessful attempts at gold-mining in the west and northwest. Hot-tempered and frightened, he wants to kill Dennin at first but ends up supporting his wife in her desire to try Dennin fairly. He performs the hanging.

Dennin   Dennin, an Irishman, has not visited Ireland and his mother in 15 years. He schemes to kill his partners and take the gold; he succeeds in killing two of them but is tried and executed by the two survivors.

Dutchy and Harkey   Dutchy, a German immigrant, and Harkey, a cocky Texan, partner with Dennin and the Nelsons to mine gold in the Klondike. They hit a successful placer mine and celebrate their success. They are murdered by Dennin for their share of the gold.

Negook   Negook refuses to help the Nelsons because he does not know who the murderer was:

> "Much wind," the Indian remarked by way of salutation. "All well? Very well?"
>
> Hans, still grasping the gun, felt sure that the Indian attributed to him the mangled corpses. He glanced appealingly at his wife.
>
> "Good morning, Negook," she said, her voice betraying her effort. "No, not very well. Much trouble."
>
> "Good-by, I go now, much hurry," the Indian said, and without semblance of haste, with great deliberation stepping clear of a red pool on the floor, he opened the door and went out.
>
> The man and woman looked at each other.
>
> "He thinks we did it," Hans gasped, "that I did it." (*Stories,* 1,007).

"The Unparalleled Invasion" (1910)

Included in the collection *The Strength of the Strong,* the futuristic DYSTOPIAN story "The Unparalleled Invasion" first appeared in *McClure's Magazine* 35 (July 1910). It is a fantasy/satire of future Western plans to use germ warfare against CHINA, a technology they then all secretly seem to plan to turn upon their Western neighbors. Though it is sometimes cited as an instance of London's fomenting fears of the Yellow Peril, in actuality it is a sardonic portrait of Western fears of the East that points to a lack of understanding of other cultures as the motive behind such monstrous notions as genocide. Understanding this story hinges upon understanding its mordant irony.

SYNOPSIS

Presented as a fairly dry historical excerpt from Walt Mervin's vaguely titled book from the future, *Certain Essays in History,* "The Unparalleled Invasion" is set in the year 1976. It tells of how in the past decades, the West (the United States and Europe) came to see China as an emerging threat to world stability and makes the decision to pre-empt China's further development through biological warfare. China's progress had been too swift for the West, beginning with its development after the RUSSO-JAPANESE WAR of 1904, in which, for the first time in modern memory, an Asian power had beaten a European—and white—one, an actual event London covered in his war correspondence from KOREA for the HEARST newspapers in 1904.

After JAPAN beats Russia, it absorbs the Western ideas it needs and sets about trying to build an empire. In the story, Japan attacks China, whose 400 million citizens possessed "mental processes" that "were the same" as theirs: "The Japanese thought with the same thought-symbols as did the Chinese" (*Stories,* 1,235–1,236). In 1922, Japan goes to war against China, and over the course of half a year loses to China Manchuria, KOREA, and Formosa (today Taiwan). However, China's strength is not just in its military might; it lies mainly in population numbers: "the real danger lay in the fecundity of her loins, and it was in 1970 that the first cry of alarm was raised. For some time all territories adjacent to China had been grumbling at Chinese immigration; but now it suddenly came home to the world that China's population was 500,000,000. She had increased by a 100 million since her awakening. Burchaldter called attention to the fact that there were more Chinese in existence than white-skinned people" (*Stories,* 1,238). By the year 1970, China is threatening to spill over its borders. That same year, when FRANCE fights for Indochina, China sends an army of 1 million men, and "The French force was brushed aside like a fly." France's 250,000 troops are "swallowed up in China's cavernous maw" (*Stories,* 1,239). Having defeated the Europeans, China proceeds to absorb more of her neighbors: Thailand, Burma, the Malay Peninsula, the southern reaches of Siberia, Nepal,

Bhutan, northern India, Bokhara, Afghanistan, Persia, Turkestan—indeed, all of Central Asia.

The year 1975 brings the Great Truce, in which universal peace is declared. Yet in secret the armies of Russia, Austria, Germany, Italy, Greece, and Turkey are mobilized and head for the Chinese borders. Over 50,000 armed merchant steamers are sent by various nations to points along China's coastline. On May 1, 1976, an airplane drops thousands of tubes of fragile glass vials full of disease-bearing microbes over China. All China is bombed with the glass tubes, which are filled with dozens of deadly germs; within six weeks most of Peking's 11 million people are dead of epidemics of malaria, smallpox, scarlet fever, yellow fever, cholera, and even bubonic plague. Nearly the same holds true in the countryside among the peasants: The Chinese government and infrastructure are destroyed as millions flee their farms in panic. If they reach the borders they are slaughtered by Western troops. Soon China is an empty wilderness. Western troops clean up by executing all survivors, then proceed on a five-year "sanitation" project of the country.

However, the extermination of the Chinese does not solve any of the political battles among the Western powers. GERMANY and France renew an old grudge over the territories of Alsace and Lorraine. In 1987, the Great Truce having been dissolved, the Convention of Copenhagen calls for all nations to "solemnly [pledge] themselves never to use against one another the laboratory methods of warfare they had employed in the invasion of China" (*Stories,* 1,246), but the story clearly implies that they soon will.

COMMENTARY

London's irony often goes undetected by his critics, and this story furnishes a perfect example. Unless his reader understands that he is being ironic, London cannot accomplish his goal of satirizing—and bemoaning—the state of affairs internationally and humanly. In this sense he resembles MARK TWAIN in his attack on the West in particular and on human nature in general. The decision of the Western powers to use germ warfare against an ever-multiplying Chinese population is presented with bitter cynicism:

And then began the great task, the sanitation of China. Five years and hundreds of millions of treasure were consumed, and then the world moved in—not in zones, as was the idea of Baron Albrecht, but heterogeneously, according to the democratic American programme. It was a vast and happy intermingling of nationalities that settled down in China in 1982 and the years that followed—a tremendous and successful experiment in cross-fertilization. We know to-day the splendid mechanical, intellectual, and art output that followed. (*Stories*, 1,245–1,246)

But the story itself is at odds with such projections: it not only praises some of the cultural values London admired in the Chinese and Japanese, but also displays his suspicion of the motives for Western governments' self-proclaimed humanistic values. After all, as a socialist, London expressed kinship with socialists around the world (especially, at several points, those in Japan and Asia) in overthrowing the militaristic national powers.

The central theme of "The Unparalleled Invasion" is of a lack of common speech. As he would so eloquently express in his 1915 speech to the PAN-PACIFIC UNION in HONOLULU, "The Language of the Tribe," wherein London calls for Asians learning English and English-speakers learning Asian languages, here he demonstrates the results of a lack of understanding among nations. As the narrator in "The Unparalleled Invasion" admits:

It was all a matter of language. There was no way to communicate Western ideas to the Chinese mind. China remained asleep. The material achievement and progress of the West was a closed book to her; nor could the West open the book. Back and deep down on the tie-ribs of consciousness, in the mind, say, of the English-speaking race, was a capacity to thrill to short, Saxon words; back and deep down on the tie-ribs of consciousness of the Chinese mind was a capacity to thrill to its own hieroglyphics; but the Chinese mind could not thrill to short, Saxon words; nor could the English-speaking mind thrill to hieroglyphics. The fabrics of their minds were woven from totally different stuffs.

They were mental aliens. And so it was that Western material achievement and progress made no dent on the rounded sleep of China. (*Stories*, 1,234–1,235)

This story is instructive to read along with London's Russo-Japanese War correspondence and his two essays on the rise of Asia, "The Yellow Peril" and "If Japan Awakens China," and it makes an interesting comparison to "Goliah" with its main character's mad scheme to make peace in the world by annihilating those he deems unfit.

London seems prescient in forecasting the coming conflict between the United States and Japan and, later perhaps, that still not fully realized between the United States and China.

CHARACTERS

Li Tang Fwung The "power behind the Dragon Throne," he is the Chinese spokesman to the Western powers who warns them,

"We are the most ancient, honourable, and royal of races. We have our own destiny to accomplish. It is unpleasant that our destiny does not tally with the destiny of the rest of the world, but what would you? You have talked windily about the royal races and the heritage of the earth, and we can only reply that that remains to be seen. You cannot invade us. Never mind about your navies. . . . Our strength is in our population, which will soon be a billion. Thanks to you, we are equipped with all modern war-machinery. Send your navies. We will not notice them. Send your punitive expeditions, but first remember France." (*Stories*, 1,240)

Jacobus Laningdale "But there was one scholar China failed to reckon on—Jacobus Laningdale. Not that he was a scholar, except in the widest sense. Primarily, Jacobus Laningdale was a scientist, and, up to that time, a very obscure scientist, a professor employed in the laboratories of the Health Office of New York City" (*Stories*, 1,241). Jacobus has the idea that germ warfare could work, as he advises the president of the United States.

President Moyer He listens to the germ warfare suggestions of Laningdale and dispatches an aide to Europe to present the idea in diplomatic circles. Moyer may be said to have instigated the germ warfare plot.

Rufus Cowdery "Rufus Cowdery, Secretary of State, left Washington, and early the following morning sailed for England. The secret that he carried began to spread, but it spread only among the heads of Governments. Possibly half-a-dozen men in a nation were entrusted with the idea that had formed in Jacobus Laningdale's head. Following the spread of the secret, sprang up great activity in all the dockyards, arsenals, and navy-yards. The people of France and Austria became suspicious, but so sincere were their Governments' calls for confidence that they acquiesced in the unknown project that was afoot" (*Stories*, 1,241).

FURTHER READING

Berkove, Lawrence I. "A Parallax Connection in London's 'The Unparalleled Invasion.'" In *American Literary Realism* 24, no. 2 (winter 1992): 33–39.

The Valley of the Moon (1913)

First serialized in Cosmopolitan, *The Valley of the Moon* is London's testament to the healing power of Sonoma Valley and his Beauty Ranch, as well as a testament to his wife, Charmian London, the model for its heroine, Saxon Brown Roberts. Saxon leads her husband, Billy, out of the labor strife of Oakland into a new life in Sonoma Valley, to the country where they may start anew. Though they encounter many immigrants on their journey, in an important sense they are immigrants too. Saxon is fond of recalling her pioneer English ancestry, what she thinks of as Anglo-Saxon, but theirs is a modern struggle to live in a modern West. Furthermore, unlike the usual American bildungsroman, this is *her* story, not his. Like Dede Mason of *Burning Daylight,* Saxon "reforms" her man into a man of the soil, not the city. Through her, as Jeanne Campbell Reesman notes, the novel enacts a search for "a

middle landscape of pastoral harmony and the urge for individual freedom within community, and it follows the wounded retreat from oppression with the re-discovery of the land" (Reesman, "Jack London's New Woman," 40).

Charles L. Crow has observed that California literature is mainly one of disillusionment: "Things did not work out here, after all." However, there is a set of works involving the San Francisco Bay Area where "a perfect home place" is realized after a radical "transformation of the self." *The Valley of the Moon* is the "first major narrative in this visionary tradition" (Crow, "Homecoming," 1–2). Yet for Crow it is "a flawed, hybrid work," beginning in the naturalist mode but turning halfway through into romance. For Billy and Saxon, historical forces may have "destroyed the promise of California," but in breaking free by leaving the mode of Naturalism for a romantic dream, they "begin their journey of ascent, and are granted at last a vision of reconciliation and wholeness, of a perfect California home" (Crow, "Homecoming," 5). Oakland was just another brutal industrial town in which dreams are ruined, like those in the East, like those in Europe, from which generations of migrants fled." Volume 1 appropriately ends with the image of a linnet in a cage, an echo of *McTeague* (Crow, "Homecoming," 5). But toward the end of Volume 2 and throughout Volume 3, this naturalistic story of class aspiration is realized through a romantic return to the land, if tempered by Realism. If at first Saxon is the idealist and Billy the pragmatist, by the end of the book Billy's far-fetched dreams of wealth in Sonoma are offset by Saxon's realistic views.

SYNOPSIS

Book I

The book opens in the laundry where Saxon works, where a woman collapses on the factory floor with labor pains, then moves to her ugly rooms in the home of her brother and sister-in-law, where the latter, Sarah, scolds her for her attendance at dances and picnics, such as the one scheduled at Weasel Park with the bricklayers.

At the picnic, Saxon meets the golden-haired Billy Roberts, a teamster, and the two fall in love.

As she contemplates this potential escape from her toil at the laundry, she imagines him as her savior:

> So blond was he that she was reminded of stage-types she had seen, such as Ole Olson and Yon Yonson; but there resemblance ceased. . . . [H]e had none of the awkwardness of the Scandinavian immigrant. On the contrary, he was one of those rare individuals that radiate muscular grace through the ungraceful man-garments of civilization. . . . She felt, rather than perceived, the calm and certitude of all the muscular play of him, and she felt, too, the promise of easement and rest. (15–16)

Saxon sees Billy as a man, "a protector, something to lean against." She tells him of her "Saxon" ancestors:

> "They were wild, like Indians, only they were white. And they had blue eyes, and yellow hair, and they were awful fighters."
>
> As she talked, Billy followed her solemnly, his eyes steadily turned on hers.
>
> "Never heard of them," he confessed. "Did they live anywhere around here?"
>
> She laughed.
>
> "No. They lived in England. They were the first English, and you know the Americans came from the English. We're Saxons, you an' me, an' Mary an' Bert, and all the American that are real Americans, you know, and not Dagoes and Japs and such." (21–22)

Billy recalls that his father was from Maine, adopted by a gold-miner who fought against the Modocs; among NATIVE prisoners is a white child, to whom the miner gives his name, Roberts. "'They figured he was about five years old. He didn't know nuthin' but Indian.'" Billy says his mother came from Ohio and describes his parents' migration west. Both their fathers fought in the Civil War. Their friends Mary and Bert are surprised by their sudden recognition of each other: "'They're thicker than mush in no time,'" he grumbles; "'You'd think they'd know each other a week already'" (22–23).

Contained here are suggestions of London's own heritage: WILLIAM CHANEY, his probable biological father, was from Maine; "Billy" of course is a dimin-utive for William. JOHN LONDON, his stepfather, came from Pennsylvania and fought in the Civil War, as did Alonzo Prentiss, husband of his wet-nurse and foster mother, Mrs. VIRGINIA PRENTISS, who made the only real heroic westward trek of any of them, from slavery to CALIFORNIA. London was lectured by his mother FLORA LONDON (who hailed from Ohio) on her Anglo-Saxon pioneer ancestors. Despite his poor grammar, Billy is well-spoken, dignified, quiet, and in control. However, after their marriage, as Saxon takes over the management of their relationship, he recedes into immaturity and impulsiveness. At first Saxon sees her race pride as her source of strength; later her understanding of community will be broadened by other immigrant groups. Just as Billy's father was raised as a Native child, Saxon likes to pull out of her chest of drawers not only her Anglo-Saxon mother's poems but also "a little red-satin Spanish girdle, whale-boned like a tiny corset, pointed, the finery of a frontier woman who had crossed the plains. It was hand-made after the California-Spanish model of forgotten days. . . . Saxon kissed the little, red satin Spanish girdle passionately," storing it away again "in haste, with dewy eyes, abandoning the mystery and godhead of mother and all the strange enigma of living" (51). The Spanish girdle connects her to an older California, a forecast of her appreciation for the diverse "races" she and Billy encounter on their journey.

Book II

At the end of Book I, Billy proposes and Saxon happily accepts. Book II finds Saxon and Billy a newly married couple. Their landlady, Mercedes Higgins, shows Saxon how to wear lingerie to keep her husband's interest. As Saxon's mentor, however, she soon exerts a negative influence. Her neighbors suspect her of witchcraft: her face is "withered as if scorched in great heats," while her black eyes speak of an "unquenched inner conflagration" (133–134). Mercedes' father was an IRISHMAN and her mother Peruvian, and in London's ethnic stereotyping this makes her "hot-blooded on both sides; and she has lived in every part of the world, including the Klondike and the South Seas." She hopes to convey her worldly experience to Saxon, especially how to "hold a man, and subtly dominate him," a power she equates "with the life force itself," but in the end Saxon rejects her. For one thing, she has no pity for the workers beaten by mobs: "'Most men are born stupid,'" she declares. "'They are the slaves. A few are born clever. They are the masters'" (179). Saxon "is horrified by Mercedes' contemptuous dismissal of the working class," comments Charles N. Watson, Jr. (Watson, 203–204; *Valley*, 182).

Bert and Mary get married, and Saxon becomes pregnant. Their happiness, however, is threatened by the growing strife between capitalists and labor. There are several conversations about the political situation, in which Tom, Saxon's brother and a socialist, joins in. As they argue about immigrants in America, conditions around them deteriorate until they start to feel hunger. One day, a riot suddenly erupts between armed private guards and striking workers. Bert is killed. Saxon has a miscarriage, and Billy decides to join the strike. Billy becomes more and more depressed and angry, and Saxon feels herself pulling away from him. Yet she sympathizes with him and blames his state on the strike:

> One thing, however, Saxon saw clearly. By no deliberate act of Billy's was he becoming this other and unlovely Billy. Were there no strike, no snarling and wrangling over jobs, there would be only the old Billy she had loved in all absoluteness. This sleeping terror in him would have lain asleep. It was something that was being awakened in him, an image incarnate of outward conditions, as cruel, as ugly, as maleficent as were those outward conditions. But if the strike continued, then, she feared, with reason, would this other and grisly self of Billy strengthen to fuller and more forbidding stature. And this, she knew, would mean the wreck of their love-life. Such a Billy she could not love; in its nature such a Billy was not lovable nor capable of love. And then, at the thought of offspring, she shuddered. It was too terrible. And at such moments of contemplation, from her soul the inevitable plaint of the human went up: *Why? Why? Why?* (218).

Desperate for money, Billy breaks his promise to Saxon and enters a prizefight. He begins to drink and threaten everyone around him. He is beaten terribly and returns home a wreck. Eventually Billy is jailed.

For many long months Saxon fends for herself, mourning her lost baby and her husband:

> Looking thus at life, shorn of its superrational sanctions, Saxon floundered into the morass of pessimism. There was no justification for right conduct in the universe, no square deal for her who had earned reward, for the millions who worked like animals, died like animals, and were a long time and forever dead. Like the hosts of more learned thinkers before her, she concluded that the universe was unmoral and without concern for men. (255)

But Saxon refuses to give in to despair; feeding herself with mussels gathered from the bay, she begins to regain her usual strength:

> There must be such a way out. When canal boys and rail-splitters, the lowliest of the stupid lowly, as she had read in her school history, could find their way out and become presidents of the nation and rule over even the clever ones in their automobiles, then could she find her way out and win to the tiny reward she craved— Billy, a little love, a little happiness. She would not mind that the universe was unmoral, that there was no God, no immortality. . . .
>
> How she would work for that happiness! How she would appreciate it, make the most of each least particle of it! But how was she to do it, where was the paths she could not vision it. Her eyes showed her only the smudge of San Francisco, the smudge of Oakland, where men were breaking heads and killing one another, where babies were dying, born and unborn, and where women were weeping with bruised breasts. (256)

While Billy is in jail, Saxon takes to combing the rocks of the Bay edge for mussels to eat. Saxon's "way out" is inspired not by the ideology of SOCIALISM she debates with Tom, but by a young boy in his skiff Saxon meets one day when she is foraging for mussels. He shares his sailing and fishing knowledge with her and answers her questions:

> "What do I want?" he repeated after her.
>
> Turning his head slowly, he followed the skyline, pausing especially when his eyes rested landward on the brown Contra Costa hills, and seaward, past Alcatraz, on the Golden Gate. The wistfulness in his eyes was overwhelming and went to her heart.
>
> "That," he said, sweeping the circle of the world with a wave of his arm. . . . "Don't you sometimes feel you'd die if you didn't know what's beyond them hills an' what's beyond the other hills behind them hills? An' the Golden Gate! There's the Pacific Ocean beyond, and China, an' Japan, an' India, an' . . . an' all the coral islands. You can go anywhere out through the Golden Gate—to Australia, to Africa, to the seal islands, to the North Pole, to Cape Horn. Why, all them places are just waitin' for me to come an' see 'em. I've lived in Oakland all my life, but I'm not going to live in Oakland the rest of my life, not by a long shot. I'm goin' to get away." (263–264)

Crow sees this adventurous boy—an incarnation of London—as a "counterpoint" to the dominant "deterministic message" of the novel (Crow, "Homecoming," 5–6). Certainly the desire to experience foreign lands is bound up with Saxon's sense of personal freedom, if not so much in her husband and his peers. She has new hope: "Oakland is just a place to start from" (270).

When Billy returns from prison, and as Saxon and Billy talk of leaving Oakland, Bert complains that Americans have been "forced" off their land, alluding to and land-grabbing by the Southern Pacific Railroad and the use of immigrant labor: "'We cleared it, an' broke it, an' made the roads, an' built the cities. And there was plenty for everybody. And we went on fightin' for it. I had two uncles killed at Gettysburg'" (174). But Saxon answers, "'And if they'd been smart they'd a-held on to them'" (174). Saxon admires her female forebears' "hard-working, hard-fighting stock" (103) Saxon works to construct a new identity as a California woman.

Book III

Saxon envisions a new start in the country for herself and for Billy when he is released. She persuades him to leave Oakland to look for a better life as a farmer: "'we want to know all about all kinds of land, close to the big cities as well as back in the mountains'" she urges (305). Her goal of personal freedom and their goals as a family lie in knowledge of new places and people. When they ride the rail car as far as San Leandro and get off, Billy's only comment is, "'Gee!—this must be the Porchugeeze headquarters'" (303). When he refuses to ask questions, Saxon decides she will: "'We've got to win out at this game, and the way is to know. Look at all these Portuguese. . . . What made the Americans clear out? How do the Portuguese make it go? Don't you see, We've got to ask millions of questions'" (305). Saxon has already observed that some "Americans live like pigs." A telephone lineman answers their queries about why immigrant groups have flourished on farms while white "Americans" have not: "'We don't use our headpieces right. Something's wrong with us,'" he says (310). Billy seems to find confirmation of his class and race prejudices on the journey, while Saxon learns from a new perspective. Billy wants to be a bonanza king like Elam Harnish: "'Just the same,' Billy held stubbornly, 'large scale's a whole lot better'n small scale like all these dinky gardens'" (304–305).

The pair make their way to San Jose, where they meet Mrs. Mortimer, an independent woman farmer who employs Chinese workers and has learned much from their horticultural practices. She becomes a mentor to the Roberts. As Billy and Saxon wander, over and over again they learn that the Anglo-Saxon "race" "lost the land," as Crow points out, "because they were not worthy of it, did not farm it with ecological respect, and thus fell victim to the Naturalistic forces of the city" (Crow, "Homecoming," 6). Mrs. Mortimer teaches them that "the true farming of California is small, intensive, in the style of the Asians and non–Anglo-Saxon Europeans who have inherited the land, not the style of the bonanza ranchers, about whom Norris wrote, who earlier had raped it," argues Crow ("Homecoming," 6).

Next, a new friend they make, Benson, similarly urges:

> "We'll soon enter the valley. You bet I saw. First thing, in Japan, the terraced hillsides. Take a hill so steep you couldn't drive a horse up it. No bother to them. They terraced it—a stone wall, and good masonry, six feet high, a level terrace six feet wide; up and up, walls and terraces, the same thing all the way, straight into the air, walls upon walls, terraces upon terraces. . . . Same thing everywhere I went, in Greece, in Ireland. . . . They went around and gathered every bit of soil they could find, gleaned it and even stole it by the shovelful or handful, and carried it up the mountains on their backs and built farms—BUILT them, MADE them, on the naked rock. . . . "My God!" Billy muttered in awe-stricken tones. "Our folks never done that. No wonder they lost out." (365)

Benson serves as a useful history lesson, "'It was our folks that made this country,' Billy reflected. 'Fought for it, opened it up, did everything—But develop it,' Benson caught him up. 'We did our best to destroy it, as we destroyed the soil of New England.'" Retorts Billy, "'We'll never be goin' around smellin' out an' swipin' bits of soil an' carryin' it up a hill in a basket. The United States is big yet. I don't care what Benson or any of 'em says, the United States ain't played out.'" But Saxon reminds him, "'We're getting an education'" (365–366).

The farmer-poet Mark Hall, whom the Roberts encounter in Sonoma, tells them his theory of the history and fate of the American West, echoing London's favorite agricultural themes:

> "When you think of the glorious chance," he said. "A new country, bounded by the oceans, situated just right in latitude, with the richest land and vastest natural resources of any country in the world, settled by immigrants who had thrown off all the leading strings of the Old World and were in the humor for democracy. There was only one thing to stop them from perfecting the democracy they started, and that thing was greediness.

> "They started gobbling everything in sight like a lot of swine, and while they gobbled democracy went to smash. Gobbling became gambling. . . . They moved over the face of the land like so many locusts. They destroyed everything—the Indians, the soil, the forests, just as they destroyed the buffalo and the passenger pigeon. Their morality in business and politics was gambler morality. Their laws were gambling laws—how to play the game. . . . And democracy gone clean to smash." (413–414)

When Billy and Saxon encounter wealthy Chinese merchants and prosperous Greek fishermen in a seaside village, Billy's disgust is again contrasted with Saxon's curiosity. There they meet another farmer-poet and his wife, Jack and Clara Hastings, who, like Mark Hall, lament the white "land-hogs" who have "abandoned farms by the tens of thousands." Clara Hastings remarks, "'All the old farms are dropping into ruin'" and mentions one farm, once a "perfect paradise" (it sounds like London's BEAUTY RANCH): "There were dams and lakes, beautiful meadows, lush hayfields, red hills of grape-lands, hundreds of acres of good pasture, heavenly groves of pines and oaks, a stone winery, stone barns, grounds—oh, I couldn't describe it in hours. When Mrs. Bell died, the family scattered, and the leasing began. It's a ruin to-day. 'It's become a profession,'" Hastings tells the Roberts, in which the "'movers . . . lease, clean out and gut a place in several years, and then move on. They're not like the foreigners, the Chinese, and Japanese, and the rest. In the main they're a lazy, vagabond, poor-white sort, who do nothing else but skin the soil and move, skin the soil and move'" (432–433).

After wandering to Sacramento, Napa Valley, Ukiah, and Redding, the couple keeps considering where they might settle, but no spot is just right. On the way they continue to look at various immigrant groups' farming practices and learn from them. Billy takes whatever work as he can get, but Saxon persuades him not to enter the BOXING ring again. Buying two horses and a wagon, Billy takes up drayage. Eventually, they take up the Hastings' invitation to visit Sonoma Valley, which is a NATIVE word for "valley of the moon." There, they find their "natural" home. The book closes with Saxon, pregnant, full of hopes for their new life in the beautiful valley; meanwhile, when Billy gazes at the mountain, all he dreams of is money to be earned by mining clay out of it.

COMMENTARY

The Valley of the Moon is nearly all dialogue. This is appropriate to the many questions Saxon asks while they are on the road, the debates on socialism back in the city, and the dialectical manner in which social conditions are analyzed overall. Saxon asks intelligent questions of everyone they meet on their journey and then has to explain the answers to Billy. Like a frontier or pioneer hero, she is able to learn and adapt, putting aside her prejudices when they get in her way. She is proud of her "Saxon" heritage, but she learns to adapt to ethnic others and learn from them instead of rejecting them on racial grounds. We are perhaps to infer that her experience with class warfare back in Oakland has made her less rigid in her social ideas. She is thus a model of Darwinian evolutionary fitness and ADAPTATION.

Billy seems to be diminished over the course of the novel; at the beginning he is strong and sure, and Saxon is thrilled to be protected by his strength. But over the course of events, Saxon emerges as the stronger of the two. In the end, Billy and Saxon find their home, but they see it differently: Saxon gravitates toward the valley's natural beauty and peace and plans to farm the land, while Billy is bent on large-scale development through horse breeding, drayage, and excavating clay for a brick manufacturer, which, Crow argues, "links him with the capitalists of Oakland whom he earlier had fought." He seems to be unable "to follow his own vision" (Crow, "Homecoming," 7–8), but of course it is really Saxon's vision that has led them to a new start. COMMUNITY versus INDIVIDUALISM, the openness to racial "others" versus traditional racism and suspicion of foreigners, are gendered and opposed in this novel, and so are Saxon and Billy's differing concepts of what nature offers. The romance of nature is clearly undercut in the novel's conclusion, in which Saxon, still full of hopes for living in nature, is silenced by Billy's descriptions of future wealth from the clay mine. One is tempted at first to see Billy's plans as practical and Saxon's musings on her pregnancy as merely romantic, but the entire narrative has demonstrated the opposite: Saxon wants simply to live, Billy to dream of riches.

In creating this novel, London was inspired by a story in the SATURDAY EVENING POST, LeRoy Armstrong's "The Man Who Came Back: Two Twentieth Century Pilgrims and Where They Landed"; he tore out the story and penciled in its margins, "Novel Motif" (Watson, 187–188). A Chicago typesetter, Armstrong was persuaded by his wife to search for a new home in the West. Relating the death of their baby, labor disputes, and the loss of his job, his drinking and loafing, he tells how Mary, his wife, wanted to imitate their settler forebears and head west. They take a train to Colorado and then walk for 1,000 miles over the Rockies, stopping here and there to work. At last they find their valley and have another baby. *The Valley of the Moon* certainly derives from "the 'back to the land' stories," Watson observes; the Londons' "preoccupation with barrenness and fertility" may have led London "to make a significant departure" from Armstrong, replacing the male point of view with the female, subordinating Billy to Saxon, who leads him to their valley. Her "penetration and sensitivity . . . serve as a corrective to Billy's emotional gyrations and egotistical bluster" (Watson 189, 194–195). Watson notes that "Many readers, viewing Saxon's emotions in light of later manifestations of Germanic and Anglo-American racism, . . . find her adulation of the 'land-hungry Anglo-Saxon' ominous"; she does not escape "the taint of racism, nor does London himself." He also attributes much of their racism to the "perennial form of working-class paranoia, . . . aggravated during periods of economic hardship when the competition for jobs is the most fierce. The same impulse appears in Bert and Billy's lament for their kind as "'the last of the Mohegans'" (*Valley*, 155). However it is in gender that Watson most effectively locates Saxon and Billy's differences on race: "London carefully distinguishes . . . between Saxon's pride of ancestry" and the "belligerent chauvinism of Billy and Bert." Saxon often remains "aloof" when the others, including Billy, complain about immigrants. When Billy grumbles that "'the free-born American ain't got no room left in his own land,'" Saxon replies, "'Then it's his own fault'" (*Valley*, 303; Watson, 195).

CHARACTERS

Saxon Brown Roberts   Saxon is the descendant of a frontier calvary officer and an early California poet. She is fiercely devoted to her Anglo-Saxon pioneer ancestry, possibly because that is all she really has, as she lives in poverty with her brother and sister-in-law in a slovenly apartment, working long days as an ironer of fancy starch in a laundry. When she meets Billy Roberts, she recognizes that she needs a man—this strong man—to take care of her. Saxon has a great deal of vision, hope, and endurance, and she, not her husband, ends up saving the couple from the dying city into a new life in the beautiful Sonoma Valley.

elderly laundrywoman   As Saxon works in the laundry ironing fancy starched pieces, a young coworker, Mary, encourages her to attend the bricklayers' picnic at Weasel Park, while she and Saxon observe an elderly coworker go into labor and be dragged off the factory floor.

Mary   Mary is Saxon's friend who encourages her to attend the bricklayers' picnic. She marries Bert Wanhope but becomes his widow when he is killed in a labor riot.

Sarah Brown   Sarah is Saxon's sister-in-law, with whom she lives. She is bitter and coarse and keeps a dirty, unhappy house. She is jealous of Saxon's beauty and her invitations to dances. She feels trapped by marriage and children and resents Saxon's still being single. She gloats when Billy is arrested.

Bert Wanhope   Bert is Mary's boyfriend who meets up with her and Saxon at the bricklayers' picnic. Bert is known for his temper. Bert flirts with Mary but hasn't yet asked her to marry him. He eventually does, and they are married soon after the Robertses. Bert is killed in a labor riot.

Billy Roberts   A former prizefighter, "Big Bill Roberts," or Billy, is a teamster. He meets Saxon at the bricklayers' picnic and the two fall in love. Saxon eventually persuades Billy to leave strike-torn Oakland and move to a farm in Sonoma Valley. However his dream is not farming there, but mining. Billy seems quite mature early in the novel but becomes more boyish as it progresses.

Tom Brown   Saxon's brother and Sarah's husband, Tom is a gentle soul who attends socialist meetings and believes in human and economic progress. Unlike him, Saxon is not prepared to wait for the eventual revolution. He and Saxon have several heated conversations about her plans to leave Oakland.

Irishman   At the bricklayers' picnic he starts to antagonize Billy, then recognizes him as the former fighter, whom he respects. The Irish at the picnic are portrayed as drunken and free with their oaths and fists.

Charley Long   A big thug who wants to marry Saxon. When he finds out she is seeing Billy, he vows to beat him. Long has already beaten up one of Saxon's admirers; he sickens her with his crude language and behavior. Billy scares him off when he accosts him. Later, when Billy is in jail, he again tries to win her, but she brushes him off.

Mercedes Higgins   Part Irish and Peruvian-Spanish, the exotic Mercedes is the Roberts's landlady in Oakland. She instructs Saxon on how to keep her man interested through feminine wiles and fancy lingerie. She at first seems like a good friend to Saxon, but she cheats Saxon out of the price of the fancywork she has been making and Mercedes has been selling. Her advice on men mirrors her avarice and untrustworthiness; according to her, a woman must spin constant illusions of herself to keep her man. Mercedes sees life in a naturalistic way.

James Harmon   Harmon is a fireman who boards with the Roberts when they are forced by Billy's strike to take lodgers. He comes and goes, and they rarely see him, but Billy objects to having him there. One day when Billy finds him talking to Saxon—one day when Billy is drunk—Billy attacks him and drives him out, slugging him first. Billy is arrested.

Roy Blanchard The son of a wealthy man, Blanchard is out to make a name for himself by breaking the teamsters' strike. He has a policeman try to beat Billy, and when Billy sees him one day he threatens to get him. Blanchard later tries to help Saxon, but he is refused.

Bud Strothers, Maggie Donahue, and Mrs. Olsen Neighbors who look in on Saxon while Billy is in jail. Bud Strothers brings messages from Billy in jail. Strothers continues to correspond with Billy about happenings in Oakland after the Robertses leave Oakland.

John, or "Johnnie" The boy Saxon encounters on the Bay; from his tiny skiff he imagines seeing the whole world outside the GOLDEN GATE. His vitality and sense of adventure encourage Saxon to persevere and to leave Oakland for a better place. He is an image of Jack London, who was called "Johnnie" or "Johnny" as a boy.

Anson, Jackson, Billy, and other teamsters Some of the Oakland and San Francisco teamsters who get into a fight. This is yet one further illustration of why the Robertses need to leave Oakland.

lineman The Robertses encounter a lineman eating his lunch in San Leandro. A native of the area, he explains to them how the land prices have been driven up by the overuse of land by the Portuguese. He is the first to sound the theme that the whites have been lazy and that the immigrants have been working overtime. Opposed to this idea, however, is that such overproduction eventually depletes the soil.

Mrs. Mortimer A woman farmer living alone near San Jose, she employs CHINESE gardeners and has learned greatly from them. She counsels Billy

and Saxon about their plans for a farm. Saxon is thrilled to see that she has an autographed copy of her mother's book of poetry.

Constable Elderly railyard constable who tries to arrest Billy and Saxon for vagrancy. He is a comical threat, and Billy scares him away, calling him "Whiskers."

Benson A farmer near San Jose whose farm Billy works on for awhile. He kindly gives them a ride in his motorcar to San Juan, then rides on the train with them to Pajaro Valley, where they hope to work in an orchard. He discusses the savvy methods of the immigrant Slavs and Japanese who have driven out "American" farmers from valley after valley.

Jim Hazard A man who dives into the big surf at Carmel; Billy and Saxon introduce themselves, and Hazard recognizes Billy from his prizefighting days. A football coach, he is the picture of health. He later joins in the Abalone Eaters' celebrations.

Mark Hall The Robertses encounter him at Bierce's Cove north of Carmel. He too recognizes Billy. Hall is a poet and a Jack London figure. From him they learn to capture abalone and more about the land. They are joined by Hall's artist friends, the Abalone Eaters. Billy boxes with one of them, Pete Bideaux, the "Iron Man." The Robertses stay with him in his "shack" in Carmel.

Mrs. Hall Mark Hall's wife, she is an image of CHARMIAN KITTREDGE LONDON. She admires Saxon and Billy for their youth and courage. She and her husband leave the Robertses when they travel to New York.

Hafler Billy and Saxon stay in his "Marble House" in Carmel when they return after a trip south. He explains what he knows about the land, taking Billy on a long ramble around Carmel.

Gunston A commission merchant Billy and Saxon meet in Monterey; he informs them of how the Chinese have become "potato kings" through thrift and clever land use. He mentions terracing, an innovation London observed in KOREA and JAPAN and carried out on his BEAUTY RANCH.

Jack and Clara Hastings Another couple resembling the Londons, the Hastings meet Billy and Saxon in Monterey and invite them aboard their yacht to go to Rio Vista. Jack is a famous writer whom Billy recognizes from his reportage of the RUSSO-JAPANESE WAR. Clara is his graceful and athletic wife. Jack sounds bitter about the way the pioneers in California have been abusing the land. He names the magical valley they search for the valley of the moon and invites them to Sonoma Valley where their ranch is located.

Mr. and Mrs. Hale Annette and Edmund Hale are another contented London-like couple; they live in a rustic home called "Trillium Covert" and house the Robertses as they make plans to live in Sonoma Valley. The Hales help them figure out how to buy their Madrono Ranch.

FURTHER READING

Campbell, Donna. "Jack London's Allegorical Landscapes: 'The God of His Fathers,' 'The Priestly Prerogative,' and *The Valley of the Moon.*" In *Literature and Belief* 21, nos. 1–2 (2001): 59–75.

Crow, Charles L. "Homecoming in the California Visionary Romance." *Western American Literature* 24 (1989): 1–19.

Gair, Christopher. "'The Way Our People Came': Citizenship, Capitalism, and Racial Difference in *The Valley of the Moon.*" In *Rereading Jack London.* Edited by Leonard Cassuto and Jeanne Campbell Reesman. Stanford, Calif.: Stanford University Press, 1996.

O'Donnell Arosteguy, Katie. "'Things Men Must Do': Negotiating American Masculinity in Jack London's *The Valley of the Moon.*" *Atenea* 28, no. 1 (June 2008): 37–54.

Reesman, Jeanne Campbell. "Jack London's New Woman in a New World: Saxon Brown Robert's Journey into the Valley of the Moon." In *American Literary Realism* 24, no. 2 (winter 1992): 40–54.

———. *Jack London's Racial Lives.* Athens: University of Georgia Press, 2009.

Watson, Charles N., Jr. *The Novels of Jack London: A Reappraisal.* Madison: University of Wisconsin Press, 1983.

"War" (1911)

Never published in serial form in the United States, this gem of a story appeared in England in *Nation* (July 29, 1911). It was included in *The Night-Born.* As a piece of antiwar literature, it compares well with MARK TWAIN's "The War-Prayer" and "A Private History of a Campaign That Failed," AMBROSE BIERCE's "Chickamauga," and STEPHEN CRANE's *The Red Badge of Courage.*

SYNOPSIS

In a time of war, a young calvaryman scouts the woods and pastures for signs of the enemy, careful not to ride in the open. He comes upon a stream, from which he is desperate to drink in the hot weather, but he sees a man with a ginger beard kneeling on the opposite bank, filling up a water bottle. The next day, he comes upon a deserted farmhouse where men have obviously been camping; two bodies hang outside it, near a set of fresh graves. Moving through the orchard next to the house, the young man gathers apples and fashions a bag for them out of his shirt. A group of enemy soldiers suddenly appears, and the young man barely escapes their bullets as he races away on his horse. However, after they have emptied their guns, he looks back to see the man with the red beard kneeling and leveling his gun for a long shot. The young man is killed by the man, and his apples spill to the ground.

COMMENTARY

Since the time, place, and other details of the war are unspecified, the story takes on a timeless dimension, like "To Build a Fire"; what is important is not the particulars of who is at war with whom, but the eternal nature of war in which a young man, innocently picking apples, is gunned down by the enemy. The contrast between such details as the apples and the beauty of the woods around the young man with the seemingly inevitable fact of death is a powerful one. While NATURE shows her fecundity with images of great forests and the golden pollen that hangs in the air, men kill each other as strangers.

CHARACTERS

young calvaryman   In the first paragraph, the narrator stresses the young man's lonely scouting expedition and characterizes him as both a normal young man and an extremely watchful one: "He was a young man, not more than twenty-four or five, and he might have sat his horse with the careless grace of his youth had he not been so catlike and tense. His black eyes roved everywhere, catching the movements of twigs and branches where small birds hopped, questing ever onward through the changing vistas of trees and brush, and returning always to the clumps of undergrowth on either side" (*Stories*, 1,726).

man with ginger beard   Soldier on the enemy side who is first seen as he fills his water bottle by a stream, then by the young man again as he flees the farmhouse. He takes careful aim and shoots the young man from his saddle from a great distance.

enemy combatants   Several mounted men who have been occupying the farmhouse and presumably killed its inhabitants; when the young man is killed at the end, they cheer: "And they, watching at the house, saw him fall, saw his body bounce when it struck the earth, and saw the burst of red-cheeked apples that rolled about him. They laughed at the unexpected eruption of apples, and clapped their hands in applause of the long shot by the man with the ginger beard" (*Stories*, 1,731).

"The Water Baby" (1918)

Published posthumously first in COSMOPOLITAN 65 (September 1918) and then in *On the Makaloa Mat*, London's last story is one of his finest, and it reveals the soul-searching he was undergoing in his

final illness and following his reading of the works of CARL JUNG, especially the idea of the collective unconscious. It also reflects his knowledge of the MYTHOLOGY and folk tradition of HAWAI'I.

SYNOPSIS

The author steps through the mask in this story as a HAOLE kama'āina who goes out fishing one day with old Kohokumu: *Lakana* was London's Hawaiian name, and *Kohokumu* means "tree of knowledge" in Hawaiian. Lakana loses patience with Kohokumu's constant chanting of the deeds of the Hawaiian demigod, Maui. One of the primary myths of Maui is that he snared the SUN, the sun of course being a symbolic presence in London's work from the KLONDIKE stories on. As James McClintock has observed, "London explicitly links Kohokumu with the most common natural archetype which Jung identifies with the oedipal myths—that of the sun (the hero and libido energy) setting (dying) in the sea (the womb) and rising in the morning (being reborn)" (McClintock, *Strong Truths*, 337). But here the sun is not the dominant force, as much as it beats down on Lakana. Kohokumu tells how Maui caught the sun to slow it down so that his mother's *tapa* cloth could dry, how he "fished up dry land from ocean depths with hooks made fast to heaven" (*Stories*, 2,484). Lakana compares Maui to Prometheus, but unlike Prometheus, who stole from heaven, Maui steals from the depths of the maternal sea: "Caught is the land beneath the water / Floated up, up to the surface" (*Stories*, 2,486). Lakana moans: "My head ached. The sun glare on the water made my eyes ache, while I was suffering more than half a touch of mal de mer." He drifts off into a half-slumber, but is startled awake "to the stab of the sun" when Kohokumu shouts, "'It's a big one,'" having caught a huge squid. He places "his lean, hawklike face into the very center of the slimy, squirming mass, and with his several ancient fangs bit into the heart and life of the matter" (*Stories*, 2,486).

While he admires the old Hawaiian's fishing skills, he finds his religious chants intolerable. But Lakana's surmise that Kohokumu's beliefs are only "a queer religion" is met with Kohokumu's eloquent retort:

"When I was young I muddled my head over queerer religions," old Kohokumu retorted. "But listen, O Young Wise One, to my elderly wisdom. This I know: as I grow old I seek less for the truth from without me, and find more of the truth from within me. Why have I thought this thought of my return to my mother and of my rebirth from my mother into the sun? You do not know. I do not know, save that, without whisper of man's voice or printed word, without prompting from otherwhere, this thought has arisen from within me, from the deeps of me that are as deep as the sea. I am not a god. I do not make things. Therefore I have not made this thought. I do not know its father or its mother. It is of old time before me, and therefore it is true. Man does not make truth. Man, if he be not blind, only recognizes truth when he sees it. Is this thought that I have thought a dream?" (Stories, 2,488–2,489)

Kohokumu is willing to give over his identity to a collectivity and to change shapes like the trickster Maui, as at the same time he evolves greater self-understanding. He tells of a dream in which he is a lark, flying toward the sun, "'singing, singing, as old Kohokumu never sang.'" Kohokumu wonders if his dream is real and whether he and Lakana are merely part of a dream Maui is having (Stories, 2,489). Then he begins to tell the tale of Keikiwai, the Water Baby, a trickster who, using his knowledge of the language and ways of sharks, is able to trick the sharks guarding the bay where the lobsters are and retrieve lobsters for his father the chief. To get the sharks out of the way so he can slip in and get a lobster, he throws a stone into the water first instead of jumping in. When they all rush to attack what they think is the Water Baby, he gets out and tells them that the one with the shortest tail is his friend and has betrayed the rest, and he repeats this charm, a trick of evidence at which there is no dispute—one will always have the shortest tail—but in which there is no truth. The one with the shortest tail is there to blame, and blamed he is, until the 40 sharks are gone, the last having burst from eating all the others. The bursting shark with its "proof" is a brilliant symbol of the futility of relying only on the surface facts of life and not their deeper meanings.

Lakana loses control of the narrative when Kohokumu forces him to hear out the story of the Water Baby, and Lakana's last word in the story is his interjected But—, to which Kohokumu pays no attention, completing the Keikiwai story. The reader does not finally know what, if anything, Lakana has learned:

"Hold, O Lakana!" he checked the speech that rushed to my tongue. "I know what next you would say. You would say that with my own eyes I did not see this, and therefore that I do not know what I have been telling you. But I do know, and I can prove it. My father's father knew the grandson of the Water Baby's father's uncle. Also, there, on the rocky point to which I point my finger now, is where the Water Baby stood and dived. I have dived for lobsters there myself. It is a great place for lobsters. Also, and often, have I seen sharks there. And there, on the bottom, as I should know, for I have seen and counted them, are the thirty-nine lava rocks thrown in by the Water Baby as I have described."

"But—" I began. . . .

"Of course I know. The thirty-nine lava rocks are still there. You can count them any day for yourself. Of course I know, and I know for a fact." (Stories, 2,493)

Kohokumu's trick of using empirical knowledge to prove his story even when the story itself defeats all such designs has silenced Lakana, for after that, who is to say what is true and what is not?

COMMENTARY

Like "The Red One," this is the story of a dying man and what A. Grove Day calls "a Jungian parable" (Day, Introduction to Stories of Hawaii, 18). "The Water Baby" is a story about knowledge, and it questions all of London's previous beliefs in knowledge systems that failed to fulfill him. It is less a contest between Western and Hawaiian ways of knowing than an admission that such opposed epistemologies can be explored from a broader perspective.

In late June 1916, when London read Jung's *Psychology of the Unconscious,* he found new perspectives on the dying and resurrected god, whether Jesus or an ancient sun-god, and arguments for the positive function of religious or spiritual belief. Evidently, an important passage was Jung's allusion to the story of Jesus and Nicodemus (John 3:2–8) which London had marked and read at least from the time of the SNARK.

> [Nicodemus] came to Jesus by night, and said unto him, Rabbi, we know that thou art a teacher come from God: for no man can do these miracles that thou doest, except God be with him.
>
> Jesus answered and said unto him, Verily, verily, I say unto thee, Except a man be born again, he cannot see the kingdom of God.
>
> Nicodemus saith unto him, How can a man be born when he is old? can he enter the second time into his mother's womb, and be born?
>
> Jesus answered, Verily, verily, I say unto thee, Except a man be born of water and of the Spirit, he cannot enter into the kingdom of God.
>
> That which is born of the flesh is flesh; and that which is born of the Spirit is spirit.
>
> Marvel not that I said unto thee, Ye must be born again.
>
> The wind bloweth where it listeth, and thou hearest the sound thereof, but canst not tell whence it cometh, and whither it goeth: so is every one that is born of the Spirit.

London also underscored Jung's interpretation, "Think not carnally or thou are carnal, but think symbolically, then thou art spirit" (Jung, *Psychology of the Unconscious,* 252–253). Religious myth, London read, gives human beings "assurance and strength, so that [they] may not be overwhelmed by the monsters of the universe." The symbols of religion may be misleading, but religion is *"psychologically true,* because it was and is the bridge to all the greatest achievements of humanity" (Jung, *Psychology of the Unconscious,* 262). As an artist who had always relied on myth—first from HOMER and MILTON in the KLONDIKE work, then on the BIBLE in the South Seas tales—London responded to Jung's search for individuation through embrace of the spirit via the medium of the archetype and embracing the "collective unconscious" as a source for the integration of the individual soul. He was struck by Jung's connections between a hidden past or "race" memory and the evolution of the individual and also by the role of the Mother in the unconscious. As Jung says, "We have dug down into the historic depths of the soul, and in doing this we have uncovered a old buried idol, the youthful, beautiful, fire-encircled and halo-crowned sun-hero, who, forever unattainable to the mortal, wanders upon the earth, causing night to follow day; winter, summer; death, life; and who returns again in rejuvenated splendor and gives light to new generations." Whoever renounces the chance to experience contact with this unconscious self in the depths of the maternal "commits a sort of self-murder" (Jung, *Psychology of the Unconscious,* 115–117).

In translator and editor Beatrice Hinkle's introduction, London underscored passages of how repressed feelings create the "hidden psyche," recalling his comments to MABEL APPLEGARTH, ANNA STRUNSKY WALLING, and others that no one could know his inner self. He jotted notes on "the often quite unbearable conflict of [a man's] weaknesses with his feelings of idealism," and marked this passage: "Those who have been able to recognize their own weaknesses and have suffered in the privacy of their own souls, the knowledge that these things have not set them apart from others, but that they are the common property of all and that no one can point the finger of scorn at his fellow, is one of the greatest experiences of life and is productive of the greatest relief" (Hinkle, in Jung, *Psychology of the Unconscious,* ix, xiv, et passim). Charmian London saw "The Water Baby" as a Jungian model of the mind "subtly presented through the medium of Hawaiian mythology, . . . clearly a symbolic representation of the Rebirth, the return of the Mother" (Charmian London, *Book of Jack London,* 2, 357–359). As Charmian records London's great discovery: "'I tell you I am standing on the edge of a world so new, so terrible, so wonderful, that I am almost afraid to look over into it'" (Charmian London, *Book of Jack London,* 2, 322–323). He also told her, "'For the first time in my life, I see the value of the confessional'" (Charmian London, *Book of Jack London, 2*, 353).

Jung's influence on this story has been recognized by London biographers. Richard O'Connor sees it as evidence that London found a new approach that would "vitalize his work" and give his life a new "more significant direction," an understanding that could change humanity's way of "thinking about itself, its purposes and its destiny" (O'Connor, *Jack London: A Biography*, 366–367). Day sees its significance in how "the ponderings even of a lowly old Polynesian may have meanings still to be discovered by the psychologists" (Day, *Introduction to Stories of Hawaii*, 18–19). For Earle Labor and Jeanne Campbell Reesman, London's search for meaning in the face of an increasingly materialistic modern world in this story draws from both 19th-century NATURE symbolism and looks forward to the emptiness of T. S. Eliot's *The Waste Land* (1925), an emptiness Eliot also sought to counter by returning to ancient mythologies. (Labor and Reesman, *Jack London*, 128). Labor sees in London's last stories a metamorphosis: "London the popular writer and hardcore materialist is becoming Jack London the deliberate mythmaker and spiritual philosopher." The twin influences of Jung and Hawai'i caused his work to undergo a "'sea-change'" (Labor, "Jack London's Pacific World," 218–219). Elsewhere, Labor remarks, "In the tradition that included James Fenimore Cooper before him and William Faulkner after him, London was acutely sensitive to the tragic consequences of the white man's inevitable civilization and corruption of the wilderness" (Labor, "Paradise Almost Regained," 43).

"The Water Baby" was finished just after two other confessional stories, "Like Argus of the Ancient Times" and "When Alice Told Her Soul." In this final story, London as author symbolically retreats at the wisdom of the "Other," as the white man John Lakana's world-weary tone gives way to the old Hawaiian fisherman Kohokumu's hoarse chanting, as though in the end, to have a chance to find himself, the narrator has to relinquish the most precious piece of his identity, his own voice. Weighted with the conventional, Lakana loses control of the story to Kohokumu. Lakana is con-

fronted by the unconscious as the scientist Bassett is in "The Red One." As Bassett respected Ngurn, Lakana is beaten by Kohokumu's knowledge.

Two kinds of knowledge—"factual" and mythic—are shown as relative in Kohokumu's tale (Reesman, "Problem of Knowledge"). As Jessica Greening Loudermilk observes, Kohokumu is Lakana's superior in the story not merely because he is Hawaiian and can trace his genealogy, rather "he is closer to London's supraracial ideal of the Hawaiian." But London's "epistemological play" in this story "reveals a new preoccupation with much larger, more universal" concerns than race: "In this, as in all the Jungian stories, London looks for something more real and universal than race as a basis for identity or knowledge" (Loudermilk, *Ka Aina Ko Pono*, 100–102).

"The Water Baby"'s secret power is language. The story is almost all dialogue and debate (Romjue, "London's Use of Hawaiian Mythology," 1–2). Though Kohokumu is the master and Lakana the student, Lakana resists true dialogue because he does not admit that Kohokumu's categories are not reducible to his. He tries to place Maui in terms of such modern frames as labor unions. In contrast, Kohokumu argues that we can only tell stories of Maui, not "prove" him, because people do not make the facts and cannot determine whether they are true or not.

Such relativity is also evident in the story's reliance upon POLYNESIAN myths. Maui is the trickster hero of the South Pacific. Abandoned by his own kind and raised by gods, who taught him their secrets, he soon defined them and begin a career of adventures in which he pulls up the earth, raises the sky, and catches the sun in a trap to lengthen the day. He steals fire and breaks other taboos. As Laura Makarius emphasizes, Maui possesses an exceptional share of *mana*, or life force, and the ability to make use of it to alter the existing order of the world (Makarius, "Myth of the Trickster," 76–79).

Many of the stories of *On the Makaloa Mat* are grounded in precontact Hawaiian beliefs and cast key characters as Hawaiians. However, as Jane Murphy Romjue emphasizes, "Only in 'The Water Baby' does London write his own truly Hawaiian tale. Here he includes lines from chants and specific allusions to key Hawaiian myths and characters, incorporates the structure of the *ho'opa'apa'a* (riddling contest) and makes traditional Hawaiian religious beliefs, such as the legend of the *aumakua*, an integral part of the action" (Romjue, "London's Use of Hawaiian Mythology," 2). Romjue identifies four separate traditional Hawaiian chants in "The Water Baby." First there is an excerpt, as Kohokumu mentions, from "'Queen Liliuokalani's own family *mele*'" (*Stories*, 2,484), a reference to the exiled queen's 1897 translation of the Hawaiian creation chant:

> Maui became restless and fought the sun
> With a noose that he laid.
> And winter won the sun,
> And summer was won by Maui. (*Stories*, 2,484)

This chant was important in establishing the queen's royal heritage as she faced dethronement, and it is reflected in Kohokumu's claims that he is related to Keikiwai (genealogy was extremely important to Hawaiians and made up the content of most of their chants). The second chant is from the "Chant of Kuali'i," which also praises Maui and traces his genealogy. The third chant is the second part of a chant called the "Pule He'e," used by the *kahuna* (priests) for the healing of the sick, ritual involving the sacrifice of a *"he'e"* or squid. The fourth chant invokes the god Lono, revered as the god of healing by the Hawaiians. Lono is also the master of the riddling contest (Romjue, "London's Use of Hawaiian Mythology," 2–4). In "The Water Baby" the riddler structure is in place with Lakana's "attempt at one-upmanship" reflected in his framing of Hawaiian myths within Western ones, yet as Romjue notes, from the beginning "he seems clearly bested here by the simplicity and directness of older, apparently wiser Kohokumu." "'And what could I reply?,'" Lakana complains; "'He had me on the matter of reasonableness'" (*Stories*, 2,485). As Romjue emphasizes, Kohokumu's victory in the *ho'opa'apa'a* is unexpected: "The Hawaiian riddling contests frequently end with a young, clever lad outwitting the seemingly older, wiser opponent" (Romjue, "London's Use of Hawaiian Mythology," 7). London also uses "The Legend of Aiai," and the legend of Punia for details of the fishing

trip. Aiai inherits four magic objects with which he could control the fish when the fish god dies, a decoy stick, a cowry shell, a hook, and a stone which could lure fish, especially a giant octopus. Keikiwai, the Water Baby, a Punia trickster, is a strong child who by 10 years old, had the strength of a man. The shark chief comes to where Punia's father fishes and with his 10 loyal sharks begin to kill and eat the father and others. Punia uses his wits to avenge his father, luring the sharks into the bay by throwing rocks in the water they mistake for Punia. One by one he turns them against one another (Romjue, 7–8).

What makes "The Water Baby" in particular so significant in London's fiction is precisely that it is located in an attempt to narrate from within the "Other" culture by having its characters speak for themselves, rely upon traditional myths, and best the white man.

CHARACTERS

Lakana "Born in the Islands myself," Lakana narrates, "I know the Hawaiian myths better than this old fisherman, although I possessed not his memorization that enabled him to recite them endless hours (*Stories*, 2,484). But though he makes this claim and he speaks Hawaiian, he does not appreciate Kohokumu's chanting because he has a headache and a hangover. He tries to fit Hawaiian myths into his own Western stereotypes, but Kohokumu has the last word.

Kohokumu Kohokumu is a figure of Jung's Wise Old Man archetype: "Now Kohokumu was a bore, and I was squeamishly out of sorts with him for his volubleness, but I could not help admiring him as watched him go down. Past seventy years of age, lean as a spear, and shriveled like a mummy, he was doing what few young athletes of my race would do or could do. It was forty feet to bottom" (*Stories*, 2,486).

FURTHER READING

Day, A. Grove. Introduction to *Stories of Hawaii* by Jack London. Honolulu, Hawaii: Mutual Publishing Co., 1985, 3–20.

Jung, Carl Gustav. *Psychology of the Unconscious: A Study of the Transformations and Symbolisms of the*

Libido—A Contribution to the History of the Evolution of Thought. Edited and translated by Beatrice Hinkle. New York: 1916. Reprint edited by William McGuire. Princeton, N.J.: Princeton University Press, 2001.

Labor, Earle. "Jack London's Pacific World." In *Critical Essays on Jack London.* Edited by Jacqueline Tavernier-Courbin. Boston: G. K. Hall, 1983, 205–222.

———. "Paradise Almost Regained." Review of *Stories of Hawaii* by Jack London. Edited by A. Grove Day. *Saturday Review* (April 3, 1965): 43–44.

Labor, Earle, and Jeanne Campbell Reesman. *Jack London, Revised Edition.* New York: Macmillan (Twayne U.S. Authors Series), 1994.

London, Charmian Kittredge. *The Book of Jack London.* 2 vols. New York: Century, 1921.

Loudermilk, Jessica Greening. *Ka Aina Ka Pono: Jack London, Hawai'i, and Race.* M. A. Thesis, University of Texas at San Antonio, 2006.

Makarius, Laura. "The Myth of the Trickster: The Necessary Breaker of Taboos." In *Mythical Trickster Figures: Contours, Contexts, and Criticisms.* Edited by William J. Hynes and William G. Doty. Tuscaloosa: University of Alabama Press, 1997, 66–86.

McClintock, James I. *White Logic: Jack London's Short Stories.* Grand Rapids, Mich.: Wolf House, 1975. Reprinted in 1997 as Jack London's *Strong Truths: A Study of the Short Stories.* East Lansing: Michigan State University Press, 1997.

O'Connor, Richard. *Jack London: A Biography.* Boston: Little, Brown, 1964.

Reesman, Jeanne Campbell. "The Problem of Knowledge in Jack London's 'The Water Baby.'" In *Western American Literature* 23 (fall 1988): 201–215.

Romjue, Jane Murphy. "Jack London's Use of Hawaiian Mythology and Legends in 'The Water Baby.'" Paper delivered at the Sixth Biennial Jack London Society Symposium, October 2002, Lihue, Kauai.

"The Whale Tooth" (1909)

"The Whale Tooth" is one of the stories in *South Sea Tales*; it was first published as "The Mission of John Starhurst" in England in *The Bournemouth Visitor's Directory* (December 29, 1909) and then in the United States in *Sunset* magazine 24 (January 1910). It is a black humor tale in which a MISSIONARY is tricked by Figians into serving as their supper.

SYNOPSIS

John Starhurst, a missionary, is determined to preach the gospel and convert all of Viti Levu, FIJI:

> The hard-worked, fever-stricken missionaries stuck doggedly to their task, at times despairing, and looking forward for some special manifestation, some outburst of Pentecostal fire that would bring a glorious harvest of souls. But cannibal Fiji had remained obdurate. The frizzle-headed man-eaters were loath to leave their fleshpots so long as the harvest of human carcasses was plentiful. Sometimes, when the harvest was too plentiful, they imposed on the missionaries by letting the word slip out that on such a day there would be a killing and a barbecue. Promptly the missionaries would buy the lives of the victims with stick tobacco, fathoms of calico, and quarts of trade beads. Natheless the chiefs drove a handsome trade in thus disposing of their surplus live meat. Also, they could always go out and catch more. (*Stories,* 1,492–1,493)

Undaunted, Starhurst sets out from Rewa Village into the mountain jungles. The king of Reva tries to dissuade him, for though the level of CANNIBALISM in Rewa is high, it is even worse in the jungle. The king worries that after the mountain dwellers "*kai-kai,*" or eat the missionary, they may come down the mountain to make war on him. But Starhurst will not listen to him nor to the traders:

> John Starhurst was not a fanatic. He would have been the first man to deny the imputation. He was eminently sane and practical. He was sure that his mission would result in good, and he had private visions of igniting the Pentecostal spark in the souls of the mountaineers and of inaugurating a revival that would sweep down out of the mountains and across the length and breadth of the Great Land from sea to sea and to the isles in the midst of the sea. There were no wild lights in his mild gray

eyes, but only calm resolution and an unfaltering trust in the Higher Power that was guiding him. (*Stories*, 1,493)

Only one man supports his quest, Ra Vatu, a convert who lends him a canoe. But Ra Vatu has dark motives; he sends a henchman, Erirola, who carries a whale tooth with him:

> It was a magnificent tooth, fully six inches long, beautifully proportioned, the ivory turned yellow and purple with age. This tooth was likewise the property of Ra Vatu; and in Fiji, when such a tooth goes forth, things usually happen. For this is the virtue of the whale tooth: Whoever accepts it cannot refuse the request that may accompany it or follow it. The request may be anything from a human life to a tribal alliance, and no Fijian is so dead to honor as to deny the request when once the tooth has been accepted. (*Stories*, 1,495)

Starhurst is accompanied by another convert, Narau. The first village they come to is ruled by a chief named Mongondro: "Mongondro was a sweet-tempered, mild-mannered little old chief, short-sighted and afflicted with elephantiasis, and no longer inclined toward the turbulence of war. He received the missionary with warm hospitality, gave him food from his own table, and even discussed religious matters with him" (*Stories*, 1,495). Later, when Starhurst and Narau are gone, Erirola appears and offers Mongondro the tooth, but he refuses it. In fact, village after village rejects the tooth when "they divined the request that would be made" (*Stories*, 1,496).

Now deep in the mountains, Starhurst comes upon Gatoka, the village ruled by Buli, a fearsome chief. However Erirola has already arrived ahead of him and has successfully given the whale tooth to Buli. Erirola tells Buli that he can do what he likes with the missionary, but he must save his boots for Ra Vatu. When Starhurst appears, he says he is sent by God. Buli is unimpressed; as a strongman tries to club Starhurst and Narau hides, Starhurst begs for his life. Buli then takes up his club and threatens Starhurst, who now realizes that he is about to die:

Bareheaded, he stood in the sun and prayed aloud—the mysterious figure of the inevitable white man, who, with Bible, bullet, or rum bottle, has confronted the amazed savage in his every stronghold. Even so stood John Starhurst in the rock fortress of the Buli of Gatoka.

"Forgive them, for they know not what they do," he prayed. "O Lord! Have mercy upon Fiji. Have compassion for Fiji. O Jehovah, hear us for His sake, Thy Son, whom Thou didst give that through Him all men might also become Thy children. From Thee we came, and our mind is that to Thee we may return. The land is dark, O Lord, the land is dark. But Thou art mighty to save. Reach out Thy hand, O Lord, and save Fiji, poor cannibal Fiji." (*Stories*, 1,498)

As the Fijians sing their death song, Starhurst is struck down; begging them to drag him softly to the oven, he hears them praise him as a strong man and Narau as a coward who will only report the incident.

COMMENTARY

Gary Riedl and Thomas R. Tietze interpret "The Whale Tooth" as a story about interpreting a text. The "text" of the whale tooth follows Starhurst into the jungle, a text that he is unaware of and would not understand if he saw it. As in "The Chinago," which also features competing "texts," "power and not justice is the issue; reliance on text to provide meaning and its propensity to engender violence is the theme. And in both the inability of interacting cultural groups to understand/interpret each other's texts results in death." As they conclude, "Throughout both stories, texts are represented as creations mistakenly interpreted and acted upon. Whether they are spoken, written down, remembered, imagined, or predicted, these varying kinds of interpretable materials run counter to the facts of the character's experience." Thus, "the tales may be seen to present the kind of subject matter that anticipates by a generation and a half the academic discussions of postmodern critics. The one thread that seems to run through all of our contemporary poststructuralist conflicts is the unreliability of texts—whatever they might be—to mediate meaning—whatever that is—from 'writer' to 'reader'" (Riedl and Tietze, "Misinterpreting the Unreadable," 516).

CHARACTERS

John Starhurst Starhurst is a missionary who attempts to convert the bush tribes of Fiji and instead meets his death at the hands of Buli, chief of Gatoka. Whether he was merely naïve about the danger he faced or motivated only by faith, he fails in his mission.

king of Rewa Chief of the village where the church is located, he tries to talk Starhurst out of entering the bush, but Starhurst will not listen to him.

Ra Vatu Ra Vatu pretends to be a convert to CHRISTIANITY but secretly resents Starhurst for once challenging him. He schemes to send his man into the bush after the missionary with a whale tooth and instructions that whoever receives it should kill Starhurst, but save his boots for Ra Vatu.

Narau A young convert who accompanies Starhurst deep into the jungle. He is terrified when Starhurst is killed and hides among the women. He is vilified as a coward by the tribe at Gatoka.

Erirola Cousin of Ra Vatu, Erirola follows Starhurst and Narau into the bush carrying a whale tooth, which he will use to get some chief to kill and eat Starhurst.

Mongondro A chief Starhurst encounters early in his journey who is friendly to him and interested in religion. When Erirola offers him the tooth, he refuses.

Buli Buli accepts the whale tooth and kills and cooks Starhurst. He alone of the chiefs is not afraid of the whites. He kills Starhurst with his gigantic war club.

FURTHER READING

Riedl, Gary, and Thomas R. Tietze. "Misinterpreting the Unreadable: Jack London's 'The Chinago' and 'The Whale Tooth.'" *Studies in Short Fiction* 34, no. 4 (fall 1997): 507–518.

"What Life Means to Me" (1906)

London wrote this essay for COSMOPOLITAN; the magazine had requested a number of prominent American writers to contribute articles with the theme in the title. London was concerned that the Hearst-owned magazine would not print such a strongly socialist article, but it did. CHARMIAN KITTREDGE LONDON recorded that in the essay "one reads what is perhaps his most impassioned committal of himself as a rebel toward the shames and uncleanness of the capitalist system. . . . His challenge is flung to that thin and cracking upper crust as he saw it" (Charmian London, *Book of Jack London*, 2, 106).

The essay begins with London's dream of escaping the working class:

> I was born in the working-class. Early I discovered enthusiasm, ambition, and ideals; and to satisfy these became the problem of my child-life. My environment was crude and rough and raw. I had no outlook, but an uplook rather. My place in society was at the bottom. Here life offered nothing but sordidness and wretchedness, both of the flesh and the spirit; for here flesh and spirit were alike starved and tormented. (*Revolution*, 293)

Thus as a child he dreamed of the delights of the upper class:

> Above me towered the colossal edifice of society, and to my mind the only way out was up. Into this edifice I early resolved to climb. Up above, men wore black clothes and boiled shirts, and women dressed in beautiful gowns. Also, there were good things to eat, and there was plenty to eat. This much for the flesh. Then there were the things of the spirit. Up above me, I knew, were unselfishnesses of the spirit, clean and noble thinking, keen intellectual living. (*Revolution*, 293)

However, London relates that he learned how hard it was to move up in society. He was never going to get ahead through manual labor—muscle, he notes, is a commodity that can be used up. Thus he turned to oyster pirating, hoboing, and crime. Fearing where this life would lead, he returns to manual labor but is routinely cheated of wages and overworked. Imprisoned for vagrancy in Erie County, New York, he was "scared into thinking": "I had been born in the working-class, and I was now, at the age of eighteen, beneath the point at which I had started. I was down in the cellar of society, down in the subterranean depths of misery about which it is neither nice nor proper to speak. I was in the pit, the abyss, the human cesspool, the shambles and the charnel-house of our civilization" (*Revolution*, 299).

He returned to CALIFORNIA and hit the books: "If I could not live on the parlor floor of society, I could, at any rate, have a try at the attic. It was true, the diet there was slim, but the air at least was pure. So I resolved to sell no more muscle, and to become a vender of brains" (*Revolution*, 300). He also discovered SOCIALISM:

> I joined the groups of working-class and intellectual revolutionists, and for the first time came into intellectual living. Here I found keen-flashing intellects and brilliant wits; for here I met strong and alert-brained, withal horny-handed, members of the working-class; unfrocked preachers too wide in their Christianity for any congregation of Mammon-worshippers; professors broken on the wheel of university subservience to the ruling class and flung out because they were quick with knowledge which they strove to apply to the affairs of mankind (*Revolution*, 301–302)

When he at last becomes successful as a writer and enjoys the privileges of success, he becomes disillusioned by the hypocrisy, greed, and moral blindness of the upper crust. In the end, he resolves to rejoin the working class: "There I am content to labor, crowbar in hand, shoulder to shoulder with intellectuals, idealists, and class-conscious workingmen, getting a solid pry now and again and setting the whole edifice rocking. Some day, when we get a few more hands and crowbars to work, we'll topple it over, along with all its rotten life and unburied dead, its monstrous selfishness and sodden materialism. Then we'll cleanse the cellar

and build a new habitation for mankind, in which there will be no parlor floor, in which all the rooms will be bright and airy, and where the air that is breathed will be clean, noble, and alive" (*Revolution*, 308).

FURTHER READING

Foner, Philip S., ed. *Jack London: American Rebel—A Collection of His Social Writings Together with an Extensive Study of the Man and His Times*. New York: Citadel Press, 1947.

London, Charmian Kittredge. *The Book of Jack London*. 2 vols. New York: Century, 1921.

London, Jack. *No Mentor but Myself: A Collection of Articles, Essays, Reviews, and Letters, by Jack London, on Writing and Writers*. New York: Kennikat Press, 1979. Reprinted in expanded edition as *No Mentor But Myself: Jack London on Writers and Writing*. Edited by Dale L. Walker and Jeanne Campbell Reesman. Stanford, Calif.: Stanford University Press, 1999.

Sinclair, Upton. *The Cry for Justice: An Anthology of the Literature of Social Protest*. Introduction by Jack London. Philadelphia: John C. Winston, 1915.

"When Alice Told Her Soul" (1918)

First published in COSMOPOLITAN 64 (March 1918) and included in the collection *On the Makaloa Mat*, "When Alice Told Her Soul" is a comic tale of what happens in HONOLULU when a well-known hula mistress becomes religious and confesses all of her sins, naming those men and women who sinned with her.

SYNOPSIS

Alice Akana, the 50-year-old mistress of a hula house, is known for her "tight tongue"; she knows many secrets about the lives of many of HAWAI'I's most prominent men and women. One day she attends a revival meeting run by Abel Ah Yo, and she is converted. However she refuses to take the last step to salvation, confessing all of her sins publicly. She knows of crooked land deals, stolen inheritances, corrupt politicians, and of course various kinds of carnal behavior. All the elite of Honolulu wait in fear that she will confess, and one after another they bring her expensive gifts.

Abel Ah Yo tries everything to make her confess, and then, learning of her fear of volcanoes and earthquakes, devises a fiery sermon comparing Hell to the pit of Kilauea and describing eternity as as long in years as there are grains of sand on Waikiki. Terrified by what she has heard, Alice confesses, naming names, pointing out people in the audience one by one. At the end of the story, some wealthy clubmen form a committee to send another potential convert who knows too much about them back to the mainland.

COMMENTARY

Though it is largely a comedy, "When Alice Told Her Soul" also addresses some of the more serious themes of the Hawaiian stories: the colonization of Hawai'i by the British and Americans, the way religion is used as a form of power over simple people, the hypocrisy of the "missionary crowd." There is also emphasis in the story on race. Abel Ah Yo's ancestry includes CHINESE, Portuguese, Scottish, and Hawaiian; though London dwells on how this racial combination gives Abel Ah Yo a canniness and flexibility that allow him to convert a pure-blooded Hawaiian like Alice and embarrass the white elite by having Alice reveal their secrets. One of his secrets is his ability with four languages:

When it came to word wizardry, he had Billy Sunday, master of slang and argot of one language, skinned by miles. For in Abel Ah Yo were the five verbs, and nouns, and adjectives, and metaphors of four living languages. Intermixed and living promiscuously and vitally together, he possessed in these languages a reservoir of expression in which a myriad Billy Sundays could drown. Of no race, a mongrel par excellence, a heterogeneous scrabble, the genius of the admixture was superlatively Abel Ah Yo's. Like a chameleon, he titubated and scintillated grandly between the diverse parts of him, stunning by frontal attack and surprising

and confounding by flanking sweeps the mental homogeneity of the more simply constituted souls who came in to his revival to sit under him and flame to his flaming. (*Stories*, 2,422)

Furthermore, "Abel Ah Yo believed in himself and his mixedness, as he believed in the mixedness of his weird concept that God looked as much like him as like any man, being no mere tribal god, but a world god that must look equally like all races of all the world" (*Stories*, 2,422). The narrator asks, "What chance had Alice Akana, herself pure and homogeneous Hawaiian, against his subtle, democratic-tinged, four-race-engendered, slang-munitioned attack?" (*Stories*, 2,423). Likewise, Alice's telling has the effect of uniting classes and races:

Word came, via telephone, almost simultaneously to the Pacific and University Clubs, that at last Alice was telling her soul in meeting; and, by private machine and taxi-cab, for the first time Abel Ah Yo's revival was invaded by those of caste and place. The first comers beheld the curious sight of Hawaiian, Chinese, and all variegated racial mixtures of the smelting-pot of Hawaii, men and women, fading out and slinking away through the exits of Abel Ah Yo's tabernacle. But those who were sneaking out were mostly men, while those who remained were avid-faced as they hung on Alice's utterance. (*Stories*, 2,431)

The story also references the importance of storytelling in Hawaiian culture and the influence of CARL JUNG's concept of the confessional on London.

CHARACTERS

Alice Akana "For Alice Akana was fifty years old, had begun life early, and, early and late, lived it spaciously. What she knew went back into the roots and foundations of families, businesses, and plantations. She was the one living repository of accurate information that lawyers sought out, whether the information they required related to land-boundaries and land gifts, or to marriages, births, bequests, or scandals. Rarely, because of the tight tongue she kept behind her teeth, did she give them what they asked; and when she did was when only equity was served and no one was hurt." From her girlhood, Alice lived "a life of flowers, and song, and wine, and dance; and, in her later years, had herself been mistress of these revels by office of mistress of the hula house" (*Stories*, 2,421).

Abel Ah Yo "Now Abel Ah Yo, in his theology and word wizardry, was as much mixed a personage as Billy Sunday. . . . The Pentecostal fire he flamed forth was hotter and more variegated than could any one of the four races of him alone have flamed forth. For in him were gathered together the cannyness and the cunning, the wit and the wisdom, the subtlety and the rawness, the passion and the philosophy, the agonizing spirit-groping and the legs up to the knees in the dung of reality, of the four radically different breeds that contributed to the sum of him. His, also, was the clever self-deceivement of the entire clever compound" (*Stories*, 2,422).

Cyrus Hodge Hodge is a sugar magnate who stops his chauffeured car to pick up Alice and give her a ride. He reminds her that he was just a boy when he frequented her hula house. He is the first of many to beg her indulgence.

old friend of Alice's Another man who begs Alice not to reveal his secrets, this "old friend" reminds her that he always played "square" with her: "He was building a magnificent house on Pacific Heights, but had recently married a second time, and was even then on his way to the steamer to welcome home his two daughters just graduated from Vassar. 'We need religion in our old age, Alice. It softens, makes us more tolerant and forgiving of the weaknesses of others—especially the weaknesses of youth of—of others, when they played high and low and didn't know what they were doing'" (*Stories*, 2,426).

senator, lawyer They are part of a group of men who seek out Alice and ask her not to betray them; they complain that their sins were merely those of youth.

Mary Mendana, Elvira Miyahara Makaena Yin Wap It is not only men who seek Alice out to ask her not to tell on them: "Mary Mendana, wife of the Portuguese Consul, remembered her with a five-dollar box of candy and a mandarin coat that would have fetched three-quarters of a hundred dollars at a fire sale. And Elvira Miyahara Makaena Yin Wap, the wife of Yin Wap the wealthy Chinese importer, brought personally to Alice two entire bolts of pina cloth from the Philippines and a dozen pairs of silk stockings" (*Stories*, 2,427).

Stephen Makekau He is a young man in the audience whom Alice identifies with this confession: "'You think this man, Stephen Makekau, is the son of Moses Makekau and Minnie Ah Ling, and has a legal right to the two hundred and eight dollars he draws down each month from Parke Richards Limited, for the lease of the fish-pond to Bill Kong at Amana. Not so. Stephen Makekau is not the son of Moses. He is the son of Aaron Kama and Tillie Naone. He was given as a present, as a feeding child, to Moses and Minnie, by Aaron and Tillie'" (*Stories*, 2,432).

MacIlwaine MacIlwaine is the chief of detectives and a friend of Colonel Stilton's, whom he hears exposed by Alice's confession.

Colonel Stilton He too is exposed by Alice: "'There is a banker in Honolulu. You all know his name. He is 'way up, swell society because of his wife. He owns much stock in General Plantations and Inter-Island. . . . His name is Colonel Stilton. Last Christmas Eve he came to my house with big aloha" (love) "and gave me mortgages on my land in Iapio Valley, all cancelled, for two thousand dollars' worth. Now why did he have such big cash aloha for me? I will tell you.'" And tell she did, throwing the searchlight on ancient business transactions and political deals which from their inception had lurked in the dark (*Stories*, 2,432).

Jim and Lizzie Lokendamper, Azalea Akau Alice's confession reveals that Jim Lokendamper has a secret wife, Azalea Akau, and he has been giving her large sums of money. Lizzie, upon hearing this, attacks Azalea. Alice also tells of Azalea's sins.

Colonel Chilton, Bob Cristy, Lask Finneston, Gary Wilkinson These clubmen respond to Alice's confession by worrying that an old beach-comber, John Ward, also knows too much about them and their shady business dealings, and so they form a committee to send him to the mainland.

"When the World Was Young"

First published in SATURDAY EVENING POST 183 (September 10, 1910), and then included in *The Night Born,* this is one of London's stories of ATA-VISM, comparable to his novella *Before Adam* in its presentation of modern man reverting to a primitive self. In certain respects, it also forecasts crossings-over of cultures by heroes in later stories, especially two written in London's last year, "The Red One" and "The Water Baby." But mostly it is a "what-if" science fiction story, somewhat influenced by CHARLES DARWIN's ideas of racial inheritance.

SYNOPSIS

A Mill Valley, CALIFORNIA, night patrolman, Dave Slotter, is attacked and trailed by a frightening apparition, whom he then seeks, a huge blond man with amazing powers of strength and agility, wearing only goatskins. Slotter escapes him and manages to identify the wild man as James J. Ward of the firm Ward, Knowles, and Co. He goes to Ward's office to confront him, probably to black-mail him, but Ward easily frightens him off. Ward tries to reconcile or at least keep satisfied his two selves, one the suited-up businessman of daylight and marriage to Lilian Gersdale and one the night-born atavism of a Teutonic *Übermensch*. (Ward only sleeps in the mornings.) Toward the end of the story a grizzly bear menaces Ward and his party:

> Lilian, clutching the railing so spasmodically that a bruising hurt was left in her finger-ends for days, gazed horror-stricken at a yellow-haired, wild-eyed giant whom she recognized as the man who was to be her husband. He was swinging a great club, and fighting furiously and calmly with a shaggy monster that was bigger than any bear she had ever seen. One rip of the beast's claws had dragged away Ward's pajama-coat and streaked his flesh with blood. (1,702)

Never has Lilian dreamed of "so formidable and magnificent a savage lurked under the starched shirt and conventional garb of her betrothed. And never had she had any conception of how a man battled. Such a battle was certainly not mod-ern; nor was she there beholding a modern man, though she did not know it. For this was not Mr. James J. Ward, the San Francisco businessman, but one, unnamed and unknown, a crude, rude savage creature who, by some freak of chance, lived again after thrice a thousand years" (*Stories,* 1,702). When the bear rips apart a dog, "Then the human brute went mad. A foaming rage flecked the lips that parted with a wild inarticulate cry, as it sprang in, swung the club mightily in both hands, and brought it down full on the head of the uprearing grizzly. Not even the skull of a grizzly could withstand the crushing force of such a blow, and the animal went down to meet the worrying of the hounds (*Stories,* 1,702–1,703). At the end, the narrator tells us:

> The early Teuton in him died the night of the Mill Valley fight with the bear. James J. Ward is now wholly James J. Ward, and he shares no part of his being with any vagabond anachro-nism from the younger world. And so wholly is James J. Ward modern, that he knows in all its bitter fullness the curse of civilized fear. He is now afraid of the dark, and night in the forest is to him a thing of abysmal terror. His city house is of the spick and span order, and he evinces a great interest in burglarproof devices. His home is a tangle of electric wires, and after bed-time a guest can scarcely breathe without setting off an alarm. Also, he had invented a combination keyless door-lock that travelers may carry in their vest pockets and apply immediately and successfully under all circumstances. But his wife does not deem him a coward. She knows

better. And, like any hero, he is content to rest on his laurels. His bravery is never questioned by those friends who are aware of the Mill Valley episode." (*Stories*, 1,702–1,703)

However, we are also told he does not dare visit his wife after dark.

COMMENTARY

Not only does this melodramatic tale reference the idea of extreme fitness and themes of Darwinian evolution and the genetic throwback, but it also suggests the ideas of SIGMUND FREUD and CARL JUNG, both of whom argued for the importance of the unconscious self. London often used the idea of the atavism in his work, which he sometimes called "the abysmal brute." Atavisms can be positive or negative in his writings, including his boxing coverage: Generally those which are Nordic are positive while those which are hairy and dark are negative. There is a fantasy figure for London in Ward: He is built, blond, rich, independent yet married, ruthless, and unconstrainable. And yet even in this idealized personification he seems at the best delusional and one-dimensional, at the worst, really dangerous. The conclusion of the story is about his being tamed. Contemporary readers may compare this ending with that of Anthony Burgess of *A Clockwork Orange* or Chuck Palahniuk in *Fight Club*, but London's readers would have also seen this ending as somewhat sad and ironic. Of what exactly is the protagonist cured?

CHARACTERS

James J. Ward A successful business tycoon who runs his empire and his marriage by day and runs wild in the forests at night as his half-naked other self, an atavism of the Teutonic savage.

Dave Slotter The night-patrolman who is hunted by Ward in his wild identity one night throughout Mill Valley. He finds out who Ward is and unsuccessfully attempts to confront him.

Professor Wertz He recognizes in young Ward's chants and songs ancient tongues including early German and TEUTON. He mistakenly believes Ward has studied these tongues and is withholding his knowledge of them from him.

Lee Sing Lee Sing is "the Chinese cook and factotum, who knew much about the strangeness of his master, who was paid well for saying nothing, and who never did say anything" (*Stories*, 1,699).

Lilian Gersdale As Ward's wife, whom he never sees after 8 P.M. in the evening, she is accompanied by her mother and brother visiting at the Ward estate when Ward battles the bear. She is amazed to witness the true identity of her husband.

White Fang (1906)

Though London said that it was a sequel to *The Call of the Wild*, and though it reverses the former novel's tale of a tame DOG finding his wild self in its portrayal of a vicious wolf-dog being tamed by the love of a kind master, *White Fang* is one of London's most naturalistic works and quite different in tone from the earlier book. Its opening paragraph sets the tone:

> Dark spruce forest frowned on either side the frozen waterway. The trees had been stripped by a recent wind of their white covering of frost, and they seemed to lean toward each other, black and ominous, in the fading light. A vast silence reigned over the land. The land itself was a desolation, lifeless, without movement, so lone and cold that the spirit of it was not even that of sadness. There was a hint in it of laughter, but of a laughter more terrible than any sadness—a laughter that was mirthless as the smile of the Sphinx, a laughter cold as the frost and partaking of the grimness of infallibility. It was the masterful and incommunicable wisdom of eternity laughing at the futility of life and the effort of life. It was the Wild, the savage, frozenhearted Northland Wild. (3)

While *The Call of the Wild*'s NATURALISM is tempered by a plot based in romance, *White Fang* is brutal and bloody in its portrayal of the hero's life until he meets Weedon Scott. Though both books are read to children, parents should stay clear of *White Fang* until the children are older. *White Fang* has been made into many films, including a sanitized one by Disney Studios. The films never replicate the violent struggles of the novel among man, dog, wolf, and the WHITE SILENCE of the Arctic shown in the book. Its ending, while redemptive, does not answer the problem of the violence (among men, not WOLVES) nor human greed, though it does supply the happy ending desired by readers.

SYNOPSIS

Part 1: The Wild

Two men, Bill and Henry, transport to a trading post below the Arctic Circle the body of a companion, Lord Albert, to be shipped back to England for burial. But they are tracked by a pack of hungry wolves who, in spying these men, have come upon the first sign of life in a long time in the famine of the terrible Arctic winter. A brave she-wolf who is part dog invades their camp by night and lures their dogs away: "The animal was certainly not cinnamon-colored. Its coat was the true wolf-coat. The dominant color was gray, and yet there was to it a faint reddish hue—a hue that was baffling, that appeared and disappeared, that was more like an illusion of the vision, now gray, distinctly gray, and again giving hints and glints of a vague redness of color not classifiable in terms of ordinary experience" (26–27). She is able to communicate with the dogs, unlike other wolves, because of her half-dog ancestry. All but two of the eight dogs are killed, and Bill is killed and eaten. Henry hides the coffin in a tree and departs for the trading post. Just as Henry is about to be attacked by the wolves, he is rescued by soldiers who are looking for Lord Albert.

Part 2: Born of the Wild

White Fang is the pup of One Eye and the she-wolf who harassed Bill and Henry. One Eye leads her and the other wolves away from the soldiers who come after Lord Albert and discover Henry: "Running at the forefront of the pack was a large gray wolf—one of its several leaders. It was he who directed the pack's course on the heels of the she-wolf. It was he who snarled warningly at the younger members of the pack or slashed at them with his fangs when they ambitiously tried to pass him. And it was he who increased the pace when he sighted the she-wolf, now trotting slowly across the snow" (49).

Thereafter, One Eye has to fight off other males for her; proving himself, he is chosen. She and One Eye go off to hunt together: "They ran side by side, like good friends who have come to an understanding" (57). She becomes pregnant, and they find a cave where she bears her pups. One day, One Eye does not return from hunting. Their five cubs learn from their first hours and days the terrible hardship of famine and all but White Fang die of starvation. White Fang ventures forth from the cave and in doing so he learns how to kill for himself. Although his mother is not always there to teach him—she is out looking for food—his natural instincts lead him to kill some ptarmigan chicks. He enjoys the sensation of killing as well as the meat. As accomplished as he feels, he is frightened by the shadow of a hawk. Just as in killing the chicks, his instincts guide him to take cover; the hawk takes the mother ptarmigan. He learns the first law of the wild: eat or be eaten.

Part 3: The Gods of the Wild

Over a period of months, as White Fang grows stronger and bigger, he learns of another "kind," humans. He and his mother, searching for food, come upon a NATIVE hunting party. One of them calls to White Fang's mother by the name "Kiche." (They are also the ones who name the gray cub "White Fang.") White Fang is confused when his mother greets the men and when they do not attack her. His mother lies down in front of them, submitting. She and White Fang follow them back to their camp. White Fang does not know that before he was born, his mother lived with the Natives. Now, living among them, White Fang learns a new law: obey the strong and oppress the weak.

> And so it was with White Fang. The man-animals were gods unmistakable and unescapable. As his mother, Kiche, had rendered her allegiance to them at the first cry of her name, so he was beginning to render his allegiance.

He gave them the trail as a privilege indubitably theirs. When they walked, he got out of their way. When they called, he came. When they threatened, he cowered down. When they commanded him to go, he went away hurriedly. For behind any wish of theirs was power to enforce that wish, power that hurt, power that expressed itself in clouts and clubs, in flying stones and stinging lashes of whips. (130)

Since the "man-gods" are strong, he has to obey them; when he finds the man-gods' dogs weak, he attacks them. Kiche is taken away on a trading trip by some of the men. White Fang misses his mother and also his life with her in the wild, but he stays among the Natives. The narrator implies that it is the one-quarter dog in him that keeps him there.

White Fang matures over the next several years. (His mother has been sold away and will not come back, though he does meet up with her again.) His master, Gray Beaver, shows him no affection but only demands obedience; he brutally punishes White Fang for any insubordination. Yet he has his kind moments: "Nay, Gray Beaver himself sometimes tossed him a piece of meat, and defended him against the other dogs in the eating of it. And such a piece of meat was of value. It was worth more, in some strange way, than a dozen pieces of meat from the hand of a squaw. Gray Beaver never petted nor caressed. Perhaps it was the weight of his hand, perhaps his justice, perhaps the sheer power of him, and perhaps it was all these things that influenced White Fang" (141–142). White Fang accepts his punishment from the man but not from his other dogs, who hate him as a wolf. They torment him until he fights back and kills his opponents. More than once, his wolf snarl alone stops them in their tracks:

As for snarling, he could snarl more terribly than any dog, young or old, in camp. The intent of the snarl is to warn or frighten, and judgment is required to know when it should be used. White Fang knew how to make it and when to make it. Into his snarl he incorporated all that was vicious, malignant, and horrible. With nose serrulated by continuous spasms, hair bristling in recurrent waves, tongue whipping out like

a red snake and whipping back again, ears flattened down, eyes gleaming hatred, lips wrinkled back, and fangs exposed and dripping, he could compel a pause on the part of almost any assailant. (146–147)

When famine strikes again, White Fang goes into the wild to live. When it passes, he goes back to Gray Beaver and travels with him to Fort Yukon, where Gray Beaver becomes addicted to whiskey.

Part 4: The Superior Gods

At Fort Yukon, White Fang sees his first white men, and realizes what a low place Gray Beaver occupies among them:

To be sure, White Fang only felt these things. He was not conscious of them. Yet it is upon feeling, more often than thinking, that animals act; and every act White Fang now performed was based upon the feeling that the white men were the superior gods. In the first place he was very suspicious of them. There was no telling what unknown terrors were theirs, what unknown hurts they could administer. He was curious to observe them, fearful of being noticed by them" (195–196).

Gray Beaver trades White Fang to a dog-fight manager, Beauty Smith, for a bottle of whiskey. Smith—called "Beauty" because he is so deformed—is a sadistic master who beats White Fang and starves him to make him fight harder:

He was a small man to begin with; and upon his meagre frame was deposited an even more strikingly meagre head. Its apex might be likened to a point. In fact, in his boyhood, before he had been named Beauty by his fellows, he had been called "Pinhead." . . . Nature had given him an enormous prognathous jaw. It was wide and heavy, and protruded outward and down until it seemed to rest on his chest. . . . This jaw gave the impression of ferocious determination. But something lacked. Perhaps it was from excess. Perhaps the jaw was too large. At any rate, it was a lie. Beauty Smith was known far and wide as the weakest of weak-kneed and snivelling cowards. To complete his description, his teeth were large and yellow, while . . . His eyes were yellow and muddy, as though Nature had run short on pigments and squeezed together the dregs of all her tubes (204).

White Fang develops a fearsome reputation on the dog-fighting circuit, killing all the dogs put in with him: "Under the tutelage of the mad god, White Fang became a fiend" (215). However, in his last fight he is about to lose to a bulldog named Cherokee when Weedon Scott, a gold prospector, stops the fight and takes White Fang to his cabin. Scott works White Fang on his dogsled team but also teaches him that not all men are cruel masters; eventually, he even teaches him love. Weedon Scott and his friend Matt realize how intelligent White Fang is.

Part 5: The Tame

With Scott, White Fang finds that "Like had been replaced by love. And love was the plummet dropped down into the deeps of him where like had never gone. And responsive, out of his deeps had come the new thing—love. That which was given unto him did he return. This was a god indeed, a love-god, a warm and radiant god, in whose light White Fang's nature expanded as a flower expands under the sun" (260). Scott, whom the narrator calls the "Love-Master," takes White Fang to his home in CALIFORNIA, where White Fang becomes part of the family and even learns to get along with other dogs. He mates with one of Weedon Scott's dogs. She has a litter of puppies, and through this White Fang achieves another kind of love—the love of a father for his children. White Fang at first feels out of place, and the Scott family does not entirely believe that he is tamed. However, he proves himself by saving Scott family members twice, the first time going for help when Scott falls off his horse and breaks his leg. He earns even more approval and the sobriquet "Blessed Wolf" when he attacks and kills an escaped convict trying to murder Weedon Scott's father, Judge Scott, for a wrongful conviction perpetrated by a corrupt police force, further emphasizing the theme of human corruption due to greed. One presumes White Fang went on to live a happy and productive life as the "Blessed Wolf."

COMMENTARY

White Fang is in many ways the opposite of *The Call of the Wild*, which tells the story of a domestic dog's transformation into the leader of a pack of wolves, divorcing himself from humans forever—to become his true self. (Interestingly, the last chapter of Part 5 of *White Fang* is called "The Sleeping Wolf," which was London's original title for *The Call of the Wild*.) In *White Fang*, a wild wolf becomes a loyal domestic pet. Throughout the book, London successfully narrates the mind of White Fang and other animals. He convincingly portrays the life of the NORTHLAND and the sharp contrast not only of civilized versus wild lives, but also their relativity. Most of the men who are White Fang's masters are cruel to White Fang, demonstrating moral laxity and debased behavior. White Fang does not reject the pure and morally clean life of the wild, but is more or less forced to do so. However, when he defends his loving master, Weedon Scott, he demonstrates his evolved ability and ADAPTATION to the world of men—men who are capable of treating him fairly. London's three great values expressed in the Northland fiction, JUS-TICE, COMMUNITY, and IMAGINATION, are all realized in the mature White Fang. Thus, both tales are Darwinian in scope, showing the survival potential of those who are able to follow instinct but also adapt to a changing environment.

CHARACTERS

Bill Bill is one of the two men guiding the sled at the opening of the novel. He is clever and resourceful as ties the dogs up every night to keep them from escaping as they are pursued by the pack of wolves. However, he is also capable of acting rashly, as when he confronts the wolves with only three cartridges in his rifle. Bill is killed by the wolf pack.

Henry Bill's partner, he helps guide the sled containing the body of Lord Albert. He is presented as a good companion and a man with tremendous endurance. By using fire to scare the wolves, he is able to keep them away, at least for a time.

One Eye One Eye is a full-blooded wolf and White Fang's father and a seasoned veteran of the wolf pack. He uses his wits to gain advantage over the other males trying to mate with Kiche and wins her. He is shown as a good father to his pups and a good provider, even when famine is all about them. He disappears on a trip to hunt for food.

Kiche Part-wolf and part-dog, she is White Fang's mother. She knows the world of men because she was reared in the Indian camp by Gray Beaver; her knowledge of men allows her to overcome Henry and Bill. She is a good mother who takes risks to bring White Fang food. Eventually, as they are starving, she returns to Gray Beaver's camp and brings White Fang with her. She is sold by Gray Beaver.

Fatty Fatty is the first sled dog of Bill and Henry's to run away to join the wolf pack. He is portrayed as foolish and is not a favorite of the men.

Frog Frog is the second sled dog to run away to the wolves. Unlike Fatty, he is shown as very intelligent; Bill and Henry cannot understand why he ran.

Spanker Spanker is the third sled dog to run away to the wolves. He has the aid of One Ear, who chews through Spanker's leather fastenings to help him escape.

One Ear One Ear is one of Bill and Henry's sled dogs; when the sled tips over he is surrounded by wolves. Bill chases after him with his rifle, but neither of them survives the wolves' furious attack.

young leader, young three-year-old-wolf They vie with One Eye for Kiche and One Eye kills them for it.

Lynx Kiche and White Fang are nearly killed when they have to fight with a lynx who has stolen into their cave. Having lost one of her kittens to Kiche, the lynx seeks revenge. Interestingly, the fight between the wolf and the lynx was the source of President THEODORE ROOSEVELT's charge that London was a "nature-faker," a charge London answered in his essay "The Other Animals," in which he gives examples of such confrontations.

White Fang's brothers and sisters White Fang's brothers and sisters die for lack of food, making White Fang Kiche's only surviving pup; he is saved when she takes him to live with the Natives.

White Fang White Fang does not appear until almost halfway through the novel, when he is born in a cave, the offspring of a she-wolf, Kiche, and One Eye, a full-blooded wolf. He is the only cub in a litter of five to escape the red tint of his mother's coat that betrays her heritage of a life alongside man and his campfire, a foreshadowing of the cub's future as a tame house dog. White Fang discovers the world around him with the help of his mother. He grows hard and cruel under several uncaring masters. He is a dangerous animal until his final master, Weedon Scott, teaches him love.

Gray Beaver The Native man Gray Beaver is Kiche's former master. He becomes a good master to White Fang and treats him fairly. There is no affection between White Fang and Gray Beaver, but there is loyalty. Gray Beaver disciplines White Fang with a club when needed, but he also provides positive encouragement with gifts of meat. However, due to his drinking debts, he is forced to sell White Fang to Beauty Smith.

Lip-lip Lip-lip is a big dog who torments White Fang at the Native village. His treatment makes White Fang withdraw from the other dogs. Lip-lip provokes them to attack White Fang, and as a result White Fang becomes vicious with the other dogs.

Mit-sah He is the son of Gray Beaver and another good master. He helps alienate the other dogs from Lip-lip, who, though he continues to dominate all the other dogs, faces opposition from them when he tries to torment White Fang. They hate him because Mit-sah, seeing the danger White Fang is in, puts Lip-lip at the head of the string of sled dogs, making them all jealous.

Beauty Smith An evil master who is despised by man and dog alike, he treats White Fang cruelly.

Taking White Fang from Gray Beaver as payment for liquor, he makes money out of dog fighting. He tortures White Fang to keep him vicious for fighting.

Three Eagles   Three Eagles buys Kiche from Gray Beaver in the settlement of one of Gray Beaver's many debts.

Kloo-kooch   Gray Beaver's wife, she is kind to White Fang, even though other tribe members reject him.

boy   This boy, while cutting up moose meat, corners White Fang and menaces him with a club for eating some leftover meat, which White Fang knows is his right. White Fang bites him.

Baseek   He is an experienced dog in the Native village, and he tries to steal White Fang's meat. However, White Fang fights and beats him, now that he has become full-grown.

Tim Keenan   Keenan is the owner of a bulldog named Cherokee, whom he selfishly uses to make money in the dogfights. He worries about the health of his own dog, but only so he can continue to profit from him.

Cherokee   A large bulldog, he is the only dog who is able to defeat White Fang. In their match, he closes his massive jaws on White Fang's throat and holds on. Only Weedon Scott's interruption of the fight saves White Fang's life.

Weedon Scott   Saving White Fang from death in a fight, Scott introduces him to love and true loyalty, for White Fang a whole new world. Unlike those who have come before, he is a kind, loving master, something White Fang knows nothing of. He takes White Fang with him back to California, where White Fang becomes a beloved member of Scott's family. White Fang saves Scott's father from a criminal intruder and earns the name "Blessed Wolf."

Major   Major is one of Scott's sled dogs, and he tries to steal meat from White Fang. White Fang easily kills him.

Matt   Weedon Scott's business partner, he too takes good care of White Fang, though he never develops a close relationship with him. He is moved when he notices White Fang's grief when Scott is away.

Collie   Despite her name, Collie is a sheep dog owned by the Scott family. Jealous of White Fang, she taunts and attacks him; at their very first introduction she jumps on him and knocks him down. Only slowly does a friendship develop between them.

Weedon Scott's mother   She is nearly attacked by White Fang when she greets her son after his long absence; White Fang is threatened by her touching Scott. After that, she does not trust White Fang—however, when he captures the convict Jim Hall she changes her mind.

Dick   A deerhound at Scott's California place, he attacks White Fang. Though afterward he tries to befriend White Fang, White Fang will have none of it.

Judge Scott   The judge is Weedon Scott's father, who, like his mother, is not sure he can trust White Fang. He believes that wolves such as White Fang cannot be trained, though he does observe Scott train White Fang not to attack chickens. When White Fang captures Jim Hall, the Judge then trusts him.

Beth Scott, Mary Scott   Beth is Weedon Scott's sister who trusts White Fang from the moment she meets him. She is the one who learns from White Fang that Weedon has been injured. She seems to have an intuitive sense of White Fang's mind and behavior. Mary is his sister too.

Alice Scott   Alice is Weedon Scott's wife. She is very mistrustful of White Fang and wishes her husband had not brought him home.

Weedon Scott, Jr., and Maude Scott   Weedon Scott's son and daughter, they too fear the wild wolf in White Fang and wonder about their father's judgement.

Jim Hall   Hall is a convict who escaped because he was not guilty of the crime for which he was sentenced by Judge Scott, who did not know of the police plot to pin the crime on Hall. Hall is out for revenge on Judge Scott, because he mistakenly thinks he was part of the conspiracy. He breaks into the Scotts' home and attacks him.

FURTHER READING

Labor, Earle. "Jack London's Mondo Cane: 'Bâtard,' *The Call of the Wild,* and *White Fang.*" In *Critical Essays on Jack London.* Edited by Jacqueline Tavernier-Courbin. Boston: G. K. Hall, 1983, 114–130.

Wilcox, Earl. "Le Milieu, Le Moment, La Race: Literary Naturalism in Jack London's *White Fang.*" In *Jack London Newsletter* 3 (1970): 42–55.

"The White Silence" (1899)

First published in OVERLAND MONTHLY 33 (February 1899), "The White Silence" is one of London's starkest portrayals of the awful challenges the NORTHLAND poses to those who would travel there: the incredible cold, the lack of sun, the scarcity of game, and above all the looming WHITE SILENCE. These challenges are not only physical but ethical.

SYNOPSIS

Two men, the Malemute Kid and Mason, travel with Mason's NATIVE wife, Ruth, across a vast wasteland of frozen silence. At the beginning of the story they discuss how low they are running on food and how the dogs are misbehaving, especially one in particular, Carmen. They decide that the other dogs will probably kill her, and they plan to eat her if that happens. Trying to get the sled up a steep bank, Mason's snowshoes get tangled in the harness and it slides all the way to the bottom. Furious, Mason beats Carmen nearly to death, then feels remorseful. A short time later, a gigantic tree falls on Mason and crushes him. Ruth and the Malemute Kid tend to him, wrapping him in warm furs, placing him on a bed of boughs, and building a fire. But they realize that Mason will die in a few days and that he cannot travel. The Kid

begs him to try, but it is hopeless. The Kid goes off with his rifle to try to kill a moose but returns empty-handed to find the dogs attacking Ruth. The dogs kill the wounded Carmen, and the Kid skins her and stores the meat. They have also gotten into their store of dried salmon and eaten it all. There is only a small amount of flour left. Mason asks the Kid to take care of his wife and take her to the Southland to live and also to take care of the child she is carrying. Mason asks the Kid not to leave him alone to die but to shoot him. As Ruth heads out with the sled, the Kid waits for several hours, then he builds a cache for Mason using two pine trees; at the end of the story, "At high noon the sun, without raising its rim above the southern horizon, threw a suggestion of fire athwart the heavens, then quickly drew it back. Malemute Kid roused and dragged himself to his comrade's side. He cast one glance about him. The White Silence seemed to sneer, and a great fear came upon him. There was a sharp report; mason swung into his aerial sepulcher, and Malemute Kid lashed the dogs into a wild gallop as he fled across the snow" (*Stories,* 149).

COMMENTARY

"The White Silence" is one of London's most naturalistic stories. Suddenly, the tree falls on Mason, one of the many disasters that can occur on the Long Trail. The three travellers face other hardships and are nearly starving, but this incident results in Mason's death. Though his death is meaningless in the face of the White Silence, he is mourned by his wife and the Kid. The most positive aspect of the story is the friendship shown to Mason by the Kid, who follows his friend's wishes and shoots him out of mercy. The Malemute Kid is one of London's code heroes, as he displays resourcefulness, courage, and BROTHERHOOD. He appears in several stories. But the main character in the story is not human, it is the White Silence itself, described in one of London's most eloquent passages:

> The afternoon wore on, and with the awe, born of the White Silence, the voiceless travelers bent to their work. Nature has many tricks wherewith she convinces man of his fin-

ity,—the ceaseless flow of the tides, the fury of the storm, the shock of the earthquake, the long roll of heaven's artillery,—but the most tremendous, the most stupefying of all, is the passive phase of the White Silence. All movement ceases, the sky clears, the heavens are as brass; the slightest whisper seems sacrilege, and man becomes timid, affrighted at the sound of his own voice. Sole speck of life journeying across the ghostly wastes of a dead world, he trembles at his audacity, realizes that his is a maggot's life, nothing more. Strange thoughts arise unsummoned, and the mystery of all things strives for utterance. And the fear of death, of God, of the universe, comes over him,—the hope of the Resurrection and the Life, the yearning for immortality, the vain striving of the imprisoned essence,—it is then, if ever, man walks alone with God. (*Stories*, 143–144)

The typical KLONDIKE theme of the presence of the SUN at a critical moment occurs at the end of the story. It suggests a sense of hope ("the Resurrection and the Life") even amid such bleakness.

CHARACTERS

Malemute Kid The Malemute Kid is a seasoned veteran of the trail. He embodies London's NORTHLAND CODE through his loyalty to his trail mates. When Mason becomes so angry he nearly kills Carmen, the Kid does not judge his friend. In the end, he shoots Mason, as requested, and puts his body into a high cache in the trees. One is certain he will take care of Ruth and her baby.

Mason Mason travels with the Malemute Kid and Ruth. He is crushed by a giant tree that falls on him. He is originally from Tennessee, and as he dies he travels back in time to his youth.

Ruth Ruth is Mason's wife; from him she has received love and good care; back in her Native settlement women are treated little better than dogs. She mourns her husband but is able to return to the trail. She, like the Kid, is a figure of strength and determination to survive.

"The Wit of Porportuk" (1906)

First published in the *New York Times Magazine* (December 1906), this grim story of love and revenge was included in the collection *Lost Face*. At 10,000 words, it is one of London's longest KLONDIKE stories.

SYNOPSIS

"The Wit of Porportuk" is a dark tale of a 16-year-old NATIVE girl, El-Soo, of Holy Cross Mission who is a fine student and who hopes to complete her education in the United States. She is very intelligent, excelling all the other girls in reading and writing English, singing, art, and mathematics. Her father, Chief Klakee-Nah, summons her to his camp Tana-naw Station, on a bend of the YUKON RIVER. He is dying and owes many debts to an old man, Porportuk. Porportuk wants to marry El-Soo, but she does not want him; she prefers a younger man, Akoon, who is a renowned seal hunter and has traveled widely, even to Siberia and Japan.

Klakee-Nah owes Porportuk $15,967.75. He jokes that he will pay him in his next life. Porportuk covets the chief's belongings, his house, his mines, and his share in a steamer, the *Koyokuk*, but finds they are worthless; the ship, for example, has long ago sunk. To save her father, El-Soo sells herself at a public auction; her action is intended to allow him safe passage to the next world. Akoon, however, who loves her, says he will kill whomever is the high bidder. Porportuk is the high bidder, promising $26,000. He pays the chief with banknotes and mortgages, but El-Soo tears them up; when he presents gold, she throws it into the Yukon.

El-Soo runs away and is followed by Akoon, and they travel by canoe up the Porcupine River and on foot across the Rockies to the Mackenzie River, where they fall in with a group of Mackenzie Natives. Porportuk overtakes them there and presents his case to a Native council; the council agrees that El-Soo is Porportuk's property: "'It is just,' the old men said" (*Stories*, 1,169). But instead of merely claiming her, Porportuk tells Akoon that he has changed his mind about her. As an old man he knows he cannot keep up with her, especially if she keeps running away: "'Never will she run away from you'" (*Stories*, 1,169). He shoots El-Soo through both ankles with his rifle so she will never walk again, let alone run. Porportuk asks the old men of the native council, "'Is it just?'" "'It is just,' the old men said. And they sat on in silence" (*Stories*, 1,169).

COMMENTARY

Like many of the stories concerning Natives in London's works, in "The Wit of Porportuk" the presence of whites in the NORTHLAND is present but not at the center of the tale. True, it is partly because she has learned white ways and become educated that she does not want to marry Porportuk (she could go to the United States instead), but her real reason is not her education but her love for Akoon. This story resembles a Native trickster folk tale, with the trickster character present in both El-Soo and Porportuk. It may be that London heard such a tale told when he was in the Northland. The matter of El-Soo is handled by Native, not white, justice, and in the Native way a council of old men has the deciding vote. But at the same time as these folk elements are present, it also contains references to Shakespeare: a young Indian boy is called a "Caliban," for example. But it is not *The Tempest* one thinks of, but *The Merchant of Venice*. Again, like many Klondike tales, this one involves disputes among young women and their father-figures when it comes to marriage.

CHARACTERS

El-Soo El-Soo is a Native girl whose mother has died; she becomes "a Mission girl" when she is taken by a nun, Sister Alberta, to Holy Cross Mission. El-Soo is an intelligent girl and makes the nuns proud of her: "El-Soo was quick, and deft, and intelligent; but above all she was fire, the living flame of life, a blaze of personality that was compounded of will, sweetness, and daring" (*Stories*, 1,149). Though she is not fond of rules, she studies to learn to read and write: "She led the girls in singing, and into song she carried her sense of equity. She was an artist, and the fire of her flowed toward creation. Had she from birth enjoyed a more favorable environment, she would have made literature or music" (*Stories*, 1,149). She has to auction herself off to pay her father's debts; she is won by old Porportuk, but she prefers a younger lover, Akoon. For her disloyalty, Porportuk shoots both her ankles so she literally cannot run away anymore.

Klakee-Na Father of El-Soo and chief of the Tana-naw; but because he is deeply in debt to Porportuk he worries that he will not be allowed into the next world. He awards El-Soo to Porportuk for the sum of $26,000 when El-Soo holds an auction with herself as the prize to raise money for her father. She thinks that her lover, Akoon, will win. When Porportuk wins, she runs away with Akoon but is caught and shot by Porportuk.

Sister Alberta Nun who takes charge of El-Soo and is heartsick that she wishes to return to her village: "Much to the despair of the Sisters, the brand plucked from the burning went back to the burning. All pleading with El-Soo was vain. There was much argument, expostulation, and weeping. Sister Alberta even revealed to her the project of sending her to the United States. El-Soo stared wide-eyed into the golden vista thus opened up to her, and shook her head. In her eyes persisted another vista. It was the mighty curve of the Yukon at Tana-naw Station" (*Stories*, 1,150).

Young Native Man He travels from Tana-naw to the Mission to tell El-Soo her brother has died and that her father is ill. Since she has been so gently reared, he appears dirty: "He was a Caliban-like creature, primitively ugly, with a mop of hair that had never been combed" (*Stories*, 1,150). For his part, he looks disapprovingly at El-Soo.

Porportuk A wealthy old man of the Tana-naw, Porportuk is owed $15,000 by the chief. When El-Soo auctions herself off, he wins, but she flees from him. He eventually catches her and maims her legs in retribution.

Akoon Akoon is El-Soo's lover; he is a strong and handsome seal hunter who has traveled the world. Akoon threatens to shoot whoever wins El-

Soo in her auction, but instead he runs away with her. He is given her in the end by Porportuk.

Tommy "Tommy, the little Englishman, clerk at the trading post, was called in by El-Soo to help. There was nothing but debts, notes overdue, mortgaged properties, and properties mortgaged but worthless. Notes and mortgages were held by Porportuk. Tommy called him a robber many times as he pondered the compounding of the interest" (*Stories,* 1,156).

crowd at the auction "Surrounding El-Soo stood the four old slaves of her father. They were age-twisted and palsied, faithful to their meat, a generation out of the past that watched unmoved the antics of younger life. In the front of the crowd were several Eldorado and Bonanza kings from the Upper Yukon, and beside them, on crutches, swollen with scurvy, were two broken prospectors. From the midst of the crowd, thrust out by its own vividness, appeared the face of a wild-eyed squaw from the remote regions of the Upper Tana-naw; a strayed Sitkan from the coast stood side by side with a Stick from Lake Le Barge, and, beyond, a half-dozen French-Canadian voyageurs, grouped by themselves" (*Stories,* 1,159).

Captain He is captain of the steamer on which Akoon works; he is angry that Akoon abandons his post as seal hunter and runs away up the Yukon with El-Soo. "'Queer beggar,' he sniffed to himself" (*Stories,* 1,165).

council of old men The old men's council of the MacKenzie Natives hear Porportuk's claim on El-Soo and rule that he is just both in claiming her and then in shooting her and giving her to Akoon.

"The Yellow Peril" (1904)

The essay "The Yellow Peril" first appeared in HEARST SYNDICATE newspapers when London returned from covering the RUSSO-JAPANESE WAR in KOREA in June 1904. It was included in *Revo-*

lution. It is one of the most often misunderstood works of London's.

The phrase, Yellow Peril, was current in London's day, especially on the West Coast. The idea was that by sheer numbers Asians would soon overpower the West, and it was routinely invoked in anti-immigration legislation and rhetoric. It ranged from legitimate fears of JAPANESE expansionism all the way to lurid magazine tales of American women captured in Chinatown and sold into "white slavery." But London's essay is a critique of the whole idea, not a testament to it.

London does describe the Koreans as weak under Japanese domination, but he is generally not critical of the Japanese or CHINESE; those cultures he admires, though he does characterize the Chinese as, for the time being, less clever than the Japanese, who, he believes, will one day dominate them. He also attributes the cleverness of the Japanese largely to their adoption of Western technology. For example, "The Chinese is the perfect type of industry. For sheer work no worker in the world can compare with him. Work is the breath of his nostrils. It is his solution of existence" (*Revolution,* 274). As to the Japanese, "To-day, equipped with the finest machines and systems of destruction the Caucasian mind has devised, handling machines and systems with remarkable and deadly accuracy, this rejuvenescent Japanese race has embarked on a course of conquest, the goal of which no man knows. The head men of Japan are dreaming ambitiously" (*Revolution,* 278–279). London opines that the Japanese will take over and "manage" China, until China catches up to them and throws them out. But though he compares Western imperialism with Asian expansion, he makes a sort of apology for Westerners because they are "spiritual":

Back of our own great race adventure, back of our robberies by sea and land, our lusts and violences and all the evil things we have done, there is a certain integrity, a sternness of conscience, a melancholy responsibility of life, a sympathy and comradeship and warm human feel, which is ours, indubitably ours, and which we cannot teach to the Oriental as we would teach logarithms or the trajectory of projectiles.

That we have groped for the way of right conduct and agonized over the soul betokens our spiritual endowment. Though we have strayed often and far from righteousness, the voices of the seers have always been raised, and we have harked back to the bidding of conscience. The colossal fact of our history is that we have made the religion of Jesus Christ our religion. No matter how dark in error and deed, ours has been a history of spiritual struggle and endeavor. We are preeminently a religious race, which is another way of saying that we are a right-seeking race. (*Revolution*, 285).

This rings rather hollow, but then he goes on to relate a conversation he had with an American woman who says the Japanese "'have no soul'" (*Revolution*, 286). He begs to differ:

This must not be taken to mean that the Japanese is without soul. But it serves to illustrate the enormous difference between their souls and this woman's soul. There was no feel, no speech, no recognition. This Western soul did not dream that the Eastern soul existed, it was so different, so totally different.

Religion, as a battle for the right in our sense of right, as a yearning and a strife for spiritual good and purity, is unknown to the Japanese. . . . Yet [they have] a religion, and who shall say that it is not as great a religion as ours, nor as efficacious? As one Japanese has written:—

"Our reflection brought into prominence not so much the moral as the national consciousness of the individual. . . . To us the country is more than land and soil from which to mine gold or reap grain—it is the sacred abode of the gods, the spirits of our forefathers; to us the Emperor . . . the bodily representative of heaven on earth, blending in his person its power and its mercy."

The religion of Japan is practically a worship of the State itself. Patriotism is the expression of this worship. (*Revolution*, 286)

London concludes,

No great race adventure can go far nor endure long which has no deeper foundation than material success, no higher prompting than conquest for conquest's sake and mere race glorification. To go far and to endure, it must have behind it an ethical impulse, a sincerely conceived righteousness. But it must be taken into consideration that the above postulate is itself a product of Western race-egotism, urged by our belief in our own righteousness and fostered by a faith in ourselves which may be as erroneous as are most fond race fancies. So be it. The world is whirling faster to-day than ever before. It has gained impetus. Affairs rush to conclusion. The Far East is the point of contact of the adventuring Western people as well as of the Asiatic. We shall not have to wait for our children's time nor our children's children. (*Revolution*, 288–289)

As East Asia scholar Daniel Métraux has observed, it is a mistake to assume London was a proponent of Yellow Peril fears; though he criticizes various aspects of Asian cultures, on the contrary, his essay, like its companion piece "If Japan Awakens China," takes a dispassionate view of the strengths of Asia compared to the United States. It also argues against misunderstanding and for learning how the "Other" thinks. London advocated that Americans should learn Japanese and Chinese and Asians should learn English; only then will the different "sides" truly comprehend each other. Many of London's predictions about the future of Asian expansion actually came true, including the Japanese invasion of China and the Japanese showdown with the United States in World War II. As Métraux notes,

During and after his time in Korea and Manchuria, London developed a thesis that postulated the rise, first of Japan and then of China, as major twentieth century economic and industrial powers. London suggested that Japan would not be satisfied with its seizure of Korea in the Russo-Japanese War, that it would in due course take over Manchuria, and would then seize control of China with the goal of using the Chinese with their huge pool of labor and their valuable resources for its own benefit. Once awakened by Japan, however, the Chinese would oust the Japanese and rise as a major industrial power whose economic prowess would cause the West so much distress. (Métraux, "Jack London and the Yellow Peril," 31)

FURTHER READING

London, Jack. *Jack London Reports: War Correspondence, Sports Articles, and Miscellaneous Writings.* Edited by King Hendricks and Irving Shepard. Garden City, N.Y.: Doubleday & Co., 1970.

Métraux, Daniel. "Jack London and the Yellow Peril." In *Education About Asia* 14, no. 1 (spring 2009): 29–33.

Tsujii, Eiji. "Jack London and the Yellow Peril." In *Jack London Newsletter* 9, no. 2 (May–August 1976): 96–98.

PART III

Related People, Places, and Topics

adaptation   Adaptation is one of the basic processes by which an organism survives in its habitat. Adaptation by NATURAL SELECTION was one of CHARLES DARWIN's key principles of EVOLUTION. Adaptation is an important quality of many of London's heroes and heroines, from the two "Incapables" of "In a Far Country" to the successful adaptations of Buck in *The Call of the Wild* and Saxon Brown Roberts in *The Valley of the Moon*.

agrarianism   Agrarianism emphasizes how the quality of life could be improved both physically and psychologically if people turn to country life, e.g., working with livestock (ranching) or cultivating land (farming). London saw himself as an agrarian by moving back to the land on his ranch and pursuing sustainable, organic techniques. His three CALIFORNIA novels, *Burning Daylight*, *The Valley of the Moon*, and *The Little Lady of the Big House*, feature agrarianism as a saving choice for their protagonists.

Alaska Territory   The northwest boundary of the North American continent, Alaska is the largest U.S. state, formerly colonialized by Russia from 1733 until 1867. The United States bought it from Russia on March 30, 1867, for $7.2 million (about 2 cents per acre). Alaska's first capital was New Archangel on Kodiak Island; it was moved to Juneau in 1912. On May 11, 1912, Alaska began to be administered by the United States; on January 3, 1959, Alaska was recognized as the 49th U.S. state; in 1968, oil was discovered at Prudhoe Bay; and in 1977, the Trans-Alaskan Pipeline was completed. Alaska and the neighboring Canadian territory of the YUKON were the settings for the 1897–98 GOLD RUSH.

alcohol, alcoholism   London was an alcoholic whose disease rapidly accelerated when he was in his 30s. He began to drink as a child, and it really took hold of him when he began OYSTER PIRATING and hung around the saloons on the OAKLAND waterfront; he had to drink and buy drinks for others to keep up his manly status among the pirates. One night, drunk, he decided to drown himself in SAN FRANCISCO BAY, but was rescued just in time.

On other occasions he drank until he nearly died. His struggles with alcohol as an adult are told in *John Barleycorn*. His drinking was a source of great concern to Charmian, his second wife, but until his last year he never gave it up. Among his characters, alcoholism is considered a grave character flaw, as in the David Grief stories.

anarchists   Anarchists are followers of a political philosophy that considers compulsory government to be unnecessary and harmful to individual freedom. London portrays anarchists in such stories as "The Minions of Midas," and one of his friends was the famous anarchist EMMA GOLDMAN.

androgyny   Androgyny refers to the capacity of a person to display male and female characteristics. In London's works, it is generally positive. The NEW WOMAN had made her way into American culture, and, in CHARMIAN KITTREDGE LONDON, he was married to one. Examples of androgynous characters London created include Frona Welse of *A Daughter of the Snows*, Joan Lackland of *Adventure*, and Maud Brewster of *The Sea-Wolf*—and also Wolf Larsen of *The Sea-Wolf*.

Anglo-Saxons   Descendants of Germanic tribes, Anglo-Saxons invaded southeast Britain from the early fifth century B.C.E.; their English nation lasted until the Norman conquest of 1066. In the United States at the turn of the 19th century, practitioners of "scientific RACIALISM" argued that only Americans with "Anglo-Saxon" blood could be true Americans, excluding most obviously blacks and Asians, but also Germans (believe it or not) to IRISH, Jews, and Italians, for example. London as a youth prided himself on his Anglo-Saxon heritage, but he did not really know who his father was, and his mother was of WELSH descent (at that time, CELTS were not thought to be fully white).

Applegarth, Mabel   Mabel Applegarth (1873–1915) was introduced to Jack London by her brother, Ted Applegarth, an early friend. She was London's first serious love and the model for Ruth Morse in *Martin Eden*. He met her in 1895 when she was a student at the UNIVERSITY OF CALIFORNIA. Her refinement and literary taste captivated him.

Arthurian legend   The legend of King Arthur and his knights of the Round Table at his court in Camelot has existed for more than a thousand years. Its creators—Geoffrey of Monmouth, Robert de Boron, Chrétien de Troyes, and Sir Thomas Malony—conjured a world of courtly love and chivalric virtue. The legend primarily consists of two larger stories, that of Arthur and Camelot, and that of various knights on quests, such as the quest for the Holy Grail. London uses elements of the Arthurian legend in several works and is especially fond of the name "Percival" for characters who lack moral agency. (Percival was the Arthurian knight who failed to ask the right questions of the grail objects.)

Aryans   A term originating in the Sanskrit language to denote speakers of a prevalent North Indian language. During the early 1900s, with the "Scientific" debates over race, it evolved to describe the superiority of Northern Europeans, the Aryan race. It was a term later used by the Nazis. London read racialist texts on Aryans and understood them as the progenitors of ANGLO-SAXONS.

atavism   Atavism means the occurrence of a trait that has not occurred in several generations, a throwback to a primitive ancestor. London believed that atavisms often dwelt inside modern humans. This is especially the case with his descriptions of fighters (*The Game, The Abysmal Brute*). In *Before Adam*, he explores over caveman progenitors. The term was used by Cesare Lombroso in the 1870s to explain the causes for criminal deviances and by SOCIAL DARWINISTS to describe the reappearance of primitive traits in "inferior races." Works that feature atavism include *Before Adam, The Scarlet Plague*, and "When the World Was Young."

Atlantic Monthly   An American literary and cultural magazine founded in Boston by James Russell Lowell, Ralph Waldo Emerson, and Henry Wadsworth Longfellow in 1857. The magazine published works by MARK TWAIN and Jack London,

along with nearly every other major fictionist of the day. When London sold the *Atlantic* his first story, "An Odyssey of the North," published in the January 1900 number, he had "made it" in terms of literary respectability. His editor at the *Atlantic* was Bliss Perry (1860–1954).

Beauty Ranch   In June 1905, having become engaged to his second wife, CHARMIAN KITTREDGE LONDON, London moved up to SONOMA VALLEY, where he fell in love with its beauty and way of life. Relying on large advances from MACMILLAN, London first purchased the 129-acre Hill Ranch, which became the nucleus of what would develop into his nearly 1,400-acre Beauty Ranch. On the grounds were numerous stone farm buildings and the buildings of a former sherry vineyard. The Londons lived in a cottage on the ranch and brought ELIZA LONDON SHEPARD there to act as its superintendent. Over the years, London became a successful farmer with organic techniques. He built a manure pit and a pig "palace." He terraced the mountainside as he had seen done in Asia. The ranch produced numerous crops including grapes, and London raised prize livestock. In 1913, his newly constructed dream home, WOLF HOUSE, burned. Today, most of the ranch is JACK LONDON STATE HISTORIC PARK, where visitors can admire the beauty of the valley and visit the buildings, including the cottage, refurbished and open to the public. Charmian's "House of Happy Walls," built after Jack's death, is the park museum. The ranch plays a significant role in his literary works, especially *The Little Lady of the Big House*.

Bêche-de-Mer English   Bêche-de-mer is a type of sea cucumber traded in the South Seas; the name also designates the pidgin English (a combination of English and Malay) spoken in the southwestern Pacific, particularly in places like New Guinea and the SOLOMON ISLANDS. For example, in *The Cruise of the* Snark, London's chapter on Bêche-de-Mer English includes the following example: "Limited vocabulary means that each word shall be overworked. Thus, *fella*, in beche de mer, . . . is used continually in every possible connection. Another overworked word is *belong*. Nothing stands alone. Everything is

Jack London rides out on his ranch, which overlooks Sonoma Valley, ca. 1910. *(Huntington Library)*

related. The thing desired is indicated by its relationship with other things. A primitive vocabulary means primitive expression; thus, the continuance of rain is expressed as *rain he stop* . . . [F]or instance, a native who desires to tell you that there are fish in the water and who says *fish he stop*. It was while trading on Ysabel island that I learned the excellence of this usage. I wanted two or three pairs of the large clam shells (measuring three feet across), but I did not want the meat inside. Also, I wanted the meat of some of the smaller clams to make a chowder. My instruction to the natives finally ripened into the following: 'You fella bring me fella big fella clam—*kai-kai* he no stop, he walk about. You fella bring me fella small fella clam—*kai-kai* he stop' [*kai-kai* means to eat] (*Cruise of the Snark*, 297–298).

Bible, as influence   Despite his insistence that he was a materialist without belief in God or an afterlife, London's writings were heavily influenced by the Bible. Biblical allusions abound in his work, especially in the South Seas tales, in which he was also influenced by his reading of Christian MISSIONARY accounts. That London had read and knew well the Bible is clear from the numerous references he makes, especially to the New Testament. As a small child he was helped to read by his African-American foster mother, Mrs. VIRGINIA PRENTISS, with the King James version; King James English appears throughout his works, especially as used to convey the speech of NATIVES in the NORTHLAND. In the South Seas works, one finds allusions to the pearl of great price ("The House of Mapuhi"), the parable of the builder ("The House of Pride"), the benevolence of Christ ("The Seed of McCoy"), the parable of the prodigal son ("In a Far Country"), Jesus's advice to Nicodemus ("The Water Baby"), and the crucifixion (*The Star Rover*). The copy of the Bible London brought aboard the SNARK is heavily annotated.

Bierce, Ambrose   Ambrose Gwinnett Bierce (1842–1913?) was a satiric American writer whose specialties included journalism and short fiction. Having served in the Civil War, he often wrote of man's cruelty to man; he became known as "Bitter Bierce." He disappeared in Mexico in 1913 where he went to join the MEXICAN REVOLUTION and was never seen again. In addition to his friendship with MARK TWAIN, Bierce was a friend of London and

GEORGE STERLING, and with them attended the BOHEMIAN GROVE "Hijinks" each year. London and Sterling corresponded often about Bierce, especially his faults. He also complained to Charmian in 1910 just before he was to leave for the Hijinks about an argument he and Bierce had and what he will do when he sees him: "Damn Ambrose Bierce. I won't look for trouble but if he jumps me, I'll go him a few at his own game. I can play-at and abuse just for the pure fun of it. If we meet, and he's introduced, I shall wait & watch for his hand to go out first. If it doesn't, hostilities begin right there" (*Letters*, 915).

Big Island (Hawai'i)   On all three of his lengthy stays in HAWAI'I, London spent time on the Big Island. He visited huge ranches like the Parker Ranch and the Balding Ranch, visited Kona and Hilo, as well as the volcanoes, rode cane flumes down mountains, and learned much of old Hawaiian folktales and customs. "The Sheriff of Kona" is one of his stories set on the Big Island.

blackbirders   *Blackbirder* is a term used to describe slavers and recruiters in the South Pacific. Representing various plantations, white men would land on an island and either "recruit," signing men up for long labor contracts, or simply kidnap men and consign them to slavery on the plantations. The Londons sailed aboard one such ship, the MINOTA, while they visited the SOLOMON ISLANDS. On the island of MALAITA, they and the crew were nearly overrun by islanders.

Black Cat   The *Black Cat*, a literary magazine, began publication in 1895, edited by H. D. Umbstaetter in Salem, Massachusetts. It featured fantasy and science fiction stories and welcomed submissions from first-time writers. London sold his short story "A Thousand Deaths" to the magazine in 1899; though he had been sending out dozens of stories, they all met with rejection until this. He was paid $40, and this helped him decide once and for all to abandon WAGE SLAVERY and a proffered post office job and turn to full-time writing.

Bohemian Club/Bohemian Grove   The Bohemian Club is a private men's club in San Fran-

cisco, founded in 1872 by journalists, artists, and musicians who wished to promote BROTHERHOOD among themselves as "bohemians." Later it began to accept businessmen and entrepreneurs as permanent members. London was a member, as was his close friend poet GEORGE STERLING. Every year, the club hosted a two-week-long retreat called the "Hijinks" at the Bohemian Grove north of the city. Members carried out all sorts of games and performances, drank, sang, composed poetry, ran naked, and even cross-dressed. It was highly secretive and banned women or outsiders of any kind.

Bonanza Creek   A stream in western YUKON, Canada, that rises near DAWSON and flows 20 miles northwest to the Klondike River. In August 1896, George Carmack discovered a large bed of gold there, which set off the Alaska GOLD RUSH into the KLONDIKE. London prospected on Bonanza Creek, but by the time he and the others in the rush arrived there, all the good claims were staked.

Bond family (Judge Hiram Gilbert Bond, Louis Bond, and Marshall Bond)   Louis and Marshall Bond were two gold prospectors from Santa Clara, CALIFORNIA, whom London knew and teamed up with in the KLONDIKE. Their DOG, Jack, was the inspiration for Buck in *The Call of the Wild*. Their father, Judge Bond, is the model for the judge in *The Call of the Wild*, Buck's first owner, and the judge's fine home is modeled on the real judge's home in Santa Clara.

Bora Bora   A French Polynesian island first inhabited in the fourth century and named *Kaka'u*. France made Bora Bora a protectorate after Abel Aubert Dupetit Thouars expelled British MISSIONARIES in Tahiti in 1842. Bora Bora was London's favorite port of call on the SNARK voyage; there he enjoyed bountiful hospitality and friendship, especially with a man from a nearby islet, Tahaa, named TEHEI. Tehei became for a time the pilot on the *Snark* and is the model for Otoo in "The Heathen."

bourgeois   A member of the middle or merchant class known as the bourgeoisie whose power and or status are not achieved through aristocratic heritage, but through money gained from employment or ownership of a means of production. In general, the bourgeoisie supported the American and French revolutions to overthrow ancient laws that upheld aristocracy and hindered a capitalist society. As a socialist, London casts the bourgeoisie as the enemy of WORKING CLASS people; even though they were not the immensely wealthy class such as Rockefeller, Gould, and Morgan, they supported the status quo as a privileged upper middle class because they owned capital. London attacks their false pieties in *Martin Eden* in particular.

boxing   By London's day, pugilism as practiced by gentleman boxers had transformed into a spectator sport for the masses. Fighters' careers were eagerly followed by fans, and the practice of prizefighting led to larger and larger purses for the winners. London was an amateur boxer, often boxing with Charmian, and much of his early newspaper correspondence consists of prizefight stories for newspaper sports sections. In this, he was acquainted with many of the leading names of the ring in his day, especially when he covered the world heavyweight fights between JACK JOHNSON and TOMMY BURNS (1908) and Jack Johnson and JIM JEFFRIES (1910). His coverage of these fights demonstrates his knowledge of the sport and his ability to provide exciting play-by-play description.

Brett, George P.   George Platt Brett (1859–1936) was the president of MACMILLAN Company, London's longtime publisher. In December 1901 he wrote to London requesting submissions. In that letter, he noted that London's stories "seem . . . to represent very much the best work of the kind that has been done on this side of the water" (*Letters* 267). London and Brett became close professional friends and worked brilliantly together, as their many letters over the years reflect. To Brett, London wrote of his dearest achievements and dreams, the ranch, the SNARK voyage, WOLF HOUSE—but also to request large advances to pay for his dreams. Brett was a most obliging publisher, and he advanced London considerable sums for these endeavors. Their faith in each other truly paid off.

brotherhood   Brotherhood is an extremely important theme in London's works. First appearing in the NORTHLAND CODE of trail mates in his KLONDIKE stories, it is a constant focus. It is portrayed directly in such tales as "To the Man on Trail" and "The White Silence," and portrayed in its absence in such grim stories as "Love of Life" or "In a Far Country." It also plays an important role in many other works, from the brotherhood of Koolau's band of lepers, to the brotherhood of David Grief with the islanders he befriends, to the Brotherhood of Man in *The Iron Heel.* On the negative side, brotherhood is the value missing in other works, such as "The House of Pride." In *A Daughter of the Snows*, Gregory St. Vincent's betrayal of a partner is what forever banishes him from the affections of the heroine, Frona Welse. Brotherhood is of course part of London's SOCIALISM.

Burbank, Luther   Burbank was a botanist and horticulturist (1849–1926) who invented new strains and varieties of plants. Burbank, who lived in Santa Rosa, CALIFORNIA, was a neighbor and friend of London's who admired his youthful vigor and personality. Burbank advised London on horticulture on the ranch, using such plants as spineless cactus for animal food that he had innovated in his studies. Burbank's "Training of the Human Plant" influenced London's RACIALISM, as it emphasizes improving the human species if first cousins are prohibited from marrying.

Burns, Tommy   Tommy Burns (1881–1955), born Noah Brusso, was a Canadian world heavyweight champion boxer. He traveled the globe 11 times defending his title. He was always viewed as the underdog due to his small build, but he was predicted to win when he lost the title to JACK JOHNSON in Sydney, Australia, in January 1909, making Johnson the first black heavyweight champion. According to London's newspaper coverage of the event, Burns never had a chance against the far-superior Johnson, though he had voiced the opinion that any white man could beat a black man in the ring. Responding to Burns and the crowd's racial epithets Johnson in turn taunted him throughout the match and merely toyed with him, until suddenly knocking him out cold.

California California means many things in London's works. It was the state of his birth and where he resided nearly all of his life. He built his BEAUTY RANCH in SONOMA VALLEY and engaged in some of the most advanced farming techniques then known. London sought adventure in the KLONDIKE and the South Seas, but with the exception of HAWAI'I, which he also loved, he really only found a home— a healing home—in California, where the climate and a diet of fresh food helped him recover from the illnesses he contracted on the SNARK voyage. London saw California as a land of rich opportunities, its farms bucolic and productive, its cities places where he could mingle with the most exciting citizens, especially writers and artists. He uses the urban set-ting of San Francisco in numerous works ("South of the Slot," "The Night-Born," *Burning Daylight*) and the countryside in even more ("All Gold Canyon," *The Valley of the Moon, The Little Lady of the Big House*). California offered millions the promise of a new life in its fertile valleys. It was the West in all its legendary promise, and its GOLDEN GATE opened the way for London's Pacific adventures, as its rivers and bays gave him sailing practice for that voyage and in recreation in years after.

cannibalism On the SNARK voyage, the Londons and their crew visited numerous spots in the South Pacific in which CANNIBALISM was still practiced, from the Marquesas in the east to the Solomons in the west. In *The Cruise of the* Snark, London bemoans the fact that unlike MELVILLE, he was not actually able to witness the practice himself. Most

Marquesans perform the Tahitian hula to Hawaiian music, which plays on an American phonograph in Nuku Hiva, 1907. *(Huntington Library)*

Jack London wearing a skirt made of human hair, Marquesas Islands, 1907 *(Huntington Library)*

often in the South Seas, cannibalism was practiced against enemies, and, sadly, children. London read in one of the MISSIONARY accounts aboard the *Snark* of a particular practice in FIJI: the captives, usually women, had their arms and legs broken and were tied down in a shallow stream, where they would become tenderized. As souvenirs from the voyage, London brought back a skirt made of Marquesan scalps and a large calabash that had been used as a dish to serve "long pig," or humans. Many works mention cannibals: "Mauki," "The Whale Tooth," "The Red One," and *Adventure.*

Cape Horn   Cape Horn is the most southerly tip of South America, marking the northern edge of

the Drake Passage. Before the completion of the Panama Canal in 1914, ships had to round the Cape between the two oceans. As the waters and weather conditions there are treacherous, ships struggled or even sank in the attempt. The Londons journeyed on one of the last sailing ships to cross the Horn, the *DIRIGO*, in 1912, from Baltimore to SAN FRANCISCO; it took the sailors weeks to battle their way through gigantic waves, terrible cold, and freezing winds. London portrays the perilous passage in the story "Make Westing."

capitalism   Capitalism is a market-based economic system in which the means of production of goods is privately owned as well as operated under competitive conditions; workers are paid set wages, while the owners reap profits. It developed beginning in the 16th century in Europe. The Scottish philosopher Adam Smith is often credited with inventing capitalism in 1776. For London as a socialist, capitalism was a corrupt economic system that exploited the masses for the wealth of the few. It is important to point out that though London made huge sums of money in the capitalist marketplace of bookselling, he himself was not a capitalist. He believed that by putting his books out in front of the most people possible that he was spreading his gospel of SOCIALISM, using the tools of capitalism. London also was an artisan who dealt in his own brains and work.

Carmel-by-the-Sea   In the beachside arts community of Carmel, near Monterey, CALIFORNIA, London found friends and fun on his visits there with "the Crowd," which included poet GEORGE STERLING, writer Mary Austin, and painter Xavier Martinez. Sterling had a home there that London often visited. The group would camp on the beach, sing songs and tell tales, and catch and cook abalones.

Carroll, Lewis   Lewis Carroll (1832–98) (Charles Lutwidge Dodgson) wrote his nonsense poem "The Hunting of the Snark" in 1874. The poem describes the voyage of an unfit crew to find an unthinkable creature. London named his yacht the *SNARK* after Carroll's nonsense poem. Perhaps no yacht had ever been so aptly named, the poem predicts *Snark*'s trickiness and CAPTAIN ROSCOE EAMES's incompetence, as in "Fit the Second, The Bellman's Speech":

> He had bought a large map representing the sea,
> Without the least vestige of land:
> And the crew were much pleased when they
> found it to be
> A map they could all understand.
>
> "What's the good of Mercator's North Poles
> and Equators,
> Tropics, Zones, and Meridian Lines?"
> So the Bellman would cry: and the crew would
> reply
> "They are merely conventional signs!
>
> "Other maps are such shapes, with their islands
> and capes!
> But we've got our brave Captain to thank:
> (So the crew would protest) "that he's bought
> us the best—
> A perfect and absolute blank!"
>
> This was charming, no doubt; but they shortly
> found out
> That the Captain they trusted so well
> Had only one notion for crossing the ocean,
> And that was to tingle his bell.
>
> He was thoughtful and grave—but the orders
> he gave
> Were enough to bewilder a crew.
> When he cried "Steer to starboard, but keep
> her head larboard!"
> What on earth was the helmsman to do?
>
> Then the bowsprit got mixed with the rudder
> sometimes:
> A thing, as the Bellman remarked,
> That frequently happens in tropical climes,
> When a vessel is, so to speak, "snarked."
>
> But the principal failing occurred in the sailing,
> And the Bellman, perplexed and distressed,
> Said he had hoped, at least, when the wind
> blew due East,
> That the ship would not travel due West!

The *Snark* was a "Boojum," as named in the poem, but despite all its deficiencies (and its captain's) it did take the crew across the wide Pacific.

cavemen   Cavemen and women appear in several of London's works, most memorably in *Before Adam* and "The Strength of the Strong." London uses this character as a primitive but describes traits as human as modern people's. London was interested in ATAVISM, or reversion to the primitive, and his study of DARWIN led him to imagine links between modern humans and ancient ones. From CARL JUNG, London absorbed the idea that all humanity is one through the collective unconscious, and this helps explain why he so often turns to atavistic figures, such as the businessman who runs naked at night in "When the World Was Young."

celebrity   London was one of the first modern celebrities and, after MARK TWAIN, in his day the best-known American writer. Because of his life of adventure, he himself, and not just his characters, was admired by millions as the perfect example of the American hero. At the HUNTINGTON LIBRARY, there are dozens of huge ledger books filled with his press clippings; just about anything he did was fodder for the daily press. When he covered the JACK JOHNSON world heavyweight fights in 1908 and 1910, his picture, and not TOMMY BURNS's or JIM JEFFRIES's, would run alongside their opponent. Ridiculous stories circulated about London, how he had wrestled or boxed with all the greatest fighters, how he had fought off bears and WOLVES in the NORTHLAND, how he rode with PANCHO VILLA. What he actually did was news enough, but his biography has always been exaggerated by his fame. In *Martin Eden*, which later made people believe the false story of London's suicide, Martin reacts against the cult of celebrity when he becomes famous as a writer. But London was shrewd about his fame; he knew what would sell books and was not ashamed to use his own life as a part of the celebrity machine. He remains today the most widely known American writer in the world.

Celts   "Celt" describes the ethnicity of a group of tribal societies in Central Europe beginning in the Iron Age. They expanded to the west in Ireland, Scotland, France, and Spain and east as far as present-day Turkey. In London's time, the term referred mostly to the IRISH, who were seen as undesirable immigrants on the East Coast of the United States. Racialists placed Celts below ANGLO-SAXONS as not quite white, some texts compared their racial shortcomings with those of blacks. London's mother was of WELSH descent, something he sometimes forgets when he mentions his Anglo-Saxon ancestors. Perhaps thinking of his mother, he names his heroine in *A Daughter of the Snows* Frona Welse, but he describes her as pure Anglo-Saxon. Celts were not discriminated against so much on the West Coast. They generally appear in his works, however, as somehow just outside the pale, as with the Irish fight promoters in "The Mexican" or the Irish toughs in *The Valley of the Moon.*

Century Company The American publishing company the Century Company was founded in 1881. Originally a subsidiary of Charles Scribner's Sons, it first published *Scribners Monthly;* this magazine was renamed the *Century Illustrated Monthly Magazine.* The company also published *St. Nicholas Magazine* for children. It included a book imprint. London published dozens of stories in *Century Magazine,* but its press published his books *The Cruise of the* Dazzler, *John Barleycorn, The Abysmal Brute, The Night-Born, Smoke Bellew,* and *The Mutiny of the* Elsinore. After *The Cruise of the* Dazzler was published, London signed a long-term contract with MACMILLAN, which he thought did superior work, especially in the actual paper and cover quality of a book. However, after a spat with Macmillan in 1913, London temporarily returned to Century. *Century Magazine* was edited by Richard Watson Gilder, and there is quite a bit of correspondence between him and London. *Century Magazine* is where his most famous story, "To Build a Fire" (1908), first appeared.

Chaillu, Paul Belloni du Paul Belloni du Chaillu (1835–1903) was a French-American anthropologist and author of several adventure books for young reader. He became known in the 1860s for exploring and proving the existence of gorillas and the Pygmy people in central Africa. As a child, London was a devoted reader of his books, many of which were set in Africa.

Chaney, William Henry A native of Maine, William Henry Chaney (1821–1903), London's probable father, was an itinerant astrologer, lecturer, and author who called himself "Professor" Chaney. Before he drifted west, he had fled the life of manual labor on farms and in factories; indeed, his plan was to join the river pirates of the Mississippi and Caribbean. However, this failed, as did a law career and a career as a journalist. After several marriages and moves, he landed in the bohemian life of San Francisco. He lived with Flora Wellman, London's mother, in 1874–75. But when he learned that she was pregnant, Chaney, aged 55 and uninterested in being a father, told Flora to get an abortion. When she refused, he left her. Until the age of 21, London thought his stepfather, JOHN LONDON, was his father. When he learned about Chaney, he wrote to ask him if he were his father, but Chaney denied it, claiming he was sterile. Whether or not this was true, he probably believed himself incapable of being a father, since none of his former wives or girlfriends had become pregnant. There is some evidence Flora had other lovers, so we will never really know who London's father was.

chechaquo A Chinook NATIVE term meaning "newcomer," it was used in the NORTHLAND as opposed to a SOURDOUGH, or old-timer. The man in "To Build a Fire" who dies because he refused the old-timer's advice to take a companion on the trail, is a *chechaquo,* as are the hapless prospecting party of Hal, Charles, and Mercedes in *The Call of the Wild.* The price for a *chechaquo* who is not willing to learn from the sourdoughs is almost always death in London's works, as in "In a Far Country."

child labor In 1910, there were over 2 million children under the age of 15 working in industrial jobs. London was himself a child laborer, and he knew well the terrible cost on the body and mind of a young child working in a factory or mine. His most memorable portrait and attack on child labor is "The Apostate," in which a boy already an old man and on his way to an early death runs away from the factory and his family.

Chilkat-Tlinglits   The   Chilkat-Tlinglits   are Tlinglits who settled at the Chilkat River in southeastern Alaska, which is about 50 miles long, flowing southward to the Lynn Canal. Tlinglits are indigenous people who live in a complex hunter-gatherer society traced through the lineage of mothers. They appear as especially fierce NATIVES in several London stories.

Chilkoot Pass Beginning near SKAGWAY, ALASKA, the Chilkoot Pass is a 3,500-foot-high mountain pass that reaches through the Coast Mountains in Alaska, British Columbia, and Canada. The trail was a route used not only by the Tlingits but also later during the 1897–98 KLONDIKE GOLD RUSH by the prospectors. It was a punishing climb, and those who managed it had to return time and time again to the base to collect the next load; the Royal Canadian Mounted Police would not let anyone cross the border at the top who did not have at least one ton of supplies. As the weather grew colder, ice steps were carved on the trail; if a man fell out of step he had to descend to the base and start all over again, for none of his fellows would let him "cut" back in the line.

China and the Chinese London's primary interest in China and the Chinese appears in his RUSSO-JAPANESE WAR correspondence when he is in Manchuria; in his warnings of Chinese world dominance in "The Yellow Peril" and "The Unparalleled Invasion"; and in clever stories of Chinese-Americans in HONOLULU. "Chun Ah Chun" tells of a rich Chinese man who easily overcomes the stupid race prejudice of the whites in Honolulu society. "The Tears of Ah Kim" is a humorous tale of traditions old and new in conflict within a prospective groom's family. London believed Asia posed a threat to the West, but he advocated for mutual understanding, especially through his membership in the Honolulu-based PAN-PACIFIC UNION and Hands-Around-the-Pacific movement.

Christianity   Though London often stated that he had no interest in religion and that as a materialist he rejected metaphysics and spirituality, in examining his works one feels he could not have been more wrong. Because he detested his mother's séances and fake spirituality, and because he felt that the church ignored social justice, he declared that he did not believe in GOD or in an afterlife. However, his statements are belied by so much in his career. Like MARK TWAIN, he might dismiss God and Christianity in one place, and then betray deep attraction to the Christian story in another. The South Seas tales in particular are full of allusions to Christ, and such allusions occur throughout the KLONDIKE fiction. *The Star Rover* consists in part of segments of a "Christ novel" he worked on for many years but never finished as such. London was in part taught to read by VIRGINIA PRENTISS using the King James Bible and was as an adult a frequent and careful reader of scripture, as the many annotations in his bibles attest. If he thought the church did not do enough for social justice, he often described Christ as the model and even God mankind must strive for. This is particularly the case in much of his socialist writings, which were influenced by Christian socialists of the day. He also created several Christ figures in his stories, as in "The Seed of McCoy." Like Twain, he seems to have drawn deeply from the well of allusions and meaning in Christianity—especially alluding to Christ's parables—if he rejected organized Christianity as a falsehood.

Christmas Day December 25 was in ancient Rome the feast day of Old SOL, a god who combined attributes of Apollo and Jove, a sun god who watched over the deeds of men and judged them. London must have been captivated by this myth, because he uses Old Sol and Christmas Day in numerous KLONDIKE stories. The SUN typically appears and disappears according to what is transpiring among men on earth, just as the elements reflect the discord and strife of men in *King Lear*. Several stories occur on December 25, such as "The Devil's Dice-Box" and "To the Man on Trail," but the day and Old Sol are referenced throughout the NORTHLAND fiction. London's acquaintance with it shows his interest in Christianity but more so his reading of Greek and Roman MYTHOLOGY.

Christy, Howard Chandler Christy (1873–1952) was an American artist and illustrator most famous for the "Gibson Girl" image in illustrated magazines, World War I posters, historical paintings, and his illustrations in the New York restaurant Café des Artistes. He illustrated many of London's periodical stories in such magazines as *Scribner's, Harper's,* and COLLIER'S WEEKLY and such serialized novels as *Burning Daylight.* His work is picturesque and romantic, especially of women, and his watercolor strokes show a dashing sense of modern style.

Cole Grammar School Located in OAKLAND, Cole Grammar School is where London attended school from 1887 until his graduation from the 8th grade in 1891. While in school he worked as a paperboy, discovered the Oakland Public Library, and bought himself a small skiff and learned to sail. He also worked after school in a cannery and engaged in OYSTER PIRATING while a student.

Collier's Weekly *Collier's Weekly* was an important outlet for Jack London's works. It was an American magazine founded in 1888, which published until 1957. It prided itself on investigative journalism, called muckraking at the time. By 1903, it was edited by Norman Hapgood, who invited London to write an eyewitness account of the SAN FRANCISCO EARTHQUAKE, which London did. Later, in 1914, *Collier's* commissioned London to cover the MEXICAN REVOLUTION. The magazine had great influence on public opinion, helping to gain passage of such legislation as the Pure Food and Drug Act (1906). Later writers such as Ernest Hemingway and Sinclair Lewis were also published in *Collier's.*

community Related to London's concept of BROTHERHOOD, community is one of the three most important themes in his fiction, along with IMAGINATION and JUSTICE. From his socialist writings and speeches to his stories and novels, London promotes ideals of community over individuality or oppressive oligarchies. Throughout his career, he

seemed imaginatively to want to join diverse communities around the world and experience them from the inside out; this he accomplishes with characters as diverse as lepers, society ladies, cavemen, prospectors, cannibals, artists, and, of course, DOGS, as in *The Call of the Wild* and *White Fang,* which are both to a large extent about adapting to fit into a new community. The NORTHLAND CODE meant never abandoning your trail mate, and the code of David Grief in the South Seas stories meant social justice for all. London's KLONDIKE stories offer fascinating glimpses into NATIVE communities and communal ways, as did his Hawaiian stories. It is one of London's highest ideals.

Conrad, Joseph Joseph Conrad (1857–1924) was born Josef Teodor Konrad Koreniowski in Poland. After a maritime career, Conrad taught himself several languages and became an English-language novelist who mainly wrote about aspects of colonialism and life at sea, while also delving into the human soul. He became a British subject in 1886. He wrote books, short stories, and memoirs, his most famous work being *Heart of Darkness* (1901). London admired Conrad's work and wrote to praise him; Conrad also wrote to London to tell him how much he liked his work. The two writers shared similar themes: the journey into the racial as well as spiritual "heart of darkness," adventure stories of the high seas, and probing psychological portraits of naturalistic characters.

Cook, Captain James Cook (1728–79) was a British ship captain and explorer and first European to explore the eastern coastline of Australia, the Hawaiian Islands, and New Zealand. As a cartographer, he put several islands on the map by recording their longitude and latitude during three exploratory voyages. As a young boy, London devoured Captain Cook's books and dreamed of following his trail in the South Seas. Cook was an inspiration for his adventures, as well as his scientific discoveries and his interaction with islanders. Unfortunately, despite his generally fair dealings with islanders (at least according to European standards), Cook met his death at the hands of Hawaiians on the BIG ISLAND over a dispute. London met an old man in HAWAI'I who claimed that his great-great-grandfather ate the toe of Captain Cook.

Coolbrith, Ina   Ina Donna Coolbrith (1841–1928) was an American poet and librarian, and a key figure in the San Francisco literary world. She was the first poet laureate of California (first poet laureate of an American state). When London was a youth, she was the librarian at the Oakland Public Library, and she helped guide his early reading interests and encouraged his writing. He wrote admiringly of her all of his life and credited her with his literary awakening.

Cosmopolitan   London published dozens of works in *Cosmopolitan* (founded 1886), at the turn of the century a serious literary magazine. He corresponded frequently with its editors, Bailey Millard, Roland Phillips, and Edgar G. Sisson. Among his contributions were *The Road,* "What Life Means to Me," *Smoke Bellew, The Little Lady of the Big House,* "My Hawaiian Aloha," "On the Makaloa Mat," and "When Alice Told Her Soul." *Cosmopolitan* also published his unfinished novel *Cherry* as *Eyes of Asia,* completed by CHARMIAN KITTREDGE LONDON. Parts of *The Cruise of the* Snark also appeared in *Cosmopolitan.*

Coxey's Army   Coxey's Army, named after its leader, the populist Jacob Coxey, mounted a protest march on Washington, D.C., by unemployed workers in 1894. The purpose of the march was to protest unemployment and petition for the creation of jobs through the improvement of roads. It was the first significant popular demonstration against Washington. One hundred men began the march in Massillon, Ohio (interestingly, the birthplace of Jack London's mother), on March 25. Other groups joined until there were 6,000 men. The march ended with the arrest of Coxey and others for walking on the grass of the U.S. Capitol. London joined up with a branch of Coxey's Army in April 1894, leaving OAKLAND with a buddy to ride the rails. Before reaching Washington, London split off from the group and visited the Midwest and New York State. He writes of his experiences on the march in *The Road* and *John Barleycorn.*

Crane, Stephen   With London, FRANK NORRIS, and THEODORE DREISER, Crane was one of the best-known American naturalists. Like London and Dreiser, he started off in newspapers muckraking, and like London he had a great sympathy for the residents of ghettos. Crane's *Maggie: A Girl of the Streets* (1896) compares well with London's *Martin Eden* and "The Apostate," while his eerie and confused racial story "The Monster" invites comparison with London's racialized heroes. Crane's classic of NATURALISM "The Open Boat" compares well with London's "To Build a Fire" and other stories of the struggle for survival. Especially notable is Crane's insistence in this story on the importance of the BROTHERHOOD of men, similar to London's NORTHLAND CODE. Like London and Norris, Crane died very young, and we are deprived of what he might have continued to write afterward. Like London, despite his naturalism, he uses romantic forms in his works, especially in his imagery. His most popular work is his antiwar novel, *The Red Badge of Courage* (1895).

credo   Although there is no copy of this credo in London's handwriting or typing, it is mentioned in various places both by him and by newspaper reporters. Whether it consists of London's exact words or is an extrapolation invented by a journalist who interviewed him, it is a memorable statement of his blazing energy and vitality:

> I would rather be ashes than dust!
> I would rather that my spark should burn out in a brilliant blaze than it should be stifled by dry-rot.
> I would rather be a superb meteor, every atom of me in magnificent glow, than a sleepy and permanent planet.
> The function of man is to live, not to exist.
> I shall not waste my days trying to prolong them.
> I shall use my time.

Father Damien (Saint Damien of Molokai)   Father Damien (1840–89) was a Roman Catholic priest born in Belgium. He became a missionary of the Congregation of the Sacred Hearts of Jesus and Mary. He was canonized, or declared a saint, on

October 11, 2009. He won recognition for his ministry to people with LEPROSY (now called Hansen's disease), especially those in HAWAI'I who had been taken to a government-sanctioned medical quarantine community on the island of Molokai. He eventually contracted and died of the disease. When he arrived, Molokai's leper settlement at Kalauapapa was a nightmare of dissolution and disorder; he built a church and organized the lepers into a prosperous community. London admired him greatly and writes of his achievements in *The Cruise of the Snark*, which also offers a humanistic view of these people so shunned by society.

Darbishire, George On the voyage of the *SNARK*, the crew stayed five months in the SOLOMON ISLANDS, with their home base at PENDUFFRYN PLANTATION on the island of GUADALCANAL. This copra plantation was run by George Darbishire and his wife, Helen, along with their partner, Tom Harding, and his wife, the countess Eugenie. By all accounts, Darbishire was a pitiless master of his slaves and workers. There are a number of photographs of him with Harding and the *Snark* crew. In one, he is dressed as a woman; it seemed that he liked to do this and raided Charmian's clothes. He was killed along with his wife and eaten by his workers in 1914, which the Londons learned of from a missionary's letter.

Darwin, Charles Darwin (1809–82), an English naturalist, began by studying plants and animals of his father's garden. He attended medical school at the University of Edinburgh. He received a Bachelor of Arts from Christ's College, Cambridge. Instead of practicing medicine, he embarked on a sea voyage on the HMS *Beagle* that lasted for five years, beginning in 1831. On this voyage, he collected fossils and studied the distribution of wildlife. Four Fuegians were kidnapped and taken to England by the captain of the *Beagle*. Darwin accompanied them on their return to Tierra del Fuego and noticed that the difference between human races lay in culture and not race. Darwin did not share the racist beliefs of his time, especially not those of his follower HERBERT SPENCER.

In 1838, Darwin theorized that EVOLUTION occurred through NATURAL SELECTION and that all species, whether human, animal, or plant, have a common ancestor from which they evolved. He published his book *On the Origin of Species* in 1859. Other famous publications by Darwin are *The Descent of Man, Selection in Relation to Sex,* and *The Expression of the Emotions in Man and Animals*. When he died he was buried in Westminster Abbey.

London read and studied Darwin's *Origin of Species* and *Descent of Man* early on and continued to use Darwinian ideas in his fiction throughout his career. Darwin was of enormous importance to London and other naturalists; his emphasis upon the "struggle for survival" and natural selection based on adaptability of organisms reverberated throughout the world, challenging traditional beliefs, especially religion, as it located human behavior in biology. It is important to recognize that there were many competing interpretations of Darwin's thought in London's day, including those of Herbert Spencer and THOMAS HENRY HUXLEY. Spencer tried to apply Darwinian thought, which he misinterpreted as "survival of the fittest" (his famous phrase, not Darwin's), to society, arguing that in the struggle of the races the white race would naturally prevail and lead the world into benevolent SOCIALISM. Huxley, a more traditional Christian, rejected Spencer's RACIALISM and instead pointed out that NATURE is no moral model and humankind needs ethics to guide them even in the face of pitiless and relentless evolution. London at first admired Spencer, then rejected him and turned to a more Huxleyan interpretation of evolution.

Works that particularly evoke a Darwinian worldview range from his essay "The Human Drift" to his stories "The Law of Life" and "In a Far Country." Adaptability such as Darwin described is one of the most important qualities of London's heroes and the lack of it contributes to the failure of his nonheroes.

Dawson, Yukon Territory Dawson City is in Yukon, Canada, and was named after the Canadian geologist George M. Dawson in 1897. The town was Yukon's capital in 1898–1952. The town became known during the KLONDIKE gold rush in 1896–98, but the city was not incorporated until 1902. Jack London lived in Dawson from October 1897 until June 1898 and used it frequently throughout his works. In many Klondike works, he mentions food shortages and resultant diseases in Dawson. London reached Dawson after struggling up steep passes, long lakes, rapids, and miles of snow on poorly marked trails. He seems to have spent a lot of time in its taverns and cabins talking to old-timers and hearing their tales, rather than spending much time out in the cold prospecting. Works with significant settings in Dawson include *Burning Daylight*, *The Call of the Wild*, and "The League of the Old Men."

Debs, Eugene V. Eugene Debs (1855–1926) was an American union leader and a founder of the International Labor Union and the Industrial Workers of the World (IWW). He ran for U.S. president five times, once for the Social Democratic Party and four times for the SOCIALIST LABOR PARTY. He was arrested and sent to prison twice for his political beliefs, once in 1894 and again in 1918. London's story "The Dream of Debs" tells of a workers' revolution so complete it could only be a socialist dream. Obviously, London admired Debs and shared his socialist views.

determinism Determinism is the philosophical view that every event, including human ideas, behaviors, and actions, is causally determined by prior events. In other words, there is no GOD guiding destiny nor any other benevolent guiding force behind NATURE. Things happen because other things cause them to happen; there is no inherent meaning in these events. London believed himself to be a materialistic determinist, especially in socialist and economic matters, but he belies his divorce from metaphysics and romance in work after work. London was an amalgam of different and conflicting ideas. Though he claimed to be a determinist, he uses multiple allusions and themes that relate to ethics, morality, and CHRISTIANITY. Toward the end of his life, he abandoned his determinism to embrace the more spiritually oriented

thought of CARL JUNG, who argued for a collective unconscious that unites all human beings and a system of archetypes they mostly all recognize. Though the principles of determinism are important to such novels as *The Iron Heel* and *Martin Eden*, they compete with more individualistic, even spiritual, counter-themes.

Dirigo A four-masted steel barque built in 1894 by Arthur Sewall & Co., of Bath, Maine, the *Dirigo* was one of the last steel-hulled four-masted sailing vessels in the American fleet of trading ships. The Londons boarded it in the winter of 1912 in Baltimore and sailed aboard as crew members around CAPE HORN to San Francisco. London later used elements of the *Dirigo* voyage in *The Mutiny of the Elsinore*, and Charmian wrote a still-unpublished account, *The Log of the Dirigo*. It was for them a pleasant break from telegrams, phone calls, interviews, and press. Accompanied by their valet from the SNARK days, YOSHIMATSU NAKATA, they wrote, exercised, and performed shipboard duties; Charmian nursed the captain, who was dying of stomach cancer. Their crossing of Cape Horn was dramatic, delayed by weeks, and dangerous, but they were proud to have been aboard a sailing vessel that managed it. However, they had been having difficulties in their marriage largely due to London's drinking and the loss of their baby girl JOY LONDON in 1910. On the voyage he swore not to drink, and didn't, and they planned and conceived another child, who was later lost to miscarriage. London resumed ALCOHOL once they got home, and they remained childless.

dogs To many casual readers of Jack London, he is the guy who wrote the dog books, *The Call of the Wild* and *White Fang*. Though dogs are important elements in his work—as are WOLVES—they are actually pretty scarce when one contemplates his 50-odd books. But they are memorable; generations of readers the world over have identified especially with Buck of *The Call of the Wild*. London's choice of a canine hero allows him to universalize the story of development the novel tells. London took the wolf as a TOTEM figure, signing letters to his friend GEORGE STERLING as "Wolf" and using that name with his wife, who also called him "Mate." London always had dogs on the ranch and knew their habits well. In the KLONDIKE he used sled dogs and so could write about their work and behavior. Today, London critics have examined the Darwinian role of dogs and wolves in his fiction. Besides the two famous novels, short stories such as "Bâtard" and "Brown Wolf" convey London's various impressions of dogs and men.

Dreiser, Theodore   Dreiser (1871–1945) was an American novelist and journalist who used NATURALISM, like London, to portray not the moral code of characters but their determination against great forces beyond their control. They seek to rise in society; sometimes their plans are in tune with the times (*Sister Carrie*) while at other times, as hard as the protagonists try to achieve, their own weaknesses undermine them (*An American Tragedy*). Both London and Dreiser faced charges of moral impropriety, and both of them defended passionately the freedom of the author to write about whatever he pleased and fought against censorship.

Dyea Beach   Dyea Beach near SKAGWAY, ALASKA, was the dropping-off point for many of the gold rushers, including London. Ships unceremoniously dumped prospectors and their gear into NATIVE boats hired for transport for the fortunate; for the unfortunate the crews simply dumped men and supplies into the marsh. Klondikers would have to make their way to shore and hire horses and Natives to help them transport their outfits to the base of the CHILKOOT PASS. London usually describes Dyea, as in *The Call of the Wild*, as a bedlam of men, horses, and packs all swarming to get to shore. Today, it is a peaceful, wildflower-strewn meadow at the base of the famous pass.

dystopian fiction   Dystopian fiction is a genre in which a dark and terrible future is foreseen, based on contemporary trends, in contrast to the UTOPIAN novel with its hopeful vision of social change. In realistic, naturalistic, and science fiction at the turn of the century and beyond, it was a popular and critically acclaimed genre. London's *The Iron Heel* and *The Scarlet Plague* are dystopian novels. GEORGE ORWELL, who admired London, wrote the famous dystopian novel *1984* (1949), which furthered some of London's fears of coming dictatorship by a fascist oligarchy.

Eames, Ninetta Wiley   Ninetta was the sister of CHARMIAN KITTREDGE LONDON's mother, Dayelle "Daisy" Wiley Kittredge. When Dayelle died, Ninetta took Charmian into her home and raised her from toddlerhood. The two were very close, though the Londons and the Eames became more distant following ROSCOE EAMES's poor performance as captain of the SNARK and Ninetta's botching of London's business affairs while on the voyage. Ninetta introduced Charmian to Jack in 1904 at WAKE-ROBIN LODGE in GLEN ELLEN; Charmian helped Ninetta write a profile on London for the OVERLAND MONTHLY.

Eames, Roscoe   Eames was married to CHARMIAN KITTREDGE LONDON's aunt, NINETTA WILEY EAMES, who helped the Londons manage their interests while they were on the SNARK voyage. Roscoe signed on as captain of the *Snark*, but within days of sailing through GOLDEN GATE was discovered to know nothing at all of NAVIGATION and little of seamanship. London took over as captain and fired Eames in HONOLULU.

Erie County Penitentiary   In June 1894, London, having abandoned COXEY'S ARMY, visited the Midwest and New York State. One evening, he camped out at Niagara Falls, wanting to see the falls at sunrise. He was arrested as a vagrant and sentenced to one month in the Erie Country Penitentiary. There, he saw horrors and experienced the bottom of the social pit, inspiring him to return to CALIFORNIA and his books, to try to find a way besides crime or menial labor to rise from his circumstances. He relates many of his prison experiences in *The Road*, but said also that most of them were unprintable.

Eskimos   Eskimos are some of the indigenous peoples of eastern Siberia, ALASKA, Canada, and Greenland. There are two main groups, the Inuit

(Arctic regions of Canada, Greenland, and Alaska) and the Yupik (Alaska and far east Russia). A third related group is the Aleut. London portrays Eskimo characters in several stories, most notably "Nambok, the Unveracious."

eugenics   Eugenics is a belief system, popular at the turn of the 20th century as part of racialist studies and pseudoscience, which posits that the quality of human life can be improved by discouraging the reproduction of people with genetic defects or undesirable racial traits and the encouraging of the reproduction of people with "good" genetics and "good" racial traits. The philosophy was inspired early on by the selective breeding in animals and a better understanding of genetics. DARWIN's cousin Francis Galton and Stanford University professor DAVID STARR JORDAN influenced London's thinking on eugenics.

evolution   Evolution is the theory that originated in the 19th century after scientists studying fossils and diverse living organisms came to the conclusion that the different species had changed during the course of time. Evolution is a minor change that takes place in genes of an organism between generations, but can produce considerable changes in the species over an extended period of time and even create a new species. What causes the changes, or "mutations," organisms undergo was unclear until the theories of natural selection of CHARLES DARWIN and Alfred Wallace. There are two major processes operating in evolution, one that constantly introduces new variations and one that makes them either more common or uncommon. NATURAL SELECTION plays an important role in evolution because it results in good traits being passed on and bad traits disappearing by means of a theory called the survival of the fittest. (This was HERBERT SPENCER's phrase as a follower of Darwin; Darwin's original phrase was "the struggle for survival.") Today, literary Darwinism is a fast-emerging field of literary study that examines Darwinian patterns in literature, arguing that much of literature has a purpose in evolutionary fitness. London was heavily influenced by Darwin, Spencer, and another interpreter of Darwinism, THOMAS HENRY

HUXLEY. Some of London's more Darwinistic stories include "The Law of Life," *The Call of the Wild,* and *The Scarlet Plague.*

Examiner **(San Francisco)**   This newspaper began production in 1865, and in 1880 it was acquired by William Randolph Hearst's father and given to him. It published many of Jack London's articles, especially his early sports reporting and his RUSSO-JAPANESE WAR correspondence. It also published work by AMBROSE BIERCE, MARK TWAIN, and other budding Bay Area writers. Like its rival the CHRONICLE, it covered London in whatever he did. He published several important interviews and essays in the *Examiner,* including "The Yellow Peril." The *Examiner,* like all Hearst syndicate papers, was known for its sensationalistic "yellow journalism" and support for U.S. imperialism.

Fiji   This island nation, the Republic of Fiji Islands, is in the South Pacific. It was settled by forerunners of POLYNESIANS around 3500–1000 B.C.E. Fiji gained its independence from Great Britain in 1970. London devotes a chapter to Fiji in *The Cruise of the* Snark and set the story "The Whale Tooth" there. He annotated several MISSIONARY books in his library about CANNIBALISM in Fiji.

film adaptations   Starting as early as 1907, London's works were made into films. Early silent films of *The-Sea Wolf, A Piece of Steak, To Kill a Man, John Barleycorn, Burning Daylight,* and others appeared, directed by the leading names of the day: D. W. Griffith, Hobart Bosworth, and Victor Fleming. There are hundreds of films based on London's works, not to mention television shows, and they reflect the films of directors around the globe. London was one of the first American writers to become conscious of the role that film would play with his works. His works have often been described as having a certain cinematic quality, and he once wrote a novel based on a screenplay (*Hearts of Three*). He engaged in complex negotiations with directors, studios, and producers, including a few protracted lawsuits over copyright. Notable films include:

The Call of the Wild (1935). Twentieth Century Fox. U.S.A. Directed by William A. Wellman. With Clark Gable, Loretta Young, and Jack Oakie.

The Sea-Wolf (1941). Warner Brothers. U.S.A. Directed by Michael Crutiz. With Edward G. Robinson, Ida Lupino, John Garfield.

Jack London (1943). United Artists. U.S.A. Directed by Alfred Santell. With Michael O'Shea, Susan Hayward, Louise Beavers, and Virginia Mayo.

The Fighter. (1952). United Artists. U.S.A. Directed by Herbert Kline based on "The Mexican." With Richard Conte, Vanessa Brown, Lee J. Cobb.

Jack London's Tales of the Klondike (1981). Seven-part 50-minute television series. Canada. Produced by William McAdam/Prime Time/Norfolk Communications. Orson Welles narrates.

White Fang (1991). Disney. U.S.A. Directed by Randal Kleiser. With Klaus Maria Brandauer, Ethan Hawke, and Seymour Cassell.

Fish Patrol   The California Fish Patrol operating out of San Francisco in London's day was a sort of Coast Guard for the Bay Area. One of their occupations was catching illegal oystermen who roamed in gangs to steal oysters from company beds. London himself was one of these pirates, but when he realized where his life of crime would inevitably lead, he switched sides and joined the Fish Patrol. He writes of these times in his stories of adventure collected in *Tales of the Fish Patrol.*

Fiske, John   John Fiske (1842–1901) was a Harvard historian and philosopher and friend of Stanford president DAVID STARR JORDAN who attempted to fuse HERBERT SPENCER with CHRISTIANITY. Under the influence of Jordan, London as a young man embraced Fiske, but soon rejected him. In his *Outlines of Cosmic Philosophy* (1874), like Spencer, Fiske proposed the European ideology of the ARYAN to organize a universal body of truth obtained by science. Fiske thought of Indo-European languages as descended from a single ancestral language traceable to the legendary Aryans of the Hindu Vedas. Though London rejected Fiske's ideas, he used some of them in forming certain "degenerate" characters as ATAVISMS, such as the dark, hairy antagonist in *The Game* (1905) or the chauffeur in *The Scarlet Plague.* One of Fiske's ideas was based on phrenology, or the shape of the skull; Fiske thought that differences in skull shape among the races indicated inferiorities and superiorities. London sometimes praises symmetrical features and derides asymmetrical ones as evidence of a lower order.

Ford, Alexander Hume   At first a newspaperman in Chicago, by 1907 Ford (1868–1945) was an entrepreneur in HONOLULU who met London upon his arrival and introduced him to many powerful people in Honolulu. In April 1908, Ford took the Londons on a tour of the Ewa plantations, designed to impress London with Hawaii's agricultural productivity; however, London was more interested in the plight of the exploited field-workers brought to the islands from CHINA, JAPAN, Portugal, and elsewhere. This experience helped inspire the stories he wrote critical of HAWAI'I's HAOLE control of the islands. However he and Ford remained fast friends. Ford had London speak to many organizations in Honolulu and invited him to join the PAN-PACIFIC UNION with its "Hands-Around-the-Pacific" aims of promoting friendly business relationships across the Pacific Rim, especially with Japan. As a promoter of SURFING (including promoting the careers of George Freeth and Duke Kahanamoku and helping found the Outrigger Canoe Club), Ford also helped teach London how to surf; despite a terrific sunburn on his first day out, London fell in love with the sport and helped popularize it on the West Coast when he returned from the SNARK voyage. Ford wrote a moving obituary of London after his death.

Foss, Daniel   In early fall 1809, mariner Daniel Foss set sail for the Friendly Islands (now called the Tonga Islands) by way of the Cape of Good Hope. It was the beginning of a six-year ordeal that would lead him through shipwreck, near-starvation, CANNIBALISM, years of solitude, and, finally, a well-earned rescue. On November 25, the *Nego-ciator*, Foss's ship, hit an iceberg and sank within minutes. Foss climbed into a small lifeboat with 20 other shipmates. By January 10, 1810, Foss and two others were the only survivors, and they were starving. Finally, they drew lots to determine who would be sacrificed for the survival of the remaining two. The ship's surgeon lost. He opened an artery in his left arm, and Foss and his fellow survivor nourished themselves on their companion's blood as he quietly died. Coming upon an island, the boat wrecked on the rocks, and Foss alone survived. The island was small with no sign of life except shellfish. Foss discovered the body of a dead seal, then later discovered a large herd of seals. He used an oar to kill them for food. The oar became his handiest tool and eventually a journal on which he carved letters telling his story. Foss was marooned for six years. In 1816, he was rescued and returned home to Maryland. He is the basis for the character in *The Star Rover* who is marooned on an island.

French   London is enormously popular in France, as numerous editions, critical books, articles, conferences, exhibits, and films attest. In Europe in general, he is read as more of a socialist writer than he is in the United States. French characters appear in his work, however, largely as stereotypes: the comical Baron de Coubertin in *A Daughter of the Snows*; the vicious colonizers of TAHITI in "The Chinago"; the heavily accented FRENCH-CANADIAN VOYAGEURS in the KLONDIKE tales; and the Renaissance swordsmen of *The Star Rover*. London's NATURALISM was heavily influenced by the French novelist ÉMILE ZOLA.

French-Canadian voyageurs   Migrating from eastern Canada where they served as crews aboard canoes that took parties of hunters out for furs, voyageurs in London's KLONDIKE fiction are largely stereotypes of the coarse, swarthy, hard-living French-Canadians who traveled the NORTHLAND either hunting for furs or carrying mail and supplies. No one could match them for their endurance on the trail. The characters François and Perrault of *The Call of the Wild* are voyageurs; they are kindly enough to Buck and the other dogs. In contrast,

in "Bâtard," Black Leclère deliberately tortures his dog and pays a terrible price. London pays careful attention to the speech of the French-Canadians: After the puppy Bâtard bites Leclère, he remarks, "'Dat fo' w'at Ah lak heem. 'Ow moch, eh, you, M'sieu'? 'Ow moch? Ah buy heem, now; Ah buy heem queek.'"

Freud, Sigmund   Freud (1856–1939) was a famous Austrian neurologist and founder of the psychoanalytic school of psychology. His best-known theories are those of the unconscious mind, repression, and the practice of psychoanalysis. Freud used the id, ego, and superego to explain his theory of the unconscious mind, wherein the id is desire, the instinct or basic drives, which are unconscious; the superego is the moralistic aspect of the psyche, which is mostly unconscious; and the ego the part of the psyche that tries to balance the id and the superego and is half in the conscious mind. Psychoanalysis is the treatment of patients who are repressed, i.e., who are involuntarily holding desires, impulses, fantasies, etc., in their unconscious; these are uncovered through dialogue between the patient and the psychologist. Freud believed sexual desire is the primary motive for life and should be addressed by psychoanalysis. Freud often used the interpretation of dreams as a treatment that could access the unconscious.

The obvious place in London's works that Freud occupies is in the story "The Kanaka Surf," about the perverse love/hate relationship a couple share. He studied Freud's *Three Contributions to the Theory of Sex,* a 1916 book he quotes directly in the story but also alludes to in *The Little Lady of the Big House.* In his personal copy of the book, he marked passages on perversions, erogenous zones, infantile object selection, and the differentiation between men and women. He also read Freud's *Selected Papers on Hysteria and Other Psycho-neuroses,* a 1912 pamphlet. London read *The Psychoanalytic Review* each month when it came out and considered himself knowledgeable about the new science of psychology and psychiatry. In his last year, he became fascinated by the psychoanalytic theory of Freud's fellow-researcher CARL JUNG.

Germans Germans are presented in two quite different ways among London's characters. On the one hand, London admired the Teutonic race to which he believed he belonged, especially the Vikings; derived from the TEUTONS was Anglo-Saxonism, a set of ideas of enormous interest to racialists, or race scientists, who, following HERBERT SPENCER, believed that only Anglo-Saxons were truly white. However, modern Germans were a different matter, and these are usually stereotyped in his fiction as slow-witted, or even brutal and drunken. The most important version of this is the psychopathic sadist Max Bunster of "Mauki."

Glen Ellen, California A small, bucolic hamlet in SONOMA VALLEY, at the base of Sonoma Mountain and the location of Jack London's BEAUTY RANCH. Glen Ellen is surrounded by lushforests, mountains, and vineyards; through it wanders Sonoma Creek, bordered by redwoods, oaks, madrones, and manzanita. London learned of Glen Ellen through his second wife, Charmian, whose aunt and uncle ran a small inn for vacationers from the city. It appears as a setting in many of his works, including "Told in the Drooling Ward," "Brown Wolf," and *The Valley of the Moon.*

God Like MARK TWAIN, London's attitude toward God was conflicted, to say the least. On one hand, he rejected the idea of God as a fiction; as a materialistic monist he did not believe in a spiritual or metaphysical realm or in the afterlife. And yet, God is a constant presence in his fiction, either as "God" or as a GREEK or Roman deity like SOL. God witnesses the doings of men. Two passages indicate how God often appears in his works. The first is from "In a Far Country." The conclusion of the story finds Percy Cuthfert freezing to death after he has murdered his partner; throughout the story the two "Incapables," as London calls them, ignore the rules of God and man and fail to adapt to the KLONDIKE—they even commit all the seven deadly sins:

> Hark! The wind-vane must be surely spinning. No; a mere singing in his ears. That was all,—a mere singing. The ice must have passed the

latch by now. More likely the upper hinge was covered. Between the moss-chinked roof-poles, little points of frost began to appear. How slowly they grew! No; not so slowly. There was a new one, and there another. Two—three—four; they were coming too fast to count. There were two growing together. And there, a third had joined them. Why, there were no more spots. They had run together and formed a sheet.

> Well, he would have company. If Gabriel ever broke the silence of the North, they would stand together, hand in hand, before the great White Throne. And God would judge them, God would judge them!

The second is the famous passage from "The White Silence" that puts man in his place in the cosmic scheme of things:

> The afternoon wore on, and with the awe, born of the White Silence, the voiceless travelers bent to their work. Nature has many tricks wherewith she convinces man of his finity,—the ceaseless flow of the tides, the fury of the storm, the shock of the earthquake, the long roll of heaven's artillery,—but the most tremendous, the most stupefying of all, is the passive phase of the White Silence. All movement ceases, the sky clears, the heavens are as brass; the slightest whisper seems sacrilege, and man becomes timid, affrighted at the sound of his own voice. Sole speck of life journeying across the ghostly wastes of a dead world, he trembles at his audacity, realizes that his is a maggot's life, nothing more. Strange thoughts arise unsummoned, and the mystery of all things strives for utterance. And the fear of death, of God, of the universe, comes over him,—the hope of the Resurrection and the Life, the yearning for immortality, the vain striving of the imprisoned essence,—it is then, if ever, man walks alone with God.

Golden Gate Before the Golden Gate Bridge was finished in 1937, Golden Gate referred to the natural opening between SAN FRANCISCO BAY and the Pacific Ocean. Before the bridge, only ferries connected Sausalito with San Francisco, and in and out of the bay came ships from all over the world. London often mentions the Golden Gate (called that because it led to the riches of the Orient) in his sailing stories; a memorable passage in *The Valley of the Moon* indicates its symbolic importance for him. A little boy in a small sailboat describes his feelings about it to the novel's heroine:

> "That," he said, sweeping the circle of the world with a wave of his arm . . . "Don't you sometimes feel you'd die if you didn't know what's beyond them hills an' what's beyond the other hills behind them hills? An' the Golden Gate! There's the Pacific Ocean beyond, and China, an' Japan, an' India, an' . . . an' all the coral islands. You can go anywhere out through the Golden Gate—to Australia, to Africa, to the seal islands, to the North Pole, to Cape Horn. Why, all them places are just waitin' for me to come an' see 'em. I've lived in Oakland all my life, but I'm not going to live in Oakland the rest of my life, not by a long shot. I'm goin' to get away." (*Valley of the Moon*, 263–264)

Goldman, Emma   Goldman (1869–1900) met London, in the company of ANNA STRUNSKY, in spring 1898 after he returned from the KLONDIKE. She visited the BEAUTY RANCH in the summer of 1910. At her request, in 1912, London wrote an introduction to the prison memoir by her friend the anarchist Alexander Berkman. Neither she nor Berkman were pleased at what he wrote, largely because he did not embrace the anarchist worldview and did not accept assassinations as a valid political strategy, and it was unpublished. It can be found at http://www.jacklondons.net/writings/Nonfiction/bookForwards/unpublishedBookforwards.html.

gold rush   In 1896 a small group of prospectors found a large gold deposit on BONANZA CREEK near the Klondike River and the town of DAWSON. When word reached the outside world, excitement spread rapidly. The United States had been suffering from recessions and bank failures in the 1890s, and unemployment was widespread. Most people who headed to the YUKON went not for

adventure but because of desperate finances. On July 15, 1897, a ship carrying a load of successful prospectors and their bags of gold landed in San Francisco, and then more landed two days later in Seattle, setting off the stampede in the fall and winter of 1897–98. As many as 40,000 people headed north, where they faced conditions they had never dreamed of, including near-starvation when resources were so limited and so many newcomers arrived. Most arrived by steamer from San Francisco or Seattle, and most disembarked at DYEA BEACH near SKAGWAY, ALASKA. From there they had to haul their one ton of supplies each (mandated by the Canadian Royal Mounted Police to get into Canada) over the forbidding CHILKOOT PASS, then stop to build boats and rafts to carry them on the chain of lakes and rivers they had to follow, then finally onto dogsleds for the long trek to Dawson. Thousands of men, women, DOGS, and HORSES perished in the attempt, especially when they used the WHITE PASS, also known as the Dead-Horse Pass, instead of the Chilkoot. Once in Dawson, they had to survive the long winter before they could prospect in the spring. Scurvy and other diseases ran rampant, and many were swindled by unscrupulous Dawsonites. The GOLD RUSH was not a romantic adventure but a desperate attempt by dispossessed people. Most came back with little but stories, the best claims staked by old-timers before they ever arrived. One of London's most detailed and dramatic narratives of the gold rush is his late short story "Like Argus of the Ancient Times," but of course it is a subject in nearly all his KLONDIKE fiction.

Greeks   Greeks and Greek culture occupy a central place in London's works. From very early on in his reading he was fascinated with Greek religion and MYTHOLOGY and was especially influenced by HOMER's *Odyssey*, especially in the KLONDIKE stories, one of which is "An Odyssey of the North." Like many educated people in his day, he believed that Northern European culture was created out of Greek and Roman traditions, such as SUN worship. He saw, like the racialists, the tradition of classical antiquity reborn as the mythology of the ARYANS. His NORTHLAND CODE of the TRAIL is influenced by

Greek ideas of BROTHERHOOD and hospitality. His best friend, the poet GEORGE STERLING, was given the nickname "Greek" by London, who signed his own letters to Sterling "Wolf." London traced his interest in WOLVES to stories of wolves and Apollo. Heroes like the Malemute Kid, Sitka Charley, and David Grief display Greek virtues of a sound body and sound mind, selflessness, and willingness to fight for freedom within their communities. As a socialist, London admired Athenian democracy. In the young fighters he describes, he often sees the Greek ideal of the male body. Greek myths are everywhere in his fiction. However, modern Greeks seem to be a different story. Billy Roberts complains about their presence in the coastal towns of CALIFORNIA, and London's young heroes of *Tales of the Fish Patrol* vie with Greek fishermen for control of the oyster beds. One story, "Demetrios Contos," tells of a boy's rescue from drowning by a Greek fisherman; this is based on a real incident in which London tried to drown himself but was miraculously pulled out by a passing Greek fisherman. London had a young Greek-American friend, Spiro Orfans, for a while but the two had a falling-out and London wrote him vociferous letters, one of which reminded him that Greeks today are "mongrels" from every nation, not the noble race of ancient times.

Guadalcanal   "Discovered" by the Spanish in 1568, Guadalcanal (local name Isatabu and sometimes spelled by London Guadalcanar) is a 2,510-square-mile jungle island in the SOLOMON ISLANDS. The deadly World War II Guadalcanal campaign took place on and around the island. Today contains the national capital of the Solomon Islands, Honiara. In London's day, it was an island of savage head-hunting, CANNIBALISM, and constant war among bush and "salt-water" tribes, and the site of Western colonization in the form of mining and copra plantations (copra being the dried kernel of the coconut, used for oil). The Londons stayed at a copra plantation there for five months at the end of 1908; they had the experiences of witnessing the management of native workers by whites; white BLACKBIRDING, or slaving ships; and rampant disease and dissolution among the whites. Their hosts were TOM HARDING and GEORGE DARBISHIRE, partners

in PENDUFFRYN PLANTATION. They visited much of the Solomons, but one wonders why they lingered there so long when London seemed to hate and fear the Solomons as much as he did. There, they contracted numerous tropical illnesses, the worst, yaws or Solomon Island sores, a flesh-eating bacteria. London treated his own and the crew's yaws with corrosive sublimate of mercury, which worked, but which in London's case did permanent damage to his kidneys. Stories set in Guadalcanal include *Adventure* and "The Red One."

Haeckel, Ernst   Ernst Haeckel (1843–1919) wrote to London on July 8, 1907, thanking him for his copy of *Before Adam*. But as early as March 1, 1900, London had written to his friend CLOUDSLEY JOHNS of Haeckel's widely circulated idea that *ontogeny recapitulates phylogeny*; that is, the development of an animal embryo traces the evolutionary history of its species. In *History of Creation* (1876) and *The Riddle of the Universe* (1900), Haeckel also claimed that nonwhites were incapable of inner culture and of higher mental development. He invented what he called MONISM to study the world, including animals, human beings, and society, as an evolutionary whole. London at first found Haeckel "unassailable" (*Letters*, 163–67) and called himself a Haeckelian "monist" (*Letters*, 589–590). Eventually, he rejected most of his ideas but hung on to the notion of monism, that everything could be explained by a single (materialist) view of the world.

Haleakala   "The House of the Sun," as Haleakala means, is a huge cloud-wrapped volcano on the island of Maui. London and his wife took a horseback camping trip in the crater of Haleakala in 1907 when the SNARK visited Maui. London devotes a chapter of *The Cruise of the* Snark to the awesome sights of the crater. Haleakala figures in the legends old Kohokumu recites in the story "The Water Baby." London also made numerous photographs of the volcano.

half-breed   In general, a derogatory term used to describe people of mixed race. In London's work, a paradox occurs with half-breeds. On one hand, in his scientific RACIALISM, London wrote disparagingly of half-breeds as "mongrels," as in the MEXICAN REVOLUTION correspondence. He spoke of the scientific breeding of pure strains on his ranch. However, once again London's contradictions surface. In so many of his stories, half-breeds or mongrels are the heroes, in *The Call of the Wild* and *White Fang,* in KLONDIKE characters like Sitka Charley or Li-Wan, in Martha Scandwell and her sister in "On the Makaloa Mat," or in the beautiful mixed-race children of Chun Ah Chun.

haole This is the Hawaiian word for a Caucasian, or white person. It is applied without too much prejudice, unlike honky or gabacho. Haoles who lived in HAWAI'I for a long time and acquired its ways are called haole kama'āina, which means longtime resident and is a very positive term. London was conscious of his status as a haole *malahini* (or newcomer), but he aspired to be kama'āina. Most of his friends in HONOLULU were haole kama'āina, wealthy descendants of the original missionary and trader colonizers of the islands. The status of being haole is explored in such stories as "Aloha Oe," "The House of Pride," "On the Makaloa Mat," and "Good-By, Jack."

Harding, Tom Harding and his partner GEORGE DARBISHIRE and their wives, plus a French plantation manager, Bernays, ran PENDUFFRYN PLANTATION on the island of GUADALCANAL in the SOLOMON ISLANDS, and hosted the Londons for five months in late 1908. Harding's wife was the Castilian countess Eugenie. In her *Log of the* Snark, Charmian describes Harding as "a handsome Englishman, of height and weight, with blue eyes and black lashes and hair, a cupid-bow mouth with even teeth and a small moustache. He is clad in white 'singlet' and white lava-lava with coloured border, and barefoot. On his head is an enormous Baden-Powell, and in his ears are gold rings which lend a Neapolitan touch, while from his neck depends a gold chain locket in which he carries a miniature of his wife" (*Log of the* Snark, 368–369). Harding and Darbishire were the models for several dissolute whites in the South Seas, in "The Inevitable White Man," "Mauki," and "Yah! Yah! Yah!"

Hawai'i The importance of Hawai'i to London's life and works cannot be overstated. From his first visit aboard the *SOPHIA SUTHERLAND* as a young sailor before the mast in 1893 to the miraculous landing of the *SNARK* there in 1907 to his extended stays in 1915–16, London loved Hawai'i, its people, climate, land, and culture. Upon his death, his admirers there sent an ilima lei to accompany his body to the grave, and in its newspaper columns and magazines appeared many heartfelt tributes and obituaries. London saw Hawai'i in several positive ways: It was a place of peaceful racial blending; it had ancient traditions and customs of great interest, it was beautiful, serene, and most of all healing, especially in his last visits there. In Hawai'i London set some of his best and most antiracist stories: "The House of Pride," "Koolau the Leper," and "The Water Baby." London learned to surf, read stories on the beach to his friends and the beach boys, sailed Hawai'i's beautiful blue waters, toured its magnificent volcanoes, met hundreds of its people, including field hands and Hawaiian royalty. He made many friends among HONOLULU's elite white barons, but angered them with his stories of lepers and oppressed field-workers. He visited the leper colony at Kalaupapa on MOLOKAI twice and wrote of his visits to try to abet the widely held prejudices against lepers. He visited KAUAI with a congressional delegation and the BIG ISLAND to stay on vast ranches and explore Hilo and Kona. His essay "My Hawaiian Aloha" speaks of his love of Hawai'i, as do the chapters set there in *The Cruise of the* Snark and his many Hawaiian stories. He was invited to join the Outrigger Canoe Club and the PAN-PACIFIC UNION. He also helped popularize SURFING on the American West Coast. He was captivated by Hawaiian legend and folklore and learned a great deal of it, as is demonstrated in stories like "The Water Baby" and "Shin Bones." Overall, he saw Hawai'i as a paradise of beauty and cultural history but one doomed by the incursions of the white West and the modern.

Haymarket Riots The Haymarket Riots occurred on May 4, 1886, in Chicago, when someone supporting the striking workers at Haymarket Square threw a bomb at the police who were breaking up the meeting. After the explosion and gunfire, eight police officers and an unknown number of civilians were dead. Four of the eight anarchists tried for murder were put to death and one committed suicide in prison. These pivotal events are mentioned in several of London's socialist short stories but especially referenced in the riot scene in *The Iron Heel*.

Haywood, Bill ("Big Bill" Haywood) William Dudley Haywood (1869–1928) was an important member of the American labor movement and a leader of the Western Federation of Miners and the Industrial Workers of the World (IWW), which he helped found. He was also a member of the executive committee of the Socialist Party of America and involved in several labor battles. Haywood's involvement in violence led to several prosecutions. His trial for the murder of Frank Steunenberg in 1907 (of which he was acquitted) drew national attention; in 1918, he was one of 101 IWW members convicted of violating the Espionage Act of 1917. While out of prison during an appeal of his conviction, Haywood fled to Russia, where he spent the remaining years of his life. Hayward is mentioned in socialist stories and is part of the inspiration for "Big Bill" Totts in "South of the Slot."

health and disease For someone identified with healthful vitality and masculine achievement, London suffered throughout his life from illnesses and died at the early age of 40. Though of only medium build, London had as a young man an extraordinary body that could overcome deadening physical toil, from the industrial hellholes of OAKLAND, to the frozen goldfields of the North, to the rigors of the life of the sailor, to ranching, boxing, swimming, SURFING, and so on. However, London abused his body with excess: ALCOHOL, cigarettes, undercooked duck, overwork, and tropical diseases. It was the latter that was to cause his early death: Afflicted with yaws, or Solomon Island sores, London treated himself with large doses of corrosive sublimate of mercury, which, eight years later, destroyed his kidneys. He was tormented in the last few years

of his life by the effects of kidney disease: He became nauseated often, suffered from diarrhea, tooth decay, headaches, weight gain, appendicitis, a strange peeling of the skin of his hands (caused by the mercury), and many other complaints. He drank too much and smoked too much and in his last years took little exercise. London makes health and disease a prominent part of his South Seas writing. At the time, there were prevailing Western stereotypes of the peoples of the South Seas. Generally, women were portrayed as exotic and alluring, shown in staged postcard shots as bare-breasted and usually preparing food. Island men were shown as either savage warriors or diseased. All of these stereotypes invited the West to "intervene" in such a God forsaken place. London's photographs from the South Seas go against this: he shows normal-looking people, often with names, going about their daily business. Nonetheless, he repeatedly laments the devastation brought upon South Seas islanders by diseases brought by whites, particularly in his chapter on the MARQUESAS in *The Cruise of the* Snark:

> When one considers the situation, one is almost driven to the conclusion that the white race flourishes on impurity and corruption. Natural selection, however, gives the explanation. We of the white race are the survivors and the descendants of the thousands of generations of survivors in the war with the micro-organisms. Whenever one of us was born with a constitution peculiarly receptive to these minute enemies, such a one promptly died. Only those of us survived who could withstand them. We who are alive are the immune, the fit—the ones best constituted to live in a world of hostile micro-organisms. The poor Marquesans had undergone no such selection. They were not immune. And they, who had made a custom of eating their enemies, were now eaten by enemies so microscopic as to be invisible, and against whom no war of dart and javelin was possible. On the other hand, had there been a few hundred thousand Marquesans to begin with, there might have been sufficient survivors to lay the foundation for a new race—a regenerated race,

if a plunge into a festering bath of organic poison can be called regeneration. (*Cruise of the Snark*, 170–171)

That London here racializes illness fits with this theme throughout the South Seas works; ironically in the end, he had to face up to the fact that as a white man his body was unfit for this environment, a failure he took hard—after all, what is the master race of ANGLO-SAXONS to do when it is so clearly handicapped? Perhaps this realization helped him envision his South Seas heroes as largely NATIVE.

Hearst Syndicate   London worked for the Hearst Syndicate run by William Randolph Hearst (1863–1951), most notably when he went to Korea to cover the RUSSO-JAPANESE WAR in 1904. London published hundreds of stories in Hearst-run newspapers like the *EXAMINER* (SAN FRANCISCO), and was even cited is some critiques of Hearst's "yellow journalism." The career of Jack London and the enormous reach of Hearst were together a modern media phenomenon. Hearst wanted to sell papers, and London sold papers. As far as is known these two powerhouses never met, but they would have had much to say to each other about modern mass media and communication.

Henderson Creek   Jack London staked a gold claim in DAWSON for the left fork at Henderson Creek in October 1897. While working this claim, London made his headquarters in a cabin owned by his friend, Charles Taylor, where he spent the long winter of 1897–98. An inscription, "Jack London, miner, author," was found in a cabin there and believed by some to be authentic (most London scholars believe it was merely a publicity stunt when the cabin was "discovered"). London sets several KLONDIKE stories in the vicinity of Henderson Creek.

homelessness and hobos   In the 1890s, city neighborhoods, country roads, boxcars, and docks were filled with homeless men and women, battered from the economic panics of 1893 and 1896. Thousands were hungry, homeless, and unemployed, due to crises involving national debt and the gold standard. This is the main reason many desperate people headed north for the ALASKA GOLD RUSH in 1898. London joined a group of hoboes, COXEY'S ARMY, who decided to join up with a march of jobless men on Washington, D.C., in 1894, experiences he writes of in such works as "The Hobo and the Fairy" and *The Road*. He stayed with the "Army" until Hannibal, Missouri, when he started out on his own to visit the Midwest and New York. He was arrested as a vagrant and placed in the ERIE COUNTY PENITENTIARY for a month, which led to his awakening as a miserable member of the social pit. He returned home to CALIFORNIA and, as he said, "opened the books" to make something more of himself than a hobo or WORK-BEAST in a factory. London had great affection and sympathy for hoboes, and several of the friends he met "on the road" visited him at the Ranch throughout his life, such as the famous hobo of the time, "A No. 1." Perhaps some of his sympathies lay in his own experience as a child, not of sheer homelessness, but of poverty and privation, as well as constant moves as his parents tried one venture after another or moved down in circumstances. London, it may be observed, though he valued home, never stayed in one for long before heading out onto the road once more.

Homer   The ancient GREEK epic poet of the eighth century B.C.E. was the reputed author of *The Iliad* and *The Odyssey*. His influence upon London was profound. London evidently read Homer early on, for his first KLONDIKE stories reflect Homer's stories of Agamemnon, Troy, Odysseus, Telemachus, and Penelope. He uses myths Homer relates of Olympian gods Hermes and Apollo and such older figures as the titan Prometheus. He was particularly attracted to the SUN-myths of Apollo and Zeus. In London's Klondike stories, men struggle with the environment and sometimes with each other, and their battles are enacted in what approaches epic form. Surely, *The Call of the Wild* borrows from the epic, wandering, ultimately successful hero. "An Odyssey of the North" retells the homecoming of Odysseus with great attention paid to the structure and tone of the epic poem.

Honolulu When London first arrived in Honolulu, the capital of HAWAI'I and the main city, located on the island of OAHU, he rapidly realized how widely his trip had been publicized in newspapers there—when the *SNARK*, after a monthlong voyage from San Francisco, was sighted coming into Honolulu Harbor and Pearl Harbor, boats came out loaded with cheering citizens brandishing newspapers with headlines of the Londons being lost at sea. He was royally entertained by the elite of Honolulu, including royalty itself. He was wined and dined and invited to exclusive enclaves such as the Outrigger Canoe Club. He was the darling of Honolulu socialites and the press. However, after a visit to some plantations with immigrant workers on the west or "Ewa" side of the island, he began to write his Hawaiian stories attacking the white Western colonizers and looking at Hawai'i through the eyes of her nonwhite immigrants. Afterward many in Honolulu shunned him, especially his former good friend, LORRIN THURSTON, publisher of the *Honolulu Daily Advertiser.* However, he continued to have many friends and came back in later years to visit them.

horses London as a boy hated the countryside and everything associated with it. But while a correspondent in KOREA in 1904 covering the RUSSO-JAPANESE WAR, London found it necessary to learn to ride horses both to try to get to the frontlines and to amuse himself when prevented from doing so. In Seoul, he bought his first horse, which he named Belle, from the former Russian ambassador to Korea, a tall Cossack. Though he complained about this horse and the small Korean ponies he also mastered, London had begun what would be a lifelong love affair with horses. When, soon after his return, he began buying his SONOMA VALLEY BEAUTY RANCH and married CHARMIAN KITTREDGE LONDON, an expert horsewoman, he practiced and became a fine horseman himself. He bred Shire stallions—the death of his favorite, Neuadd Hillside, in 1916 a terrible blow—as well as purebreds like his beloved Washoe Ban. Numerous works contain descriptions of horse-riding on the ranch, "Told in the Drooling Ward," "Planchette," *John Barleycorn, The Little Lady of the Big House.* In *The Valley of the Moon,* Billy Saxon is a horse-teamster, and in London's KLONDIKE writings are narratives of the terrible treatment horses received in the GOLD RUSH.

human documents A literary term at the turn of the last century used and reused by writers from Edmond de Goncourt and Alphonse Daudet in France, to Sarah Orne Jewett and Jack London in the United States. The common idea is that the human face in a portrait tells a story, a narrative of a life told in a visualized moment in time. London used the term to describe his photographs and PHOTOJOURNALISM. Unlike anthropological, scientific, colonial, touristic photographers of his time—who looked for images of nonwhite NATIVE peoples of the day—London photographed nonwhite Natives, not as types, but as individuals, without fake poses or backdrops, normal people going about normal business. He also made many portraits of Natives as people and not types. Jewett used the term to describe a series of photographic portraits of great men at different times of their lives in *McClure's Magazine* in 1893.

Huntington Library A private, nonprofit institution, the Huntington was founded in 1919 by Henry E. Huntington, a successful figure in railroad companies, utilities, and real estate holdings in Southern CALIFORNIA. Huntington had great interest in books, art, and gardens. He put together the beginnings of one of the finest research libraries in the world, a stunning art collection, and famous botanical gardens with plants from all across the globe. The library's collection of rare books and manuscripts in the fields of British and American history and literature is unmatched, with 6 million items. The largest single literary collection at the Huntington is the Jack London Collection, made up of manuscripts, letters, diaries, files, annotated books, notes, clippings, and much more, even including London's death mask.

Huxley, Thomas Henry An English biologist, Huxley (1825–95) was an early promoter of the evolutionary theory of CHARLES DARWIN. Huxley differed from Darwin's other great champion, HERBERT SPENCER, a sociologist who promoted Darwinism as "SOCIAL DARWINISM," in which he applied Darwin's findings to organizing society. Huxley was one of Darwin's first adherents; he was even called Darwin's bulldog. He rejected Spencer's social Darwinism, calling it "reasoned savagery." After London encountered Huxley, he turned a much more critical eye on Spencer. Like Darwin himself, London was never comfortable with the amoral aspects of EVOLUTION. Huxley was troubled by Spencer's "survival of the fittest" as the only possible conclusion as evolution applied to human society (that phrase was actually Spencer's; Darwin wrote "the struggle to survive"). London agreed: He upheld the individual, championed the underdog, and was an avowed socialist. London repeatedly shows in his fiction that merely surviving isn't everything and that what might make one fittest in one environment would not in another, and, most of all, that there is a crucial moral dimension to understanding evolution and its impact on humanity.

Huxley most memorably voiced his disagreement with Spencer in "Evolution and Ethics," the 1893 Romanes lecture at Oxford University. Huxley saw nature as unsuitable as a moral guide for humans. SOCIAL DARWINISM was a "fallacy," for social progress really means "a checking of the cosmic process at every step and the substitution for it of another, which may be called an ethical process; the end of which is not the survival of those who may happen to be the fittest, but of those who are ethically the best." He insists, "Let us understand, once for all, that the ethical progress of every society depends, not on imitating the cosmic process [of evolution], still less in running away from it, but in combating it." There would always be a contest between the "State of Nature" and the "State of Art of an organized polity," and this would continue until the State of Nature eventually prevailed (*Evolution and Ethics and Other Essays* [New York: Appleton, 1915], 33–35). Though humanity cannot be comforted with visions of an ultimately victorious battle, London agreed with Huxley that nevertheless it must proceed with ethics as the standard for civilization.

imagination   One of the most important elements of ADAPTATION and survival for characters in London's works is the imagination. Along with a sense of JUSTICE and a belief in COMMUNITY, the imagination appears throughout his works as the mark of a superior—and surviving—individual. As an artist with an enormous imagination, London creates believable characters across the globe and through the centuries, from prize fighters, the Romans who crucified Christ, a SOLOMON ISLAND cannibal, a young couple in OAKLAND caught up in labor violence the slum-dwellers of 20th-century LONDON, ENGLAND. He had an uncanny ability to try to imagine a culture or character from the inside out; no other American writer of his day gave direct voice to such a diverse group of narrators and storytellers. This is particularly important because most of these characters are nonwhite and represented points of view unfamiliar to most readers. And surely no one could transport readers to the frozen NORTHLAND or exotic South Seas better than London. In certain characters, the importance of using their imaginations is key to their survival: in Buck in *The Call of the Wild*, Saxon Brown Roberts in *The Valley of the Moon*, Johnny in "The Apostate," the title character in "Mauki," and Felipe Rivera in "The Mexican." Another interesting example is the unnamed protagonist of "Love of Life," who, even though he is nearly certain that his partner Bill has abandoned him with a broken ankle in the vast reaches of tundra they were crossing, still keeps hoping that Bill is waiting for him up the trail; this imaginative hope helps him keep going, even though he soon stumbles upon Bill's bones. In contrast, the man in "To Build a Fire" dies because, as the narrator emphasizes, he was "without imagination."

Indians   *See* NATIVES.

individualism   Individualism is a very broad concept but one with particular relevance to London's beliefs. As a political philosophy, individualism emphasizes independence and self-reliance. Every individual is unique and should be able to pursue whatever goals and desires he or she wants, without interference from society. Individualism is opposed to collectivism, especially SOCIALISM, which upholds the communal good over individual goals. London entertained both of these philosophies, opposed though they are. He was heavily influenced by the socialism of KARL MARX but also the superman hero of FRIEDRICH NIETZSCHE. Though he never gave up the idea of both personal heroism and individualism as a driving force in his life and work, he described himself as a socialist and said that he had rejected Nietzsche. But the conflict between individualism and socialism confuses some of his best works, such as *The Sea-Wolf* and *Martin Eden.* In the former novel, Wolf Larsen, a brutal sea captain and proponent of Nietzsche, is supposed to be the villain, but he is much more interesting than the (anti-individualist) young couple who oppose him. London's readers admired Martin Eden as the very type of the individualist bildungsroman hero; his suicide disappointed them. London claimed Martin died because he did not embrace socialism, but that alternative is not really presented to him in the book. London's contradictions reflect the lively debate about such philosophies during his time.

Intercollegiate Socialist Society   On September 12, 1905, a small group of socialists (including Jack London, UPTON SINCLAIR, and Clarence Darrow) met at Peck's Restaurant on Fulton Street in New York City. Out of this meeting came the Intercollegiate Socialist Society, founded for the purpose of promoting an interest in SOCIALISM among college men and women. London was chosen president, Sinclair, vice president. Members included William Dean Howells, Lincoln Steffens, Thorstein Veblen, and Edwin Markham. The Rand School of Social Science became the New York headquarters of the society. Harvard College was selected as the primary center for promoting socialism on college campuses. By 1915, the Society had chapters on 60 campuses. London went on a multistate lecture tour for the society beginning in October 1905, spanning several months; he lectured dozens of times throughout the Midwest and Northeast. He was a hit even among the privileged audiences of students at Yale and Harvard, but he was excoriated by the conservative press for bringing socialism to the nation's campuses.

international reputation   London is probably the most popular American writer in the world; his works have been translated into more than 100 languages. There are numerous complete editions from foreign presses, and he is the subject of exhibits, symposia, and political debates in dozens of countries today. With the Internet, it is easier to track his readership at home and in other countries. His positioning against the rising Hitler in 1930s socialist and communist newspapers in France was the subject of one recent exhibit, while a new bibliography of his extensive translations into Mongolian has also recently been made available (it goes back to 1907 and contains dozens of translations). There are dozens of Jack London Societies around the world, most notably in FRANCE and JAPAN, and there are excellent Web sites on London in many languages. In general, he is read abroad less as the author of DOG books and more as a socialist thinker and activist. But it is undoubtedly his combination of accessibility and universal themes—not to mention adventure—that continue to draw readers. International scholars are engaging more and more their American counterparts in debating London's ideas in an international forum. More than any other American writer of his day—London portrayed believable characters from many cultures.

Irishmen   Irishmen are usually portrayed in London's works as stereotypes, such as the crooked fight promoters of "The Mexican." The only exception to this is in the strange story "Samuel," set on a remote Scots-Irish island. In it, London paints a moving portrait of a Scots-Irish woman and uses heavy dialect, which he patiently learned from a Scots-Irish sea captain. Though his own mother was of WELSH ancestry, London sometimes regarded CELTS in general as less than ANGLO-SAXONS, and they do not play a large role in his work.

Irving, Washington   Irving (1783–1859) was an American author who wrote numerous books and stories, including *Tales of the Alhambra,* a collection of romantic essays and short fiction pieces published in 1832, set in the abandoned palace the Alhambra in Granada, Spain. As a boy, London was captivated by Irving's *Alhambra,* as he details in *John Barleycorn*. Perhaps his later tendencies toward ROMANTICISM and interest in faraway places were kindled in part by this magical book.

Jack London State Historic Park   Jack London State Historic Park is located south of State Highway 12 off Arnold Drive, two miles from the center of the small town of GLEN ELLEN, CALIFORNIA, in SONOMA VALLEY. Featured exhibits on 830 acres of London's original BEAUTY RANCH property include the cottage where he lived and wrote, the ruins of his dream home, WOLF HOUSE, his grave, the Pig Palace, two unique silos, stone barns, ruins of a former winery, the House of Happy Walls Museum, and nine miles of hiking and riding trails. Docents conduct guided tours of certain park highlights every weekend. The cottage has been beautifully restored and reopened to the public. So many of London's works evoke the beauty of the ranch, and visitors will not be disappointed. In fact, many say they never really knew London until they visited his ranch.

Japan and the Japanese   Japan and the Japanese occupy an important place in London's canon, though his attitude toward them seems conflicted. On one hand, he wrote touching early stories about the lives of everyday Japanese based on his visit to YOKOHAMA in 1893 on the *SOPHIA SUTHERLAND*, and his very last work was about a Japanese-American young woman, *Cherry*. But largely because of the mixed portrait of the Japanese in his RUSSO-JAPANESE WAR correspondence and even more so because of a pair of essays, "The Yellow Peril" and "If Japan Awakens China," most people thought he was anti-Japanese. However, the story is much more complicated than that. In the war correspondence he complains bitterly about the Japanese army's censorship of his work and what he saw as their cruelty to their own men and yet he writes admiringly of their courage and discipline. In his fiction, he presents fully realized, sympathetic Japanese characters, especially in the Hawaiian stories. In his personal life, he was much loved by his Japanese servants, especially YOSHIMATSU NAKATA, who joined the Londons on the *SNARK* and *DIRIGO* voyages and wrote a moving memoir about London.

London is extremely popular in Japan, and several Japanese scholars have published books on him. The Jack London Society of Japan is large and very active, second only to the one in the United States. London believed Japan would become America's main rival unless a friendship was achieved; in 1915 he gave his speech "The Language of the Tribe" to the PAN-PACIFIC UNION in HONOLULU on the topic of Japanese-U.S. friendship, advocating that schoolchildren in both countries be taught each other's language.

Jeffries, James J. ("Jim" Jeffries)   Jeffries (1875–1953) was a world heavyweight BOXING champion. He was a heavy, strong fighter with tremendous stamina. Winning the heavyweight title, he defended it seven times before retiring in 1904. However, in 1910 he unwillingly came out of retirement—to fight the African-American boxer JACK JOHNSON. The nation went mad with race rhetoric and hysteria: Jeffries was dubbed the "Great White Hope." No one thought Johnson could beat him, but Johnson did so easily in Reno on July 4, 1910. The unthinkable had happened: A black man had beaten the Great White Hope himself. For his pains, Johnson was forever after persecuted by the U.S. government in various ways, while Jeffries was invited to the White House by THEODORE ROOSEVELT as the "white" world heavyweight champion. London had met Jeffries earlier but was rebuffed by him in Reno. London described him as grim and taciturn, Johnson as wary, alive, and in complete control of his body and emotions. London praised Johnson in his newspaper reportage after Jeffries's defeat. He had wanted Jeffries to win, but he recognized Johnson's superior talent.

Johns, Cloudesley   Johns (1874–1948) was a beginning writer and socialist born in San Francisco. He served as a newspaperman in Los Angeles, then joined the *San Francisco Post* as reporter, city editor, and music, drama, and literary critic. He wrote London a note of encouragement on his short fiction in February 1899, and the two became close pen pals and friends. As budding writers, they shared ideas, techniques, and philosophies in numerous letters over many years. London often gave Johns advice on writing, and Johns was a good critic of London's work. They exchanged both manuscripts and personal news, as well as differing views on world events and social justice.

Johnson, Jack Arthur John Johnson (1878–1946), also known as "Papa Jack," was born in Galveston, Texas, and after a youth of wandering, began to box and eventually became the world heavyweight BOXING champion. He was the first African American to win the title, and his subsequent victory as a black man over the "Great White Hope," boxer JIM JEFFRIES, set off a firestorm of racist reaction around the country. He was hounded by the FBI, denounced on the floor of Congress, and eventually arrested on a specious charge of taking a woman across the Illinois state line for the purpose of prostitution (she was his white wife). Johnson beat the Canadian TOMMY BURNS in Australia in 1908, first winning the title, then Jeffries in Reno, Nevada, in 1910. Riots broke out all over the country after the latter fight, leaving dozens dead and many more wounded when the police and white crowds tried to subdue the African Americans celebrating in the streets. London covered both matches, and, though he confessed he had wanted the white man to win, he is unsparing in his praise of Johnson's ability and superior brain. Johnson was arguably the best heavyweight of his generation. He kept his title until 1915, when, after having fled the United States for Canada, Europe, and Mexico, he agreed to a shortened prison term if he would fight Jess Willard in Cuba for the title. Many think he threw the fight to close the deal. Once out of prison, his life deteriorated into the spectacle of him, broke, allowing boys at state fairs to punch him in the stomach for a nickel. He loved women, liquor, and fast cars, but his luck was running out. He was killed in an automobile accident in Raleigh, North Carolina. London admired Johnson not only for his magnificent physique and finely honed fighting skills, but also for his witty repartee in the ring and as an underdog—both things London identified with. London was the most famous and widely syndicated reporter at the Johnson fights, and his

Publicity photograph of Jack Johnson *(Huntington Library)*

headlines about Johnson's unflappable "golden smile" appeared around the world. The protagonist—and, oddly, antagonist—in "The Mexican" is inspired by Johnson.

Johnson, Martin Martin Elmer Johnson (1884–1937) was a teenaged employee in his father's Independence, Kansas, jewelry store when he read of Jack London's planned around-the-world cruise. He wrote to London offering his service on the crew of the SNARK. He described himself as, like London, a "rolling stone" in search of adventure. London received hundreds of such offers, but for some reason he liked Martin's tone and wrote back asking him if he could cook. Martin replied that he could, and he was accepted. Martin worked hard before he left for the London ranch learning to cook from a short-order diner cook. Martin signed on the *Snark* and served on it until the voyage ended in 1909. He wrote his own account of the voyage, *Through the South Seas with Jack London* (1913), and after the voyage he traveled the Midwest with his glass lantern slide show of his *Snark* adventures; like London he was an excellent photographer. Martin married Osa Johnson (née Leighty, 1894–1953), and the two forged a celebrity team of world adventurers and explorers, traveling to such faraway places as the NEW HEBRIDES, the SOLOMON ISLANDS, Africa, and Borneo. They were among the first wildlife cinematographers and made dozens of films. Their adventures on their twin airplanes—one painted with leopard spots and one with tiger stripes—were chronicled in the press worldwide. Martin died when a plane he was on crashed near Newhall, California; he was on his way to visit the widowed CHARMIAN KITTREDGE LONDON at the BEAUTY RANCH. After his death, Osa published her memoir of their lives together, *I Married Adventure* (1940).

Jordan, David Starr Early on, London met and read David Starr Jordan (1851–1931), the first president of Stanford University, who helped introduce SOCIAL DARWINISM and EUGENICS to the United States, and who would become London's friend and mentor. They met in OAKLAND during Jordan's lecture series on EVOLUTION, published as *The Days of a Man: Memories of a Naturalist, Teacher and Minor Prophet of Democracy* (1922). In Jordan's earlier *Foot-notes to Evolution* (1898), London encountered the ideas of Francis Galton, a cousin of DARWIN's who was inspired by SPENCER to outline basic eugenic principles. Galton and Jordan's ideas figure strongly in *The Kempton-Wace Letters* in Wace's comparison of human mating to stock breeding (*Kempton-Wace Letters*, 32). In *The Call of the Nation* (1910), Jordan urged eugenics as a matter of national security. Jordan argued against U.S. imperialism abroad, as he felt war would draw the best to go fight, hence leaving the unfit at home to procreate. In *Imperial Democracy* (1899), "inferior" races are seen as incapable of self-government, while the white race is possessed of the polit-

ical genius necessary for an effective society. In his admiration for boxers and other athletes, London followed Jordan's interest in the physical culture movement, as outlined in Jordan's *The Strength of Being Clean: A Study of the Quest for Unearned Happiness* (1900). From Jordan, London learned of August Weisman's *Essays Upon Heredity and Kindred Biological Problems* (1891), which inspired *Before Adam*'s racial memories (or "germ plasm"). During the Spanish-American War, Jordan argued that "the Anglo-Saxon or any other civilized race degenerates in the tropics," a notion that London would comfort himself with when he had to abandon the *Snark* voyage due to illness. Jordan also introduced London to the works of JOHN FISKE, ERNST HAECKEL, and others.

journalism Like so many other writers, and like the other naturalists, London got his start in writing largely in journalism, contributing sports coverage, human interest essays, and war correspondence to a wide range of magazines and newspapers. He covered the RUSSO-JAPANESE WAR for the HEARST SYNDICATE, the JACK JOHNSON world heavyweight fight in 1908 for the *NEW YORK HERALD* syndicate, the SAN FRANCISCO EARTHQUAKE and MEXICAN REVOLUTION for *COLLIER'S*. His stories and photographs appeared in newspapers the world over. He was one of the first and best-known photojournalists of his day. London was a constant subject himself in the mass media, as his tens of thousands of press clippings at the HUNTINGTON LIBRARY attest. In addition, he was an avid reader of the mass media, and he often chose story ideas from the columns of newspapers. He was one of the most widely recognized celebrities of his times.

Jung, Carl G. Carl Gustav Jung (1875–1961) was a Swiss psychiatrist, and the founder of Jungian psychology. His practice is called analytical psychology, which seeks to integrate the driving forces that are at the core of human behavior. With FREUD, he was considered the first modern psychologist to emphasize understanding the psyche through exploring the worlds of dreams, art, MYTHOLOGY, religion, and philosophy. Although he was a practicing clinician, he also explored Eastern and Western philosophy, alchemy, astrology, sociology, as well as literature and the arts. His greatest contribution includes the concept of psychological archetypes, the collective unconscious, synchronicity, and individuation.

Archetypes are near-universal symbols that reflect both the psyche and the imagination. They can be perceived in myths, symbols, rituals, and basic human instincts. Jung took Freud's theory of the unconscious one step further by differentiating between the personal and collective unconscious. The personal unconscious is personal and confined to an individual, while the collective unconscious is part of the unconscious mind of all of humanity arising from ancestral experiences. Jung's concept of synchronicity conjoins the experience of two or more events that did not occur by chance. Jung also theorized that in order for a person to become whole he or she has to undergo the process of individuation, which happens when one transforms one's psyche by taking the personal and collective unconscious and bringing them into the consciousness. Jung describes this process as healing because it is a journey to find the self and the divine.

Jung emphasized the importance of balance and harmony, warning that modern people depend too heavily on science and logic and would benefit from integrating spirituality and appreciation of unconscious realms. For him the psyche consisted of separate parts, the *shadow* (like Freud's id, the "dark side"), the *persona* (like Freud's ego), and the *anima* (the soul, portrayed as feminine in the male psyche); integration is necessary for a person to become whole. Jung had been a protégé of Freud's but eventually broke with him, seeking a more spiritual dimension to psychology than Freud allowed.

London first encountered Jung when he read *Psychology of the Unconscious* (1912) in translation in the summer of 1916, though he seems to have been employing archetypes and other Jungian patterns before he read him (making Jung's point that archetypes are instinctual). London was deeply struck by Jung's notion of a collective unconscious and thus the interrelatedness of all humankind, and he wrote several stories specifically influenced by Jung's ideas, notably, "The Bones of Kahekili," "When Alice Told Her Soul," and "The Water

Baby." There has been a great deal of scholarship in London studies on his mythic dimensions as influenced by Jung. In Jung, London seems to have found answers for long-troubling questions, especially about the universal relatedness of people rather than their divisions by race or class. Jung also helped him tap the ancient legends of HAWAI'I for their mythic power, which informs many of his late Hawaiian tales.

justice With the IMAGINATION and COMMUNITY, justice is the third major value in London's works. London's heroes have a strong sense of justice, and numerous stories show justice being tried and tested. London uses GREEK and Roman myths about the judgment of the gods on the deeds of men and women. Partners resolve or fail to resolve disputes, provisions are divided, men are hung for their crimes, tribal members are banished, wives are paid for, gambling debts sorted out. Sometimes "rough" justice is served, as in "Mauki," "In a Far Country," "The Feathers of the Sun," or "The Unexpected." Villains are unmasked, the innocent protected, the heroic rewarded. Many stories have as their plot varying degrees of justice, including also the miner's court in *A Daughter of the Snows*, the French colonial tribunal in "The Chinago," the unexpected resolution of "The Master of Mystery" and "A Hyperborean Brew." *The People of the Abyss* is an outcry for social justice, as is *The Iron Heel* and London's other socialist stories, speeches, and essays. "The Law of Life" explains NATURE's harsh justice in leaving the old and ailing behind. David Grief roams the South Seas setting things right. Sometimes, the story is of injustice: "The Mexican," "The Chinago," "The White Man's Way," "The House of Pride." And sometimes notions of justice are forged in action and go against the usual standards of justice: "The Wit of Porportuk," "The League of the Old Men," "Mauki."

Kaluaikoolau (Koolau) Koolau (d. 1896) is the hero of one of KAUAI's great legends. A native of Waimea, Koolau was a cowboy and an expert rifleman, well liked and respected. In 1892, after learning that he and his young son had contracted LEPROSY, Koolau fled with his son and his wife

Pi'ilani deep into Kalalau Valley, located on the remote Na Pali coast, one of several deep and all but inaccessible valleys that fan out like accordion folds of lush blue and green. Koolau was initially promised the company of his wife and son in Molokai, but, at the docks, when denied, he fled and resisted. The valley had become a refuge for Hawaiians afflicted with leprosy. Like Koolau, they preferred hiding out here than enduring forced separation from their loved ones. In June 1893, Koolau shot and killed a sheriff LOUIS STOLZ and two provisional government soldiers who had been sent to arrest him. Before they came, the authorities had become so frustrated that they had the U.S. Navy shell the valley. Koolau vowed never to be taken alive; he thus became a powerful symbol of resistance for many Hawaiians in the years following the overthrow of Queen Liliuokalani. Koolau died and was buried in Kalalau Valley by Pi'ilani, their son having already died. London first heard the Koolau story from BERT STOLZ, son of the murdered sheriff. One would think London would have formed a negative view of Koolau from this, but he instead wrote a story passionate with anticolonial feeling and great admiration for the heroic leper holdouts. Pi'ilani, when she emerged from the bush several months after Koolau's death, dictated her story to a missionary, Glen Sheldon. This version was translated and published in English by Francis Frazier as *The True Story of Kaluaikoolau: As Told by His Wife, Piilani* (2001). London's story strips away the religious framework of Pi'ilani's version, indeed, eliminates Pi'ilani altogether, and focuses upon Koolau as a revolutionary hero who had received injustice and fought back. Some of London's most lyrical descriptions of the Hawaiian landscape and flora appear in this story, along with his unflinching descriptions of the lepers, and, perhaps most important, his unsparing critique of the whites who brought in leprosy and also took over all the islands. In his speeches to his followers, Koolau is an eloquent critic of HAWAI'I's losses.

kama'āina In HAWAI'I, this means one who belongs to the land, either a native or an immigrant who understands and loves Hawai'i and its ways. London aspired to be kamaaina, as he writes in several letters and essays. The opposite is malihini, which means newcomer. The land, or *'āina,* is an extremely important element in Hawaiian religion and tradition. Another expression that conveys one's right to belong in Hawai'i is being "on the mat," as in "On the Makaloa Mat." HAOLES, or whites, could be kamaaina with the right attitude and long years of residence, like Lakana in "The Water Baby" or Roscoe Scandwell of "On the Makaloa Mat."

kanaka *Kanaka* in Hawaiian means a man. It is used without prejudice by Hawaiians and whites. London uses the term in a number of Hawaiian stories and in *Adventure,* where it is used more broadly to mean any POLYNESIAN man.

Kauai Kauai, the oldest and greenest of the Hawaiian Islands, is the fourth largest. It was also the most independent, having never been conquered, only joining the Hawaiian kingdom in 1810. London visited Kauai as a guest of a congressional party on a junket to study Kauai's water resources. He gave an interesting interview to a Rev. John Lydgate there published in the *Garden Isle,* the island newspaper, in which he connects his being partly raised and much loved by VIRGINIA PRENTISS to his feeling for nonwhite heroes. He set one of his most famous stories, "Koolau the Leper," on Kauai's Na Pali coast, in Kalalau Valley.

Kipling, Rudyard Kipling (1865–1936) was a British author and poet who was born in Bombay, India, and lived there until the age of six; he returned at the age of 17. He is best known for his work *The Jungle Book* (1894), a set of classic children's tales set in India. Kipling received the Nobel Prize in literature in 1907. He was also known for his war poems and stories. London was early on greatly influenced by the fiction of Kipling; he carefully studied Kipling's subjects, point of view, structure, and dialogue in crafting his own first stories. He also absorbed Kipling's hero, the white male conqueror, though he interrogated this figure as well—as did Kipling. From Kipling, he also learned how to universalize his tales through broad adventure, wide-ranging locales, and, of course, animal heroes.

Klondike The Klondike, especially as used in London's works, refers to a particular region of the YUKON TERRITORY near DAWSON, northwest of the rest of Canada and east of the Alaskan border, where a few streams off the Klondike River yielded great amounts of gold to a few early prospectors beginning in August 1896. When this was made public, the ALASKA GOLD RUSH of 1897–98 was on. The original name of the region was Tr'ondëk, but early gold seekers could not pronounce the name and changed it to Klondike. London was one of the many people participating in the gold rush, and many of his works were inspired by the experiences he had, such as *Burning Daylight* and dozens of short stories. In 1897, London journeyed the hard miles to reach the Klondike and spent that winter there; though he found little gold, the Klondike afforded him his first real artistic resource. He went on to write so many stories about the Klondike (and even in his last months) that he is probably one of the most important popularizers of the term, even today. London had a cabin on HENDERSON CREEK near the Klondike River, but he evidently spent more time swapping stories in the taverns of Dawson than actually mining. On a 1,500-mile raft trip up the YUKON RIVER that spring to reach ST. MICHAEL on the Bering Sea and begin the journey home, though he was sick with scurvy, he began a YUKON DIARY, which led to his first submissions of short stories about his adventures and observations.

Korea Mostly based on his RUSSO-JAPANESE WAR correspondence (since he did not really feature Koreans in his fiction), London's attitude toward Korea and toward Koreans was largely pity, mixed with critique of their docility with the what he saw as the superior JAPANESE. But this attitude in some dispatches is belied by much in others: his sensitive photographs about the hardships of Korean refugees on the roads and beggars young and old in SEOUL, his writings about the disruptions of once-peaceful Korean villages, his careful study of some Korean phrases to make a petition to a *yang-ban*, or

tribal leader. London's photographs of Koreans during this war speak much more to his sense of them as suffering human beings and not pawns in a game of war. He took hundreds of photographs of young girls begging, families struggling down muddy and frozen roads, once-proud village leaders subjected to servitude. Interestingly, London is quite popular in Korea and is the subject of numerous editions, scholarly books, and conferences there.

labor unions, strikes Labor unions are the organizations of workers who join together to achieve goals such as increased wages, creation of new jobs, and the safety of the workplace. Labor strife and union organization were prominent features of London's times. He treats strikes and uprisings memorably in many works, most notably in *The Iron Heel,* "South of the Slot," and "The Dream of Debs."

leprosy Leprosy, today called Hansen's disease, is technically known as a chronic granulomatous disease of the peripheral nerves and mucosa of the upper respiratory tract with skin lesions as the primary external symptom; it is caused by the bacteria *Mycobacterium leprae* and *Mycobacterium lepromatosis.* Untreated, it can progress to cause permanent damage to the skin, nerves, limbs, and eyes, causing facial sores and rotting extremities. Leprosy has been recorded for 4,000 years, but only in the 20th century was a cure found. London and his wife visited the LEPER COLONY on the island of MOLOKAI at Kalaupapa, established by FATHER DAMIEN, a Belgian priest, a few decades earlier and now run by the Hawaii Board of Health, whose director, Lucius Pinkham, was a friend of London's. Pinkham asked him to go there and write a positive story about the settlement to help dispel the irrational fear of lepers. London did so, in "The Lepers of Molokai," reprinted in *The Cruise of the* Snark. London's sympathetic, warm, and even humorous account of how his suppositions were overturned by his visit there went a long way to help humanize these people. He and Charmian attended a rodeo on the Fourth of July and were impressed with the lepers' sense of COMMUNITY and their enjoyment of their lives. London's humane photographs of the lepers also reveal his liking for them and his admiration for their heroic and joyful spirit. The Londons visited again in 1915.

Lewis, Sinclair Lewis (1885–1951) was an American author and the first American to receive the Nobel Prize in literature in 1930. Besides writing novels, he also wrote short stories and plays that analyzed American society and critiqued CAPITALISM. Lewis's earliest published creative work—romantic poetry and short sketches—appeared in Yale literary magazines. After graduation he drifted, seeking a writing career. While working for newspapers and publishing houses (and for a time at the CARMEL-BY-THE-SEA writers' colony), he learned to turn out popular stories that were eagerly purchased by a variety of magazines. Lewis sold some plots to Jack London, including the plot for the unfinished novel *The Assassination Bureau, Ltd.*, later finished by another writer. Save this one, London did not use Lewis's plots, though he was influenced by a few of his ideas.

London, Becky (Becky "Bess" London Fleming) London's second child, Becky London (1902–92), was born on October 20, 1902, while London was in Europe following his stint in LONDON, ENGLAND, to write *The People of the Abyss*. She was still an infant when his marriage broke up in 1903. In contrast to her older sister, JOAN LONDON, who criticized her father, Becky remained loyal to him, though her relationship with him was not as involved as Joan's, who carried on a lifelong letter correspondence with him and who later became his biographer and carried on his socialist work. Becky graduated with a degree in history and a teaching certificate from the UNIVERSITY OF CALIFORNIA. She took up secretarial work to support herself. She became pregnant out of wedlock and when the baby, Jean, was born in 1924 the family covered up her pregnancy and announced that she was raising an adoptee. She married Percy Fleming in 1927, and they had a son, Guy. Especially after Joan's death in 1971, Becky's public profile grew; when Percy died, London aficionado Russ Kingman and his wife Winnie invited Becky to live with them in GLEN ELLEN. The Kingmans' Jack London Bookstore was visited by numerous London scholars and fans, who were fortunate to get to meet Becky. She was an active member of the Jack London Foundation until her death.

London, Bess (Elizabeth "Bessie" Maddern London) Elizabeth Maddern, later Bess or Bessie Maddern London (1876–1948), was London's first wife. She grew up in OAKLAND, where her father was a plumber. In the mid-1890s, she met London when he sought a mathematics tutor to help him prepare for the entrance exams to the UNIVERSITY OF CALIFORNIA. She became engaged to a friend of Jack's, Fred Jacobs, but Jacobs was killed on his way to fight in the Spanish-American War. Jack had had love affairs with MABEL APPLEGARTH and ANNA STRUNSKY. Proposing to Anna one afternoon, he was angered at her coyness. He suddenly proposed to Bess and married her within the week. He told her the marriage was not based on love but science, the position his Herbert Wace espouses in *The Kempton-Wace Letters*. Bess presumably agreed, although she was in love with him. She did her best to help him entertain his friends from the "Crowd," a collection of Bay Area bohemians. Bess's life centered on her home and their daughter Joan and helping Jack by typing and editing his manuscripts. She did not like his friends and did not understand his artistic side. Soon London, his marriage crumbling, believed he was still in love with Anna, who came to the house to work on their collaborative book. With Bess pregnant a second time, London left for England where he wrote *The People of the Abyss*. When she learned of Bessie's second pregnancy, Anna broke off their relationship. In 1903, London fell in love with Charmian and left Bess and their two daughters. The divorce granted in 1905 was contested, though London agreed to pay heavy alimony and child support. Bess, furious and jealous, would not allow the girls to visit Jack at the ranch if Charmian were there. He in turn complained about her attitude and both argued over money. His will left a bequest to his daughters but not to Bessie. In 1938, a stroke left her bedridden, paralyzed, a condition in which she would remain for 10 years until her death.

London, Charmian Kittredge Charmian Kittredge London (1871–1955) was London's second wife. His marriage to his first wife disintegrating, London fell in love with Charmian, the niece of NINETTA WILEY EAMES and the daughter of the California poet DAYELLE WILEY (with her husband Captain Willard Kittredge), in 1904. They had met in March of 1900 when Ninetta Eames interviewed him for OVERLAND MONTHLY. Less than a month later, he married Bess. However, it became clear, despite their two daughters, that Jack and Bess were an ill-fitted match. London had dreamed of a "man-comrade," an androgynous woman with whom he could share equally his life and especially adventures, but Bessie was interested in her home and children and was not the mate-woman vivacious Charmian would be. Where Bessie was reserved and conventional, Charmian was outgoing, sexually uninhibited, and used to supporting herself. She was a lifelong believer in exercise and an outstanding horsewoman. After their marriage, Charmian pluckily joined in all of his adventuring, especially when she was first mate of the SNARK. Throughout their marriage, Charmian tried to get her husband to live a healthier life; for instance, on the DIRIGO voyage, when he wasn't looking she threw his alcohol and cigarettes overboard. In addition to her athleticism, Charmian was a very feminine woman and dressed beautifully; she was a talented pianist and loved the arts.

Charmian was a friend of Bessie's, and Bessie confided in her that she thought Jack was having an affair with Anna, but it was by then Charmian. Their love affair was passionate and grew very fast. Jack told Bessie he was leaving her. At this point, London left for KOREA, but when he returned a divorce petition was waiting for him naming Anna as correspondent. Jack and Charmian took great pains to conceal their relationship, but they married the day after the divorce became final, on November 19, 1905, while London was on tour for the INTERCOLLEGIATE SOCIALIST SOCIETY. Their was an exceptionally happy marriage, though not without its difficult moments, especially their failure to have children. Charmian was often troubled by Jack's unhealthy habits, especially drinking and smoking.

Charmian would go on to become his love companion and an integral part of his career. She kept his files, handled his correspondence and submissions, typed his stories, and, most important, she saved everything. London had the habit of throwing his notes and manuscripts away, but Charmian not only saved them all, but she also carefully placed his photographs in photo albums, preserving them as well. Thus the huge Jack London Collection at the HUNTINGTON LIBRARY is there in large part because of her careful stewardship of London's career. This stewardship was maintained by ELIZA LONDON SHEPARD and her family. Charmian was also an author, writing three books about Jack London including her biography of him.

One of London's many love letters to Charmian gives us a sense of their relationship:

> My thoughts are upon you always, lingering over you always, caressing you in a myriad ways. . . . Ah Love, it looms large. It fills my whole horizon. Wherever I look I feel you, see you, touch you, and know my need for you. . . . I love you, you only &wholly. . . . [E]ach moment I am robbed of you, each night & all nights I am turned away from you, turned out by you, give me pangs the exquisiteness of which must be measured by the knowledge that they are moments and nights lost, lost, lost forever. (*Letters*, 391).

London's letters to Charmian are a remarkable record of the most important relationship of his life. He had numerous loving pet names for her. London responded to Charmian's maturity as a lover and a partner, and she would prove to be the great love he felt had always eluded him. After his death, Charmian and Eliza struggled, especially during the Great Depression, to hang onto London's copyrights and save the ranch from foreclosure. To both of them and to Eliza's descendants, her son IRVING SHEPARD and her grandson Milo Shepard, readers of Jack London owe a tremendous debt.

London, England In 1902, on his way to cover the Boer War in South Africa as a war correspondent, when London reached London, England, he found out that the war had ended. Instead of returning home, he briefly toured the Continent then lived disguised as a homeless American sailor so that he could observe the conditions of the poor in London's grimy East End. Out of this experience came *The People of the Abyss*. London's chapters and his photographs outline in stark detail the horrors of the East End. London was profoundly shocked that the greatest empire on the planet could do no better for its citizens; after all, these were London's real-life examples of ANGLO-SAXONS. He advocated SOCIALISM as a means to address their plight and also suggested they emigrate to the American West where they might have a chance at health and happiness. London also visited Kent, where he picked hops.

London, Flora Wellman (mother) Flora Wellman (1843–1922) was born in Massillon, Ohio, to well-to-do parents Marshall and Eleanor Garret Jones Wellman. Her father made his fortune in canal-building, contracting, and wheat. Flora's mother died when she was four, and she was replaced by a stepmother, Julia Hurtzthal. There were already five children, and Julia had four more with Marshall. They lived in an elegant mansion of 17 rooms on the best street in town. Flora's childhood was thus one of comfort. She wore fine clothes and had tutors as well piano and speech lessons. At age 12, she contracted typhoid, which stunted her growth and damaged her vision. She never grew over five feet tall. Then, three years later, the financial crisis of 1858 sank her father's fortune. This reversal may explain why she suddenly left Ohio and headed west. For a decade her whereabouts are not clearly established. She did volunteer as a nursemaid in the Civil War. In the early 1870s, she appears in records of a boardinghouse in Seattle. There she met WILLIAM CHANEY, an itinerant astrologer who called himself "Professor" Chaney and who had had several wives already. His progressive beliefs appealed to Flora. In 1874, they moved to San Francisco, where Chaney lectured on astrology and Flora taught music and was a publisher's assistant. Having been interested for a long time in spiritualism, the belief that through a medium the spirits of the dead could speak to the living, she held séances for money. The couple supported the liberal social causes of the day, including rights for women, blacks, and the working class. They were known around the Bay Area as believers in free love and a bohemian lifestyle. But it all came to a halt when Flora became pregnant. When she told Chaney, according to her he told her to get an abortion, which she refused. He left her, and she shot herself in the head (the wound was a mere grazing), all covered in lurid detail by the newspapers: On June 4, 1875, newspapers headlined, A DISCARDED WIFE. Flora moved in with friends and gave birth to son John Griffith Chaney on January 12, 1876. Chaney never admitted paternity, claiming he was sterile and could not have been the father. Flora was very weak after the birth and could not nurse her son, and so he was given over to nurse to VIRGINIA PRENTISS, an ex-slave and African-American neighbor who lost a son to stillbirth the night London was born; this was the custom in those days.

On February 19, 1877, Flora married carpenter JOHN LONDON, a widower with two young daughters. He was disabled from his time in the Union army in the Civil War and this meant that he was not physically able to work as he would like. The family struggled for years as they tried various schemes to support themselves: farms, a store, boardinghouse, these ideas nearly all Flora's. They moved numerous times. In addition, Flora took in sewing, held her séances, and taught piano. Her son spent a good deal of time at the home of Mrs. Prentiss, whom he regarded as a second mother. Flora was not an emotionally demonstrative person and was caught up in her feverish attempts to gain income. London felt throughout his life that she did not love him, and he sharply criticized her for her coldness. However, she was the person who urged him to send his story "Typhoon Off the Coast of Japan" to the *San Francisco Call*, resulting in a cash prize and his first publication. Yet London could not forgive her lack of maternal love; he told CHARMIAN KITTREDGE LONDON he never received a caress from her, while he was warmly loved by Mrs. Prentiss. Like Jack, Jennie disapproved of Flora's séances and constant fly-by-night financial schemes. London left both homes for the waterfront and the road; but as a man he supported both

Flora and Jennie and their families. When London was divorced by Bess, Flora sided with her and even lived with her and her granddaughters, who also described her as cold and remote. At the age of 21, discovering Chaney's identity, London's feelings for her took another blow when he found out she had lied to him all these years about his parentage. Suffering with arthritis, Flora spent her final years in the company of Jennie Prentiss, who eventually lived with her. She died on January 4, 1922, having outlived her son. Her independence and drive characterized her as well as him, her willingness to try out new things and to struggle against all odds. She is almost certainly a model for Frona Welse in *A Daughter of the Snows,* both for her fiery independence and also, unfortunately, her racism, which she taught her son. But it was her reticence when it came to showing him affection that left the deepest impression on him.

London, Joan Miller (daughter)   Joan London (1901–71) was the eldest daughter of Jack and BESS LONDON, his first wife. She was the author of *Jack London and His Times* (1939), a biography of her father. Her other works include a memoir *Jack London and his Daughters* (1990, with her son, Bart Abbott), which explores the effects of divorce on children, using her family as an example, and *So Shall Ye Reap: The Story of César Chávez & the California Farm Workers Movement* (1970, with Henry Anderson). Like London, she was a socialist and focused on that dimension of his career. When Joan was born, London so adored her that he kept a photo album of her called "Joan's Book," with photos and funny captions of the curly-haired little girl. After London left Bess, Joan, who was only two-and-a-half, and her baby sister BECKY LONDON, lived with their mother. They looked forward to their father's visits. Unfortunately, his access to them was restricted by their mother, who never got over her fury at him; she would not let the girls visit him if Charmian were present, further alienating Joan from him, for as the older child, she took her mother's side and developed mixed feelings for her father. London loved being involved in the girls' school lives, and Joan in particular he encouraged as a writer. He always challenged both of them to

do their best, but especially Joan. How sad, then, that as he became more and more sick and embittered, in 1914 he broke off ties with Joan in a very cruel letter comparing her to a ruined colt—ruined, that is, by her mother. He forced her to choose, and she chose Bess. However, by the time of his death, the daughters and their father had reconciled; his last letter is to Joan making plans for a picnic at Lake Merritt in OAKLAND.

Joan shared many of her father's gifts; she was extremely intelligent, a disciplined writer, and a ceaseless campaigner for SOCIALISM. In high school she edited the literary magazine. Just after her father died, she enrolled at the UNIVERSITY OF CALIFORNIA, majoring in history. After graduation as a Phi Beta Kappa, she married Park Abbott, and had a son, Bart. They divorced after three years and shared custody of the boy. Joan began speaking for various organizations on such topics as feminism, socialism, and her father. She made friends with Charmian, who served as a valued mentor. Joan would have two more husbands. After her 1934 divorce from her second husband, Charles Malamuth, a Russian scholar, Joan moved to Hollywood, where she ran a secretarial service and represented the work of other writers. Returning to San Francisco, she worked for the maritime union and corresponded with Leon Trotsky and

Joan London (right), her son Bart Abbott (left), and Clark Gable discuss the 1935 film adaptation of *The Call of the Wild. (Huntington Library)*

other socialists who had known her father, including Cesar Chavez. She also published her socialist biography of her father. She became an editor and librarian for the California Labor Federation and was active in Citizens for Farm Labor; she and her third husband, Charles Miller, were investigated by the FBI for her activism. Joan died in January, 1971, of throat cancer. Though she championed her father's socialism and wrote one of the first biographies of him, she had a very fraught relationship with him; for one thing, as a writer, she felt she was working in her father's shadow. As a girl she was always trying to please him, but she harbored deep resentments. Like him, she was an ALCOHOLIC. But unlike her sister Becky, who simply adored her father and did not compete with him, Joan carried on his public work as a socialist and reformer.

London, John   John London (1828–97) was a native of rural Pennsylvania, where he worked on the family farm and later for the railroad. He married Anna Jane Cavett and farmed in the Midwest. He and Anna Jane had a large family, with 11 babies born. With the outbreak of the Civil War, he enlisted with the 126th Illinois Volunteers and fought in several battles. Measles and pneumonia contracted during the war left him disabled, with only one lung. He was honorably discharged, and the family settled in Iowa. John was a hunter as well as a farmer, working with the local Pawnees. In 1873, Anna Jane died of tuberculosis, leaving him with three small children still at home, a son, Charles, and two daughters, Ida and Eliza.

Hoping to find an easier life than farming and hunting on the prairie, he moved to CALIFORNIA, where his son died. He placed the girls in an orphanage while he tried to get work in San Francisco. He worked with an African-American man, Alonzo Prentiss, who introduced him to FLORA WELLMAN. They married on February 19, 1877, blending their families, Flora's boy Johnny and John's Eliza and Ida. Due to his physical limitations, John had trouble keeping work, and so Flora threw herself into plans for getting ahead. They tried the grocery business, poultry raising, farming, boardinghouses, and, due to the failure of most of these ventures and the hard economic times, they moved often. Though for the most part they lived a fairly stable life of the working class, they were also often close to poverty. (John was eventually able to collect a disability pension from his service in the army, and he also worked as a night watchman in the OAKLAND port). Like VIRGINIA PRENTISS, Eliza furnished Jack with motherly love and attention, Flora too distracted by making ends meet to offer her son much affection. John too was very fond of the boy and gave him love and attention.

Johnny, as he was called in the London home (Mrs. Prentiss claimed she gave him the name "Jack"), believed until the age of 21 that John London was his natural father. He loved John, and John taught him SAILING, fishing, and hunting birds. Johnny accompanied John to the waterfront SALOONS, where he learned of the exciting life at sea and its adventures. In 1897, just before he left for the GOLD RUSH, London learned the truth about his origins. He was furious with Flora for not telling him the truth, but he continued to love John. John died that fall while London was in the KLONDIKE, meaning that upon his return from the NORTHLAND, London was the family's breadwinner. No one will ever really know who Jack London's father was; some believe that WILLIAM CHANEY, who believed himself sterile, left Flora because he was certain her baby was not his. The baby may even have been John's.

London, Joy   Joy London, Jack and Charmian's only child, was born on June 20, 1910, but died after only 40 hours. The birth was difficult and the placenta had to be surgically removed. It is possible that the birth was botched by the doctors, but whatever the cause, her death devastated her parents. Charmian fell into a long depression, and Jack, about to go away to cover the JACK JOHNSON-JIM JEFFRIES world heavyweight championship, got into a brawl in a tavern in OAKLAND. He did not want to leave Charmian, but she urged him to go. The couple also experienced miscarriages and never had another child.

Long Sickness   This term London uses to describe his bout with depression in 1904–05, as his marriage was collapsing, and his ALCOHOLISM as described in *John Barleycorn,* in which he also refers to the WHITE LOGIC of alcoholism. The term appears throughout his work to describe depression.

Lord Howe Atoll In the short story "Mauki," London sets the main action of the story, Mauki's being tormented by Max Bunster and his revenge, on Lord Howe Atoll:

> If one leaves Meringe Lagoon, on Ysabel, and steers a course due north, magnetic, at the end of one hundred and fifty miles he will lift the pounded coral beaches of Lord Howe above the sea. Lord Howe is a ring of land some one hundred and fifty miles in circumference, several hundred yards wide at its widest, and towering in places to a height of ten feet above sea-level. Inside this ring of sand is a mighty lagoon studded with coral patches. Lord Howe belongs to the Solomons neither geographically nor ethnologically. It is an atoll, while the Solomons are high islands; and its people and language are Polynesian, while the inhabitants of the Solomons are Melanesian. . . . Nobody ever comes to Lord Howe, or Ontong-Java as it is sometimes called. Thomas Cook & Son do not sell tickets to it, and tourists do not dream of its existence. Not even a white missionary has landed on its shore (*Stories,* 1,538–1,539).

Also called Ontong Java Atoll and Luangiua, it is one of the largest atolls on earth. The Londons visited it on the *SNARK* cruise in late 1908 and heard the true story of the trader's incorrigible cook, MAUKI. The choice of setting for "Mauki" on Lord Howe is also because of its remoteness and barrenness. The Moongleam Soap Company that owns Mauki's contract thinks he will never be able to escape from there as it is so remote.

MacLean, Captain Alex Alex MacLean (1858–1914) was the inspiration for the character Wolf Larsen in *The Sea-Wolf.* He was a skillful sea captain and a colorful adventurer whose escapades in the 1880s in the Pacific sealing trade laid the foundation for his status as a folk hero. As captain of the sealing schooner *Carmencita,* MacLean was accused of poaching and piracy. In a 1905 letter, London answers a query on MacLean from the editor of the *EXAMINER* (San Francisco). London responds that though he never met MacLean he did base Wolf Larsen on him (*Letters,* 492). In an article called "London's Sealing Sea Wolf an Outcast on the Deep" (*Chicago Record-Herald,* January 29, 1906), London commented that "McLean [sic] had a big record as a rough character and was known as the worst man, so far as physical violence was concerned, among the seal hunters" (*Letters,* 492).

Macmillan Company London's long and productive relationship with the company that published most of his books began when its publisher, GEORGE P. BRETT, wrote to London in January 1902 asking for work he might care to submit. Save for a brief interlude when London left Macmillan for CENTURY, Macmillan was his publisher and Brett his editor. Macmillan advanced London great sums of money to finance his pet projects, such as WOLF HOUSE and the SNARK. Macmillan was founded in 1843 by Daniel and Alexander Macmillan, two brothers from Scotland. The British house published such authors as Charles Kingsley, Thomas Hughes, Christina Rossetti, Matthew Arnold, LEWIS CARROLL, ALFRED, LORD TENNYSON, Thomas Hardy, and RUDYARD KIPLING. George Edward Brett opened the first Macmillan office in the United States in 1869, and Macmillan sold its U.S. operations to the Brett family, George Platt Brett, Sr., and George Platt Brett, Jr., in 1896, resulting in the creation of an American company, Macmillan Publishing.

Malaita Malaita, the most populous and one of the largest of the SOLOMON ISLANDS, is tropical, densely forested, and mountainous. On its southwest end is the Indispensible Strait, dividing it from GUADALCANAL. In London's day, it was feared by white men as the most dangerous of the Solomons; the labor "recruiting" they engaged in on the islands did not go smoothly on Malaita, where, between intertribal wars and conflicts with whites, there was much bloodshed and brutality. The Londons traveled aboard a BLACKBIRDER or slaver while visiting the Solomons and were nearly overrun with Malaitans when their ship was for a while marooned on a reef. But they also visited the women's market on Malaita where London made a number of photographs. In the story "Mauki," the title character is from Port Adams on Malaita:

—[a place] so savage that no traders nor planters have yet gained a foothold on it; while, from the time of the earliest bêche-de-mer fishers and sandalwood traders down to the latest labor recruiters equipped with automatic rifles and gasolene engines, scores of white adventurers have been passed out by tomahawks and soft-nosed Snider bullets. So Malaita remains to-day, in the twentieth century, the stamping ground of the labor recruiters, who farm its coasts for laborers who engage and contract themselves to toil on the plantations of the neighboring and more civilized islands for a wage of thirty dollars a year. The natives of those neighboring and more civilized islands have themselves become too civilized to work on plantations. (*Stories*, 1,532)

mammon   mammon is a term used in the BIBLE to mean material wealth, especially as wealth is venerated instead of GOD by those guilty of avarice. Mammon is sometimes personified as an evil deity. In Matthew 6:19–21, 24 (and elsewhere in Matthew and Luke), Jesus warns his followers,

"Lay not up for yourselves treasures upon earth, where moth and rust doth corrupt, and where thieves break through and steal: But lay up for yourselves treasures in heaven, where neither moth nor rust doth corrupt, and where thieves do not break through nor steal: For where your treasure is, there will your heart be also. . . . No one can serve two masters, for either he will hate the one and love the other; or else he will be devoted to one and despise the other. You can not serve both God and mammon."

In the Middle Ages, mammon was personified as a demon or the very devil himself. Though there was no ancient god with the name, he is personified as a wicked god or fallen angel in Edmund Spens-

er's *The Faerie Queene*, Milton's *Paradise Lost*, and by St. Thomas Aquinas. London would have been acquainted with him from the Bible and also *Paradise Lost*; he uses the term frequently to describe the greed of gold-hunters, and he indirectly alludes to the figure of Mammon in Milton's hell at the end of his story "To Build a Fire."

Manifest Destiny   Manifest Destiny is the 19th-century idea in the United States that it was not only destined but also divinely ordained to take over the North American continent, from the Atlantic seaboard to the Pacific Ocean, followed by Canada, Mexico, Cuba, and Central America. Manifest Destiny justified the genocide against NATIVES.

Mariposa   In December 1907, while in Papeete, TAHITI, London found that his business affairs back in CALIFORNIA needed his immediate attention. He and Charmian decided to take a break from the SNARK voyage and took the ship *Mariposa* back to the states in early January. They visited old friends, London sorted out his finances, and they shopped. They returned to Tahiti on the *Mariposa* in February. In Spanish *mariposa* means "butterfly," and perhaps this is a reason he used the name for the ship Martin Eden boards for the MARQUESAS, and from which he jumps to his death in the sea—he had flown too close to the "light" of celebrityhood.

Marquesas Islands   These Polynesian islands with their high mountains and lush valleys lie in the eastern South Pacific. The main settlement is TAIOHAE on the island of NUKU HIVA. Populated with POLYNESIANS coming from the west in their canoes around 100 B.C.E., they were "discovered" by Europeans in 1595 when Spanish explorer Álvaro de Mendaña de Neira landed, naming them after his patron, Marquis of Cañete, viceroy of Peru. Of the island groups of the Pacific, the Marquesas suffered the greatest population loss from diseases brought by Westerners in the 16th century; there was once a population numbering over 100,000, but only 20,000 by the middle of the 19th century, when HERMAN MELVILLE described them as beautiful and strong people in his book *Typee*—though he did admit that they were cannibals. By the time Jack London, having read of the Marquesas in *Typee* and been inspired by that book to undertake the SNARK voyage, arrived 50 years later there were only 2,000 or so left. As he relates in *The Cruise of the* Snark, everywhere they were dying of tuberculosis, smallpox, and common viruses to which they had no immunity. He was deeply struck by this tragedy, noting that only those Marquesans who had some mixed blood in them had a chance of surviving the white man's microbes.

Marx, Karl Marx (1818–83) was a German philosopher, political economist, and historian whose ideas as in such books as *The Communist Manifesto* and *Das Kapital* forever changed the way the world would study labor and capital. Father of both SOCIALISM and communism, Marx believed that history was a long series of class struggles, and that the present economic system of capitalism (and the bourgeois class) would one day be overthrown by its workers (the proletariat) and a socialist state introduced in which the means of production would be owned by the workers. As a young man London read him eagerly and was deeply influenced by his thought. Like Marx, he thought that revolution would have to be violent, that capital would never give up its grip on labor willingly. Both Marx and London thought in terms of an international working class that would refuse to fight the nationalistic wars of the upper and bourgeois class and would band together to usher in a new world. London remained devoted to Marx's ideas until his death.

materialism The philosophy of materialism asserts that only matter exists, that all phenomena including consciousness have material causes. Materialism dismisses idealism and spirituality as fictions. London declared himself early on a "materialistic monist," one who believed everything was related by deterministic forces within matter and that there was no god or afterlife. However, he consistently betrays this stance in his romantic and even spiritual descriptions of people and places in his fiction, and his frequent references to the soul, to GOD, and to heaven. Socialism both addressed

his interest in the materiality of life and gave him a higher purpose.

Mauki After getting lost en route in an attempt in fall 1908 to visit LORD HOWE ATOLL, the SNARK crew eventually found it and stayed at the home of a local white trader. London heard tales of the crimes of their host's Malaitan cook, Mauki, which intrigued him, and so he met and talked with Mauki on September 28. Mauki was serving several sentences for committing various crimes, including murder, theft, and escape. The trader made a regular practice of beating him and other servants and showed off the graves of his three former wives, whom he also beat, just as he continued to beat his present three wives for not making copra fast enough. Charmian remarks on the disparity between this young cook's crimes—"murders, escapes in handcuffs, thefts of whaleboats—a history of bloodcurdling crimes and reprisals too long to go into," with his "mild" face and even "deceptive weak prettiness" (*Log of the* Snark, 445). London created in his fictional Mauki a strong and determined young chief who gets his revenge upon the whites who enslaved him and returns home to rule over his people.

McClure, Phillips and Co. S. S. McClure paid London monthly advances while he wrote *A Daughter of the Snows*, which he later sold to J. B. Lippincott Co. for publication in 1902. McClure, Phillips published *The God of His Fathers* in 1901; throughout his career London published chapters and stories in *McClure's Magazine*.

Melanesians Melanesia is a subregion of what is today referred to as the continent of Oceania from the western Pacific Ocean eastward to FIJI, comprising most of the islands just north and northeast of Australia. Melanesians are the inhabitants of the region, which includes the islands of New Guinea, Vanuatu, New Caledonia, the SOLOMON ISLANDS, and other smaller islands. The name Melanesia comes from Greek and means "islands of the black-skinned people," a term was first used by Jules Dumont d'Urville in 1832 for this grouping of islands distinct from Polynesia and

Micronesia. Today the term is rejected by some Melanesians because they see it as racist. In London's *The Cruise of the* Snark, he sharply distinguishes between Polynesians and Melanesians; the darker skin color of the latter and their wilder ways, including continuing to practice CANNIBALISM and head-hunting, made them fearful. London thought of the Polynesians, who were lighter in color, as superior to the "blacks" of Melanesia. In addition, he blamed the Solomon Islands for his final illnesses aboard the SNARK, especially yaws or Solomon Island sores.

Melville, Herman   Melville (1819–91) was an American novelist, short story writer, poet, essayist, and author of *Moby-Dick,* sometimes said to be the greatest American novel. Ironically, it was not recognized as such in Melville's lifetime; it was rediscovered in the 1920s. He became famous with his first novel, *Typee,* based on his own experiences living among the cannibals of NUKU HIVA in the MARQUESAS, but afterward he struggled for literary recognition. In retaliation for the poor reception of *Moby-Dick,* he wrote *Pierre,* a bloody, sensationalistic potboiler he threw in the critics' faces as what he supposed they wanted. Like his friend Nathaniel Hawthorne, Melville is considered a "dark" romantic—as they agreed, they would write out of the "blackness" of life and "Say NO in thunder" to the Victorian pieties of their day. They sought to expose both national and personal psychological conflicts in their characters and cast doubt on the accepted religious beliefs of their time. Melville was London's most significant literary forebear in the South Seas. London was clearly influenced by Melville's novels *Typee, Omoo,* and *Moby-Dick.* Reading *Typee* as a boy inspired London the man to undertake his SNARK voyage; however, when he arrived at the actual TYPEE VALLEY on the island of Nuku Hiva in the Marquesas, he was bitterly disappointed. Where Melville described a few thousand well-built, handsome people living in their lush valley, London only encountered abandoned *pae-paes* (or stone platforms on which huts were built) and the coughs and moans of the few remaining Typeeans, nearly all dying of white man's diseases.

Mexican Revolution   The Mexican Revolution began in 1910 with an uprising led by Francisco I. Madero against the dictator Porfirio Díaz. Díaz brought modern industrial progress to his country but at the cost of human rights and democracy. The revolution developed into a multisided civil war. Madero took office in 1910 but was forced to resign in 1913 by Victoriano Huerta and his supporters. Madero was assassinated in 1913. Huerta was seen by many as having taken illegal possession of presidential power. Venustiano Carranza, supported by other leaders such as PANCHO VILLA and Emiliano Zapata, refused to accept Huerta as president. Huerta fled in 1914, and Carranza became president but was also driven out by Villa and Zapata in 1915. Carranza returned to power by election in 1917 but assassinated in 1920.

In early 1913, Huerta conspired with U.S. ambassador Henry Lane Wilson to remove Madero from power. When Huerta became president, most nations around the world acknowledged him as the rightful leader. However, U.S. president Woodrow Wilson refused to recognize Huerta's government. The United States was eager to install someone who would support American oil interests. Carranza led the opposition against Huerta, calling his forces the Constitutionalists, with the secret support of the United States. In April 1914, U.S. opposition to Huerta had reached its peak when American forces seized and occupied the port of VERACRUZ, cutting off arms from Germany. In July, Huerta fled to Spain. London covered the U.S. invasion of Veracruz and various battles between Constitutionalists and Huerta's forces in his Mexican Revolution war correspondence of 1914, published in COLLIER'S. London had earlier supported the peasants in their revolutionary struggle for freedom, a topic which is at the center of his story "The Mexican," and he made speeches calling upon his brother revolutionists to prevail. However, by 1914, he became very critical of the revolutionary leaders and the entire revolution itself. This disappointed his socialist readers back home, who saw him as siding with the American oil companies.

Milton, John   Milton (1608–74) was one of the greatest poets in the English language and author of the epic *Paradise Lost* (1667), one of London's favorite works of literature; he alludes to it often in his writing and carried it with him as one of only three books he took into the KLONDIKE, the other two being *Origin of Species* and a guidebook to the YUKON. He read amazed miners excerpts of the poem around the fire at night. London modeled some of his prose on Milton's poetic style and diction and reread the poem throughout his life.

Minota The *Minota* was a BLACKBIRDER, or slaver ship, captained by a Captain Jansen and operating in and around the SOLOMON ISLANDS. In fall 1908, the Londons, who were visiting the Solomons, went on an excursion on the ship and were nearly overrun and killed by islanders on MALAITA when the ship grounded on a reef. The local missionary and another ship captain saved the day, but headlines appeared that the Londons had been eaten by cannibals. The crew were a rough lot, and perhaps because of this Charmian "rescued" a terrier pup from the captain's chambers and brought her aboard the SNARK. Named "Peggy," she became a favorite pet at the BEAUTY RANCH.

missionaries Nearly from the time of the major "discoveries" of South Sea islands in the 18th century, Europeans and Americans sent missionaries all across the Pacific to Christianize the "benighted heathens" who lived on the islands. Catholic and Protestant missions spread, eventually even on the most "savage" islands. Protestantism especially found a ready hold, and it reigns today as the most common religious preference. To prepare for the SNARK voyage, London read dozens of missionary accounts and made notes for story ideas. He learned a great deal from these, for while they object to the savagery of the natives, they also, especially when written by a well-educated missionary, record the traditions, customs, and languages of South Sea islanders. Many of these books and his annotations may be examined at the HUNTINGTON LIBRARY. There are humorous and dark stories about missionaries, such as "The Whale Tooth." However the topic of missionaries in HAWAI'I had a different resonance to it; there he observed that the missionaries' descendants

had gobbled up for themselves much of the land and riches of Hawai'i; they were not interested in souls, but in workers who would make them rich. Still today, HONOLULU business and society are dominated by the rich white descendants of those early missionary families. Percival Ford is a negative figure of this class, pious but without a soul. In FATHER DAMIEN London found the very opposite, the model of the missionary who cares for his flock; Father Damien settled the Kalaupapa leper colony in MOLOKAI.

Molokai leper colony On the peninsula of Kalaupapa on the island of Molokai was located a settlement of lepers forced to leave their homes when they contracted the disease. At first it was a nightmare of outlawry and desperation; people were just thrown off ships because it was impossible to land. There they would stay until they died, escape prevented by the dangerous seas and a sheer wall of mountain at their back. When FATHER DAMIEN, a Belgian priest, arrived in 1873, he set about creating a peaceful settlement and dealt with the lawbreakers. He built a church and a happy settlement. At its peak, about 1,200 men, women, and children were in exile on Molokai. The isolation law remained in effect until 1969, when it was finally repealed. Today, about 20 former sufferers of LEPROSY—now known as Hansen's disease—continue to live there, and it is now part of Kalaupapa National Historical Park. In London's day, there was still irrational fear of lepers, but he and Charmian visited the colony for its Fourth of July parades, music, and rodeo in 1908. As he relates in *The Cruise of the* Snark, he found not monsters and despair, but light-hearted, communally sound, and productive people. Asked by his friend, Lucius Pinkham, head of the board of health in HAWAI'I, to write sympathetically and honestly of their state to dispel prejudice about leprosy around the world, he did in "The Lepers of Molokai." They visited again in 1915. London made many photographs of the lepers, but they are unlike the medical mug shots the lepers were used to posing for. London shows them going about their daily activities like anyone else; he pictures the leper band and the gifted trick rodeo riders and women stunt riders.

His words and images went a long way to dispelling notions about leprosy.

monism   Monism is the philosophical view that sees unity within a field where it is not expected, such as the theological idea that there is only one GOD, but that that one God has different manifestations in different religions. London interpreted monism to mean that there was a single explanation for all of life on earth, which he saw in CHARLES DARWIN, HERBERT SPENCER, and ERNST HAECKEL. London was fond of overarching definitions, but he eventually gave up the idea of monism.

Morrell, Ed.   Ed. Morrell was the name used by a man born Edward Brennan in Pennsylvania. Using the name Ed Martin, he migrated to CALIFORNIA, where he worked odd jobs and robbed trains on the Southern Pacific Railroad as a sort of modern-day Robin Hood. He was convicted of grand larceny and was sentenced to two years in SAN QUENTIN PRISON. Upon his release in 1893, he went to Fresno and assumed the name of Ed. Morrell. He and another man robbed trains but were caught. Morrell spent more than 15 years in San Quentin prison and more than five years in solitary confinement, mostly restrained in a modified straitjacket. He and his wife later wrote a book about his ordeal called *The 25th Man.* London met him when he visited the ranch in November 1911 and again in March of 1914; he found Morrell's story fascinating and used it in *The Star Rover.* London supported legislative efforts to make the straitjacket and other cruel punishments in prisons illegal. London also pressed to work against another feature of the prison system, the rule that if an inmate assaults another or a guard he may receive the death penalty.

Mountain Meadows Massacre   London sets chapters of *The Star Rover* in the Mountain Meadows Massacre, told from the point of view of a boy, Jesse Fancher. MARK TWAIN also uses the incident in *Roughing It.* The massacre happened on September 11, 1857, when a wagon train of Fancher-Baker emigrants from Arkansas passed through Mountain Meadows, Utah, a territory controlled by the local Mormon militia. About 120 people including women and children were killed. Only 17 children under the age of 8 were taken alive and distributed in the Mormon community. The Mormons paid some Paiute NATIVES to assist them in the slaughter and dressed up as Natives themselves to carry out the attack.

mutiny on the *Bounty*   The mutiny on the *Bounty* was led by Fletcher Christian against William Bligh on April 28, 1789. The ship was on a breadfruit expedition when the mutiny occurred 1,300 miles off the TAHITI coast. The mutineers placed Bligh and his officers in a small boat with provisions; miraculously, they survived. The mutineers took Tahitian wives and eventually fled to the remote island of PITCAIRN, where they remained. The character McCoy who pilots a burning ship through dangerous waters in "The Seed of McCoy" is supposed to be a descendant of the *Bounty* mutineers and their Tahitian wives.

mythology   Perhaps no other American writer demonstrated a greater mythopoeic imagination than Jack London. Throughout his career he drew upon diverse mythologies, especially GREEK, Roman, Norse, Native American, Hawaiian, and POLYNESIAN. Late in life, he read the works of CARL JUNG and found his ideas on the collective unconscious and archetypes a rich source for his last Hawaiian stories. Whether in allusions to the Roman sun god SOL, legends of the Hawaiian demigod Maui, Northwest NATIVE trickster tales, or Homeric plot structures, London drew on a huge array of myths gleaned from his reading. One of his most consistent mythic elements is of the archetypal feminine, Jung's anima, or Great Mother. One sees this especially in stories like "The Night-Born," "Samuel," and "The Water Baby." London's male heroes follow mythic models, such as Naass in "An Odyssey of the North," Tarwater in "Like Argus of the Ancient Times," or, of course, Buck in *The Call of the Wild.* In that novel, the myth of the hero is most clearly presented: It is Buck's realization of the "other world" of the primitive past that leads him to find his true self. The critic Earle Labor has been the primary scholar to address London's use of myth. It is significant that one of the writers most famous for his NATURALISM was also driven by a mythic sense of the past in the present as well as the interconnectedness of all people in all cultures through shared myths; his mythic imagination is also his romantic imagination.

Nakata, Yoshimatsu Nakata (1889–1967) was a young JAPANESE man in HONOLULU who was hired to serve as London's valet when the SNARK reached Honolulu in 1907. Nakata also accompanied the Londons on the voyage of the DIRIGO, where he began typing for London. He was much loved by the Londons, and his memoir of his time with them shows that he cared deeply for them too. He was to stay with the Londons until 1916 when he returned to Honolulu and became a dentist. The *Jack London Journal* 7 (2000) issue features a history of Nakata. In the late 1930s, the psychologist Barry Stevens interviewed him and prepared the book-length account as "A Hero to His Own Valet." She also had a brief meeting with Sekine, who was London's valet in the final months of his life, and included these notes in the manuscript.

Napa Valley Napa Valley is located about 70 miles north of the San Francisco Bay area. The first Europeans to explore the valley were Francis Castro and Father Jose Altimura in 1823, who found six NATIVE tribes in the valley. The Londons were fond of riding over the steep passes from SONOMA VALLEY into Napa. Today, Napa is an upscale region with fine restaurants and inns and some of the most famous wineries in the world.

Natives London's KLONDIKE stories reference numerous Native tribes in the Pacific Northwest and the YUKON: Chilkoots, Chilkats, Tlingits, Tagish, Tanana, Sticks, and others. His stories dramatize the changes wrought upon the Natives by the traders and gold prospectors who increasingly filled the region, especially those of *Children of the Frost*: diseases and alcohol, loss of hunting and fishing grounds, loss of women to white husbands, collapse of traditional tribal ways. Indeed nearly all of London's Klondike stories feature Natives, and several, such as "The Master of Mystery," are clearly based on Native folktales. Upon leaving the

Klondike in 1898, London floated up the YUKON RIVER on a raft to ST. MICHAEL on the Bering Sea; along the way he noted in his YUKON DIARY the pitiful condition of the Natives he encountered, and these observations were his first Klondike writings. London uses King James English to convey the primitive nobility of his Native speakers. But he saw the Natives as ultimately doomed by the superior force of the whites; in such stories as "Li Wan the Fair" and "The League of the Old Men," London presents their situation as tragic. He paid careful attention to their customs, names, and history in his stories.

nativism Nativism was a turn-of-the-century movement that favored established inhabitants over immigrants. The term was usually not used by nativists themselves, but by their opposition. Nativists usually called themselves merely patriots. Nativism played a big part in anti-immigration legislation such as the Chinese Exclusion Act of 1882 and the Gentleman's Agreement of 1908 restricting JAPANESE emigration.

naturalism Naturalism is a movement that began in France during the mid-19th century inspired by ÉMILE ZOLA's novels and essays, especially *Thérèse Raquin* and its preface and the essay "Le Roman Experimental." It continued strongly until World War I, especially in the United States. In his essay, Zola explains that naturalist writers should subject believable characters and events to experimental conditions. Zola explains his idea of DETERMINISM, by which a person's fate is determined by his or her genetic heritage and environment. Determinism presents a character as pulled down by the past or beaten by a force he or she cannot overcome, such as poverty, bad genes, or criminality. Often society is to blame, but characters have to deal both with outside forces and inner weaknesses, and because they sometimes act like animals, they are also responding to the forces of NATURE. Thinkers who influenced naturalism include CHARLES DARWIN, SIGMUND FREUD, and KARL MARX. Naturalism in a sense is both an extension of and a reaction against REALISM, which is similar to naturalism in that they both aim to portray realistic everyday life, but different in that naturalism attempts to find out scientifically the forces underlying human nature that influence or drive people's actions, not just observe the surfaces of actions and personal thoughts. Where realism portrays the middle classes, naturalism tends to show the lives of the downtrodden. The characters' struggles are stark and their situations unforgiving. Naturalism treats characters and their reactions to certain situations as case studies in which the author's tone is distant and objective. Naturalistic writers offer what they think of as objective truth and also, displaying its inherent ROMANTICISM, a more subjective version of truth. FRANK NORRIS, who, along with London, THEODORE DREISER, STEPHEN CRANE, and Edith Wharton, was a major American naturalist, believed naturalism also partakes of romanticism. Naturalism seeks not so much to show a "man versus nature" scenario, but to reveal the conflicts within human nature. Scientific principles and ordinary people in extraordinary circumstances are the themes that drive naturalistic literature, which often follows a narrative of descent, in which a character starts off at one point and goes downhill from then on no matter what he or she does. Naturalism relies on attention to detail, the latter sometimes called "the documentary eye." Naturalistic stories generally do not have any heroes.

natural selection   The principal of natural selection was advanced by CHARLES DARWIN and first published in his book *On the Origin of Species* in 1859. Natural selection is a process in which traits that are a benefit to the survival or success of an organism are passed on from generation to generation and become more common in the population of an organism. Natural selection is the key to EVOLUTION and led HERBERT SPENCER to introduce the phrase "the survival of the fittest" because that is what natural selection guarantees. Since natural selection occurs via mutations in organisms that over time confer a survival advantage, it is random and thus challenges the idea that GOD intervenes in life on earth.

nature   Jack London is frequently described as a nature writer. Certainly, his stories of the Far North

evoked a sense of nature not common in fiction of the time: for him, nature was far from the romantic construct of the literature of previous generations, but, as in "To Build a Fire" or "The White Silence," a remote and uncaring nature as imagined by Darwinism and naturalism. And yet London imbues nature with terrific symbolic power: in the judgment it exacts in "In a Far Country," in the maternal sea of "The Water Baby," in the healing valleys and mountains of CALIFORNIA. The stories "All Gold Canyon" and "The Night-Born" contrast the "man-meanness" of cities with the awesome beauty and power of nature. But we must not forget that London's main subject was human nature, in all its glories and failures. Thus he was not a "nature writer" like John Muir or Mary Austin, but a writer who used the backdrop of nature from the YUKON to the South Seas as a stage upon which humans confront each other or test themselves. There are many passages evocative of the power of nature in his work, such as this one from "All Gold Canyon":

> It was the green heart of the canyon, where the walls swerved back from the rigid plan and relieved their harshness of line by making a little sheltered nook and filling it to the brim with sweetness and roundness and softness. Here all things rested. Even the narrow stream ceased its turbulent down-rush long enough to form a quiet pool. Knee-deep in the water, with drooping head and half-shut eyes, drowsed a red-coated, many-antlered buck.
>
> On one side, beginning at the very lip of the pool, was a tiny meadow, a cool, resilient surface of green that extended to the base of the frowning wall. Beyond the pool a gentle slope of earth ran up and up to meet the opposing wall. Fine grass covered the slope—grass that was spangled with flowers, with here and there patches of color, orange and purple and golden. Below, the canyon was shut in. There was no view. The walls leaned together abruptly and the canyon ended in a chaos of rocks, moss-covered and hidden by a green screen of vines and creepers and boughs of trees. Up the canyon rose far hills and peaks, the big foot-hills, pine-covered and remote. And far beyond, like

clouds upon the border of the sky, towered minarets of white, where the Sierra's eternal snows flashed austerely the blazes of the sun. (*Stories*, 1,017).

Nature Man (Ernest Darling) As a young man, Darling was ill and found he had to escape mental and physical breakdown at his physician father's home in Oregon. His illness was called neurasthenia, and was cured not by the many medical treatments he underwent, but by his rebellion against them. Darling headed to TAHITI, where he went about in a red loincloth preaching SOCIALISM. He built a terraced farm in the wilds above the harbor. The Londons visited him in Papeete in Tahiti, and London admired his spirit. However, alarmed at his unconventional lifestyle, even for Tahiti, and his socialism (he flew a red flag in front of his shack), the local French authorities seized the farm, on

Ernest Darling, "Nature Man," Tahiti, 1907 *(Huntington Library)*

which he had grown papayas, avocados, breadfruit, mangoes, bananas, and coconuts, and they blocked the road to his farm. In Nature Man, London saw a dualistic figure: Though Darling seemed the very model of the white man who had "crossed the beach" and entered the Tahitian community, living as the Tahitians did, he was rejected. In trying to enter into community with the islanders, Darling forgot about the French colonial bureaucracy and French nationalism, and he did not realize that the locals too would view him with suspicion. Nature Man is a romantic dream of nature defeated by the everyday political realities of life in the South Seas.

navigation When the *SNARK* sailed through the GOLDEN GATE on April 23, 1907, bound for HAWAI'I 2,100 miles away, she had no navigator. London hired Charmian's uncle ROSCOE EAMES as captain and navigator. However, it soon became apparent that Eames knew nothing of navigation. London had to teach himself while at sea, a difficult skill he was very proud to have acquired. In *The Cruise of the* Snark's chapter 4, "Finding One's Way About," London details the arduous crash course he undertook:

> I shall describe how I taught myself navigation. One whole afternoon I sat in the cockpit, steering with one hand and studying logarithms with the other. Two afternoons, two hours each, I studied the general theory of navigation and the particular process of taking a meridian altitude. Then I took the sextant, worked out the index error, and shot the sun. The figuring from the data of this observation was child's play. In the "Epitome" and the "Nautical Almanac" were scores of cunning tables, all worked out by mathematicians and astronomers. It was like using interest tables and lightning-calculator tables such as you all know. The mystery was mystery no longer. I put my finger on the chart and announced that that was where we were. I was right too. . . . I had exploded the mystery, and yet, such was the miracle of it, I was conscious of new power in me, and I felt the thrill and tickle of pride. And when Martin asked me, in the same humble and respectful way I

had previously asked Roscoe, as to where we were, it was with exaltation and spiritual chest-throwing that I answered in the cipher-code of the higher priesthood and heard Martin's self-abasing and worshipful "Oh." As for Charmian, I felt that in a new way I had proved my right to her; and I was aware of another feeling, namely, that she was a most fortunate woman to have a man like me. . . .

Proud? I was a worker of miracles. I forgot how easily I had taught myself from the printed page. I forgot that all the work (and a tremendous work too) had been done by the masterminds before me, the astronomers and mathematicians, who had discovered and elaborated the whole science of navigation and made the tables in the "Epitome." I remembered only the everlasting miracle of it—that I had listened to the voices of the stars and been told my place upon the highway of the sea. (*Cruise of the* Snark, 51, 55)

New Hebrides (Vanuatu)   New Hebrides is the colonial name given in the 19th century to the group of islands in the South Pacific known today as the nation of Vanuatu. London visited and photographed the New Hebrides on the SNARK trip.

New Woman   New Woman describes women, who at the turn of the century went against the spoken and unspoken rules and limitations the white male-dominated society imposed on them—

A New Hebrides family shows off their possessions. *(Huntington Library)*

a new feminist ideal. New potential for women is apparent in the fiction of Kate Chopin, Sarah Orne Jewett, Charlotte Perkins Gilman, Henry James, William Dean Howells, Jack London, and THEODORE DREISER, among many others. The New Woman was independent, educated, athletic, and daring. She might be portrayed as a Gibson girl in magazines or as a gritty heroine in works such as London's *Burning Daylight*. CHARMIAN KITTREDGE LONDON was a New Woman who significantly influenced her husband's conception of women of the modern age; she was one of the first women in CALIFORNIA to ride astride, not to mention serving as first mate of the SNARK. She was accomplished as well at the piano and other arts.

New York Herald The *New York Herald* was a major newspaper in New York City that existed between 1835 and 1924, when it was bought by the *New York Tribune* and renamed the *New York Herald Tribune*. Its international edition later became the English-language *International Herald Tribune*. In London's day, the newspaper was considered to be the most sensationalistic of the leading New York papers. Its ability to entertain the public with daily news made it the leading circulation paper of its time. For the *Herald*, London contributed coverage of the 1908 world heavyweight match between JACK JOHNSON and TOMMY BURNS. It also was the site of the first publication of the short story "Lost Face."

Nietzsche, Friedrich Wilhelm Nietzsche (1844–1900) was a German philosopher and philologist. He wrote numerous works, mostly essays, on religion, morality, culture, philosophy, and science and exerted enormous influence upon his contemporaries and followers; his influence continues to pervade existentialist and postmodernist thinking. Nietzsche promoted the philosophy of INDIVIDUALISM and rejected religion, SOCIALISM, and democracy. A key element of Nietzsche's philosophy is the "will to power," which he believed was a more important element than ADAPTATION to survive. He believed that the struggle to survive is a secondary drive, less important than the desire to expand one's power. His figure of the Übermensch,

often translated as "superman" (though in German the word "mensch" is gender-neutral), exemplified his ideas about the individual as hero. London did not read Nietzsche until 1906, but he fell heavily under his influence for a time. Eventually, he gave Nietzsche's individualism up in favor of socialism. Wolf Larsen, though created before London knew much about Nietzsche, is a clear specimen of the superman, with all his self-destructive traits; Martin Eden is a failed example of a superman.

Norris, Frank Benjamin Franklin Norris, Jr. (1870–1902), was an American novelist, short story writer, essayist, and critic, a naturalist writer known for his novels *McTeague: A Story of San Francisco* (1899) and *The Octopus: A California Story* (1901), as well as numerous short stories and essays published in the San Francisco literary magazine *The Wave*. In his works, he depicts the suffering of his characters often caused by their own greed or corruption, but more often by their genetics and social circumstances, such as poverty or alcoholism, huge forces well beyond their control. Norris's idea of naturalism, derived from ÉMILE ZOLA, is that it is a form of ROMANTICISM, since larger-than-life things happen to its characters. He often employed the naturalist "narrative of descent" and seems distant and even amused by the sufferings of his characters. Unlike London, Norris freely employed racial stereotypes, such as the Jew Zerkow in *McTeague* and McTeague's Irishness, as well as the Mexicans of *The Octopus*. Of all the naturalists, Norris came from the highest social class and graduated from Harvard; this may explain some of his remoteness from his characters as well as his sense of them as romantic. London reviewed *The Octopus* favorably and admired Norris's work.

Northland When London, his characters, and his readers speak of the Northland, they mean the vast area where his stories were set, present-day ALASKA and the YUKON TERRITORY. From Juneau and SKAGWAY all the way to the Arctic Circle, London uses various aspects of the Northland setting in his tales: the terrible cold, the barren wastes, the sea, the mountains, and the NATIVES. He opposes the harsh lessons of the Northland to the easy lives of the SOUTHLAND and underscores it as a place where men, women, and DOGS are tested to their limits. He was also responsive to its beauty: shining white mountains, dark blue seas, roaring rivers, and the aurora borealis.

Northland code   London's characters in the Northland live or die by what London presents as a Northland code. This code is based on BROTHERHOOD and COMMUNITY. Among its precepts are never travel alone from "To Build a Fire"; never abandon a trail mate as in "Love of Life"; never kill a partner as in *A Daughter of the Snows;* offer hospitality to strangers as in "A Klondike Christmas"; and learn to adapt to circumstances, which the incapables of "In a Far Country" fail to do. As London put it, "In the Klondike nobody talks. Everybody listens. There you get your perspective. I got mine." Instances in which various heroes adhere to the code include "The White Silence," "To the Man on Trail," and "Siwash."

Nuku Hiva   Nuku Hiva is the largest of the MARQUESAS ISLANDS, part of French Polynesia. HERMAN MELVILLE's *Typee* is set in a valley on Nuku Hiva, Taipivai Valley, on the eastern side of the island. ROBERT LOUIS STEVENSON's first landfall on his Pacific voyage aboard the *Casco* was on the north side of the island. Having read Melville and Stevenson, London was inspired to undertake his SNARK journey. After a treacherous 61-day crossing from HAWAI'I, the *Snark* arrived in TAIOHAE on December 6, 1907. The party visited Taipivai; both there and in Taiohae they noticed how the islanders, described as beautiful, noble, and happy by Melville, were dying off from white man's diseases, mostly tuberculosis. Thus, London's time in the Marquesas was hardly the romantic idyll he envisioned, but an up-close look at the ravages undergone by the islanders, a pattern he would continue to observe on the voyage.

Oahu   Oahu is the third largest island in HAWAI'I and the location of the state capital HONOLULU, which is located on the southeast coast of the island. Oahu is also the home of Pearl Harbor. The Londons spent a great deal of time on Oahu,

especially in Honolulu, which they first visited on the *Snark* in 1907 and then again for longer periods in 1915–16. In 1907, Oahu was the *Snark*'s first landfall after 30 days at sea. They lived at Pearl Lochs and on Waikiki Beach. London spends several chapters of *The Cruise of the* Snark on Oahu, describing mountains and forests and beaches, but also exploitative plantation labor. The latter gave rise to his Hawaiian short stories critical of the missionary-descended white elite of the islands who wrested power away from the Hawaiians and took over much of the land, building agricultural and trading empires. London set several Hawaiian stories on Oahu, especially in Honolulu: "The House of Pride," "When Alice Told Her Soul," and "On the Makaloa Mat," to name a few.

Oakland, California   In London's day, Oakland was a fast-growing, highly diverse, working-class city with a very busy port. London lived in Oakland on and off as a child and a man. Today, Jack London Square on the Oakland waterfront and Heinold's Tavern commemorate the importance of Jack London to Oakland, as does a reading room named for him at the Oakland Public Library. London returned to high school after his sailing and hoboing adventures, graduating from Oakland High School in 1896 to enter the University Academy in Alameda to cram for entrance exams to the University of California. London was a frequent contributor to the *Aegis*, the high school literary magazine. A book called *The Jack London Homes Album*, by Connie Johnson and Homer Haughey, lists the various residences London occupied in Oakland.

The Odyssey   The *Odyssey* is one of two major ancient Greek epic poems attributed to HOMER, a sequel to the *Iliad*, the other work ascribed to him. Probably composed near the end of the eighth century B.C.E., the *Odyssey* tells the story of Odysseus, who spent 10 years trying to return home to his island of Ithaca from the Trojan Wars, all the while contending with angry gods and grumbling men, sorceresses such as Circe and monsters like the Cyclops. Odysseus survives by using his wits; Homer calls him "wily Odysseus." Once home, he disguises himself as an old shepherd and secretly meets his son, Telemachus. His home is filled with suitors for the hand of his long-suffering wife, Penelope, who has been feeding and entertaining them but keeping their proposals on hold. Following a contest of bow and arrows, Odysseus reveals himself to the suitors and kills most of them. London was influenced by the *Odyssey*'s myth of the return home and the code of honor among Odysseus's men and family. He characteristically uses Homeric imagery and structure in "An Odyssey of the North," "The Son of the Wolf," and "Like Argus of the Ancient Times."

Oppenheimer, Jake Oppenheimer was a prisoner who was serving a life sentence at SAN QUENTIN for murders. He continued his career as a murderer in prison. A new law was passed in 1901 imposing the death penalty on prison inmates who murdered or attempted murder while in prison. Oppenheimer was tried under the new legislation in 1907 and sentenced to death. London uses Jake Oppenheimer as a character in *The Star Rover*. With ED. MORRELL he is a friend of the protagonist. London actively campaigned against the law that condemned him, and it was eventually lifted.

Orwell, George Eric Arthur Blair, or George Orwell (1903–50), was an English author whose works emphasized social injustice, democratic SOCIALISM, and opposition to totalitarianism. He is best known for his 1945 work *Animal Farm*. Orwell admired London and wrote essays about his works.

Ouida (Marie Louise de la Ramée) Ouida was the pen name of a French-English writer of historical romances, Marie Louise de la Ramée (1839–1908). London's favorite book as a child was Ouida's *Signa* (1875), a tragic tale of a gifted young Italian musician. London's copy lacked the last chapters and so until he was an adult he did not know that the heroic young man actually dies in the book. It was an early inspiration for the artist in him. She is best remembered today for her *Dog of Flanders and Other Stories* (1872). De la Ramée was also an animal rights activist; at one time she owned 30 DOGS.

Overland Monthly A monthly magazine started by a publisher with the *Californian* in 1880 and renamed *The Californian and Overland Monthly* in 1882. The magazine eventually became the most prestigious literary magazine west of the Rockies. It became the *Overland Monthly* in 1883. It merged with *Out West* in 1923, and the publication ended in 1935. London published numerous stories in the *Overland Monthly*, especially early on, and publication there at that time in his career was a huge break for him. Among his stories that appeared there were one of his first, "The Men of Forty-Mile," and later "The White Silence," "To the Man on the Trail," "The Son of the Wolf," and many more. The *Overland Monthly* gave Jack London his first real literary exposure.

oyster pirating As a teenager, London borrowed $300 from VIRGINIA PRENTISS and bought himself a small sloop, on which he learned to sail the tricky waters of SAN FRANCISCO BAY. Soon, he fell in with a group of criminals who were oyster pirates, sneaking out to company-owned oyster beds at night, collecting oysters, then selling them on the docks. Though it sounds like a rather tame kind of piracy, these were hardened, older men who had been engaged in all sorts of criminal and gang activity. Trying to keep up with their dangerous choices and especially their drinking frightened London and, after a few near-death experiences, he left the oyster pirates and joined the California Shore Patrol who went after the pirates. London writes about his oyster pirating and shore patrol duty in *Tales of the Fish Patrol* and *John Barleycorn*.

panic of 1893 The panic of 1893 was a U.S. economic depression, beginning with the Philadelphia and Reading Railroad bankruptcy in 1893, which caused a series of bank failures. People withdrew all their money from the banks and caused bank runs. The economy did not begin to recover until 1896 after William McKinley was elected. People had no work, they starved, and their children died—it was a terrible time. London was a young man during this time, and his seeking odd jobs, sailing jobs, and hoboing—as well as the attempt to find gold in the KLONDIKE—attest to the effects of the panic on him, and he was representative of many. Fighting the gold versus the silver standards and negotiations among labor, capital, industry, and municipal entities were often difficult and even violent, with strikes and general unrest. In the West, many farmers lost their farms, and others were taken over by the Southern Pacific Railroad, as London relates in *The Valley of the Moon*. The economy experienced 10 years of rapid growth when the Klondike GOLD RUSH helped to restore the confidence of the American people, until, that is, the panic of 1907.

Pan-Pacific Union The Pan-Pacific Union, sometimes known as the Hands-Around-the-Pacific movement, was an organization founded in HONOLULU by leading businessmen eager to promote trade with Asia, especially JAPAN. HAWAI'I territorial governor Walter F. Frear was a founding member. It had a building in Honolulu and sponsored conferences, luncheons and dinners, and other events for visiting foreigners; it published the *Mid-Pacific Magazine*, which ran several articles on London. Woodrow Wilson was invited to be its honorary president. Though it was primarily aimed at protecting American business interests, it also promoted peace and cooperation among the nations. London was invited to address the group and in 1915 delivered his speech "The Language of the Tribe," which proposed that American students learn Japanese and Japanese students English.

Paumotu Archipelago Paumotu Archipelago, also called the Tuamotus, is comprised of about 80 atolls or coral islands in French Polynesia, the largest collection of atolls in the world. The archipelago was first discovered by Ferdinand Magellan in 1521. It became well known in Europe during the 1800s for its pearls. In London's *The Cruise of the* Snark, the Paumotus present extreme challenges in sailing through their shallow reefs and hidden islands. In "The Seed of McCoy," the title character nimbly pilots the burning ship through waters like these.

Penduffryn Plantation This copra plantation on the island of GUADALCANAL in the SOLOMON ISLANDS was home to the Londons and their crew

for five months in 1908 toward the end of the SNARK cruise. London's *The Cruise of the* Snark portrays its inhabitants, the co-owners GEORGE DARBISHIRE and TOM HARDING and the enslaved working for them. Photographs and comments by London illustrate the harsh life on the plantation and the harsh treatment of the workers. He sets several works there, *Adventure*, *Jerry of the Islands*, and *Michael, Brother of Jerry* (the last two are children's works). The photographs London made of Darbishire and Harding and their wives indicate a certain debauched quality in these white masters; for one thing, Darbishire liked to stay drunk and to cross-dress, raiding Charmian's trunk. One afternoon there was a costume party accompanied by generous amounts of liquor and hashish. In 1914, a letter from the local missionary informed the Londons that Darbishire and his wife had been attacked and eaten by their workers.

photojournalism London might be described as a photojournalist or certainly a proto-photojournalist, since the practice was still in its infancy in his day. Early photojournalism largely consisted of war photography. London's friend James Henry "Jimmie" Hare (1856–1946) first gained a reputation for war photography in the Spanish-American War in 1898. London produced photographic work as good as anyone's, though it was also different, less interested in the "news" of the photograph than in the human subjects. Whereas much of Hare's Russo-Japanese War photography shows sunken ships, bombed buildings, and mangled artillery, London's work is almost exclusively focused on the human face and the body. London's photo journalism included his war correspondence in Korea in 1904 and in Mexico in 1914. Working during the first true mass media era, London saw the increasing use of photographic images in newspapers and magazines. Technological, social, and economic developments furthered photography, especially in the printing of photographic images as halftones and the development of faster-speed films and handheld cameras. The halftone process enabled photographs to be reproduced economically; with their wide distribution, newspapers and picture magazines were available to nearly anyone. For

London, the most important technological innovations were the portable folding cameras introduced at the turn of the 20th century such as the Eastman Kodak 3A. The smaller handheld cameras, faster films, and faster lenses allowed photographers greater freedom of movement and subject matter. In place of glass plates, the folding camera contained flexible roll film, enabling the photographer to make a series of photographs on the same roll. Thus, London was a pioneer nearly at the inception of modern popular photography.

Pitcairn Island   Pitcairn, Henderson, Ducie, and Oeno Islands are a group of four volcanic islands in the southeastern Pacific Ocean and the last remaining British overseas territory in the Pacific. The descendants of the *Bounty* mutineers live on the islands, where their ancestors fled with their Tahitian wives after the mutiny. Pitcairn is small, lacking in many resources, and remote. From the time of the mutineers' arrival, it has been a scene of discord and misrule. The gentle, Christlike pilot McCoy in "The Seed of McCoy" tells of the horrors that occurred on the island in the past, as the mutineers and their descendants fought one another.

plantation labor   Throughout the South Seas, from HAWAI'I to the SOLOMON ISLANDS, London observed systems of plantation labor by islanders working for whites. In Hawai'i, it was the sugarcane and pineapple fields, in the Solomons it was copra (the dried kernel of a coconut, used for making oil). For the laborers it was a hard life and they were often treated unfairly. Sometimes, the labor was recruited and work contracts were signed spelling out the pay and the length of service; at other times, especially in the Southwest Pacific, BLACKBIRDERS, or slavers, simply kidnapped islanders and enslaved them. Such plantation labor is an important element in such tales as "The Chinago" and "Mauki." In Hawai'i, terms and conditions for workers were much better.

Poe, Edgar Allan   Since Poe is often thought of as the father of the short story, and since London was one of the best short fictionists of his day, it is not surprising that London was influenced by Poe.

In his essay "The Terrible and Tragic in Fiction," London defends Poe and all horror writers as telling important truths about life and staying true to their artistic calling. Like Poe, London was a painstaking craftsman in his stories, and like Poe he knew how to go for the single effect. In Baltimore, just before leaving on the *DIRIGO* in 1912, London posed for a photograph at Poe's grave.

Polynesians   Polynesia (which means "many islands") is a region of Oceania comprising over 1,000 islands scattered over the central and southern Pacific Ocean. Polynesia is generally defined as the islands within the Polynesian triangle with its corners at HAWAI'I, New Zealand, and Easter

Portuguese laborers and children on a sugar plantation, Oahu, Hawaii, 1907 *(Huntington Library)*

Island. Other main island groups located within the Polynesian triangle include SAMOA, Tonga, the Cook Islands, and French Polynesia (including the MARQUESAS and the Society Islands). "Polynesia" refers to one of the three parts of Oceania (the others being Micronesia and MELANESIA), whose precolonial population generally belongs to one big ethno-cultural family which carried out centuries of maritime migrations. Between about 3000 and 1000 B.C.E., speakers of Austronesian languages originating on the island of Taiwan, spread through island Southeast Asia. A civilization called the Lapita culture began to spread; between about 1300 and 900 B.C.E., the Lapita culture reached as far as FIJI, Tonga, and Samoa. In this region, true Polynesian culture developed. Around 300 B.C.E., this new people spread eastward from Fiji, Samoa, and Tonga to the Cook Islands, Tahiti, the Paumotus, and the Marquesas, eventually going as far east as Rapa Nui (Easter Island), as far north as Hawai'i, by C.E. 500, and as far west as New Zealand (C.E. 1000). The migrations of these Polynesians, who navigated tremendous distances in their canoes, steered by the stars and the currents, are nothing short of astonishing, considering that they colonized most of the Pacific Ocean. London admired Polynesians and cast many as characters; he was frightened of the darker and more primitive Melanesians and rarely makes them heroes. Heroic Polynesians in his works include Otoo in "The Heathen," Joe Garland in "The House of Pride," Mapuhi's mother in "The House of Mapuhi," and McCoy in "The Seed of McCoy." London developed a deep interest in Polynesian MYTHOLOGY and used it in many tales, such as "The Water Baby" and "Shin Bones."

Prentiss, Virginia Virginia Prentiss (ca. 1882–1922) was born a slave on a plantation in Virginia and was later a slave on a plantation near Nashville, Tennessee. Escaping during the Civil War, she married Alonzo Prentiss and moved to OAKLAND, where she became a pillar of the black community and church. On the night London was born, she suffered a stillbirth in the same hospital. When FLORA WELLMAN LONDON could not provide milk or care for her baby, he was given to Mrs.

Prentiss to wet-nurse, as was the custom in those day. She loved the boy and more or less raised him for his first years of life; throughout his youth he would live with her for periods of time. Where he found his own mother cold, he had only loving memories of Mrs. Prentiss. She baked for him, took him to church and school, helped teach him to read using the King James BIBLE. She may have even been the one who named him "Jack"; he was called Johnny in the London home, but Mrs. Prentiss called him her little "jumping jack." For many years, the two families lived near one another in Oakland and its environs. The Prentiss family was more stable emotionally and financially than the Londons. Mrs. Prentiss lent him money to buy a boat to sail on SAN FRANCISCO BAY. When Alonzo and then the children died, London supported her. She cared for his two daughters both during his marriage to BESS MADDERN LONDON and after the divorce. Eventually, she lived with Flora in Oakland. She also cared for Charmian after the loss of her baby, Joy. She died in 1922 at the Napa State Hospital. London wrote glowing tributes to her and inscribed each of his books to her. She was a strong woman, proud of her race, and we may infer that from her London derived much of the antiracism of his stories. Jeanne Campbell Reesman's book *Jack London's Racial Lives* (2009) contains a full discussion of her role in his life, as does Clarice Stasz's *Jack London's Women* (2003).

prizefighting *See* BOXING.

proletarian A proletarian is a member of the laboring class. KARL MARX used the term to identify the working class of a capitalist society that does not own the means of production and thus, in order to earn money, must sell their labor. London identified himself as a member of the WORKING CLASS but not as a proletarian. As an artist and public figure, he could speak out for his class but because of his writing he was not as oppressed as they were. He believed that one day the proletariat would rise up in worldwide socialist revolution to wrest power from the capitalist oligarchies that controlled the wealth of the world and its armies.

Pyongyang, Korea   Spelled "Ping-Yang" by London in his RUSSO-JAPANESE WAR correspondence, Pyongyang is the present-day capital of North Korea. Though he was largely prevented from photographing and writing about battles during the war by the Japanese army, ahead of other correspondents, he finally managed to move past Ping-Yang and cross the Yalu River into Manchuria, where he witnessed the buildup to a major battle. At one point, detained at Ping-Yang, London wrote to Charmian to describe the forlorn village in which he is being held (Poval Colli, near Ping-Yang), its people "scared to death." He reports, "We storm the village—force our way into the stables—capture 25 lbs. Barley hidden in man's trousers—and so forth and so forth, for two mortal hours—chatter and chin-chin to drive one mad. And this is but one of the days" (*Letters*, 416).

racialism   Racialism, sometimes call scientific racialism, was a pseudoscience popular at the turn of the 20th century. Its proponents were whites who argued that only the white race would survive; the inferior races would be eliminated by natural selection. It thus became an ideology that supported nativism, anti-immigration measures, imperialism, and EUGENICS. It was used to support political or ideological positions of racial supremacy in Nazi Germany. It is now obsolete as far as serious scientists are concerned. London was initially attracted to the doctrines of racialists, including those of his friend, Stanford University president DAVID STARR JORDAN, and he read widely in the field. But though he sometimes propounded racialist ideas in his nonfiction and some novels, in his short fiction there is little trace; instead, he privileges nonwhite characters and makes them narrators, speaking for themselves. Major figures in scientific racialism included Arthur Gobineau, Madison Grant, Benjamin Kidd, HERBERT SPENCER, and Francis Galton.

racial memory   CARL JUNG used the term *racial memory* as a concept in his psychological theories. The concept suggests that memories, feelings, and ideas are inherited from generation to generation as part of the collective unconscious. This memory is present in a person at birth without having been created through a sensory experience. According to Jung, racial memories are incorporated into the genetic code of a species that shared those common memories and then passed on. People of various cultures can recognize such near-universal symbols as archetypes and myths, as of the SUN or creation. London invokes the idea of racial memory in such works as "When the World Was Young" and *Before Adam.*

realism   Realism is the literary movement that reacted against ROMANTICISM at a time of political and social upheavals. Romantic writers of the early 19th century offered their audiences an escape from the world, but realist writers wanted to offer a more middle-class and everyday truth, in part in order to encourage liberal reforms. The realist movement began in France and spread through Russia, England, and the United States. Like naturalist writers, realist writers tried to give the factual elements of a story in an objective and unbiased manner. This included both psychological characterizations (like Henry James), and the outward lives of the middle class (William Dean Howells). MARK TWAIN furnished a different kind of realism, more rooted in the American frontier. Their themes explored class conflict, aspects of life in the city and countryside, philosophy and morality, and marriage and family. Setting is very important in realist novels, and writers documented every aspect of it. In representing characters from different backgrounds, writers had to pay great attention to dialogue in order to capture different dialects and speech patterns. Naturalism departs from realism in several ways, but one of the most important is in its focus on the lives of the underclass with all of its brutality. Naturalism is influenced by Darwinism in a way that realism is not.

reincarnation   In *The Star Rover*, London portrays a fictionalized version of the real-life experiences of ED. MORRELL, confined in a straitjacket for many terrible years in SAN QUENTIN PRISON. Morrell claimed he learned to use "astral projection" (out of body experience) to visit his previous lives—in order to survive in the jacket. He believed in reincarnation, the idea that an essential part of a living being, the soul, survives death and is reincarnated or reborn in a new body whether human or animal in another place and time. Once the soul or spirit enters the new body, a new personality is developed without the complete loss of the prior personality. London himself did not believe in astral projection or reincarnation.

Río Blanco   In 1908, during the MEXICAN REVOLUTION, there was a strike put down with much bloodshed by General Porfirio Díaz at the Río Blanco textile mills, which were owned by German and Spanish companies. The strike was directed by two exiles who had fled across the border to St. Louis, Enrique and Ricardo Magon, who published and smuggled across the border a little revolutionary weekly called *Regeneracion,* the voice of the Mexican Liberal Party, which had been crushed by Díaz. In his story "The Mexican," London shows us Felipe Rivera's memories of the massacre, which included his parents. This memory is why he seeks revenge against the government through the revolution. Felipe's father, Joaquin Fernandez, published a little revolutionary newspaper from his home.

Roamer   London was often happiest when he was on the water. After the cruise of the SNARK, in 1910 he asked his former brother-in-law Ernest Matthews to keep an eye out for a bargain. Together, they met William H. Craig, the owner of the *Roamer.* London paid $175 for the 40-year-old sailboat, with large sails and a large cabin. She maneuvered easily in the tricky waters of SAN FRANCISCO BAY and the SACRAMENTO DELTA. Her large sails meant that she could move in the lightest breeze. The Londons never grew tired of the *Roamer* and spent months at a time aboard her. Jack's writing and Charmian's typing took up their mornings, but in the afternoon they fished, hunted ducks, swam, lounged on deck, played cards, or talked. A favorite pastime was reading aloud to each other. Whenever he needed to get away and relax, he turned to the *Roamer.*

romanticism   Though he thought of himself as a materialist and determinist and identified with the naturalist movement in literature, London wrote works which nearly all contain elements of romanticism, the literary movement of the early 19th century that emphasized the importance not of neoclassical norms but of strong personal emotion as the true source of aesthetic experience, privileging horror and the supernatural, NATURE as the sublime, the picturesque, a new emphasis on human psychology, a "natural" as opposed to a conventional language. Jacqueline Tavernier-Courbin's *The Call of the Wild: A Naturalistic Romance,* argues for London as a writer who melded the genres of romance and naturalism to achieve new effects. Certainly *The Call of the Wild* is realistic and naturalistic, but Buck's transformation into his true self is a romantic bildungsroman, as Romantics stressed the importance of individual insight and the hero's development. Romantic artists who influenced London include EDGAR ALLAN POE, Nathaniel Hawthorne, Washington Irving, Goethe, Mary Shelley, John Keats, ALFRED, LORD TENNYSON, and the Brownings. Works that particularly reveal a romantic view of life include "The Son of the Wolf," "The Story of Jees Uck," *A Daughter of the Snows, The Sea-Wolf, Martin Eden,* "The Night-Born," "The Hobo and the Fairy," "By the Turtles of Tasman," *Burning Daylight,* and *The Valley of the Moon.*

Roosevelt, Theodore   Roosevelt (1858–1919) was the 26th president of the United States, in office from 1901–09. Roosevelt's ideas of winning of the west and the strenuous life influenced London, as did his championing of NATURE conservancy, including beginning what would later be the national park system. London would have also found congenial—for the most part—Roosevelt's views on how immigrants had to become Americans and participate in democratic institutions. As an outdoorsman like London, he promoted a new ideal of masculinity. He was famous for his service with the Rough Riders in Cuba during the Spanish-American War. With a strong hand he regulated corporations and promoted job safety—what he called the Square Deal—for average Americans. Had London read much of

Frontispiece of *The Star Rover* (Macmillan, 1915): "'You are a man,' she completed. 'Not even in my sleep have I ever dreamed there was such a man.'" *(Huntington Library)*

Roosevelt's many historical works, he would also have realized that Roosevelt was a great writer and fine historian. However, when Roosevelt wrote a scathing review of London's *White Fang,* calling London a "nature-faker," London fired back with his essay "The Other Animals." Roosevelt objected to London's having a lynx fight with WOLVES, but London stated that he had observed it himself. Perhaps, given the size of these men's personalities, there just wasn't room enough on the national stage for both of them. Nevertheless, Roosevelt managed to convince the Japanese to let Jack London out of jail when he was in KOREA.

Russia and the Russians   Russia and the Russians appear in several London works, *A Daughter of the Snows,* the RUSSO-JAPANESE WAR correspondence,

and various KLONDIKE tales. London, like many in the West, was shocked when JAPAN defeated Russia in the 1904 war; it was the first time in modern history that an Asian nation defeated a European one. In his war correspondence, London identifies with the "white" Russians and is shocked to see them killed and imprisoned by the Japanese. While in SEOUL, he bought his first horse, Belle, from the former Russian ambassador. Russia occupied ALASKA and the YUKON beginning in the early 19th century, before it was taken over by England and the United States. Russians had forts and fishing camps down the coast of northern CALIFORNIA; Fort Ross near Bodega Bay is one of them. London agreed with the NATIVES that the Russians had been cruel conquerors, and he contrasts the actions of Anglo-Americans with them, though in truth they were little different as exploiters of NATIVE lands and fishing grounds. Most Russians in the Northwest were fur hunters and traders.

Russo-Japanese War   For the HEARST SYNDICATE, London traveled to KOREA to cover the Russo-Japanese War in January 1904. By steamer, train, junk, and small sailboat, he made his way to the frozen coast of Korea and roamed with the Japanese Army all the way to the Yalu River, the border with Manchuria, where he witnessed parts of a major battle. However, censored for the most part by the Japanese army, London was frustrated that he saw so little action. Instead, he turned to subject matter behind the lines, the ruined Korean villages, refugees, the sore feet of green Japanese soldiers, the beggars of SEOUL. His dispatches and PHOTOJOURNALISM convey this human element. The Russo-Japanese War is not well-remembered today, but its repercussions were felt for a long time. JAPAN had defeated CHINA in 1895, but FRANCE and GERMANY helped Russia pressure Japan into accepting only money instead of territory. Nicholas II of Russia borrowed from France for this and also to finish the Siberian railway eastward, which opened up badly needed trade routes. The terminus of the railway was to be located in Port Arthur (now Lüshun), a southern port of Manchuria, as Russia needed a warm-water port. Russia occupied Manchuria to protect the railway, all the way to the Yalu River, the border with Korea. Korea was the object of imperialist ambitions of both Russia and Japan and each built up arms. The United States and Great Britain supported the Japanese. Russians and Germans sought to control the Chinese, and the Chinese begged Japan to save it from the Russians. Russia experienced open revolt. A war with the Japanese was seen by the czar's advisers as an ideal distraction; everyone believed the tiny country would be demolished. Neither did Russians dream Japan would make the first move, but on February 8, 1904, Japan invaded Russia at Port Arthur, sinking most of the Russian navy and setting up a base on an island nearby. If this defeat was not ultimately decisive militarily, it was major news around the world. Among other things, it was a cause of the 1905 Russian Revolution. Though early in the war the American position was pro-Japanese, following the war, Americans turned anti-Japanese, echoing the anti-Asian panic of the 1880s–90s. The Russo-Japanese War was a racial war of many complexities, beginning with U.S. and British support for an Asian nation against a white one, then resulting in severe anti-Asian feeling in the States and in Europe at its conclusion.

Sacramento Delta   The Sacramento–San Joaquin River Delta is a huge inland river delta and estuary off SAN FRANCISCO BAY. At its western edge, it is bordered by the Central Valley and the confluence of the Sacramento and San Joaquin Rivers; it lies just east of where the rivers enter Suisun Bay (an upper arm of San Francisco Bay). The city of Stockton is located on the San Joaquin River on the eastern edge of the delta. This is the largest estuary on the U.S. West Coast. The rivers exit the Central Valley through the Coast Range via the narrow Carquinez Strait, which leads to San Francisco Bay and ultimately the Pacific Ocean. The delta consists of small natural and man-made channels (sloughs), creating a system of isolated lowland islands and wetlands defined by levees. As a youthful oyster pirate, London once threw himself into the water at Benicia in the delta and was rescued by a passing Greek fisherman. As a man, he and his wife sailed their boat the *Roamer* in and out of its sloughs, visiting friends, fishing, swimming, relaxing, and reading.

sailing   From his boyhood, London loved sailing. He sailed boats of all descriptions during his life and even shipped aboard large craft like the SOPHIA SUTHERLAND and DIRIGO. His most famous sailboat was the ketch rig the SNARK, but he also adored his ROAMER, on which he sailed the waters of SAN FRANCISCO BAY and the SACRAMENTO DELTA. OAKLAND, where he largely grew up, had a bustling international harbor, to which he was drawn. Whether a teenaged OYSTER PIRATE on San Francisco Bay, a nervous captain and navigator in such dangerous South Seas as the PAUMOTO reefs, or a man of leisure on the *Roamer*, London loved sailing. In *The Cruise of the* Snark's opening chapter, he explains how he and Charmian thrilled to the seafarer JOSHUA SLOCUM's three-year voyage in his boat the *Spray*, and how they conceived their plan of a seven-year, round-the-world voyage:

> But to return to the *Snark*, and why I, for one, want to journey in her around the world. The things I like constitute my set of values. The thing I like most of all is personal achievement—not achievement for the world's applause, but achievement for my own delight. It is the old "I did it! I did it! With my own hands I did it!" But personal achievement, with me, must be concrete. I'd rather win a water-fight in the swimming pool, or remain astride a horse that is trying to get out from under me, than write the great American novel. Each man to his liking. Some other fellow would prefer writing the great American novel to winning the water-fight or mastering the horse. (*Cruise of the* Snark, 3)

He also confesses

> The trip around the world means big moments of living. . . . Fallible and frail, a bit of pulsating, jelly-like life—it is all I am. About me are the great natural forces—colossal menaces, Titans of destruction, unsentimental monsters that have less concern for me than I have for the grain of sand I crush under my foot. . . . They are the cyclones and tornadoes, lightning flashes and cloud-bursts, tide-rips and tidal waves, undertows and waterspouts, great whirls

and sucks and eddies, earthquakes and volcanoes, surfs that thunder on rock-ribbed coasts
and seas that leap aboard the largest crafts
that float, crushing humans to pulp or licking
them off into the sea and to death. . . . In the
maze and chaos of the conflict of these vast
and draughty Titans, it is for me to thread my
precarious way. The bit of life that is I will exult
over them. . . . It is good to ride the tempest
and feel godlike. I dare to assert that for a finite
speck of pulsating jelly to feel godlike is a far
more glorious feeling than for a god to feel godlike. Here is the sea, the wind, and the wave.
Here are the seas, the winds, and the waves of
all the world. Here is ferocious environment.
And here is difficult adjustment, the achievement of which is delight to the small quivering
vanity that is I. I like. I am so made. It is my
own particular form of vanity, that is all. There
is also another side to the voyage of the Snark.
Being alive, I want to see, and all the world is a
bigger thing to see than one small town or valley. (*Cruise of the* Snark, 5)

St. Michael, Alaska   St. Michael is a city near
Nome, Alaska. It is located at the southeastern
end of Norton Sound. During the GOLD RUSH, St.
Michael, at the delta of the YUKON RIVER, was a
destination from which one could return home, as
steamers came and went from its port. It was also
the home of a Catholic mission. London floated on
a raft up the Yukon in 1898 to leave the KLONDIKE,
picking up a ship at St. Michael. In his writings he
refers to it as "St. Michael's."

saloons   In *John Barleycorn*, London writes of
how part of being a man was drinking in saloons;
taken to his first ones by his stepfather JOHN LON-
DON, even as a boy London knew the value of
the male companionship there. At Croll's Tavern
in Alameda and Heinold's in OAKLAND, London
drank with men much older than he and learned
to buy rounds. As he relates in *John Barleycorn*, this
led to an early addiction to ALCOHOL. He also frequented the saloons of DAWSON, listening to old-
timers' tales. Interesting scenes set in saloons occur
in *Burning Daylight* and the KLONDIKE stories. He

wrote in the opening chapter of *John Barleycorn*
that he had written it to support the temperance
movement and close the saloons.

Samoa   Today the Independent State of Samoa
governs the western part of the Samoan Islands. In
1722, Jacob Roggeveen was the first European to
come upon the Samoan Islands. The United States,
Britain, and Germany took interest in the islands,
and all three countries formed alliances with local
tribal leaders, causing an eight-year civil war in
which the three countries supplied their allies with
arms, training, troops, and warships. The civil war
ended after a gigantic storm destroyed most of the
warships. After Britain gave up its claim to the
Samoan Islands, they were divided into two parts,
the eastern part, known as American Samoa, and
the western part, known as German Samoa. The
Londons and their crew visited Samoa on the cruise
of the *SNARK*. They were entertained by island royalty and visited ROBERT LOUIS STEVENSON's home
in Apia, Vailima. London made many photographs
of Samoa, including a number of portraits.

San Cristoval   London uses this spelling for the
island of San Cristobal, today known as the island
of Makira, the largest island of the Makira-Ulawa
Province in the SOLOMON ISLANDS. It is east of
GUADALCANAL and south of MALAITA. The boy
Mauki and his companions eat in "Mauki" is not of
their Malaitan island; he is a "San Cristoval boy,"
and thus, within their traditional ethics, fair game.

San Francisco Bay   San Francisco Bay, at 1,400
square miles, drains approximately 40 percent
of CALIFORNIA; into it flow the Sacramento and
San Joaquin Rivers from the Sierra Nevada. With
Suisun Bay and San Pablo Bay, an entire group of
bays are often referred to as San Francisco Bay. San
Francisco Bay is surrounded by a region known as
the San Francisco Bay Area, dominated by the cities of San Francisco and OAKLAND. By his teenaged
years, London was an experienced sailor on the
treacherous waters of the bay.

San Francisco Chronicle   The *San Francisco
Chronicle* is northern California's largest newspaper.

It was founded in 1865 as *The Daily Dramatic Chronicle* by teenage brothers Charles de Young and Michael H. de Young. In London's day, it was the largest newspaper on the West Coast. London wrote several articles for the *Chronicle,* and it kept up-to-date his latest endeavors, with featuring him throughout his life as a sort of Western hero. It is owned by the Hearst Corporation, for which London also worked.

San Francisco earthquake   On April 18, 1906, San Francisco was wrecked by a great earthquake beginning at 5:13 A.M. Then, it was almost totally destroyed by raging fires that burned for four days. Thousands of people died. Damage was estimated at $500,000,000 in 1906 dollars. Awakened by the earthquake at their SONOMA VALLEY ranch, Jack and Charmian rode their horses to the top of Sonoma Mountain and were shocked to see the red sky above San Francisco, burning 50 miles away. When they reached San Francisco, London photographed the terrible effects of the quake and he returned later to document the city's slow recovery in an article for COLLIER'S MAGAZINE, "The Report of an Eyewitness." Charmian's diary entry for the day begins with the one word "Earthquake" (in red) and continues: "Mate [Jack] and I spent night in burning streets," she wrote, "terrific experience. Napped on a doorstep til dawn" (Charmian Kittredge London, Diary, 1906. Jack London Collection, Henry E. Huntington Library, San Marino, California). She recorded their impressions of Broadway when they left the ferry and "all night roamed the city of hills, prey to feelings that cannot be described" (Charmian Kittredge London, *Jack London,* 2: 141). She recalls, "We must have tramped forty miles that night. Jack's feet blistered, my ankles were become almost useless" (Charmian London, *Jack London,* 2: 143). She mourned, "Oh, the supreme truth of desolation and pain, that night of fire and devastation." As London recorded in his *Collier's* article: "Not in history has a modern imperial city been so completely destroyed. San Francisco is gone. Nothing remains of it but memories and a fringe of dwelling-houses on its outskirts. Its industrial section is wiped out. Its business section is wiped

out. Its social and residential section is wiped out. The factories and warehouses, the great stores and newspaper buildings, the hotels and the palaces of the nabobs, are all gone. Remains only the fringe of dwelling houses on the outskirts of what was once San Francisco." He added, "There was no opposing the flames. There was no organization, no communication. All the cunning adjustments of a twentieth century city had been smashed by the earthquake. The streets were humped into ridges and depressions, and piled with the debris of fallen walls. The steel rails were twisted into perpendicular and horizontal angles. The telephone and telegraph systems were disrupted. And the great water-mains had burst. All the shrewd contrivances and safeguards of man had been thrown out of gear by thirty seconds' twitching of the earth-crust" (*Jack London Reports,* 351–352).

San Francisco Morning Call   As a teen London won a story contest in the *Morning Call,* with "The Story of a Typhoon Off the Coast of Japan." The *Morning Call* was published from 1856–95. It operated under various names until it merged with the *San Francisco Bulletin.* MARK TWAIN once worked for the *Morning Call.*

San Quentin prison   San Quentin State Prison is in Marin County, CALIFORNIA. Opened in July 1852, it is the oldest prison in the state. It is the location of California's only death row for male inmates, at one point the largest in the United States. London was a critic of the California penal system, including San Quentin. He set his novel *The Star Rover* in its basements and dungeons. During London's time, the warden at San Quentin made frequent use of straitjackets and other forms of torture.

Santa Clara Valley   The "sun-kissed Santa Clara Valley," as London calls it in the opening of *The Call of the Wild* at Judge Miller's bucolic country home, refers to a region of CALIFORNIA that lies south of the SAN FRANCISCO BAY. Today largely known as Silicon Valley, the county seat is San Jose. In London's day, it was known as the Valley of Heart's Delight, with its miles of farms and orchards. For London, it represented the fruitful and peaceful life of the SOUTHLAND. In the KLONDIKE, he met the Bond brothers and from their dog, Jack, and their descriptions of their father, Judge Bond's, place in Santa Clara, he imagined the opening of *The Call of the Wild*:

> Buck lived at a big house in the sun-kissed Santa Clara Valley. Judge Miller's place, it was called. It stood back from the road, half-hidden among the trees, through which glimpses could be caught of the wide cool veranda that ran around its four sides. The house was approached by graveled driveways which wound about through wide-spreading lawns and under the interlacing boughs of tall poplars. At the rear things were on even a more spacious scale than at the front. There were great stables, where a dozen grooms and boys held forth, rows of vine-clad servants' cottages, an endless and orderly array of outhouses, long grape arbors, green pastures, orchards, and berry patches. Then there was the pumping plant for the artesian well, and the big cement tank where Judge Miler's boys took their morning plunge and kept cool in the hot afternoon. (*The Call of the Wild*, 1)

Saturday Evening Post The *Saturday Evening Post* is a bimonthly American magazine. Beginning publication in 1821 as a four-page newspaper, it became the most widely circulated weekly, gaining status under longtime editor George Horace Lorimer (1899–1937). The *Post* published current events, editorials, human interest pieces, humor, illustrations, a letter column, poetry (including work written by readers), cartoons, and stories. It was known for commissioning illustrations and original works of fiction. Curtis Publishing Company stopped publishing the *Post* in 1969, but it was revived in 1971 as a quarterly publication. Today, the *Saturday Evening Post* magazine is published six times a year. *The Call of the Wild* first appeared in five serialized issues in the *Post*, for which Jack London was paid $750. MACMILLAN bought the book rights 22 days later for only $2,000! London also published numerous stories in the *Saturday Evening*

Post, notably "The Devil's Dice Box," "South of the Slot," "A Piece of Steak," and "The Hobo and the Fairy."

Savard, Louis Savard was a fellow prospector London knew in the KLONDIKE who may have inspired such characters as François and Perrault in *The Call of the Wild* and even Black LeClére in "Batard." Charmian writes about Savard in her *Book of Jack London* (vol. 1, 238 ff).

Scandinavians London admired the Teutonic blond hero and what he thought of as his Viking ancestors who mingled with ANGLO-SAXONS to create modern Anglo-Saxons. Several of his characters imagine their racial past as marauding Vikings, such as Frona Welse in *A Daughter of the Snows*. But in that novel is also a vignette of several strapping Scandinavians who try to rescue a drowning man and are themselves drowned, hardly a portrait of heroic might. London uses the myths of the Norse throughout his stories, as in "The Son of the Wolf" and *The Valley of the Moon*.

scotch shepherd dog In *The Call of the Wild*, the narrator tells us that Buck is the son of a St. Bernard and a scotch shepherd. For the latter, London may have had in mind the small, collielike Shetland sheepdog, sometimes called a Scotch Shepherd. Since these only weigh 14 to 30 pounds, they don't seem like likely candidates for Buck's parentage. Some dog classifications call the collie a "scotch shepherd." London may then mean a St. Bernard and a collie, but it is hard to be sure. It is worth noting that as much as London worried about the interbreeding of races or animals, his greatest hero is of mixed-race.

Seoul, Korea Today, Seoul is the capital of South Korea, but in London's times it was the entire country's capital. London spent much time in Seoul, often against his will—being prevented from getting to the front-line stories of battles by the Japanese army. Left with time on his hands, he roamed the streets of Seoul and took hundreds of photographs of its varying classes as they were affected by the RUSSO-JAPANESE WAR of 1904.

From child beggars to once-proud elders, he captured with his camera and pen both individual and cultural stories of war and displacement. In Seoul, he gave a command performance, reading *The Call of the Wild* to officers of the Japanese army at the Seoul YMCA. He learned to ride his first horse. He spent much of his time in Seoul in his hut writing of his experiences.

Shepard, Captain James H.   Shepard was ELIZA LONDON SHEPARD's husband and Jack London's would-be partner in the KLONDIKE; when they arrived there, however, Shepard realized he was not up to the climbing of the CHILKOOT PASS and returned home. The Shepards divorced in 1915; in 1913, Shepard threatened Eliza with a gun and was ordered off the ranch by Jack London.

Eliza London Shepard (stepsister)   Eliza (1866–1939) was born to Midwestern farmers John and Anna Jane London. When she was eight years old, her mother died of tuberculosis, and her father took her and her sister Ida, as well as their brother Charles, west to CALIFORNIA to start a new life. He placed them in an orphanage while he sought work in San Francisco. In 1877, Eliza was reunited with her father, who had married FLORA WELLMAN LONDON. She became stepsister to baby Johnny. She was kind and loving to him, unlike his mother, and she became his lifelong best friend. She served as ranch superintendant, a role especially critical when he was away traveling, and, after his death, she worked side-by-side with Charmian in the struggle to preserve the ranch and his copyrights during the Great Depression.

When she was 16, the family took in sea captain JAMES SHEPARD as a boarder. Although he was over twice her age and widowed with children, she married him and settled nearby, perhaps to escape Flora. In 1899 they had a child, Irving. She continued to love and support London. In 1897 James Shepard partnered with London to strike out for the Klondike gold fields. However, he realized he was unfit and returned home.

After Eliza's marriage broke up, in 1910 she and her son Irving came to live on the BEAUTY RANCH, where Jack hired her as both ranch superinten-

dant and foreman on the building of WOLF HOUSE. She was practical, hard-headed, and devoted. She proved exceptional at all her duties, supervising workers, handling accounts, keeping up with legal matters. In May 1913 James appeared on the ranch with a gun and threatened to shoot her. Jack and an assistant grabbed the gun from him and threw him off the ranch; in 1915 he divorced her for desertion. Following London's death, Eliza and Charmian became even closer friends and business partners, handling such matters as the business of the ranch and book and film rights contracts. During the 1920s she served as national president of the Woman's Auxiliary to the American Legion and spent 1926 in Washington, D.C., where she also participated in the Woman's Labor Congress. She was also active in the Daughters of the American Revolution. When Eliza died she was praised in the press as a patriotic woman who loved the outdoors. London loved Eliza and was always grateful to her. She also contributed to his artistic work: it was she who assembled the first of the London photo albums by pasting and captioning his photographs from *The People of the Abyss* into an album for him.

Shepard, Irving   Irving Shepard (1900–55) was ELIZA LONDON SHEPARD and JAMES SHEPARD's only son and Jack London's step-nephew. He grew up on the BEAUTY RANCH and sent important papers and books of London's to the HUNTINGTON LIBRARY, a practice followed by his son, Milo Shepard. It has been the Shepard family's charge to preserve the ranch and London's literary legacy. Irving coedited *Letters from Jack London* with King Hendricks in 1965. He also donated items to the Utah State University Library, following an earlier bequest by Charmian. Shepard thought of himself as a farmer and a country man, but like his son Milo, he helped make available to scholars today many treasures from Jack London's life and career, including such gems as Charmian's diaries, manuscripts, and unpublished letters.

Sinclair, Upton   Upton Sinclair, Jr. (1878–1968), was a Pulitzer Prize–winning, American author who wrote more than 90 books. He won wide fame in the first half of the 20th century, particularly for his

1906 muckraking novel, *The Jungle*. The book dealt with conditions in the U.S. meatpacking industry, causing a public uproar that contributed to the passage of the Pure Food and Drug Act and the Meat Inspection Act in 1906. London reviewed Sinclair's *The Jungle* favorably and thought of him as a fellow socialist. London contributed the introduction to Sinclair's manifesto *The Cry for Justice* (1915).

Skagway, Alaska In several works, such as *The Call of the Wild* and "Like Argus of the Ancient Times," London relates how would-be prospectors were put off steamers at DYEA BEACH near Skagway, to struggle in the marsh and mud to get their supplies ashore. In earlier times, Skagway was the home of the Tlingit people, who fished, hunted, and traded, due to their strategic location. Skagway was incorporated in 1900 but shortly before that was a sort of wild west town of saloons, gambling, and drink, run by a criminal gang headed by one "Soapy" Smith. The KLONDIKE GOLD RUSH changed the little settlement forever. In July 1897 the steamer *Queen* docked with the first boatload of prospectors. More ships brought more miners into the new town; there, they had to prepare for the 500-mile journey to the goldfields above the CHILKOOT PASS. The population increased to 30,000, mostly American prospectors. Some realized how difficult the route to the goldfields and would be decided to stay behind to supply goods and services to miners. These were the people who became rich. Stores, saloons, and offices increasingly lined the muddy streets. Skagway is a popular stop on cruise ship trips to Alaska.

Slocum, Captain Joshua As told in his 1899 book, *Sailing Alone Around the World*, Slocum (1844–1909) was a Canadian-American adventurer, a writer, and supposedly the first man to sail single-handedly around the world. He disappeared in November 1909 while aboard his sailboat, the *Spray*. His book was the inspiration for the Londons' eventual cruise of the SNARK. Slocum left Boston, Massachusetts, in 1895 and returned to Newport, Rhode Island, in 1898, having sailed 46,000 miles. In November 1909, Slocum set sail for the West Indies and South America to explore the Orinoco, Rio Negro, and Amazon Rivers. He was never heard from again.

Sloper, Ira Merritt One of Jack London's partners in the KLONDIKE, along with Fred Thompson and Jim Goodman. As CHARMIAN KITTREDGE LONDON records in her biography of her husband, Sloper was especially helpful in building the rafts and boats the party needed to journey on lakes and rivers on their way to DAWSON. Sloper is thought to be the model for London's character the Malemute Kid.

Snark The *Snark* was a 43-foot sailboat, ketch-rigged, that London had built in 1906–07 for his proposed round-the-world cruise. Unfortunately, London had the bad luck to be building a boat after the SAN FRANCISCO EARTHQUAKE, when supplies and labor were scarce. Though he ordered the best materials, the *Snark* was actually poorly built and gave the crew many problems on their first crossing to HAWAI'I. Having collided with a barge just before she was finished, the *Snark* suffered a two-inch warp on one side. Only days after leaving the GOLDEN GATE, she displayed a number of problems, which London writes about in his chapter "The Inconceivable and Monstrous" in *The Cruise of the Snark*. The wood planks, full of butts, leaked; the head malfunctioned; water ran into the coal supply and food; the main engine fell off the mount, as did the launch engine. But most serious of all, she wouldn't come about or heave to, making the 30 days to Hawai'i full of danger in large troughs and storms. But she took the intrepid crew to Hawai'i and the South Seas, and once repaired in Hawai'i she maneuvered just fine. The *Snark* was abandoned in Sydney Harbor when London became ill and was hospitalized in late 1908. She was stripped of her furnishings; the story goes that she became a BLACKBIRDER and was eventually scuttled. A few of the fittings the *Snark* are at the House of Happy Walls Museum at JACK LONDON STATE HISTORIC PARK in GLEN ELLEN, CALIFORNIA.

Social Darwinism Social Darwinism is the concept that the theory of natural selection is applicable to social phenomena, including racial divisions.

It was popular in the United States as early as 1877. Other names besides Darwin's that were often invoked by Social Darwinists are Thomas Malthus, Francis Galton (Darwin's cousin known for his theory of EUGENICS), and HERBERT SPENCER, another disciple of Darwin's who predicted an eventual future for the dominant white race in SOCIALISM. Spencer is best known for the phrase "survival of the fittest," which was his interpretation of Darwin's actual phrase, "the struggle to survive." Galton argued that not only physical traits are passed on from generation to generation but also mental qualities, so that social morals had to adapt change to prevent the overbreeding of the "less fit." Social Darwinism is criticized not only for racism, imperialism, and aspects of eugenics, but for advocating strength over such social forces as ethics. London at times sounded like a Social Darwinist, but gave up Spencer's ideas of applying Darwin's model to human relationships, though the latter continued to influence his works.

socialism Socialism refers to an economic system in which the means of production are under common ownership of the people with equal individual access to the resources. Socialism arose as a response to the industrial revolution as a political philosophy designed to help the WORKING CLASS. Socialist political movements developed in England and France between the 1820s and 1850s with an abundance of different systems designed by people such as Robert Owen, Joseph Fourier, KARL MARX, and Friedrich Engels. At that time, members of the middle class who wanted to improve the conditions of the working class developed a utopian socialism that depended upon patrons for the formation of model communities, but these projects largely failed. Engels and Marx began constructing a more radical socialist theory by attacking utopianism and proclaiming that the entire ruling class has to be overthrown in order to create a new socialist society that could function without economic exploitation or the domination of the state. Britain and GERMANY began to develop socialism between 1870 and 1914, bringing about reforms in education, insurance, public health, and public utilities and transportation. The socialism of Western Europe spread to RUSSIA, which was also industrializing, but Russian socialists embraced the more radical revolutionary socialism of Marxism. Socialism played an important role in U.S. politics only for a short time and never really caught with the larger public on as it had in Europe and Asia. London was a socialist all of his life and a member of the SOCIALIST LABOR PARTY. Socialism furnished him with themes and subjects central to his work, such as in *The Iron Heel* and stories such as "South of the Slot" and "The Dream of Debs."

Socialist Labor Party The Socialist Party of America, in which Jack London was an active member, was a democratic socialist political party in the United States, formed in 1901 by a merger between the new Social Democratic Party of America and disaffected elements of the Socialist Labor Party, which had split from the main organization in 1899. The SLP drew support from trade unionists, progressive social reformers, populist farmers, and immigrant communities. As a presidential candidate, EUGENE V. DEBS won over 900,000 votes in 1912 and 1920, while the party also elected members of the U.S. House of Representatives and numerous state legislators and mayors. The party's opposition to American involvement in World War I, led to defections and even persecution, as did divisions as to how to judge Russia's Bolshevik Revolution in 1917 and the establishment of the Communist International in 1919. After the 1920s, the Party's appeal was weakened by the popularity of Franklin Roosevelt's New Deal.

Sol Sol, or Old Sol, was a Roman god of the SUN, akin to the GREEK gods Zeus and Apollo, and the Greek mythological figure of Helios, who drives the sun's chariot across the heavens each day. Sol was viewed as a judger of men; his all-seeing eye of heaven especially records and judges evil deeds. In London's KLONDIKE fiction, Sol is mentioned numerous times as a judging eye. He appears when something bad is about to happen and observes it. Sol's feast day was December 25, and so CHRISTMAS DAY appears in connection with him in London's work. His number was seven, which also constitutes a pattern in the Klondike fiction.

Solomon Islands   Today, the Solomon Islands are part of Melanesia, east of Papua New Guinea, consisting of nearly 1,000 islands. Together, they cover a landmass of 10,965 square miles. The capital is Honiara, located on the island of GUADALCANAL. The Solomon Islands are believed to have been inhabited by MELANESIAN people for thousands of years. Great Britain established a protectorate over the Solomon Islands in the 1890s, but when London visited, the Solomons were thought of as one of the wildest and most dangerous places on earth, full of warlike tribes, headhunters, and cannibals—and this was true. The Londons lingered there for five months, however, the same amount of time as they had spent in HAWAI'I. They stayed on a copra plantation, PENDUFFRYN, and toured the many islands. Their long stay is odd, given London's condemnation of the Solomons as a place he wouldn't send his worst enemy. Sailing with the crew of the MINOTA, A BLACKBIRDER, or slave ship, they were nearly overrun on the island of MALAITA when the ship hit a reef. London sets many of his works in the Solomons, including "Mauki," *Adventure,* "The Inevitable White Man," and "The Red One."

Sonoma State Home   Sonoma State Home, in GLEN ELLEN, CALIFORNIA, was once California's primary facility for the care of the developmentally disabled and mentally retarded. Originally a private institution, it was taken over by the state in 1885 and until 1909 was known as the California Home for the Care and Training of Feeble-minded Children. It is now called Sonoma Developmental Center and is the oldest facility in California established specifically for serving the needs of individuals with developmental disabilities. The facility opened its doors to 148 residents on November 24, 1891. Originally located in Vallejo and Santa Clara, the home was later moved to its present location. In 1953, Sonoma State Home became Sonoma State Hospital, and in 1986, the name was changed to Sonoma Developmental Center. Over the years, the facility has expanded several times. London set his story "Told in the Drooling Ward" there; its grounds border his ranch.

Sonoma Valley   Sonoma Valley bears a NATIVE name that means valley of the moon; if one drives north through the valley at certain times one

George and Helen Darbishire and workers at Penduffryn Plantation, Guadalcanal, 1908 *(Huntington Library)*

sees the moon rise and set seven times behind the mountains. Sonoma Valley is home to some of the earliest vineyards and wineries in the state, some of which survived the phylloxera epidemic of the 1870s and the impact of Prohibition. Today Sonoma Valley is home to some of the finest wineries in the state. London built his ranch on Sonoma Mountain near the town of GLEN ELLEN; on 1,400 acres he farmed organically and raised livestock. Sonoma meant home and health and happiness to London, and from his travels he was always eager to return to its beauties and ease of life. He set many works there, notably the three "Sonoma" novels, *Burning Daylight, The Valley of the Moon,* and *The Little Lady of the Big House.*

Sophia Sutherland   The *Sophia Sutherland* was a North Pacific sealing schooner that sailed out of San Francisco. In 1893, London took a seven-month voyage on her, and when he returned he won first prize in a contest for writing the best descriptive article in the SAN FRANCISCO MORNING CALL for his "Story of a Typhoon off the Coast of Japan." London proved himself among the experienced sailors aboard and later used some of what he learned in *The Sea-Wolf.*

Sourdough   A "sourdough" means an old-timer in the KLONDIKE, someone tested and experienced, with considerable wisdom about survival in the NORTHLAND. London listened to the stories of sourdoughs in the taverns of DAWSON and used many of their reminiscences in his stories. The name comes from a leavening used to make their bread. The best-known sourdough in his work is the old-timer from SULPHUR CREEK in "To Build a Fire"; he warns the protagonist, "Never travel alone," but the man does so anyway, at the cost of his life.

Southland   In London's KLONDIKE fiction, Southland refers to the lower 48 states. The implication is that residents of these states are outsiders who do not understand survival in the NORTHLAND, as depicted in his story "The Sunlanders."

Spencer, Herbert   Herbert Spencer (1820–1903) was an English philosopher who influenced not only philosophy, but politics, economics, sociology, psychology, and literature. Spencer's first major work was *The Proper Sphere of Government,* a collection of letters that presented his concept of INDIVIDUALISM. Spencer is best known for his phrase "survival of the fittest," which was his term for what DARWIN called "natural selection" or "the struggle to survive." Spencer first used the term in 1864 after he read Darwin's *On the Origin of Species* and wrote and published his *Principles of Biology* (1864). Spencer extended Darwin's theory of evolution into sociology. EVOLUTION for "The survival of the fittest" was described by Spencer as the evolutionary system in which the best individuals, the best species, and the best races would survive by having acquired the best characteristics needed for survival. Other individuals, species, and races would die off, which was the way it was designed by NATURE. This concept is the foundation for RACIALISM. Other works Spencer is known for are *Principles of Psychology* (1855) and *Progress: Its Laws and Cause* (1857). London was heavily influenced by Spencer's theories, especially his racialism. As a young man, London was enraptured by Spencer's seemingly complete model of the world and was also a believer in SOCIAL DARWINISM. Spencer sought to apply the evolutionary ideas of Charles Darwin to society, arguing that the eventual future would be for whites only and would evolve into a socialist form of government. Darwin repudiated Spencer's racialist ideas. Eventually London had enough of him too, when he turned to Thomas Henry Huxley's more humane interpretation of Darwin's theories. Martin Eden become enamored of Spencer but does not give him up in favor of socialism, as London did.

Sterling, George   George Sterling (1869–1926), a California poet, was celebrated during his lifetime as one of the greatest American regional poets, but outside of California he never gained much fame. Sterling became a significant figure in Bohemian literary circles in northern California early in the 20th century and helped develop the artists' colony in CARMEL-BY-THE-SEA, along with AMBROSE BIERCE and Jack London. The hamlet had been discovered by Charles Warren Stoddard and others, but Sterling made it famous. He lived there six years and was called the uncrowned king of Bohemia.

Sterling and London formed a very close friendship; there are dozens of letters between them, and they signed their letters to each other "Greek" (Sterling) and "Wolf" (London). London trusted Sterling as a critic of his writing and had him copyedit *The Sea-Wolf.* CHARMIAN KITTREDGE LONDON was a bit jealous of their closeness and never bonded with Sterling, though she and his wife, Carrie, were good friends.

Sterling joined the BOHEMIAN CLUB and participated in their theatrical productions each summer at the Bohemian Grove. For the main Grove play in 1907, the club presented *The Triumph of Bohemia,* Sterling's verse drama of the battle between the "Spirit of Bohemia" and MAMMON for the souls of the grove's members. Bierce arranged for the publication of Sterling's poem "A Wine of Wizardry" in the September 1907 number of COSMOPOLITAN, which afforded Sterling some national notice.

Sterling was a heavy drinker and his wife left him, later committing suicide. Sterling was probably using opium and other narcotics. He carried a pill of cyanide for many years. In November 1926, he used it at his residence at the San Francisco Bohemian Club.

Stevenson, Robert Louis   Robert Louis Stevenson (1850–94) was a Scottish author who wrote novels, poems, essays, short stories, short story collections, and children's literature, including the boys' adventure classics *Treasure Island* and *Kidnapped.* Much of his writing was based on his travels. While traveling, he met important people with whom he became close friends and who influenced him, such as authors Henry James, Edmund Gosse, Leslie Stephen and Charles Warren Stoddard (who was coeditor of the *Overland Monthly*); he also befriended and King Mataafa of Samoa, and King Kalakaua of the Hawaiian islands. London read and was influenced by Stevenson's *Tales of the South Seas.* When the SNARK visited Apia, SAMOA, the Londons made a pilgrimage to Stevenson's home there. Stevenson had moved to Samoa in 1890 and was active in local politics and culture. There, he was known as Tusitola, the storyteller.

Stewart River   The Stewart River flows east to west south of DAWSON, through the towns of McQuestion, Mayo, and Stewart Landing. It is 331 miles long, rising in the Mackenzie Mountains, central YUKON TERRITORY, Canada, and flowing generally west to the Yukon River south of Dawson. The river is navigable for most of its length. It was a river in which prospectors, including Jack London, panned for gold.

Stolz, Louis and Bert   Louis Stolz was the sheriff of KAUAI who tried to apprehend the leper KOOLAU in Kalalau Valley, where he had fled. Stolz was killed by a bullet from Koolau's rifle. His son, Bert Stolz, was a crew member aboard the SNARK, and told London the story. But London's story makes Koolau the hero ("Koolau the Leper") and does not seem to mourn Stolz.

Strunsky, Anna   See WAILING, ANNA STRUNSKY.

Sulphur Creek   Sulphur Creek, a branch of Dominion Creek, a tributary of the Indian River near Dawson in the KLONDIKE region, was the site of a gold rush in 1897. Sulphur Creek is home to the wise old-timer in "To Build a Fire." Interestingly, the story is full of references to sulphur, whether the burning fistful of matches dropped in the snow by the protagonist or the brimstone of hell. Sulphur is the only other yellow mineral besides gold.

sun   *See also* SOL. The sun is an important element in both London's KLONDIKE fiction and his South Seas fiction. In the Klondike, it functions as Old Sol, appearing just when something profound is about to happen, judging the deeds of men. This is especially prominent in "The Devil's Dice Box" and "In a Far Country." London was interested in the mythology of Apollo, the judge of men who has to set things right. In the South Seas, the sun is the enemy who must be defeated by white man, whose skin cannot take its actinic rays. David Grief, called "a son of the sun," is immune to its rays and tans and moves about as he will, a sort of fantasy figure for London, whose own body was severely damaged by the South Seas sun.

sun dogs Prominently featured in such tales as "The Sun-Dog Trail," sun dogs (scientific name *parhelion*, plural *parhelia*, for "beside the sun"), also called mock suns, comprise a particular type of ice halo around the SUN. A colored patch of light to the left or right of the sun, 22 (or more) degrees distant, and at the same distance above the horizon as the sun, is a sun dog. It is the most commonly seen of ice halos. Sun dogs are thought to presage some terrible event in many cultures.

supermen Many believe London advocated the solitary conquering superman as his hero, but this is incorrect. Though London has many strong and individualistic heroes (Buck, Martin Eden, David Grief), he believed in SOCIALISM and so argued in his fiction for the importance of the group, the pack, the trail mate, the COMMUNITY. This was the important aspect of London that was misunderstood by the young man Chris McCandless who, in the 1990s, set out to Alaska to live "in the wild" away from everyone, as detailed in Jon Krakauer's book *Into the Wild*. London himself learned the price that comes with trying to be a superman: working too hard, living too hard, and lack of exercise led to his early death. As he demonstrates, especially in his late South Seas tales, living means living within multiple communities and not alone, a lesson he also absorbed from CARL JUNG's works in his last year.

surfing London learned surfing on Waikiki Beach in 1907 upon the SNARK's first call in HONOLULU; as teachers he had ALEXANDER HUME FORD and George Freeth. Duke Kahanamoku also surfed with them. London got a terrible sunburn his first day out but did manage to ride some waves. He helped popularize surfing in travel articles like "My Hawaiian Aloha" and in *The Cruise of the* Snark. As he described a Hawaiian surfer:

> And suddenly, out there where a big smoker lifts skyward, rising like a sea-god from out of the welter of spume and churning white, on the giddy, toppling, overhanging and downfalling, precarious crest appears the dark head of a man. Swiftly he rises through the rushing white.

His black shoulders, his chest, his loins, his limbs—all is abruptly projected on one's vision. Where but the moment before was only the wide desolation and invincible roar, is now a man, erect, full-statured, not struggling frantically in that wild movement, not buried and crushed and buffeted by those mighty monsters, but standing above them all, calm and superb, poised on the giddy summit, his feet buried in the churning foam, the salt smoke rising to his knees, and all the rest of him in the free air and flashing sunlight, and he is flying through the air, flying forward, flying fast as the surge on which he stands. He is a Mercury—a brown Mercury. His heels are winged, and in them is the swiftness of the sea. In truth, from out of the sea he has leaped upon the back of the sea, and he is riding the sea that roars and bellows and cannot shake him from its back. But no frantic outreaching and balancing is his. He is impassive, motionless as a statue carved suddenly by some miracle out of the sea's depth from which he rose. And straight on toward shore he flies on his winged heels and the white crest of the breaker. There is a wild burst of foam, a long tumultuous rushing sound as the breaker falls futile and spent on the beach at your feet; and there, at your feet steps calmly ashore a Kanaka, burnt, golden and brown by the tropic sun. Several minutes ago he was a speck a quarter of a mile away. He has "bitted the bull-mouthed breaker" and ridden it in, and the pride in the feat shows in the carriage of his magnificent body as he glances for a moment carelessly at you who sit in the shade of the shore. He is a Kanaka—and more, he is a man, a member of the kingly species that has mastered matter and the brutes and lorded it over creation. (*Cruise of the* Snark, 75–76)

Swinburne, Algernon Charles Algernon Charles Swinburne (1837–1909) was a controversial English poet. Though he was admired as an exquisite versifier and inventor of a new poetic form, the roundel (a variation of the French rondeau), he was thought of as decadent and dangerous; he was an ALCOHOLIC and sexual masochist and an anti-religionist. Ironically, Ruth Morse is reading his poem "Dolores" in the opening chapters of *Martin Eden*; perhaps in her bourgeois education she does not know much of his life. His poetic works include: *Atalanta in Calydon* (1865), *Poems and Ballads I* (1866), *Songs before Sunrise* (1871), *Poems and Ballads II*, (1878) *Tristram of Lyonesse* (1882), *Poems and Ballads III* (1889), and the novel *Lesbia Brandon* (published posthumously).

taboos   Since he writes about indigenous tribal peoples, London was sensitive to the importance of taboo among them. A taboo prohibits various types of human activity; it is both sacred and forbidden. Breaking the taboo is considered punishable by society. The term appears in many POLYNESIAN cultures. In those cultures, *tabu* (or *tapu* or *kapu*) often has specific religious associations. CAPTAIN JAMES COOK introduced the word into English in 1777 after returning from the South Seas. In "Mauki," the title characters "tambos" direct his ethical compass; he nearly fails in his last escape attempt because he has a taboo against touching a woman.

Tahiti   Tahiti was first sighted by a Spanish ship in 1606, but no European went ashore until Samuel Wallis in 1767. Tahiti is part of French Polynesia in the archipelago of the Society Islands; it was made a possession of France after Louis-Antoine de Bougainville circumnavigated the island between 1766 and 1769. He described the island as a utopia or earthly paradise without the corruption of civilization, but Tahiti's idyllic society was corrupted by the Europeans who followed JAMES COOK after he set up camp in 1769. The Europeans introduced venereal disease, influenza, and ALCOHOL into Tahiti's society, which decimated its population. The SNARK arrived in Tahiti on December 27, 1907. They stayed until January 13, 1908, when the Londons took the steamer MARIPOSA back to San Francisco to deal with financial and business problems. While in Papeete, they made the acquaintance of Ernest Darling, known as the NATURE MAN, and London devotes most of his chapter on Tahiti to him. London also set his story of a doomed field worker "The Chinago" in Tahiti.

Taiohae   Taiohae, located on a wide bay of the same name on the NUKU HIVA, is the principal settlement of Nuku Hiva and the capital of the MARQUESAS ISLANDS. On either side of the entrance to its bay are two small islands, the Sentinels. Muake, a mountain rising behind the town to an elevation of 2,835 feet, dominates the background. When London arrived there on the SNARK in 1907, he had been drawn by MELVILLE's depictions of the people of the Taipivai Valley (Typee). But in Taiohae he found only dying islanders infected with white man's diseases. The only men fit for work were mixed-blood people with partial immunities. London and Charmian rented a house in the town and explored TYPEE VALLEY.

Tehei of Tahaa   Tehei was a resident of the island of Tahaa, near BORA BORA, when the Londons visited in 1908. He came aboard the SNARK as a pilot for a time. The crew enjoyed a splendid luau at Tehei and his wife, Biihura's home on Tahaa, which makes up a chapter of *The Cruise of the* Snark, "The High Seat of Abundance." London modeled his character Otoo in "The Heathen" after Tehei and also photographed him.

Tennyson, Alfred, Lord   Alfred Tennyson, the first Baron Tennyson (1809–92), was the Poet Laureate of the United Kingdom and a fellow of the Royal Society. He is also one of the greatest English-language prels. Among his works are "The Lady of Shalott," "Ulysses," "In Memoriam A. H. H.," "Maud," and "Crossing the Bar." London read and admired Tennyson throughout his life.

Teutons   The Teutons are an ancient Germanic tribe often mentioned by GREEK and Roman authors. They are believed to have lived in Jutland and given their name to a region in northern Denmark called Thy. Before 100 B.C.E., the Teutons migrated to the Danube Valley and attacked Roman Italy but were beaten by Gaius Marius in the Battle of Aquae Sextiae in 101 B.C. St. Jerome wrote about the Teuton women who were captured in the battle and committed mass suicide including the murder of their children. London identified as an ANGLO-SAXON and inheritor of Teutonic or

Viking adventurers. However, in his works Teutons do not always fare well: the drowned Scandinavians in *A Daughter of the Snows* or the white men who die out in the South Seas.

Thoreau, Henry David   Henry David Thoreau (1817–62) was an American author whose best-known works are *Walden* (1854) and *Civil Disobedience* (1849). Thoreau was considered one of the leading transcendentalists of his time who believed in living his life simply in peace with nature, as well as resistance to civil government.

Thurston, Lorrin   Lorrin Andrews Thurston (1858–1931) was a lawyer, politician, and businessman born and raised in HAWAI'I. The grandson of two of the first MISSIONARIES to Hawai'i, Thurston played a leading role in the American overthrow of the Hawaiian Kingdom, dethroning Queen Lili'uokalani and creating the Republic of Hawaii. He published the *Pacific Commercial Advertiser* (later the *Honolulu Advertiser*, to which he contributed opinion columns) and owned other companies. From 1906 to 1916, he lobbied national politicians to create a national park to preserve the Hawaiian volcanoes. He was an important promoter of Hawaiian business and tourism. He became a friend of London's when the SNARK arrived in 1908, introducing him to important people and setting up lecture opportunities for the famous author. However, they had a falling out personally and in print when London published his Hawaiian stories, later collected in *The House of Pride*. To show missionary descendants as cruel masters of indigenous people and to write stories about lepers sent Thurston into a series of furious articles against London in the *Advertiser*, to which London hotly responded. Both felt betrayed. The two men never really made up the break.

totems   A totem describes a broad and diverse set of practices and ideas. A totem is a sacred entity to a family, clan, or tribe, usually a figure, sometimes an animal, sometimes some other element of the natural world. Totems watch over those who hold them sacred. The word is of Ojibwa origin, but totemistic ideas occur in other NATIVE groups and around the world in many cultures. London was aware of Native totems in the NORTHLAND and uses them in many stories. For himself, as in "The Son of the Wolf," he adopted the wolf as his totem. He signed his letters to his friend GEORGE STERLING as "Wolf." His dream home in SONOMA VALLEY he named WOLF HOUSE, and he had a favorite DOG, Brown Wolf, also the title of one of his stories. In his fiction he seems to have seen something in the wolf pack that evoked both timelessness and primitivism, but also cooperation and COMMUNITY.

the trail   The trail in the KLONDIKE fiction is literally where much of the action in the stories takes place, but it has a figurative role as well as a metaphor of the journey of life and the struggle to survive. When men struggle across the vast north, confronting many obstacles and dangers and proving themselves to their group, there is a spiritual dimension to this voyage. Perhaps borrowing from the *Odyssey*, London makes trails a centerpiece of many of his best works: "The Devil's Dice Box," "An Odyssey of the North," *The Call of the Wild*, and "Like Argus of the Ancient Times." The trail is also where the NORTHLAND CODE of BROTHERHOOD is tested; those who stay with their trail mates survive, those who depart on their own die, as in "To Build a Fire." Leaving a partner behind on the trail is a great sin, as in "Love of Life." In a broader sense, the trail suggests London's lifelong love of roaming and adventuring, whether riding boxcars as a hobo, sailing the South Seas, or prospecting in the YUKON.

Twain, Mark   Twain (1835–1910) and London were the two most popular writers of their day, though Twain had quite a head start on London and was better supported by the Eastern elite of such magazines as *Harper's* and ATLANTIC MONTHLY. But both were born poor, grew up in the west, started out as journalists, wrote about particular regions, wrote juvenile fiction as well as that for adults, were highly critical of capitalist and bourgeois society, and spent a lifetime traveling to faraway places. Their images and their books were everywhere, and each man was constantly the subject of newspaper and magazine articles. It is interesting to read them comparatively; for example, *The Call of the Wild* and *Adventures of Huckleberry Finn*, perhaps America's two greatest claims to world novels. Twain was reportedly jealous of London's royalties and speculated that one day a real socialist from RUSSIA would find him and take them away!

Typee Valley   Known locally as Taipivai, this lush valley on the Marquesan island of NUKU HIVA was made famous by HERMAN MELVILLE in his 1846 novel *Typee: A Peep at Polynesian Life*, loosely based on the adventures of Melville and a companion when they jumped ship from the American whaler the *Acushnet* at Nuku Hiva in 1842. Melville spent three weeks in Taipivai. His narrator and stand-in, Tommo spends much longer. Tommo, is at first frightened of the Typeeans, whom he believes to be cannibals. But as he lingers there, he falls in love with the people, whom he describes as tall, noble, and beautiful. It is with some reluctance that he escapes. When London visited Taipivai 50 years later, these people were nearly all gone, having succumbed to the white man's diseases. Only those with some mixed blood were able to survive.

University of California, Berkeley   London attended the University of California, Berkeley, for one semester, but he lived in and around the town off and on in his early life. He claimed not to have learned anything from the professors he saw as stuffy and outmoded, but he dropped out not because he did not like it but because he ran out of money. He uses the university as a setting in several works, including *The Kempton-Wace Letters*, "South of the Slot," and *The Scarlet Plague*. Some of his earliest stories written for the Oakland High School literary magazine, *Aegis*, feature what he imagined then as the life of well-to-do college men and women. Today, the university's Bancroft Library contains a large collection of Jack London papers, photographs, and other materials.

utopian literature   Utopia is a name taken from a book by Sir Thomas More (1478–1535), *Utopia* (1516). It is defined as an ideal or perfect place or state or any visionary system of political or social perfection. In literature, it refers to a detailed description of a state ordered by a system the author proposes as a better way of life than any known to exist. The objectives of the utopian novel were political, social, and philosophical. London wrote more DYSTOPIAS, or dark visions of the future, than he did utopias, but his California novels propose the rural life as a sort of utopian antidote to the evils of the big city.

Veracruz, Mexico   The city of Veracruz is a major port city on the Gulf of Mexico in the Mexican state of Veracruz. The metropolitan area is Mexico's second largest on the gulf coast and an important port. In 1914, during the MEXICAN REVOLUTION, it was occupied by the United States for seven months in the Second Battle of Veracruz because of the Tampico Affair, an altercation between American sailors and the Mexican troops of General Victorio Huerta. London and his wife traveled from Galveston aboard a ship with Major General Frederick Funston's men; London covered the U.S. invasion in his correspondence for COLLIER'S.

Villa, Pancho   José Doroteo Arango Arámbula (1878–1923), better known as Pancho Villa, was a Mexican revolutionary general and for a time provisional governor of Chihuahua. As the leader of the División del Norte (army of the North), he was feared by Americans who several times tried to catch him. Villa was enormously popular among ordinary Mexicans. When Francisco Madero was president of Mexico, one of his commanders started a revolt, and Villa defended him; along with General Victoriano Huerta, who would become president. However, Huerta brought Villa up to a firing squad on false charges; Villa was saved by a letter of pardon from Madero. Villa continued to lead raids against Huerta and even over the border in the United States. Headlines during the revolution claimed that Jack London was riding with Villa.

wage slavery   This is a term London often used to describe the life of the child laborer, factory worker, or other manual worker who earns only enough to survive and is exploited by his employer. It was the realization while in ERIE COUNTY PENITENTIARY that unless he could find a way to use his brains and not his body to earn a living he would end up broken like the men he encountered there. He had heard VIRGINIA PRENTISS's story of escaping slavery in the South, and in such works as *The Call of the Wild* the impulse to escape from a life of meaningless toil is the cry of the individual self to be fulfilled. London depicts wage slavery in many works, most notably "The Apostate."

Wake-Robin Lodge   In May 1903, Jack made his first visit to GLEN ELLEN, CALIFORNIA, camping on the grounds of NINETTA WILEY EAMES's country house, Wake-Robin Lodge. Ninetta was Charmian's aunt and introduced her niece to London when she interviewed him for OVERLAND MONTHLY. There Jack and Charmian fell in love. Charmian described the summer of 1903 in her *Book of Jack London:* "Here a congenial company of acquaintances met in the summers, making merry in the incomparable woods bordering Graham and Sonoma Creeks, swimming in the pools, tramping, boxing, fencing, kiting, and gathering about the campfire at dusk for discussion and reading" (*Book of Jack London,* 1: 392). It was at a table outside by the creek that London wrote his novel *The Sea-Wolf.* A year later, following his divorce, London spent a week at Wake-Robin Lodge, and "his regard for the beautiful mountainside had only extended," wrote Charmian. By the following summer, he had committed himself to both Charmian and Glen Ellen. In June 1905, he purchased the Hill Ranch for $7,000, beginning the building of his BEAUTY RANCH.

Walling, Anna Strunsky   Anna Strunsky (1879–1964), was born in RUSSIA to a Jewish family. They fled Europe for the United States in 1893. By high school, Anna, a very intellectual and socially aware young woman, joined the SOCIALIST LABOR PARTY. In December 1899, at an SLP meeting, Anna, then attending Stanford University, from which she was graduated in 1900, met Jack London. They spent enormous amounts of time together discussing political issues as part of a wider group of San

Anna Strunsky Walling, ca. 1903   *(Huntington Library)*

Francisco intellectuals known as the Crowd. On a biking trip in the Berkeley hills, London suddenly proposed marriage to Anna. Having been brought up as a genteel young lady, she played coy. She said she had to go cover revolutionary developments in Russia. Angry, his former math tutor and friend, London impulsively married Bess Maddern, less than a week later. Three years later, Strunsky and London anonymously published a collaborative novel in the form of letters, *The Kempton-Wace Letters* (1903). The book is devoted to a debate on the nature of love in which one correspondent, Dane Kempton, defines the ideals of love as romantic, while the other, Herbert Wace, contends love is essentially biological. Their feelings for each other revived during this project, London told Anna that he wanted out of his marriage and to marry her. This time she accepted. However, while London was in LONDON, ENGLAND, writing *The People of the Abyss*, Anna discovered that Bess was pregnant with their second child, and she broke off their plans. They remained close friends throughout their lives. Anna wrote reviews of his books and a moving obituary. She also wrote a memoir of her time with London that was never published. She married the American socialist and labor leader William English Walling in Paris in 1906. They had several children. In 1915, Anna published her only novel, *Violette of Père Lachaise*. Anna's role as author in the socialist movement was overshadowed by her husband's work and the duties of motherhood. Their life together was unhappy; for one thing, as she hints in her memoir, she was still in love with London. Anna died in 1964.

Welsh   The Welsh as CELTS occupy a good deal of London's thoughts on race in general and his own personal ancestry in particular. His mother, Flora Wellman, was of Welsh ancestry. He has Frona and Jacob Welse in *A Daughter of the Snows* as ANGLO-SAXONS or Vikings, but he also names them as Welsh. Celts were discriminated against in London's day (especially on the East Coast) and were not considered fully white. Thus the discrepancy in this novel indicates some sort of indecision on London's part as to the role that being a Celt played in his own life.

White Logic   This is the name London assigns to his ALCOHOLISM. As he defines it in *John Barleycorn*:

> I am aware that within this disintegrating body which has been dying since I was born I carry a skeleton, that under the rind of flesh which is called my face is a bony, noseless death's head. All of which does not shudder me. To be afraid is to be healthy. Fear of death makes for life. But the curse of the White Logic is that it does not make one afraid. The world-sickness of the White Logic makes one grin jocosely into the face of the Noseless One and to sneer at all the phantasmagoria of living. (*John Barleycorn*, 315)

When he looks in the mirror, he sees this death's head looking back at him, but still he drinks.

Toward the conclusion of the book, he has a dialogue with the White Logic:

> Bog-lights, vapours of mysticism, psychic overtones, soul orgies, wailings among the shadows, weird gnosticisms, veils and tissues of words, gibbering subjectivisms, gropings and maunderings, ontological fantasies, pan-psychic hallucinations—this is the stuff, the phantasms of hope, that fills your bookshelves. Look at them, all the sad wraiths of sad mad men and passionate rebels—your Schopenhauers, your Strindbergs, your Tolstois and Nietzsches.
>
> "Come. Your glass is empty. Fill and forget."
>
> I obey, for my brain is now well a-crawl with the maggots of alcohol . . . (*John Barleycorn*, 329)

White Pass (Dead-Horse Trail)   As described by Jack London in several KLONDIKE works, the White Pass or Skagway Trail wandered 45 miles from SKAGWAY to Lake Bennett as one of the two passes that opened up the interior of the YUKON. Lower in elevation than CHILKOOT PASS and supposedly suitable for stock animals to pack supplies, the trail turned to horror as men and animals struggled through swamps, high mountains, deep canyons, huge boulders, and thick forests. Hundreds of streams had to be crossed, with flooding after heavy rains. The trail soon became deeply rutted and muddy under the feet and hooves of thousands. It became so narrow that two animals had trouble passing each other. Eventually, they simply walked over and through the dead and dying horses and mules that littered the trail. Most of the 3,000 horses used on the trail died in Dead Horse Canyon, and the heaps of carcasses left travelers with a horrendous sight. In 1898, the White Pass and Yukon Railroad Company was formed, and despite the dangers, managed to construct a railway which opened in July 1900, opening up the YUKON like never before. Even today, riders on the train can spot the traces of fallen horses and equipment on the treacherous trail.

White Silence   London uses this term to indicate how far away and uncaring NATURE is in the

NORTHLAND. It refers to the weird silence that could settle on travelers as they journeyed over empty, frozen spaces. In the short story "The White Silence," London memorably describes man's sense of humility in the face of the awful power of nature:

> The afternoon wore on, and with the awe, born of the White Silence, the voiceless travelers bent to their work. Nature has many tricks wherewith she convinces man of his finity,— the ceaseless flow of the tides, the fury of the storm, the shock of the earthquake, the long roll of heaven's artillery,—but the most tremendous, the most stupefying of all, is the passive phase of the White Silence. All movement ceases, the sky clears, the heavens are as brass; the slightest whisper seems sacrilege, and man becomes timid, affrighted at the sound of his own voice. Sole speck of life journeying across the ghostly wastes of a dead world, he trembles at his audacity, realizes that his is a maggot's life, nothing more. Strange thoughts arise unsummoned, and the mystery of all things strives for utterance. And the fear of death, of God, of the universe, comes over him,—the hope of the Resurrection and the Life, the yearning for immortality, the vain striving of the imprisoned essence,—it is then, if ever, man walks alone with God. (*Stories,* 144–145)

Wilde, Oscar   Oscar Fingal O'Flahertie Wills Wilde (1854–1900), one of the leading celebrities of his day, was an IRISH playwright, poet, and author of numerous short stories and plays and one novel. Known for his wit, he became one of the most successful playwrights of the late Victorian era in London, with such favorites as *The Importance of Being Earnest.* He was part of the aesthetic and decadent movements. His career included being a reviewer for the *Pall Mall Gazette* (1887–89) and the editor of the *Woman's World.* When he was accused of indecency with a young noble man by that man's father, he was convicted of sodomy and sent to Reading Gaol for two years' hard labor. This broke his health, and he left England for the continent, where he died soon after. Though London also admired his plays and poetry, he was most affected by a pamphlet Wilde published in 1891 called "The Soul of Man Under Socialism." London's heavily annotated personal copy is among his papers at the HUNTINGTON LIBRARY. Wilde's idea of SOCIALISM was a bit different from London's, but it interested London. Wilde's view in the pamphlet is more like a libertarian point of view or an anarchic one. Wilde criticizes what society sees as altruism in helping the poor which spoils them and also prevents them from exercising their talents. Charity will not transform the poor; only a reorganization of society. In a socialist society, artists in particular would be free to exercise their talents. Socialism will thus lead to INDIVIDUALISM when individuals no longer fear poverty and starvation.

Wiley, Dayelle ("Daisy" Wiley)   Daisy Wiley (?–1876) was CHARMIAN KITTREDGE LONDON's mother. She migrated west in a wagon train from Wisconsin with her parents and two sisters, Ninetta and Tissie; Daisy kept a journal in which she details their trip. Daisy eventually arrived in southern CALIFORNIA, where she met and married a cavalry captain, Willard "Kitt" Kittredge. They had one daughter, Charmian. After her birth, they moved to San Francisco. Daisy, who was a poet whose work appeared in *Godey's Lady's Book,* suffered from depression and turned to opiates; she died in 1876. Ninetta took Charmian into her home and raised her. Daisy is the model for Saxon Brown Roberts's mother in the *Valley of the Moon,* in which Saxon imagines her as the model of a Western pioneer woman.

Wolf House   Construction on Jack and CHARMIAN LONDON's dream house began in April 1911, under the direction of architect Albert Farr of San Francisco. To save it from earthquakes, it was built on a huge floating slab large enough to support a 40-story building. Redwood trees, many still covered in their own bark, red volcanic rocks, blue slate, huge boulders, and cement were chosen for primary building materials. The roof was of Spanish tile. London's design called for 15,000 square feet of living space in a four-story building, with 26 rooms and nine fireplaces. He envisioned it as unpretentious, spacious, and natural. Redwood

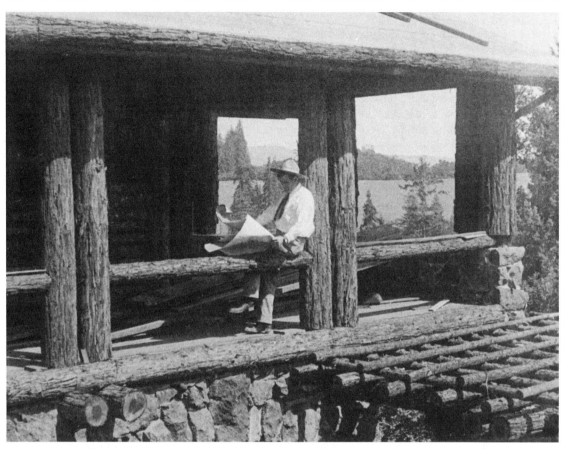

Jack London reviewing plans for Wolf House, 1913 *(Huntington Library)*

tree posts upheld the porte-cochère and porches. Inside the rafters were of natural logs. The home was designed to be a writer's castle, but also a place where London's many friends could be hosted, thus there are very public spaces in the house and very private ones. London's writing lair, at the top of a tower, was his retreat; it was 19 by 40 feet with a library of the same size directly under it, connected by a spiral staircase. Here he would have room at last to house his entire library. The living room was 18 by 58 feet, two stories high with redwood balconies nearly all the way around. A huge stone fireplace was set at the end of the room. Wolf House was also supposed to be easy to take care of; it had its own hot water, laundry, heating, electric lighting, vacuum and refrigeration plants, a dairy room, root cellar, and wine cellar.

On a hot August evening in 1913, Wolf House burned to the ground; the cause is thought to have been spontaneous combustion from rags soaked in linseed oil left in the house. The cost was an estimated $75,000 in 1913 dollars. London purchased an insurance policy several weeks before the fire and collected about $10,000. He vowed to rebuild Wolf House, but did not have nearly enough money to do so. Instead, he built an annex to the cottage, where he worked for the next three years until he died in 1916.

wolves *See also* DOGS. London's personal TOTEM and a figure in numerous stories, wolves are the very essence of life in the NORTHLAND. They form a danger to everyone who takes to the trail, reflecting the primitive and untamed in the wild, but they are also often a model for how humans can survive in the wild. London writes attentively of pack behavior, especially in *The Call of the Wild* and *White Fang*. It is as the symbolic "law of life" that wolves attack old Kooshkosh in "The Law of Life"; it is as the naturalistic force of survival of the fittest that the wolf trails the man in "Love of Life." London signed his letters "Wolf" and named his house WOLF HOUSE. In "The Son of the Wolf," Scruff Mackenzie takes as his totem the wolf as against the NATIVES' raven. In so many of London's works, the wolf represents a kind of freedom to be found in the wild, as is the case with Buck.

Woman's Home Companion *Woman's Home Companion* was a successful American monthly publication, published from 1873 to 1957; climbing to a circulation of 4 million during the 1930s and 1940s. Among the contributors to the magazine were Shirley Jackson, Anita Loos, John Steinbeck, and P. G. Wodehouse. Jack London published works in *Woman's Home Companion*, including chapters from *The Cruise of the* Snark and the story "The Apostate."

Woodruff, Charles Colonel Charles Edward Woodruff (1860–1915), a surgeon with the U.S. Army Medical Corps, published a book in 1905 called *The Effects of Tropical Light on White Men*, which argued that while the white man may roam much of the world and conquer it, he is unsuited by his fair skin to work in the Tropics. Based on his observations while serving in the Philippines, he explained how the sun's damaging rays affect whites in the South Seas and argued against white settlements there. After his own trials with the tropical sun during the SNARK voyage, London read Woodruff's book and was much relieved. The failure of the voyage was not his fault, but the fault of his skin. Like London at times, Woodruff was a racialist, but ironically, his findings demonstrate that the white man is not always superior, which contradicted RACIALISM.

work-beast *See also* WAGE SLAVERY. London uses this term to describe those who toil either as animals (*The Call of the Wild*) or like animals ("The Apostate") in a corrupt capitalist system.

No matter how hard they work, they are only tools for those who own their labor. This figure comes up throughout London's KLONDIKE, socialist, and Pacific fiction, in which different kinds of work-beasts are presented. Though London valued hard work and WORKING CLASS people, he rejected such toil as ruinous to the individual.

working class London was a proud member of the working class, as he sets forth in essays such as "What Life Means to Me" and "How I Became a Socialist." Working class are those who work for wages, usually at manual labor. They occupy a position between the middle and lower class; in contrast to the economic and educational resources of the middle and upper classes, working class people in London's day struggled to survive. Working classes are mainly found in industrialized economies and in urban areas. Some of London's working class heroes are Big Bill Totts in "South of the Slot," Ernest Everhard in *The Iron Heel*, and Johnny in "The Apostate." Despite his high earnings for his writings, London always identified with the working class.

the writing game London made no secret that he wrote for money. He saw himself as an artist and craftsman who figured out the writing game in his first years of writing, and he became adept at negotiating the best deals for himself. Despite his statements that he wrote only for money, London's works belie this. London always needed money for his grandiose personal projects, such as the SNARK and the ranch and so from time to time he wrote potboilers. The vast majority of his work, however, is anything but. Perhaps London's avowals that he wrote for cash reflect his WORKING CLASS roots; he certainly did not think of himself as an effete writer of the ivory tower, but a writer for the people. As Martin Eden reflects, the important thing was not really the money, but what it could provide in what London called "big moments of living" in *The Cruise of the* Snark's opening chapter. London despised the greed and corruption of the robber barons and other capitalists of his day, intent only on profit at the expense of workers. Thus, he did not worship money, but only wanted what it could provide for his "moments of living."

Jack London and his favorite Shire stallion, Neuadd Hillside, ca. 1913 *(Huntington Library)*

Yalu River, Battle of the   The Battle of the Yalu River during the RUSSO-JAPANESE WAR was the one battle London managed to cover in his war correspondence. It took place from April 30 to May 1, 1904, and was the first major land battle of the war. It was fought near Wiju (modern-day Uiju, North Korea) at the border between KOREA and CHINA. Hundreds of RUSSIAN and JAPANESE soldiers died in the battle; as London notes, the Japanese sacrificed its soldiers in their determination to win. The carnage was sickening to London, and he was shocked by the defeat of the whites, the Russians, by an Asian nation, as was the Western world. The defeat of the Russians removed the falsehood that the small nation of Japan would be easily defeated and that the war would be short.

Yeehat Indians   The Yeehat Indians are a fictional NATIVE tribe who massacre John Thorn-

ton and his dogs near the end of *The Call of the Wild*. London had heard tales of especially savage Natives in the interior of the YUKON. Though Buck takes his terrible revenge on the Yeehats when he returns to camp and finds them there, they are the ones who keep his legend alive in their stories of the great wolf-dog who leads the pack.

Yokohama, Japan   London first visited the port city of Yokohama when he sailed as an able seaman aboard the North Pacific sealing ship, the *SOPHIA SUTHERLAND*, in 1893. He set three of his earliest stories there, all sensitive portraits of ordinary JAPANESE people. He returned again en route to KOREA as a war correspondent in the RUSSO-JAPANESE WAR in 1904. His previous experiences in 1893 in the waterfront bars helped him gather information when he passed through on his way to Korea.

Young, Egerton R.   Young (1840–1909) was a traveler and author of books on the NORTHLAND. According to an article by I. A. M. Bosworth called "Is Jack London a Plagiarist?" in the *Independent* magazine, Young accused London of plagiarizing *The Call of the Wild* from his own book *My Dogs in the Northland* (1902). London wrote a letter to the *Independent*'s editor in response pointing out that he had written to Young to thank him for his source material and defending himself from the charge. He noted that he and Young had used some of the same sources in their depictions of DOGS and WOLVES in the Northland.

Youth's Companion   The *Youth's Companion* (1827–1929) was an American children's magazine published for more than 100 years until it merged with *American Boy* in 1929. Early issues centered on religion and advice for clean living. In the 1890s, its content was reconceptualized to focus upon adults as well as children with articles contributed by writers such as Harriet Beecher Stowe, MARK TWAIN, Emily Dickinson, Booker T. Washington, and Jack London. London published numerous stories in *Youth's Companion*, notably the first (1902) version of "To Build a Fire," several of the *Tales of the Fish Patrol* stories, and many early KLONDIKE stories such as "Chased by the Trail."

Yukon diary   On his trip up the YUKON RIVER to head home from the KLONDIKE, London began keeping a diary of the people and places he encountered, noting the difficulties of NATIVES whose lives had been so disrupted by the coming of the whites. He especially remarked on the sorry state of Native women who had been "married," then abandoned by white men. This diary, which has never been published, is included in the Jack and Charmian London Collection at Utah State University. Charmian recorded many of the diary's entries (*Book of Jack London* 1: 248ff.).

Yukon River   The Yukon River has its source at the Llewellyn Glacier at the southern end of Atlin Lake, British Columbia, and flows into Lake Laberge north of Whitehorse. Half is located in ALASKA, and the other half divided between British Columbia and the YUKON TERRITORY in Canada. It is the longest river in Yukon and Alaska and was once the main means of transportation, especially during the KLONDIKE GOLD RUSH (1896–1903). Riverboats were used until the Klondike Highway was completed in the 1950s. In the summer of 1898, London floated 1,500 miles up the river on a raft to ST. MICHAEL, Alaska, where he caught a ship for home. On this trip, he kept a YUKON DIARY, his first Klondike writing. This mighty river figures in numerous London works, especially *A Daughter of the Snows*, "To Build a Fire," "Chased by the Trail," and "Like Argus of the Ancient Times."

Yukon Territory   Yukon Territory, created in 1898, is the smallest and westernmost of Canada's three federal territories. The first half of the 19th century marked the beginning of European incursions into the Yukon Territory. The Hudson's Bay Company created trading posts throughout the Yukon in the 1840s for explorers and traders. American traders expelled the Hudson's Bay Company in 1869 after ALASKA was purchased by the United States. Most of London's Northland stories are set in the Yukon Territory.

Zola, Émile   Zola (1840–1902) was a French writer and one of the most important practitioners of NATURALISM. He was a prolific author of novels exposing social injustices and also inner forces such as genetics that could doom an individual. His best-known novels are *Thérèse Raquin*, *Germinal*, and *L'Assomoir*.

Zola is today perhaps most well known for "J'Accuse . . ." a letter to the president of France he published in 1898 in the Paris newspaper *L'Aurore*. At the risk of his career and his life, Zola defended Alfred Dreyfus, a French army engineer wrongly accused of treason. Zola accused the French army of anti-Semitism and obstruction of justice. For his pains, he was brought to trial for criminal libel. However, Dreyfus was pardoned. London was heavily influenced by Zola. Of particular importance was Zola's combination of ROMANTICISM and naturalism.

PART IV

Appendices

CHRONOLOGICAL BIBLIOGRAPHY OF JACK LONDON'S WORKS

Novels

The Cruise of the Dazzler. New York: Century, 1902.

A Daughter of the Snows. Philadelphia, Pa.: J. B. Lippincott, 1902.

The Call of the Wild (novella). New York: Macmillan, 1903.

The Kempton-Wace Letters (with Anna Strunsky). New York: Macmillan, 1903.

The Sea-Wolf. New York: Macmillan, 1904.

The Game (novella). New York: Macmillan, 1905.

White Fang. New York: Macmillan, 1906.

Before Adam. New York: Macmillan, 1907.

The Iron Heel. New York: Macmillan, 1908.

Martin Eden. New York: Macmillan, 1909.

Burning Daylight. New York: Macmillan, 1910.

The Abysmal Brute (novella). New York: Century, 1913.

Adventure. New York: Macmillan, 1911.

The Valley of the Moon. New York: Macmillan, 1913.

The Mutiny of the Elsinore. New York: Macmillan, 1914.

The Scarlet Plague. New York: Macmillan, 1915.

The Star Rover. New York: Macmillan, 1915.

The Little Lady of the Big House. New York: Macmillan, 1916.

Jerry of the Islands. New York: Macmillan, 1917.

Michael Brother of Jerry. New York: Macmillan, 1917.

Hearts of Three. New York: Macmillan, 1920.

The Assassination Bureau [completed by Robert L. Fish]. New York: McGraw-Hill, 1963.

Cherry [unfinished last novel by Jack London]. Edited by James Williams. *Jack London Journal* 6 (1999): 4–76.

Short Fiction Collections

The Son of the Wolf. Boston: Houghton Mifflin, 1900.

Children of the Frost. New York: Century, 1902.

The God of His Fathers. New York: Century, 1901.

The Faith of Men & Other Stories. New York: Macmillan, 1904.

Tales of the Fish Patrol. New York: Macmillan, 1905.

Moon-Face & Other Stories. New York: Macmillan, 1906.

Love of Life & Other Stories. New York: Macmillan, 1907.

Lost Face. New York: Macmillan, 1910.

When God Laughs and Other Stories. New York: Macmillan, 1911.

South Sea Tales. New York: Macmillan, 1911.

The House of Pride and Other Tales of Hawaii. New York: Macmillan, 1912.

A Son of the Sun. Garden City, NY: Doubleday, Page & Company, 1912.

Smoke Bellew. New York: Century, 1912.

The Night-Born. New York: Century, 1912.

The Strength of the Strong. New York: Macmillan, 1914.

The Turtles of Tasman. New York: Macmillan, 1916.

The Red One. New York: Macmillan, 1918.

On the Makaloa Mat. New York: Macmillan, 1919.

Dutch Courage and Other Stories. New York: Macmillan, 1922.

Plays

Scorn of Women. New York: Macmillan, 1906.

Theft: A Play in Four Acts. New York: Macmillan, 1910.

The Acorn-Planter: A California Forest Play—Planned to Be Sung by Efficient Singers Accompanied by a Capable Orchestra. New York: Macmillan, 1916.

Daughters of the Rich: A One-Act Play. [Curtain-raiser written under London's name with his permission by Hilda Gilbert]. Edited by James E. Sisson. Oakland, Calif.: Holmes Book Company, 1971.

Gold. [with Herbert Herron]. Edited by James Sisson, 1972.

Nonfiction Books

The People of the Abyss. New York: Macmillan, 1903.

War of the Classes. New York: Macmillan, 1905.

The Road. New York: Macmillan, 1907.

The Cruise of the Snark. New York: Macmillan, 1911.

John Barleycorn: Alcoholic Memoirs. New York: Century, 1913.

Fiction and Nonfiction Collections

Revolution and Other Essays. New York: Macmillan, 1910.

The Human Drift. New York: Macmillan, 1917.

Letters

The Letters of Jack London. Edited by Earle Labor, Robert C. Leitz, III, and I. Milo Shepard. 3 vols. Stanford, Calif.: Stanford University Press, 1988.

Notable Modern Editions

The Complete Short Stories of Jack London. Edited by Earle Labor, Robert C. Leitz, III, and I. Milo Shepard. 3 vols. Stanford, Calif,: Stanford University Press, 1993.

The Call of the Wild: Annotated and Illustrated. Edited by Dan Dyer. Norman: University of Oklahoma Press, 1997.

Jack London's Tales of Cannibals and Headhunters: Nine South Seas Stories by America's Master of Adventure. Edited by Gary Riedl and Thomas R. Tietze. Albuquerque: University of New Mexico Press, 2006.

Jack London on the Road: The Tramp Diary and Other Hobo Writings. Edited by Richard W. Etulain. Logan: Utah State University Press, 1979.

Jack London Reports: War Correspondence, Sports Articles, and Miscellaneous Writings. Edited by King Hendricks and Irving Shepard. Garden City, N.Y.: Doubleday & Co., 1970.

No Mentor but Myself: A Collection of Articles, Essays, Reviews, and Letters, by Jack London, on Writing and Writers. Edited by Dale L. Walber. New York: Kennikat Press, 1979. Reprinted in expanded edition as *No Mentor But Myself: Jack London on Writers and Writing.* Edited by Dale L. Walker and Jeanne Campbell Reesman. Stanford, Calif.: Stanford University Press, 1999.

Sporting Blood: Selections from Jack London's Greatest Sports Writing. Edited by Howard Lachtman. Novato, Calif.: Presidio Press, 1981.

Stories of Hawaii. Edited by A. Grove Day. Honolulu: Mutual Publishing Company, 1994.

BIBLIOGRAPHY OF
SECONDARY SOURCES

Books on London

Bykov, Vil. *In the Steps of Jack London.* Edited by Earle Labor, Susan Nuernberg, and Hensley Woodbridge. Translated by Julia Istomina. In The World of Jack London. URL: http://www.jacklondons.net. Accessed June 19, 2010.

Cassuto, Leonard, and Jeanne Campbell Reesman, eds. *Rereading Jack London.* Stanford, Calif.: Stanford University Press, 1996.

Day, A. Grove. *Jack London in the South Seas.* New York: Four Winds Press, 1971.

Foner, Philip S., ed. *Jack London: American Rebel—A Collection of His Social Writings Together with an Extensive Study of the Man and His Times.* New York: Citadel Press, 1947.

Gair, Christopher. *Complicity and Resistance in Jack London's Novels: From Naturalism to Nature.* Lewiston, N.Y.: Edwin Mellen, 1997.

Hamilton, David Mike. *"The Tools of My Trade": Annotated Books in Jack London's Library.* Seattle: University of Washington Press, 1986.

Haughey, Homer L., and Connie Kale Johnson. *Jack London Homes Album.* Stockton, Calif.: Heritage Publishing, 1987.

———. *Jack London Ranch Album.* Stockton, Calif.: Heritage, 1985.

Hedrick, Joan D. *Solitary Comrade: Jack London and His Work.* Chapel Hill: University of North Carolina Press, 1982.

Hodson, Sara S., and Jeanne Campbell Reesman, eds. *Jack London: One Hundred Years a Writer.* San Marino, Calif.: Huntington Library Press, 2002.

Johnston, Carolyn. *Jack London—An American Radical?* Westport, Conn.: Greenwood, 1984.

Kingman, Russ. *Jack London: A Definitive Chronology.* Middletown, Calif.: Rejl, 1992.

———. *A Pictorial Life of Jack London.* New York: Crown, 1979.

Labor, Earle. *Jack London.* New York: Twayne Publishers, 1974.

———. *Jack London: An American Life.* New York: Farrar, Straus & Giroux, 2011.

Labor, Earle, and Jeanne Campbell Reesman. *Jack London, Revised Edition.* New York: Macmillan (Twayne U.S. Authors Series), 1994.

Lasartemay, Eugene P., and Mary Rudge, *For Love of Jack London: His Life with Jennie Prentiss—A True Story.* New York: Vantage, 1991.

London, Charmian Kittredge. *The Book of Jack London.* 2 vols. New York: Century, 1921.

———. *Jack London in Aloha-Land.* Reprinted. New York: Kegan Paul, 2002.

———. *Our Hawaii.* New York: Macmillan, 1917.

———. *The Log of the* Snark. New York: Macmillan, 1915.

———, ed. *The New Hawaii, Containing My Hawaiian Aloha.* London: Mills and Boon, Ltd., 1923.

London, Joan. *Jack London and His Daughters.* Introduction by Bart Abbott. Berkeley: Heyday Books, 1990.

———. *Jack London and His Times.* New York: Doubleday, 1939. Reprinted with new introduction by the author. Seattle: University of Washington Press, 1968.

Loudermilk, Jessica Greening. *Ka Aina Ka Pono: Jack London, Hawai'i, and Race.* M. A. Thesis, University of Texas at San Antonio, 2006.

McClintock, James I. *White Logic: Jack London's Short Stories.* Grand Rapids, Mich.: Wolf House, 1975.

Reprinted in 1997 as *Jack London's Strong Truths: A Study of the Short Stories*. East Lansing, Mich.: Michigan State University Press, 1997.

Nakada, Sachiko. *Jack London and the Japanese: An Interplay Between the West and the East*. Yamanashi-ken, Japan: The Central Institute, Jorinji Zen Monastery, 1986.

Nuernberg, Susan, ed. *The Critical Response to Jack London*. Westport, Conn.: Greenwood Press, 1995.

O'Connor, Richard. *Jack London: A Biography*. Boston: Little, Brown, 1964.

Ownbey, Ray Wilson, ed. *Jack London: Essays in Criticism*. Santa Barbara, Calif.: Peregrine Smith, 1978.

Reesman, Jeanne Campbell. *Jack London's Racial Lives*. Athens: University of Georgia Press, 2009.

———. *Jack London: A Study of the Short Fiction*. New York: Macmillan (Twayne Studies in Short Fiction Series), 1999.

Reesman, Jeanne Campbell, Sara S. Hodson, and Philip Adam. *Jack London, Photographer*. Athens: University of Georgia Press, 2010.

Sciambra, Joseph C. "From Herbert Spencer to Alfred Schultz: Jack London, His Library, and the Rise of Radical Racialism in Turn of the Century America." M.A. Thesis, Sonoma State University, 1977.

Sherman, Joan. *Jack London: A Reference Guide*. Boston: G. K. Hall, 1977.

Stasz, Clarice. *American Dreamers: Charmian and Jack London*. New York: St. Martin's, 1988.

———. *Jack London's Women*. Amherst: University of Massachusetts Press, 2001.

Stone, Irving. *Sailor on Horseback: The Biography of Jack London*. Cambridge, Mass.: Houghton Mifflin, 1938.

Tavernier-Courbin, Jacqueline. *The Call of the Wild: A Naturalistic Romance*. New York: Twayne, 1994.

———, ed. *Critical Essays on Jack London*. Boston: G. K. Hall, 1983.

Walker, Franklin. *Jack London and the Klondike: The Genesis of an American Writer*. San Marino, Calif.: Huntington Library, 1966.

Watson, Charles N., Jr. *The Novels of Jack London: A Reappraisal*. Madison: University of Wisconsin Press, 1983.

Woodridge, Hensley C., John London, and George H. Tweney. *Jack London: A Bibliography*. George-town, Calif.: Talisman Press, 1966. Expanded and reprinted. Millwood, N.Y.: Kraus Reprint Co., 1973.

Zamen, Mark E. *Standing Room Only: Jack London's Controversial Career as a Public Speaker*. Foreword by Earle Labor. New York: Peter Lang, 1990.

Books with Significant Portions on London

Blotner, Joseph. *The Modern American Political Novel, 1900–1960*. Austin: University of Texas Press, 1966.

Boylan, James. *Revolutionary Lives: Anna Strunsky and William English Walling*. Amherst: University of Massachusetts Press, 1998.

Edmond, Rod. *Representing the South Pacific: Colonial Discourse from Cook to Gauguin*. Cambridge: Cambridge University Press, 1997.

Geismar, Maxwell. *Rebels and Ancestors: The American Novel, 1890–1915*. Boston, Mass.: Houghton Mifflin, 1953.

Homberger, Eric. *American Writers and Radical Politics, 1900–1939: Equivocal Commitments*. New York: St. Martin's, 1986.

Howard, June. *Form and History in American Literary Naturalism*. Chapel Hill: University of North Carolina Press, 1985.

Johnson, Martin. *Through the South Seas with Jack London*. New York: Dodd, Mead, 1913. Reprinted Cedar Springs, Mich.: Wolf House Books, 1967.

Martin, Stoddard. *California Writers: Jack London, John Steinbeck, The Tough Guys*. New York: St. Martin's, 1983.

McBride, Christopher Mark. *The Colonizer Abroad: American Writers on Foreign Soil, 1846–1912*. New York: Routledge, 2004.

Raskin, Jonah, ed. *The Radical Jack London: Writings on War and Revolution*. Berkeley: University of California Press, 2008.

Sinclair, Upton. *The Cry for Justice: An Anthology of the Literature of Social Protest*. Introduction by Jack London. Philadelphia: John C. Winston, 1915.

Williams, Tony. *Jack London—The Movies*. Middletown, Calif.: Rejl, 1992.

Articles in Books

Auerbach, Jonathan, ed. Introduction to *Northland Stories* by Jack London. Harmondsworth, U.K.: Penguin, 1997.

Barley, Tony. "Prediction, Programme and Fantasy in Jack London's *The Iron Heel.*" In *Anticipations: Essays on Early Science Fiction and Its Precursors.* Edited by David Seed. Syracuse, N.Y.: Syracuse University Press, 1995, 153–171.

Baskett, Sam S. "Jack London: 'In the Midst of It All.'" In *Jack London: One Hundred Years a Writer.* Edited by Sara S. Hodson and Jeanne Campbell Reesman. San Marino, Calif.: Huntington Library Press, 2002, 123–146.

———. "Sea Change in *The Sea-Wolf.*" In *Rereading Jack London.* Edited by Leonard Cassuto and Jeanne Campbell Reesman. Stanford, Calif.: Stanford University Press, 1996, 92–109.

Beauchamp, Gorman. "Jack London's Utopian Dystopia and Dystopian Utopia." In *America as Utopia.* Edited by Kenneth M. Roemer. New York: Franklin, 1981, 91–107.

Bender, Bert. "Jack London and 'the Sex Problem.'" In *Jack London: One Hundred Years a Writer.* Edited by Sara S. Hodson and Jeanne Campbell Reesman. San Marino, Calif.: Huntington Library Press, 2002, 147–188.

Berkove, Lawrence I. "Jack London's 'Second Thoughts': The Short Fiction of His Late Period." In *Jack London: One Hundred Years a Writer.* Edited by Sara S. Hodson and Jeanne Campbell Reesman. San Marino, Calif.: Huntington Library Press, 2002, 60–76.

———. "The Myth of Hope in Jack London's 'The Red One.'" In *Rereading Jack London.* Edited by Leonard Cassuto and Jeanne Campbell Reesman. Stanford, Calif.: Stanford University Press, 1996, 204–216.

Campbell, Donna M. "'The (American) Muse's Tragedy': Jack London, Edith Wharton, and *The Little Lady of the Big House.*" In *Jack London: One Hundred Years a Writer.* Edited by Sara S. Hodson and Jeanne Campbell Reesman. San Marino, Calif.: Huntington Library Press, 2002, 189–216.

DeGuzmán, María, and Debbie López. "Algebra of Twisted Figures: Transvaluation in *Martin Eden.*" In *Jack London: One Hundred Years a Writer.* Edited by Sara S. Hodson and Jeanne Campbell Reesman. San Marino, Calif.: Huntington Library Press, 2002, 98–122.

Derrick, Scott. "Making a Heterosexual Man: Gender, Sexuality, and Narrative in the Fiction of Jack London." In *Rereading Jack London.* Edited by Leonard Cassuto and Jeanne Campbell Reesman. Stanford, Calif.: Stanford University Press, 1996, 110–129.

Dickey, James. *Introduction to "The Call of the Wild," "White Fang," and Other Stories* by Jack London. Edited by Andrew Sinclair. New York: Penguin, 1981, 7–16.

France, Anatole. Preface to *The Iron Heel.* In *Critical Essays on Jack London.* Edited and Translated by Jacqueline Tavernier-Courbin. Boston: Prentice Hall, 1983, 35–37.

Furer, Andrew. "'Zone-Conquerors' and 'White Devils': The Contradictions of Race in the Works of Jack London." In *Rereading Jack London.* Edited by Leonard Cassuto and Jeanne Campbell Reesman. Stanford, Calif.: Stanford University Press, 1996, 158–171.

Giles, James R. "Assaulting the Yeehats: Violence and Space in *The Call of the Wild.*" In *Twisted from the Ordinary: Essays on American Literary Naturalism.* Edited by Mary E. Papke. Knoxville: University of Tennessee Press, 2003, 188–201.

Heckerl, David K. "'Violent Movements of Business': The Moral Nihilist as Economic Man in Jack London's *The Sea-Wolf.*" In *Twisted from the Ordinary: Essays on American Literary Naturalism.* Edited by Mary E. Papke. Knoxville: University of Tennessee Press, 2003, 202–216.

Hopkins, Lisa. "Jack London's Evolutionary Hierarchies: Dogs, Wolves, and Men." In *Evolution and Eugenics in American Literature and Culture, 1880–1940.* Edited by Lois Cuddy and Claire M. Roche. Lewisburg, Pa.: Bucknell University Press, 2003, 89–101.

Labor, Earle. "Jack London's Mondo Cane: 'Bâtard,' *The Call of the Wild,* and *White Fang.*" In *Critical Essays on Jack London.* Edited by Jacqueline Tavernier-Courbin. Boston: G. K. Hall, 1983, 114–130.

———. "Jack London's Pacific World." In *Critical Essays on Jack London.* Edited by Jacqueline Tavernier-Courbin. Boston: G. K. Hall, 1983, 205–222.

McElrath, Joseph R., Jr. "Jack London's *Martin Eden:* The Multiple Dimensions of a Literary Masterpiece." In *Jack London: One Hundred Years a Writer.* Edited by Sara S. Hodson and Jeanne Campbell Reesman. San Marino, Calif.: Huntington Library Press, 2002, 77–97.

Peluso, Robert. "Gazing at Royalty: Jack London's *The People of the Abyss* and the Emergence of American Imperialism." In *Rereading Jack London*. Edited by Leonard Cassuto and Jeanne Campbell Reesman. Stanford, Calif.: Stanford University Press, 1996, 55–74.

Phillips, Lawrence. "The Canker of Empire: Colonialism, Autobiography and the Representation of Illness: Jack London and Robert Louis Stevenson in the Marquesas." In *Postcolonial Theory and Criticism*. Edited by Laura Chrisman and Benita Parry. Cambridge, U.K.: Brewer, 1999, 115–132.

———. "Jack London and the East End: Socialism, Imperialism and the Bourgeois Ethnographer." In *A Mighty Mass of Brick and Stone: Victorian and Edwardian Representations of London*. Edited by Lawrence Phillips. Amsterdam, Netherlands: Rodopi, 2007, 213–234.

Pizer, Donald. *Realism and Naturalism in Nineteenth-Century American Literature*. Rev. ed. Carbondale: Southern Illinois University Press, 1984.

Riedl, Gary, and Thomas R. Tietze. "Fathers and Sons in Jack London's 'The House of Pride.'" In *Jack London: One Hundred Years a Writer*. Edited by Sara S. Hodson and Jeanne Campbell Reesman. San Marino, Calif.: Huntington Library Press, 2002, 44–59.

Shor, Fran. "Power, Gender, and Ideological Discourse in *The Iron Heel*." In *Rereading Jack London*. Edited by Leonard Cassuto and Jeanne Campbell Reesman. Stanford, Calif.: Stanford University Press, 1996, 75–91.

Slagel, James. "Political Leprosy: Jack London the *Kama'aina* and Koolau the Leper." In *Rereading Jack London*. Edited by Leonard Cassuto and Jeanne Campbell Reesman. Stanford, Calif.: Stanford University Press, 1996, 172–191.

Stasz, Clarice. "Social Darwinism, Gender, and Humor in *Adventure*." In *Rereading Jack London*. Edited by Leonard Cassuto and Jeanne Campbell Reesman. Stanford, Calif.: Stanford University Press, 1996, 130–140.

Tambling, Victor R. S. "Jack London and George Orwell: A Literary Kinship." In *George Orwell*. Edited by Courtney T. Wemyss and Alexej Ugrinsky. Westport, Conn.: Greenwood Press, 1987, 171–175.

Tavernier-Courbin, Jacqueline. "*The Call of the Wild* and *The Jungle*: Jack London's and Upton Sinclair's Animal and Human Jungles." In *The Cambridge Companion to American Realism and Naturalism: Howells to London*. Edited by Donald Pizer. Cambridge: Cambridge University Press, 1995. 236–262.

———. "Jack London and Anna Strunsky: Lovers at Cross-Purposes." In *Jack London: One Hundred Years a Writer*. Edited by Sara S. Hodson and Jeanne Campbell Reesman. San Marino, Calif.: Huntington Library Press, 2002, 21–43.

Walsh, Tanya. "Historical Discourses in Jack London's 'Shin Bones.'" In *Rereading Jack London*. Edited by Leonard Cassuto and Jeanne Campbell Reesman. Stanford, Calif.: Stanford University Press, 1996, 192–204.

Ward, Susan. "Ideology for the Masses: Jack London's *The Iron Heel*." In *Critical Essays on Jack London*. Edited by Jacqueline Tavernier-Courbin. Boston: Prentice Hall, 1983, 166–179.

Journal Articles (By Decade)

2000+

Bedwell, Laura. "Jack London's 'Samuel' and the Abstract Shrine of Truth." In *Studies in American Naturalism* 2, no. 2 (winter 2007): 150–165.

Berkove, Lawrence I. "*Before Adam* and *The Scarlet Plague*: Two Novels of Evolution by Jack London." In *ALN: The American Literary Naturalism Newsletter* 2, no. 1 (2007): 13–16.

———. "Jack London and Evolution: From Spencer to Huxley." In *American Literary Realism* 36 (2004): 243–255.

Bomback, Andrew S., M.D., and Philip J. Klemmer, M.D. "Jack London's 'Mysterious Malady.'" *American Journal of Medicine* 120 (2007): 466–467.

Brandt, Kenneth K. "Repudiating 'The Gladiatorial Theory of Existence': Tom King's Ethical Development in Jack London's 'A Piece of Steak.'" In *Aethlon: The Journal of Sport Literature* 20, no. 2 (spring 2003): 101–108.

Ellis, Juniper. "'A Wreckage of Races' in Jack London's South Pacific." *Arizona Quarterly* 57, no. iii (2001): 57–75.

Emmert, Scott. "The Familiar Uncommon Spectator: Jack London's Female Watchers in *The Game* and *The Abysmal Brute*." In *Aethlon: The Journal of Sport Literature* 22, no. 1 (fall 2004): 137–146.

Furukawa, Haruro, and Clara Furukawa. "Sakaicho, Hona Asi, and Hakadaki: Jack London's First Visit to Japan in 1893." *Jack London Foundation Newsletter* 17, no. 2 (April 2005): 1–8.

Heckerl, David K. "'Violent Movements of Business': The Moral Nihilist as Economic Man in Jack London's *The Sea-Wolf*." In *Twisted from the Ordinary: Essays on American Literary Naturalism*. Edited by Mary E. Papke. Knoxville: University of Tennessee Press, 2003, 202–216.

Hensley, John R. "Eugenics and Social Darwinism in Stanley Waterloo's *The Story of Ab* and Jack London's *Before Adam*." In *Studies in Popular Culture* 25, no. 1 (October 2002): 22–37.

Jaeckle, Jeff. "Patterns of Paradox in Form and Content in 'The Mexican.'" In *The Call* 11, no. 1 (2001): 2–5.

Kersten, Holger. "The Erosion of the Ideal of the Heroic Explorer: Jack London's *The Cruise of the Snark*." In *Narratives of Exploration and Discovery: Essays in Honour of Konrad Gross*. Edited by Wolfgang Kloss. Trier, Germany: Wissenschaftlicher Verlag Trier, 2005, 85–97.

Kim, Young Min. "A 'Patriarchal Grass House' of His Own: Jack London's *Martin Eden* and the Imperial Frontier." In *American Literary Realism* 34 (2001): 1–17.

Lauter, Paul. "London's Place in American Studies." In *The Call: The Magazine of the Jack London Society* 14, no. 1 (spring–summer 2003): 11–17.

Marovitz, Sanford E. "Jack London's 'The Sun-Dog Trail': A Stereoscopic View." In *Eureka Studies in Teaching Short Fiction* 7, no. 1 (fall 2006): 78–84.

———. "London in Melville's Wake: Two Sons of the Sun in Polynesia." In *The Call: The Magazine of the Jack London Society* 14, no. ii (fall–winter 2003): 3–7, 10.

McKenna, John J. "Jack London's 'The Law of Life': A 21st Century Prophesy." In *Eureka Studies in Teaching Short Fiction* 5, no. 1 (2004): 20–25.

Mitchell, J. Lawrence. "Jack London and Boxing," *American Literary Realism* 36, 3 (spring 2004): 225–243.

Monteiro, George. "Fear and Desire in Jack London's 'Law of Life.'" In *Estudos Anglo-Americanos* 27–28 (2003): 91–94.

Nakata, Yoshimatsu. "A Hero to His Valet." Transcribed by Barry Stevens. Edited by Clarice Stasz. In *Jack London Journal* 7 (2000): 26–103.

O'Donnell Arosteguy, Katie. "Things Men Must Do: Negotiating American Masculinity in Jack London's *The Valley of the Moon*." In *Atenea* 28, no. 1 (June 2008): 37–54.

Orgeron, Marsha. "Rethinking Authorship: Jack London and the Motion Picture Industry." In *American Literature* 75, no. 1 (March 2003): 91–117.

Raney, David. "'No Ties Except Those of Blood': Class, Race, and Jack London's American Plague." In *Papers on Language and Literature: A Journal for Scholars and Critics of Language and Literature* 39, no. 4 (fall 2003): 390–430.

Reesman, Jeanne Campbell. "Re-Visiting *Adventure*: Jack London in the Solomon Islands." In *Excavatio* 17: nos. 1–2 (2002): 209–237.

———. "Rough Justice in Jack London's 'Mauki.'" In *Studies in American Naturalism* 1, nos. 1–2 (summer 2006): 42–69.

———. "Socialism and Racism in the Works of Jack London." In *Excavatio* 13 (2000): 264–275.

Riedl, Gary, and Thomas R. Tietze. "Misinterpreting the Unreadable: Jack London's 'The Chinago' and 'The Whale Tooth.'" In *Studies in Short Fiction* 34, no. 4 (fall 1997): 507–518.

Rundin, John. "The Naturalist Platonism of Jack London's 'The Red One.'" In *Excavatio: Emile Zola and Naturalism* 19, nos. 1–2 (2004): 334–347.

Shillingsburg, Miriam J. "Jack London's Boxing Stories: Parables for Youth." In *Eureka Studies in Teaching Short Fiction* 5, no. 1 (fall 2004): 7–15.

Swafford, Kevin R. "Resounding the Abyss: The Politics of Narration in Jack London's *The People of the Abyss*." In *Journal of Popular Culture* 39, no. 5 (October 2006): 838–860.

Swift, John N. "Jack London's 'The Unparalleled Invasion': Germ Warfare, Eugenics, and Cultural Hygiene." In *American Literary Realism* 35, no. 1 (fall 2002): 59–71.

Whalen-Bridge, John. "How to Read a Revolutionary Novel: *The Iron Heel*." In *Jack London Journal* 5 (1998): 38–63.

Wright, Louise E. "Jack London's Knowledge of Thoreau." In *Concord Saunterer* 14 (2006): 61–72.

1990–1999

Baskett, Sam S. "Sea Change in *The Sea-Wolf*." In *American Literary Realism* 24, no. 2 (winter 1992): 5–22.

Berkove, Lawrence I. "A Parallax Connection in London's 'The Unparalleled Invasion.'" In *American Literary Realism* 24, no. 2 (winter 1992): 33–39.

———. "Thomas Stevens: London's Comic Agent of Evolutionary Criticism." In *Thalia: Studies in Literary Humor* (special issue on the humor of Jack London) 12, no. 1, 2 (1992): 15–24.

Gair, Christopher. "Hegemony, Metaphor, and Structural Difference: The 'Strange Dualism' of 'South of the Slot.'" In *Arizona Quarterly* 49 (spring 1993): 73–97.

Harvey, Anne-Marie. "Sons of the Sun: Making White, Middle-Class Manhood in Jack London's David Grief Stories and the *Saturday Evening Post*." In *American Studies* 39, no. 3 (1998): 37–68.

Labor, Earle. "The Archetypal Woman as a 'Martyr to Truth': Jack London's 'Samuel.'" In *American Literary Realism* 24, no. 2 (winter 1992): 23–32.

Phillips, Lawrence. "The Indignity of Labor: Jack London's *Adventure* and Plantation Labor in the Solomon Islands." In *Jack London Journal* 6 (1999): 175–205.

Reesman, Jeanne Campbell. "Irony and Feminism in *The Little Lady of the Big House*." In *Thalia: Studies in Literary Humor* 12, nos. 1 and 2 (1992): 33–46.

———. "Jack London's New Woman in a New World: Saxon Brown Robert's Journey Into the Valley of the Moon." In *American Literary Realism* 24, no. 2 (winter 1992): 40–54.

———. "Marching With 'the Censor': Jack London, the Japanese Army, and Cultural Production." In *Jack London Journal* 6 (1999): 135–174.

———. "'Never Travel Alone': Naturalism, Jack London, and the White Silence." In *American Literary Realism* 29, no. 2 (winter 1997): 33–49.

———. "Prospects for the Study of Jack London." In *Resources for American Literary Study* 25, no. 2 (1999): 133–158.

Shor, Fran. "*The Iron Heel*'s Marginal(ized) Utopia." In *Extrapolation: A Journal of Science Fiction and Fantasy* 35, no. 3 (fall 1994): 211–229.

Sweeney, Michael S. "'Delays and Vexation': Jack London and the Russo-Japanese War." In *Journalism and Mass Communication Quarterly* 75, no. 3 (autumn 1998): 548–558.

Tavernier-Courbin, Jacqueline. "To Love or Not To Love? Jack London and Anna Strunsky's *The Kempton-Wace Letters*." In *Symbiosis* 1, no. 2 (1997): 255–274.

Tietze, Thomas R., and Gary Riedl. "'Saints in Slime': The Ironic Use of Racism in Jack London's South Sea Tales." In *Thalia: Studies in Literary Humor* 12, nos. 1–2 (1992): 59–66.

Whalen-Bridge, John. "Dual Perspective in *The Iron Heel*." In *Thalia: Studies in Literary Humor* 12, nos. 1–2 (1992): 67–76.

Zamen, Mark E. "'The Storm of Applause': Jack London's Oratorical Career." In *Jack London Journal* 1 (1994): 235–268.

1980–1989

Hays, Peter L. "Hemingway and London." In *Hemingway Review* 4, no. 1 (1984): 54–56.

Hensley, Dennis E. "Jack London's Use of the Linguistic Style of the King James Bible." In *Jack London Echoes* 3 (July 1983): 4–11.

Kirsch, James. "Jack London's Quest: 'The Red One.'" In *Psychological Perspectives* 11 (fall 1980): 137–154. Reprinted in *The Critical Response to Jack London*. Edited by Susan M. Nuernberg. Westport, Conn.: Greenwood Press, 201–216.

Littell, Katherine M. "The 'Nietzschean' and the Individualist in Jack London's Socialist Writings." In *Jack London Newsletter* 15 (May–August 1982): 76–91.

Moreland, David A. "The Author as Hero: Jack London's *The Cruise of the* Snark." In *Jack London Newsletter* 15, no. 1 (1982): 57–75.

———. "The Quest That Failed: Jack London's Last Tales of the South Seas." In *Pacific Studies* 8 (fall 1984): 48–70.

Naso, Anthony J. "Jack London and Herbert Spencer." In *Jack London Newsletter* 14, no. 1 (January–April 1981): 13–34.

Phillips, Lawrence. "Violence in the South Sea Fiction of Jack London." In *Jack London Newsletter* 16 (January–April 1983): 1–35.

Reesman, Jeanne Campbell. "The Problem of Knowledge in Jack London's 'The Water Baby.'" In *Western American Literature* 23 (fall 1988): 201–215.

1970–1979

Baskett, Sam S. "*Martin Eden:* Jack London's Poem of the Mind." In *Modern Fiction Studies* 22 (spring 1976): 23–26.

Campbell, Jeanne. "'Falling Stars': Myth in 'The Red One.'" In *Jack London Newsletter* 11 (May–December 1978): 87–101.

Cole, Terrence. "Go Up, O Elam: The Story of Burning Daylight." In *Alaska Journal* 6, no. 4 (1976): 235–239.

Graham, Don. "Jack London's Tale Told by a High-Grade Feeb." In *Studies in Short Fiction* 15 (fall 1978): 429–433.

Labor, Earle. "From 'All Gold Canyon' to *The Acorn-Planter:* Jack London's Agrarian Vision." In *Western American Literature* 11 (summer 1976): 83–102.

Tavernier-Courbin, Jacqueline. "Jack London's Portrayal of the Natives in His First Four Collections of Arctic Tales." In *Jack London Newsletter* 10 (1978): 127–137.

Tsujii, Eiji. "Jack London and the Yellow Peril," In *Jack London Newsletter* 9, no. 2 (May–August 1976): 96–98.

———. "Jack London Items in the Japanese Press of 1904." In *Jack London Newsletter* 8, no. 2 (1975): 55–58.

Ward, Susan. "Jack London's Women: Civilization vs. The Frontier." In *Jack London Newsletter* 9, no. 2 (May–August 1976): 81–85. Reprinted in *Twentieth-Century Literary Criticism.* Vol. 9. Edited by Harold Bloom.

1960–1969

Labor, Earle. "Jack London's Symbolic Wilderness: Four Versions." In *Nineteenth-Century Fiction* 17, no. 2 (1962): 149–161. Reprinted in *Jack London: Essays in Criticism.* Edited by Ray Wilson Ownbey. Santa Barbara, Calif.: Peregrine Smith, 1978, 31–42.

———. "Paradise Almost Regained." Review of *Stories of Hawaii* by Jack London. Edited by A. Grove Day. *Saturday Review* (April 3, 1965): 43–44.

Labor, Earle, and King Hendricks. "London's Twice-Told Tale." In *Studies in Short Fiction* 4 (1967): 335. Reprinted in *The Critical Response to Jack London.* Edited by Susan M. Nuernberg. Westport, Conn.: Greenwood Press, 1995, pp. 9–16.

1950–1959

Baskett, Sam S. "Jack London's Heart of Darkness." *American Quarterly* 10 (spring 1958): 66–77.

CHRONOLOGY

1876

January 12: Jack London born in San Francisco, California, the only child of Flora Wellman, who named as his father William Henry Chaney, with whom she had lived as common-law wife in 1874–75; the infant was named John Griffith Chaney

September 7: Flora Wellman Chaney married John London, and the child was renamed John Griffith London

1878

After Jack and his stepsister Eliza suffered near-fatal attacks of diptheria, the family moved across San Francisco Bay to Oakland, where John London sold produce to local markets and ran a grocery store

1881

Family moved to a farm in Alameda

1886

March 27: Family bought a house in Oakland after living on farms in San Mateo County and Livermore

1891

Graduated from Cole Grammar School (eighth grade) and took a job in Hickmott's Cannery; a few months later, with money borrowed from Virginia Prentiss, purchased the *Razzle-Dazzle* and became an oyster pirate on San Francisco Bay

1892

Worked as a deputy patrolman for the California Fish Patrol in Benicia

1893

January–August: Served as an able-bodied seaman aboard the *Sophia Sutherland,* a sealing schooner, to Hawai'i, the Bonin Islands, Japan, and the Bering Sea

Late August: Took a job in a jute mill at 10 cents an hour for 10-hour-plus workdays

November 11: "Story of a Typhoon off the Coast of Japan" was published as the best descriptive article in a contest for young writers sponsored by the *San Francisco Morning Call*

1894

Worked as a coal heaver in the power plant of the Oakland, San Leandro, and Hayward Electric Railway

April 6: Left Oakland to join Kelly's Army, the western contingent of Coxey's Industrial Army of the Unemployed, in its march on Washington to protest economic conditions

May 25: Left Kelly's Army at Hannibal, Missouri, to begin tramping on his own

May 30: Visited World's Fair in Chicago

June 29–July 29: Arrested in Buffalo, New York, and served a 30-day sentence for vagrancy in the Erie County Penitentiary

Toured the East Coast and returned west by coal car across Canada, earning passage from Vancouver as a coal stoker aboard the SS *Umatilla.*

1895

Attended Oakland High School; published short stories and articles in the *Aegis;* participated in the Henry Clay Club; fell in love with Mabel Applegarth

1896

Joined the Socialist Labor Party in April; left high school; briefly attended the University Academy in Alameda to prepare for entrance examinations at the University of California, then with tutoring from Mabel and Ted Applegarth, Fred Jacobs, and Bessie Maddern, was admitted to the University of California

1897

February 4: Left the university after one semester and, after a brief period of writing and socialist work, took a job in the Belmont Academy laundry

July 25: Sailed with his brother-in-law, Capt. James H. Shepard, aboard the SS *Umatilla* for Port Townsend, Washington, then aboard the *City of Topeka* for Juneau, Alaska, to join the Klondike gold rush

Spent the winter in an old cabin on Split-Up Island, between the Stewart River and Henderson Creek, 80 miles from Dawson City, Yukon Territory

1898

Suffering from scurvy, left the Klondike, rafting down the Yukon River from Dawson to St. Michael on the Bering Sea; worked his way home as a coal stoker, arriving in Oakland in late July; started an intensive regimen to become a professional writer

1899

January: "To the Man on Trail" published in the *Overland Monthly,* which then requested a series of Northland stories

July 29: "An Odyssey of the North" accepted for publication in the January 1900 issue of the *Atlantic Monthly*

December: Met Anna Strunsky

Published during the year a total of 24 items, including essays, jokes, poems, and stories

1900

April 7: Married Bessie Mae Maddern

Book published: *The Son of the Wolf* (Houghton Mifflin)

1901

January 15: Birth of daughter Joan

July: First journalism assignment, covering the Third National Bundes Shooting Festival for Hearst

Defeated as Socialist Democrats' candidate for Mayor of Oakland (received 245 votes)

Book published: The God of His Fathers (McClure, Phillips)

1902

August–September: Lived in East End of London, collecting material for and writing *The People of the Abyss;* traveled in Europe for three weeks

October 20: Birth of daughter Bess (Becky)

Books published: A Daughter of the Snows (Lippincott); *Children of the Frost* (Macmillan); *The Cruise of the Dazzler* (Century)

1903

Fell in love with Charmian Kittredge; separated from Bessie London; bought the sloop *Spray* for sailing on San Francisco Bay

Books published: The Kempton-Wace Letters, with Anna Strunsky (Macmillan); *The Call of the Wild* (Macmillan); *The People of the Abyss* (Macmillan)

1904

January–June: In Korea as a war correspondent for Hearst, covering the Russo-Japanese War

June 28: Suit for divorce filed by Bessie, on grounds of desertion; Anna Strunsky named as cause of separation

Books published: The Faith of Men (Macmillan); *The Sea-Wolf* (Macmillan)

1905

February–March: Took a sailing trip up the Sacramento River on *Spray;* defeated as Social Democrat candidate for mayor of Oakland (received 981 votes)

April–September: Spent summer at Wake-Robin Lodge in Glen Ellen, Sonoma County

June 6: Purchased the 129-acre Hill Ranch, the beginning of his "Beauty Ranch"

October 18: Began socialist lecture tour of the East and Midwest

November 19: Married Charmian Kittredge in Chicago the day after the divorce from Bessie London became final

December 27: Interrupted lecture tour for a honeymoon in Jamaica and Cuba

Books published: War of the Classes (Macmillan); *The Game* (Macmillan); *Tales of Fish Patrol* (Macmillan)

1906

January 11: Returned to United States from honeymoon in Jamaica

January 19: Resumed lecture tour, giving "The Coming Crisis" before audience of 4,000 at New York's Grand Central Palace; lectured at Carnegie Hall on January 25, at Woolsey Hall, Yale University, on January 26, and at the University of Chicago on January 29; after lectures in St. Paul and Grand Forks, North Dakota (University of North Dakota), canceled tour because of illness and returned to Glen Ellen in mid-February; began building the *Snark* for projected seven-year around-the-year cruise; Reported the San Francisco earthquake (April 18) for *Collier's*

Books published: Moon-Face and other stories (Macmillan); *White Fang* (Macmillan); *Scorn of Women* (Macmillan)

1907

April 23: After repeated delays, the *Snark* sailed from Oakland for Hawai'i

May 20: Snark dropped anchor in Pearl Harbor and underwent extensive repairs while Jack and Charmian visited Hawaiian Islands

October 7: Left Hilo for Marquesas

December 6: Arrived at Nuka Hiva, Marquesas Islands

December 18–27: Sailed from Marquesas to Tahiti

Books published: Before Adam (Macmillan); *Love of Life and Other Stories* (Macmillan); *The Road* (Macmillan)

1908

January 13–February 14: Round trip from Papeete to Oakland aboard the *Mariposa* to straighten out financial affairs

April 4–May 7: Resumed *Snark* voyage, sailing from Tahiti to Samoa

May 20–27: Sailed to Fiji Islands

June 4–11: Sailed to new Hebrides

June 21–28: Sailed to Solomon Islands

November 4–14: Sailed to Australia

November 20: Hospitalized in Sydney, Australia, for double fistula operation; suffering from multiple tropical diseases

December 8: Publicly announced that *Snark* voyage was being abandoned

Purchased the La Motte Ranch

Book published: The Iron Heel (Macmillan)

1909

April 8–July 21: Returned to Oakland via Ecuador, Panama, New Orleans, and Grand Canyon; returned to Glen Ellen on July 24

October 17–November 9: With Charmian sailed the San Joaquin and Sacramento River deltas

Book published: Martin Eden (Macmillan)

1910

February 12: Hired stepsister Eliza Shepard as business manager and superintendent of ranch

May 14: Purchased 700-acre Kohler-Frohling-Tokay Ranch, expanding Beauty Ranch to nearly 1,000 acres

June 19: Daughter Joy born; she dies on June 21

July 4: Reported Johnson-Jeffries world championship fight in Reno, Nevada

October 17–November 14: With Charmian, sailed aboard the *Roamer* in the San Joaquin River delta

November 20: Architect Albert Farr visited ranch to discuss plans for Wolf House

Books published: Lost Face (Macmillan); *Revolution and Other Essays* (Macmillan); *Burning Daylight* (Macmillan); *Theft: A Play in Four Acts* (Macmillan)

1911

January 5–February 10: The Londons visited Los Angeles

April 11–May 3: Sailing trip with Charmian aboard the *Roamer* in San Francisco Bay

June 12–September 5: Drove four-horse wagon, with Charmian and manservant Nakata, on 1,340-mile trip to Oregon and back; moved from Wake-Robin Lodge to new home on Kohler Ranch

December 24: The Londons departed by rail for New York

Books published: When God Laughs and other Stories (Macmillan); *Adventure* (Macmillan); *The Cruise of the* Snark (Macmillan); *South Sea Tales* (Macmillan)

1912

January 2: Arrived in New York City

January 30: Signed publishing contract with the Century Company

March 1: The Londons sailed from Baltimore on *Dirigo* for five-month voyage to Seattle around Cape Horn

August 4: Returned to Glen Ellen; on August 5, signed five-year contract with *Cosmopolitan* for fiction

August 12: They lost second child through miscarriage

November 26–December 28: Sailed the San Joaquin and Sacramento River deltas aboard the *Roamer*

Books published: The House of Pride and Other Tales of Hawaii (Macmillan); *A Son of the Sun* (Doubleday, Page); *Smoke Bellew* (Century)

1913

April 24–30: Visited Los Angeles to discuss movie contract with Sydney Ayres and Herbert M. Horkheimer of the Balboa Amusement Producing Company

June: Resumed publishing with Macmillan

July 8: Operated on for appendicitis

August 22: Wolf House destroyed by fire

October 5: With Charmian attended Grauman's Imperial Theatre in San Francisco to see premier of Bosworth, Inc.'s *The Sea-Wolf,* the first feature-length film produced in America

October 18: Began *Roamer* cruise of San Joaquin and Sacramento River deltas

December 11: Met with Ed. Morrell at Saddle Rock Restaurant in Oakland to get story of his prison experiences, used in *The Star Rover*

December 14–16: Visited Los Angeles for copyright trial arising out of dealings with Balboa Amusement Producing Company; ruling was in London's favor

Books published: The Night-Born (Century); *The Abysmal Brute* (Century); *John Barleycorn* (Century)

1914

January 8–February 20: Ended *Roamer* cruise to travel to New York City to discuss business affairs

April 7: Tom Wilkinson and William Beatly visited ranch to discuss the Jack London Grape Juice Company; articles of incorporation filed on July 16; the company failed in 1915

April 18: With Charmian left Oakland for Veracruz, Mexico, via Houston and Galveston, to report the U.S. occupation for *Collier's*

May 30: Suffered attack of acute dysentery

June 18: Returned to Glen Ellen

October 4: With Charmian departed on *Roamer* cruise of the Sacramento and San Joaquin River deltas

Books published: The Strength of the Strong (Macmillan); *The Mutiny of the Elsinore* (Macmillan)

1915

January 15–17: Visited Winter Carnival at Truckee

January 31: Returned to Glen Ellen from *Roamer* cruise

February 12: Suffered attack of acute rheumatism

February 23: The Londons sailed on SS *Matsonia* for five-month stay in Hawai'i after visiting Panama-Pacific Exposition in San Francisco on February 22

July 23: Returned to Glen Ellen

December 16: Sailed on SS *Great Northern* to Hawai'i

Books published: The Scarlet Plague (Macmillan); *The Star Rover* (Macmillan)

1916

July 26: Sailed from Honolulu to San Francisco on SS *Matsonia*

September 3: Attended California State Fair at Sacramento; stricken there with acute rheumatism in left foot; returned to Glen Ellen on September 16

October 26: Attended trial in Santa Rosa over water rights suit filed by Edward and Ninetta Payne

November 8–14: Second trial in Santa Rosa over water rights suit settled in London's favor; on November 10 suffered slight attack of ptomaine poisoning

November 16: Newsreel of London at ranch made by Gaumont Company; film shown on December 16

November 21: Suffered again from stomach disorder and complained about inability to sleep

November 22: Found unconscious in bed by servant Sekine; died at 7:45 P.M. after repeated attempts to revive him failed; death attributed to "uraemia following renal colic. Duration one plus days. Contributor chronic intestinal nephritis. Duration three years."

Books published: The Acorn-Planter: A California Forest Play (Macmillan); *The Little Lady of the Big House* (Macmillan); *The Turtles of Tasman* (Macmillan)

Books published posthumously: The Human Drift (Macmillan, 1917); *Jerry of the Islands* (Macmillan, 1917); *Michael, Brother of Jerry* (Macmillan, 1917); *The Red One* (Macmillan, 1917); *On the Makaloa Mat* (Macmillan, 1917); *Hearts of Three* (Macmillan, 1920); *Dutch Courage and Other Stories* (Macmillan, 1922); *The Assassination Bureau* (completed by Robert L. Fish; McGraw-Hill, 1963)

INDEX